Humphrey Bogart's image in the poster designed by Waldemar Świerzy for the film retrospective "The Cinema According to Chandler." The event was organized in the fall of 1988 by the Film Society (Film Club) "Kinematograf -75" (Poznań, Poland), which was run by Jacek Jaroszyk (President, see dedication) and the author (Vice-President). The team had previously organized two other retrospectives related to the subject matter of this book: "The Films of Gary Cooper" (in May 1986) and "The Films of Humphrey Bogart" (in January 1987).

FOUR HOLLYWOOD LEGENDS IN WORLD LITERATURE

References to Bogart, Cooper, Gable and Tracy

Henryk Hoffmann

Foreword by Maria Cooper Janis

BearManor Media

Albany, Georgia

Four Hollywood Legends in World Literature: References to Bogart, Cooper, Gable and Tracy
Copyright © 2016 Henryk Hoffmann. All Rights Reserved.

No part of this book may be reproduced in any form or by any means, electronic, mechanical, digital, photocopying or recording, except for the inclusion in a review, without permission in writing from the publisher.

Published in the USA by
BearManor Media
P.O. Box 71426
Albany, GA 31708
www.BearManorMedia.com

On the cover: Humphrey Bogart in *Casablanca* (WB, 1942/3), Gary Cooper in *High Noon* (Stanley Kramer-UA, 1952), Clark Gable in *Gone with the Wind* (MGM, 1939) and Spencer Tracy in *Boys Town* (MGM, 1938)—all publicity shots.

Softcover Edition
ISBN-10: 1593931816
ISBN-13: 9781593931810

Printed in the United States of America

Table of Contents

Dedication   vii
Foreword   ix
Introduction   xiii

Part One: Humphrey Bogart		1
I.	References to Bogart's Films	2
II.	References to Bogart: the Man, the Actor, the Celebrity	193
III.	List of References (Found) to Bogart and His Films	243
IV.	Credits of Bogart's Films <u>Referenced</u>	267
V.	Bogart's Monographic Bibliography	279
Part Two: Gary Cooper		283
I.	References to Cooper's Films	284
II.	References to Cooper: the Man, the Actor, the Celebrity	423
III.	List of References (Found) to Cooper and His Films	475
IV.	Credits of Cooper's Films <u>Referenced</u>	495
V.	Cooper's Monographic Bibliography	507
Part Three: Clark Gable		509
I.	References to Gable's Films	510
II.	References to Gable: the Man, the Actor, the Celebrity	627
III.	List of References (Found) to Gable and His Films	691
IV.	Credits of Gable's Films <u>Referenced</u>	713
V.	Gable's Monographic Bibliography	723
Part Four: Spencer Tracy		725
I.	References to Tracy's Films	726
II.	References to Tracy: the Man, the Actor, the Celebrity	811
III.	List of References (Found) to Tracy and His Films	847
IV.	Credits of Tracy's Films <u>Referenced</u>	861
V.	Tracy's Monographic Bibliography	871

Epilogue: Final Remarks and Conclusions   873
Overall Bibliography (Reference Sources)   881
Index   911

*This book is dedicated to
Jerzy Hoffmann, Jacek Jaroszyk,
Roman Kopytko and Bernard Sołtysiak
– four people that share my passion for the works of the four legends*

Foreword by Maria Cooper Janis

I do not think it is being prejudiced to say that I find the premise and ideas behind Henryk Hoffmann's new book on Hollywood legends unique, fascinating, and very worthwhile-reading for the general public and film buffs alike. To put the body of an artist's work in the context of not only his times, but the public tastes, to learn about his colleagues and the political forces that are acting all around him, is a stage that helps us understand more deeply the nature and scope of that person's talents and artistic challenges. Bogart, Cooper, Gable, and Tracy are all great film names and legends, no doubt, and this unique approach to understanding and examining the professional lives of these actors, I feel, is refreshing and starts one thinking in more depth about the impact of the people we designate "stars" or "legends."

Gary Cooper's screen persona and Gary Cooper the man, husband, father, the friend, were integrated into a seamless whole in his person—without artifice. I would like to share a quote from my father that illustrates his thinking:

"I don't like to see exaggerated airs and exploding egos in people who are already established.... No player ever rises to prominence solely on his or her extraordinary talent. Players are molded by forces other than themselves. They should remember this and at least twice a week drop down on their knees and thank Providence for elevating them from cow ranches, dime store ribbon counters, and bookkeeping desks."

In addition to testifying to my father's modesty and humility, this quotation proves that Gary Cooper, just like probably the other three actors, was not aware of his role as an idol, neither did he anticipate the impact that his films would have on future generations. Times have certainly changed and the movies of our different decades reflect that. It is quite unbelievable to learn, for instance, that in some circles, in its day, one of my father's most-loved films, *Mr. Deeds Goes to Town*, was perceived to have "Communist leanings."

It pleases me to see the wide range of my father's work given an exploration via the interesting film synopses and excerpted texts from other authors and their books. In his film roles, he was certainly more than a "one trick pony." For example, I have always felt his ability in the area of comedy roles was too much overlooked by both the studios and the public. Due to his versatility he was able to move easily from Western star to "dashing romantic leading man" to war hero to, as he would put it, "plain, average Joe American."

It is also interesting to see how the various Cooper characters in all the different films have evoked such emotional and creative responses in others and have found their way into authors' minds and their own stories. It is like a "happy haunting"—this Cooper persona following these other creators, maybe challenging them or annoying them, whatever it is that keeps resonating then and now, some seventy years plus after the majority of Gary Cooper movies were made. The characters he portrayed seemed to get under people's skin and provide a vehicle or jumping-off point for their own stories and imagination.

Clearly, as Mr. Hoffmann illustrates, Gary Cooper became a metaphor in people's minds. The film star in his various roles, it seems, somehow went deeper. The man himself, not the actor, but a simple and complex human being who always felt "damn lucky" for all the good breaks in life he had been given. To be relevant some fifty years after your career is finished is a testimony to some underlying basic principles. In the mega television series *The Sopranos*, even Tony Soprano refers to Gary Cooper as if he were talking through some of his life problems with his shrink! "High Noon" itself and Gary Cooper have become an absolute part of the lexicon in American writing. "To be high-nooned" is even given a definition referring to the film in the dictionary—Life imitates Art. Movies have a magical way of staying with the viewer long after the film has been seen. A mere few words enduringly tell the listener volumes "like Gary Cooper walking down the street in *High Noon*." It evokes emotions and memories. No more need be said.

Introduction

They were all born within a period of two years, between 1899 and 1901; they started their film careers roughly within a period of five years, between 1925 and 1930; and all four of them died prematurely—approximately within a period of ten years, between 1957 and 1967. All four won multiple Academy Award nominations in the Best Actor category (only!) and all received at least one Oscar; all became legends in their life time—legends that kept growing in size, complexity and propagation area years after their demise. Despite the fact that their careers significantly overlapped, Humphrey Bogart, Gary Cooper, Clark Gable and Spencer Tracy were hardly ever in each other's way. Cooper and Gable did compete at some point for the higher rank as a superstar, but, frankly, they were never serious contestants for the same part in a movie, maybe except for the role of Rhett Butler.

The four actors' relaxed and unthreatened coexistence in the professional

Hollywood environment can be explained by means of the relatively clear differences in their screen personae. Despite their physical resemblance, both tall and strikingly handsome, Gable and Cooper were notably different in their ways to prove themselves as heroes and to win a woman's heart. Loud, talkative and rough toward both men and women, Gable was almost the opposite of Cooper's taciturn, modest, gentle and sensitive personality. Tracy's forte was his wit and sophistication, combined with the ability to tackle highly intellectual challenges. And Bogart, probably the toughest of the four—on the surface at least—was frequently reluctant to admit his inclination for sentimental and unselfish acts. Working under contract for different studios was an additional factor allowing their friendly coexistence. Gable and Tracy were both hired primarily by MGM, but from the start they were compatible and co-starred as friends instead of being onscreen or off-screen rivals; Bogart worked mostly for Warner Brothers, and Cooper's best years were associated with his Paramount contract. Thus, they created their remarkable performances mostly away from each other (Cooper never shared credits with any of the other three), in films that make the history of Hollywood, each having at least one signature title: Bogart his *Casablanca*, Cooper his *High Noon*, Gable his *Gone with the Wind* and Tracy his *Boys Town*. Although they have been known for years by their one-word nicknames derived from their either last (Bogie or Bogey, Coop, Gabe) or first (Spence) names, the four actors also belong to the relatively small group of movie stars (including Chaplin, Garbo, Dietrich, Monroe, Brando, Nicholson, De Niro and a few others) who can be unambiguously referred to by mentioning only their last names.

While the actors' personae were considerably different, their careers had several common denominators. Each of them specialized in one or two genres, but all proved to be diverse actors playing in a variety of films. Bogart is remembered for a significant number of gangster roles (especially from the early stage of his career) and (later on) for other crime subgenres, but the other three actors did also, more than once, visit that area—Cooper in *City Streets* and *The Naked Edge*; Gable in *The Secret Six*, *A Free Soul* and *Manhattan*

Introduction

Melodrama, and Tracy in *20,000 Years in Sing Sing*, *Riffraff* and *They Gave Him a Gun*. While every fourth movie in Cooper's filmography is a western, Gable made eight (quasi-) westerns, and both Bogart's and Tracy's names appear in the credits of four. Gable was admired in a host of memorable romantic comedies—from *It Happened One Night* and *Forsaking All Others* to *Teacher's Pet* and *It Started in Naples*, but so were Cooper (e.g. in *Desire*, *Mr. Deeds Goes to Town*, *Ball of Fire* and *Love in the Afternoon*) and Tracy (*Libeled Lady* and most of his films co-starring Katharine Hepburn), while even Bogart, admittedly cast against type, appeared in but a few comedies (such as *Swing Your Lady*, *Sabrina* and *We're No Angels*). Tracy's filmography includes an impressive number of prestigious productions involved in serious political, social and/or moral issues, e.g. *Fury*, *The Seventh Cross*, *The Last Hurrah* and most of his films directed by Stanley Kramer, but the work of each of the other three actors also includes at least a few such pictures. To carry the list of similarities even further, all four actors appeared in war movies, in sea pictures, in movies focused on sports (albeit not always as sportsmen) and in courtroom dramas or films including one or more memorable scenes taking place in court. All played pilots, doctors and men of the press, and all—interestingly—made memorable movies set in Europe, Africa and Asia. Three of the actors have given superior performances in Ernest Hemingway screen adaptations—Cooper, a long-time friend of the writer, in *A Farewell to Arms* and *For Whom the Bell Tolls*, Bogart in *To Have and Nave Not* and Tracy in *The Old Man and the Sea*. Gable has never played a Hemingway character, but many of his roles—e.g. in *Mogambo*, *Soldier of Fortune* and *The Misfits*—have conspicuous traits of a Hemingway hero.

Humphrey Bogart, Gary Cooper, Clark Gable and Spencer Tracy managed to reach positions at the very top in the American movie industry, which is proven—among other things—by certain statistics. All four actors have repeatedly appeared on the list of the Top Money Making Stars. There was one year—1948— showing all four on the list (Cooper as #5, Bogart #7, Gable #8, Tracy #10)—and as many as eight years listing the names of three: 1941 (Gable #2, Tracy #6, Cooper #8), 1942 (Gable #3, Cooper #4,

Tracy #11), 1943 (Cooper #6, Bogart #8, Gable #11), 1944 (Cooper #2, Tracy #5, Bogart #7), 1945 (Tracy #5, Bogart #6, Cooper #7), 1947 (Cooper #4, Bogart #5, Gable #7), 1949 (Cooper #6, Bogart #10, Gable #11) and 1955 (Cooper #5, Bogart #9, Gable #11). Furthermore, in the 1997 poll of *Entertainment* magazine, Bogart was selected as #1, Cooper as #18, Gable as #8 and Tracy as #15 movie star of all time. The American Film Institute's 1998 List of America's 100 Great Movies includes four pictures starring Bogart (*Casablanca*, *The African Queen*, *The Maltese Falcon* and *The Treasure of the Sierra Madre*), two Gable films (*Gone with the Wind* and *Mutiny on the Bounty*), one movie with Cooper (*High Noon*) and one with Tracy (*Guess Who's Coming to Dinner*). Moreover, the AFI's 2005 List of the Top 100 Movie Quotes includes six quotations from *Casablanca*, three from *Gone with the Wind*, and one from *The Maltese Falcon*, *To Have and Have Not*, *The Treasure of the Sierra Madre* and *The Pride of the Yankees*.

Understandably, all of the actors worked with the best Hollywood directors, but—strangely—there is only one director, Raoul Walsh, that worked with each of them. John Ford collaborated with three of them (Bogart, Tracy and Gable), and so did Frank Capra (Gable, Cooper, Tracy), Victor Fleming (Cooper, Tracy, Gable), Michael Curtiz (Tracy, Bogart, Cooper), William A. Wellman (Tracy, Cooper, Gable), Sam Wood (Tracy, Cooper, Gable), King Vidor (Tracy, Gable, Cooper), Delmer Daves (Bogart, Cooper, Gable) and Edward Dmytryk (Bogart, Tracy, Gable). The major directors that worked with two of them include W. S. Van Dyke (Gable, Tracy), Richard Boleslawski (Gable, Cooper), Frank Borzage (Tracy, Cooper), Jack Conway (Gable, Tracy), Henry King (Cooper, Tracy), Fritz Lang (Tracy, Cooper), Howard Hawks (Cooper, Bogart), Fred Zinnemann (Tracy, Cooper), William Wyler (Cooper, Bogart), John Huston (Bogart, Gable) and Billy Wilder (Bogart, Cooper). Alfred Hitchock's prime coincided with that of the four actors, but, strangely, none of them ever worked with the master of suspense.

Among female co-stars, there is none that had the honor of working with all four of the male megastars. Those that appeared opposite three of the

Introduction

actors include Joan Crawford (Gable, Cooper and Tracy), Claudette Colbert (Gable, Cooper, Tracy), Loretta Young (Tracy, Gable, Cooper), Ingrid Bergman (Tracy, Bogart, Cooper), Barbara Stanwyck (Cooper, Bogart, Gable) and Deborah Kerr (Gable, Tracy, Cooper). The list of actresses that played with two of the stars is long: Sylvia Sidney (Cooper, Tracy), Helen Hayes (Cooper, Gable), Bette Davis (Tracy, Bogart), Marlene Dietrich (Cooper, Tracy), Marion Davies (Cooper, Gable), Jean Harlow (Gable, Tracy), Carole Lombard (Gable, Cooper), Myrna Loy (Gable, Tracy), Hedy Lamarr (Tracy, Gable), Katharine Hepburn (Tracy, Bogart), Teresa Wright (Cooper, Tracy), Lana Turner (Gable, Tracy), Ava Gardner (Gable, Bogart), Lauren Bacall (Bogart, Cooper), Claire Trevor (Bogart, Tracy), Grace Kelly (Cooper, Gable) and Audrey Hepburn (Bogart, Cooper). Interestingly, there are two major male stars that happened to play opposite three of the actors— Fredric March, who shares film credits with Bogart, Cooper and Tracy, and Burt Lancaster, who appeared in movies with Cooper, Gable and Tracy.

The exceptional position, superior status and everlasting popularity of the four stars have been indirectly confirmed by the movie industry itself—e.g. through an homage to Bogart in several movies, such as Jean-Luc Godard's *Breathless* (1960), Robert Moore's *The Cheap Detective* (1978) and Carl Reiner's *Dead Men Don't Wear Plaid* (1982), in addition to Herbert Ross's *Play It Again, Sam* (1972) and Robert Day's *The Man with Bogart's Face* (1980), two films based on literary works discussed in the book, or in Sidney J. Furie's biographical picture *Gable and Lombard* (1976)—as well as in several non-cinematic areas. Bogart and Cooper have both been honored with postal stamps in the "Legends of Hollywood" series, issued in 1997 and 2009, respectively. Furthermore, Cooper's image appeared on the stamp of *Beau Geste* and Gable's on the stamp of *Gone with the Wind*—both issued in the four stamp series commemorating the year 1939, Hollywood's *annus mirabilis* (1990). Bogart, Cooper and Gable are mentioned in popular song lyrics: Bogart in several, including Fraternity Band's "Don't Bogart Me" (also known as "Don't Bogart That Joint," 1968), Suzanne Vega's "Freeze Tag" (1985) and Bon Jovi's "Captain Crash and the Beauty Queen of Mars" (2000);

Four Hollywood Legends

Cooper in the revised, 1946 version of "Puttin' on the Ritz", written by Irving Berlin and originally published in 1929 (it was performed by Gable in the film *Idiot's Delight* with the original lyrics which obviously do not mention Cooper) and in "La Dernière Séance" (1977) sung by Eddy Mitchell; and Gable also in several, including "Dear Mr. Gable" ('You Made Me Love You') sung by Judy Garland in the movie *Broadway Melody of 1938* (1937) and "Camelot" from *Monty Python and the Holy Grail* (1975). Bogart and Tracy were both honored with a street name—103rd Street between Broadway and Amsterdam Avenue was renamed "Humphrey Bogart Place," and Tracy has a street in Iowa City, Iowa.

With all this said, it is worth pointing out that literary references are probably the ones which most unambiguously and most objectively reconfirm the greatness of the four stars. While the overall number of literary (mostly narrative but, occasionally, also lyrical) works (novels, short stories, plays, poems and some nonfiction books) containing references to the four actors and their films is overwhelming, the validity of the data is strengthened by the time span of the sources: a great deal of them were published in the last two decades and quite a few (referring to each of the actors) within the last five years; which means that numerous writers—either old or young—remember and respect those stars many years, half a century in some cases, after they died. The authors whose works are quoted in the book include a large number of highly acclaimed American writers—such as F. Scott Fitzgerald, John O'Hara, Budd Schulberg, Herman Wouk, J. D. Salinger, James Jones, James A. Michener, Jack Kerouac, Charles Bukowski, Kurt Vonnegut, John Updike, Philip Roth, William Styron, Don DeLillo, Thomas Pynchon, Tim O'Brien and Paul Auster—and a significant number of foreign writers from Canada, Europe, South America and Australia.

One more thing that all of the four actors have in common is that each has at least four (over a dozen, in Bogart's case) literary works using his name as the title or a part of it, alluding to his film in the title and/or using the actor as one of the major characters. Interestingly, in the Bibliography (Reference Sources) there are eighteen items (by sixteen authors) with

Introduction

references to all four stars—two works by George Baxt and Andrew J. Fenady, and one by James Scott Bell, Marisa de los Santos, Michael B. Druxman, John Gregory Dunne, Elizabeth Hay, Stuart Kaminsky, Adam Kennedy, Michael Malone, Martha Sherrill, Rachel Shukert, John Updike, Gore Vidal, Joseph Wambaugh and James Neel White. Moreover, ten other authors—Loren D. Estleman, William Goldman, Oscar Hijuelos, Stephen King, Laura Lippman, James A. Michener, Robert B. Parker, Lawrence Sanders, Budd Schulberg and Stuart Woods—refer to all four actors in different books. Thus, the total number of writers (that I know of) who recognized the existence of all the four movie stars in narrative works—in one way or another—is twenty-six. As some authors have referenced three of the actors (e.g. William Bernhardt, Fannie Flagg, Greg Iles, Susan Isaacs, Jack Kerouac, Elmore Leonard, Larry McMurtry, John O'Hara, Thomas Pynchon, Adriana Trigiani, Donald E. Westlake and Herman Wouk), some two and some only one, the total number of writers quoted in the book is nearly three hundred, while the overall number of their literary works listed in the Bibliography (Reference Sources) is almost twice as high, close to six hundred.

The book consists of four parts, each part devoted to one actor and each having five identical sections. In the first section, references to the actor's films are discussed; the second section presents references to the actor himself; the third section shows the complete list of references to the actor and his films (such a list, in addition to offering a clear picture of which writers and to what extent favor each actor, is justified by the fact that not all excerpts found in the resources are presented in the first two sections—either because of their relative insignificance, the lack of an English translation in case of foreign-language works, repetitiveness and/or abundance in a given work); the fourth section offers the credits of the films referenced (in order to avoid unnecessary repetition in the expository film descriptions in the first section); and the fifth section offers the actor's complete monographic bibliography (which seems appropriate considering the kind of reference book it aspires to be). The name of an actor when mentioned within a quoted passage in his <u>own</u> part is always in **bold print** and <u>underlined</u>, just like all the titles of his films. **Bold print** itself is used for a given movie's other members of the cast and crew and for any related key words/phrases/clauses/sentences, such as character names, unique locations or dialogue lines quoted from that film—in addition to the names of the other three stars and/or their films mentioned in excerpts <u>outside</u> of their own parts. The information about the original written sources is provided in three different places. The Overall Bibliography (References Sources) contains the author's name, the title of the literary work, and then the information about the specific edition that was quoted (in order to make it possible for the reader to find the exact quotes). On the other hand, in the text of Sections I and II and in the list of references to an actor and his films (Section III in each part) the year of its copyright/original publication is provided instead (to give the reader an accurate idea about the time relation between the book and the film or between different references).

In the title of the book the actors are referred to as 'legends.' And while they certainly deserve such an honor, there are other epithets appropriate in this context: the stars can be called 'icons,' 'household names,' 'cultural symbols' or 'sociological phenomena.' There is no doubt that the actors have become a vivid part of modern English language. Cooper deserves the credit for 'Nope,' and 'high noon,' having irreversibly invaded the vernacular, is widely used in both casual communication and multiple works of both fiction (as proven by the content of this publication) and nonfiction (e.g. *High Noon in Southern Africa: Making Peace in a Rough Neighborhood* by Chester A. Crocker, 1993; *High Noon on the Electronic Frontier: Conceptual Issues in Cyberspace* by Peter Ludlow and Mike Goodwin, 1996; or *High Noon: 20 Global Problems, 20 Years to Solve Them* by Jean-Francois Rischard, 2007) to designate a deadline, a showdown or any other form of imminent challenge, confrontation or threat—whether in the area of personal, national or global safety, in the field of social, economic or technological problems, or in the recently popular subject of weather and ecological issues. 'Bogarting' is a slang term connoting at least a couple of different things; and if anyone says, "We'll always have Paris," "Frankly, my dear, I don't give a damn" or

Introduction

"Long live the little difference!" most cultured people, at least at a certain age, know where these quotations come from.

Having started cults in various circles all over the world, Bogart, Cooper, Gable and Tracy are names that keep reemerging in everyday conversations, in journalism (e.g. in an assay on "Sartre and Camus in New York," published in *The New York Times*, July 15, 2012), in music (not only in song lyrics, but also in major concerts, e.g. Andrea Bocelli: Love in Portofino, on August 11, 2012, where Bogart and Gable appear in the kaleidoscopic montage among the celebrities visiting the Italian fishing village over the years), in movies, on postal stamps and in literature. Thus, the information contained in the book offers one more significant and precious data base for assessing the *impact factor* of each of the actors and his films; at the same time, it constitutes a unique documentation of and a commentary on the golden era of Hollywood created by representatives of another medium both during that era and years after it became a time long gone, a time evoking reflections and nostalgia. Moreover, without a doubt, the book provides a precious source for further studies of the complex and bilateral relationship between film and literature.

In lieu of Acknowledgments, I would like to express my indebtedness to a number of people without whose cheering, sacrifice and help the book would never have been completed. I am grateful to my family, in particular to my wife Betsy, for continuous support and understanding, to my friends Jacek Jaroszyk and Sean Francis for important leads, and, especially, to Maria Cooper Janis and Stephen Humphrey Bogart, for their encouragement, guidance and endorsement of the idea through their own written contributions to the final product.

Part One
HUMPHREY BOGART

Humphrey Bogart's publicity shot.

Born: Humphrey DeForest Bogart; December 25, 1899; New York City, New York

Died: January 14, 1957; Los Angeles, California

Spouses: Helen Menken (1926-1927, divorced); Mary Philips (1928-1937, divorced); Mayo Methot (1938-1945, divorced); Lauren Bacall (1945- his death; two children: son Stephen Humphrey and daughter Leslie Howard)

Academy Award: The African Queen (1951)

Academy Award Nominations: Casablanca (1943), *The Caine Mutiny* (1954)

I. REFERENCES TO BOGART'S FILMS

The overwhelming number of Bogart's movies referenced in narrative literature is a direct consequence of the actor's immense recognition and popularity among certain writers—such as George Baxt, Lawrence Block, Stuart M. Kaminsky, Elmore Leonard, Marcia Muller, Robert B. Parker, John Updike, Joseph Wambaugh and several others. While Block holds the record of mentioning the biggest number of Bogart's films in one book, it is because of Baxt's amiable series of mysteries set in the old Hollywood that quite a few of the actor's early movies get some well-deserved attention in narrative fiction. Baxt is also one of the three authors that make a reference to *Up the River*, a minor picture which is significant because of being the very first feature-length film in the careers of both Bogart and Spencer Tracy.

Up the River **(1930).** This mild crime drama with humorous elements is a generally forgotten movie. It was probably first alluded to in James A. Michener's novel *The Drifters* (1971) due to the fascination for Bogart and Tracy that Harvey Holt, a war hero, tech rep and regular participant in Pamplona bull chases, repeatedly expresses in front of the narrator and other characters, an international group of young runaways who clearly do not share his views and taste. While the allusion in Michener's book is quoted in Part Four (on Tracy), below is the excerpt from George Baxt's novel *The Humphrey Bogart Murder Case* (1995), in which Bogart is one of the major characters, helping Detective Herbert Villon solve the complicated murder mystery. The other real-life celebrities that play notable roles in the book include Dashiell Hammett and Lillian Hellman. Despite the novel's setting in the heart of the movie industry, the references to *Up the River* (a movie directed by John Ford), and many other films for that matter, are seldom closely related to the storyline even though Bogart's third wife, Mayo Methot, mentioned in the following excerpt, is involved in the plot in a significant way:

> Mayo Methot, the third **Mrs. Humphrey Bogart**. **Bogie**, **Spencer Tracy** dubbed him that when both made their feature-length film debuts back in 1930 in John Ford's prison comedy, *Up the River*. **Tracy** did well after it, **Bogie** didn't [p. 5].

The Petrified Forest **(1936)**. Bogart's first picture after his forced five-year period on the stage was *The Petrified Forest*, adapted from the play that provided the actor with an important break on Broadway. He gave a charismatic performance as gangster Duke Mantee, opposite Leslie Howard as Alan Squier, and it was thank to Howard's support that Bogart subsequently got the part also in the screen version of the play. And the first reference to *The Petrified Forest*, found in Evan Hunter's *The Blackboard Jungle* (1955), a realistic and moving story of a young teacher, Richard (Rick) Dadier, is related as much to the play as it is to the film. Rick, who—in the difficult post-World War II reality—finds a job at a vocational school in New York, faces a lot of challenges from his students. In his first attempt at taking control over his class, he cashes on his acting experience, and, in the evenings, contemplates about his situation, analyzing examples from the classics.

> "You ever try to fight thirty-five guys at once, teach?"
>
> . . .

He walked directly to the boy, pushed his face close to his, and said, "Sit down, son, and take off that hat before I knock it off."

He said it tightly, said it the way he's spoken the lines for **Duke Mantee** when he'd played *The Petrified Forest* at Hunter [p. 76].

The fact that Rick had modeled his performance in the school production on Bogart's in Archie Mayo's screen version of the play, rather than in the stage production, is indirectly confirmed in the next excerpt from the book, which relates a scene that takes place about twenty pages later. After a rape attempt on Miss Hammond, which was bravely and effectively stopped by Rick, Alan Manners, a skeptical teacher who is planning to leave Manual Trades for an all-girls school, sarcastically refers to Rick as an eager hero and Humphrey Bogart:

> "I'll get out, don't worry." Manners said, examining his classic profile in the mirror over the sink. "And I'll think of you playing **Humphrey Bogart** back here."
>
> "Come on," Rick said. "We'd better get upstairs."
>
> "I can see why things happen to you," Manners said knowingly, lifting his briefcase from the window-sill. "You're too damned eager."
>
> "Me?" Rick said. "I'm not eager. I'm **Humphrey Bogart**"
>
> [pp. 94-95].

And so Rick assumes the image and is, for the time being, content and unworried:

> He was **Humphrey Bogart** all through that day. He had no trouble at all during the first three periods, even though he could sense resentment on the other side of his desk. He tried to forget the resentment, and he kept the classes pinned

down with an iron fist, never once forgetting he was **Humphrey Bogart**. . . . He made a mental note to tell Anne to stop worrying as soon as he got home, and when the bell sounded at the end of his duty period, he dropped the **Humphrey Bogart** role and headed straight for the teachers' lunchroom [p. 95].

American poster for Archie Mayo's *The Petrified Forest* (1936).

FOUR HOLLYWOOD LEGENDS

In Irwin Shaw's novel *Rich Man, Poor Man* (1970), Bogart and the film are mentioned in a passage where a newly married couple, Captain (Willie) and Mrs. (Gretchen) Abbott, go to the movies after making love in a hotel:

> They didn't want to leave each, so they went over to Broadway and had orangeades at a Nedick stand, faint taste of tropics in a Northern latitude, then continued on to 42nd Street and went into an all-night movie and sat among derelicts and insomniacs and perverts and soldiers waiting for a bus and watched **Humphrey Bogart** playing **Duke Mantee** in *The Petrified Forest*.
>
> When the picture ended, they still didn't want to leave each other, so they saw *The Petrified Forest* over again [p. 152].

The allusion to the film in James A. Michener's novel *The Drifters* (1971) is very brief:

> 'Did you see the time when he fought with **Leslie Howard** in the desert?' [p. 506]

In William Styron's novel *Sophie's Choice* (1978), the film is mentioned within a description of a Nazi doctor as he is remembered by Sophie:

> Very "Nordic"-looking, attractive in a thin-lipped, austere, unbending way, the young officer had treated her frostily during their brief meeting, almost to the point of contempt and boorishness; nonetheless, she could not help but be taken by his arresting handsomeness, by—surprisingly—something not really effeminate but rather silkily feminine about his face in repose. He looked a bit like a militarized **Leslie Howard**, whom she had had a mild crush on ever since *The Petrified Forest*. Despite the dislike he had inspired in her, and her satisfaction

in not having to see this German officer again, she remembered thinking about him later rather disturbingly: If he had been a woman, he would have been a person I think I might have felt drawn to [p. 481].

A clearly non-sequitur reference to *The Petrified Forest* appears in Stuart M. Kaminsky's mystery *Smart Moves* (1986). During a rehearsal at Bert Williams Theatre, a Nazi agent named Povey is out to kill and he is stopped by private eye Toby Peters, his friend Alex Albanese and singer Paul Robeson. The struggle with the unsuccessful assassin is followed by a conversation between the narrator (Peters) and two FBI agents, nicknamed (in a very likely allusion to Hammett's partners in *The Maltese Falcon*) Spade and Archer, which includes a reference to the movie, rather than the play, as the characters mentioning it are more likely to be familiar with the film:

> I turned and looked into the audience area, where Spade and Archer sat on folding chairs watching my performance on stage. Spade held up my holster and pistol, the missing prop.
> "Do Duke Mantee," Spade said.
> "***Petrified Forest***," prompted Archer.
> "I know," I said, stepping off the platform and reaching for my holster and pistol. Spade held it out for me [p. 73].

As the brief quotation related to *Up the River* from Baxt's *The Humphrey Bogart Murder Case* (1995)—see above—is continued, the narrator provides information about Bogart's subsequent work:

> He floundered around in small parts, mostly as gangsters until the opportunity to portray **Duke Mantee** on Broadway in ***The Petrified Forest***, a thinly disguised character inspired by the 1934's public enemy number one, John Dillinger. **Leslie Howard** starred in the play and when **Jack Warner** asked him

to re-create the role in film he refused to do so unless **Bogart** was signed for **Mantee. Bogart** stole the film from its costars, **Howard** and the volatile **Bette Davis. Bogie** didn't look back after that though he often wanted to. **Warner**'s kept him in supporting roles with an occasional lead in a B low-budget film. **Bogart** with his complaints for better treatment joined **Miss Davis** and Jimmy Cagney as major thorns in **Jack Warner**'s side [p. 5].

An allusion to Bogart's part in the film appears in Bill Crider's *We'll Always Have Murder: A Humphrey Bogart Mystery* (2001), a book which is significant for using Bogart as a part of the subtitle and as one of the major characters (he helps private eye Terry Scott, the narrator, in the investigation) and for containing references to the actor's thirteen movies. The allusion takes place in a conversation between Scott, Bogart, and a cop named Congreve:

> Congreve's face was almost maroon. I hoped he wasn't going to pop a blood vessel and ruin **Bogart**'s carpet.
> "I know what you're thinking," I told Congreve. "It's right out of some bad movie."
> "You'll never get away with this," **Bogart** said, right on cue in his best **Duke Mantee** voice. "I'll get you if it's the last thing I do" [p. 147].

Bullets or Ballots **(1936).** The major real-life character in Stuart M. Kaminsky's *Bullet for a Star* (1977) is Errol Flynn. Nonetheless, many other movie stars get mentioned, and, in the following scene, containing a reference to this William Keighley's film (featuring both Bogart and Edward G. Robinson), it is Robinson that gives advice to private eye Peters:

> "By the way, I think you should take care of that back. It could be something serious. If you'd like the name of a good

orthopedic man, let me know. I used him myself when I took a bad fall in the death scene of ***Bullets or Ballots*** [p. 59].

Humphrey Bogart (with unidentified players) in a scene from William Keighley's *Bullets or Ballots* (1936).

***Black Legion* (1937).** Archie Mayo's *Black Legion* is the first (chronologically speaking, based on the release date) of the twenty-six Bogart movies referenced in Lawrence Block's mystery *The Burglar Who Thought He Was Bogart* (1995). The reason for the abundance of such references in the book is a Bogart film festival in New York attended by protagonist Bernie Rhodenbarr, a bookstore owner in daytime and a burglar at night (also the narrator), at first with Ilona Markova, a mysterious woman he met in his bookstore, and later with Carolyn Kaiser, his good lesbian friend. The context of the following scene is a double feature show at the Musette for which Ilona does not show up:

> At the refreshment stand a tall guy with a goatee but no mustache said, "All by yourself tonight."
> I'd seen him and his dumpling of a girlfriend just about every night, but this was the first time either of us had spoken. "All alone," I agreed. "She said she might have to work late. She might still turn up."
> We talked about the film we'd just seen [*Passage to Marseille*], and about the one coming up. Then I went back to my seat and watched **_Black Legion_** [p. 138].

***Marked Woman* (1937).** This almost completely forgotten movie, directed by Lloyd Bacon, is referenced by George Baxt in *The Humphrey Bogart Murder Case* (1995) as the author continues his monographic sketch on Bogart, which, in this case, offers also some information about the actor's private life, his relationship with his wife in particular:

> "Goddamn you, I'm always sticking my neck out for you and what do I get for it? Do I get any gratitude? All I get is the chop! I got you into **_Marked Woman_**, didn't I?"
> "Four years ago! And playing an over-the-hill whore!" [p. 11]

As **Bogart** became more successful, **Mayo** felt herself slowly but surely shunted to the background. As **Bette Davis** had told her when they were filming *Marked Woman*, "There's nothing more unnecessary than a Hollywood wife" [p. 23].

Kid Galahad **(1937).** Using a story that has been frequently recycled by Warner Brothers, this gangster/boxing drama directed by Michael Curtiz is mentioned—together with William Wyler's *Dead End*—by Baxt in *The Humphrey Bogart Murder Case* (1995), in a sentence which in fact focuses on *The Wagons Roll at Night*, a movie made four years after these two.

Bogie had balked at doing this one, not because of the actress, whom he had supported in *Dead End* four years earlier, but because *Wagons* was a remake of the **Edward G. Robinson** and **Bette Davis** melodrama of four years earlier, *Kid Galahad*, in which **Bogart** had been the villain. **Bogart** thought there was something incestuous about it [p. 12].

Dead End **(1937).** In addition to the reference in George Baxt's mystery (see above), Wyler's outstanding gangster drama *Dead End* is also mentioned in Stuart M. Kaminsky's *Bullet for a Star* (1977) and Lawrence Block's *The Burglar Who Thought He Was Bogart* (1995). The context of the scene in *Bullet for a Star* is private investigator Peters checking in at a hotel and offering—in the role of the narrator—some similes to the reader:

I had no luggage, but I paid cash, and the woman at the desk appreciated being compared to Joan Crawford. Most of the women in Los Angeles thought they looked like Jean Harlow, Joan Crawford, Joan Blondell or Olivia DeHavilland [misspelled]. The Joan Crawford behind the desk looked more like **Marjorie Main** in *Dead End*.

. . .

A relatively old lady of the evening walked past me down the hall. She didn't look as good as **Marjorie Main** in *__Dead End__*. I gave her a polite smile and shrugged at the phone indicating I was too busy [p. 125].

Joel McCrea as Dave Connell and Humphrey Bogart as 'Babe Face' Martin in a scene from William Wyler's *Dead End* (1937).

While the above excerpt is focused on an actress playing a minor character in the film, some important details about the movie itself are offered in *The Burglar Who Thought He Was Bogart*:

> In **Dead End**, **Bogart** plays Baby Face Martin, a gangster making a sentimental visit to his boyhood home on the Lower East Side. By the time it's over he's been slapped by his mother, **Marjorie Main**, and shot dead on a fire escape by **Joel McCrea**. There were a lot of other good people in the movie, including **Claire Trevor** and **Sylvia Sidney** and **Ward Bond**, along with **Huntz Hall and** Leo Gorcey, who evidently wandered over from the Bowery. **Lillian Hellman** wrote the screenplay and **William Wyler** directed, but my favorite credit was costumes, by someone named **Omar Kiam**.
> During **Bogie**'s death, Ilona reached over and took my hand.
> She held it through to the end of the picture, and when she came back from the ladies' room at intermission she reached to take my hand in both of hers [p. 93].

Swing Your Lady **(1938).** Directed by Ray Enright, this unremarkable comedy is a minor item in Bogart's filmography—comedy was not his forte. The film, along with another one, is briefly mentioned in Block's novel *The Burglar Who Thought He Was Bogart* (1995), typically in a conversation between Bern and Carolyn:

> "What's the program for tonight?"
> "*The Caine Mutiny*," I said, "and *Swing Your Lady*."
> "I remember *The Caine Mutiny*. He was great in that, playing with those marbles."
> "Ball bearings, I think they were."

"I'll take your word for it. What's the other one? *Swing Your Partner?*"

"**Swing Your Lady**."

"I never heard of it."

"Nobody did. **Bogart**'s a wrestling promoter in the Ozarks."

"You're making this up."

"I am not. According to the program, **Reagan** has a small part."

"**Reagan? Ronald Reagan?**"

"That's the one."

"Well, at least it's only a small part. Wrestling in the Ozarks. And square dancing, I'll bet. Why else would they call it **Swing Your Lady**?"

"You're probably right" [p. 79].

Men Are Such Fools **(1938).** Another mediocre movie, this one directed by Busby Berkeley, was mentioned early in Block's book *The Burglar Who Thought He Was Bogart* (1995) as part of an introduction of the Bogart film festival:

> In the past fifteen days I had watched thirty movies, all of them either starring or featuring **Humphrey Bogart**. Some of them were films that everybody knows, like **The Maltese Falcon** and **Casablanca** and **The African Queen**, and others were movies that nobody's ever heard of, like **Invisible Stripes** and **Men Are Such Fools** [p. 42].

The Amazing Dr. Clitterhouse **(1938).** Directed by Anatole Litvak, this relatively interesting gangster comedy-drama is referenced in Bill Crider's already mentioned novel *We'll Always Have Murder: A Humphrey Bogart Mystery* (2001). In the quoted passage, the actor is given a chance to reveal the secret of his professional success:

"It's not easy to do," I said.

"I did it," **Bogart** said. He wasn't bragging, just making a comment. "I told Barbara how I did it. It worked for me, and now maybe it's worked for her."

"And what advice was that?"

"You take whatever parts they give you, and you don't complain. I did <u>*The Oklahoma Kid*</u>, and I did **Dr. X**, I did <u>*The Amazing Dr. Clitterhouse*</u>. I never complained. All I ever said was, 'Hand me the script'" [p. 64].

***Angels with Dirty Faces* (1938).** Michael Curtiz's excellent gangster drama is referenced in several major works. In John Updike's short story "Packed Dirt, Churchgoing, a Dying Cat, a Traded Car" (1961), an allusion to the film takes place when narrator/writer David Kern tries to fall asleep after a party and, in his thoughts, goes for a moment back to his childhood:

> The dark vibrating air of my bedroom felt like the dust of my grave; the dust went up and up and I prayed upward into it, prayed, prayed for a sign, any glimmer at all, any microscopic loophole or chink in the chain of evidence, and saw none. I remembered a movie that had frightened me as a child; in it **Jimmy Cagney**, moaning and struggling, is dragged on rubber legs down the long corridor to the electric chair. I was that condemned man [p. 110].

Stuart M. Kaminsky mentions the film in his mystery *Tomorrow Is Another Day* (1995), in a scene which takes place at the Academy Awards dinner, where private eye Toby Peters (the narrator) hopes to catch a dangerous murderer:

> I looked around for someone who might be Spelling, but it was tough to see much till they all sat down. I did see **Jimmy**

Cagney biting his lower lip and smiling, his eyes fixed on MacDonald. He'd failed as best actor a few years ago in *<u>Angels with Dirty Faces</u>*. *Variety* and the *Hollywood Reporter* had him neck and neck this year with Ronald Colman. *Yankee Doodle Dandy* was the sentimental favorite, but the Academy was usually in M-G-M's pocket, and *Random Harvest* looked good for Colman [pp. 187-188].

Lorenzo Carcaterra references the film in two of his books. In his nonfiction *Sleepers* (1995), a book containing several allusions to Bogart, the film is quoted in the motto:

> "Let's go say a prayer for a boy who couldn't run as fast as I could."
> —**Pat O'Brien** to **the Dead End Kids**
> in *<u>Angels with Dirty Faces</u>*

In Carcaterra's novel *Gangster* (2001), the reference to the film does not include Bogart's name either; the actor, however, is mentioned in a different part of the book. The reference to *Angels with Dirty Faces* is a part of a long passage in which the narrator, raised by gangsters, describes all the advantages (in his mind) of such an upbringing:

> I knew how the mob owned certain fighters and weight divisions and cleared out their purses long before the matches were even fought. I read about the great baseball players of the past and was told how many of them had links to organized crime. I knew all about Willie Sutton and every bank he ever held up and Two-Gun Crawley and his famous Upper West Side hostage siege, which had been the basis for the **James Cagney** movie *<u>Angels with Dirty Faces</u>*.

No young man could ever ask for a better education [p. 393].

Gary Brandner uses the title of this and a few other films at the beginning of "Heat Lightning" (2003), a short story featuring private eye Matthew Drumm, in order to define its time setting. However, while three of the movies were released before the outbreak of World War II, which time is in agreement with a previously mentioned sentence from the *Allford Courier*'s front page—"The story under the picture said FDR demanded assurance from Hitler and Mussolini that they would not attack anybody." (p. 141)—the mentioning of *Now, Voyager*, a film released in 1942, in the passage suggests that the war is already going on.

> I drained the Blatz, chipped a hunk of ice off the block, and sucked on that. I paged on through the *Courier* and stopped at the movie page with Louella Parsons's column and ads for the three theaters in Allford. The Liberty had *Now Voyager*, a Bette Davis movie you would have to break my legs and drag me into. At the Grand was **_Angels with Dirty Faces_**, which I'd seen last week. The Capitol was showing *Stagecoach*. It had John Wayne, which made it worth seeing right there. Even better, the second feature was *Charlie Chan at Treasure Island* [pp. 141-142].

The movie is also mentioned by the narrator of Dermot McEvoy's novel *Our Lady of Greenwich Village* (2008), in a passage comparing two cousins from Ireland, newspaper columnist Benedict Reilly, also known as Cyclops, and Monsignor Seán Pius Burke, also known as Johnny Pie:

> They were complete opposites. Cyclops was a character right out of **_Angels with Dirty Faces_**, while his cousin would be more comfortable singing a Bing Crosby-led choir. Cyclops

would go to Vietnam and return to a job as a copyboy at the *Daily News*. Johnny Pie would go off to college, then to seminary and graduate school [p. 113].

***King of the Underworld* (1939).** Lewis Seiler's minor thriller is mentioned twice by Lawrence Block in *The Burglar Who Thought He Was Bogart* (1995) as one of the items of the Bogart film festival. In the first excerpt, the author/narrator reveals the film's storyline:

> In ***King of the Underworld***, **Bogart** plays the title role of Joe Gurney. **Kay Francis** and **John Eldredge** play a husband-and-wife team of doctors, **Eldredge** with a mustache almost as unfortunate as **Bogie**'s in ***Virginia City***. **Eldredge** saves a wounded henchman of **Bogart**, who enlists him as the gang's doctor. When their hideout is raided, **Bogart** decides **Eldredge** must have ratted, and shoots him. **Bogart** and his men get away, but the cops arrest **Kay Francis**.
>
> Then, in what I thought was a terrific touch, **Bogart** kidnaps a writer and forces him to ghost his autobiography, planning to kill him when he's done. First, though, he busts two captured gang members out of jail, gets wounded in the process, and manages to find **Kay Francis**, who's been trying to dig up evidence that will clear her at the trial. A big help she turns out to be; she tips off the cops, infects **Bogart**'s wound, and blinds him with tainted eye-drops. He's stumbling around the hideout after her and the writer, trying to kill them even if he can't see them, when the cops burst in and gun him down [p. 252].

In the second passage, the reader listens to Bernie sharing his opinion about the movie with Carolyn Kaiser:

> We talked some about the film, and I gave her a rundown

on the first feature, ***King of the Underworld***, which she was sorry to have missed. "Except I like it better when he doesn't get killed at the end," she said. "You know me, I'm a sucker for a happy ending."

"In ***King of the Underworld***," I said, "the ending's not happy until he dies. But I know what you mean. Maybe that's why they usually show the older picture first. He tended to be alive at the end of the later ones, when he was a bigger star" [p. 256].

The Oklahoma Kid **(1939)**. There are several great westerns among the brilliant movies released in 1939, but Lloyd Bacon's *The Oklahoma Kid* is not at the top of the list, even though it was a major production. The film is mentioned in George Baxt's *The Humphrey Bogart Murder Case* (1995), and the reference is made to James Cagney, the star and hero of the picture, rather than to Bogart, who is cast here as the villain, Whip McCord.

"Yeah. I was a ghoul back from the dead. It died." He smiled. "I did a Western with **Cagney** that year. *The Oklahoma Kid*. Can you imagine me on horseback popping a six-shooter? Scared hell out of the horse. Scared hell out of **Cagney**, too [p. 64].

Another reference to Lloyd Bacon's western, this time including Bogart's name, appears in Bill Crider's book *We'll Always Have Murder: A Humphrey Bogart Mystery* (2001). In the following passage, Bogart offers important information about one of the suspects to private eye Terry Scott:

I thought I knew all the stars and near-stars, but Stoney Randall was a new name to me.

"He's a stuntman," **Bogart** said. He's doubled for me in a couple of pictures, like *The Oklahoma Kid*.

. . .

"I saw *The Oklahoma Kid*," I said. "You didn't look much like a cowboy."

"Neither did **Cagney**, and he didn't have to wear a moustache. I look like hell with a moustache, but they insisted. After all, I was the bad guy."

"The man who shot **Cagney**'s paw."

"I didn't shoot him. I got him hanged, though, so you were close" [pp. 63-64].

Dark Victory (1939). Scripted by Casey Robinson and directed by Edmund Goulding, *Dark Victory* is a memorable melodrama, even though it is not included among the top achievements of its year. The film is referenced in Truman Capote's *Answered Prayers: The Unfinished Novel* (1987), in a passage focused on gossip and minor characters:

> According to Lady Ina, Delphine Austin and Bobby Semenenko had been inseparable the past year or so, lunching every day at Côte Basque and Lutèce and L'Aiglon, traveling in winter to Gstaad and Lyford Cay, skiing, swimming, spreading themselves with utmost vigor considering the bond was not June-and-January frivolities but really the basis for a double-bill, double-barreled, three-handkerchief variation on an old **Bette Davis** weeper like *Dark Victory*: they both were dying of leukemia [p. 154].

An extensive reference to the film appears in John Irving's novel *A Prayer for Owen Meany* (1989) with voices by Johnny Wheelwright (the narrator), his grandmother, his stepfather, Dan Needham, and his friend, Owen Meany:

> But if a movie as stupid as *The Ten Commandments* could make Owen Meany murder toads by

throwing them at Mary Magdalene, a performance as compelling as **Bette Davis**'s in *Dark Victory* could convince Owen that he, too, had a brain tumor.

At first, **Bette Davis** is dying and doesn't know it. Her doctor and her best friend won't tell her.

"THEY SHOULD TELL HER IMMEDIATELY!" Owen said anxiously. The doctor was played by **George Brent**.

"He could never do anything right, anyway," Grandmother observed.

Humphrey Bogart is a stableman who speaks with an Irish accent. It was Christmas of '56 and we were watching a movie made in 1939; it was the first time Grandmother had permitted us to watch *The Late Show*—at least, I *think* it was *The Late Show*.

...

"You'd think that **Humphrey Bogart** could learn a better Irish accent than that," my grandmother complained.

Dan Needham said that he wouldn't give **George Brent** a part in a production of the Gravesend Players; Owen added that Mr. Fish would have been a more convincing doctor to **Bette Davis**, but Grandmother argued that "Mr. Fish would have his hands full as **Bette Davis**'s husband"—her doctor eventually gets to be her husband, too.

"*Anyone* would have his hands full as **Bette Davis**'s husband," Dan observed.

Owen thought it was cruel that **Bette Davis** had to find out she was dying all by herself; but *Dark Victory* is one of those movies that presumes to be instructive of the subject of how to die. We see **Bette Davis** accepting her fate gracefully; she moves to Vermont with **George Brent** and takes up gardening—cheerfully living with the fact that one day, suddenly, darkness will come.

"THIS IS VERY SAD!" Owen cried. "HOW CAN SHE NOT THINK ABOUT IT?"

Ronald Reagan is a vapid young drunk.

"She should have married *him*," Grandmother said. "She's dying and he's already dead."

Owen said that the symptoms of **Bette Davis**'s terminal tumor were familiar to him.

"Owen, you *don't* have a brain tumor," Dan Needham told him.

"**Bette Davis** doesn't have one, either!" Grandmother said. "But I think **Ronald Reagan** has one."

"Maybe **George Brent**, too," Dan said.

"YOU KNOW THE PART ABOUT THE DIMMING VISION?" Owen asked. "WELL, SOMETIMES MY VISION DIMS—JUST LIKE **BETTE DAVIS**'S!"

"You should have your eyes examined, Owen," Grandmother said.

"Owen, you *don't* have a brain tumor," Dan Needham repeated.

"I HAVE *SOMETHING*," said Owen Meany [pp. 273-274].

The Roaring Twenties **(1939).** Raoul Walsh's excellent gangster drama *The Roaring Twenties* (starring James Cagney, Priscilla Lane and Bogart) is referenced in Loren D. Estleman's *Jitterbugs* (1998), a thriller about a Detroit serial killer operating in the World War II years. The film is mentioned in a passage relating the conversation between the killer (later identified as Ladislaus Ziska) and his potential victim, a young woman named Erma:

"Someone told me once I looked like Taylor. I didn't believe her." He watched her out of the corner of his eye.

She leaned away from his arm to squint at his profile. "You

were right." She huddled back in. Her chunky heels made an irritating clacking noise on the sidewalk.

He probed. "It could have been worse. She might have said **Humphrey Bogart**."

"He doesn't look so bad. I thought he was handsome in *The Roaring Twenties*. He wore pretty suits and he wasn't as short as Jimmy Cagney. Anyway I don't see why all the girls like Robert Taylor. Van Johnson is much better looking" [pp. 60-61].

Frank McHugh (Danny Green), James Cagney (Eddie Bartlett) and Humphrey Bogart (George Hally) in a publicity shot for Raoul Walsh's *The Roaring Twenties* (1939).

Bill Crider's book *We'll Always Have Murder* (2001) contains two references to the film. The first one appears in a passage relating the dialogue between private eye Scott (the narrator), Bogart and two henchmen of mobster Charles Orsini (also known as Charlie O.), Mike and Tank:

> "Have you asked Mr. Orsini if he wants to see us?" he asked.
> "He don't want to see you," Mike said.
> Tank didn't say anything. He just nodded.
> "I think he does," **Bogart** said. I didn't interrupt. If he wanted to do the talking, that was fine with me. "Why don't you check with him."
> He looked pointedly at the phone on a wooden stand beside the door into Charlie O.'s office.
> "You got a message for him?" Mike asked.
> "That's right," **Bogart** said. His voice had roughened, and he sounded a lot more like the racketeer he'd played in *The Roaring Twenties* than usual. "I got a message for him. He'll want to hear it personally" [pp. 90-91].

Then the film is mentioned by a cop in an exchange that takes place some fifty pages later (in a continuation of the scene presented under *The Petrified Forest*):

> Even though I knew he [Bogart] was kidding, he managed to send a chill up my spine. It was no wonder Mr. Warner was willing to pay him so well.
> "Very clever," Congreve said. "You two should get Jack Warner to star you in a remake of *The Roaring Twenties*" [p. 147].

The Return of Dr. X (1939). Directed by Vincent Sherman, this minor horror is referenced in two novels using Bogart's name as part of the title and subtitle, respectively: *The Humphrey Bogart Murder Case* (1995) by George Baxt and *We'll Always Have Murder: A Humphrey Bogart Mystery* (2001) by Bill Crider (the actor is also one of the major characters in both). In the first book, the movie is mentioned (with disbelief) by Dashiell Hammett, another real-life character in Baxt's novel:

> There was a storage space to the right of the bar. The door was open and **Bogart** stood in the center of the room with his hands on his hips. "Doesn't look as though the place has been disturbed." He knelt beside the large carton that contained Jack Methot's papers. The strong cord with which the carton was bound was undisturbed. There was no sign of an attempt to cut it. Hammett was at a shelf examining scripts of **Bogart**'s earlier films. "For crying out loud, did you really do something called <u>*The Return of Dr. X*</u>?" [pp. 63-64]

In Crider's book, the title of the film (in an abbreviated version, without italics) appears in a sentence where Bogart explains one of the aspects of being a Hollywood star. The quotation is presented under *The Amazing Dr. Clitterhouse.*

Virginia City (1940). One of Bogart's three standard westerns (which number includes a B production, *A Holy Terror*, from 1931), this popular and action-packed movie was one of many films director Michael Curtiz made with Errol Flynn. The pretext for the reference to this movie in Lawrence Block's mystery *The Burglar Who Thought He Was Bogart* (1995) is once again the Humphrey Bogart film festival in New York City, which is attended by the book's narrator/protagonist, Bernie Rhodenbarn.

> "How were the movies?"
> "The movies?" I said. "The movies were great. <u>*Virginia City*</u> and <u>*Sabrina*</u>. What's not to like?"
> "<u>*Virginia City*</u>," she said. "It sounds like a western. Actually,

it sounds like a southern western, if you stop and think about it. What is it?"

"A western."

"**Humphrey Bogart** in a western?"

"**Errol Flynn**'s the hero," I said. "**Bogart**'s a half-breed bandit."

"Give me a break, Bern,"

"With a mustache and sideburns, and it is a sort of a southern western, because it's during the Civil War and Confederate sympathizers in this Nevada mining town are planning to ship a load of gold bullion to Dixie."

"But **Errol Flynn** saves the day?"

"And **Bogie**'s killed, of course. **Flynn** won't say where the gold is because he hopes it'll be used to rebuild the South after the war. That's his story, anyway. I figure he wanted a retirement fund for himself. Anyway, **Miriam Hopkins** pleads for his life and Abraham Lincoln commutes his sentence.

"Who played Lincoln?"

"I missed the credit. Not **Raymond Massey**, though" [pp. 211-212].

In George Baxt's novel *The Clark Gable and Carole Lombard Murder Case* (1997), on the other hand, the film is mentioned in reference to producer Jack Warner's thoughts about the prospects of publicity created by a murder and the location of the corpse:

> **Jack Warner**, listening in his living room, was delighted the corpse had landed just off **Miriam Hopkins**' private beach. Just the mention of her name could stimulate box office for her coming opus, *Virginia City*, in which her sparring mate was young **Errol Flynn** [p. 139].

Brother Orchid **(1940).** Lloyd Bacon's modest but pleasing morality tale, starring Edward G. Robinson as the reformed gangster, is also referenced in Block's *The Burglar Who Thought He Was Bogart* (1995), as part of a long report Bernie gives Carolyn about his movie shows:

> "**<u>Brother Orchid</u>** was pretty interesting. **Edward G. Robinson** was the star. He's a gangster, and **Bogart** takes over the mob while **Robinson**'s in Europe. He comes back and **<u>Bagart</u>**'s men try to rub him out, and he escapes and takes shelter in a monastery, where he takes the name **Brother Orchid** and spends his time growing flowers [p. 71].

They Drive by Night **(1940).** Anatole Litvak's superior crime drama about truck drivers, co-starring George Raft, Ann Sheridan and Ida Lupino, is referenced in a couple of books. In James A. Michener's novel *The Drifters* (1971), it is—as usual—a part of Harvey Holt's story:

> 'This typhoon was blowing across the Indian Ocean—heading away from us but still with a powerful sting in its tail. Snapped off the top of our tower four miles ouside of Gago Coutinho—but not all the way off. One girder refused to break loose ... kept the steel mass hanging there ... thrashing hell out of what was left. So somebody had to climb up there and cut it away. You face these things. It's like **<u>Humphrey Bogart</u>** driving that truck when he left **Ann Sheridan**'s restaurant' [p. 467].

In Marcia Muller's mystery *Where Echoes Live* (1991), the narrator/protagonist, San Francisco private investigator Sharon McCone, comes to a small town in the high desert of northeastern California (only miles from the Nevada border) to investigate a series of bizarre events, and stays in a motel with her former colleague, Anne-Marie Altman. In order to make a phone call to her company, All Souls, she is referred to the receptionist, Mrs.

Wittington, whose night habits become a pretext for mentioning a couple of films:

> "Good idea." I stood up, looked for a phone.
> "Isn't one," she said, "but you can use Mrs. Wittington's."
> I glanced at my watch, "Isn't eleven-thirty a little late to bother her?"
> "No way—she's a late-night movie buff like me. A couple of times this week IO've gone up to the lodge and watched till two with her. She loves anything bloody or with truckers in it."
> "Truckers?"
> "Uh-huh. ***They Drive by Night***, *Smokey and the Bandit*. Don't matter who's in it, how bad it is, or from what era so long as there's a truck and a hairy guy driving it" [p. 27].

The film is also referenced in *The Burglar Who Thought He Was Bogart* (1995) by Lawrence Block, in a conversation between Bernie and Carolyn, as one of two movies starring Bogart and Ida Lupino:

> "What's the other one? ***They Drive by Night***? Who's in that, if you don't mind my asking? Besides **Ida Lupino**."
> "**George Raft**," I said. "And I think **Ann Sheridan**."
> "And?"
> "And **Bogart**. He plays a one-armed truck driver. They showed ***High Sierra*** at the Musette, but on a night I couldn't go. I was stuck at that auction. And ***They Drive by Night*** never played the Musette" [p. 359].

High Sierra **(1941).** Based on W. R. Burnett's superior novel, and directed by Raoul Walsh, *High Sierra* (co-starring Ida Lupino) showed Bogart in his first leading role in a truly important movie, and thus it was only a step away from his great breakthrough in *The Maltese Falcon*. It is referenced in several works.

Stuart M. Kaminsky's *Bullet for a Star* (1977) is one of the author's many mysteries set in Los Angeles with private investigator Peters as the protagonist. When Peters tries to locate actor Harry Beaumont (a blackmail and murder suspect), he talks first to Warner Brothers gate guard Hatch and then to actor Jerome Cowan, who directs Peters to Bogart. The confrontation between Peters and Beaumont happens in the surroundings of the set of *High Sierra*.

"Seen him today?"

"No, he's on location, somewhere above Santa Barbara on a **Walsh** picture, *__High Sierra__*. Should be back tomorrow for some shooting, I think" [pp. 55-56].

Ida Lupino, carrying a dog, walked near me, and I asked for Harry Beaumont. She looked around and directed me toward a young man who said he had seen Beaumont, talking to an actor named **Cowan**. He pointed out **Cowan**, who was leaning against a tree, smoking. I recognized him. He was thin, taller than me, with a pencil-line mustache and hair thin and combed straight back.

"**Jerome Cowan**?" I said sticking out a hand.

"Right," he said, shaking my hand.

"I wonder if you can tell me where to find Harry Beaumont?"

Cowan looked at me quizzically [pp. 86-87].

As I ran out of the house, I met **Cowan** coming down the hill. Behind him and in the distance I could hear **Bogart** shouting, "All right. All right. I'll take the goddamned fall."

"You talk to Beaumont?" **Cowan** asked me.

"Briefly," I said panting.

"Mean-tempered son of a bitch, isn't he?" [p. 92].

Bogart stretched, put his hands on his hips and looked up the hill.

"It's a long one, but I think George made a mistake in turning it down," he said. I figured George was George Raft. **Bogart** confirmed it with his next words. "Now if old George will just turn down **the Falcon** role it'll be a good year's work for me."

. . .

"**Walsh**," shouted **Bogie**, "you one-eyed baboon. I'll die for you, but I'm not taking the tumble from up there."

"Fifteen minutes," shouted **Walsh**.

Bogart was shaking his head and smiling when he turned back to me.

"You know that maniac actually carries a gun on the set?" he said tilting his head toward the crowd of small people below us.

. . .

"Where are you going Edwin Booth?" cackled **Walsh**.

"My friend and I are going to the latrine together," **Bogart** said in a high falsetto. **Walsh** and the group of actors and technicians around him broke out laughing.

"And my family wanted me to be a polo player," whispered **Bogart** leading the way toward a farmhouse about fifty yards away. **Bogie** explained that the farmhouse was being used for costume changes. Beaumont had already finished his shooting for the location and was on his way back to L.A. by now if he had changed quickly.

. . .

"Harry, this is a friend of mine, Toby Peters," said **Bogart**. "I'd appreciate it if you'd answer a few questions for him."

"You know what you can do with your appreciation," Beaumont snarled.

Bogart pointed a finger at the bigger man and spoke softly.

"And you know what you can do with a mouthful of loose teeth." He turned from Beaumont to me with an amused look and whispered. "Sorry, that's the best dialogue I could come up with on short notice. It lacked a certain flair wouldn't you say, Toby?"

. . .

As I ran out of the house, I met **Cowan** coming down the hill. Behind him and in the distance I could hear **Bogart** shouting, "All right. All right. I'll take the goddamned fall" [pp. 87-92].

Andrew J. Fenady's *The Secret of Sam Marlow* (1980) offers a lengthy description of the film:

The Encore Theatre on Melrose was reprising a couple of **Bogart** classics. Actually, one was a classic—***High Sierra***; and the other was a quasiclassic—***Key Largo***. Sam had seen them both dozens of times; he had lost count. But he plunked down his two bucks, picked up a pair of popcorn cartons for another singleton and sat in an aisle seat up toward the front.

High Sierra was made and came on first. **Bogart** played **Roy Earle** and got the part because Paul Muni turned it down. Mr. Muni didn't want to die in the end. It's been rumored that George Raft, who was a bigger star than **Bogart**, also turned down the part, but Raft always denied it.

. . .

High Sierra was about an old-time gangster who had been sprung by **Big Mac**, played by **Donald MacBride**, to pull off a heist in Las Vegas. The gangster, **Roy Earle**, was hard as nails but had a soft spot for a crippled girl and a dog, a mutt named Pard. **Earle** was a crook, but he wasn't crooked. Not like a cop named **Jake Krammer**, played, naturally, by **Barton MacLane**. **Earle** also had a moll named **Marie**, played by **Ida Lupino**, who got star billing over **Bogart**. That was the last time **Bogey** ever got billed second. **Bogart**'s dialogue included the immortal line: **"I hope you're not trying to pull a fast one—'cause I don't like fast ones."** The picture was raw, rugged, violent, sensitive, and sentimental. It also featured a hotel clerk named **Louis Mendoza** who was played by a Hungarian named **Cornel Wilde** who went on to bigger and better parts for a long, long time.

Bogart did die in the end and also went on to bigger and better parts. The dog and **Ida** lived, but no so happily ever after. It was a damn good picture written by **John Huston** and **W. R. Burnett** [p. 142].

In Elmore Leonard's *LaBrava* (1983), a reference to the movie, triggered by a real-life situation similar to the plot of the film, takes place in a conversation between Joe LaBrava, an ex-Secret Service man now a photographer, ex-movie star Jeanie and old bookmaker Maurice Zola regarding one of the villains, Richard Noble:

"I'm talking about his attitude. The way he walks around the apartment, looks at my things. He's possessive and he's intimidating, without saying a word. He wants something and I don't know what it is."

"He wants *you*," Maurice said. "Guy like that, doesn't have any dough. What's he make? He wants you to keep him, buy him presents."

"I don't think so," she said. "He would've given me a few hints by now. Like he can't afford new clothes on his salary, wouldn't mind having a new car." Her eyes moved to LaBrava. "His sister's a cripple and needs an operation."

American poster for Raoul Walsh's *High Sierra* (1941).

<u>High Sierra</u>, La Brava thought.

"What he's doing, he's sneaking up," Maurice said.

Humphrey Bogart and **Ida Lupino**, LaBrava thought. He couldn't think of the name of the girl with the clubfoot [pp. 103-104].

The Humphrey Bogart Murder Case (1995) by George Baxt makes a reference to the film several times. First, the movie is mentioned in a scene where two police detectives, Marley and Gross, visit Evelyn Wood (Mayo Methot's eccentric mother; thus, Bogart's mother-in-law), who has reported that her apartment in Portland, Oregon, has been ransacked:

> "My daughter hasn't lived here in over twelve years. She hasn't visited in over five. She's in the movies.
> Marley eyes lit up. "Oh yeah? Maybe I seen her in something."
> "Her name is Mayo Methot." Her face hardened. "She's married to a bum named **Humphrey Bogart**."
> Gross's eyebrows went up. "Miss Wood, by you he may be a bum, but by me, he's one hell of a good actor. He was sure swell in *High Sierra*. Didn't you think he was terrific in that one?" [p. 3]

The dialogue is followed by some background information offered by the narrator:

> **Bogart** soon graduated to accepting other stars' rejects. When Paul Muni and George Raft refused *High Sierra*, **Bogart** inherited it. It was a surprise success [pp. 5-6].

A clearly favorable, and somewhat humorous, reference to Bogart and his film is made during a conversation between Bogart and Theda Bara's Japanese butler, Kiro:

> He realized Kito was holding a pen and an autograph album under his nose.
> "Please Mr. **Bogart**, would you sign my album?"
> "Sure," said **Bogart**, and scribbled his name.

Alan Curtis ('Babe'), Humphrey Bogart (Roy Earle) and Arthur Kennedy ('Red') in a scene from Raoul Walsh's *High Sierra* (1941).

"Oh sir, please. Above your name please write 'To my good friend Kito.'"

Bogart smiled. "No problem."

"Oh sir, you are truly my most favorite actor in all the world. I see your pictures many times. I have seen **_High Sierra_** eight times."

"No kidding? By now you should have built up an immunity to it" [p. 141].

Another reference to the film appears in Lawrence Block's *The Burglar Who Thought He Was Bogart* (1995), once again during an exchange between Bernie and Carolyn:

> "What have you got against **Ida Lupino**?"
> "Nothing, but I never knew you were such a big fan. What's the big deal about **Ida Lupino**?"
> "I always liked her," I said. "But tonight's movies are kind of special. *They Drive by Night* and *High Sierra*."
> "I'm sure they're both terrific, but . . . wait a minute, Bern. I know *High Sierra*. It's not an **Ida Lupino** movie.
> "It most certainly is."
> "She may be in it, but that doesn't make it her movie. It's a **Humphrey Bogart** movie. He's trapped on a mountain peak with a rifle, and they kill him."
> "Why'd you have to ruin the ending for me?"
> "Come on, Bern, you know the ending. You've seen the movie."
> "Not recently" [pp. 358-359].

The film is also referenced in another mystery by Block, *When the Sacred Ginmill Closes* (1986). The quoted excerpt relates the ways in which narrator/protagonist Matt Scudder handles his drinking problem:

> I took it easy with the hard booze, drank a can of ale, and made myself eat half a sandwich. I took a hot shower, and that helped, and then I ate another half-sandwich and drank another can of ale.

> I went to sleep, and when I woke up I put the TV on and watched **Bogart** and **Ida Lupino**, I guess it was, in <u>*High Sierra*</u>. I didn't pay a whole lot of attention to the movie but it was company. I went over to the window now and then and watched the rain. I ate part of the remaining sandwich, drank some more ale, and nipped a little from the bourbon bottle. When the movie ended I turned the set off and had a couple of aspirins and went back to bed [p. 122].

In Michael Walsh's printed prequel/sequel to *Casablanca* called *As Time Goes By* (1998), there are a couple of references to Bogart that are unrelated to his greatest hit. *High Sierra*, along with its stars and director, is mentioned as a sort of inside joke in the part of the book when Rick Blaine and Sam Waters look for Ilsa in London:

> As they passed through Leicester Square, Rick and Sam observed that London's pleasure district was undaunted; the dance halls were full and the cinemas were running. Rick noticed that the Astor was playing <u>*High Sierra*</u>. "STARRING **HUMPHREY BOGART** AND **IDA LUPINO**. DIRECTED BY **RAOUL WALSH**," proclaimed the marquee. Rick could take or leave the movies. He much preferred the theater, especially musicals [p. 89].

In Bill Crider's book *We'll Always Have Murder: A Humphrey Bogart Mystery* (2001), the investigation brings private eye Terry Scott and Bogart to a movie set, where the latter talks to the little guy in charge of spiders (used as one of the props):

> The man looked up when he saw us and said, "Oh, my. Can it be **Humphrey Bogart** in person? I loved your work in <u>*High Sierra*.</u>"

"I was pretty fond of that, myself," **Bogart** said. "Especially since I almost didn't get the part."

"It would have been unthinkable to use anyone else. No one would have been right for it."

"Leslie Howard was the only one who thought so at the time" [p. 76].

The Wagons Roll at Night **(1941).** This minor melodrama, directed by Ray Enright and co-starring Sylvia Sidney, is one of many references found in George Baxt's *The Humphrey Bogart Murder Case* (1995). Needless to say, the passage refers to the great actor himself:

> He certainly couldn't depend on his agent, who was one of **Warner's** cronies. This has been a good year for him. After the surprise success of ***High Sierra*** he went into a circus movie, ***The Wagons Roll at Night***, with Sylvia Sidney starting a screen comeback after several years away in the theater [p. 12].

The Maltese Falcon **(1941).** The movie that according to many was decisive in Bogart's promotion to the leading man status is referenced in numerous works. The presented excerpts offer an abundance of information about it; thus, it is enough to say here that it was the first collaboration of Bogart with John Huston, whose script closely followed the storyline of Dashiell Hammett's novel, and whose direction was instrumental in making *The Maltese Falcon* a top example of a new genre known as film noir.

The oldest reference to the film, along with three more allusions to Bogart pictures, is Woody Allen's *Play It Again, Sam* (1968), a popular play which was soon turned into a successful movie. Huston's classic is the one that opens the play as the movie is mentioned in the initial stage directions:

ACT ONE/Scene 1

The house LIGHTS DIM and we hear the voices of **Humphrey Bogart** *and Mary Astor in a scene from*

"*The Maltese Falcon.*" *It is the scene at the end where* **Bogart** *is going to turn her in despite the fact he loves her and she can't believe it* [p. 5].

At rise ALLAN is alone in the swivel chair watching "The Maltese Falcon" on a tiny TV which sits on the

D. R. hassock. The film is in the final sequence wherein **Bogey** *tells* **Mary Astor** *that he is going to turn*

her in. The sound track precedes the Curtain for a line or two. . . . He watches a bit after the curtain is up, sighs, crosses to the set and turns it off [p. 6].

Then the film is mentioned in a conversation between Allan and Linda:

ALLAN. I thought you didn't like me so much. I thought maybe you thought I was an oddball.

LINDA. I never really knew you. I mean we never spent any time together. Dick described you as the first guy who sat through "**The Maltese Falcon**" twelve times in two weeks. Then when the four of us went out together you acted differently than now [p. 35].

Finally, the similarity between the plots of the play and the film makes the lines delivered by the character named Bogart an obvious allusion to the movie:

BOGART. You play too rough for me, Sugar. It was you that killed Johnson. Parker found out about it so you killed him too. But that wasn't enough for you. You wanted to finish me off. You knew you couldn't do it while I was facing you so you figured you'd get me to turn my back. But not me, Sugar. Now come on. You're taking the fall. (LINDA *exits, sobbing,* D. R. *slot.*) That's all there is to it [p. 53].

American poster for John Huston's *The Maltese Falcon* (1941).

In James A. Michener's novel *The Drifters* (1971), the film is mentioned by Harvey Holt in connection to his war experience:

> The tape had come to one of the songs that Holt liked most, 'Sentimental Journey,' 'I heard this for the first time in camp in Iwo Jima. I was a kid eighteen. I wondered if I would ever know any beautiful women like the ones I had seen singing with the big bands. You know, Helen Forrest and Martha Tilton. Or Bea Wain, for that matter.' He hesitated. 'It wasn't that I was afraid of being killed. I'd seen so many men get it that I knew this

was pure chance. Like **Humphrey Bogart** when he was fighting **Sydney Greenstreet** for the statue' [p. 466].

Andrew J. Fenady's *The Man with Bogart's Face* (1977) is a humorous story of a man who—through plastic surgery and determination—assumes the persona and profession of two famous characters created by Dashiell Hammett and Raymond Chandler and portrayed on the screen by Humphrey Bogart. He also assumes a new name—Sam Marlow—to disperse any doubts about his provenience. Since the book is also a mystery with a series of allusions and similarities to the genre's classics, the idea of a treasure is also borrowed, with the Eyes of Alexander modeled on the "Falcon," and the mere mention of Hammett's novel is a clear reference to its film version as well—through the multiple associations of Bogart and the protagonist. Below is one of the conclusive scenes involving Sam and Gena, his client and lover:

"Sam, how did you go with Bumbera?"
"He's pretty mad. Not as mad as Hacksaw. But they'll get over it. What're you reading?"
"One of the books from your library. It's called *The Maltese Falcon*. I'd never read it before."
"The girl goes to jail in the end."
"Sam – I never meant for anyone to get hurt" [p. 241].

In Fenady's sequel, *The Secret of Sam Marlow* (1980), the film is mentioned again in a long passage about a double feature matinee that Sam Marlow attends in the Encore Theatre. One paragraph refers to Huston's classic:

Raft did turn down *The Maltese Falcon* and doesn't deny that. His agents advised him that there was a clause in his contract stipulating he didn't have to star in a remake. *The Maltese Falcon* had already been filmed twice. Once in 1931 with Ricardo Cortez as **Sam Spade** and again under the title *Satan Met a Lady* with Warren William as the detective and Bette Davis in the female lead. The agents also advised Raft that **Huston** had never directed a feature before and all the women in the movie—**Mary Astor**, **Gladys George**, and **Lee Patrick**— were too old and nobody would come to see the picture. Bad advice [pp. 141-142].

In Stuart M. Kaminsky's *Bullet for a Star* (1977), there is a scene where private investigator Peters talks with Peter Lorre about his next movie; a comparison between the first and the third (upcoming) movie version of Dashiell Hammett's prime novel is made:

> "Mind if I ask what this office is for?" I said, looking back.
> "Not at all," said Lorre. "It's one of the first sets for a movie I'm doing. Should be shooting it in the near future. It's called *The Maltese Falcon*."
> "I saw the picture," I said. With Ricardo Cortez. Why make again?"
> "A very clever young writer named **John Huston** has convinced the studio to do it with him directing. I don't know if it's a good idea or not, but it has an excellent role for me."
> "This is something more like a detective's office than the one in the Cortez picture," I said, "but it's still a palace compared to mine" [p. 61].

The next excerpt shows Peters trying to find Harry Beaumont, a blackmail and murder suspect, on the set of *High Sierra*:

> "I wonder if you can tell me where to find Harry Beaumont?"
> **Cowan** looked at me quizzically.

"I'm a private investigator working for the studio on something rather confidential," I whispered.

"Really," he said, "I'm playing a private detective in my next picture."

We walked for a few minutes, and he said he was going to play Miles Archer, Sam Spade's partner in *The Maltese Falcon*. It wasn't a big role, but it was a good one [p. 87].

Then Peters tries to reach Hatch, the Warner Brothers gate guard who killed two men (including his own son, actor Harry Beaumont), in order to prevent him from killing Errol Flynn:

> Slowly and quietly I moved over and through the equipment and darkness to the office of **Spade and Archer**. There was a light on in the set, a single small light, but enough for me to see **Spade**'s desk.
>
> There was a man at the desk opening a drawer. As silently as I could, I moved to the sofa in Spade's office and sat, just as I was about to collapse. The man at the desk was so busy that he didn't hear me.
>
> He was my killer and I greeted him. We were old friends.
>
> "Hello, Hatch," I said softly [p. 143].

Instead of revealing the secret, Peters offers the best, somewhat illegal, solution to protect the innocent, and Errol Flynn, who comes to rescue when Hatch is about to shoot Peters, agrees to go with it:

> "Thanks," said Hatch.
>
> I asked Flynn to take the money and leave the torn negative in **Spade and Archer's** wastebasket. He supported me with one hand, and Hatch walked in front of us [p. 149].

Four Hollywood Legends

In another novel by Stuart Kaminsky, *Think Fast, Mr. Peters* (1987), Peters introduces himself to Peter Lorre, the major character in the book:

> **Peter Lorre** looked younger than I had expected. His face was an unlined as a five-year-old's and his slightly closed eyes and straight black hair falling over his forehead added to the childlike look.
> "Yes?" he asked.
> "My name's Peters," I said. "Toby Peters. We met a couple of years ago over at Warner Brothers. You were on a break on the *Maltese Falcon* set playing cards."
> He smiled up at me politely and took a drag at his cigarette but it was clear that he didn't remember me [p. 26].

As the conversation continues, Hammett's foremost detective is mentioned by name:

> "I've never met a real private detective before," **Lorre** said. "You'd think that after playing a Japanese detective and confronting **Sam Spade** I would have gone out of my way to meet someone of your profession but I never considered such first-hand knowledge necessary" [p. 28].

A lot of Peter Lorre impersonators show up for an audition at the Hitching Post Theater:

> The line of actors and would-be actors went on doing Mr. Moto, the killer in *M* in fake and real German and, God help me, doing **Joel Cairo** in *The Maltese Falcon* [p. 176]

The protagonist in Stuart Kaminsky's mystery *Lieberman's Thief* (1995) is police detective Abe Lieberman. Here is a scene relating his conversation with two murder suspects (the guilty woman in the book behaves in the same way as the guilty dame in Huston's movie):

> Betty Franklin's eyes had closed when Harvey Rozier spoke. She wrung her hands, actually wrung her hands. Lieberman couldn't remember seeing someone do that since **Mary Astor** in <u>The Maltese Falcon</u> [p. 185].

Humphrey Bogart (Sam Spade), Peter Lorre (Joel Cairo), Mary Astor (Brigid O'Shaughnessy) and Sydney Greenstreet (Casper Gutman) in a scene from John Huston's *The Maltese Falcon* (1941).

A reference to Bogart and an allusion to *The Maltese Falcon* were found in Robert B. Parker's mystery *The Judas Goat* (1978), in a scene where Spenser (the narrator/private eye) and Hawk (his associate) tail a young terrorist, Katherine Caldwell:

> I used to know a guy named Shelley Walden when I was with the cops who would get spotted tailing a guy through a rock concert. I never knew why he was so bad at it. He had

a small, innocuous look about him and he wasn't clumsy, but he couldn't keep out of sight. I tried to run this stakeout like Shelley would have.

If she spotted me when she went by she didn't let on. I knew Hawk was somewhere behind her but I didn't see him. When she went into her apartment I walked casually across the street and leaned on a lamppost and took out a newspaper and started to read it. That would have been Shelley's style. The old **Bogart** movies where he pulls back the curtain and there's a guy under a lamppost reading a newspaper. I figured she'd see that someone had been rummaging in her apartment and that would get her nervous. It did [pp. 96-97].

An allusion to the film appears also in Elmore Leonard's *LaBrava* (1983), during a chat between LaBrava, Jeanie and Maurice:

Jean got up to turn the lights on. It was her show, she had insisted on turning them off. Maurice, trapped in his recliner, extended his empty glass, and LaBrava got up to make drinks, remembering a **Bogart** line to the question, **"How do you like your brandy?" Bogart**, as **Sam Spade: "In a glass."** In that frame of mind after seeing Jean's picture [p. 255].

A chat between two major characters, Chili and Elaine, is also the context of a reference to the film which appears in another novel by Elmore Leonard, *Be Cool* (1999):

Elaine said, "You're going too fast."
Chili said, "What do you want me to do, learn to stutter?"
And Elaine said, "**Bogart** in *The Maltese Falcon*. That's the best line in the picture. Everything else is expository" [p. 156].

There is a funny reference to the movie in Joseph Wambaugh's police novel *The Secrets of Harry Bright* (1985). Harlan Penrod, the gay houseboy of millionaire Victor Watson's property, is helping two Hollywood cops, Sidney Blackpool and Otto Stringer, with the investigation of the murder of Jack Watson, the millionaire's son.

> Harlan Penrod was already waiting when at 6:30 P.M. they pulled up in front of the Watson home.
> "**Sam Spade** Junior," Otto said.
> Harlan wasn't dressed like **Sam Spade** but he did have a Burberry trenchcoat over his shoulder and it wasn't raining. Otto didn't comment, but rolled his eyes at Sidney Blackpool who, like Otto, was still dressed as a resort golfer [p. 157].

> "Well, it's all we got to start with," Sidney Blackpool said, as he drove the Toyota toward Palm Canyon Drive.
> "They didn't start with much in ***The Maltese Falcon***," Harlan remarked [p. 158].

> Five minutes later, the detectives and Harlan Penrod were in the hotel office with the night manager who was digging through the employee files, saying, "Well, we shouldn't have too much trouble, Sergeant. Hotel employees in this town have to have police identification cards. We send our people to the police when we hire them and they get their pictures and fingerprints taken. Everyone who might have access to rooms, that is: maids, bellmen, even valet parkers."
> "Our first *real* lead!" Harlan said, looking as though he'd just found the elusive **bird from Malta** [pp. 159-160].

A poignant reference to the film, commenting on some artistically uncalled-for practices, is made by a cop with acting aspirations in Wambaugh's *Finnegan's Week* (1993):

> "Okay," he said. "And maybe I can talk you into voting for Ross. He's the only thing that can save our country."
>
> "You think America's that desperate, huh?"
>
> "Absolutely," Fin said. The watershed event that signaled the imminent collapse of American civilization was the colorization of **_The Maltese Falcon_**" [p. 194].

In another police novel by Wambaugh, *Hollywood Crows* (2008), Hollywood Nate Weiss, in a conversation with two other cops, surfing enthusiasts Jetsam and Flotsam, makes a sarcastic allusion to a famous line from John Huston's classic movie, a line that is ranked #14 on the American Film Institute's List of the Top 100 Movie Quotes (2005):

> "Come to Malibu, bro," Jetsam said. "Maybe you'll have a vision too and find your true self."
>
> Nate stood up then, nodded, and said, "Am I ever glad I came here today. All this time I've been buying lottery tickets and stalking talent agents, and the answer was right before my eyes. I just couldn't see it till you sea slugs dialed me in. It all comes down to a surfboard. **The stuff that dreams are made of!**" [pp. 216-217]

There are a few references to Bogart and his films in Roderick Thorp's mystery *Rainbow Drive* (1986). *The Big Sleep* and *The Treasure of the Sierra Madre* are mentioned early in the book, *The Maltese Falcon* toward the end. The quoted passage shows policeman Mike Gallagher from Hollywood Division in action:

He still didn't know what he was going to do. At the top of the escalator, on the left, was a camera shop, empty, with two kids in open-collared, white dress shirts behind the counter. As one approached, Mike flashed his badge. "All right if I use your phone?"

"Something tells me I'll have a richer, happier life if you do."

Mike smiled in spite of himself. "It's not bad." He started to dial Kennedy and stopped. "Let me have some privacy."

The kid raised his hands and backed up, grinning. He had blue eyes and thick, dark, close-cropped hair. **"Go ahead,"** he said through his teeth, **"I won't stop you."**

Mike was listening to Kennedy's telephone ring when he realized that the kid had been doing **Bogart** in ***The Maltese Falcon***, when **Peter Lorre** as **Joel Cairo** had insisted on searching **Bogey**'s office. Kennedy said hello and Mike identified himself as he turned his forefinger and thumb into a gun and shot the kid, who doubled up with laughter [pp. 349-350].

In Thomas Pynchon's novel *Vineland* (1990), an allusion to this and a few other films appears in a passage describing the Noir Center in lower Hollywood:

Noir Canter here had an upscale mineral-water boutique called Bubble Indemnity, plus The Lounge Good Buy patio furniture outlet, **The Mall Tease Falcon**, which sold perfume and cosmetics, and a New York-style deli, The Lady 'n' the Lox [p. 326].

A brief allusion to the film appears in Dennis Lehane's *A Drink Before the War* (1994), in a scene where private investigators Patrick Kenzie and Angela Gennaro exchange ideas in their office:

We spent a good ten minutes not coming up with an answer to that one.

"Shit!" Angie said at the end of those ten minutes.

"Apt," I said. "Not too helpful though."

She lit a cigarette, placed her feet up on the desk, and stared at the ceiling. More **Sam Spade** than I'd ever be. She said, "What do we know about Jenna?"

"She's dead" [p. 169].

In *The Burglar Who Thought He Was Bogart* (1995) by Lawrence Block, the film is naturally mentioned several times. Along with Bogart and *Casablanca*, it is praised in one of many chats Bernie has with his friend Carolyn:

"After all," I said, it is **Bogart**. He's always interesting to watch even in some dog of a movie you never heard of. And when it's a picture I've seen a dozen times, well, who can get tired of *Casablanca* or *The Maltese Falcon*? They get better every time you see them" [p. 79].

That conversation is continued many pages later, but this time it is tied more closely with the events in Block's novel:

"Bern," she said gently, "don't you think that's a job for the police?"

"No, it's not. It's my job."

"How do you figure that?"

"**When your partner is killed,**" I said, "**you have to do something about. Maybe he wasn't much good and maybe you didn't like him much, but that doesn't matter. He was your partner, and you're supposed to do something about it.**"

"Gee," she said. "I never thought of it that way. I have to admit, Bern, when you put it like that it sounds so forceful and clear-cut that it's hard to argue with you."

"Why, thank you, Carolyn."

"You're welcome. '**He was your partner, and you're supposed to do something about it.**' I'll have to remember that. She looked sharply at me. "Wait a minute. Who said that?"

"I did," I said. "Just a minute ago."

"Yeah, but **Sam Spade** said it first. In *The Maltese Falcon*, when **Miles Archer** is murdered. Maybe it's not word for word, but that's exactly what he said."

I thought about it. "You know," I said, I think you're right."

She reached out a hand, laid it on top of mine. "Bern," she said, "do you want to know what I think? I think you've been going to too many movies."

"Maybe."

"You're starting to get yourself mixed up with **Humphrey Bogart**," she said, "and that can be dangerous. The line's a great one, but it doesn't fit the situation."

"It doesn't?"

"Hugo Candlemas wasn't your partner. If he was anything, he was an employer. He hired you to steal that portfolio" [pp. 159-160].

It is worth mentioning that the same line from Huston's classic is quoted once again in the book on p. 193, this time as a punchline in the relationship between Bernie and Mr. Charles Weeks.

A somewhat remote, and sarcastic, allusion to the film's character, and the actor who portrayed him in the most convincing and charismatic way, takes place in Stephen Humphrey Bogart's mystery *Play It Again* (1995), when the narrator shows matrimonial detective R.J. Brooks (a character modeled on the author himself) in action:

R.J. shifted an unlit cigar to the other side of his mouth and stepped off the fence onto a wall bracket that secured the drainpipe. He almost lost his footing as a face peered at him from a window—his reflection. **Sam Spade**, my ass. He looked more like a cat burglar with delusions of grandeur. He had his fictional mentor's devil streak, all right, and the jutting jaw line, but his eyes were cobalt blue, like his mother's; and although he could talk as tough as his crusty old man when the chips were down, he usually tried to reason his way out of scrapes before resorting to rough stuff [p. 19].

George Baxt's *The Humphrey Bogart Murder Case* (1995) contains an overwhelming number of references to the movie. It is mentioned for the first time in a chat between mother and daughter:

Only a few days ago Mayo told Evelyn that **Bogie** was rehearsing another George Raft reject, *The Maltese Falcon* [p. 6].

Then, in a conversation between the daughter, Mayo, and her husband, Bogart:

He exploded. "I am not having an affair with **Mary Astor**! She's fully booked!"
Mayo rubbed the cigarette out in an ashtray and then jumped to her feet, fists clenched. "Don't think I know what this whole *Maltese Falcon* movie is all about?"
"Sure you do. You read the script."
"*I* should be playing Astor's part!"
"Now come on, Slugger. Let's not go through that routine again" [p. 11].

Some more information is provided by the narrator on the following page:

But the film [*The Wagons Roll at Night*] did well, and now he was rehearsing **The Maltese Falcon**, the third version of Dashiell Hammett's successful novel. True, he was second or maybe third or even fourth choice for the part, and it would be the directorial debut of John Huston, who had also written the script. And a new director and an old story could be a fatal combination. **Bogart** believed in Huston, who was a friend, a poker-playing buddy, and a fellow skirt-chaser [p. 12].

At **Warners**, he found **Mary Astor** reading the script of **The Maltese Falcon** aloud to herself in one of the conference rooms occasionally used for rehearsals. Most directors rehearsed on the set and then ordered a take, but **John Huston** was taking no chances with his first film. The script was an ensemble piece, and he had pleaded with **Jack Warner** for extended rehearsal time [p. 24].

An introduction between Sydney Greenstreet and Bogart is related in the following scene:

"Ah, **Bogie**. At last!" He and **Bogart** shook hands. "I'm **Sidney** [misspelled] **Greenstreet**, the villain of the piece. I believe in a previous incarnation the part was written for a woman. Perhaps I'll use a subtle touch of effeminacy."

Mary Astor said, "You'll have a hard time getting that past the censors."

Said **Bogart**, "Sure. It'll pass. It's already in the script. **Huston**'s used it the way **Hammett** wrote it in the book. The kid traveling with **Greenstreet** and **Joel Cairo**, **Lorre**'s part. He's obviously **Gutman**'s lover."

"But he's a killer!" exclaimed **Mary**.

"But aren't most lovers?" asked **Greenstreet** [pp. 26-27].

More background information:

At **Warner Brothers**, the rehearsal had still not gotten underway. **Bogie**, **Mary Astor**, and Sidney Greenstreet were joined by director **John Huston**, son of **Walter Huston**, and three other important cast members, **Peter Lorre**, **Gladys George**, and **Elisha Cook Jr**. Miss **George** was looking painfully thin, and **Bogie** wondered if she was hooked on drugs as the rumor had it [p. 33].

Bogart, Police Detective Herbert Villon and Hazel Dickson, the cop's girlfriend and a gossip columnist, discuss the case and its similarities to the film:

Hazel said, "So that's what a cornucopia looks like. I wouldn't give it as a wedding gift to a couple I disliked."

"It's sealed," said **Bogart**. He and Villon looked at each other. "You know, Herb, at the end of *The Maltese Falcon* when they find what they really think is the bird they're looking for, it turns out to be a fake [p. 165].

In Michael Walsh's *As Time Goes By* (1998), it is clearly Hammett's original novel that is mentioned in a scene where Rick meets Ilsa in a Prague restaurant during their secret mission. In fact, it is the Czech name of the place that leads the narrator to allude to the famous detective story—undoubtedly due to Bogart's leading role in its movie version—offering, at the same time, an interesting twist:

He was meeting her at a small restaurant called U Maltézských Rytířů, an ancient barrel-shaped cellar just across the river from his hotel in the Malta Strana that had once been, or so the legend had it, a hospice of the Knights of Malta. Rick didn't know much about Malta except what he had read in *The Maltese Falcon* by **Hammett**, more than a decade ago, when he still had time to read. Despite himself, he was letting his mind drift back over the past when he spotted Ilsa walking down the stairs and into the dining room. Right away, he was back in the present [p. 285].

Michael Malone's short story "Invitation to the Ball" (1998) is a murder mystery, or rather two mysteries separated by about a hundred years and tied by the character of Mattie, a beautiful woman who turns out to be a con artist (real name: Madeline Gart) instrumental in the demise of her rich husband, Chanler Swaine. An allusion to John Huston's classic film takes place during the introduction of Mattie to Chanler by Mark Tolar, Mattie's lover and accomplice in the scheme:

> Mattie laughed. "Why do men think just because a woman's capable of adultery, she's capable of murder too?"
> "You gotta admit, Tug," Mark grinned as they followed Mattie and Chanler into the club dining room. "Mattie's right for him. Like **Bogie** says, **the stuff that dreams are made of**. Look at Channie!" Chanler was talking to the young woman with an animation unusual for him. She nodded, smiling as they went [p. 260].

Michael Malone's novel *The Four Corners of the Sky* (2009), brimming with movie references, mentions five Bogart films, and *The Maltese Falcon* is alluded to in two separate places. The first excerpt is the final part of a telephone conversation between Sam Peregrine, protagonist Annie's aunt and adoptive mother, and Miami cop Daniel Hart, who—although he is chasing Annie's con artist father—is going to end up marrying the criminal's daughter.

> "My brother is not a criminal and my name's Peregrine. Sam Peregrine."

The pleasant voice returned. "Ah, Sam, like Grace Kelly, Tracy Samantha Lord."

"What?"

"*High Society. Philadelphia Story.*"

Sam gripped the phone. "You like old movies?"

"Love 'em."

"Wait a minute. How old are you, Mr. Hart?"

"Twenty-six."

"That's a good age. Don't waste it."

"**Stuff that dreams are made of.**" He hung up.

Sam recounted the conversation. "If I'd known he was a cop, I wouldn't have told him about St. Louis" [pp. 168-169].

The second passage, including a paraphrase of the same quotation (or, rather, its original version of whose provenience—Shakespeare's *The Tempest*—Sam is clearly unaware), relates another telephone conversation. This time Sam's interlocutor is Raffy Rook, a Cuban con man working with Annie's father, Jack:

That was her dream now that Annie and Jack had reconnected. To bring Jack back home.

"'**We are such stuff that dreams are made on**,' Sam," Raffy told her.

"Oh yes, **_The Maltese Falcon_**," she replied, to his confusion, for he knew as little about the movies as she knew of Shakespeare [p. 397].

Bill Crider's book *We'll Always Have Murder: A Humphrey Bogart Mystery* (2001) has two references to the film. Both take place during conversations between private eye Terry Scott (the narrator) and Humphrey Bogart, who is helping the former with the investigation. In the second excerpt, the person tied is mobster Charlie O.'s henchman Mike.

"You're stubborn, too," **Bogart** said. "You can take that however you want."

I sat down in a chair and said, "You play your cards too close to the vest, **Bogart**, and I'm not sure why. Maybe you do have something to hide. Or maybe you were just trying to give me to Congreve. What do you think this is—*The Maltese Falcon*? Do you think because somebody was killed, we have to give the cops a fall guy? Do you figure me for **Wilmer**? If you do, you're wrong all the way. We don't have to give anybody to the cops, because we didn't kill anybody. And I'm damned sure not **Wilmer**" [pp. 148-149].

"I didn't think so. Charlie O. would never trust a gunsel like you."

When I called him a gunsel, he strained so hard that he almost broke loose. However, we'd used our neckties to bind his hands and feet, and they were made of silk. He didn't stand a chance.

"You think he knows what *gunsel* mean?" **Bogart** asked.

"Maybe he saw *The Maltese Falcon*," I said. "I'm pretty sure he didn't read the book."

"Hardly anybody who saw the movie or read the book knew, either." **Bogart** grinned. "I'll bet Bob Carroll would know" [p. 217].

A reference to the film appears in Martha Sherrill's *My Last Movie Star* (2002) as part of a dream experienced by journalist Clementine James (the book's narrator):

I was walking down a street. It was dark, foggy. It was Ed's street, in the Eighties on the East Side, and in my dream I stepped inside the shining lobby of his apartment building and found **Mary Astor** standing at the door to the elevator looking at me with the meek, intense stare of hers. It was that ***Maltese Falcon*** gaze; she seemed guilty of something. She was wearing a felt hat. She smiled thinly. She handed me a copy of her book [p. 213].

In Terrill Lee Lankford's Hollywood novel *Earthquake Weather* (2004), the film's screenplay is mentioned as one of many remarkable achievements of the past which the book's protagonist and narrator, young "creative executive" Mark Hayes, rightly admires:

> A pile of screenplays on the coffee table had become a sea of screenplays on the floor. These weren't screenplays that I was covering for my job, but two dozen or so of my favorite works of the past, scripts I could pick up and read whenever I needed to cleanse my palate after covering something particularly noxious. *Chinatown, Lawrence of Arabia, The Long Goodbye, Sunset Boulevard, Body Heat, Cutter and Bone, Some Like It Hot,* ***The Maltese Falcon****, Paper Moon, My Bodyguard, The Last Detail, North by Northwest:* there wasn't a loser among them. That stack of scripts was my compass. I referred to it whenever I felt myself getting lost in the morass of works by lesser word slingers. Reading screenplays of that quality made me feel like Salieri in a roomful of Mozarts [p. 22].

A reference to Bogart and the film was also found in *Hey There (You with the Gun in Your Hand)* (2008), one of the Rat Pack mysteries by Robert J. Randisi. In the quoted passage, Frank Sinatra is revealing his two new acting projects (which did materialize in reality) to Eddie Gianelli, the narrator/protagonist, pit boss at the Sands Casino in Las Vegas:

> "That came out last year," he said, handing me the glass. "I'm thinking of makin' a movie out of it. I'd play the lead, Tony

Rome, a Miami private eye. There's another one, too, came out last month. It's called *The Lady in Cement*."

"Sounds interesting," I said. Any parts for the other guys?"

"Naw," Frank said, sitting in an armchair across from me. "Well, maybe Nick Conte." I just need somebody to play the cop. Nick looks like a cop."

"Wait a minute," I said. " 'Tony Rome' is the P.I.? And the author is Anthony Rome?"

"It's a pen name," Frank said. "The guy's real name is Marvin Albert. I've talked to him once, already." He leaned forward, picked the book up, looked at it, put it down and said, "It's gonna be good. Kinda like **The Maltese Falcon** my buddy **Bogey** made, only in this one the guy's *ex*-partner is killed, and there's no Falcon, just a pin, a piece of jewelry. It's gonna be good," he said again [p. 9-10].

The most recent allusion to the picture was found in Robert K. Tanenbaum's mystery *Betrayed* (2010), in a scene where Todd Fielding, a not-so-tough private eye, is waiting for a client's visit in his office:

Fielding glanced around the office in anticipation of the arrival of his beautiful client. He tossed and old pizza box off the couch, unlatched the door, leaving it open just a crack, and then half sat, half leaned against the front of the desk with what he though was his finest **Humphrey-Bogart**-as-**Sam-Spade** pose. He was concentrating on the type of smile he should employ—*friendly, suggestive, but not gloating, I think*—so at first, he didn't grasp the enormity of the situation [p. 293].

All Through the Night **(1942).** Vincent Sherman's light espionage comedy is referenced in two mysteries. In Stuart Kaminsky's *Think Fast, Mr.*

Peters (1987), private eye Peters, trying to locate Peter Lorre, talks to Mike Durban, a Warner Brothers security guy:

> "**Peter Lorre,**" I said. "Is he working a picture with you?" Or do you have a number on him?"
> "He was here back at Christmas. Something like ***All Through the Night***, but I hear he's over at Universal on something. Nice man. Took Bill for eight bucks and some change at poker one noon before he took off. Nice man though. You want a number, you say?" [p. 19]

In Marcia Muller's *Trophies and Dead Things* (1990), Sharon McCone, staff investigator at All Souls Legal Cooperative, is asked by Hank Zahn, senior partner of the company, to help him with clearing up the apartment of a client who has been murdered. In the process, McCone comes across some film books, videos and movie memorabilia:

> Finally on the bottom shelf I found a few volumes on film: guides to serials, crime movies, and *film noir*, plus a few books about old TV series such as "Perry Mason." I boxed them all, then turned to the videotapes.
> There were hundreds of them, stacked against the wall behind the TV: **Bogart, Tracy** and Hepburn, Barbara Stanwyck, William Powell, Cary Grant; a full run of Charlie Chans and Mr. Motos and the Topper series; westerns, comedies, drama. Not one of them had been produced later than the mid-fifties. It made me wonder if Hilderly hadn't been trying to pretend the sixties and seventies and eighties had never happened.
> After I boxed the tapes, I looked around for what Hank had called "the other stuff." There wasn't much of it. A water-stained lobby card for a **Bogart** movie called *All Through the Night*, framed but with badly cracked glass [p. 12].

The Big Shot **(1942).** Directed by Lewis Seiler, this minor crime drama is one of Bogart's many films referenced in Lawrence Block's *The Burglar Who Thought He Was Bogart* (1995). The movie is summarized in an extensive passage offered by the narrator as part of his report on the Bogart retrospective:

> In **_The Big Shot_**, **Humphrey Bogart** plays **Duke Berne**, a career criminal who's trying to go straight because a fourth felony conviction will put him in prison for life. But he can't stay away from it, and goes in on the planning of an armored-car heist. The head of the gang is a crooked lawyer, and the lawyer's wife is **Bogart**'s old sweetheart. *She* won't let **Bogie** risk his life, and keeps him from participating in the robbery by holding him in his room at gunpoint. A witness picks him out of a mug book anyway, which strikes me as questionable police work, but that's my professional point of view showing.
>
> The lawyer's jealous, and screws up **Bogie**'s alibi, and he winds up going down for the count. There's a prison break, and **Bogie** gets away, but one thing after another goes wrong, until finally **Bogie** hunts down the rat lawyer and kills him. He's shot, though, and dies in the hospital.
>
> That was the first picture, and I'd never seen it before. I got caught up in it, too, and maybe that was why I didn't eat much of the popcorn, or it may have been because I'd been munching peanuts at the Bum Rap [pp. 343-344].

Casablanca **(1942/43).** Completed and premiered in 1942 and running for Academy Awards against movies released in 1943 (in which competition it won three Oscars—for best picture, director and script—and four additional nominations), Bogart's seal of fame and, at the same time, one of the biggest hits of all time, *Casablanca* is referenced in countless literary works, out of which over one hundred have been collected for this publication. Because the film is also the most represented item on the American Film Institute's List of the Top 100 Movie Quotes (with six lines), I have decided to arrange the references here first according to specific quotations, and, after that, according to the usually applied chronological criterion.

The #5 quote ("Here's looking at you, kid.") was found in a few works, the first one of which is Steve Shagan's *City of Angels* (1975). The following passage, relating a conversation between two cops, is a good example of an indirect praise of Bogart:

> Louis was standing at the window. Phil said, 'Hiya, pal.' He crossed to the steel cabinet, opened the top drawer, took out the Bushmills and two glasses, and came around behind his desk. 'Come on, Louis, have a drink.' Phil filled the glasses halfway. Louis sat in the battered chair in front of the desk. He picked up his glass and, imitating **Bogart**, said, **'Here's looking at you, sweetheart.'**
>
> Phil drank with him and said, 'Don't make fun of my hero."
> 'He was my hero, too,' Louis said. 'Him and John Garfield.'
> Phil looked surprised. 'You're too young to know Garfield.'
> 'The late show' [p. 74].

In Andrew J. Fenady's already quoted novel *The Man with Bogart's Face* (1977), there is also a brief allusion to *Casablanca*—through this very well-known line, here uttered by Sam Marlow to Gena Anastas (whom he chose not to send to jail):

> "Sam."
> "Yeah?"
> She lifted the sheet that covered her and was naked before him.
> "Shut up, Sam, and come to bed."

Humphrey Bogart as Rick Blaine and Ingrid Bergman as Ilsa Lund in a scene from Michael Curtiz's *Casablanca* (1942/3).

He lifted the glass of brandy toward his lips. "Yeah – **here's looking at you, kid**" [p. 243].

The line is quoted twice in Robert B. Parker's mystery *The Judas Goat* (1978), both times during a romantic scene between Spenser and Susan:

I poured some champagne in her glass and mine. I put the bottle down, raised the glass and said, **"Here's looking at you, kid"** [p. 165]

"Did William Powell take Myrna Loy to a Dunkin' Donut shop?"

"He didn't know enough," I said. I raised my coffee cup toward her.

She said, **"Here's looking at you, kid."**

I said, "How did you know what I was going to say?"

"Lucky guess," she said [p. 169].

John Updike alludes to the film in several works. His short story "Tristan and Iseult" tells about a patient of a dental hygienist and his reaction to the surroundings, the description of which gives a pretext to allude to a couple of Bogey's films and two of his co-stars:

Heaven here was a ceiling of acoustical tiles, perforated irregularly in order to entertain trapped eyes like his. The angelic music was from an "easy listening" station—every third tune, it seemed to him, that nonsensical croon about **Key Largo, Bogie** and **Bacall, here's looking at you, kid, have it all** [pp. 148-149].

Christina Skye, in her novel *Going Overboard* (2001), quotes three famous lines from *Casablanca*.

Two of them, #5 and #43 on the List, are quoted during an animated discussion between the book's two major characters, Carly Sullivan and Ford McKay, just before they decide to watch the movie together:

"No way." Carly slid the tape back into its slot. "It you want classic, there's only one choice. Great plot, an amazing cast, and music that lingers." She moved along the alphabetized rows, selected a tape, and waved it at McKay. "The best of the best, as fresh today as it was in 1942. Won three Oscars. **'Here's looking at you, kid.'** "

" **'We'll always have Paris,'** " McKay countered. "Okay, **Bogie** works for me. Take a seat. Archer gave me full operating instructions. He even made us food."

When Carly was comfortable in the front center seat, he flicked a remote and sent the room into darkness. Without a word he handed her a bowl of popcorn drowning in decadent swirls of butter, then eased her back against his shoulder as stirring strains of music filled the room.

In minutes Carly was swept away to **Rick**'s smoky café in war-torn **Casablanca** [p. 137].

A paraphrase of the #5 quotation appears in James Scott Bell's novel *Try Darkness* (2008), where narrator/lawyer Ty Buchanan investigates a murder of a young woman/single mother, and, in checking the background of one of the suspects, TV celebrity Todd McLarty, he gets invited to the studio:

The taping I'd been invited to was at the **Warner Bros. Studios** in Burbank. They shot *Casablanca* here. Now it was home to *Men in Pants*.

Here's looking at crud, kid [p. 205].

Michael Malone's *Time's Witness* (2002) is a mystery set in Hillston, North Carolina, and narrated by police chief Cuddy Mangum. The two references to the film (quoting two lines, #32 and #5 on the List) take place on two different occasions—one during an exchange between two cops, the other one, mentioning the movie several times, at the conclusion of a cops' party:

On my way out, I passed Sergeant Fisher with a chest-high stack of arrest files. "Any luck, Sergeant?"

He scratched at gray stubble on his black cheek. "Nothing but alibis tighter'n a bank on a dollar. Looks like most of these Klanners work Saturday jobs."

"Well, just keep on **rounding up the usual suspects**. Like the movie says. You know, I met this girl, thought I looked like **Humphrey Bogart**."

He kept going. "Can't help you. White people all look alike to me" [p. 120].

Nora said. "My God, look at that TV! They said it'd be *big*, but—"

Rolling the console toward the wall, Justin called over his shoulder, "Quick, plug it in. *__Casablanca__*'s on Channel Seven at 11:30. Or are you feeling tired, Cuddy?"

"*__Casablanca__*'s what we were going to say we came over to watch."

I said, "Fine, I've seen it."

Justin started yanking jacks out of my old TV set. "Oh, you love *__Casablanca__*. You always cry at the noble stuff. **'Here's mud in your eye, kid.'**"

"Oh, Jesus!" I plugged the VCR unit into the new model. **"'Here's looking at you, kid. *Here's looking at you, kid!*'"**

"See!" Justin grinned. "He loves the movie [p. 531].

The #20 quote ("Louis, I think this is the beginning of a beautiful friendship.") is also very popular among writers. A paraphrase to it was found in Robert Ludlum's novel *The Matlock Paper* (1973), in a scene where the book's protagonist, Professor James Matlock, intentionally makes Mr. and Mrs. Beeson "high":

Once on the first plateau, it wasn't too hard for Matlock to imitate his companions and then convince Beeson to go for another dosage.

"Where's the almighty discretion, Doctor?" Chuckled Beeson, sitting on the floor in front of the couch, reaching occasionally for one of his wife's legs.

"You're better friends than I thought you were."

"Just **the** *beginning* **of a beautiful,** *beautiful* **friendship.**" The young wife slowly reclined on the couch and giggled. She seemed to writhe and put her right hand on her husband's head, pushing his hair forward.

Beeson laughed with less control than he had shown earlier and rose from the floor. "I'll get the magic then."

When Beeson walked into his study, Matlock watched his wife. There was no mistaking her action. She looked at Matlock, opened her mouth slowly, and pushed her tongue out at him. Matlock realized that one of Seasonal's side effects was showing. As was most of Virginia Beeson [p. 68].

In Lawrence Block's shorty story "Some Days You Get the Bear," included in the collection of the same name (1993), a reference to the film (including two quoted lines, #32 and #20) becomes a part of the description of a special day (when he finds a threatening addendum to a sign over the cash register of a hardware store) in the life of the protagonist, a movie and book reviewer:

It happened finally on an otherwise unremarkable day. He'd spent the whole day working on a review of a biography (***Sydney Greenstreet****: The Untold Story*), having a lot of trouble getting it the way he wanted it. He had dinner alone at the Greek place down the street and rented the video of **_Casablanca_**, sipping jug wine and reciting the lines along with the actors. The wine and the film ran out together [p. 189].

> "Hey, there," he said. "Time to **round up the usual suspects**. Can't sleep either, can you, big fellow?"
>
> He took the bear and got back into bed with it. He felt a little foolish, but he also felt oddly comforted. And he felt a little foolish *about* feeling comforted, but that didn't banish the comfort.
>
> With his eyes closed, he saw **Bogart** clap **Claude Rains** on the back. **"This could be the start of a beautiful friendship," Bogart** said.
>
> And before he could begin to figure it all out, Paul fell asleep [p. 190].

The last line is quoted again (or somewhat misquoted again) in Block's Bernie Rhodenbarr mystery *The Burglar Who Traded Ted Williams* (1994)—as usual to illustrate the "one hand washes the other" relationship:

> "And he'd have hated to part with those dimes."
>
> "Now he won't have to. But he'd better figure on keeping them out of sight for a year or two."
>
> "I'll make sure he knows that." A slow smile spread on his face. "What's the line from ***Casablanca***? At the very end, **Bogart** to **Claude Rains**."
>
> **"This could be the start of a beautiful friendship."**
>
> "Indeed. And a profitable one. Get some sleep, Bernie. I've a feeling the next few days are going to be busy ones" [p. 206].

The film is referenced by Block again, with the same line, in *Small Town* (2003), in a passage where the book's protagonist, writer John Blair

Creighton, is hooked by the movie on television on the night preceding an important (for him) auction. The same line as above is quoted here; this time more correctly:

> He'd been up late the night before, fooling around on the computer; then channel surfing. AMC was running **_Casablanca_**, and he told himself he'd just watch it for a few minutes, but he'd never been able to turn that film off and couldn't this time, either. He got misty when they played "La Marseillaise," the way he always did, and he was still there and still paying attention when **Bogart** told **Claude Rains** that it looked like **the beginning of a beautiful friendship** [p. 189].

In Stuart Woods's *L.A. Times* (1993), there are three allusions to the movie. The first one, focused on the description of the main character's apartment, is mentioned in the same excerpt as one including Gary Cooper's *For Whom the Bell Tolls* (and presented there). The second one appears when studio head Leo Goldman explains some of his policies to his newly hired producer, Michael Vincent:

> I swear to God. What makes a blockbuster a blockbuster changes so quickly that it scares me to death. My idea of a nightmare is a movie—any kind of movie—that goes into production without a perfect script. I know, I know, **_Casablanca_** started without a finished script, but that's a very wild exception [p. 80].

The last excerpt, not mentioning the title but using the very well-known quotation, is a part of a conversation between a cop and a sociopath producer. Policeman Ricardo Rivera accepts a well-paid position at the studio in return for not revealing Michael Vincent's involvement in a murder:

"That sounds good," Rivera said, sticking out his hand. "As **Bogart** said to **Claude Rains, I think this could be the beginning of a beautiful friendship**" [p. 188].

In his political thriller *Mounting Fears* (2009), Stuart Woods gets back to the latter quotation, which is an illustration of some writers' inevitable tendency to repeat themselves. However, while the context of the reference is somewhat different, the irony of its content is the same in both novels as both the men speaking the line end up being murdered by the addressees of the quote. Here, Ned Partain, a journalist of the *National Inquisitor*, is thrilled to have found somebody in Panama City that can help him locate the man he is looking for, ex-CIA assassin Teddy Fay. Little does he know that the person he is speaking to is the same one he is interested in finding (obviously using a fake name, Larry Toms).

"Let me buy you a drink," Teddy replied, signaling the bartender.
"If you could help me find this guy, there would be a reward," Ned said. "My paper is very generous."
Teddy looked at the photo again. "You know, I think I've seen this guy right here in Panama City."
"Larry, my friend," Ned said, "**this could be the beginning of a beautiful friendship**, as **Claude Rains** said to **Bogey**."
"You know," Teddy said, "it might be at that" [p. 138].

Another paraphrase of the line appears in Bill Crider's *We'll Always Have Murder: A Humphrey Bogart Mystery* (2001), as part of the conclusive passage, where the two protagonists, Scott and Bogart, say goodbye to each other and go their separate ways:

Bogart grinned again.

"I'll see you around, kid," he said.

He turned and walked away. With his raincoat and hat on, he looked just as he had at the end of **_Casablanca_** when he and **Claude Rains** had walked away from the camera. I wondered what had happened to **Rick** and **Louis Renault** after that night, whether they'd really had that **beautiful friendship**.

Probably not, I thought, and I drove my new, slightly damaged, Packard down the rain-washed street [pp. 219-220].

Loren D. Estleman's *Something Borrowed, Something Black* (2002), a mystery about the last job of a retired and newly married hit man, Peter Macklin, contains one insignificant reference to the film and one quotation of the famous line from the movie. The circumstances of the quotation are rather unusual, because the line is said by Laurie, the wife of the protagonist, to a gangster's henchman, who is supposed to "take care" of her during the time Macklin is away to perform the job:

Their meals came. She waited impatiently while the waiter set everything out and determined that nothing else was needed. When he was gone—she didn't know if it was anger at Peter that made her say it, or delight at the absurdity of her companion—she leaned forward and said, "Abilene, **I think this is the beginning of a beautiful friendship**."

He let his jaw slide. She laughed at him [p. 60].

One more reference to that particular line was found in James Scott Bell's mystery *Final Witness* (1999). Russian hit man Grigory Viazmitin, known as The Man and hiding behind the name Fred Stefanos, terrorizes student lawyer Rachel Ybarra, who works for the L.A. prosecutor. Here is one of their more friendly conversations, which takes place before Viazmitin reveals his intentions:

"I know about you."

"Yes?" Rachel answered, not knowing exactly what he meant.

"Yes I do. You're part of a Christian group at the university."

"That's right."

"And you take that nonsense seriously?"

"Yes."

"Here at the close of the twentieth century? Someone with your obvious intelligence? Why do you cling to it?"

"I believe in it."

"Like a child believes in Santa Claus?"

"No. Like someone who trusts his parents."

"You intrigue me."

"You intrigue *me*."

Stefanos issued a short laugh. "Then we intrigue each other. **This should be the start of a beautiful friendship**" [p. 130].

One of the very first references to *Casablanca* was found in Sue Kaufman's novel *Diary of a Mad Housewife* (1967), at the conclusion of a scene where the book's narrator, Tina, and her husband Jonathan go out to eat and to a movie. The passage includes a line that is ranked #28 on the list ("Play it again, Sam. Play 'As Time Goes By.'"):

> We went to an Italian movie in a theater near the restaurant. It was our Italian evening. It was only 10:15, much too early to go home, where we'd only have to be alone with each other. The movie was terrible, even though Mastroianni had the male lead, and I came out with a splitting headache. When we got home we found Mrs. Prinz stretched out asleep on the couch in the den, her skirt hiked way up, while across the room a rerun of **Casablanca** flickered on the TV. **Bergman** was saying to **Bogart**, "**Kiss me! Kiss me as if it were the last**

time!" and while that epic embrace took place, Mrs. Prinz rolled over and let out a volley of snores, completely drowning out **"As Time Goes By"** [p. 66].

An allusion to the film, through the lyrics (or their paraphrase) of the famous song, appears also in Herman Raucher's novel *Summer of '42* (1971). The song is sung by the fifteen-year-old protagonist, Hermie, which is understandable as he is a regular patron at the local movie theater; however, in the summer of 1942 it was still a few months before the film was released. Thus, even though Hermie may have been familiar with the song—it was much older than the movie—the references to Rick and Sam are definitely anachronistic. Anyway:

In the shower and out he sang **"As Time Goes By"** as only he could.

You must remember this, a kiss is still a kiss;
A guy is just a guy.
The fundamental things apply
As time flies by.

Play it again, Sam.

And when two lovers, woo, they still say
I love you,
A guy is just a guy.
The world will always welcome lovers,
As time flies by.

Sing it again, **Rick**.

Moonlight and love songs, jealousy and hate,

Hearts full of passion, lovers need a mate;

His sister was knocking at the door. Fuck her. Big finish.

Woman needs man and man must have
a date . . .
On that you can rely [pp. 128-129].

Humphrey Bogart and Dooley Wilson (Sam) in a scene from Michael Curtiz's
Casablanca (1942/3).

Casablanca as a whole is artistically paraphrased by one of the movie's most devoted admirers, Woody Allen, in his play whose title itself, *Play It Again, Sam* (1968), is an allusion to a very well-known melodramatic scene from Curtiz's classic. To make things absolutely clear, Allen names one of his main characters 'Bogart' and mentions *Casablanca* twice (pp. 7 and 55), but the specific references to this film are not as interesting as those to three other Bogart pictures—*The Maltese Falcon*, *To Have and Have Not* and *The African Queen*—and the quotations referring to those can be found in the respective places of the book.

A complex reference to the film, with a few lines quoted, appears in Steve Shagan's novel *Save the Tiger* (1972). In the following passage the book's protagonist, Harry Stoner, talks to his business partner, Phil Greene:

> "Phil, you remember **_Casablanca_**? This scene . . . Rick's club. Closed . . . four in the morning . . . Dooley Wilson's playing that song. **_Bogie_** is sitting at the bar, smoking, watching his reflection in the mirror. Everything's been building to this moment; then **Bergman** floats in behind **_Bogie_**. Christ, you can almost smell her perfume . . . She gets close . . . she whispers, **'Hello, Rick.' _Bogie_** doesn't move. Keeps smoking. **Bergman** moves a little closer. She says, **'You remember Paris, Rick?'** . . . Now he takes the cigarette out of his mouth; never looks at her. He says, **'Yeah, I remember Paris. You wore blue and the Germans wore grey.'"**
>
> Phil said, "I don't think it happened that way. I think they met downstairs, in the casino."
>
> With a tinge of anger, Harry replied, "Well, that's the way I remember it." Then he softened. "Who wrote those things and where did they go? What happened to them?"
>
> Phil nodded. "I know what you mean" [p. 135].

Then an allusion is made to the movie when the narrator relates Harry reminiscing about the war:

> It was **Casablanca**, late November 1942. But there was no **Rick's**, no **Bogart**, no **Bergman**; and they weren't playing **"As Time Goes By."** Harry was on a last pass. They were moving out to Tunisia in twenty-four hours. He was wandering through the narrow Moorish streets, not far from the waterfront and sipping cheap Algerian wine from a bottle wrapped in an empty Red Cross doughnut bag [p. 221].

Lawrence Block mentions *Casablanca* in several of his novels. The context of the reference in *The Burglar Who Painted Like Mondrian* (1983), where two of the famous lines are mentioned, is bookstore owner/burglar Bernie Rhodenbarr making a phone call from the scene of murder to Ray Kirschmann, a pragmatic and slightly corrupt cop:

> "What I figured. Where are you?"
> "In the belly of the beast. Listen, I've got a job for you, Ray."
> I already got a job, remember? I'm a police officer."
> "That's not a job, it's a license to steal. What's that line in *Casablanca*?"
> " **'Play it again, Sam.'** "
> "Actually he never says it exactly that way, It's **'Play it, Sam,'** or **'Play the song, Sam,'** or some variation like that, but he never says, **'Play it again, Sam.'** "
> "That's really fascinating, Bern."
> "But that wasn't the line I meant. **'Round up the usual suspects.'** *That's* the line I meant. And that's what I want you to do" [p. 257].

In his mystery *When the Sacred Ginmill Closes* (1986), Block quotes some well-known lines from the film again in a scene that, naturally, takes place in a bar. The book's narrator/protagonist, ex-cop Matt Scudder, asks bartender Billie to replay a record which he finds fascinating probably due to its philosophical and decadent lyrics:

"**Play that again**," I said.
"Wait. There's more."

*And so we'll drink the final toast
That never can be spoken:
Here's to the heart that is wise enough
To know when it's better off broken*

He said, "Well?"
"I'd like to hear it again."
" '**Play it again, Sam. You played it for her, you can play it for me. I can take it if she can.**' Isn't it great?"
"**Play it again**, will you?" [p. 117]

A rather unusual reference to the same scene in the film, somewhat sarcastic and self-pitying on the narrator's part due to a sad farewell to a beauty speaking with a foreign accent, appears toward the end of Block's *The Burglar Who Thought He Was Bogart* (1995):

Play the song, I thought. Where the hell was **Dooley Wilson** when you needed him?
"And then you came along," she said, and reached out a hand to touch my face, and smiled that smile that was sad and wise and rueful. "And I fell in love with you, Bear-naard."
"And once we were together..."

"Once we were together we had to be apart. I could be with you once and keep you as a memory to warm me all my life, Bear-naard. But if I had been with you a second time I would have wanted to stay forever."

"And yet you came here tonight."

"Yes."

"Where do you go from here, Ilona?"

"To Anatruria. We leave tomorrow. There's a night flight from JFK."

"And the two of you will be on it."

"Yes."

"I'll miss you, sweetheart."

"Oh, Bear-naard . . ." [pp. 346-447].

In one more quotation coming from a book by Block, this one, *Hit Parade* (2006), featuring hit man John Keller, the author goes back to the line he quoted over twenty years ago in quite a different kind of novel. The quotation is triggered by a sign with the actor's name used by a driver waiting for the protagonist outside the Detroit Airport:

> He hadn't checked a bag, so he hoisted his carry-on and walked straight to where the drivers were waiting and scanned the signs for one bearing the name **BOGART**. He didn't know why they'd picked that name, which could only invite unnecessary conversational overtures from strangers, twisted-lip imitations: **"Play it again, Sam. You played it for her, now you can play it for me."** But that was their choice, **Bogart**, and there'd been no time to talk them out of it, let alone to rent a car and drive to Detroit.
>
> Time, Dot had told him, was of the essence. So here he was, fresh off a bumpy flight, and looking for a sign with **BOGART** on it. He found it right off the bat, and when his eyes moved

from the sign to the man who was holding it, the man was looking right back at him, with an expression on his face that Keller found hard to read.

He was a short, stocky guy, who looked as though he spent a lot of time at the gym, lifting heavy objects. He said, "**Mr. Bogart**? Right this way, sir" [pp. 129-130].

In Thomas Pynchon's novel *Vineland* (1990), the famous song from the film is mentioned as part of the ad hoc repertoire of a band:

> The band was a twist-era puttogether, two saxes, two guitars, piano, and rhythm. From somewhere mildew-prone and unvisited, the hotel staff had brought piles of old-time Combo-Ork arrangements of pop standards, including Thanatoid favorites like "Who's Sorry Now?," "I Gotta Right to Sing the Blues," "Don't Get Around Much Anymore," and the perennially requested **"As Time Goes By"** [p. 225].

Stephen Humphrey Bogart, in his mystery *Play It Again* (1995), alludes to *Casablanca* in three different ways. First, he uses a memorable line from the film as the title of his novel (and refers to it again on page 66), then he calls the protagonist's cat Ilsa (pages 42-46), and, finally, he inserts the movie's famous vocabulary in an old letter from the protagonist's father to his mother (clearly modeled on Bogart and Bacall):

> Some of the boys upstairs at the studio are very worried about you having this kid. They say it will kill your career, and do a lot of damage to mine. You don't want that, any more than I do, **kiddo**.
>
> . . .
>
> How about it, **kid**? [p. 88]

Stephen Bogart does exactly the same in his second R.J. Brooks mystery, *The Remake: As Time Goes By* (1997), where the private investigator, still having the cat named Ilsa (p. 166), tries to stop the shooting of a remake of a famous 1940s' film (starring his deceased parents) and solves a series of murders of people associated with the movie project by a maniac who claims he has identical intentions as R.J. By calling the classic movie *As Time Goes By*, Stephen Bogart makes it a clear allusion to *Casablanca* despite the fact that it was Ingrid Bergman, not Lauren Bacall, that appeared opposite his (the author's and his protagonist's) father in the original film. Here are some excerpts from the novel that further support such an interpretation of the allusion:

> He gave his dry hacking little laugh again and lurched sideways. "***As Time Goes By*** means something, Brooks. Something special, pure, *good*. Not just to me, but to all of us, our whole culture. Millions of people, all around the world. Because it stood for something. It was a rallying cry for the last great moral battleground—and the good guys *won*. It was important, goddammit—maybe one of five or six movies in history that are really *important*" [p. 206].

The above opinion was expressed by Ed Minch, one of the suspects due to his open attack on the idea of the remake. The second excerpt relates a conversation between R.J., Henry Portillo (R.J.'s "Uncle" Hank) and Mary Kelley (the daughter of the remake's producer and her ex-husband, William Kelley, the avenging murderer):

> Portillo said nothing for a moment, then, "What did you have in mind?"
> "A press release from the studio. We get them to announce they're shooting a new version of the airport scene from ***As Time Goes By***."

"Oh, God, I *love* that scene," Mary gushed.

R.J. grinned. "Everybody loves that scene, kid. That's why I picked it. Maximum instant publicity. Everybody will be on hand for the shoot, from Janine Wright on down. And if I'm a killer trying to get Janine Wright, I'll be there, too" [p. 259].

The last quotation is the description of the event announced in the previous excerpt:

> Three huge wind machines couched in an arc around the set. Nosing in between them was the front end of an airplane, what looked like a DC-3. The nose and windshield were there, perched above the soundstage. Behind them was nothing, no tail section, no wings. The airplane was chopped off weirdly in accordance with movie-making logic; if the shot only shows the nose, you don't need the whole damn plane.
>
> R.J. knew what the set-up meant. From the other machines and technicians standing around, R.J. could see they were all set to re-create the famous scene. Wind, rain, and heartache.
>
> R.J. had seen the original maybe a hundred times. His mother and father facing each other on the runway, the wind and rain whipping around them, the fate of the world hanging in the balance, as they said good-bye. He still couldn't watch it without getting a lump in his throat, and he wasn't the only one. It was maybe the most famous movie scene of all time [pp. 268-269].

In *What We Do for Love* (1997), an original book written and illustrated by Ilene Beckerman, the film is mentioned as an inspiration of one of the narrator/protagonist's fantasies:

> I'd be **Ingrid Bergman** with <u>**Bogart**</u> in <u>*Casablanca*</u> and **Sam** would be at the piano playing **"As Time Goes By."** Then I'd get on the plane with **Paul Henreid** [p. 54].

Michael Walsh's novel *As Time Goes By* (1998) is an acknowledged allusion, in fact a sequel and a prequel (due to a number of flashbacks set in various places between 1931 and 1938) to the extremely popular movie. It borrows the names of the main characters—Rick, Ilsa, Victor Laszlo, Louis Renault and Sam Waters—from the film, and it makes the provenience absolutely unambiguous by means of the subtitle (A novel of *Casablanca*) and the title itself, referring to the song written by Herman Hupfeld in 1931 and made internationally famous by the film. The song, which plays such a dramatic role in the movie, is mentioned inside the book four more times, the first and second times during a scene in London, then twice in the flashbacks set in New York in 1935 (before and after the death of Lois, the woman Rick loved deeply):

> He smoked and drank for a time in silence. Sam continued to improvise at the keyboard. Unconsciously he let his fingers slide over **"As Time Goes By."**
> "Knock it off," objected Rick, but Sam interrupted him quickly.
>
> . . .
>
> "Tell you the truth, I don't much care for it. But it was always one of your favorites."
> "And hers," Rick said. "So cut it out."
> "I hear you, Mr. Rick," said Sam, continuing to play, "but I ain't listening to you."
> "You're fired," said Rick.
> "I believe that when you give me that damn raise you been promisin' me," said Sam.

"He'll never fire you, Sam," said Ilsa. "You play **'As Time Goes By'** too beautifully for him ever to do that."

Once more she came to him out of the darkness, an angel in white, as she had done in his café in Casablanca [pp. 149-150].

Sam started to play his signature tune, and the crowd applauded. The tinkling of the ivories was the only sound in the joint. Nobody was allowed to talk when Sam Waters played. Especially when he played **"As Time Goes By"** [p. 301].

His last view of the club was the awning, and the poster in front, the poster he had printed up just the other day, which advertised "Tonight in person. Lunceford and **Hupfield (misspelled)**, together again. Performing your favorite songs, including the hit, **'As Time Goes By'**! With Sam Waters at the piano" [p. 334].

Another song tied to *Casablanca*, "Knock on Wood," is referenced in one of the earlier flashbacks set in New York in 1932:

He [Rick as the runner of the Tootsie-Wootsie Club for gangster Solomon Horowitz] kept the songwriters paid and mostly sober. He made sure the pianists knew which songs were the most popular. Once in a while he even let a customer sing along, especially when that colored boy Sam Waters was at the keyboard playing **"Knock on Wood."** He kept his gat in his trousers or in the pocket of his dinner jacket just as smooth as silk and nobody the wiser, not even the cops who came there to drink and ogle [pp. 221-222].

Bill Crider's novel *We'll Always Have Murder* (2001) includes three allusions to the film, and one of them has already been presented. Here are the other two, which, in fact, take place earlier in the book than the other one.

The first one is made—consciously and purposefully—by television actor Slappy Coville when he meets Bogart (and Scott, the narrator) in Chasen's:

> When he saw us headed toward him, he launched into one of the worst **Bogart** impersonations I'd ever heard.
>
> "Look who's here," he said. " **'Play it Sam. If she can stand it, I can. Play it.'**"
>
> There was a busty blonde in the circular booth beside him, and she laughed loudly. Either she thought he was wonderful or she'd had far too much to drink [p. 114].

A paraphrase of another line from the movie is used by Bogart himself when he addresses stuntman Stoney Randall with justified accusations:

> "I always thought I could trust you, Stoney," he said, "but you really let me down when you killed Burleson. Especially when you tried to frame me for it. You should have known that **I play the sap for nobody**" [p. 181].

Ace Atkins's novel *Robert B. Parker's Lullaby* (2012) includes many witty conversations between friends and associates Spenser and Hawk. Here is one with an allusion to the film by means of the famous line:

> "Wired?" Hawk said.
>
> "They got more bugs in that place than a bait shop."
>
> "Bait shop do have lots of bugs."
>
> "We pull this off, maybe you and I go fishing."
>
> "*'We'll take the car and drive all night,'*" Hawk said. "*'We'll get drunk.'*"
>
> **"Play it, Sam."**
>
> **"Yes-suh, Mr. Rick."**
>
> Hawk began to whistle **"As Time Goes By"** [p. 289].

The #32 quote ("Round up the usual suspects.") was found in three books. It is a part of a passage at the very end of Joseph Wambaugh's novel *The Glitter Dome* (1981), in a relaxed conversation among the cops. The quoted line is a response to the Weasel's quotation from *Gone with the Wind*:

> "**Round up the usual suspects**," said the Ferret, sounding just like **Claude Rains** [p. 298].

In George Baxt's mystery *The Greta Garbo Murder Case* (1992), the line is used by Police Detective Herbert Villon when he talks to some Hollywood people (working on a fictitious project, *Joan the Magnificent*) about the first victim:

> Lisa complimented her on the smart suit she was wearing. Alysia thanked her. Haines in his smart-aleck way asked the lawmen, "You guys got any hot leads?"
> Villon folded his arms and said, "We're **rounding up the usual suspects**" [p. 133].

Three movies starring Bogart are referenced in Christina Skye's novel *Going Overboard* (2001). Two lines from *Casablanca* have already been presented. The other line from the film is quoted by McKay about a dozen pages later, when he, a Navy SEAL on a secret mission, and Nigel Brandon, the governor-general of Santa Marina, discuss the measures that need to be taken in order to counteract serious crimes:

> "Since I can't do anything more here, I'm returning to Bridgetown. Daphne and I are staying in a friend's town house there for the moment."
> "Well guarded, I hope."
> "You may be certain of that. Crime seems to be becoming a problem everywhere."

"Then **round up the usual suspects**," Mc Kay suggested, recalling the worldly police chief in <u>*Casablanca*</u>. "If your normal criminal elements aren't involved, they might know who is" [p. 149].

The #43 quote ("We'll always have Paris.") appears in several works. It was found in Lawrence Block's *The Burglar Who Thought He Was Bogart* (1995), where *Casablanca* is mentioned several times. Most of the references are included in quotations presented under other movies. Below is a part of the dialogue between Bernie Rhodenbarr and Ilona Markova, taking place in Bernie's bookstore and leading to the couple's first date, after they discovered their shared fascination with Bogart films:

"Oh, yes. Very romantic." A knowing smile played on those lips. "Take me out this evening."
"Wherever you say."
"Not to Paris," she said. "That would be romantic, wouldn't it? If we were to meet like this, and tonight we flew to Paris. But I don't want you to take me to Paris, not yet."
"Paris can wait."
"Yes," she said. "**We'll always have Paris**. Tonight you may take me to the movies" [p. 62].

In James Scott Bell's already cited mystery *Final Witness* (1999), both the movie and the line are mentioned during a telephone conversation between the male protagonist, FBI agent Jeff Bunnell, and a New York reporter whom he asks for help:

A moment later he heard her voice. "Hello?" Amy Alford said.
"Is this New York's most famous reporter?" Jeff asked.
"Jeff?"

"Surprised?"

"Surprised enough to hang up."

"Don't."

"Give me one god reason."

"Paris?"

A pause. "What are you talking about?"

"It's romantic."

"Then I haven't got time."

"Remember in *__Casablanca__*? **__Bogie__** tells **Ingrid Bergman**, **'We'll always have Paris.'** The pleasant memories" [p. 251].

A reference to the same line takes place in Bell's *No Legal Grounds* (2007), but this time it is the villain who uses the quotation. The protagonist is Sam Trask, a middle-aged lawyer who—in addition to facing problems with his teenage daughter—has to find a way to stop the harassment by an old sociopathic college friend, Nicky Oberlin. Here is one of their conversations that takes place during one of their few relatively civil encounters:

"Nicky, let me just put it this way: I really appreciate the fact that you looked me up after all these years, that you wanted to get together and all that, but right now I just don't have time to fit in any new social relationships. I've got family things going on and law things going on; you know how it is. So let's just leave it at that, and remember the old times."

Pause. "You mean **we'll always have Paris**?"

"What was that?"

"You know, that line from *__Casablanca__*? **Bogart** says it to **Bergman** just before he dumps her on the plane."

"Oh, yeah. Right."

"Well, sorry, Sam. I'm not getting on the plane" [pp. 50-51].

Robert K. Tanenbaum's mystery *Betrayed* (2010) contains three references to the film, all connected dramatically and all quoting the same line. The first one takes place in a scene where newsstand vendor Dirty Warren has a chat with Michelle Oakley, a beautiful woman he would subsequently be accused of murdering:

> Seeing his discomfiture, Michelle touched his arm. "Sorry, I shouldn't have put you on the spot. I'm sure you have a lovely wife."
> Warren shook his head. "No . . . whoo . . . no wife."
> "A girlfriend, then? I mean, since me," she said with a giggle.
> Again the head shake, but he managed a smile. "No, not since you. But **we'll always have Paris.**"
> Michelle guffawed loudly enough that several people nearby looked over with distaste. "Still a movie buff, eh?" she said. I remember when we used to go to the movies; you would know everything there was about the film. I always found that so fascinating. So let's see if I can get this. The film is <u>*Casablanca*</u>, and <u>**Humphrey Bogart**</u>'s character . . . um . . ."
> "**Rick Blaine**," Warren said helpfully.
> "Right, **Rick**, but don't tell me the rest. **Rick** says **'We'll always have Paris'** to <u>**Ingrid Bergman**</u>'s character, **Ilsa Lund**" [pp. 118-119].

The second reference appears in a passage where Marlene Ciampi, Judge's Karp's wife trying to solve the murder case, reads a note sent to Warren (now in jail) by Michelle.

> It had been addressed to **Rick Blaine**, and the return address said it had been sent by **Ilsa Lund**. *Why are those names familiar?* She'd looked up at a poster from the movie <u>*Casablanca*</u>, starring <u>**Humphrey Bogart**</u> and **Ingrid Bergman**. *As **Rick Blaine** and*

Ilsa Lund. She'd smiled. *That was a nice touch, Michelle. Now let's see what you sent Warren* [p. 320].

Finally, the movie is mentioned in the book's closing scene, where Warren, now cleared of all charges, sets a trap for the real killer but gives up the revenge at the last moment:

> As he'd waited in the park with Grale, Booger, and the Mole People, Warren had imagined the blood of Williams spilling on the ground. But now he sighed and shook his head. "No, but thank you, David," he said. "He's all ... whoop ... yours."
> With that, he turned away. He was no killer, and hic cat, Brando, was waiting for him. *Maybe I'll watch* **Casablanca** *again*, he thought as a shooting star crossed the sky. "**We'll always have Paris**," he said aloud, and walked into the night [p. 359].

Jodi Picoult's psychological thriller *House Rules* (2010) tells a story about the troubled family of Jacob Hunt, a teenage boy with special gifts, attributed to Asperger's syndrome, and a fascination with forensic analysis. The book contains two allusions to the film. The first one is a part of a passage in which the boy's mother (Emma, the narrator of that chapter) describes how she feels about his syndrome:

> When Jacob says things like this—truths so raw most of us won't even admit them in silence, much less speak them out loud—he seems more lucid than anyone else I know. I do not believe my son is insane. And I do not believe that his Asperger's is a disability, either. If Jacob didn't have Asperger's, he wouldn't be the same boy I love so fiercely: the one who watches **Casablanca** with me and can recite all of **Bogey**'s dialogue; the one who remembers the grocery list in his head when I've inadvertently left it sitting on the counter; the one

who never ignores me if I ask him to get my wallet out of my handbag or run upstairs to get a ream of paper for the printer [p. 273].

The second allusion, a rather non-sequitur quotation of the line from the movie, takes place during the panic and commotion caused by Jacob's 15-year-old brother Theo's escape by an airplane (as he is afraid to be suspected of murdering Jess Ogilvy). While the passage is narrated by Jacob himself, his interlocutor is lawyer Oliver Bond:

> I don't like to think of Theo on a plane; I don't like planes. I understand Bernoulli's principle, but for the love of God, no matter how physical forces are being exerted on the wings for lift, the hardware weighs a million pounds. For all intents and purposes, it should fall out of the sky.
>
> My mother takes the phone and starts to dial a long-distance number. It sounds like the notes of a game show theme song, but I can't remember which one.
>
> "Christ," Oliver says. He looks at me.
>
> I don't know how I'm supposed to respond. **"We'll always have Paris,"** I say [p. 348].

The last of the quotes making the List of the Top 100, #67 ("Of all the gin joints in all the towns in all the world, she walks into mine."), is also recognized in literature. It is an illustration of the author's déjà vu-kind of sensation related to a locale in Nelson DeMille's mystery *The General's Daughter* (1993):

> The O Club at Hadley is vaguely Spanish in architecture, perhaps Moorish, which may have been why <u>*Casablanca*</u> popped into my mind, and I quipped out of the side of my mouth, **"Of all the joints in the world, she walks into mine"** [p. 3].

In Sandra Brown's mystery *Smash Cut* (2009), there is a scene in a bar where sociopath Creighton Wheeler (who also happens to be a movie freak) tries to get acquainted with Ariel Williams, an ex-girlfriend of the man whom he hired to kill his uncle. Wheeler quotes the line from *Casablanca*, which the young woman does not recognize:

> When he reached her, he said nothing at first, letting his eyes do the talking for him. He looked into her face as though visually eating it up. Women loved that.
> Then he leaned toward her to make himself heard. "**Of all the gin joints, in all the towns, in all the world, she walks into mine.**"
> She blinked several times, looking apprehensive and confused. "Excuse me?"
> Not a **Bogie** fan. Too bad. "What would you like?"
> "Apple martini?" [p. 98].

The remaining references to *Casablanca* are presented chronologically, even though some of them may include other lines from the film, lines that did not make the list.

While most references to Bogart films in James A. Michener's novel *The Drifters* (1971) are clearly favorable, as they are made by Holt, the reference to *Casablanca* shows ambivalence, as two extreme opinions are presented:

> Later, when they said that the trouble with the American motion picture was that it lacked relevancy, Holt asked if they didn't think that sometimes the good American movies sort of summed up the feeling of a generation, and wasn't that relevant. When they asked for an example, he said, 'Like at the beginning of World War II, when we fellows were all chopped up about strange lands and death and what courage was and we saw

Humphrey Bogart mixed up with all sorts of cross currents, in a strange land, but doing what he could to save **Ingrid Bergman** ...'

One of the young men snapped his fingers and said, 'My God! He means *Casablanca*,' and a girl said, 'Like wow! That turkey.'

'It related to the mood ... well, the mood my friends were in.'

'Mr. Holt,' Gretchen explained, '*Casablanca* was a mishmash of clichés, made solely to earn a lot of money from starry-eyed young fellows like yourself. It succeeded. But don't ask us to take it seriously. The people who made it didn't.'

I expected Holt to blow his stack, but instead he sat back and listened, and after a while he heard a beauty of a statement, an insolent provocation to which he would often refer [pp. 551-552].

In Donald E. Westlake's humorous *Jimmy the Kid* (1974), the author's recurring gang of characters—Dortmunder, Kelp, May, Murch and his Mom—executes a kidnapping caper in accordance with a novel and encounter a series of unpredicted adventures due to the unusual traits of the victim, 12-year-old Jimmy Harrington. The book they model their caper on is non-existent *Child Heist* by Richard Stark (one of the author's pennames—a clear inside joke on his part). While wandering all over New Jersey in search of an abandoned farm house, the gang hides in the woods.

In the deep dark woods they huddled around the television set, for warmth as much as for entertainment. The movie now was *Captain Blood*, Errol Flynn's first picture, directed by **Michael Curtiz**, best known for *Casablanca*. Jimmy was pointing out to an uncaring audience how the obsessive close-ups of Flynn from a low-angle camera made him separate from and above the surrounding action when Kelp came blundering back through the woods to say, "Well, I finally found something. It wasn't easy out here, let me tell you."

It was now shortly after dawn; *Captain Blood* would soon be giving way to *Sunrise Semester* [p. 179].

An extensive and insightful allusion to the films with multiple references to Bogart's name appears in Tim O'Brien's Vietnam War memoir *If I Die in a Combat Zone* (1975)—as part of the author/narrator's complex reflections, later mixed with the description of one of the characters (Captain Johansen):

> Before the war, my favorite heroes had been make-believe men. Alan Ladd of *Shane*, Captain Vere, **Humphrey Bogart** as the proprietor of Café d'Americain, Frederic Henry.
>
> . . .
>
> To a man, my heroes before going to Vietnam were hard and realistic. To a man, they were removed from other men, able to climb above and gaze down at other men. **Bogie** in his office, looking down at roulette wheels and travelers.
>
> . . .
>
> To a man, my heroes were wise. Perhaps Vere was an exception. But when he allowed Billy Budd to die, he was at least seeking justice, tormented by a need for wisdom, even omniscience. But certainly Shane and **Bogart** and Henry had learned much and knew much, having gone through their special agonies.
>
> And each was courageous. **Bogie**. How could a man leave **Ingrid Bergman**, send her away, even for the most noble of causes?
>
> . . .
>
> He was blond. Heroes somehow are blond in the ideal. He had driven racing automobiles as a civilian and had a red slab of

scarred flesh as his prize. He had medals. One was for killing the Viet Cong, a Silver Star. He was like Vere, **Bogie**, Shane, and Frederic Henry, companionless among herds of other men, men lesser than he, but still sad and haunted that he was not perfect [pp. 142-144].

In John Gregory Dunne's Los Angeles novel *True Confessions* (1977), a double reference to the film appears in connection with Lois Fazenda, a murdered prostitute: first in a paragraph summarizing the information on her life, then in a passage focused on two different photographs published in the same newspapers, one of the photos owned by her father and one by Sammy Barron, a midget living in a trailer:

> Lois Fazenda also did two days as an Arab extra in *Casablanca* at **Warner Brothers**. Her only other movie work was being eaten out in a film directed and associate-produced by Timothy Mallory [p. 175].

> He had a graduation picture of Lois Fazenda wearing a white cap and gown and it was published in the *Express*, the *Times*, the *Herald*, the *Daily News*, the *Examiner* and the Long Beach *Press-Telegraph*. Sammy Barron had a photograph of Lois Fazenda in the Arab costume she wore during her two days of extra work on *Casablanca* at **Warner**'s. It was printed in the *Express*, the *Times*, the *Herald*, the *Daily News*, the *Examiner* and the Long Beach *Press-Telegraph* [pp. 176-177].

Bogart's name is mentioned along with an allusion to *Casablanca* in Robert B. Parker's mystery *The Judas Goat* (1978), in a scene where Spenser, having arrived in London, gets himself ready for the job:

I looked at myself in the mirror over the bureau. I turned up the collar. Elegant. Clean-shaven, fresh-showered, with a recent haircut. I was the image of international adventurer. I tried a couple of fast draws to make sure the shoulder holster worked right, did once perfect **Bogart** imitation at myself in the mirror, **"All right, Louis, drop the gun,"** and I was ready for action [pp. 42-43].

The film is also referenced in Andrew J. Fenady's *The Secret of Sam Marlow* (1980), in a scene set in a Santa Monica Disco Dis-Co Club, where stuntman Will Catcher offers help to Sam who, in the eyes of Walter, the manager, does not behave properly:

"This clown's trying to break up the party."

"He's a friend of mine, Walter."

An ally. The odds shrunk some. But not enough. Not in this joint abounding in bouncers.

"I don't care if he's the King of Bulgaria," Walter observed.

"Things are very bad in Bulgaria. The devil has people by the throat," Sam remarked.

"What?" Walter looked puzzled.

"That's a line from *Casablanca*. You see there was this young girl . . ."

"This guy's nuts," Walter said to Catcher. Then, to Sam, "Out!" [p. 147]

In William Goldman's psychological thriller *Control* (1982), a reference to the film—through a misunderstanding and also by way of another Ingrid Bergman picture—appears unexpectedly within an action scene:

Eric moved with silent grace onto the fifteenth floor, gun ready. No movement, nothing. The place was totally empty and totally dark—except for the light rising from the elevator shaft. It was like a glimpse of some other world, some eerie world, a **Bergman** film. He said that last to Haggerty, who was beside him now.

Haggerty nodded. "Right. Yeah. *Gaslight*. I get what you mean. I loved her in that but she was great in *Casablanca* too."

Eric decided to leave well enough alone [p. 163].

Barbara Taylor Bradford referenced *Casablanca* in a few novels. In her book *Remember* (1991), the film is mentioned in a conversation between job partners and lovers, war correspondent Nicky Wells and photographer Cleeland Donovan. The film is compared to Clark Gable's *Somewhere I'll Find You*, a movie they are watching:

> "Hey, Nick, this is really sappy," Clee muttered at one moment, looking at her from the corner of his eye.
> "I know. A lot of old movie are."
> "Not *Casablanca*, that's held up pretty well" [p. 130].

In another novel by Bradford, *Letter from a Stranger* (2012), the reason for mentioning the movie is a comparison between the cities of Casablanca and Istanbul. The protagonist, documentary filmmaker Justine Nolan, ends up in the capital of Turkey in search of her dear grandmother, whom she has believed to be dead for ten years, and has a chat with a life-long friend of her grandma, Anita:

> Sitting back in her chair, Anita paused for a moment, and then said, "Istanbul was a city of intrigue during the Second World War. Turkey was a neutral country, and the likes of dispossessed royalty and riffraff from every country gathered here—"She cut herself off, and was thoughtful for a moment, before asking, "Did you ever see that old movie, *Casablanca*?"

"Of course! It's famous, and one of my all-time favorites. Very romantic, and oh boy, **Ingrid Bergman** was gorgeous," Justine replied. "Are you trying to tell me that Istanbul was like Casablanca in those days?"

"Exactly; it was intriguing, dangerous, fascinating."

"I can just imagine" [pp. 246-247].

There are as many as four allusions to the movie in Umberto Eco's novel *Foucault's Pendulum* (1988)—all mentioning Rick's Café. The one quoted below appears in a passage relating a discussion about masonry. The reference is made by Jacopo Belbo, one of the three Garamond Press/Manutius editors (the other two being narrator Casaubon and Diotallevi), obsessed with The Plan (a conspiracy allegedly originated by the Templars and spanning over centuries) and, eventually, destroyed by its forces, at this point represented anonymously by a mysterious man calling himself Agliè:

"Masonry was like **Rick's** in **Casablanca**," Belbo said. "Which turns upside down the common view that it is a secret society."

"No, no, it's a free port, a Macao. A façade. The secret is elsewhere."

"Poor Masons."

"Progress demands its victims. But you must admit we are uncovering an immanent rationality of history" [pp. 434-435].

Joseph Wambaugh's Palm Springs mystery *Fugitive Nights* (1992) includes a reference to the picture in a scene where middle-aged drinking cop Lynn Cutter, Officer Nelson Hareem and ex-cop and private investigator Breda Burrows discuss one of the hypotheses about the suspect in a case on which they collaborate:

"Why, Nelson?" Breda asked. Not that it makes any real difference in my life. But why? I'm curious."

"The coins in the mouth were the first tipoff," Nelson said. "The old Indian at the reservation said it proves he's a man a the desert."

"I see. He couldn't be a man of the Mexican desert?"

"At first I thought so, till Lynn found this." Nelson handed a dime-sized coin to Breda. "It's Spanish. *Diez pesetas*. See the profile of King Juan Carlos? I figure the guy flew to Mexico on Iberia Airlines by way of Spain. I figure he's from Algeria, maybe Morocco. That's right near Spain."

"I know. I saw ***Casablanca***," Breda said [p. 122].

In Stuart Woods's *Strategic Moves* (2011), the screening of the film becomes just a matter-of-fact event when a group of associates from a security company named Strategic Services, including its Chairman and CEO Mike Freeman and the book's protagonist, Stone Barrington, take a trip on a C-17 plane from New York City to Baghdad:

> After they had cruised for a few minutes, Stone, Holly, and Todd Bacon followed Mike Freeman from the cockpit to the Airstream trailer, where they settled into chairs and Mike gave them a choice of movies. They settled on ***Casablanca***.
>
> . . .
>
> Stone hadn't seen the movie for years, and he enjoyed it as much as the first time he'd experienced it. When the titles came up at the end, Stone checked the moving map, which showed another ninety minutes of flight time to the Azores [p. 104].

John Updike mentioned Bogart and *Casablanca* in several works. In "Morocco" (1979), a short story about an American family of six spending an unfortunate vacation in Morocco, an allusion to the film appears as part of a description of a place, "some dusty small city, perhaps Safi" (p. 12), where the narrator (the father) runs a red light and worries about the consequences:

> We were already on the outskirts of town, and no police car was giving chase. The empty green pastures, the smooth empty road reclaimed us. Our prolonged struggle down the coast was rerun backwards. Here was the little restaurant in the meadow on the cliff. Here was the place where everybody refused to eat the liver sandwiches that the one-eyed man had cooked for us on a charcoal burner set up beside the road. Here was **Casablanca**, which didn't look at all like **the movie**. And here was Rabat [p. 13].

Updike's story "Cruise" is focused on a couple of participants in a Mediterranean cruise, Calypso and Neuman, both between divorces, who have a brief love affair. A reference to the classic movie takes place when Neuman, suffering from sea-sickness, tries to persuade Calypso not to have fun on her own:

> "Don't go to the lounge," he begged, feeble and green-faced yet sexually jealous. "There's a hard-drinking crowd up there every night. Hardened cruisers. Good-time Charlies. Tonight they're having a singalong, followed by a showing of *__Casablanca__*. Whenever they show *__Casablanca__* on one of these boats, all hell breaks loose [p. 285].

The references to the film in Updike's novel *In the Beauty of the Lilies* (1996) are a result of young Essie entertaining the idea of becoming a movie star:

> Essie would experiment in front of the mirror with putting her hair up like Rita Hayworth's in *My Gal Sal* or Bette Davis in

The Little Foxes and *Now, Voyager*, or looser like Greta Garbo's in *Two-Faced Woman* or **Ingrid Bergman**'s in <u>*Casablanca*</u> [p. 261].

"Oh, I do things like this," Essie said, and edged closer with a tilted head. She pictured **Ingrid Bergman** in <u>*Casablanca*</u>, the scene where she pulls a gun on him, in the room above Rick's with the Venetian blinds, and he says in his beautiful white tuxedo jacket, *Go ahead and shoot. You'll be doing me a favor*, and she can't and their profiles merge, her tearstained cheeks shining, her hair rimmed with light and slightly out of focus, her lips numb and thick and a little bit open, as she desperately surrenders herself in a war-torn world [p. 266].

The main character in many mysteries by Scottish writer Ian Rankin is Inspector John Rebus. In *Mortal Causes* (1994), he disappoints his girlfriend, Dr. Patience Aitken, by renting the wrong kind of movies and is subsequently challenged [p. 79] to name five out of his favorite black-and-white films. The titles come back slowly to him, but the Humphrey Bogart classic (along with a Billy Wilder old movie) hits him relatively soon, but under rather unusual circumstances:

> Rebus heard about it on the morning news. The radio came on at six twenty-five and there it was. It brought him out of bed and into his clothes. Patience was still trying to rouse herself as he placed a mug of tea on the bedside table and a kiss on her hot cheek.
> '*Ace in the Hole* and <u>*Casablanca*</u>,' he said. Then he was out of the door and into his car [p. 86].

In James W. Hall's mystery *Mean High Tide* (1994), the film and its two leading stars are mentioned more than once; the first time when Sylvie talks to Thorn:

"You ever see **_Casablanca_**, Thorn? **Humphrey Bogart, Ingrid Bergman?**

Thorn didn't answer.

"First movie I ever saw. I was only eight, nine. My mother took me. I remember her crying in the dark. Me on one side of her, my sister, Gwyneth, on the other, and Mother crying between us.

Thorn watched Sylvie's eyes cloud, watched her begin to breathe her mouth.

"We sat through that movie twice. The second time, all of us cried. **Humphrey Bogart** so bitter and hard on the outside, but turning out to be a hero after all. **Ingrid Bergman** making him love her, and turning him into a hero, making him do what she wanted him to do. All three of us sat there and cried and I decided right then, Thorn, right at that exact second that I was going to have to learn how to be a woman like that if I was going to survive in the Winchester family. I was gonna have to learn how to be **Ingrid Bergman**. That's what all three of us were thinking. How the hell do we turn Harden into **Humphrey Bogart**? [pp. 237-238]

Then when Sylvie talks to her mother:

"**_Casablanca_**," Sylvie said. "You remember that afternoon we went to see **_Casablanca_**, Mommy? How we all cried. You remember that?

. . .

"Remember how **Humphrey Bogart** turned to mush at the end of the movie? How **Ingrid Bergman** wrapped him around her finger? Is that why you cried, Mother? Thinking about Daddy, wishing you could turn him to mush. I know that's why *I* cried" [pp. 341-342].

"This was right after we saw **_Casablanca_**. You found where Daddy hid the car keys, and we drove into town when he was away. Remember? That was a big day. The day you found those keys. And after that I became Sylvie the movie maker. Sylvie the mogul. Remember? Lights, camera, action" [p. 345].

Finally, when the narrator takes over, with Sylvie and her mother being still in the same room:

> All Sylvie could do was go over it again in her mind, go over those few years before her mother left. Go over and over that time again, looking for what went wrong. Remembering the stories, trying to understand them. Trying to decipher that movie too, **_Casablanca_**, another fairy tale. Maybe that would explain.
>
> . . .
>
> But it was Sylvie's own fault. Men only accomplished the things women urged them to. If it weren't for **Ingrid Bergman**, **Humphrey Bogart** would have stayed in the same bar forever. Cold and dead inside
> [pp. 359-360].

Kinky Friedman's mystery *God Bless John Wayne* (1995) includes a reference to the movie in a scene where the book's narrator, private eye Kinky Friedman, flies to Florida to continue his investigation and ends up sitting in a Cuban bar:

> I got out the envelope and set it down on the bar next to the glass of Mount Gay. It was a moment fraught with destiny, and I was the only one in the place who realized it. In fact, I was very damn near the only one in the place. The jukebox had suddenly gone autistic on me and the bartender had taken to swatting

the occasional fly like the guy in *Casablanca* with the funny hat. Maybe it was the calm before the storm [p. 79].

A brief reference to the film and one of its supporting players appears in Jeffrey Deaver's crime novel *The Bone Collector* (1997). The excerpt is a part of a scene where and police detective Paulie Sellitto visits Lincoln Rhyme, a physically crippled criminologist, to talk about the difficult case:

> "Hit me again, Lon."
> Rhyme drank through a straw, Sellitto from a glass. Both took the smoky liquor neat. The detective sank down in the squeaky rattan chair and Rhyme decided he looked a little like **Peter Lorre** in *Casablanca* [p. 225].

Pete Hamill, in his novel *Snow in August* (1997), mentions Bogart three times and *Casablanca* once. The reference to the film, quite original, is a part of the passage where young Michael Devlin and his mother Kate finally hear, in their New York apartment after World War II, the story of the demise of Rabbi Hirsch's wife Leah. While the facts are obviously presented by Judah Hirsch, the original narrative recounts the tale as it is imagined by Michael:

> He was with Rabbi Hirsch on the steps of the synagogue as frightened Jews arrived in Prague from a place called the Sudetenland, to sleep on floors or in wagons, and together they heard Hitler ranting on the radio that the Sudetenland was German. Everybody wanted visas to America, like **Ingrid Bergman** in that movie *Casablanca*. But Michael heard them saying that the Americans didn't want any more Jews. And wondered if this was because in America there were also people who painted swastikas on synagogues [p. 236].

Four Hollywood Legends

In Elizabeth Hay's "Sayonara" (1997), a short story set in Toronto and Ottawa, narrator/protagonist Bethie shares with the reader and analyzes different stages of her strange friendship or relationship with her boss, Leonard Brooks. One of the nights after work, he invites her to his place to watch a movie:

> It was nearly midnight and everyone else had gone home. Leonard came over to my desk with his coat on. His small round face was tired and in need of a shave, but he looked keyed-up and strangely intent.
> "You have to go?" I said.
> "Yes," he said. And you have to come with me." His words were firm and deliberate. I think he had practiced that line.
> "*Casablanca*," I said, and his face fell.
> "Damn Richard." Richard had taped a note to the cafeteria wall saying the movie would be on at midnight.
>
> . . .
>
> Outside it was dark and cool. We walked under leafy trees beside large old houses that were very quiet, but not as quiet as we were. The only word in my head was *tired*. In his apartment I sat on the sofa, he took the armchair and murmured much of the dialogue: **"Maybe not today, maybe not tomorrow, but soon and for the rest of your life"** [pp. 137-138].

As many as six allusions to the film appear in Elizabeth Hay's *Garbo Laughs* (2003), a novel set in Ottawa. The Gold family, especially Harriet and her teenage children, Kenny and Jane, are fascinated with old movies and have a regular Friday night shows shared with their friends of similar interests. The first allusion, emphasizing the romantic flavor of the film, is presented in Part Four (on Tracy, under *Woman of the Year*); the last one (on p. 273) is the song "As Time Goes By," unambiguously alluding to the movie. The second one is a rarely quoted line, mentioned as part of Harriet's reflections about the effect of video:

> She was thinking about the disease of video love. How it had changed her life, perhaps more than anything else had. The ability to see Cary Grant's face, a certain look on his face, over and over again. To see Fred Astaire, the "beautiful mover," walking alone on a train platform and singing "All by Myself." To hear the intonation Kevin Kline gives "I want you." Or George Peppard gives "Will you marry me?" Or **Humphrey Bogart** gives "**The Germans wore grey, you wore blue**" [pp. 128-129].

The next excerpt is one of many letters that Harriet writes to Pauline Kael and never sends:

> *Dear Pauline,* she would write in her notebook, thinking about the insidious nature of attraction, *Who are the most memorable lovers, and why? The ones we're ashamed of, that's who and that's why. The ones we're angry at ourselves for liking. The ones who excite our resistance, which breaks down over time. The stronger the resistance, the more complete the breakdown and the more memorable the affair. Think of screen lovers. I do. Cary Grant and Ingrid Bergman in* Notorious. *Burt Lancaster and Gina Lollobrigida in* Trapeze. **Humphrey Bogart** *and* **Ingrid Bergman** *in* **Casablanca**. *Colin Firth and Jennifer Ehle in* Pride and Prejudice. *Now why are they memorable? Because the woman gets under the man's skin. She puts him off balance and makes him angry: angry to find himself attracted to someone he'd missed* [p. 150].

A debate whether *Casablanca* is a better film than *The Godfather* is stirred up by young Kenny and joined by his mother, his father (Lew) and his great aunt (Leah):

> Kenny poured Cheerios recklessly into a bowl and Harriet, standing at the stove, heard them spill from counter to floor like a broken string of pearls. "Kenny," she groaned.
>
> He picked some of them up and said, "In this magazine's top-100 list, **Casablanca** beats out *The Godfather*. Do you approve of that?"
>
> Leah came into the kitchen in her dressing gown and Harriet poured a cup of coffee. "It depends," she said. "One has a clam on the heart..."
>
> . . .
>
> Kenny tapped his mom on the shoulder. "You should have an opinion," he said. "You have to have a preference. You can't like them the same. **Casablanca**'s number two. *The Godfather*'s number three."
>
> "What's number one? Not *Citizen Kane*."
>
> "Yeah."
>
> "God."
>
> By now Lew was in the kitchen too. "But *Citizen Kane* stinks," he said, which gave Kenny his Jack Frame foothold.
>
> . . .
>
> Leah said, "They're wrong about **Casablanca**. *The Godfather* is the better movie [p. 155].

Harriet mentions the movie again in another "letter" to Pauline Kael, the one she writes on the day she hopes to meet the famous critic by her aunt's arrangement:

> *Dear Pauline, Leah claims to know you, but then she claims to know everyone. I hardly expect to see you today, but I can't help*

thinking about what I'll ask, if by some miracle you're actually here. Cary Grant, first and foremost. We'll talk about him. Then why you're impervious to the charms of **Casablanca** *but susceptible to the dubious appeal of* Tequila Sunrise [p. 231].

The film is also mentioned in Ralph Peters's thriller *The Devil's Garden* (1998). Lt. Colonel Evan Burton, in his relentless search of a senator's daughter who was kidnapped from a refugee camp in Azerbaijan, checks numerous probable places and talks to many people. The following excerpt is a part of a scene where Burton goes to Charley's American Bar and Grill in Teheran:

> The parking lot mixed old Volgas with new Volvos, Chaikas with BMWs and Jeeps, and there were enough milling bodyguards to form a platoon. A weightlifter beside the front door prissed in a burnt-orange, double-breasted suit with a lump under the left shoulder large enough to be a light artillery piece.
> "Looking good, Shamil," Burton told him. "The girls can run, but they can't hide."
> "I introduce you to good girl," Shamil told him, but Burton was already inside and heading for the stairs. He could hear the noise from the bar already—Texas laughter, North Sea crude joke, Parisian declarations, and universal bombast. Charley's was **Rick's** from *__Casablanca__* for the nineties, where polo shirts substituted for **Bogart**'s white dinner jacket and the in-crowd played oil deals for hundreds of millions instead of roulette for a handful of francs [p. 56].

Susan Isaacs, in her epic mystery *Red, White and Blue* (1998), mentions *Casablanca* twice. The reason for including the film (along with another classic) in the following passage is to describe investigative reporter Lauren Miller's first impressions after her arrival in Jackson Hole, Wyoming:

> However, she also knew that the total permanent population of the town of Jackson was five thousand.
> It was this Pop. 5,000 that stuck in Lauren's mind. A cute numeral. She'd pictured setting down on a bumpy landing strip, then walking into a rinky-dink shack with a ceiling fan, an amalgam of *Stagecoach* and **_Casablanca_** [p. 210].

The reason for the second reference is to describe Lauren's state of mind, and the similarity of the situation in the book and in the film, in view of the approaching and inevitable goodbye between her and Charlie, the man she considers her true love:

> She won't let him go the airport with her. No **_Casablanca_** scenes, she tells him. She carries her duffel bag and laptop to the Jeep. They do not kiss goodbye. They are crying. Their faces are soaked, and their noses are running. They hug. He says, "I'll love you for the rest of my life." She says, "I'll love you too, the same way" [p. 398].

In Elmore Leonard's *Be Cool* (1999), a reference to the film is made by Hy Gordon, who describes the home of NTL Records:

> "When I was at Casablanca," Hy Gordon said, "you walk in off Sunset you were in **_Casablanca_** the movie, **Rick**'s place. They had a stuffed camel in the lobby, palm trees, cane furniture, disco turned way up they piped through the offices" [p. 191].

In another novel by Leonard, *Djibouti* (2010), the film is mentioned again, this time in reference to Hollywood's unwritten policy about movie titles in a scene where Dara Barr, a documentary filmmaker, and her unusual assistant, Xavier LeBo, discuss the chances of their ambitious project about modern ship hijacking:

> "I see myself sitting in a studio exec's office," Dara said. He's got my screenplay in front of him. Or it might be a treatment."
> "What are you callin it?"
> "*Djibouti*. They'll want to change it to something else, tell me foreign words don't sell as features."
> "Like **Casablanca**, Xavier said. "They don't like *Djibouti*, go indie. Get financing from some rich guy loves you or the story" [p. 169].

Muriel Barbery's *Gourmet Rhapsody* (2000) is a novel written from various points of view and presenting the protagonist, food critic Pierre Arthens, by several different voices. A reference to *Casablanca* appears in a section narrated by ... a cat named Rick:

> Why Rick? you may ask. I myself often wondered, but as I have no words with which to formulate the question, it went unheeded until one December evening about ten years ago, when a little redheaded woman, who used to come to the house to have teas with the Maître, asked, as she gently stroked my neck, where my name had come from. (I liked her, that lady, she always had a slightly musky fumet about her, very unusual for a woman, as most of her sex are inevitably smeared with heavy, heady perfumes, lacking that little scent of venison in which a cat—a real cat—can find just what he's looking for.) He replied, "It's after the character **Rick** in **Casablanca**, he's a man who knows how to give up a woman because he would rather have his freedom." I could sense that she stiffened a little. But I could

also appreciate that aura of manly seduction with which the Maître gratified me through his offhand reply [p. 120].

In Vincent Lardo's *McNally's Alibi* (2002), an Archy McNally novel based on the character created by Lawrence Sanders, a reference to *Casablanca* is triggered by a discussion about Helmut Dantine:

> We watched *Hotel Berlin*, and it was as campy and enjoyable as I remembered it from previous screenings in New York and New Haven at cinemas that specialize in showing movies that were made before they became something called "films."
>
> I didn't tell Georgy about **Dantine**'s marriage to the oil baron's daughter, leaving ancient gossip and scandals to the master, Decimus Fortesque.
>
> Instead, I showed off and said, "Did you know that **Helmut Dantine** was in *Casablanca*?"
>
> "No."
>
> "He was." I nodded sagely. "Might have been his first film. He plays **Jan Brandel**, the Bulgarian who tries to win **Rick**'s roulette table to save his wife's virtue. A bit part for which he didn't get a credit."
>
> Georgy was impressed. "I'll rent *Casablanca* for our next night at the movies" [pp. 308-309].

An unusual reference to the film can be found in Martha Sherrill's novel *My Last Movie Star* (2002). The speaker in the quoted passage is Tallulah Bankhead, one of the deceased actresses paying a ghostly visit to the book's narrator, journalist Clementine James:

> "God, I was watching TV the other night," Tallulah continued, "and there he was, that fucking **Paul Henreid** propped up in a dinner jacket looking embalmed. He looked

one hundred. Two hundred. And he was desperately trying to be **Paul Henreid** again, as though anybody cared. He was gassing on about *Casablanca* and how it was written into his contract that **Victor Laszlo** wind up with **Ilsa** at the end, but once filming began, he started to worry. And with good reason, darling. *Nobody wants Ilsa to wind up with him instead of Bogart.* That's the beauty of the picture. But **Paul** was babbling on, oblivious of this—such a hideous bore and pompous windbag" [p. 195].

The reference to the picture in Stuart M. Kaminsky's *Mildred Pierced* (2003) appears in a scene at the Warner Brothers Studios, where private investigator Peters is looking for Joan Crawford who is in danger; a killer posing as a policeman is about to abduct her:

> There was a table and six chairs and a rack of costumes. **Michael Curtiz**, who had just been assigned *Casablanca* when I was fired, was standing with a clipboard talking to a girl in a gray suit who was taking notes. He was about my height, had a receding hairline, and was wearing a frown [pp. 208].

In Linda Barnes's Carlotta Carlyle mystery *Deep Pockets* (2004), the ex-cop/private investigator is hired by Harvard Professor Wilson Chaney to find his blackmailer and she soon realizes that the case is more complicated than it appears to be at first. When woken up by her client demanding to hear the results, she reminisces about her old naïve days:

> When I started at the Academy, I thought cops had it for ex-offenders. The whole cop attitude, I thought, reeked of that final scene in the old film *Casablanca*, the one where the French cop says, "Round up the usual suspects." The French cop knows who did it, knows who killed the nasty Nazi major, but the usual

guys are gonna get rousted, and probably one of them will wind up doing the time [p. 88].

Australian Markus Zusak's inspirational novel *I Am the Messenger* (2002) is a story of how young cabdriver Ed Kennedy's life becomes meaningful through the guidance of a series of mysterious messages that he keeps receiving. A reference to *Casablanca* (and another classic film) appears in the context of Ed's attempt at following the instructions of one of such messages:

>There's only Bell Street now, and I go there in the afternoon. Number 39 is an old, jaded cinema that you walk down into. There's an old terrace house above it, where a board sits glued to the awing. Today, the lettering says **Casablanca** 2:30 p.m. and *Some Like It Hot* 7 p.m. As you walk down, there are posters of old movies displayed in the windows. The paper is yellow on the edges, and when I walk in, there are more inside [p. 248].

There are two relatively original references to the film in Rupert Holmes's mystery *Where the Truth Lies* (2003). Both of the quoted excepts relate a dialogue between the book's narrator, young journalist O'Connor, and actor/singer Vince Collins (with Lanny Morris, another major character, mentioned in the second excerpt), even though the scenes take place in completely different stages of the story:

>As I laughed, I leaned against a brownstone wall and a piece of its plaster broke off behind me. He reached out to study to study me and ushered me to where Euclid Avenue made a T-shaped intersection with French Street.
>
>"And, uhhh, 'you must remember this,'" Vince murmured, gesturing to a lovely brownish-gray boulevard that revealed itself as we turned the corner. It was a location from **Casablanca**,

one that had been etched into my retinas years ago. The current moniker of "the Burbank Studios" had made me forget that this was still *that* Warner Bros., and this corner was where **Rick** and **Ilsa** had first been in love, in flashback, within a few steps of the Arc de Triomphe."

"I'm in the same French street where **Bogart** and **Bergman** were," I murmured.

"It's just plaster of Paris." He smiled. Oh, what a clever lad he was he, who had displayed in several of his films the same gruff masculine hurt that **Bogart** had patented a generation earlier. It made me remember that Vince was a movie star. When I was nine, I'd seen this same man embrace Lizabeth Scott and Martha Hyer on corners exactly like this. I'd stared at the screen, twenty-five-cent bag of popcorn in my hands, my eyes and palms growing damp [p. 20].

It was three twenty-four, and if Lanny was even a minute early, this wasn't going to work. I strolled back from the bathroom and found Vince staring at the view that filled his wide windows, a veritable relief map of downtown Los Angeles. He gazed thoughtfully at nothing in particular. I adopted the most casual, glib manner I could muster, considering that I wanted to make like **Peter Lorre** in *Casablanca* and beg, "**Rick**, hide me!"

"Sorry if I was long," I said breezily.

Vince half-smiled. "You never hear *men* apologizing on that account." He stepped away from the window [p. 238].

James Neel White's *I Was a P-51 Fighter Pilot in WWII* (2003) is a nonfiction book subtitled "A Collection of hard-to-find Stories about Aviation in The Piston-Powered Era 1903-1945." A reference to the film appears in Chapter 45—1942, the first Year of America's War—in a passage where the author offers some personal information about the time before he became a fighter pilot in the 352nd Fighter Group:

> I was a soda jerk. The ice cream store was furnished with white French-style wire chairs. I was told to meet the public with a smile and keep the place spotless. It was there that I acquired my love for hot-fudge sundaes. With my trusty flashlight, I ushered moviegoers down dark aisles to vacant seats in the Auditorium Theater. At that time, **Casablanca** with **Humphrey Bogart** and **Ingrid Bergman** was a hit [p. 177].

In Jeffrey Cohen's Aaron Tucker mystery *A Farewell to Legs* (2003), there are two insightful references to *Casablanca*, both made by the wisecracking protagonist, who also happens to be the narrator of the book:

> I started in on the third act of the mystery screenplay. Screenwriting, for those of you sensible enough never to have tried it, is traditionally done in three acts. And the acts are defined in no better terms than those of **Julius Epstein**, who, with his brother **Philip** and **Howard Koch**, wrote a little picture called **Casablanca** that you might have seen, so he should know.
>
> "In the first act," Epstein said, "your main character gets caught up a tree. In the second act, people come out and throw rocks at him. And in the third act, he gets down out of the tree" [p. 64].
>
> . . .
>
> I sat down at the kitchen table and slammed my fist down like **Bogart** in **Casablanca**, except I wasn't mad at **Ingrid Bergman**. Why hadn't I just gotten up the courage to go talk to those parents? Was there still time to call them on the phone and tell them to ask their kids if they were delinquents? This was probably going to lead to Anne losing her job after her contract

was up, and after all my talk about what a good friend I am and how I appreciate all she's done for Ethan, I had done nothing [pp. 228-229].

There is an extensive and beautiful reference to the film in Marisa de los Santos's *Love Walked In* (2005). First mentioned on p. 73 as one of the bullets assessing narrator/protagonist Cornelia Brown's *Date Seven*, the movie used as notation is elaborated on and quoted by Cornelia a few pages later:

> Not *Casablanca*: "The chief beauty of the duck is that it can wait," Martin told me, mid-kiss, and this is the point at which the camera turns away, maybe running over the sensual lines of the Art Deco and Modernist furniture, taking a peek at the street beneath the window, resting on the duck cooling in its pan, before switching off altogether [p. 76].

> I'm not sure why. But just afterward, before either of us had even caught our breaths, I looked at his faultless profile, at his lashes resting on his cheeks, and at the hollow at the base of his throat that is one of my favorite parts of the human anatomy as it is one of everyone's favorite parts of the human anatomy, and in the presence of all this loveliness, the words that came into my head were these: **"Who are you? And what were you before? And what did you do and what did you think?"** Except that when **Rick** says this to **Ilsa** in the Paris flashback, you know that they already know everything that matters about each other. You know because you've seen them together in **Casablanca**, seen **Rick**'s eyes when she walks into the room in her white dress, his dark, broken, longing gaze, and you've seen her tilt her face up to see him, her eyes lit with tears, and you understand that, in spite of Nazis and husbands and distance

and leave-takings and history, they are connected to each other in the deepest way and for all eternity [p. 77].

But Marin, Martin, Martin. As I lay there thinking the "Not *Casablanca* thoughts, Martin did something that pushed all of those thoughts not out of, but certainly to the back of, my mind, to a shadowed little corner where their own mothers wouldn't recognize them. Martin propped himself up on one elbow and, seriously and with great care, began to run his finger lightly over my face. He did this for a long time, and in his eyes and in his fingertip was reverence, just the sweetest kind of awe. My bones and skin turned under his touch [pp. 78-79].

A reference to the film (and a few other classics) on a diametrically different note appears later in the book, when Cornelia's life is at a different stage:

Now, Voyager, Splendor in the Grass, Dr. Zhivago, Roman Holiday, even *Casablanca*—of course, *Casablanca*. All those films in which the woman doesn't get her man, those films of yearning unsatisfied, hearts unappeased. You like them; I've liked them too. But I'll tell you what: try belonging body and soul to man who will never belong to you; see how well you like those films then [pp. 230-231].

A brief reference to the film, related to the habit of smoking, appears in another novel by Marisa de los Santos, *Falling Together* (2011). The context of the passage is a telephone call that one of the protagonists, Will Wadsworth, reluctantly makes to Sam Dehnam-Drew to inquire about a mutual friend from the past:

Samantha Dehnam-Drew made will want to smoke. Not in the same way that *Casablanca* made him want to smoke every time he saw it; chiefly because he was sitting on his back steps not seeing Samantha, just talking to her on the phone, but her luxurious, intriguingly placed inhaling pauses and her drawn-out velvet exhales sounded so satisfying that Will could feel them in his own chest [p. 168].

F. Paul Wilson's *Infernal* (2005) is a Repairman Jack novel about the mystery behind 'Lilitongue,' a device capable of "eluding all enemies." In the following passage protagonist Jack and Gia, the woman he loves and is going to have a baby with, are about to watch some films in order to forget about the imminent threat of Jack's existence in this world. Jack has taken "the Stain" from Gia after she took it from her daughter Vicky, and now he is expecting to be taken away by Lilitongue:

"So the films help distract me. They make it easier for me. But if they don't make it easier for you—"

"No-no. They distract me too. What else do you have?"

"Well, I brought *Citizen Kane*."

"We must have watched that four times in the last year. I'm tired of it."

Jack never tired of it—every time he watched it he found something new—but let it slide. He looked through the short stack of tapes.

"*Casablanca*?" he said and realized immediately what a bad choice that was.

"Dear God, no. That final good-bye scene . . . I can't handle that. Too close to home."

"All right then, I've got **Gone with the Wind**, **The Maltese Falcon**, and *To Kill a Mockingbird*."

"All too much like real life. I need some sort of fantasy—far, far from reality."

"How about *The Wizard of Oz*? That far enough?"

"Perfect. I could use—" [pp. 335-336]

Dermot McEvoy's novel *Our Lady of Greenwich Village* (2008) contains a couple of allusions to the film through the line about "rounding the usual suspects" (pp. 33 and 115), quoted by different characters, and two unambiguous references. The first one is a part of the description of Aloysius Hogan, the proprietor of The Moat, a famous bar in Greenwich Village:

> Not lacking in ego, he saw himself as **Humphrey Bogart** in *Casablanca* with the Moat being his Café Américain [p. 25].

The second one is a part of a comparison between overly pragmatic journalists and Captain Louis Renault which Wolfe Tone O'Rourke, Democratic candidate for Congress for New York's 7th Congressional District, makes during a television show:

> "I'll watch mine, if you watch yours." O'Rourke was just getting going. "As I told that imbecile over at Fox, the people own these airways, not you, not Murdoch, not General Electric. You and the rest of the journalist frauds couldn't wait to air Clinton's semen story, but when the language gets a little raunchy, you're like **Claude Rains** in *Casablanca*—'shocked, shocked'—that such filth could be going on the airways" [p. 223].

In Thomas Pynchon's mystery *Inherent Vice* (2009), an allusion to the film (and to *Mildred Pierce*, another movie directed by Michael Curtiz) appears in a scene where private eye Doc Sportello's lawyer Sauncho talks about Hollywood studios and refers to the storylines of the two Warner Brothers' classics from the 1940s:

> "It was a class-action suit waiting to happen," Sauncho protested. "If it isn't us, it'll be somebody else. And think of the potential. Every studio in town's vulnerable. Warners! What if

you could find enough pissed-off viewers who *don't* want **Laszlo and Ilsa to get on the airplane together?** Or what if they want Mildred to strangle Veda at the end, like she does in the book? A-and—" [p. 360]

In Marcia Muller's mystery *Coming Back* (2010), Ted Smalley, staff investigator Sharon McCone's gay office manager, and his significant other, Neal Osborn, include a viewing of the classic film in their plans for the evening:

> He began straightening his desk. He and Neal planned a quiet evening at home tonight. Neal's lasagna—he'd taken over the cooking when he closed his secondhand bookshop and become an online seller—and a remastered DVD of **_Casablanca_** that a friend had given them for Christmas. Domesticity—that suited them best [p.58].

Fannie Flagg's novel *I Still Dream About You* (2010) is set in Alabama, and its protagonist, Maggie Fortenberry, a seemingly happy wife and mother, has a life full of surprises. In the following scene, including a less known quotation from the film, she struggles with problems related to her job as a realtor:

> Of course, this meant another delay on her river plans, but she couldn't be selfish about it. As really inconvenient as the timing was, she realized that just like **Humphrey Bogart** said at the end of the movie **_Casablanca_**, her plans **didn't mean a hill of beans in the big scheme of things**. This was something bigger than she was. Birmingham had lost so many landmarks in the past, and if she could just find the right buyer, the delay would be well worth it. Despite herself, she couldn't help but feel a little excited. This was Crestview [pp. 157-158].

A rather unusual reference to the film was found in William Peter Blatty's mystery *Dimiter* (2010). Neurologist Dr. Moses Mayo has a modest office at Hadassah Hospital in Jerusalem, which is decorated in an original way: two quotations by Israeli humorist Ephraim Kishon are accompanied by two American pictures:

> Prominently centered between a travel poster of Carmel, California, and a photo of the fog-shrouded lovers' farewell at the end of the film **Casablanca**, the advisories steadied Mayo's walk through the world [p. 86].

Later in the book, nurse Samia Maroon talks to Mayo about a mysterious volunteer named Wilson:

> "Wouldn't hurt if he'd shave off that beard. It covers too much of his face. Oh, what's this? Does this mean something? What? Is it a line from the movie?" She was pointing to a caption in bold block letters that Mayo had inscribed beneath the **Casablanca** photo:
>
> **I NEVER MAKE PLANS THAT FAR AHEAD** [pp. 93-94]

And, further on:

> A faraway melancholy painted Mayo's eyes as for a moment he stared at the **Casablanca** photo, and from there he turned his gaze on the Europa cigarette butts bent and mounted in an ashtray on his desk, and from there to the blackness outside his window, wishing it were dawn when the U.N. Headquarters building could be seen high on a hilltop to the east in Ein

Kerem where John the Baptist had been born, thus permitting the neurologist his customary smile upon reflecting that the rise on which the building now stood was the biblical Hill of Evil Counsel [p. 100].

In a dream, policeman Sgt. Major Meral sees his friend, Mayo Moses, now dead, in the burial chamber of Christ:

> Then a grating, rumbling sound filled the crypt as large sections of the wall slid away and out of sight to reveal a narrow secret room in which Moses Mayo stood staring out at Meral. Wrapped completely in white burial cloths underneath, Mayo wore a slouch hat and a belted trench coat that resembled **Humphrey Bogart**'s in the film *Casablanca* [p. 250].

In Stephen King's novel *11/22/63* (2011), a reference to the film is a part of a lengthy passage in which the book's narrator/protagonist describes the appearance of Sadie, the woman he loves:

> There were plenty of good-looking women in the Dallas Auditorium on fight night, but Sadie got her fair share of admiring glances. She had made herself up carefully for the occasion, but even the most skillful makeup could only minimize the damage to her face, not completely hide it. Her dress helped matters considerably. It clung smoothly to her body line, and had a deep scoop neck.
>
> The brilliant stroke was a felt fedora given to her by Ellen Dockerty, when Sadie told her that I had asked her to go to the prizefight with me. The hat was an almost exact match for the one **Ingrid Bergman** wears in the final scene of *Casablanca*. With its insouciant slant, it set her face off perfectly ... and of course it slanted to the left, putting a deep triangle of shadow over her bad cheek [p. 651].

Action in the North Atlantic **(1943).** A brief reference to this engaging World War II picture, directed by Lloyd Bacon and co-starring Raymond Massey, was found in James A. Michener's novel *The Drifters* (1971), once again as a digression made by Harvey Holt:

> An assistant faces a difficult job transporting a heavy piece of equipment to an outpost: 'You saw how **Humphrey Bogart** and **Raymond Massey** took their ship to Murmansk' [p. 462].

Thank Your Lucky Stars **(1943).** Bogart is one of many Warner Brothers stars playing themselves in this entertaining compilation, which was directed by David Butler. The film is referenced in Stuart M. Kaminsky's *To Catch a Spy* (2002), a Los Angeles mystery beginning on December 31, 1943. In the following passage, narrator/protagonist Peters describes a New Year's party organized by his landlady, Mrs. Plaut:

> Anita and I had sat together, talking about high school, past spouses, her daughter, the war, and which movie we were going to see on Thursday, her day off. The choice was hers. She said she wanted to see *Thank Your Lucky Stars*, the war-effort musical with **Humphrey Bogart**, Eddie Cantor, Bette Davis, Errol Flynn, Olivia de Havilland, Ida Lupino, Dennis Morgan, and John Garfield. I told her Davis and Flynn had both been clients of mine. She was impressed [p. 18].

Sahara **(1943).** Directed by Zoltan Korda, who also co-wrote the script based on an episode in a Soviet movie, *Sahara* is a superior World War II drama, referenced in two novels and one poem. The allusions to the film in Steve Shagan's novel *Save the Tiger* (1972) are all connected and all resulting from the fact that in a bar visited by protagonist Harry Stoner and his business partner, Phil Greene, a television set is on and the movie is playing:

Bogart was making an heroic stand in the **Sahara**. All he had going for him was a tired Sherman tank and a fistful of men against a brigade of Afrika Corps Panzers. The preoccupied crowd at the bar were unaware that only **Bogie** stood between the Germans and Cairo. Except Harry. He popped some roasted peanuts in his mouth as he watched the action on the large screen from a booth not far from the television set.

Phil sipped his vodka and said, "We should check the mezzanine."

"What for? Rico's handling it. Leave him alone. It's his moment."

"You've got to heal this thing with Meyer and Rico."

But Harry was in the **Sahara**. He was with **Bogie** [pp. 134-135].

Bogart walked out of the fort toward the Panzer captain. They were both carrying white flags. The German column was in desperate need of water and they thought **Bogie** had a hidden well.

Phil was on his second Smirnoff.

Harry was walking alongside **Bogie**, carrying the BAR low; it would rise to the left when he pulled the trigger. If **Bogie** needed help, he could chop the German in half in three seconds [pp. 137-138].

Bogart and the Panzers had been temporarily done in by a cat commercial [p. 141].

An unusual reference to the film appears in the third stanza of Arthur L. Clements's poem "Why I Don't Speak Italian" (1988):

> In wartime movies my buddies and I saw
> white-skinned Germans stand firm and doomed
> while a tan Italian surrendered in the **Sahara** to **Bogart**,
> sang *Aïda*, and fixed the stalled American tank [p. 83].

In Loren D. Estleman's already mentioned novel *Jitterbugs* (1998), the picture is mentioned in a passage relating the serial killer's attempt to get away from the cops:

> At length he poked the bayonet under his belt, slating the blade backward, and clambered up onto a fender. The day's humidity had condensed into droplets on the smooth metal; the moisture seeped through his clothes, chilling him with the thrill of risk. He was **Humphrey Bogart** in *Sahara*, the lone survivor of his unit wiped out in North Africa, becoming one with his tank, prepared to sell his life dear [p. 296].

Passage to Marseille **(1944).** Bogart's first collaboration with Michael Curtiz after *Casablanca*, *Passage to Marseille* is a rewarding World War II adventure, featuring French actress Michele Morgan and some of the actors from the previous hit. In Lawrence Block's *The Burglar Who Thought He Was Bogart* (1995), the film is one of many in the Bogart retrospective:

> The first feature, *Passage to Marseille*, was made in 1944, not long after *Casablanca* and obviously inspired by it, although the credits said it was based on a book by **Nordhoff** and **Hall**. (You remember them, they wrote *Mutiny on the Bounty*.) **Bogart** plays a French journalist named **Matrac** who's on Devil's Island when the movie opens, framed for murder and serving a life sentence. He and four others escape, only to be picked up on the high seas by a French cargo ship. Of course the convicts want to go fight for France—has there ever been anyone as fiercely patriotic as a criminal in a Hollywood movie?—but France has just surrendered, and **Sydney Greenstreet** wants to turn the ship over to the Vichy government. His attempted mutiny is thwarted, and **Bogart** and his buddies join a Free French bomber squadron in England. His plane is the last to return

from a mission, and after it lands his crewmates bring him off, dead.

Well, hell, he died for a good cause, and until then he got to spend time with **Claude Rains** and **Peter Lorre** and **Helmut Dantine** and, well, all the usual suspects. It wasn't the best film he ever made, but it was a quintessential **Bogart** role, the hard-bitten cynicism shielding the pure idealist, the beautiful loser coolly victorious in defeat [p. 137].

To Have and Have Not **(1944).** An important film in Bogart's career for more than one reason, *To Have and Have Not* (co-starring Lauren Bacall, in her first screen appearance, and Walter Brennan) was scripted by Jules Furthman and William Faulkner and very loosely based on Ernest Hemingway's novel of the same name. It is also one of the two pictures Bogart made with Howard Hawks, both outstanding, both brimming with memorable scenes and both enhanced by the incredible onscreen (and off-screen) chemistry between the leading stars (Bacall also plays in the other).

An interesting, because including a twist, allusion to the film appears in Woody Allen's *Play It Again, Sam* (1968), during a conversation between Allan and Bogart. (The line quoted below in part, and in excerpts from other works in full, ranked #34 in the American Film Institute's List of the Top 100 Quotes, 2005.)

BOGART. (*Crosses* D. L.) Relationship? Where'd you learn that word? From one of those Park Avenue headshrinkers?"

ALLAN. I'm not like you. At the end of **"Casablanca,"** when you lost **Ingid Bergman**, weren't you crushed?"

BOGART. (*Crosses* U. L. *steps*) Nothing that a little bourbon and soda wouldn't fix.

ALLAN. See, I don't drink. My body will not tolerate alcohol.

BOGART. Take my advice and forget this fancy

relationship stuff. The world is full of dames. **All you got to do is whistle.** (**Bogart** *exits* U. R. *slot, DREAM LIGHT FADESA.*) [pp. 7-8]

In James A. Michener's novel *The Drifters* (1971), Harvey Holt compares his annual running in front of bulls in Pamplona to what Bogart's character does in the film:

'Just like **Humphrey Bogart** running his boat out of Cuba,' Holt said reflectively. 'No great sweat if that's your job.'

'I thought it was Errol Flynn who had the boat in Cuba,' Monica said.

'That time he told **Lauren Bacall** to whistle,' Holt explained.

'Oh, you mean a movie! Never saw it.'

The others hadn't seen it either, and Holt asked, 'You mean to tell me not one of you saw one of the greatest dramatic moments in movie history ...'

'**Bogart** didn't make any movies during the last decade,' Gretchen said. 'At least I don't remember any.'

'He's been dead twelve years,' Holt said 'When was it made?' he asked me. 'That great **Hemingway** story?'

'I saw it in Libya during the war.'

Holt said he couldn't believe it had been so long ago [p. 505].

Adam Kennedy's novel *Just Like Humphrey Bogart* (1978) is rich in film allusions, especially to Bogart whose name is even used as part of the book's title. Two of the actor's movies mentioned by name are reinforced by

a detailed description of his face in a lengthy passage focused on the lonely New York City days of narrator/protagonist Duffy Odin:

In the past weeks, to kill the time, days and evenings, I had spent long hours watching movies, most often in a theatre on Eighty-sixth Street, a place that showed films of the thirties and forties, a new double bill each day. The game was to go without knowing, to avoid the cinema advertisements in the newspaper, to approach the theatre with your eyes on the sidewalk, not seeing till you stepped up to the box office what was playing.

"What's the program tonight?" I said to the woman in the ticket cage.

"There's a poster right behind you."

"I know. But I'd rather have you tell me."

"*__The Big Sleep__* and *__To Have and Have Not__*." She tore a ticket off the roll and pushed it toward me. I pushed it back and said, "No, thanks. Not tonight."

I went to the theatre next door, another revival house. Six Woody Woodpecker cartoons on the bill. And five short films, silent, with Laurel and Hardy. But before I walked away from the first theatre, I stopped to look at **Bogart**'s picture, blown up, grainy, the head four feet tall.

I studied the face, narrow and pinched, the eyes wet-looking, angling down to their outside corners, the anxious forehead, the questioning eyebrows and the ordinary nose, cheeks furrowed on either side, the long upper lip over prominent teeth, saliva always at the corners of the mouth and in the voice, the spoiled lower lip, and the small chin scored with a soft dimple.

I stood for a long time, studying that face, examining its details, trying to see behind it, trying to learn something. Finally I gave up, walked into the theatre next door, and concentrated fully on Laurel and Hardy [pp. 159-160].

Janet Leigh's Hollywood novel *House of Destiny* (1995) has several references to Bogart, the first one of which is connected with this movie. The scene is a conversation (about their respective plans for the night of April

25, 1944) between two friends and business partners, Wade Colby and Jude Abavas:

> Wade shrugged apologetically, caught in the act. "I had hoped not to give you time to think. Or be alone. And of all nights, I promised **Jack Warner** I'd go to his screening of ***To Have and Have Not***. Why don't you come with Joyce and me? Forget the work! We can do that tomorrow."
>
> "No, my friend. But I thank you, more than I can ever say, believe me. And I'll be fine, honest. I think I need to be by myself for a while. And you need to get dressed and go. I hear the picture is hot stuff—**Bogart** and this **Bacall** girl really heat up the screen, they say. Don't forget the juicy parts. I want all the details in the morning [p. 129].

The film, along with *The Maltese Falcon*, is mentioned in Christina Skye's novel *Going Overboard* (2001), in the excerpt relating the protagonists' reaction to their watching of *Casablanca*. Below is Carly's voice. Ford's is presented in Part Two of the book (under *High Noon*).

> They were arguing even before the final credits began.
> "No way. **Bogart** was good, but he was better in *****To Have and Have Not*****. And what about *****The Matlese Falcon*****?" Carly huffed [p. 137].

In Bill Crider's already cited novel *We'll Always Have Murder* (2001), a reference to the film is made by Bogart himself when he is telling narrator/protagonist Terry Scott about the beginning of his relationship with Lauren Bacall:

> "Your wife knew you and **Miss Bacall**?"
> "She didn't know, but she suspected. Betty and I were filming *****To Have and Have Not*****. Sluggy kept calling the set after

I'd left to find out where I'd gone. She was always told that I was 'out with the cast.' Before long, everybody was calling Betty *The Cast*. Naturally Sluggy was suspicious" [pp. 11-12].

A reference to Lauren Bacall and Hoagy Carmichael in the film was found in Judith Ryan Hendricks's *Bread Alone* (2001), a novel set first in Los Angeles, then in Seattle. The players are mentioned in a scene where the recently divorced narrator/protagonist, Wynter Morrison (Wyn), is taken by Mac to dinner at Lofurno's, a restaurant which reminds Wyn of a movie set for a speakeasy:

> He laughs. "This place is sort of a throwback. The food's great, though. And so's Arlene. The singer."
> "She looks like she's through for tonight."
> He shakes his head. "She's just taking a break. She'll sing till everybody's gone. Her voice reminds me of **Lauren Bacall**. Was it ***To Have and Have Not*** where she sang?"
> " 'Am I Blue.' And **Hoagy Carmichael** played the piano." I look at the open menu [pp. 186-187].

In Ed McBain's 87th Precinct novel *Eat Ollie's Book* (2002), the reference to the film has a character of an inside joke played out by two cops, Carella and Kling, as they bring their homicide investigation to the Offices of the deceased Councilman Lester Lyle Henderson:

> Behind each desk sat the so-called T-Generation, kids who had come of age when the terrorists bombed America, none of them older than twenty-five, all of them staring at their computers as if transfixed, fingers flying, performing God only knew what political tasks for their now deceased leader. None of them looked up as Carella and Kling worked their way to the

rear of the room where three identical doors sat like props in a stage farce. One of them bore a plaque that read: A. PIERCE.

"**Lauren Bacall**," Carella said. "***To Have and Have Not***."

Kling looked at him.

"The next line is, '**You know how to whistle, don's you Steve? You just put your lips together and blow.**'"

"Oh," Kling said, "Yeah," and knocked on the door.

"**Bogart**'s name was **Steve**," Carella explained. "In the picture."

"Come in," a voice called.

Alan Pierce was a man in his late thirties, Carella guessed, old by comparison to the cadre of kids manning the computers outside [pp. 137-138].

A reference to the film in Lawrence Block's *Small Town* (2003) appears in a scene where writer John Blair Creighton and folk-art dealer Susan Pomerance have a relatively intellectual conversation, following a rather disappointing love-making, and the song "Rosalie's Good Easts Café" triggers their discussion about what she can or cannot remember based on her age:

"I can see why you like that song. I mean, besides the fact that it's terrific. It's a novel, isn't it?"

"That's exactly what it is. There was a DJ who played that cut all the time. He got in trouble, because he wasn't getting enough commercials in, but he played it anyway. You're too young to remember."

"The other day your lawyer told me I was too young to remember ***To Have and Have Not***. The movie, not the novel. I remember it just fine."

"Because they show it on television. That album was

released in 1973. Were you listening to much country music in 1973?" [p. 348]

Elmore Leonard's mystery *Up in Honey's Room* (2007) is set during World War II. The author makes a reference to the film, through his protagonist, U.S. Deputy Marshal Carl Webster, in a scene where Webster relates to FBI agent Kevin Dean the circumstances in which he got shot:

> Carl said, "You know what a Duck is? Not the one you eat, the kind you drive. She goes on land or water, looks like a thirty-foot landing craft with tires. We're coming back from the supply depot on Manus, the main island, with stores and a hundred and fifty cases of beer. We take the Duck into the water for forty yards and we're back on Los Negros. A minute later there's rifle fire, four shots coming out of the bush and I'm hit. Right here in the side, the fleshy part, the first time in my life I was ever shot. The two guys with me hit the deck. One of 'em, George Klein, had fallen in love with **Lauren Bacall** the night before watching <u>*To Have and Have Not*</u> on a sixteen-millimeter projector. It's the picture **Lauren** says to **Humphrey Bogart**, '**You know how to whistle, Steve?**' If he wants her for anything. "**You put your lips together and blow.**' The other one aboard the Duck, a fella named Elmer Whaley from someplace in Arkansas, me and Elmer were sucking on Beech-Nut scrap during the trip [p. 81].

An interesting reference to the film, focused mostly on the assets of Lauren Bacall, appears in Elmore Leonard's novella "Comfort to the Enemy" (2009), in a passage where Carl Webster shares with Louly a peaceful episode from his World War II experience:

> After that tender moment he said, "They gave us the carbine and a steel helmet. Once in a while they'd announce

General Quarters over the PA and we'd go down to the beach and wait for something to happen. The thing the helmet was good for, it held two cans of beer in chipped ice we'd each take to the show at night. We're Seabees, so we made seats with arms and a back that would hook on to the plank nailed to a log – rows of hard boards going back from the screen. It rained it didn't matter, we'd go to the show. One night I was with this young Seabee, George Klein from Chicago, in the rain watching **Lauren Bacall** in her first movie, *To Have and Have Not* where she tells **Humphrey Bogart** if he wants anything just whistle? **Lauren Bacall** says to him, **"You know how to whistle, Steve. You put your lips together and blow."** And George Klein went crazy. At that moment he fell in love with **Lauren Bacall** and kept saying, "We're the same age. You know it? Look at her. **Lauren Bacall** and I are the exact same age" [p. 104].

The movie is also alluded to in a scene where Webster tells Narcissa Raincrow, his father's girlfriend, about his encounter with Honey Deal:

"Here's Honey, the best-looking girl I ever met, or the second best."

"She look like a movie star?"

"**Lauren Bacall**. 'You know how to whistle, Steve?' Honey sounds like her, her voice."

"They call her **Betty**, her friends."

"She takes off her blouse."

"She's wearing a brassiere?"

"It's white. She puts her hands behind her back to unhook it and says . . ." Carl paused. "She uses an obscene word."

The fifty-four-year-old Creek woman who looked somewhat like a heavy Dolores Del Rio said, "Which one, *fuck*?"

"Yeah" [pp. 274].

The same line from the film is quoted also in Michael P. Naughton's *Deathryde: Rebel Without a Corpse* (2008), a novel that additionally includes multiple allusions (starting on p. 15) to *The Big Sleep*, essentially through the name of the unusual services (*The Big Sleep Celebrity Death Tours*), and a double reference to *The Enforcer*. In fact the excerpt quoted below is a continuation of the first passage quoted under *The Enforcer*:

> Dean picked up a *Hollywood Reporter* from the nightstand and said, "So how is acting coming?"
>
> Stanwyck hated those earth shattering kind of Q and As.
>
> "I had a casting director tell me to lose the grandmother garb and get real the other day, she said. "Can you believe that? They have no respect for old Hollywood."
>
> Dean grabbed his keys, half-listening.
>
> "I'll bet Garbo is turning in her grave over today's young Hollywood."
>
> Dean bent over the bed and kissed her goodbye and said, "Thanks for the roll in the hay."
>
> She did one of the worst impersonations of **Lauren Bacall** he had ever heard and said in an overly dramatic tone, **"You know how to whistle, don't you?"**
>
> Dean didn't respond [p. 79].

Conflict **(1945).** Directed by Curtis Bernhardt, and co-starring Alexis Smith and Sydney Greenstreet, this superior crime drama is referenced in Lawrence Block's *The Burglar Who Thought He Was Bogart* (1995). The film is just mentioned, like many others, as part of Bern's report to Carolyn about the Bogart retrospective:

> We ate some more of the daily special, sipped some more celery tonic. Then she said, "Bern, what did you see last night?"

"*The Roaring Twenties*," I said.

"Again? Didn't you see that Monday night?"

"You're absolutely right," I said. "They tend to run together in my mind." I closed my eyes for a moment. "*Conflict*," I said.

"*Conflict*?"

"And *Brother Orchid*."

"I never heard of either of them."

"Actually, I may have seen *Conflict* years ago on late-night TV. It was vaguely familiar. **Bogart**'s in love with **Alexis Smith**, who's his wife's younger sister. He hurts his legs in a car crash, but then he hides the fact that he's recovered so that he can kill his wife."

"Bernie—"

"**Sidney** [misspelled] **Greenstreet**'s the psychiatrist who sets a trap for him. See, the way he does it . . . " "You don't care, do you?"

"Not hugely" [pp. 70-71].

The Big Sleep (1946). This is the second, and, unfortunately, last Bogart-Hawks collaboration, in which the actor is cast (the only time in his career) as Philip Marlowe, Raymond Chandler's charismatic private investigator. It was written by the same team as *To Have and Have Not* (joined by Leigh Brackett), and this time the script was based on a novel by another great author (his probably prime achievement despite the unresolved confusion in its storyline), and thus both movies are excellent examples of a situation where one major author (Faulkner in this case) works on a text created by another major author (Hemingway and Chandler, respectively). The film was already mentioned twice, within the references presented under *To Have and Have Not*.

American poster for Howard Hawks's *The Big Sleep* (1946).

An extensive reference to the film appears in Andrew J. Fenady's *The Man with Bogart's Face* (1977). The context is a conversation including private eye Sam Marlow, Elsa Borsht and two cops, Lt. Marion Bumbera and Det. Sgt. Horace Hacksaw:

> "Miss Borsht, I'll station a team of officers outside. You won't be bothered again."
> "She's gonna spend the night at my secretary's place," said Sam. "She can't sleep in this mess."
> "Good idea." Bumbera nodded. "But I'll leave the team at the house anyhow in case –"
> "No, Sam, I'm going to stay here."
> Sam shrugged.
> "The boys'll be outside. Come on, Hack. What a screwed-up situation."
> "Hell," smiled Sam, "you think this is screwed up? You ever see a picture called *The Big Sleep*? 1946, **Warner Brothers**. You could sit through it eighty-eight times and still not know what the plot was. **Faulkner, Leigh Brackett**, and **Jules Furthman** wrote the script, and it's a cinch they never talked to each other. I think each one did every third page on his own and **Howard Hawks** just shot it and hoped for the best. **Bogart** and **Bacall** were great but I'll bet they didn't know what it was about either unless they read the book" [pp. 135-136].

Additional allusions to this film, by means of addressing Bogart's Marlowe's tendency to pull at his ear lobe, appear in both *The Man with Bogart's Face* (p. 25-26) and *The Secret of Sam Marlow* (pp. 6, 35, 61, 107, 151 and 155).

The reference to the film in Roderick Thorp's mystery *Rainbow Drive* (1986) takes place in a scene where policeman Mike Gallagher visits the film studio Galaxy International, during a screening, to see German star Gretchen Heidl and, inevitably, meets the studio boss, Norman Birnbaum:

"Good morning, Mr. Birnbaum," she said as softly as Mike had ever heard her.

"Good morning, Gretchen."

Mike wanted to be careful. He moved his foot over onto Gretchen's and pressed gently as he reached around to Birnbaum. "Barney Phillips, Mr. Birnbaum. How are you?"

Birnbaum extended a limp, thin-boned hand. "Mr. Phillips." He gestured toward the small screen. "A brave role for Dick, don't you think? Imagine **Humphrey Bogart** camping it up like that."

"He did, in *The Big Sleep*. In Arthur Geiger's bookstore." Mike went into a lisp. **"Do you have a *Ben Hur*--?"**

Birnbaum offered a small smile. "When I started in this business, no one knew anything about its history. Now you youngsters quote the classics scene by scene" [p. 83].

James Grady's suspenseful novel *Thunder* (1994) contains references to numerous films and to as many as four pictures starring Bogart. They are all listed together as items in the collection of Frank Mathews, a murder victim whose townhouse is being searched by CIA agent John Lang:

The floor-to-ceiling shelves of videocassettes reflected Frank's best-known passion: movies.

"Not this new crap," Frank once told John: "Classics."

Alan Ladd and Veronica Lake in *The Glass Key* and *The Blue Dahlia*. **Bogart** in *To Have and Have Not*, *The Big Sleep*, *The Maltese Falcon*, *Casablanca* [p. 95].

The passage is quoted in this entry for a reason; this movie version of the Raymond Chandler classic is mentioned again about a hundred pages later:

Friday night. Cold. Empty. End of the real-world workweek.

John and Phuong used her father's two VCRs to copy the covert surveillance segment into three of his movies: *The Glass Key*, *Chinatown*, ***The Big Sleep*** [p. 205].

In Lawrence Block's *The Burglar Who Thought He Was Bogart* (1995), the film is referenced—just like most of the other Bogart movies—during an exchange between Bernie and Carolyn:

> The second picture was ***The Big Sleep***, and whoever put the program together had been having fun, combining two pictures with near-identical titles. But of course this was the classic, based on the **Chandler** novel with a screenplay by **William Faulkner**, starring **Bogie** and **Bacall** and featuring any number of good people, including **Dorothy Malone** and **Elisha Cook, Jr.** I won't summarize it for you, partly because the plot's impossible to keep straight, and partly because you must have seen it. If not, well, you will [p. 344].

John Updike, in his novel *In the Beauty of the Lilies* (1996), uses a couple of Bogart films to embellish a descriptive passage about Essie when she was still young, not aware of her future career as a movie star, in her room of her parents' house in Basingstoke, Delaware:

> Then with her eyes she did crisscrosses on the shadowy ceiling in the bed next to her. The light from the street below came in through the Venetian blinds like that scene in ***Casablanca*** or for that matter ***The Big Sleep*** with **Humphrey Bogart** not so handsome this time and *The Killers* with Burt Lancaster as this broken-down boxer destined to be killed [pp. 276-277].

Humphrey Bogart as Philip Marlowe and Lauren Bacall as Vivian Rutledge in a publicity shot for Howard Hawks's *The Big Sleep* (1946).

There are a few references to the film and to its main character in Bill Crider's novel *We'll Always Have Murder* (2001). The first one appears within the description of Bogart in a scene where he is introduced to the book's narrator/protagonist, private eye Terry Scott:

> He had luggage under his eyes and looked as if he needed a shave, but there was nothing new in that. He appeared that way sometimes in the movies, too. He was wearing a dark suit and tie that looked like what he'd worn in ***The Big Sleep***, right down to the white pocket hanky. Since actors (though not actresses) had to provide their own wardrobes, it might well have been the same clothing. On the third finger of his right hand he wore a gold ring set with a large ruby [p. 6].

An obvious allusion to the movie takes place in one of the first conversations between Scott and Bogart:

> "It's a question about a movie."
> "Forget it. I don't know who killed **Sternwood**'s chauffeur, and neither did **Raymond Chandler** when we asked him about it. **William Faulkner** was on the set, and he's the one who was stumped in the first place. If he and **Chandler** couldn't figure it out, nobody could."
> "I guess it doesn't matter in the long run, then."
> "Not when you're sleeping **the Big Sleep**, Junior" [pp. 14].

Some forty pages later, the film comes up again in a conversation between the two men:

> "Nobody's going to get hurt," I said.
> "Besides, you're not a real detective. You're just a guy who cleans up messes. What do you know about murder?"

"I saw *The Big Sleep*," I said.

"That won't help you much. Nobody knows what the hell happened in that picture" [p. 53].

An extensive passage with multiple references to the film includes two gay guys, Bernie and Evan, who help Bogart and Scott after the two detectives survive a car accident:

> His passenger, Bernie, got out as well. He was smaller than the driver, and he was wearing a suit and a tie painted with what must have been a tropical sunset. His hands fluttered when he talked.
>
> "Oh, **Mr. Bogart**," he said, "I'm *such* a fan of your movies. You were absolutely wonderful in *The Big Sleep*. Wasn't he, Evan? Wasn't he absolutely wonderful? And your wife, **Miss Bacall**, is simply gorgeous. Isn't she gorgeous, Evan?"
>
> . . .
>
> "You know what I liked about *The Big Sleep*?" Bernie said as we drove off. He was turned in the seat so he could look at us. "I simply *loved* the part where you went into the bookstore to ask for the copy of *Ben Hur*."
>
> **Bogart** pushed up the brim of his hat.
>
> "The *Ben Hur* 1860?" **Bogart** said in the same milquetoast voice he'd used in the movie, and I thought Bernie was going to swoon. "The one with the erratum on page one-sixteen?" [pp. 164-165]

The Two Mrs. Carroll **(1947)**. Peter Godfrey's disappointing mystery (co-starring Barbara Stanwyck and Alexis Smith) is mentioned in Bill Crider's *We'll Always Have Murder* (2001), in one more exchange between the two protagonists, Scott and Bogart:

Bogart grinned. "And they're absolutely correct. Bit I earned the right to be one. Let me tell you something, Junior. When I came to this town, I took every role they offered me and never complained. Even after I started to make a name for myself, I still took whatever they told me to. 'Just give me the script,' that was all I ever said. But it's not that way any longer. I have a little power now, and I'm finally using it. There are some people who don't like it. Fuck 'em."

He took a deep drag on his cigarette. The coal glowed brightly.

"If that's true," I said, "why did you make **_The Two Mrs. Carrolls_**?"

"Jesus," **Bogart** said, and laughed again. "Your needle is almost as sharp as mine. I made that thing two years ago for that bastard **Harry Cohn**, and I should have known better. **Harry Cohn** was reason enough to avoid it, and playing an English painter was another. Even **Harry** didn't want to release it, which tells you a lot. But he finally did, greedy son of a bitch" [pp. 31-32].

Then it is referred to again in a conversation with Peter Lorre:

> The police were always willing to play along with the studios up to a certain point. The point wasn't always the same, but we hadn't reached it in this case.
>
> **Bogart** had finished with his breakfast, and he'd started on the second martini and a Chesterfield for dessert.
>
> "And did you kill him, **Bogie**?" Lorre asked. "This Burleson, I mean."
>
> **Bogart** blew out a stream of smoke and said in the same lousy British accent he'd tried in **_The Two Mrs. Carrolls_**, "I did,

old boy. Hit him squarely between the eyes with a stale crumpet. It was either him or me, you see" [pp. 58-59].

***Dark Passage* (1947).** Written (from a novel by David Goodis) and directed by Delmer Daves, the film (co-starring Lauren Bacall) is referenced in several works.

The title of the film is mentioned just next to an allusion to *Casablanca* in a passage that appears in Stephen King's epic *The Stand* (1978) as part of a character description:

> Harold tries sometimes to be icy, so sophisticated—he always seems to me like a jaded young writer constantly searching for that special Sad Café on the West Bank where he can idle the day away talking about Jean-Pierre Sartre and drinking cheap plonk—but underneath, well covered, is a teenager with a far less mature set of fantasies. Or so I believe. Saturday matinee fantasies for the most part: Tyrone Power in *Captain from Castile*, **Humphrey Bogart** in ***Dark Passage***, Steve McQueen in *Bullitt*. In times of stress it's always this side of him which seems to come out, maybe because he repressed it so severely as a child, I don't know. Anyway, when he regresses to **Bogie**, he only succeeds in reminding me of that guy who played **Bogie** in that Woody Allen movie, ***Play It Again, Sam*** [p. 552].

In "Ghosts" (1986), the central novella of Paul Auster's *The New York Trilogy*, the movie is mentioned in a series of titles (for some reason not italicized) which private investigator Blue enjoys watching in the dark movie theaters:

> Blue is fond of the movies, not only for the stories they tell and the beautiful women he can in them, but for the darkness

of the theater itself, the way the pictures on the screen are somehow like the thoughts inside his head whenever he closes his eyes. He is more or less indifferent to the kinds of movies he sees, whether comedies or dramas, for example, or whether the film is shot in black and white or in color, but he has a particular weakness for movies about detectives, since there is a natural connection, and he is always gripped by these stories more than by others. During this period he sees a number of such movies and enjoys them all: Lady in the Lake, Fallen Angel, **Dark Passage**, Body and Soul, Ride the Pink Horse, Desperate, and so on [pp. 190-191].

The protagonist in Marcia Muller's mystery *While Other People Sleep* (1998) is detective Sharon McCone whose job in this one is to find out the reasons for the strange behavior of her gay office manager, Ted Smalley. She gets a message from his boyfriend, Neal Osborn, which includes a reference to the movie:

> At eleven, long after I'd ended the surveillance and gone home to filed further calls from my puzzled family members, Neal phoned. Ted had announced he was going to a special midnight screening of **Humphrey Bogart**'s *Dark Passage*, and, no, he didn't want company. It sounded like a ploy to get away for a couple of hours; Ted was a big **Bogart** fan and could probably recap the film's plot to back up his story [p. 104].

In another mystery by Muller, *Coming Back* (2010), the movie is mentioned again, this time as a part of the description of the place where Ted Smalley lives:

> His building was an Art Deco classic that had been used as a location in the **Bogart**-Bacall film *Dark Passage*. Ted

loved living in a place built in what he considered his favorite twentieth-century era. Maybe he should tap into the styles of that time for his next fashion statement—smoking jackets, hats, suits nipped in at the waist [p.110].

Bogart, as one of the characters in Bill Crider's *We'll Always Have Murder* (2001), mentions the movie himself when talking about his wife and their professional plans:

> "Where is she?"
>
> "In New York, doing a short publicity tour and visiting her mother. In a few weeks, we're going to be shooting a picture together. It's called **Dark Passage**. Betty wanted to see her mother before we got started, and the studio wanted to get her picture in the New York papers. **Dark Passage** is going to be a good picture, and a popular one, too, if people can get over the idea that a man would actually have plastic surgery and choose to wind up looking like me" [p. 30].

The Treasure of the Sierra Madre (1948). Based on a remarkable novel by B. Traven, this superior study of human greed, obsession and paranoia won three Academy Awards, two for John Huston (script and direction) and one for his father, Walter Huston (supporting actor). A line from this film ("Badges? We ain't got no badges! We don't need no badges! I don't have to show you any stinking badges!") ranked as #36 on the American Film Institute's List of the Top 100 Movie Quotes. It is also referred to in several literary works presented throughout this entry.

Possibly the first reference to the film appears in Jack Kerouac's *Desolation Angels* (1960):

> "Charly"," I say, "there's lots of uranium in the dry mountains of Chihuahua I bet"

"Where's that?"

"South of New Mexico and Texas, boy—dintya ever see *Treasure of the Sierra Madre* that picture about the old coot prospector who outwalk'd the boys and found gold, a reglar mountain goat of gold and they first met him in Skidrow Flophouse in his pee-jamas, old **Walter Huston**?" [p. 87]

A direct reference to the storyline itself appears in Andrew J. Fenady's mystery spoof *The Man with Bogart's Face* (1977):

> Both men went to the table, set down their suitcases, and opened them. Both were filled with currency.
> "Well," said Sam, "it looks like it'll spend all right. Close 'em up, boys. Wouldn't want a sudden gust of wind to blow any of it away, like in *The Treasure of the Sierra Madre* [pp. 222-223].

The film is referenced in Sam Shepard's *Motel Chronicles* (1982), an illustrated memoir in the form of a collection of untitled tales and poems. The movie is mentioned by the narrator in an entry dated 4/14/1982 but focused on a trip through the Southwestern area that took place in 1957.

> The combination of the heat, not eating, the speed and then the whiskey on top of it made me just about lose my cookies. But I held it all in somehow. The all of a sudden Ed's Uncle gets this brilliant idea. 'Let's go shoot Jackrabbits!,' he says. 'You wanna?' And his whole face lit up almost exactly like **Walter Houston**'s [misspelled] face in *Treasure of the Sierra Madre*. In fact he reminded me a whole lot of **Walter Houston**. Kind of like a little leprechaun. He got real excited and ran into his kitchen and started pulling boxes of 22. long ammo out of the

Walter Huston (Howard), Humphrey Bogart (Dobbs) and Tim Holt (Curtin) in a scene from John Huston's *The Treasure of the Sierra Madre* (1948).

cupboards and then brought out these three pistols that he kept in a green canvas bag under his bed [p. 95].

In Roderick Thorp's novel *Rainbow Drive* (1986), two L.A. policemen discuss a murder investigation strategy, and it leads to a quotation from the famous movie:

"Let's see how the wind blows," Mike said. "I think I can go to the end of the day before I have to surface. The gal I spoke to was more interested in protecting herself than remembering my name, and I'll bet you a dollar, the receptionist turns over the tape just because I ask for it. She **don' need no steenking bodge**."

Dan grinned. He had taught Mike the line from *The Treasure of the Sierra Madre*, using it, in fact, when he had to pound on some asshole [pp. 55-56].

In Clive Cussler's novel *Sahara* (1992), a reference to the film appears in a scene following protagonist Dirk Pitt's encounter with a prospector who reveals an unbelievable story about a mysterious Civil War ironclad:

"I can't guarantee the Lincoln legend," the Kid said adamantly, "but I'll bet Mr. Periwinkle and the remains of my grubstake, the *Texas* and the bones of her crew, along with the gold, lie here in the sand somewhere. I've been roamin' the desert for five years searchin' for her remains and by God I'm gonna find her or die tryin'."

Pitt gazed at the shadowed form of the old prospector in sympathy and respect. He rarely saw such dedication and determination. There was a burning confidence in the Kid that reminded Pitt of the old miner in ***Treasure of the Sierra Madre*** [p. 256].

In his Matthew Hope novel *Gladly the Cross-Eyed Bear* (1996), Evan Hunter (writing as Ed McBain) has Hope's associates, Warren Chambers and Toots Kiley, encounter drug smugglers while sailing on their fishing boat (on Florida waters):

> Warren was standing outside the closed and locked door to the head, listening to Toots taking her morning pee inside there, when he heard the boat approaching. He looked up curiously, and then, as the sound of the motor got closer and closer, he realized the boat was pulling alongside, and he was starting topside when he heard a voice shouting in a Spanish accent, "Allo, anybody aboar?"
>
> He went up the latter to the cockpit.
>
> A bearded man who looked like one of the banditos in **Treasure of the Sierra Madre** was already aboard. Big toothy smile in his scraggly beard. Wearing chinos, thong sandals, and a loose white fisherman's shirt bloused over the trousers [p. 254].

In Hunter's novel *The Moment She Was Gone* (2002), the narrator, Andrew Gulliver, talks about the strange habits of his father, a painter:

> I sometimes thought he never slept. All he did was paint and smoke his little Brazilian cigars, which he called in a thick Spanish accent, "gringo steenkers," blowing out clouds of smoke and grinning like one of the banditos in **Treasure of the Sierra Madre** [p. 67].

A more subtle reference to the movie appears in Martha Sherrill's novel *My Last Movie Star* (2002), an interesting book about a young movie star and a journalist (the narrator) writing a celebrity profile about her:

> Ed gazed at me in a disconnected way, and then he smiled. The look in his eyes was desperate, like something out of **The Treasure of the Sierra Madre** [p. 26].

James Lee Burke's *Bitterroot* (2001) is a novel set in the Bitterroot Valley of Montana. Its protagonist is former Texas Ranger Billy Bob Holland who, in the following scene, is discussed by a reporter and a federal agent. Their conversation leads to a rhetorical question about a line uttered by one of Bogart's best movie characters:

> "Billy Bob's got a nice office on the town square. People respect him. That's more than I can say about some folks," Lucas replied.
> "You see *Treasure of the Sierra Madre*?" the agent said. "**Humphrey Bogart** plays this worthless character named **Fred C. Dobbs**. He's always saying, 'Nobody's putting anything over on **Fred C. Dobbs**.' What do you think that line means? I never really figured it out" [p. 234].

Burke returns to the movie *The Treasure of the Sierra Madre* and its paranoid character in his novel *Rain Gods* (2009), which is set in a small Texas town near the Mexican border. This time the pretext for the reference is the fact that one of the book's characters has a name strikingly similar to the name of the character played by Bogart, and "another" character has the same name as the one used by the author of the novel. The conversation cited below is between Sheriff Hackberry Holland and Deputy Sheriff Pam Tibbs:

> He put his thumb on the edge of one name. She stood behind him, leaning down, one arm propped on his desk, her arm touching his shoulder.
> "**F.C. Dobbs**. What's remarkable about that?" she said.
> "You remember the name **Fred C. Dobbs**?"
> "No."
> "Did you see *The Treasure of the Sierra Madre*?"
> "A long time ago."
> "**Humphrey Bogart** played the role of a totally worthless panhandler and all-around loser whose clothes are tatters and his lips are so chapped they're about to crack. When he thinks

he's about to be slickered, he grimaces at the camera and says, 'Nobody is putting anything over on **Fred C. Dobbs**.'"

"Collins thinks he's a character in a film?"

"No, Collins is a chameleon and a clown. He's a self-educated guy who believes a library card makes him more intelligent that an MIT graduate. He likes to laugh at the rest of us."

"Maybe F.C. Dobbs is a real person. Maybe it's just coincidence."

"There are no coincidences with a guy like Jack Collins" [p. 392].

Two minutes later, she came back into his office. "The first name is actually the initial **B**, not 'Bee' with a double *e*. The last name is **Traven**, not Travis...."

But he wasn't thinking about her chagrin. "Collins sold the land to himself. He laundered his name and laundered the deed."

"I'm not following you at all."

"**B. Traven** was a mysterious eccentric who wrote the novel *The Treasure of the Sierra Madre*" [p. 394].

These revelatory lines cast a different kind of light on the description of Jack Collins that appears a few pages earlier in the book:

It was the way Collins breathed and the image the sound conjured up from the Hollywood of years gone by. Collins seemed to draw his air across his teeth. His mouth became a slit, his speech laconic and clipped, his face without expression, like a man speaking not to other people but to a persona that lived inside him. Perhaps speaking like a man who had a nervous twitch, who was wrapped too tight for his own good, who was at war with the Fates.

A man with dry lips and a voice that rasped as if his larynx had been fried by cigarettes and whiskey or clotted with rust. A man who wore his hair mowed on the sides and combed straight back on top, a man who wore a hat and clothes from another era, his narrow belt hitched tightly into his ribs and his unpressed slacks tucked into western boots, perhaps like a prospector of years past, his whole demeanor that of tarnished frontier gentility [p. 391].

Humphrey Bogart and Walter Huston in a scene from John Huston's *The Treasure of the Sierra Madre* (1948).

In Stuart M. Kaminsky's mystery *Midnight Pass* (2003), a reference to the film and some names related to it is made by the book's narrator, process server Lewis Fonesca, after a hard day (the excerpt has two errors: Curtain is misspelled; Fernandez should be Alfonso Bedoya):

I hadn't slept much the night before. I pulled down the shades, climbed into bed around two, and turned on a tape of ***The Treasure of the Sierra Madre***. I watched **Walter Huston** do his dance on the mountain and call Curtain and Dobbs damned fools for not knowing they were standing on top of gold. I watched **Emilio Fernandez** say, "Badges, badges, we don't need no stinkin' badges." I said it along with him.

I made it to the end of the tape and immediately fell asleep [pp. 259-260].

A suspenseful and, at the same time, funny reference to the film appears in Stuart Woods's thriller *Short Straw* (2006). Cupie and Vittorio, two men hired by Santa Fe lawyer Ed Eagle, try to bring his wife safely back from Mexico, watching for cops and kidnappers, and encounter some suspicious-looking Mexicans in a black SUV during a necessary stop on the road for Barbara Eagle to go pee in the bushes:

"Buenos dīas, señores," the man in the passenger seat said. He was middle-aged, mustachioed, bad teeth.

"Hiya," Cupie yelled, smiling, too. "You speak the English?"

"Of course, señor," the man replied. "Do you need help?"

"We're just looking for the best way to Juárez."

"You go straight ahead, all the way to Tijuana, then turn right on highway number two, and the way takes you all the way to Juárez."

Cupie looked at the map, puzzled. "Wouldn't it be shorter to go more cross-country?"

"Yes, señor, but the roads are not so very good, and, of course, there are the bandits."

"Oh, I see. Well, it sounds more exciting that way. Thanks very much."

> The rear window of the Suburban slid down a couple of inches and a pair of eyes appeared, looking into the rear seat of the Toyota, then it slid up again.
>
> "Adiòs, señores," the front passenger said. "Vaya con Dios!" The Suburban roared away.
>
> "Speaking of bandits," Vittorio said, "the guy looked just like the bandit in <u>***Treasure of the Sierra Madre***</u>. The '**We ain't got no steenking badges**' guy."
>
> "Yeah, and his intensions are pretty much the same." Cupie looked over to see Barbara coming [pp. 102-103].

The line quoted above is also used in James Scott Bell's mystery *Try Dying* (2007), in a scene where lawyer Ty Buchanan looks for a man who may help him explain the circumstances of his fiancée's death in an unusual accident:

> I bellied up to the bar at the opposite end, aware of the looks I was getting, and stayed there until the glum bartender headed my way. He was short and dark, with a thick black moustache. He didn't say anything, just flicked his head a little to indicate he was listening.
>
> "I'm here to see Tomas Estrada," I said.
>
> After a moment's hesitation, the bartender said, "See your badge."
>
> "**We don't need no stinking badges**."
>
> He glared, confused.
>
> "I'm not a cop," I said [p. 86].

Michael Malone, in his novel *The Four Corners of the Sky* (2009), refers to the film through two different quotations. The first excerpt, revealing the habits of Sam and Clark, the adoptive parents of protagonist Annie, includes also a line from *Casablanca*:

The famous lines of movies gave them a language that made them feel closer. If Sam wanted a drink, she'd growl in Garbo's voice, "'Give me a whiskey and don't be stingy, baby.'" If Clark was battling a Christmas tree into its stand, he'd snarl like **Bogie**, "**Nobody gets the best of Fred C. Dobson.**" When Sam played on the piano the song Jill had loved most, "Wind Beneath My Wings," Clark shouted, "**Don't play it again, Sam!**" and Sam yelled back, "'Are you talkin' to *me?*'" They were particularly fond of movies in which incompatible misfits, who'd been given each other by the accidents of life, became friends, to the good of both [pp. 184-185].

The other passage comes from a funny scene where Annie and Raffy, Jack's 'associate,' try to visit Annie's con artist father, Jack, who is hiding incognito in Golden Days (a nursing home), and are stopped by Chief Hospital Administrator M.R. Skippings:

> But in M.R. Skippings's pink-stucco universe it was. "Are you refusing to show me those badges?"
> Annie grinned. "Are you really actually saying to me 'show me you badges,' I mean actually really?" The elevator doors opened. Chamayra stepped out of the car. She looked at them horrified but didn't speak and trotted quickly away down the hall. Annie shoved Raffy inside the elevator, jumping in with him. Skippings struggled to wedge open the doors.
> Annie smiled at her pleasantly. "'**We don't need no badges. I don't have to show you any stinking badges!**'" The doors closed. "*Treasure of the Sierra Madre*," she explained to the wide-eyed Raffy as they descended. "I could feel it coming. That's the correct quote; most people get it wrong" [p. 315].

FOUR HOLLYWOOD LEGENDS

Key Largo **(1948).** Scripted (from the play by Maxwell Anderson) by Richard Brooks and John Huston (the film's director), *Key Largo* is a superior crime drama with an all-star cast including Bogart, Lauren Bacall, Edward G. Robinson, Lionel Barrymore and Claire Trevor (in an Oscar-winning supporting role). The oldest reference to the movie probably comes from Andrew J. Fenady's novel *The Secret of Sam Marlow* (1980). The excerpt below is a continuation of one long passage partially presented in the entries on *High Sierra* and *The Maltese Falcon*:

> Ironically, the lead in **_Key Largo_** had been played on broadway by the same fellow who turned down **_High Sierra_**, Paul Muni.
>
> **_Key Largo_** was suspiciously similar in plot to **_The Petrified Forest_**. A gangster and his boys take over a small isolated hotel and hold hostages until they make a deal and hotfoot it away. In this case they hot-boated it away—or tried. **Bogart** and **Edward G. Robinson** reversed the roles they had played plenty of times in the thirties. This time **Bogart** was the hero and **Robinson** the **Mantee**-like gangster with Mafioso overtones. And this time **Bogey** blasted **Robinson** full of lead instead of vice versa. Good cast—**Lauren Bacall, Lionel Barrymore, Claire Trevor** as the moll this time, who won an Academy Award mostly due to the lousy was she sang "Moanin' Low." Also **Thomas Gomez, Marc Lawrence,** and **Harry Lewis,** who now owns all the Hamburger Hamlets and is a millionaire.
>
> The picture missed the mark a little, but **Bogart** and **Bacall** didn't. Sam had timed it just right. As the **Max Steiner** music swelled and **Bogey** steered the "Santana" back to Key Largo and **Bacall**, Sam ran out of popcorn [pp. 142-143].

American poster for John Huston's *Key Largo* (1948).

The film is referenced in Susan Isaacs's mystery *After All These Years* (1993), in a scene where the narrator/protagonist, Rosie Myers, framed for murdering her estranged husband, is eavesdropping on a conversation between her high school boyfriend Tom Driscoll, and Jessica, Richie Myers' girlfriend conducting a financial research for Tom:

> From the way Jessica used her body, you'd have thought she'd spent two years studying **Lauren Bacall** in <u>*Key Largo*</u> instead of earning a master's in finance. But if I had to put money on what she had that hooked successful men like Carter, Richie, and Nicholas Hickson, I'd have to say that the erotic aspect—the legs, the sultry walk, the glossy, perpetually parted lips—was only half of it. The other fifty percent was a cold mind so much like her conquests' minds that when they took her to bed, they could be making love to themselves [p. 209].

A clear allusion to the film appears in Stephen King's *Bag of Bones* (1998), in a passage describing narrator/protagonist Mike Noonan's arrangements for a trip:

> On my way back home, I passed The Shade, Derry's charming little revival movie house, which has prospered in spite of (or perhaps because of) the video revolution. This month they were showing classic SF from the fifties, but April was dedicated to **Humphrey Bogart**, Jo's all-time favorite. I stood under the marquee for several moments, studying one of the Coming Attractions posters. Then I went home, picked a travel agent pretty much at random from the phone book, and told the guy I wanted to go to Key Largo. Key *West*, you mean, the guy said. No, I told him, I mean **Key Largo**, just like in the movie with **Bogie** and **Bacall**. Three weeks. Then I rethought that. I was wealthy, I was on my own, and I was retired. What was this "three weeks" shit? Make it six, I said [pp. 83-84].

Humphrey Bogart

In John Grisham's novel *The Brethren* (2000), two letters—one being the initial response (by Al Konyers) to a letter written by three imprisoned judges (under the name of Ricky) as part of their scam, and the other one being one of the judges' responses to Al's letter, as a continuation of their scam—include a reference to Bogart and three of his films:

Dear Ricky:

Hello. My name is Al Konyers. I'm in my fifties. I like jazz, old movies, **Humphrey Bogart**, and I like to read biographies. I don't smoke and don't like people who do. Fun is Chinese take-out, a little wine, a black-and-white western with a good friend. Drop me a line.

Al Konyers [p. 152]

Dear Al:

Thank you for your last letter. It means so much to me to hear from you. I feel like I've been living in a cage for months, and I'm slowly seeing daylight. Your letters help to open the door. Please don't stop writing.

I'm sorry if I've bored you with too much personal stuff. I respect your privacy and hope I haven't asked too many questions. You seem like a very sensitive man who enjoys solitude and the finer things of life. I thought about you last night when I watched *__Key Largo__*, the old **Bogart** and **Bacall** film. I could almost taste the Chinese carry-out. The food here is pretty good, I guess, but they simply can't do Chinese.

I have a great idea. In two months when I get out of here, let's rent *__Casablanca__* and *__African Queen__*, get the carry-out, get a bottle of nonalcoholic wine, and spend a quiet evening on the sofa. God, I get excited just thinking about life on the outside and doing real things again.

...

Thanks, friend.

Love, Ricky [pp. 163-164]

The movie is also mentioned in Bill Crider's *We'll Always Have Murder* (2001), as one of several opinions expressed by the fans of Bogart, one of the book's main characters. Here it is Harry, a guard of Club Sappho, that gets the privilege of meeting the legendary star:

"You're always full of the blarney, Mr. Scott. And who's the fella you have with you? He looks familiar."

"**Humphrey Bogart**," I said, "meet Harry."

They shook hands, and I thought I noticed **Bogart** wincing just a bit at Harry's grip, though he tried not to show it."

"I'm a big fan," Harry told **Bogart**. "I really loved *Key Largo*. Your wife, **Miss Bacall**, she's really something" [p. 120].

In Stuart M. Kaminsky's *The Dead Don't Lie* (2007), an Abe Lieberman mystery set in Chicago, police officer Lieberman has a conversation with his grandson Barry while taking a bath (and his wife Bess is sleeping in the bedroom):

Abe nodded toward the closed door a few feet behind him, beyond which Bess lay sleeping.

"You look like **Edward G. Robinson** in *Key Largo*," said Barry. "When he took a bath."

"The difference is he was round, had a big cigar, and a drink. I am lean with a glass of water over there on the sink in case I feel dehydrated" [pp. 20-21].

***Knock on Any Door* (1949).** This memorable courtroom drama is the first one out of several Bogart films referenced in Andrew J. Fenady's *The Secret of Sam Marlow* (1980). The characters mentioned in the excerpt are private detective Sam Marlow and his beautiful ex-client, Gena Anastas, who is one of the major characters in Fenady's previous Sam Marlow novel, *The Man with Bogart's Face*.

> Pantheon Pictures was about a fifteen-minute drive to Sam's Larchmont office. During the drive, Sam reflected on the fact that it had been a good year. Except for two deaths. Gena Anastas, a girl he probably was in love with, had died. She liked to drive fast—and she died fast. There was a quote from a **Bogart** movie, **<u>Knock n Any Door</u>**: " . . . **live fast, die young and have a good-looking corpse.**" Gena's corpse wasn't good looking. It was just about midnight when she pranged her seventy-five-thousand-dollar sardine can into a boulder in Malibu and bounced down a cliff into the Pacific Ocean. They couldn't get her until noon the next day. Not a good-looking corpse [p. 24].

Although it is true that the film, directed by Nicholas Ray, made the line famous, the credit should in fact go to Willard Motley, the author of the original novel, where the line is uttered repeatedly by Nick Romano, the tragic youngster.

Tokyo Joe **(1949).** This minor item in Bogart's filmography, together with *Chain Lightning* (another picture directed by Stuart Heisler and one that Bogart made next), is mentioned twice in Lawrence Block's *The Burglar Who Thought He Was Bogart* (1995), in a telephone conversation between Bernie and Carolyn, during which the reader finds out for the first time about the Humphrey Bogart film festival:

> "We're going to the movies."
> "Oh," she said. "Well, that's always a good choice on a first date. What are you going to see?"

"A double feature. ***Chain Lightning*** and ***Tokyo Joe***."

"Did they just open?"

"Not exactly."

"Because I never heard of them. ***Chain Lightning*** and ***Tokyo Joe***? Who's in them? Anybody I ever heard of?"

"**Humphrey Bogart**."

"**Humphrey Bogart**? The **Humphrey Bogart**?"

"It's a film festival," I explained. It's at the Musette Theater two blocks from Lincoln Center. Tonight's the first night, and I'm meeting her at the box office at a quarter to seven" [pp. 64-65].

In a Lonely Place **(1950).** Directed by Nicholas Ray and co-starring Gloria Grahame, this outstanding psychological drama is referenced extensively in two different books. In James A. Michener's novel *The Drifters* (1971), the whole movie show, taking place in an unusual environment, is related by narrator Fairbanks:

> Perhaps enjoy is not the word. He lived each moment of the film with terrible intensity, giving me the impression that for him this was something more than another in the distinguished chain of **Bogart** movies. I had not seen it before nor even heard of it, and in subsequent weeks when I spoke of my experience in other camps I found no tech rep who had heard of it either. It was excellent. **Bogart** was a film writer in Hollywood, accused of murder and trusted only by **Gloria Grahame**. As the first spasmodic reels unfolded, you got the idea that it was just another murder mystery and that **Miss Grahame** was certain to save **Bogart** from the electric chair or gas chamber or whatever it was that California used. In the long intervals between reels we discussed this probable development with the German rubber man, who said approvingly, 'It takes the Americans or

the French to put together a really good *policier.*' I asked if he thought that **Bogart** had been involved in the murder of the young woman, and he said, 'Never. Not in an American film. In a French film, yes.'

This type of opinion held through the first intermission, but I noticed that Holt did not react to the guesses. He was the only one present who knew how the film came out, and he took quiet satisfaction in eavesdropping on our wrong guesses, for during the fifth intermission the German and I confessed that we had been mistaken. This was something more than a mere *policier*. It was a character study of the film writer in conflict with the likable girl who was befriending him. 'I have the curious feeling,' the German whispered as we looked out toward the jungles that encroached upon Pakanbaru, 'that **Mr. Bogart** is not going to get the girl this time. He's truly psychotic . . . something like your friend Holt.'

And in the last reel **Bogart** did become the archetype of a tech rep—lonely, embattled, obstinate, totally incapable of understanding a woman—so that in the final shot he stalked off-camera, a defeated, bitter man taking his battle to some other terrain populated with other actors whom he would be incapable of understanding or adjusting to.

...

On the long drive back to Holt's camp I said, 'I didn't catch the name of that movie.'

'*In a Lonely Place*,' he said. He rarely used the names of movies. In future conversations this would be spoken of as 'that time when **Humphrey Bogart** kicked away the love of **Gloria Grahame**.' He thought that **Bogart** should have received an Oscar for this film. '**Miss Grahame**, too, for that matter, but she got one that time when she was Dick Powell's wife.' This missed me, but before I could query him, he added reflectively, 'Funny,

Powell was a screenwriter too. I guess **Miss Grahame** goes for screenwriters' [pp. 464-465].

Gloria Grahame as Laurel Gray and Humphrey Bogart as Dixon Steele in a scene from Nicholas Ray's *In a Lonely Place* (1950).

It is worth pointing out here that in Dorothy B. Hughes's excellent novel on which the film was based the Bogart character is not only psychotic, he is a serial killer pretending to be a writer. Also, the film which brought Gloria Grahame her only Academy Award (for a supporting actress) is Vincente Minnelli's *The Bad and the Beautiful* (1952).

A major reference to *In a Lonely Place* appears also in *The Burglar Who Thought He Was Bogart* (1995), a mystery by Lawrence Block. The context of the reference is an exchange between Bernie and an attractive and mysterious female who comes to his used bookstore to purchase a Humphrey Bogart book:

> "What I love," she said, "is what you see on the screen. *That* **Humphrey Bogart**. Rick in *Casablanca*. Sam Spade in *The Maltese Falcon*."
>
> "**Dixon Steele** in *In a Lonely Place*."
>
> Her eyes widened. "Everyone remembers **Rick Blaine** and **Sam Spade**, she said. "And **Fred Dobbs** in *The Treasure of the Sierra Madre*, and **Philip Marlowe** in *The Big Sleep*. But who remembers **Dixon Steele**?"
>
> "I guess I do," I said. "Don't ask me why. I remember titles and authors a lot, that's natural in this business, and I guess I remember character names, too."
>
> "*In a Lonely Place*. He's a screenwriter, **Dixon Steele**, do you remember? He has to adapt a novel but he can't bear to read it, and he gets a hat-check girl to come tell him the story. Then she's murdered, and he is a suspect."
>
> "But there's another girl," I said.
>
> "**Gloria Grahame**. She's a neighbor and gives him an alibi, and then she falls in love with him and types the manuscript and prepares his meals. But she sees the violence in him when his car is in an accident and he beats up the other driver, and again when he beats his agent for taking his script before it was finished. She thinks he must have killed the hat-check girl after all, and she is going to leave him, and he finds out and starts choking her. Do you remember?"
>
> Vaguely, I thought. "Vividly," I said.
>
> "And there's a phone call. The hat-check girl's boyfriend has confessed to the murder. But it's too late for them, and **Gloria Grahame** can only stand there and watch him walk out of her life forever."

"You don't need the book," I said. "Not in hardcover or in paperback. You've got the whole thing memorized."

"He is very important to me."

"I can see that."

"I learned English from his films. Four of them, I played them over and over on the VCR. I would say the lines along with him and the other actors, trying to pronounce them correctly. But I still have an accent, don't I?"

"It's charming" [pp. 60-61].

The Enforcer **(1951)**. This superior, but generally forgotten, crime drama, directed by Bretaigne Windust (with uncredited help from Raoul Walsh), is referenced in two books: LaVyrle Spencer's *Then Came Heaven* (1997) and Michael P. Naughton's *Deathryde: Rebel Without a Corpse* (2008). In Spencer's family/romance novel *Then Came Heaven*, set in a small Polish-Catholic Minnesota town, the film is mentioned in a passage relating a date of widower Eddie Olczak and Jean, formerly Sister Regina and Eddie's daughters' teacher at St. Joseph's:

"If you'd like we can drive through town first and see what's playing there, and then you can decide."

"No, the drive-in is fine."

Nevertheless, they drove through town, but the marquee said **Humphrey Bogart** in ***The Enforcer***, which put an end to that, since it was a story about killers for hire, which was sure to have a bad decency rating. So they went to the Fall Drive-in and watched Doris Day and Gordon MacRae fall in love and sing their way through a musical courtship in *On Moonlight Bay* [p. 307].

American poster for Bretaigne Windust's *The Enforcer* (1951).

The first of the two excerpts from Naughton's book is a good illustration of how a text message, or any other form of message, about a Bogie film show can change one's plans for a given night:

"I figured," Stanwyck said, "since you got your hambone boiled, now we can get to know each other a little better. I'm a rental . . . there are no late fees and there's this cool Starbucks up the street.'

Dean checked his Blackberry. Quincy texted him.

He scrolled the message:

Egyptian Theater.

7 p.m. **The Enforcer**.

Humphrey Bogart.

He holstered his Blackberry on his hip and said, "Sorry sweetheart, Daddy-o's got to go. Gotta a date with **Bogie** at the Egyptian."

Dean picked up a *Hollywood Reporter* from the nightstand and said, "So how is the acting coming?" [p. 79]

The second excerpt shows James DeRossa, also known as James Dean, the brain of an absolutely original heist, watching the movie show and meeting with one of his "associates":

Dean sat in the balcony of the Egyptian Theatre during a rare screening of the 1951 version of *The Enforcer*, starring **Humphrey Bogart**. The restored, black & white classic played to a half-full theater. Afterwards, the Egyptian was having a Q & A with some ancient cast member they dug up from the original film, but Dean was there to make the change. He watched two gangsters being interrogated on the big screen:

Bogart: "Who's the men you deliver the bodies to?"

Gangster: "The undertaker."

Dean laughed at the dialogue as he listened to the classic actors' voices echo in the Egyptian.

Detective: "What undertaker?"

. . .

Quincy sidled toward Dean and took a seat. He let out a gig sight as he plopped down. He was a big guy, looked like Bob Barker with shock white hair. Immaculately dressed—although the black trench coat was a bit much, Dean thought.

. . .

"The procession is set up at Ascension in Orange County," Dean said. "They'll be on a wild goose chase, but it's a dead end to nowhere."

Quincy glanced up at **Bogart** on the screen and said, "They've been watching us the whole time" [pp. 107-108].

The African Queen **(1951).** One more major example of the fruitful Bogart-Huston collaboration, *The African Queen* (co-starring Katharine Hepburn) is the picture that brought Bogart his only, but well-deserved Academy Award. It is one of four Bogart films referenced in Woody Allen's *Play It Again, Sam* (1968). This one is mentioned by Barbara Tyler (a minor character) in a conversation with Allan:

> BARBARA. I just did my Ph.D. on "Cinema" for the New School, and I used some of your articles for reference. They're very clever.
> ALLAN. (*PIANO MUSIC starts.*) Thank you.
> BARBARA. I particularly liked the article you wrote on **"The African Queen."**
> ALLAN. That was one of my favorite movies.
> BARBARA. It was quite a departure for **Bogart**.
> ALLAN. Well, you see the thing about **Bogart** that most people don't know is that . . . [p. 56].

The first allusion to the film in James A. Michener's novel *The Drifters* (1971) is a result of Holt's defending General MacArthur and not blaming him for a serious military mistake in Korea; the second one is one more non-sequitur digression made by Holt:

> I asked whether MacArthur could have known that the marines were marching north into the jaws of three hundred thousand enemy in single-file formation, with thirty yards between men. 'A general can't know everything. I don't fault MacArthur. It was like **Humphrey Bogart** guided his boat into those weeds with leeches. He couldn't be expected to know everything' [p. 479].

> So far as I know, at that time not one of my young friends had ever spoken the name Moçambique. It came into the conversation obliquely when Holt said, 'Watching that young lady leave for Split reminded me of how **Humphrey Bogart** decided to go down the river with **Miss Hepburn**. It was about the same, only they were much older' [p. 547].

Pat Conroy's nonfiction book *The Water Is Wide* (1972) is an account of the author's challenging job as a teacher on Yamacraw Island, off the shore of South Carolina. A reference to the movie is a part of a narrative paragraph related to Ted Stone, a picaresque and multi-skilled, if overly conservative, white man monopolizing most of the jobs available on the island:

> So I listened to Stone and was glad to be learning. He loved to talk about himself and nothing could have been more instructive to me. On a whim, he had once traveled to Florida with a group of friends, bought the boat which **Humphrey Bogart** captained in the film *The African Queen*, and brought it back to Yamacraw Island, where it survived a year then rotted slowly into oblivion. It gave me an immense thrill to think that my boat docked in the same spot which once harbored the

African Queen. It fired the Irish romanticism within me, as did Mr. Stone's accounts of the hurricane of '59 that crushed boats and docks like playthings, that uprooted oak trees as tall as towers, that incapacitated a town thirty miles from the island and made it a national disaster area [pp. 71-72].

The film, along with *Casablanca*, is also referenced in William Goldman's *Marathon Man* (1974), in a conversation between the book's protagonist, Tom 'Babe' Levy, and Peter Janeway, the Division's Commander who is also working for Kaspar Szell (the 'White Angel'):

> "And I wish you'd stop being difficult," Janeway said.
> "I haven't started being difficult," Babe replied, kind of liking the sound of his answer even as he spoke it. **Bogart** might have said something just like that. Not in any of the great ones like *African Queen* or *Casablanca*, but it was a decent-enough comeback for most of those crummy B pictures **Warners** was always sticking him in [p. 143].

Fannie Flagg's *Coming Attractions* (1981) is a novel set in the 1950s, in fact starting in 1952. Thus, a reference to *The African Queen* in that book is a plausible move on the author's part. The quoted passage describes the aftermath of young Daisy Fay's heroic deed, saving her friend Angel from drowning:

> I thought I'd just have to go ahead and drown at an early age, but then I remembered that black snake. When it me that some more of them might be in the water, I must have got the strength of a hundred, because I got loose and saved my own life.
> Angel was real sick. I never saw somebody throw up so much in my life, and we had leeches all over us just like **Humphrey**

Bogart in *African Queen*. Ugh! We took Angel back up to the Blue Gardenia Lounge and told her momma and daddy what had happened [p. 65].

Katharine Hepburn as Rose Sayer and Humphrey Bogart as Charlie Allnut in a scene from John Huston's *The African Queen* (1951).

A poignant commentary on the profession of writing, referring to a repulsive scene in the film, was found in Connie Willis's short story "Even the Queen" (1992):

> *When you're a writer, the question people always ask you is, "Where do you get your ideas?" Writers hate this question. It's like asking* **Humphrey Bogart** *in* **The African Queen**, *"Where do you get the leeches?" You don't get ideas. Ideas get you* [p. 89].

In Lilian Jackson Braun's mystery *The Cat Who Brought Down the House*

(2003), the film is mentioned as part of the upcoming program of the newly opened exclusive movie theater in Pickax:

> Back on the pavement they jabbered all the way to the Nutcracker Inn.
> He said, "I've bought a Gold Card Membership."
> "You shouldn't have, Ducky. You can see a show anytime as my guest."
> "But I wanted to be a member. How will we know what's being shown?"
> "Members get a newsletter every two months." She mentioned productions like **_The African Queen_** . . . *The Godfather* . . . *My Fair Lady* . . . *Close Encounters of the Third Kind*" [p. 174].

A lengthy reflection about Katharine Hepburn, with a brief reference to the film, appears in Elizabeth Hay's novel *Garbo Laughs* (2003), in one of many "letters" that Harriet Gold writes to Pauline Kael:

> *I don't know why, but I've been thinking about* **Katharine Hepburn***, asking myself why I find her so embarrassing that I have to look away. She's all over her own face, somehow. So aware of herself and how smart and shiny she is. Always being seen. And I agree with you that she's good, she's often very good. But I can't watch her. Ida told me that she much preferred Barbara Stanwyck.*
>
> . . .
>
> She leaned forward and added, *I do like her, however, in* **The African Queen** [p. 126].

The movie is also one of five Bogart pictures referenced in Michael Malone's novel *The Four Corners of the Sky* (2009). The excerpt offers some more information about Annie Peregrine Goode and her adoptive parents, Sam (also Annie's aunt) and Clark:

> After a while, Sam started her imitation of **Katharine Hepburn**. "'Nature, Mr. Allnut, is what we are put in this world to rise above.'"
>
> Because niece and uncle had lived for years with a woman who owned a movie store and who responded to life crises almost exclusively by quoting classic films, the inimitable **Hepburn** voice, even badly mimicked, was somehow as soothing as a lullaby.
>
> "*African Queen*," Annie said [p. 120].

Jill McCorkle's novel *Life After Life* (2013) is a compilation of current stories and flashbacks relating the complex lives and relationships of the residents and employees of Pine Haven Retirement Facility in Fulton, North Carolina. The passage below describes the relationship of Sadie Randolph, a retired third-grade teacher, and Paul, her youngest child:

> Paul is stubborn and keeps trying, but in the meantime he just reads every word of her monthly bill from Pine Haven, makes phone calls and asks lots of questions as she taught him to do and, of course best of all, sends pictures of the children and all the brochures from conventions and retreats for ophthalmologists so she can send a customer anywhere in the world. There was even one trip advertised to go down the Amazon and she pulled it out to show Benjamin and Abby just the other day because he knows that *The African Queen* is one of her favorite movies and he has promised to bring a copy for her to watch someday soon [pp. 38-39].

Deadline – U.S.A. **(1952)**. This generally forgotten drama, written and directed by Richard Brooks, is nonetheless one of the best pictures that Bogart made in the 1950s. One of the first references to the film was found in James A. Michener's novel *The Drifters* (1971); it appears in the book as another digression made by Harvey Holt:

> Once, when a woman dressmaker in Hong Kong had to go out of business because a Yugoslavian adventurer had stolen her cash, Holt sat morosely listening to Glenn Miller tapes and reflecting the matter. 'I keep thinking of the way **Humphrey Bogart** saved that newspaper for old **Ethel Barrymore**. A woman in business ought to have someone she can rely on' [p. 463].

Jon Talton's novel *Deadline Man* (2010) resembles Brooks's film in at least two ways—in the characterization of the protagonist, a tough columnist facing a challenging assignment, and in the predicament of the newspaper he works for. Some other similarities (and differences) between the book and the film (which—not unexpectedly—happens to be referenced in the passage) are presented below:

> In the newsroom, the paper is put together with the latest computer programs. Page designers do everything and more that the old printers used to handle in the back shop, the last of whom were bought out eight years ago. But the printing presses remain, the muscular manufacturing process that puts news on paper. When I started, the pressroom was grimy, the presses old, noisy as hell. It looked exactly like something out of the black-and-white movie ***Deadline USA***, where **Humphrey Bogart** as fearless editor defies a threatening mob boss. Now it's surgical-suite clean and high tech, with stainless steel catwalks surrounding Goss Uniliners that can print 80,000 copies per hour in full color. They're still loud. I can hear them—feel them—through the glass [pp. 132-133].

***Beat the Devil* (1954).** Some extensive references to this less successful collaboration of Huston and Bogart (co-starring Jennifer Jones and Gina Lollobrigida) appear in several books. The juxtaposition of opinions about this movie and *Casablanca* (see above), expressed by different characters of James A. Michener's novel *The Drifters* (1971)—Holt's "sacred" convictions contrasted by the "sacrilegious" views eagerly, and almost tactlessly, offered by some of the six young runaways— perfectly illustrates the generation gap so vividly demonstrating itself in the late 1960s:

> 'I saw him in one movie,' Yigal said. 'It was excellent.'
> 'What was he?' Holt asked.
> 'You know, that classic—***Beat the Devil***, with **Robert Morley** and that superb cast.'
> 'Oh, sure!' Monica cried. 'That wonderfully nutty thing about Tangier.'
> 'They should all have been arrested,' Holt growled.
> 'Who? **Morley** and **Bogart**?'
> 'The producer, the director, anyone responsible for such a waste of **Bogart**'s talent. That picture was a disgrace, the only poor one **Bogart** ever made.'
> 'Are you talking about the **Truman Capote-John Huston** classic?' Gretchen asked.
> Holt apparently did not recognize the names. 'What I'm talking about,' he said, 'is that miserable picture which somebody threw together and made **Bogart** look like a fool.'
> 'It's the only good thing he ever did,' Gretchen said firmly, and the others agreed.
> Holt exploded. 'You mean that piece of trash . . .'
> 'Mr. Holt, it had style, wit' [p. 506].

In Sam Shepard's short story "Lost in the Ruins" (1990), the narrator is an actor shooting a film on location in Mexico, trying to understand and feel the character he is to play:

> This is a man who wears a watch! He cares about time. He wears handmade English shoes. He's got some scratch! I stare at the shoes. They remind me of **Robert Morley** in **John Huston**'s ***Beat the Devil***. What period was that movie? Earlier. Had to be thirties; late thirties. This one is supposed to be the fifties. I remember the fifties. I lived through the fifties, but it doesn't help. My memories of the fifties have nothing to do with this character. I remember great Chevys with fins and Tijuana girls in tight split skirts. That's about it. Something about ***Beat the Devil*** strikes a chord. European sleazy characters stranded in an exotic environment. Similar to this. Dust. **Bogart**. **Peter Lorre**. Brecht. No! Not Brecht! Don't get off the track here. . . . This character is European through and through. Western. American, and gringo to the bones. He's in a foreign land, but he carries all his luggage with him; all his curse of heritage. His sense of superiority is involuntary. Intellectual. It's culturally preordained. He looks into the faces of these Indians without the slightest empathy. They are victims of culture, the same as him. Victims of the jungle; he, of the industrial age. They have nothing in common. He feels no contempt; just indifference. He's not as soft as **Robert Morley**, yet not as hard as **Bogart**. He's simply alone [pp. 206-207].

The movie is also extensively referenced in Lawrence Block's *The Burglar Who Thought He Was Bogart* (1995), where the information is provided by the narrator/protagonist, who attends the Bogart festival in New York:

> ***Beat the Devil***. Directed by **John Huston**, who shared the screenplay credit with **Truman Capote**. The cast included

Gina Lollobrigida as **Bogart**'s wife and **Jennifer Jones** as a compulsive liar married to a fake English nobleman. **Peter Lorre**'s in it as well, along with **Robert Morley** and a bunch of great character actors whose names I can never remember.

I settled into my seat, thinking that maybe this time I'd be able to understand what was going on on the screen. I must have seen the movie three or four times over the years and was never able to make head or tail out of it. Everybody was trying to hoodwink everybody else, and when **Jennifer Jones** prefaced a statement with "in point of fact" you knew for certain she was about to come up with a whopper, but beyond that I could never quite manage to follow the plot. Maybe this time will be different.

. . .

"No one can follow it," I said. "It's ***Beat the Devil***. I think they must have been making it up as they went along, and I'm positive they didn't have any prissy little rule about not having a drink when they had work to do. No worries about getting out of shape, not on that set" [pp. 253-256].

In Stuart M. Kaminsky's *Denial* (2005), a Lew Fonesca mystery, Sally Porovsky, Fonesca's good friend working for Children Services of Sarasota, conned Lew into being the Big Brother to Darrell, a thirteen-year-old boy, whose reaction to Lew's video collection is nothing but predictable:

> When I got back to the room behind my office, Darrell was looking through my videos.
> "Never heard of any of this shit," he said.
> "A gap in your education," I said.
> "This stuff all black-and-white?" he asked, holding up the box for ***Beat the Devil***.

Fred MacMurray (Lt. Tom Keefer), Robert Francis (Ens. Willie Keith), Van Johnson (Lt. Steve Maryk) and Humphrey Bogart (Lt. Cmdr. Philip Francis Queeg) in a scene from Edward Dmytryk's *The Caine Mutiny* (1954).

"Most of it," I said as I put towel, soap and shaving things on a shelf.

Darrell was shaking his head [p. 191].

***The Caine Mutiny* (1954).** Bogart's biggest hit of the 1950s, next to or opposite *The African Queen*, was based on the popular World War II book by Herman Wouk and directed by Edward Dmytryk. The all-star cast includes Van Johnson, Fred MacMurray and Jose Ferrer. One of the first references to the film was found in Stephen King's novel *Christine* (1983), and the scene where it appears is a high school football practice (the narrator is Dennis Guilder, a good friend of protagonist Artie Cunningham):

So ... another week of hell on the practice field. Another week of Coach yelling *Hit that sucker*. One day we practiced for

nearly four hours, and when Lenny suggested to Coach that
it might be nice to have some time left for doing homework,
I thought—just for an instant—that Puffer was going to belt
him one. He had taken to jingling his keys constantly from
hand to hand, reminding me of **Captain Queeg** in *The Caine
Mutiny*. I believe that how you lose is a much better index to
character than how you win. Puffer, who had never been 0-2 in
his coaching career, reacted with baffled, pointless fury, like a
caged tiger being teased by cruel children [p. 126].

The context of the reference in James W. Hall's mystery *Mean High Tide*
(1994) is a passage where the narrator describes the favorite weapon of Roy
Murtha, in reality ex-gangster Ray Bianetti:

His wire was two feet long, with the steel ball bearings
fused to each end. Similar to the steel balls **Humphrey Bogart**
played with at the end of that mutiny movie, taking the steel
balls out of his pocket in the courtroom and fondling them and
giving it all away that he was crazy. Ball bearings like **Bogart**'s,
giving Murtha something to grip, and making it possible to use
the wire like a bolo if necessary, sling it around the neck of his
victim.

Murtha understood **Bogart**'s fascination for the steel
balls. Their weight, their perfect shape, the comfort they gave
him when he rolled them in his hand. In his coat pocket the
ball bearings clinked when he walked. It was how he got his
nickname. The clink of death approaching. Of course, there
were those who said it was the steel balls hanging between Ray
Bianetti's legs that made the noise. (p. 321)

Loren D. Estleman, in his Detroit novel *Edsel* (1995), makes an analogy
between the habit of Bogart's character in the film to the behavior of J. W.

Pierpont, a private eye working for trade union boss Reuther. The observation is made by the book's narrator, journalist Connie (Constantine) Minor, now—in the 1950s, when the book is set—hired as a pitchman by Ford Corporation's lawyer, Israel Zed:

> He rolled the ball over in his palm, pushing it with his thumb. Agnes and I had gone to see *__The Caine Mutiny__* at the Roxy over Christmas and I thought of **Bogart**'s Captain Queeg and his steel ball bearings.
>
> . . .
>
> Reuther looked down, saw what he was doing with the ball, colored a little, and put it in his pocket; I guessed he's seen the same movie [p. 97].

In his novel *Gladly the Cross-Eyed Bear* (1996), Evan Hunter (writing as Ed McBain) compares the behavior of toy company tycoon Brett Toland to that of Captain Queeg in the film (or Herman Wouk's novel):

> As Bobby unwraps the hard candy, Brett tells him all about this idea he's had for a teddy bear.
> Rolling the heads between his fingers the way **Queeg** rolled the stainless-steel marbles in *__The Caine Mutiny__* (but reforming smokers can be forgiven their little physical tics), Brett says that he suddenly remembered a hymn they used to sing in church when he was a Baptist growing in Overall Patches, Tennessee ... [p. 179]

Another reference to the film was found in Stuart M. Kaminsky's Florida mystery *Vengeance* (1999). After finding Beryl Tree's missing fourteen-year-old daughter, process server Lew Fonesca finds himself in front of the *Fair Maiden* boat, owned by John Pirannes, a dangerous call-girl operator, deciding what he needs to do next in order to protect the girl from the rich, powerful and dangerous pimp:

> I opened my eyes. A man stood on the deck, legs apart. He had stepped out of an ad in one of the *Vanity Fair* magazines in my allergist's office. He was wearing white slacks, white deck shoes and a black shirt with a little white anchor over his heart. His hair was white and blowing with the breeze. His legs were apart, his hands folded in front of him. I knew who he was.
> "Permission to come aboard," I said, remembering **The Caine Mutiny** and trying to inject a hint of sarcasm into my request [p. 165].

A humorous allusion to the film appears in Dermot McEvoy's novel *Our Lady of Greenwich Village* (2008), in a scene where Congressman Swift is having sex with his chief of staff, Peggy Brogan, and is distracted by the movie *The Song of Bernadette* on the television screen:

> The vibrator buzzed as Brogan rubbed herself, then grabbed a handful of balls with her fingers, causing Swift to step up and relentlessly pound her. It was all in the balls, Brogan knew, as she pulled Swift up into her.
> "Jesus," said Swift. "My God, that feels good" as he curiously thought of **Captain Queeg** and the ball bearings [p. 46].

It is worth adding here that in the same scene, Swift, a big fan of old movies, lectures about the cast of *The Song of Bernadette* and explains to Peggy that John Ridgley appeared also in *The Big Sleep* (p. 45) and Jerome Cowan in *The Maltese Falcon* (p. 46), each time mentioning Bogie as the leading man.

Audrey Hepburn as Sabrina Fairchild and Humphrey Bogart as Linus Larrabee in a scene from Billy Wilder's *Sabrina* (1954).

***Sabrina* (1954).** In this is enormously likeable romantic comedy, directed by Billy Wilder and co-starring Audrey Hepburn and William Holden, Bogart is admittedly cast against type, but he does not spoil the fun and even offers some new angle to his part. In addition to being mentioned in Lawrence Block's *The Burglar Who Thought He Was Bogart* (1995), in a passage presented under *Virginia City*, the film is alluded to twice by Harvey Holt, a brave and patriotic tech rep, in James A. Michener's novel *The Drifters* (1971), who offers an analogy (in the first excerpt) and defends the artistic quality of the American motion picture industry (in the second one):

> Two men court the same secretary from the French embassy in Constantinople: 'You saw what happened when **Humphrey Bogart** and **William Holden** were both in love with **Audrey Hepburn**.' This other **Hepburn** he always referred to as **Audrey**. For him there was only one Miss Hepburn, the actress [p. 462].

> 'Did you see the time when he and **William Holden** were both in love with **Audrey Hepburn**?'
> 'Who directed?' Gretchen asked.
> 'Directed? Who the hell cares who directed?' [p. 506]

***The Barefoot Contessa* (1954).** Written and directed by Joseph L. Mankiewicz, and co-starring Ava Gardner, Edmond O'Brien (Academy Award) and Rossano Brazzi, the film is referenced in a few novels. Just like thirteen other Bogart pictures, it is mentioned in James A. Michener's novel *The Drifters* (1971); the first passage illustrates an analogy while the second one offers a less successful attempt by Harvey Holt to defend the American film in general:

> The agricultural attaché in the American embassy makes a damned fool of himself over a Hong Kong party girl: 'Who can explain these things? Look at the way **Humphrey Bogart**

kept coming back to **Ava Gardner** after he had made her a great actress.' This one stumped me, as did many of his references. When I asked what picture he was referring to, he said, impatiently, 'You know. The one where a voice sang "Que Será, Será" in the background' [p. 462].

'Or when he was in Europe . . . just like you kids . . . only he was in love with **Ava Gardner**?'

This last rang a bell with Cato. 'Yeah, I caught it on a late, late show one night. A prime stinker' [p. 506].

The Mambo Kings Play Songs of Love (1989) by Oscar Hijuelos is a moving account of the lives and careers of two Cuban brothers who came to New York in the late 1940s and became quite successful musicians as leaders of their band, the Mambo Kings. The older brother, Cesar, is a free spirit and has many girlfriends. With one of them, Vanna, however, he has an especially good time, their relationship lasts much longer than others, and he treats her quite decently:

Like his music, the Mambo King was very direct in those days. He and Vanna had just been out to dinner at the Club Babalú and Cesar said to her, as she chewed on a piece of plantain fritter, "Vanna, I'm in love with you, and I want the chance to show you what it's like to be loved by a man like me." And because they'd been throwing down pitchers of the Club Babalú's special sangria, and because he had taken her to a nice movie—**Humphrey Bogart** and **Ava Gardner** in *The Barefoot Contessa*—and because he had gotten her a fifty-dollar modeling fee and an expensive ballroom dress with pleated skirt so she could appear between himself and his younger brother on the cover of "Manhattan Mambos '54"; and perhaps because he was a reasonably handsome man who seemed earnest and knew, as wolves know, exactly what he wanted from her—she could see it in his eyes—she was flattered enough that when he said, "Why don't we go uptown?" she said, "Yes" [p. 17].

The reference to Mankiewicz's picture in Stuart M. Kaminsky's *Midnight Pass* (2003) is a result of process server Lew Fonesca comparing his good friend/almost girlfriend Sally Porovsky to the famous actress:

> "Come over for dinner Sunday," Sally said.
> She looked tired but she was smiling. Her skin was clear, and in the red, white, and yellow lights of the stores in the mall she reminded me of **Ava Gardner** in <u>*The Barefoot Contessa*</u> [p. 233].

The film is also alluded to in Michael Malone's novel *The Four Corners of the Sky* (2009), in a passage which offers some information about Annie's aunt Sam's intimate life:

> Meanwhile, according to Clark, Sam had never recovered from the loss of her partner, Jill, whom she'd met on a whitewater-rafting vacation in Arizona, and who'd run off with someone else after living with Sam for seven years. Sam insisted she was still willing to try again, although she claimed vaguely to friends that she'd been about as lucky in love as **the Barefoot Contessa**. Few in Emerald had any idea what she meant by this analogy, or that the role in the movie had been played by their fellow Tar Heel, **Ava Gardner** [pp. 181-182].

The Left Hand of God **(1955).** Directed by Edward Dmytryk, this unusual picture (co-starring Gene Tierney) does not compare well with the earlier Bogart-Dmytryk collaboration, *The Caine Mutiny*. It is mentioned in *The Burglar Who Thought He Was Bogart* (1995) by Lawrence Block as one of the films Bernie sees at the festival at the Musette Theater. In the following passage, the narrator/protagonist gives some background information about the film:

> The second feature was *The Left Hand of God*, one of **Bogart**'s last films. He plays an American pilot in China during the war, working for **Lee J. Cobb**, who's a Chinese warlord. **Cobb**'s men kill a priest, and **Bogart** winds up escaping in the dead priest's clothing and holing up at a mission, where he poses as the priest's replacement, reminding me a little of **Edward G. Robinson** in *Brother Orchid*.
> It all works out in the end [p. 94].

American poster for William Wyler's *The Desperate Hours* (1955).

***The Desperate Hours* (1955).** Written by Joseph Hayes from his novel and play, and directed by William Wyler, this remarkable thriller (co-starring

Fredric March and Arthur Kennedy), where Bogart is once again cast as a ruthless killer, is referenced in Greg Iles's suspenseful novel *24 Hours* (2000). Since both Iles's book and Wyler's film depict a perfect and happy family facing an unexpected terror, the complex references to the movie are not accidental. The characters in the quoted scene are Karen Jennings, the terrorized mother, and Joe Hickey, the dangerous villain:

> Karen watched the digital clock beside her bed flash over to 1:00 A.M. She was sitting in the overstuffed chair in the corner, hugging her knees; Hickey lay on the bed, his injured leg propped high on some pillows. The Wild Turkey bottle sat beside him, along with Will's .38. His eyes were glued to the television, which was showing the opening credits of *The Desperate Hours* with **Humphrey Bogart** and **Fredric March**. She was glad he hadn't yet realized there was a satellite dish connected to the bedroom television; she didn't want him flipping through to Cinemax and getting and getting more ideas from the T&A movies they seemed to run all night.
>
> "**Bogey**'s good," Hickey drawled, sounding more than half drunk. "But Mitchum was the greatest. No acting at all, you know? The real deal" [p. 174].
>
> Karen rocked slowly but ceaselessly in her chair, her arms around her shins, her chin buried between her knees. Hickey was still lying on the bed, his eyes glued to **Bogart** and **Fredric March** as they played out the final minutes of *The Desperate Hours* [p. 187].
>
> Gunshots rang from the television. **Bogey** fell to the ground. "Goddamn it, Hickey said [p. 188].

***The Harder They Fall* (1956).** Bogart's last screen appearance, which was directed by Mark Robson and co-starring Rod Steiger, is not one of the very best Bogart pictures; still, it is an ambitious and skillfully executed commentary on professional boxing. It was based on Budd Schulberg's novel of the same title, which, ironically, contains a reference to Bogart (presented in Section II). The analogy between this film and a real-life situation occurring in James A. Michener's novel *The Drifters* (1971) is a little bit stretched:

> An Indonesian government official has to make a crucial decision: 'You have to stick with it all the way, just like **Humphrey Bogart** when he was writing the truth about **Rod Steiger** and the fight racket' [p. 462].

Rod Steiger as Nick Benko and Humphrey Bogart as Eddie Willis in a scene from Mark Robson's *The Harder They Fall* (1956).

The movie is also referenced in Loren Estleman's novel *The Hours of the Virgin* (1999), in a passage where the narrator/protagonist, private eye Amos Walker, shares with the reader his little joys of Christmas:

> I don't know why I thought of it. At Christmas I'd surprised myself with the gift of a VCR, the dividend from a

credit check I'd given up on getting paid for until the mail came on December 23rd, and I started thinking about Dale and his comic strips while standing in the classics section of the video store two streets from my house, three minutes to closing on the way back from Grosse Ile. The movie I was thinking of renting was ***The Harder They Fall***, which didn't belong to the same world as Nancy and Sluggo. I wound up renting *The Adventures of Rocky and Bullwinkle* and watched it straight through at home without taking off my coat. It didn't help, although Mr. Peabody reminded me a little of Gordon Strangeways [p. 133].

Bogart made a total of about seventy-five feature films during his relatively short career, tragically ended by his untimely death. He worked with director Lloyd Bacon seven times, but the most impressive long-term collaboration the actor had with John Huston (six films, all major accomplishments made in the second stage of Bogart's career) and Michael Curtiz (also six, with *Casablanca* being the definite highlight of their collaboration). Raoul Walsh cast Bogart in three important pictures, when the actor was in the transitional period, in the years 1939 – 1941. Four other major directors—William Wyler, Howard Hawks, Richard Brooks and Edward Dmytryk—hired Bogart twice, with the artistic results remarkable in most cases. As a supporting actor Bogart appeared five times opposite Bette Davis and Ann Sheridan, and four times opposite Joan Blondell. Ida Lupino was his co-star in two of the Walsh movies, and Sylvia Sidney starred in two of the actor's films released in 1937 and 1941. Mary Astor was opposite Bogart in Huston's two early pictures, and Lauren Bacall was lucky to play opposite her fiancé/husband in five major hits, including two directed by Hawks and one by Huston. Claire Trevor shares credits with Bogart in three movies made between 1937 and 1948, and Alexis Smith in two films from the mid-1940s. Bogart's other significant female co-stars, each playing opposite him only once, include Ingrid Bergman, Michele Morgan, Lizabeth Scott, Barbara Stanwyck, Gloria Grahame, Katharine Hepburn, Audrey Hepburn, Ava

Lizabeth Scott as 'Dusty' Chandler and Humphrey Bogart as Captain 'Rip' Murdock in a publicity shot for John Cromwell's *Dead Reckoning* (1947).

Gardner and Gene Tierney. The major male stars that repeatedly appeared in Bogart films include Edward G. Robinson (five times), Pat O'Brien (four), James Cagney (three), George Brent (two) and George Raft (two).

The references presented above cover fifty-one movies (a record that is extremely difficult to match by any filmmaker), which constitute two thirds of the actor's overall filmography spanned over the twenty-seven years of his career. The picture that collected the biggest number of literary references (only in my research) is *Casablanca*, mentioned in 108 works and thus surpassed (slightly) in this respect only by *Gone with the Wind*. The other Bogart films that stand out because of the abundance of references include *The Maltese Falcon* (forty), *The Treasure of the Sierra Madre* (nineteen), *To Have and Have Not* (fifteen), *The African Queen* (thirteen), *The Big Sleep* (ten), *High Sierra* and *Key Largo* (nine each), *The Petrified Forest* (eight), *Angels with Dirty Faces* and *The Caine Mutiny* (seven each), *Dark Passage* (five) and *Sabrina* (four). While two important films —*Dead End* and *The Roaring Twenties*— appear to be somewhat neglected by writers, even though each is mentioned in three works, the three pictures that are definitely overlooked in literature are Nicholas Ray's *In a Lonely Place*, a generally underrated masterpiece referenced only in two books, and John Cromwell's *Dead Reckoning* (1947) and Michael Curtiz's *We're No Angels*, with no reference found.

With this said, it needs to be made clear that Bogart is undoubtedly and unquestionably the all-time #1 movie star as far as the number and frequency of literary references are concerned. It is evident in the books that were researched for this publication, as well as in those that I have never read or seen or even heard of. Because, based on what I hear from many people, including Stephen Bogart (a voracious reader of, primarily, mysteries), Humphrey Bogart's name (in one way or another) and many of his films keep popping up in books to such a degree that they become a part of the usual, or ordinary, language (especially in crime fiction), and the experienced reader, instead of being surprised or amused, pays no attention to them anymore.

II. REFERENCES TO BOGART: THE MAN, THE ACTOR, THE CELEBRITY

One of the first references to Bogart himself appeared in Budd Schulberg's novel *The Harder They Fall* (1947), which is ironic considering the fact that Bogart appeared in the movie version of the book less than ten years later. The following excerpt starts with a conversation between the book's narrator/protagonist, boxing press agent Eddie Lewis (portrayed by Bogart in the film), and Al Leavitt, a nosy newspaperman:

> "You wouldn't trust your own mother, would you?" I said.
> "Not if she was in the fight game," Leavitt said.
> "Come on out to Pat Drake's and cool off," I said. "Pat's throwing a little party—just four or five hundred people—up at his joint in Bel Air."
> Drake was an ex-chauffeur for Nick back in his boot days who wandered into Hollywood when things got hot in New York, started working extra and went to the top as a rival studio's answer to **Bogart** [pp. 205-206].

Humphrey Bogart's publicity shot.

The actor is mentioned by name four times in Gore Vidal's novel *Myra Breckinridge* (1968), usually together with other movie stars. Here are two excerpts worth quoting in this section of the book due to their clearly flattering character and, in case of the second one, the narrator/protagonist's prophetic abilities:

> Of all students of the Academy, only one has sought to model himself on a Forties star: the sickest of the Easterners is currently playing **Humphrey Bogart**, and he is hopeless in the part. The rest are entirely contemporary, pretending to be folk singers, cowboys and English movie actors. Needless to say, all attempts at imitating Cockney or Liverpudlian accents fail [p. 40].

> But what will the current generation think of my efforts? That is the question. I find that any reference to stars of the Forties bores them. "Who was **Gary Cooper**?" asked one young thing last night; to which another girl answered, "The one with the big ears," thinking he was **Clark Gable**! But they all find **Humphrey Bogart** fascinating and he may yet prove to be my bridge to them [p. 62].

Bogart's name is mentioned as many as three times by Muriel, the "visitor from Hollywood," in the second scene of Neil Simon's play *Plaza Suite* (1969):

> JESSE (*Lolling back on the sofa*) In this very room . . . Will you stop with the celebrity routine. Aside from a couple of extra pounds, I'm still the same boy who ran anchor on the Tenafly track team.
> MURIEL   And is living in the old **Humphrey Bogart** house in Beverly Hills [p. 544].

> JESSE Why? You never asked me that when I kissed you in Tenafly.
>
> MURIEL You weren't a famous Hollywood producer living in **Humphrey Bogart**'s house signing John Huston for your next picture in Tenafly. Can I please have your reaction to my kiss? [p. 247]

> MURIEL For seventeen years?
>
> JESSE On and off.
>
> MURIEL In **Humphrey Bogart**'s old house? I don't believe you, "Mr. International Liar." And I don't trust you. (*She gets up and again begins to gather her belongings*) And I'm not staying [p. 248].

In Ed McBain's *Jigsaw* (1970), there is a lengthy conversation between cops on duty which contains an exchange of interesting, movie-related observations:

> Meanwhile, on the ferry to Bethtown, two other cops were working very hard at sniffing the mild June breezes that blew in off the River Harb. Coatless, hatless, Carella and Brown stood at the railing and watched Isola's receding skyline, watched too the busy traffic on the river, tugboats and ocean liners, a squadron of Navy destroyers, barges and scows, each of them tooting and chugging and sounding bells and sending up steam and leaving a boiling, frothy wake behind.
>
> 'This is still the cheapest date in the city,' Brown said. 'Five cents for a forty-five minute boat ride—who can beat it?'
>
> 'I wish *I* had a nickel for all the times I rode this ferry with Teddy, before we were married,' Carella said.

'Caroline used to love it,' Brown said. 'She never wanted to sit inside, winter or summer. We always stood here on the bow, even if it meant freezing our asses off.'

'The poor man's ocean cruise,' Carella said.

'Moonlight and sea breezes . . .'

'Concertina playing . . .'

'Tugboat honking . . .'

'Sounds like a Warner Brothers movie.'

'I sometimes thought it was.' Brown said wistfully. 'There were lots of places I couldn't go in this city, Steve, either because I couldn't afford them or because it was made plain to me I wasn't wanted in them. On the Bethtown ferry, though, I could be the hero of the movie. I could take my girl out on the bow and we could feel the wind on our faces, and I could kiss her like a colored **Humphrey Bogart**. I love this goddamn ferry, I really do.'

'Yeah,' Carella said, and nodded" [pp. 249-250].

This passage, among other things, gives the readers an idea of what kind of movies were made by Warner Brothers and reminds them that Bogart seldom appeared in a color picture.

James A. Michener's novel *The Drifters* (1971) contains references to as many as fourteen Bogart films and to as many as ten Tracy pictures. The reason for such an abundance of references to the two actors' movies is partially explained in Part Four (on Tracy) and partially in the following two excerpts, focused on the convictions of Harvey Holt, an abroad working tech rep, but also a war hero, a tiger killer, a regular Pamplona runner and a big American patriot:

He lived an intense emotional life which appeared, at casual inspection, to have been structured upon the films made by these two actors. Actually, it was the other way around; American life in those years was so clear-cut, the national values so well agreed upon, that films mirrored the consensus-type of life Holt led. Instead of his aping **Tracy** and **Bogart**, they were copying him. Art thus followed life, which is the preferred sequence; today art, especially popular music, invents new patterns which students follow in enthralled obedience [pp. 462-463].

Bogart represented the man Harvey felt he was; **Tracy**, the gentleman he would have liked to be. At his frontier stations he had ample opportunity to watch his favorites in their best films, for constructions firms provided their men with five films a week, and the oldies from 1940 to 1960 predominated [p. 463].

William Goldman, in his novel *Marathon Man* (1974), in addition to referencing two Bogart films (*Casablanca* and *The African Queen*), mentions the actor himself in three other places. Bogart appears in protagonist Tom 'Babe' Levy's thoughts, clearly as a role model, during Babe's exchange with Peter Janeway, a government man who, as it turns out later, plays on both sides of the fence:

"I'll take to down to D.C., we'll keep you hidden till whatever this is is over. Anything you want, I swear, please, just tell me."

Babe didn't even hesitate. **Bogart** wouldn't have hesitated. "I wasn't upset, Mr. Janeway, I swear, it was just curiosity; now that I know, I think it's terrific. I mean, historians don't get much chance to have adventures, it's kind of a sedentary profession, you know what I mean?" Sit on your tail all day, read, read, read [p. 157-158].

Then Bogart and other tough men of the screen come to Babe's mind when he is addressing his murdered brother:

Humphrey Bogart's publicity shot.

Babe went back to his chair in the corner and sat. He cleared his mind to mourn.

No chance.

"Doc," he said out loud. "You're gonna have to give me a raincheck." Because the truth was, the terrible and very strange truth was, simply that in all his adult life, he had never had an adventure before, and the thrill of it swept all possibility of thinking far, far away. **Bogie** and Cagney, they had adventures every day of their lives. Edward G. too. And now it was his turn [p. 159].

Finally, Babe refers to the actor's heroics once again in the continuation of the above quoted scene, when he tries to decide whether he should face the imminent danger in his apartment or go out and, at the same time, get some of his favorite egg cream:

> Heart, goddammit, pounding.
> Cagney wouldn't have even thought twice, **Bogie** would have gone unarmed after the egg cream, and here was he, panicked as he crept down the reasonably well lit stairs in what he knew was a fruitless quest for a mixture of chocolate and cold milk club soda [p. 161].

In John Updike's short story "Gesturing" (1974), Richard Maple, recently separated from his wife Joan, makes mental comparisons between himself and one of his children, John, in reference to their respective youth idols and influences:

> When I was fourteen, I lay around reading science fiction. You lie around looking at *Kung Fu*. At least I was learning to read.
> "It's good," John protested, his adolescent voice cracking in fear of being distracted from an especially vivid piece of slow-motion *tai chi*. Richard, when living here, had watched the program with him often enough to know that it was, in a sense, good; the hero's Oriental passivity, relieved by spurts of mystical violence, was insinuating into the child a system of ethics, just as Richard had taken ideals of behavior from dime movies and

comic books—coolness from **Bogart**, debonair recklessness from Errol Flynn, duality and deceit from Superman [p. 806].

A reference to the actor in Updike's novel *In the Beauty of the Lilies* (1996) appears during a conversation between Essie/Alma and her agent and lover, Arnold Fineman, about the fact that she, to his surprise, did sleep with Harry Cohn:

"Who says I didn't fuck him?" Perhaps jealousy would rouse him. Her sexual failure rankled. It was like a flop at the box office; your whole self was on the line . . .
"My friend of a friend says." He sucked smoke down twice and let a thin yellow-blue vapor bounce out with his words. "Don't tell me I was misinformed." She squeezed Arnie's muscleless bare arm, in amused salute to the **Bogart** echo [p. 356].

Robert B. Parker's *God Save the Child* (1974) is the novel in which Spenser meets Susan Silverman, his girlfriend appearing in several of Parker's subsequent Spenser books. At the end of their first dinner together, in Spenser's apartment, the following conversation takes place:

"Okay," I said. "I worked. I am a sleuth, and being a sleuth I can add two and two, blue eyes. If you half expected me to make a pass and you came anyway, then you must have wanted me to do so . . . sweetheart."
"My eyes are brown."
"I know, but I can't do **Bogart** saying 'brown eyes.' And don't change the subject" [pp. 223-224].

In another novel by Parker, *The Judas Goat* (1978), there are several allusions to Bogart's movies, such as *The Maltese Falcon* and *Casablanca*. Here is a reference to the actor himself, which takes place in a London hotel where Spenser suspects being ambushed:

> I thought about shifting it to my left hand. I wasn't as good with my left hand, and I might need to be very good all of a sudden. I wouldn't be too good if my gun hand had gone to sleep, however. I shifted the thing to my left hand and exercised my right. The gun felt clumsy in my left. I ought to practice left-handed more. I hadn't anticipated a gun hand going to sleep. *How'd you get shot, Spenser? Well, it's this way, Saint Pete. I was staked out in a hotel corridor but my hand went to sleep. Then after a while my entire body nodded off. Did **Bogie**'s hand ever go to sleep, Spenser? Did Kerry Drake's? No, sir, I don't think we can admit you here to Private-Eye-Heaven, Spenser* [p. 50].

Andrew J. Fenady wrote two novels featuring a Humphrey Bogart lookalike: *The Man with Bogart's Face* (1977) and *The Secret of Sam Marlow: The Future Adventures of the Man with Bogart's Face* (1980)—both making numerous references to Bogey and his films. The former book was already quoted in such entries as *The Maltese Falcon*, *Casablanca*, *The Big Sleep* and *The Treasure of the Sierra Madre*. Below there are some of many references to the actor himself. First mentioned in the dedication—along with such names as Dashiell Hammett, Raymond Chandler, Dick Powell and Gene Tierney—the actor appears then in the expository part of the novel, which announces the protagonist's transformational operation:

> *So Dr. Inman performed the operation. Now he was about to remove the man's bandages.*
>
> *Yes – the operation was successful. The man looked exactly like* **Humphrey Bogart** [p. 7].

An allusion to Bogart's famous mannerisms, including his minor speech impediment, can be found only two pages later:

> The blond twittered and said, "I'm here about the ad you put in the paper."
> Sam lowered his weapon and twitched his upper lip. "Which ad, Duchess?" Sam was a little sibilant when he talked.
> "I put in more than one" [p. 9].

The next quotation is a nice illustration of a "what if" kind of deliberation pertaining to the history of the cinema:

> You know, Sam thought to himself, Dana Andrews was swell in *Laura* – but just think if **Bogart** had played Lieutenant McPhearson. God almighty – just think of **Bogart** smoking his cigarette and looking up at the portrait of Laura. What a love scene [p. 21].

Another allusion to one Bogart's mannerisms, most memorable from *The Big Sleep*, is made during the exchange between Sam and Elsa Borsht concerning her father, Horst:

> "You know," Sam continued, "the acoustics here are among the finest in the world."
> "Yes, I know." The redhead was still confused. "About my father –"
> "What's his first name?"
> "Horst."
> "Horst Borsht?"
> "That's right."
> "These men who've been following him." Sam pulled at his earlobe. "Have you ever seen them?"

"Yes. From a distance" [pp. 25-26].

Bogart's typical attire is described in a passage relating Sam and Gena's visit to the Wax Museum:

> In front of it was a wax figure of **Bogart**.
> **Bogey** was wearing a gray felt hat. Both hands were in the pockets of his trench coat. Both pockets had bullet holes and powder burns on them. The left sleeve also had a hole through it [p. 81].

Fenady's sequel to *The Man with Bogart's Face*, called *The Secret of Sam Marlow*, also includes multiple references to Bogart and his movies, such as *The Petrified Forest*, *High Sierra*, *The Maltese Falcon*, *Casablanca*, *Key Largo* and *Knock on Any Door*. The actor himself, again, is mentioned for the first time in the expository part of the book:

> It was a year ago that the plastic surgeon removed the bandages. The operation proved successful. Very successful. Dr. Inman's patient looked exactly like **Humphrey Bogart**. But it wasn't just the face that was changed. From now on it would be a new name and a new life. With danger, dames, and dough. Like **Bogart**. Yeah, **Bogart**. He knew how to live and love. There'd never been anyone quite like him. Until now.
> That's how Sam Marlow, private investigator, was born [p. 1].

Soon the actor's name appears again—this time in a nostalgic paragraph about Southern California of the 1930s:

> Two hours later he had driven through Palm Springs. In the early thirties, Ralph Bellamy and Charlie Farrell picked up

fifty-three acres on Indian Avenue for thirty-five hundred bucks and started the Racquet Club. **Bogart** was a good tennis player and golfer. He came down to Palm Springs quite often and played at the Racquet Club. But now Palm Springs was Dixie. The elite had moved farther east toward Rancho Mirage, Palm Desert, Indian Wells, and La Quinta [p. 3].

In another passage regarding the past, Sam reminisces about his visit to Newport to say goodbye to the dying John Wayne:

> Duke lifted his right hand. On his emaciated wrist there was still the brass bracelet given to him by the Montagnard guerrillas of Vietnam. And he managed to grin at Sam.
> "You glorious sonofabitch." Duke's voice was even coarser than usual. "You got away with it, didn't you, Trooper? Wait till I tell **Bogey**. He'll laugh like hell. You always were a glorious sonofabitch. Weren't we all—glorious sonsabitches!" [pp. 24-25]

The book contains some insightful observations about the major Hollywood studios. The paragraph about Warner Brothers, needless to say, lists Bogart as one of its greatest stars:

> Warner Brothers was the tabloid of the studios. Stories right out of the headlines, the streets and alleys. Fast-paced gangster pictures with machine-gun dialogue and editing. Social dramas and, later, historical biographies with people like George Arliss, Paul Muni, Eddie Robinson, and Johnny Garfield. And, of course, **Bogart** [p. 17].

And, in one more quotation from Fenady's novel, the narrator and/or Sam addresses the problem of the correct spelling of Bogart's nickname:

> He got into the grey coupe and started south toward Wilshire. Some spell it **_Bogie_** and some spell it **_Bogey_**. Sam preferred **_Bogey_**. No special reason, but then he didn't have to have one. A man or a woman can spell his or her name any way he or she prefers. So that closed the book on that one [p. 130].

Charles Bukowski did not appear to be a big movie buff, and his film references are relatively scarce. However, his appreciation of Bogart is quite apparent in a number of references that appear in at least a couple of his novels—*Factotum* (1975), where *Casablanca* is mentioned briefly and rather insignificantly, and *Hollywood* (1989), for the excerpt from which see Part Three, on Gable—and several short stories. (Note the spelling differences in some of Bukowski's works: he does not always start sentences with a capital letter.)

In "A Rain of Women," a story about the nameless narrator's Friday afternoon, disappointing due to the man's errands and indecisiveness which cancel pleasant opportunities, the name of the actor is mentioned twice, as the narrator's alter ego, in the conclusive paragraph:

> I walked out in the rain and back to my car, opened the trunk, threw the meat in and stood back against the wall, looking worldly, smoking a cigarette, waiting for them to run it up the rack, waiting for the first post, but I knew that I had failed, failed an easy one, failed a good one, a gift from the heavens on a shit rainy day, Los Angeles, a Friday going into evening, the cars still going by with wipers going going going, no faces behind the glass, and me, **Bogart**, me, the one who has lived, crouched up against that wall, asshole, rounded shoulders, the Benedictine monks laughing wildly as they drank their wine, all the monkeys scratching, the rabbis blessing pickles and weenies; the man of action – **Bogart**, leaning on a Biers-Sobuck wall, no fuck, no guts, it rained it rained it rained, I'll take Lumber King

in the first and parlay it to Wee Herb; and a mechanic came and got it and ran it up the rack and I looked at the clock – 5:30, it was going to be close, but somehow it didn't matter so much anymore. I threw the cigarette out in front of me and stared at it. the red glow stared back. then the rain put it out and I walked around the corner looking for a bar [p. 159].

The main characters of "Night Streets of Madness" are Bukowski himself and "the kid," a young poet to whose collection of poems the narrator has written a foreword. "The last of a drunken party," they are having a nice chat when a loud horn outside of the house ruins the moment:

"let's go out there and tell them to jam that horn up their ass," said the kid, influenced by the Bukowski myth (I am really a coward), and the Hemingway thing and **Humphrey B.** and Eliot with his panties rolled. well. I puffed on my cigar. the horn went on [pp. 160-161].

In "Animal Crackers in My Soup," the narrator (using the name Gordon Jennings) accepts an unlimited hospitality of a strange woman named Carol, who runs the Liberated Zoo. It is Carol who makes a reference to two movie stars when describing her guest:

I stretched out beside Carol. She turned on her side, resting her head upon my arm. I faced her. The whole sky and earth ran through those eyes.

"You look like Randolph Scott mixed with **Humphrey Bogart**," she said.

I laughed. "You're funny," I said.

We kept looking at each other. I felt as If I could fall down inside her eyes [p. 210].

"The Murder of Ramon Vasquez" tells a story of the titular character, an old, homosexual movie star from the silent era, who unwisely lets two young and hungry fans enter his house, offers them a meal and, as a result, gets murdered. Bogart is one of several movie stars that become the topic of the introductory conversation:

> The boys snatched at the food. It didn't take them long. The plate was clean.
> Then they started on the wine.
> "Did you know **Bogart**?"
> "Ah, only slightly."
> "How about Garbo?"
> "Of course, don't be silly."
> "How about **Gable**?"
> "Only slightly."
> "Cagney?"
> "I never knew Cagney" [p. 215].

Adam Kennedy's novel *Just Like Humphrey Bogart* (1978) starts with a reference to the movie star in the title itself due to some evident similarities between the main character, aspiring actor Duffy Odin, and Bogey's overall screen persona. A direct reference to the actor's name is also made twice in the book—in addition to the one within the excerpt presented in the entry on *To Have and Have Not*—first during a conversation between the protagonist and Hermione Wessen, a German agent living in Paris:

> Frau Wessen, the faint shadow of a mustache and husky voice on the telephone, liked by chances. "I like your future," she said. "I can help you. You remind of **Bogart** [p. 11].

The second reference to Bogart takes place during a meeting with another agent, American Asher Durst, to whom Duffy is introduced by Helen, his ex-girlfriend and presently a good friend trying to help him:

> New York is dead unless you're doing a play, or a daytime television show. A soap opera. Almost everything else is done on the Coast. I have a service office here but I spend most of my time in California. That's where the action is. And for *you*, unless you're dead-set on working in the theatre, I'd say there's no question. You should be on the Coast." He turned to Helen and said, "You're right. He does remind me of **Bogart**. Something about the mouth" [pp. 112-113].

Stuart M. Kaminsky is a big fan of Bogart and his films, which is evidenced by numerous allusions in his books. Two references to the actor were found in *Bullet for a Star* (1977). The first one appears in a scene where private eye Peters tries to locate actor Harry Beaumont (a blackmail and murder suspect, playing a state trooper in *High Sierra*) and he talks first to Warner Brothers gate guard Hatch, then to actor Jerome Cowan, and finally to Bogart:

> "Beaumont just had a few unpleasant words with **Bogie**, said Cowan, "maybe he knows which way your man went."
> I thanked Cowan who told me they were on a shooting break and **Bogart** was probably halfway up the hill. I started up the hill toward a knot of people, one of whom was talking rather loudly in a voice I recognized, a near-angry lisp.
> "Try it again, one more time," growled **Bogart**.
> I was close enough to see a wirey little guy in a state trooper's uniform lunge at **Bogart**, who laughed, jumped on top of the man and went tumbling with him into a tree.
> "That's one out of two," said **Bogie** his back against a tree and panting. "Let's leave it at that."

Four Hollywood Legends

The state trooper and two other men and a skinny woman carrying a script started down the hill. As I moved toward **Bogart**, he looked up at me.

"Don't tell me," he said lifting his upper lip in a familiar grimace of thought. "Peters, Toby Peters, used to work security at the studio." He started to get up but I motioned him back, took his hand and joined him against the tree. "Where you been?"

"Private investigator," I said. He nodded and lifted an eyebrow. **Bogie** had always looked either very gentle to me or very rough. There was no in-between. Right now he looked rough as he nervously touched the lobe of his left ear. His hair was shaved at the sides and he seemed a bit jumpy [pp. 87-88].

The second reference takes place while Peters is listening to the radio:

On KFI, Jimmy Fiddler told me that Vivien Leigh and Laurence Olivier were just married and **Humphrey Bogart**'s career was skyrocketing [p. 126].

In another mystery by Kaminsky, *Murder on the Yellow Brick Road* (1977), also set set in Los Angeles of 1940, Bogart is mentioned in a passage narrated by Peters:

From 1:30 to 3:30 in the afternoon I watched the scenery and listened to the Radio Parade for Roosevelt. Eleanor Roosevelt, Joseph P. Kennedy, Henry Fonda, Groucho Marx, Walter Huston, Katharine Hepburn, Lucille Ball and **Humphrey Bogart** all told me why I should vote for F.D.R. Since I knew **Bogart** slightly, I was impressed, but I didn't think I was even registered to vote. (p. 66)

In Kaminsky's novel *High Midnight* (1981), there is a scene where Peters is talking on the phone with Marco Hanoyez, the multiple killer, not exposed yet. Marco praises Peters for the bluff he pulled on a couple of hoodlums in order to get out of a crime scene (where their boss, Lombardi, was killed).

> "Okay," I said. "You think you know who killed Lombardi, Tillman and your brother-in-law Larry."
> "I know," he said, taking a deep breath of air. All I could smell was the dead fish. "That was a sharp trick this afternoon. You really did an act, like . . . like **Bogart** or one of those guys" p. 167].

Peters is once again the narrator in Stuart M. Kaminsky's *The Devil Met a Lady* (1993), a novel where two references to Bogart were found. Acting as a private eye, who was hired to protect Bette Davis by her second husband, Peters reveals his thoughts about the famous actress:

> The word on the lot had been that she was a decent sort, feet to the ground, who got a bad deal from the Brothers Warner. . . . Though the trades wondered what she was complaining about, the people who worked on the lot knew that she was getting paid far less than any of the male leads, including Cagney, Flynn, Raft, **Bogart**, or even Edward G. Robinson, all of whom had the right to turn down projects [p. 42].

Then Tobey Peters talks to the lady selling celebrity cookies at the bakery:

> "Howard Duff on the radio is one of my favorites," she said. "Saw a picture of him in a fan magazine. I could do a Howard Duff cookie."

"Call it a Sam Spade cookie," I suggested, putting my wallet away. "Npbody knows what Duff looks like."

"Then the customers would think it was a bad **Bogart**" [p. 49].

A nice paragraph including an original reference to Bogart appears in Lawrence Sanders's *The Sixth Commandment* (1979), where the narrator, foundation's grant investigator Samuel Todd, shares his inner thoughts with the reader:

> It was not a memory, since I was too young to recall an ancient hotel lobby like that, smelling of disinfectant and a thousand dead cigars. I could only guess I remembered the set from an old movie, and any moment **Humphrey Bogart** was going to shamble over to the enameled blonde, buy a pack of Fatimas, and lisp, "Keep the change, tweetheart" [p. 29].

George Baxt's *The Tallulah Bankhead Murder Case* (1987) makes a reference to the fights between Bogart and his third wife in a scene where Tallulah Bankhead talks to sculptor Nanette Walsh:

> She indicated Nanette's bruised face with a gentle wave of a hand. "I assume those are legacies left you by Mr. Zang. Dahling, you'd do better to use Max factor eight. It does wonders for bruises and miracles for black eyes. O got that tip from Mayo Methot." She provided in an aside, "**Bogart**'s penultimate wife" [p. 164].

Bogart's third wife is also mentioned in another mystery by Baxt, *The Humphrey Bogart Murder Case* (1995):

"Her name is Mayo Methot." Her face hardened. "She's married to a bum named **Humphrey Bogart**."

. . .

"We recognize the name, Miss Wood," said Marley, now with added exaggerated patience. He wished he could contact **Humphrey Bogart** to tell him what an overbearing bitch his mother-in-law was, though it immediately occurred to him that **Bogart** was probably well aware of it" [pp. 3-4].

In his mystery *The Greta Garbo Murder Case* (1992), Baxt mentions Bogart in three places, each time as an obvious celebrity. The first excerpt is a part of a conversation between Police Detective Herb Villon and Federal Agent Arnold Lake about Peter Lorre:

Villon said, "I know him slightly. We sweat it out in the same steambath on Thursday night where the celebrities go. You know, **Bogart**, Eddie Robinson, Vic McLaglen...." [p. 82]

The other two allusions reflect the kind of relationship that Bogart had with Erich von Stroheim in the context of Romanoff's, where von Stroheim is taking Alysia Hoffman, his lover and member of the cast:

"Come Alysia. How's about Romanoff's? I feel in a festive mood tonight. Maybe **Bogie** will be there. I enjoy trading insults with him" [p. 151].

The lady in question was reading her director's palm. The lighting at Mike Romanoff's restaurant in Beverly Hills was subdued and flattering and there was no **Humphrey Bogart** for von Stroheim to trade barbs with [p. 156].

In addition to numerous references to Bogart's pre-1942 films in George Baxt's *The Humphrey Bogart Murder Case* (1995), the name of the actor himself, either as Humphrey Bogart, Bogart or Bogie, appears on almost every page of the book as he is one of the major characters. Below there are two insightful passages referring to the actor's private life, one related by the character of Bogart himself and one by the omniscient narrator:

> "I was! I was a real mean kid." He was warming up himself, usually his least favorite subject. "I went to this very exclusive private school. Trinity. It was so exclusive, I think it didn't have an address. The kids used to beat me up." He laughed. "I suppose I wasn't exactly a charmer, what with my kind of parents and my poor sisters terrified of both of them. Poor Pat. How she suffered. I think her breakdown was a blessing [p. 25].

> Hammett and Hellman tailed **Bogart** in his car. **Bogart** was listening to the news on the radio and liking none of what he heard. Britain under bombardment, the U.S. escalating conscription. In World War I **Bogart** had been in the navy. He hated it. He was a seaman second class on the *Leviathan* and became a master at swabbing decks. An accident scarred his upper lip resulting in his slight lisp which had already become his trademark. Now he was just past forty and didn't think he'd be called up. The country was not yet at war but it was inevitable. There were rumors that President Roosevelt was listening with interest to the overtures of the British to come on in, the water's just fine.... **Bogart** thought about his fellow actors at Warner Brothers. He couldn't see Cagney, Paul Muni, George Raft, Pat O'Brien, Alan Hale bearing arms. The younger ones would be called. Bill Lundigan, Herb Anderson, and, with any luck, that pain in the backside Reagan who kept insisting one day he'd be president of the United States. **Bogart** advised him, "First learn how to act. The presidency is a great part. It's almost as good as

Hamlet." Next he tried to envision Mayo as a war wife. It wasn't easy [p. 82].

George Baxt's subsequent novel, *The Clark Gable and Carole Lombard Murder Case* (1997), contains one reference to *Virginia City* and several to Bogart. The one below appears during a chat Police Detective Herb Villon has with Mala Anouk, Nana Lewis and Nell Corday, three aspiring actresses and protégés of Carole Lombard:

> "Did Prince Mike fall all over him?" asked Herb. Mike Romanoff, who owned the famous Hollywood eatery, insisted he was a Russian Romanoff and was Hollywood's most famous inside joke. But he was popular with many stars, **Humphrey Bogart** being his biggest champion [pp. 43-44].

The actor's name is mentioned once again when the narrator offers more information about Romanoff:

> Mike Romanoff was a bogus prince and Hollywood was notorious for taking anyone and anything bogus to its heart. Mike carved his niche quickly, thanks to endorsements from the likes of **Clark** and Carole and **Humphrey Bogart** and his wife Mayo Methot, with whom he was constantly embroiled in battle [p. 128].

In the next passage, Bogart becomes one of the book's characters and participates in the conversation, along with his wife, Detective Villon and his girlfriend Hazel, Carole Lombard and F.B.I. agent Carl Arden:

> **Bogart** asked Herb Villon, "Got any suspicions you can share with us?"

"It's too soon in a murder case to share anything. Hazel, what the hell are you scribbling in that pad of yours?"

"Anything I think is usable," snapped Hazel.

"You mean salable," said Mayo.

Carl Arden's brain was whirling. The banter at the two tables was all too fast for him. This wasn't like Washington where the men dressed like floor walkers and had floor walker mentalities.

Carole asked Arden, "I think your mind's wandering. Don't let it wander too far, it might get lost."

Arden admitted, "You're all too quick for me."

Bogart said, "I think Lynton's killer was too quick for him. He wasn't murdered in his casino, eh? But he was floating in the ocean. Doing the dead man's crawl?" [pp. 131-132]

The actor appears as himself a few more times in the continuation of the scene that takes place at Romanoff's (pp. 134, 138-139), and then when he informs his wife of his decision to leave:

> **Bogart** looked at his wristwatch and said to Mayo, "Let's go home. I know it's early but we can spar a few rounds in the basement" [p. 142].
>
> [Photo 29. Caption: Humphrey Bogart's publicity shot.]

An unassuming simile involving the actor's name appears in Peter Lovesey's mystery *Diamond Solitaire* (1992), in a narrative/descriptive passage focused on the book's protagonist, detective Peter Diamond, currently working as a security guard:

> About six, no further on in his conclusions, he took the subway south and found his way to Battery Park. The Statue of Liberty was already a blue silhouette fading in the evening light.

A ferryboat came in and he watched the procedure as the iron trellis snapped back and the passengers disembarked. With a strong breeze blowing, he was glad of his raincoat—which he'd never thought of as anything like Lieutenant Columbo's. It was a trenchcoat really, well lined and with flaps that could button across the chest. With the hat, it was definitely more **Bogart** than Peter Falk [p. 252].

Two brief references to the actor were found in Dennis Lehane's *A Drink Before the War* (1994), both scenes taking place at expensive Boston hotels, the Ritz-Carlton and the Copley Plaza, respectively. The narrator is private eye Patrick Kenzie.

> My shoes clacked with military crispness on the marble floor, and the sharp creases of my pants reflected in the brass ashtrays. I always expect to see George Reeves as Clark Kent in the lobby of the Ritz, maybe **Bogey** and Raymond Massey sharing a smoke [p. 4].

> The Copley's still trying to bounce back from its status as the city's most forgotten hotel. Its latest multimillion-dollar refurbishment will have to go a long way to erase its once dark corridors and staid-to-the-point-of-death atmosphere from people's minds. They started with the bar, though, and they've done a good job. Instead of George Reeves and **Bogey**, I always expect to see Burt Lancaster as J. J. Hunsecker holding court at a table, a preening Tony Curtis at his foot. I mentioned this to Angie as we entered [p. 117].

Lawrence Block mentions as many as twenty-six of Bogart's movies in his mystery *The Burglar Who Thought He Was Bogart* (1995), almost each of them accompanied by the actor's name, which also appears independently (i.e. without being attached to any specific film) in many pages of the book. A lengthy, and extremely flattering, passage referring to Bogart is the one which relates the first encounter of the male protagonist with the main female character:

> She'd been holding a book, and she placed it on the counter where I could see it. It was Clifford McCarty's **_Bogey: The Films of Humphrey Bogart_**, the hardcover edition published thirty years ago by Citadel Press. I checked the penciled price on the flyleaf.
> "It's twenty-two dollars," I sad. "And, because I'm honest to a fault, I'll tell you that there's a paperback edition available. The title's slightly different but it's the same book."
> "I have it."
> "It's around fifteen dollars, if memory serves, and sometimes it does." I blinked. "Did you just say you have it?"
> "Yes," she said. "It's called **_The Complete Films of Humphrey Bogart_**, and your memory serves you quite well. The price is fourteen ninety-five."
> "And you already own it."
> "Yes. I want a hardcover copy."
> "I guess you're a fan."
> "I love him," she said. "And you? Do you love him?"
> "There's never been anybody quire like him," I said, which, when you come right down to it, could be said of just about anyone. "He was one of a kind, wasn't he? He had—"
> "A certain something."
> "That's just what I was going to say." The tips of my fingers rested on the book, scant inches from the tips of her fingers. Her nails were manicured, and painted a rich scarlet. Mine were not. I fought to keep my fingers from reaching out for hers, and

I said, "Uh, I have a copy of the **Jordan Manning** biography. At least I did the last time I looked."

"I saw it."

"It's out of print, and difficult to find. But I guess you already have a copy."

She shook her head. "I don't want it."

"Oh? It's supposed to be good, but—"

"I don't care," she said. "What do I care about his life? I don't care where he was born, or if he loved his mother. I don't give a damn how many wives he had, or how much he drank, or what he died of" [pp. 58-59].

Needless to say, the conversation is continued with many film titles mentioned by both parties, and the quotations are presented in Section I of Bogart's part of the book.

In addition to a reference to *Casablanca*, Ilene Beckerman's book *What We Do for Love* (1997) mentions Lauren Bacall and Bogart in the protagonist's attempt to justify her own marriage to a much older man, whose name we never find out—except for a single initial ('H'):

> I was scared to tell my grandparents. I was twenty and the Professor was thirty-seven. Lauren Bacall was twenty and **Bogart** forty-five when they got married; Mia Farrow was twenty and Sinatra fifty when they got married. But neither Lauren nor Mia were Harry and Lillie Goldberg's granddaughter [p. 38].

A reference to the whole Bogart family appears in Dominick Dunne's novel *Another City, Not My Own* (1997), in a passage describing a location in Holmby Hills. The protagonist is writer and journalist Gus Bailey:

> For the occasion at hand, a small dinner to meet Marcia Clark, the gates of Ray Stark's estate in Holmby Hills were open

as Gus drove through. There were green hedges, white flowers, and the occasional piece of sculpture on either side of the long drive. He had been there before, many times, in years gone by. He'd been there even before the Starks bought the house, when the previous owners, the film stars **Humphrey Bogart** and **Lauren Bacall**, had lived there with their two small children. "That was a long time ago," Gus said to himself [pp. 49-50].

The actor is even mentioned in Dale Furutani's mystery *The Toyotomi Blades* (1997). The context is a conversation between the narrator/protagonist, Japanese-American amateur detective Ken Tanaka, and his Japanese opponent, Hirota:

> With him standing before me, a lot of things clicked into place, but the truth was that I was very surprised to see him. However, when you're shocked, hurt, and scared spitless, a little stupid macho posturing is allowed. It comes from watching too many **Humphrey Bogart** movies. "Where did you come from?" I asked.
> "From nowhere. I am the shadow. I am the wind. The way of Ninjitsu teaches me to be invisible."
> "Ninjitsu?"
> "The way of the Ninja," Hirota said. "I was quite invisible and you walked right past me."
> I didn't believe his. It was his turn to do some macho posturing. It's a male thing [p. 197].

Humphrey Bogart's name appears in at least two novels by Oscar Hijuelos, an American author born of Cuban parents. The Pulitzer Prize-winning book *The Mambo Kings Play Songs of Love* (1989) was already mentioned in the context of a reference to *The Barefoot Contessa*. The book contains three more references to the actor himself, one in the context of

Humphrey Bogart

Nestor's painful realization that he has been left by the love of his life, María:

> One night they were supposed to see a **Humphrey Bogart** movie and meet at their usual place, in front of a bakery called De Leon's. When she failed to turn up, he walked the streets looking for her until three in the morning, and when he returned to the *solar* he told his older brother what had happened and Cesar said that there was probably a good reason why she had missed their date [p. 105].

Another one appears in a passage describing the life and favorite pastime of Cesar Castillo as an older man, after his stay in the hospital:

> And of course he liked to watch the variety shows on Channel 47 from New Jersey, a Spanish broadcasting station, his favorite being the incredibly voluptuous Iris Chacón, whose jewel-beaded hips and cleavage made the Mambo King a little delirious, and he liked the old musicals from Mexico, like the kind that his former arranger Miguel Montoya used to compose scores for: vampire Westerns and masked wrestler/detective/ nightclub singer films and the soap operas about love and family, the women young and beautiful, the men virile and handsome, while he was just an old man now, sixty-two years old but looking seventy-five. Hollywood movies also made him happy, his favorites featuring the likes of **Humphrey Bogart**, William Powell, and Fredric March, Veronica Lake, Rita Hayworth, and Marilyn Monroe [p. 267].

Finally, the actor becomes a part of a simile in a passage listing some minor characters that Cesar recalls during his extensive reminiscences in the Hotel Splendour, New York, prior to his demise:

He remembered the short priest from the local parish who resembled **Humphrey Bogart** and always seemed to be looking down women's dresses [p. 333].

The author's equally moving *Beautiful María of My Soul* (2010) is neither a sequel nor a prequel to *The Mambo Kings* as it tells a parallel story of the older book's relatively minor character, María Garcia y Cifuentes, where she leaves Nestor Castillo in the middle of their ardent relationship, causing his misery till his untimely death at thirty-one, and also serving as the inspiration of a sad love song that turns out to be the biggest hit of the band led by Nestor and his elder brother Cesar. A reference to Bogey in the latter book appears in the first chapter, in a scene where María, having left her village, is off to a new life in Havana, hitchhiking in a stinking truck carrying animals:

> They'd come to another gas station, then a fritter place, with donkeys and horses tied up to a railing (sighing, she was already a little homesick). She saw her first fire engine that day, a crew of *bomberos* hosing down a smoldering shed, made of crates and thatch, near a causeway to a beach; a cement mixing truck turned over on its side in a sugarcane field, a coiling flow of concrete spewing like *mierda* from its bottom; then more billboards, advertising soap and toothpaste, radio shows, and, among others, a movie starring **Humphrey Bogart** and Lauren Bacall, whose faces were well known to even the *guajiros* of Cuba! (Another featured the enchanting visage of the buxom Mexican actress Sarita Montiel; another, the comedian Cantinflas.) [pp. 7-8]

Because this chapter of the novel is set in 1947, the movie mentioned in the passage can be either *To Have and Have Not*, *The Big Sleep* or, most likely, *Dark Passage*, then the most recent release.

An unusual reference to Bogart appears in Kirk Douglas's novel *Dance with the Devil* (1990), in a scene where film director Danny Dennison has lunch with agent Milton Schultz:

> Milt, dressed in his loudest checkered sports jacket, and Danny, in his dark-blue blazer and gray flannel slacks, had lunch at the studio commissary before the meeting. Chomping on a "**Humphrey Bogart**" steak, Milt mumbled, "Don't say I didn't get you into the studio" [p. 101].

Stephen Humphrey Bogart makes a clear allusion to Bogart as the protagonist's (and his own) father in his mystery *Play It Again* (1995), when he describes matrimonial detective R.J. Brooks and the kind of relationship he had with his father:

> But there were some burdens you just couldn't run away from. Genetics, for one thing. Some said he had his mother's sultry mannerisms, and what he remembered of his combative father's knotted physique and eccentric lisp. But he'd also shared their devotion to strong drink [p. 19].

> He was long used to not knowing his father, who had died too long ago, when R.J. was just a kid. They hadn't had much time together, what with the old man's busy work schedule and all [p. 89].

In Janet Leigh's novel *House of Destiny* (1995), the references to Bogart are mainly related to his open opposition to the procedures of the House Un-American Activities Committee:

> Among this group were some of the most gifted talents in the film industry—Dalton Trumbo, Lester Cole, Albert

Maltz, Herbert Biberman, Eddie Dmytryk and John Howard Lawson, to name a few. In all, they were labeled the Unfriendly Ten, and then the Hollywood Ten, and had subsequently been cited for contempt by Congress. A contingent of prominent Hollywood leaders had flown to Washington to attend a session of the hearings in support of those called to testify. Included in the trip were **Humphrey Bogart**, Lauren Bacall, John Huston, Evelyn Keyes, Danny Kaye, Sterling Hayden, and June Havoc [pp. 158-159].

The trip is mentioned again several pages later in an exchange between friends and business partners Jude and Wade:

> "Oh, Jude, why can't we be as uncomplicated as Basa and Floozy! Look at them—zonked—not even the impending birth of puppies concerns them."
>
> Wade looked at Jude, a sudden shadow passing over his face. "Do you think I'm chicken-shit because I didn't go to Washington with **Bogey**'s group? You know he called."
>
> "Hell, no, Wade. I think it would have been hypocritical if you had gone. You can't pretend to be what you're not! It wasn't because you were afraid, you rightfully chose not to go because you weren't dedicated to the cause. You damn well didn't know what it was all about then, and you're still not sure about it, even now [pp. 164-165].

A reference to a certain genre of films that Bogart used to appear in, especially during the war, was found in W.E.B. Griffin's World War II espionage novel *Blood and Honor* (1996), in a self-explanatory excerpt about one of the main characters, communications expert David Ettinger:

Although he was in fact an agent of the Office of Strategic Services—and before that an agent of the U.S. Army Counterintelligence Corp—David Ettinger rarely thought of himself as a real-life version of the secret agents **Humphrey Bogart**, Alan Ladd, and other film stars portrayed in the movies [p. 497].

A minor reference to Bogart was found in Don DeLillo's lengthy novel *Underworld* (1997), in a passage describing Lenny Bruce's performance during a Carnegie Hall midnight show in 1962:

> Lenny did a fair approximation of a street preacher's voice, which was surprising, which was very unhip in fact because even if he'd started in the business as a mimic, doing Cagney and **Bogart** with German accents, and even if he updated frequently, doing contemporary types of every persuasion, it was not a white comic's option these days to do a black man's voice, was it? [p. 627]

In Pete Hamill's *Snow in August* (1997), a novel set in New York City in the years after World War II, Bogart's name appears three times. The first reference is related to the RKO on Grandview Avenue, an expensive movie theater where young Michael Devlin had been taken by his father (subsequently killed in the Battle of the Bulge) and where his mother now gets a job as a cashier:

> Still, Michael longed for the Grandview the way he sometimes longed for his father. He passed it on long walks and gazed at the murals; he studied the showcards in their glass cases, telling of coming attractions. John Garfield. Betty Grable. **Humphrey Bogart**. John Wayne. At the Venus, all the movies

were old; they returned over and over again, the images ragged and often scratched [p. 81].

Then, the actor's name is mentioned, along with James Cagney's, in a scene where Frankie McCarthy, a bully and member of the gang called the Falcons, is arrested for assaulting a Jewish candy store owner:

> The crowd laughed and so did the Falcons, who were standing just inside the door of the poolroom. A few of them rested pool cues on their shoulders like baseball bats.
> "This is a bum rap," Frankie McCarthy said, lifting chin defiantly, like Cagney or **Bogart**. "They got nothin' on me" [p. 151].

The last reference, both nostalgic and informative, is related to another movie theater, the cheap Venus, where Michael used to go on a regular basis:

> The worst news was that a fire burned out the orchestra section of the Venus and the disgusted owner just gave up and closed the place. There was talk that the Falcons had set the fire because the owner threw Tippy Hudnut out for exposing himself to a twelve-year-old girl. Nobody could prove it. Not the exposure. Not the arson. And Michael imagined a roundup of all the characters who had passed across the screen in the dark: Gunga Din and Dr. Cyclops, Ken Maynard and the Durango Kid, **Humphrey Bogart** and James Cagney, Bing Crosby and Edward G. Robinson, along with Tarzan, King Kong, Superman, the Masked Marvel, and Dick Tracy [p. 247].

Erica Jong's *Inventing Memory* (1997) is a family saga spanning about a hundred years, mostly the twentieth century, with a considerable part set in post-World War II Hollywood. Bogart is mentioned in a letter from

Salome Levitsky Wallinsky to her daughter, Sally Wallinsky Robinowitz, in a passage referring to the funeral of her mother, Sarah Solomon Levitsky, a distinguished artist:

> *The memorial service for Mama was very moving. She touched so many lives. All her old cronies were there, looking frail. And her portraits all around. I never knew she did so many. She painted everyone—Calvin Coolidge to Loretta Young;* **Humphrey Bogart** *to Edward G. Robinson; Betty Grable to Marilyn Monroe; Babe Paley to Nancy Kissinger—though (in the early years) not always under her own name* [pp. 188-189].

There is a long passage in Elliott Roosevelt's mystery *Murder in the Lincoln Bedroom* (2000) describing a special auction organized by the First Lady. Bogart happens to be one of the Hollywood guests:

> The focus of the auction was Hollywood personalities, and the master of ceremonies was to be Cecil B. DeMille. Told that the First Lady was in the room, he strode toward her, beaming.
>
> "An auspicious evening," said the most famous film director in Hollywood, the creator of overblown, tacky biblical extravaganzas—a man, however, with a sure finger on the pulse of public taste. "I can't say how grateful we are to see you here."
>
> "I am most pleased to be here, Mr. DeMille," said Mrs. Roosevelt.
>
> "Let me present someone who is glad to see you again. I believe you know **Humphrey Bogart**."
>
> **Bogart** had approached just behind DeMille and was indeed conspicuously pleased to see the First Lady.
>
> For all his tough-guy roles, **Bogart** was actually the mannerly son of a park Avenue family. His father was a surgeon, his mother a professional photographer who sold pictures of her

son to an advertising campaign for baby food. He had served in the navy in the First World War, and a wound taken when a shell hit his ship had scarred and partially paralyzed his lip—the source of the notorious **Bogart** sneer.

"It's a real pleasure, ma'am. We met when you were in California visiting Elliott," said **Bogart**.

"I remember it well, **Mr. Bogart**. I remember it very well."

Bogart, who usually let his cigarette dangle from a corner of his mouth, held it between his fingers at his left side now. Since she last saw him he had developed a reputation for drinking heavily—though that might have been just gossip; gossip being next to motion pictures the most ostentatious product of Hollywood.

"I've seen Elliott since," said **Bogart**. "At a party given by Howard Hughes at his villa in the hills. I can compliment Elliott, ma'am. When he saw what kind of party it was, he was out of there pretty quick."

"What sort of party was it, **Mr. Bogart**?"

Bogart smiled. "Oh, nothing so bad. Not an orgy, certainly. It was centered on his pool and cabanas. Some of the girls were nude in the water. Some sat around in their underthings. I actually don't think Howard Hughes would have stood for anything . . . well, you know. But Elliott, I guess, saw right off that it was nowhere for a son of the President to be in wartime when other sons were—You know what I mean."

. . .

"I had a drink with him later, before he went back to war," said **Bogart**. "He explained it just as you have said it. I didn't ask him why he had departed from the Hughes party abruptly, but I think he used good judgment. [pp. 84-86].

Some minutes later Bogart is interrogated about Elliott's participation in that same party by columnist Hedda Hopper. His response includes some Latin, but the second paraphrase contains a grammatical error (the Perfect Tense of '*maneo*' is '*mansi*,' not '*mani*.'), which, however, should be attributed to the book's author (who, nota bene, conceived the whole passage as an inside joke about himself) rather than to Bogart:

> **Bogart** smiled the distorted smile his wound had caused. "*Venit, vidit, exit,*" to paraphrase Caesar. "He came, he saw, he left. When Elliott saw the naked girls, he shook hands with Hughes, thanked him for the invitation, and left."
>
> "I must say, that's a bit disappointing," said Hedda.
>
> "I suppose it is," said **Bogart**. "As for me, '*Veni, vidi, mani.*' I came, I saw, I stayed. It was no orgy, but it was my kind of party" [p. 88].

In Lorenzo Carcaterra's *Gangster* (2001), Bogart's name pops up in a lengthy passage where the narrator presents the real gangsters' perception of Hollywood crime films and actors:

> Above all else, however, gangsters love crime movies and police shows. Angelo and Pudge both would get a big laugh as they sat back and watched Hollywood's idea of what they did for a living, their every move glamorized and overdramatized. "Most of the time, the movies and shows are so far off base it's not even worth the time it takes to sit through them," Pudge the critic would often tell me between bites of an egg roll. "Rod Steiger as Al Capone goes beyond stupid. . . . You still don't pick up anything from watching any one of them work. Not like you did with somebody like Cagney. Him you could study, take what you saw him do and bring it out to the street with you and not have to worry about getting gunned down. A couple of

other old-timers had it figured out the right way, too. George Raft was one. Paul Mini and John Garfield were two more. But **Humphrey Bogart** didn't make the final cut. None of us ever bought him as a tough guy. We never paid for his sell. To us, he always came across as a rich boy acting tough, which, from what I understand, is what he was in real life" [pp. 361-362].

While the opinion expressed here about Bogart may appear unfavorable, it needs to be realized that the judgment is most likely based on the actor's characterizations in the gangster films of the 1930s—such as *The Petrified Forest*, *Dead End*, *Angels with Dirty Faces*, *The Roaring Twenties*, etc.—where, both through the way the roles were written and through the way Bogart consciously built his performances, the dominant traits of the guys he portrayed were meanness and cowardice. At the same time, the complexity of those characterizations announced the ambiguity in the actor's future persona, which made him a megastar in the 1940s.

In Martha Sherrill's novel *My Last Movie Star* (2002), Bogart's name (and Gable's) is mentioned during an extensive discussion among several deceased actresses' ghosts (including Mae West, Greta Garbo, Clara Bow, Colleen Moore, Ginger Rogers, Billie Burke) about different cemeteries:

> "Ferncliff Cemetery is awfully nice," interjected Billie, who hadn't been following the conversation too carefully.
> "Where's that?" asked Mae.
> "New York," I said.
> "All that rain and snow," said Colleen Moore. "And who wants to wind up next to Joan Crawford?"
> I shrugged.
> "I'm in Glendale," Clara was saying to Mae. "If it's good enough for Bette Davis, it's good enough for me. **Gable**'s there. He's got a semiprivate with Carole Lombard. And **Bogart** has full private."

"Full private?" I had to ask.

"At Forest Lawn, semiprivate pretty much means you get a corridor that's roped off," Mae explained. "The fans can still come see you, but they gotta step over a rope. It works if you want to make out like you're aloof—like you're the private type—but you really aren't. With full private, you get the iron gate, the private garden, the works. Nobody can come" [p. 272].

Loren D. Estleman, in his novel *Something Borrowed, Something Black* (2002), references Bogart, along with a few other major movie stars, in the description of a poster that is mentioned in a passage relating the days the protagonist's wife Laurie was forced to spend with gangster Charles Major's henchman, Roy Skeets, alias Abilene:

Abilene, who really did know his way around Hollywood, took her to Mann's (formerly Grauman's) Chinese Theater, where she mastered the urge to try out Jean Harlow's footprints like the prototypical tourist but bought a poster in the gift shop that showed James Dean standing in the boat crossing the Delaware while John Wayne rowed and **Humphrey Bogart** draped in his trench coat over Marilyn Monroe's shoulders [p. 69].

In Lilian Jackson Braun's mystery *The Cat Who Brought Down the House* (2003), the actor becomes an item on a list of Hollywood celebrities whose signed photographs make an exhibition in the local library in Pickax:

They had seen the announcement in Friday's paper: "Autographed photographs of old movie stars from the Thelma Thackeray collection—on temporary exhibition."

Eight-by-tens in individual easel-back frames filled the shelves in two showcases: Claudette Colbert, Ronald Colman,

FOUR HOLLYWOOD LEGENDS

Groucho Marx, Joan Crawford, Fred Astaire, **Humphrey Bogart**, Esther Williams, Edward G. Robinson, and more [p. 95].

Another reference to the actor appears in James Neel White's nonfiction book *I Was a P-51 Fighter Pilot in WWII* (2003), which was already mentioned under *Casablanca*, in a passage where the author/narrator strays from the main topic and talks about his experiences in a movie theater as a teenager (in 1938):

> I went to Saturday afternoon matinees at the Auditorium Theater where they had kids perform on stage (below the silver screen) for applause more than for prizes. I watched Western serials that featured Gene Autry, Tom Mix and the Lone Ranger and blew bubbles that snapped when revolvers did. When the dust settled, they always ended up with the good guys. I liked James Cagney, **Humphrey Bogart** and Johnny Weissmuller better because they were involved in things other than horses, ranches and shootouts [p. 62].

In addition to four of his films, Bogart himself is mentioned several times in Elizabeth Hay's *Garbo Laughs* (2003), a novel focused on a couple of years in the life of a Canadian family fascinated with old movies. The first excerpt is a part of a scene set in a fruit store, where Harriet Gold meets Dinah Bloom (about to become the family's close friend) and they talk about Harriet's eleven-year-old son, Kenny:

> They push their carts to the front, where it just so happens that the most beautiful woman in Ottawa is working the cash. While they wait in line Dinah asks if Kenny is still writing his **Humphrey Bogart** stories, and Harriet tells her he's too busy listing reasons why he should see *The Godfather* [p. 84].

The next passage is a commentary on Harriet and Lew's married life, following a scene in which Harriet is depressed because of being forced to host her aunt:

> Upstairs, Lew had made the mistake of smiling a peaceable, almost begging smile, and the gap between them widened. That smile. She was married to a kind man, but did she want to be? No. She wanted a thug who would go downstairs, grab everybody by the scruff of the neck, and throw them out into the night. Where was **Humphrey Bogart** when she needed him? Where was Sir Sean? [p. 175]

One more significant reference to Bogart appears in a scene where Harriet asks her son about his favorite actors:

> "I know it breaks your heart, but no. Who are *your* top five?"
> "Marlon Brando, Al Pacino, Paul Newman, **Humphrey Bogart**, Charlie Chaplin."
> She sat up, put on her glasses and stared at him. "What happened to Frankie?"
> Kenny looked sheepish. "They're better actors," he said [p. 276].

In Marisa de los Santos's *Love Walked In* (2005), there is an insignificant reference to Bogart on p. 78 and a significant allusion to his work later in the book, when two fictitious literary characters, both portrayed by Bogart on the screen, along with the actor's prime genre, are evoked during the exchange between Cornelia Brown (the narrator) and Martin Grace:

> "So I took a rather bold step today and engaged a private investigator," said Martin.

233

Four Hollywood Legends

"You did?" I asked, and **Sam Spade, Philip Marlowe**, and every film noir detective to whom the word "hard-boiled" was regularly attached began gumshoeing his way around my mind [p. 110].

Bogart's name, along with Robert Mitchum's, is mentioned in Joseph Wambaugh's *Hollywood Station* (2006), in a passage describing an impressive and famous building in Los Angeles, seen here through the eyes of cop Brantley Hinkle:

> The Bradbury Building, at 304 South Broadway, was an incongruous place in which to house the dreaded Professional Standards Bureau, with its three hundred sergeants and detectives, including the Internal Affairs Group, all of whom had to handle seven thousand complaints a year, both internally and externally generated against a police force of nine thousand officers. The restored 1893 masterpiece, with its open-cage elevators, marble staircases, and five-story glass roof, was probably the most photographed interior in all of Los Angeles.
>
> Many a film noir classic had been shot inside that Mexican-tile courtyard flooded with natural light. He could easily imagine the ghosts of Robert Mitchum and **Bogart** exiting any one of the balcony offices in trench coats and fedoras as ferns in planter pots cast ominous shadows across their faces when they lit their inevitable smokes. Brant knew that nobody dared light a cigarette in the Bradbury Building today, this being twenty-first-century Los Angeles, where smoking cigarettes is a PC misdemeanor, if not an actual one [p. 133].

James Scott Bell's *Try Darkness* (2008) is a sequel to *Try Dying* (2007). Here there is a scene in which protagonist/narrator Ty Buchanan talks with his ex-coworker and friend Al Bradshaw, a lawyer representing a company that Buchanan is now fighting. They are not able to understand each other, and Al, in his reproach, makes an analogy to characters played by Bogart:

> "Wait a minute," he said, now looking like he'd drawn that straight and was ready to go all in. "I see. You think there could be some connection between this chick's murder and Orpheus. You really do, don't you?"
> I said nothing.
> Al was happy to go on, tilting his head back as if telling a joke to a packed house. "Yeah! You got this idea you're some kind of **Bogart** or something, and you're gonna find a conspiracy. Yeah, Ty Buchanan, supercop" [p. 66].

Bogart is mentioned in two humorous mysteries by Jeffrey Cohen, *Some Like it Hot – Buttered* (2007) and *It Happened One Knife* (2008). In the former his name pops up in a conversation between narrator/amateur detective Elliot Freed and the wife of a man that died in Elliot's movie theater:

> "You don't talk like a movie theatre owner. You talk like a detective."
> "Watch enough **Bogart** and everybody talks like a detective" [p. 111].

In Cohen's *It Happened One Knife* (2008), the reference to Bogart takes place in a scene where Elliot Freed admires the skills of fictitious comedian Harry Lillis (who turns out to be a dangerous individual):

> "What a dump!" Lillis spouted, in a perfect Bette Davis impression. I had to admire his technique: Lillis was one of the few impressionists who didn't exaggerate the voice he was doing—he went for accuracy. In the Lillis and Townes films, he had spoken lines as Cary Grant, **Humphrey Bogart**, Dean

Martin, Dwight D. Eisenhower, and on one occasion, his partner [p. 44].

Thomas Pynchon's Southern California/Las Vegas mystery *Inherent Vice* (2009) includes a passage where Doc Sportello reveals his ideas about his own profession to his associate Fritz, mentioning two literature and film characters whose names unambiguously point out at the one and only actor who has portrayed both:

> They got into face-stuffing activities for a while, forgetting if they'd ordered anything else, bringing Magda back over, then forgetting what they wanted her for. "'Cause PIs are doomed, man," Doc continuing his earlier thought, "you could've seen it coming for years, in the movies, on the tube. Once there was all these great old PIs—**Philip Marlowe**, **Sam Spade**, the shamus of shamuses Johnny Staccato, always smarter and more professional than the cops, always end up solvin the crime while the cops are followin wrong leads and getting in the way" [p. 97].

Robert Olen Butler's unique novel *Hell* (2009) tells a story about evening newscaster Hatcher McCord, who unexpectedly finds himself in Hell and meets a long list of celebrities there. Bogart, one of the other Hell inhabitants, is referenced extensively in pp. 25-36; here are some excerpts worth quoting:

> Virgil says to the man, "He's here."
> "Thanks," the man says. And from the timbre of the voice and the sibilant "s", Hatcher instantly knows who it is. **Humphrey Bogart** turns to the side to clear the door. The light falls on his creviced face, and even though his eyes are still in the shadow of his hat brim, Hatcher can see their sad, dark depth.

Virgil vanishes in the shadows. Hatcher steps forward.

"You're late," **Bogey** says.

Hatcher moves past him and into the back staircase landing of a tenement. The lightbulb juts nakedly from a fixture in a side wall, and mounting the opposite wall is a vast dark shadow of the staircase banister. Hatcher looks around him with the panic of an actor's dream. He's on and he doesn't know his lines.

Bogey steps up beside him. "Her note said 4D."

"4D," Hatcher says.

"One more thing."

"Yes?"

"Put your hat on."

Hatcher realized there's something in his hand. He looks down. He holds a gun-metal gray snap-brim fedora. He puts it on.

The rasp and hiss of a match turns his face to **Bogey**, who is lighting a cigarette. **Bogey** drags once and exhales. He reaches into his inner coat pocket and pulls out a pack of cigarettes. He flicks one partway out. It's a Camel. He offers it to Hatcher [p. 25].

Hatcher and **Bogey** are standing before the dame and she's looking at the two of them, one at a time, back and forth, like she's trying to figure out which one of them is going to throw her over his shoulder and carry her out of a burning building.

Hatcher waits for **Bogey** to do the talking, but his partner isn't saying a word.... **Bogey** doesn't act like this around dames.

Finally, **Bogey** speaks. "You're not who you said you were."

"Who'd I say I was?"

Bogey hesitates. "Nobody."

"That's me," she says.

"You're not who I thought."

"I got no control over what you think."

Abruptly **Bogey** turns to Hatcher. "You talk to her." And **Bogey** heads for the window, which looks out into utter darkness. "I thought she'd be someone else," he says, low [p. 27].

Meanwhile, **Bogey** stares into nothing out the window as if it was something, and the voice in his head speaks: *I thought it was going to be her. I don't have any reason in this forsaken town to expect anything to turn out right, but somehow I thought it was going to be baby at last.... Baby is* **Bacall**, *after all. She has a well sense of timing. So she turns, and the hair falls a little over her face but you can see both her beautiful eyes, those wide-set eyes, and she give me that little half smile and we're together again. That's what I wanted real bad* [p. 28].

Hatcher backs out of the room and gently closes the door. He steps into the stairway landing, and **Bogey** is gone. He listens for the man's footsteps below, but hears nothing. "**Bogey**?" he calls. There's no answer. Even the corridor behind is quiet. They're all suffering in silence now, and it's time to move on [p. 35].

A reference to Bogart, because of a phrase that he was known for using frequently, appears in Annalena McAfee's novel *The Spoiler* (2011), in a draft written by columnist Tamara Sim about a legendary war correspondent years past her prime:

> *Honor Tait, friend of the stars, once the Marlene Dietrich of the newsroom, would never be a GI's pin-up these days, but, for all her years, she is still what* **Humphrey Bogart** *would call a fine-looking woman. Under her corrugated skin, the cheekbones, once no doubt rendered in paint by artist lovers, are still visible, the hair, a*

formerly lustrous strawberry blonde, now a handful of white feathers scattered over the rosy dome of her scalp [p. 153].

The quotations presented in Sections I and II of this part of the book come from over 240 literary works written by more than 130 authors. The writers that have shown an especial fondness of or a consistent interest in Bogart and his films are Stuart (M.) Kaminsky (fourteen works mentioning fourteen of his films), Lawrence Block (seven/twenty seven), John Updike (seven/four), Robert B. Parker (seven/three), Martha Grimes and Greg Iles (six/three), Joseph Wambaugh (six/two), Charles Bukowski (six/one), Evan Hunter/Ed McBain (five/five), Loren D. Estleman (five/five), Michael Malone (five/five), Elmore Leonard (five/four), James Scott Bell (five/two), George Baxt (four/eleven), Stephen King (four/four), Marcia Muller (four/four), Stuart Woods (four/two) and Pete Hamill (four/one). While Block also holds the record of mentioning the largest number of Bogart movies in one work (twenty six, in *The Burglar Who Thought He Was Bogart*), the runners-up in that respect include James A. Michener's *The Drifters* (fourteen), Bill Crider's *We'll Always Have Murder* (thirteen), Baxt's *The Humphrey Bogart Murder Case* (ten), Dermot McEvoy's *Our Lady of Greenwich Village* and Michael Malone's *The Four Corners of the Sky* (five each).

As some of the books mentioned in the previous paragraph are significant for using Bogart's name as part of their titles, it is appropriate to show the complete list of the works that make a point of alluding to the actor's name or films in the title or subtitle, or using him as one of the major characters. Here they are:

Play It Again, Sam (1968) by Woody Allen, *Bullet for a Star* (1977) by Stuart M. Kaminsky, *The Man with Bogart's Face* (1977) by Andrew J. Fenady, *The Secret of Sam Marlowe: The Further Adventures of the Man with Bogart's Face* (1980) by Andrew J. Fenady, *Hubert: oder, Die Rückher nach Casablanca* (*Hubert, or the Return to Casablanca*, 1978, in German) by Peter Härtling, *Just Like Humphrey Bogart* (1978) by Adam Kennedy, *The Burglar Who Thought He Was Bogart* (1985) by Lawrence Block, *The Humphrey Bogart Murder Case*

(1995) by George Baxt, *Play It Again* (1995) by Stephen Humphrey Bogart, *The Remake: As Time Goes By* (1997) by Stephen Humphrey Bogart, *As Time Goes By* (1998) by Michael Walsh, *We'll Always Have Murder: A Humphrey Bogart Mystery* (2001) by Bill Crider and *Say It Again, Sam* (2004) by Mary McBride. The list would be considerably longer if it included the mysteries recently written by some self-published authors.

Bogart references collected for this publication are unevenly distributed in time, showing a cubic progress in numbers from only one reference found in a book from the 1940s, two from the 1950s, twenty five from the 1960s, and then growing even faster, reaching nearly seventy in the 1990s and about the same number in the first decade of the twenty-first century. With eighteen allusions already found in works from the current decade, it is safe to assume that the tendency to mention Bogart and his films in literature is definitely stable, if not increasing.

Humphrey Bogart as Sam Spade in *The Maltese Falcon* (1941) and Humphrey Bogart as Philip Marlowe is a scene from *The Big Sleep* (1946)—two films responsible for labeling the actor as the quintessential private eye.

Bogart's screen persona is dominated by complexity and ambiguity. Ironically, or symptomatically, in both his first and last movie, *Up the River* (set mostly in a prison) and *The Harder They Fall* (dealing with corruption in professional boxing), the focus is law-breaking even though in both Bogart plays an essentially decent guy. To go even further in this reasoning, the character Bogart plays in *Sabrina* (a romantic comedy!) is the one that gets the girl in the final scene of the film, but he reveals traits atypical in a crystal hero as he manipulates the situation and breaks the girl's heart in the name of helping out his financially threatened family. The dichotomy of the actor's persona is dominant in all of his roles and quite clear in the juxtaposition of the two movies which are responsible for labeling Bogart as the quintessential private investigator—*The Maltese Falcon* and *The Big Sleep*—a contrast that is carried over from the respective novels by Dashiell Hammett and Raymond Chandler. While Bogart's Sam Spade is the epitome of pragmatism, his Philip Marlowe is the Knight Errant of the modern city, usually involved in a lost cause, rarely hesitant to "stick out his neck" for a character that the reader or viewer most often does not even give a damn about. The same dichotomy, as applied to one protagonist, becomes the major strength in Bogart's characterization of Rick in *Casablanca*. Bogart appeared in numerous crime pictures, and his characters either oscillate in one direction (*High Sierra*, *Key Largo*) or the other (*Conflict*, *The Desperate Hours*), but the moral ambiguity is always there to a smaller or larger degree, with the perfect balance probably best illustrated by *In a Lonely Place*, which does not surprise if we realize the change of the ending (or rather the whole premise) from Dorothy B. Hughes's novel to Nicholas Ray's film.

The same dichotomy was brought to a higher level when Bogart's persona was expanded by such traits as obsession and paranoia. No wonder, thus, that two of Bogart's most memorable characterizations are those of Dobbs and Captain Queeg in *The Treasure of the Sierra Madre* and *The Caine Mutiny*, respectively. The complexity and richness of those characters can be challenged only by Charlie Allnut, the captain of the falling apart boat in *The African Queen*, a movie for which Bogart won his only Academy Award. Some critics commented that the Oscar granted to the actor was a gesture indirectly honoring his previous remarkable performances in movies that got to be even more appreciated by 1952. Those critics, however, were quite wrong. The greatness of Bogart's previous performances notwithstanding, the role the actor built in *The African Queen*, composed through pure exhibitionism of the protagonist's unrealized human strengths, vices, sensitivity, frailty and wisdom resulting from experience, deserved the Oscar more than anything that Bogart ever did before or after. Thus, *The African Queen*, along with some other movies that Bogart made in the 1950s, proves convincingly that the cult that started to develop around the actor in the 1940s, due to the enormous success and popularity of a significant number of his films from that period, was sealed and expanded through the amazing growth of the actor's talent, and by the time of his death the heritage that he left consisted of a multitude of extremely engaging and mature performances in a host of pictures that crowd the American Film Institute's List of the Top 100 Films of all time.

III. LIST OF REFERENCES (FOUND) TO BOGART AND HIS FILMS

While the year after the book title refers to the copyright/publication date (to provide an accurate sense of chronology), the page numbers are taken from the specific editions in which the references were found—as described in the Overall Bibliography (Reference Sources).

Woody Allen – *Play It Again, Sam* **(1968)**
- Bogart – 5-8, 18, 38, 41-46, 53-56
- *The Maltese Falcon* – 5, 6, 35, 53
- *Casablanca* – 7, 55
- *To Have and Have Not* – 8
- *The African Queen* – 56

Ace Atkins – *Robert B. Parker's Lullaby* **(2012)**
- *Casablanca* – 289

Paul Auster – "Ghosts" (1986)
- *Dark Passage* – 191

Muriel Barbery – *Gourmet Rhapsody* **(2000)**
- *Casablanca* – 120

Linda Barnes – *Deep Pockets* **(2004)**
- *Casablanca* – 88

George Baxt – *The Clark Gable and Carole Lombard Murder Case* **(1997)**
- Bogart – 44, 93, 128-129, 131-132, 134, 138-139, 142
- *Virginia City* – 139

George Baxt – *The Greta Garbo Murder Case* **(1992)**
- Bogart – 82, 151

George Baxt – *The Humphrey Bogart Murder Case* **(1995)**
- Bogart – 3-6, 10-13, 20-27, 32-35, 41-61, 63-109, 111-122, 126-144, 146-149, 153-166, 168-200
- *Up the River* - 5
- *The Petrified Forest* - 5
- *Marked Woman* – 11, 23
- *Kid Galahad* - 12
- *Dead End* - 12
- *The Oklahoma Kid* – 64
- *The Return of Dr. X* – 63-4
- *High Sierra* – 3, 5-6, 12, 141
- *The Wagons Roll at Night* – 12
- *The Maltese Falcon* – 6, 11, 12, 13, 24, 26, 33-35, 37, 42, 43, 46, 56, 112, 165, 198, 199

George Baxt – *The Tallulah Bankhead Murder Case* **(1987)**
- Bogart – 164

Ilene Beckerman – *What We Do for Love* **(1997)**
- Bogart – 38, 54
- *Casablanca* – 54

James Scott Bell – *Final Witness* **(1999)**
- Bogart – 251
- *Casablanca* – 130, 251

James Scott Bell – *No Legal Grounds* (2007)
- Bogart – 51
- *Casablanca* – 51

James Scott Bell – *Try Darkness* (2008)
- Bogart – 66
- *Casablanca* – 205

James Scott Bell – *Try Dying* (2007)
- *The Treasure of the Sierra Madre* – 86

James Scott Bell – *Try Fear* (2009)
- Bogart – 47

William Peter Blatty – *Dimiter* (2010)
- Bogart – 250
- *Casablanca* – 86, 94, 100, 250

William Peter Blatty – *Legion* (1983)
- Bogart – 134-135
- *The Maltese Falcon* – 29
- *Casablanca* – 32, 134-135

Lawrence Block – *The Burglar Who Painted Like Mondrian* (1983)
- *Casablanca* – 257

Lawrence Block – *The Burglar Who Thought He Was Bogart* (1995)
- Bogart – 29, 42-44, 53, 58-59, 60, 62-65 67, 71-72, 78-80, 92, 94, 97, 107-108, 136-139, 160, 208, 211-212, 252-253, 275, 305, 312, 343, 344, 355, 357-359
- *Black Legion* – 138
- *Dead End* – 93, 104
- *Swing Your Lady* – 79, 80
- *Men Are Such Fools* – 42
- *King of the Underworld* – 252, 256
- *The Roaring Twenties* – 70
- *Invisible Stripes* – 42
- *Virginia City* – 211-212, 252
- *Brother Orchid* – 70, 71, 94

- *They Drive by Night* – 358-359
- *High Sierra* – 358-359
- *The Maltese Falcon* – 42, 60, 79, 159-160, 193
- *The Big Shot* – 343-344
- *Casablanca* – 42, 60, 62, 79, 137, 346
- *Passage to Marseille* – 137
- *Conflict* – 70
- *The Big Sleep* – 60, 344
- *The Treasure of the Sierra Madre* – 60
- *Tokyo Joe* – 64
- *Chain Lightning* – 64
- *In a Lonely Place* – 60, 62
- *The African Queen* – 42
- *Beat the Devil* – 253-255
- *The Caine Mutiny* – 79, 80
- *Sabrina* – 211, 212
- *The Left Hand of God* – 94

Lawrence Block – ***The Burglar Who Traded Ted Williams*** **(1994)**
- Bogart – 206
- *Casablanca* – 206

Lawrence Block – ***Hit Parade*** **(2006)**
- Bogart – 129, 130
- *Casablanca* – 129

Lawrence Block – ***Small Town*** **(2003)**
- Bogart – 189
- *Casablanca* – 189
- *To Have and Have Not* – 348

Lawrence Block – "Some Days You Get the Bear" (1993)
- Bogart – 190
- *Casablanca* – 189, 190

Lawrence Block – ***When the Sacred Ginmill Closes*** **(1986)**
- Bogart – 122

- *High Sierra* – 122
- *Casablanca* – 117

Stephen Humphrey Bogart – *Play It Again* (1995)
- Bogart – 19, 89
- *The Maltese Falcon* – 19
- *Casablanca* – 42-44, 66, 88

Stephen Humphrey Bogart – *The Remake: As Time Goes By* (1997)
- *Casablanca* – 28, 34, 43, 59, 166, 187, 206, 259, 268-269

Barbara Taylor Bradford – *Letter from a Stranger* (2012)
- *Casablanca* – 246-247

Barbara Taylor Bradford – *Remember* (1991)
- *Casablanca* – 130

Barbara Taylor Bradford – *Where You Belong* (1999)
- *Casablanca* – 83

Christopher Bram – *Lives of the Circus Animals* (2003)
- *Casablanca* – 155

Gary Brandner – "Heat Lightning" (2003)
- *Angels with Dirty Faces* – 141

Lilian Jackson Braun – *The Cat Who Brought Down the House* (2003)
- Bogart – 95
- *The African Queen* – 174

Sandra Brown – *Smash Cut* (2009)
- Bogart – 98
- *Casablanca* - 98

Charles Bukowski – "Animal Crackers in My Soup"
- Bogart – 210

Charles Bukowski – *Factotum* (1975)
- *Casablanca* – 158

Charles Bukowski – *Hollywood* (1989)
- Bogart – 132

Charles Bukowski – "The Murder of Ramon Vasquez"
- Bogart – 215

Charles Bukowski – "Night Streets of Madness"
- Bogart – 160

Charles Bukowski – "A Rain of Women"
- Bogart – 159

James Lee Burke – *Bitterroot* **(2001)**
- Bogart – 234
- *The Treasure of the Sierra Madre* – 234

James Lee Burke – *Rain Gods* **(2009)**
- Bogart – 392
- *The Treasure of the Sierra Madre* – 391, 392, 394

Robert Olen Butler – *Hell* **(2009)**
- Bogart – 25-36

Truman Capote – *Answered Prayers: The Unfinished Novel* **(1987)**
- *Dark Victory* – 154

Lorenzo Carcaterra – *Gangsters* **(2001)**
- Bogart – 361
- *Angels with Dirty Faces* – 393

Lorenzo Carcaterra – *Sleepers* **(1995)**
- *Angels with Dirty Faces* – 85

Leslie Carroll – *Temporary Insanity* **(2004)**
- *The Treasure of the Sierra Madre* – 111

Arthur L. Clements – "Why I Don't Speak Italian" (1988)
- Bogart – 83
- *Sahara* – 83

Harlan Coben – *Deal Breaker* **(1995)**
- Bogart – 259
- *Casablanca* – 259

Jeffrey Cohen – *A Farewell to Legs* **(2003)**
- Bogart – 228
- *Casablanca* – 64, 228

Jeffrey Cohen – *It Happened One Knife* **(2008)**
- Bogart – 44

Jeffrey Cohen – *Some Like it Hot – Buttered* (2007)
- Bogart – 111

Max Allan Collins – *Quarry in the Middle* (2009)
- *The Maltese Falcon* – 120

Richard Condon – *Prizzi's Family* (1986)
- Bogart – 184

Pat Conroy – *The Water Is Wide* (1972)
- Bogart – 72
- *The African Queen* – 72

Bill Crider – *We'll Always Have Murder* (2001)
- Bogart – 5-7, 10-22, 30-33, 35-51, 53-59, 61-72, 74-91, 94-118, 120-123, 125-139, 145-168, 171-188, 192-215, 217-220
- *The Petrified Forest* – 147
- *The Amazing Dr. Clitterhouse* – 64
- *The Oklahoma Kid* – 63-64
- *The Roaring Twenties* – 91 – 147
- *The Return of Dr. X* – 64
- *High Sierra* – 76
- *The Maltese Falcon* – 149, 217
- *Casablanca* – 114, 181, 220
- *To Have and Have Not* – 12
- *The Big Sleep* – 6, 14, 53, 164-165
- *The Two Mrs. Carrolls* – 32, 59
- *Dark Passage* – 30
- *Key Largo* – 120

Clive Cussler – *Sahara* (1992)
- *The Treasure of the Sierra Madre* – 256

Jeffrey Deaver – *The Bone Collector* (1997)
- *Casablanca* – 225

Don DeLillo – *Underworld* (1997)
- Bogart – 627

Marisa de los Santos – *Falling Together* (2011)
- *Casablanca* – 168

Marisa de los Santos – *Love Walked In* (2005)
- Bogart – 78, 110
- *Casablanca* – 73, 76-78, 230

Nelson DeMille – *The General's Daughter* (1993)
- *Casablanca* – 3

Eric Jerome Dickey – *Resurrecting Midnight* (2009)
- Bogart – 82, 172
- *The Maltese Falcon* – 82

William Diehl – *Primal Fear* (1993)
- Bogart – 189

E. L. Doctorow – *Daniel* (1991)
- Bogart – 43

Kirk Douglas – *Dance with the Devil* (1990)
- Bogart – 101

Michael B. Druxman – *Tracy: A One-Person Play in Two Acts* (1984)
- Bogart – 34, 61, 68
- *Up the River* – 34
- *The African Queen* – 61

Dominick Dunne – *Another City, Not My Own* (1997)
- Bogart – 50

John Gregory Dunne – *True Confessions* (1977)
- *Casablanca* – 175, 177

Umberto Eco – *Foucault's Pendulum* (1988)
- *The Maltese Falcon* – 28, 227
- *Casablanca* – 54, 435, 464, 474

Loren D. Estleman – *Edsel* (1995)
- Bogart – 97
- *The Caine Mutiny* – 97

Loren D. Estleman – *The Hours of the Virgin* **(1999)**
- *Casablanca* – 60
- *The Harder They Fall* – 133

Loren D. Estleman – *Jitterbug* **(1998)**
- Bogart – 61, 296
- *The Roaring Twenties* – 61
- *Sahara* – 296

Loren D. Estleman – *Retro* **(2004)**
- *Casablanca* – 73, 199

Loren D. Estleman – *Something Borrowed, Something Black* **(2002)**
- Bogart – 69
- *Casablanca* – 48, 60

Andrew J. Fenady – *The Man with Bogart's Face* **(1977)**
- Bogart – dedication, 7, 9, 20, 26, 36, 81, 84, 92, 136, 162, 168-170
- *The Maltese Falcon* – dedication, 241
- *Casablanca* – 243
- *The Big Sleep* – dedication, 136
- *The Treasure of the Sierra Madre* – 222-223

Andrew J. Fenady – *The Secret of Sam Marlow* **(1980)**
- Bogart – 1, 3, 5, 6, 11, 17, 23, 24, 25, 35, 61, 64, 68, 69, 107, 129, 130, 134, 141, 142, 143, 151, 155, 162, 174, 177
- *The Petrified Forest* – 142
- *High Sierra* – 141, 142
- *The Maltese Falcon* – 141, 142, 156
- *Casablanca* – 147
- *Key Largo* – 141, 142, 143
- *Knock on Any Door* – 24

Fannie Flagg – *Coming Attractions* **(as** *Daisy Fay and the Miracle Man***) (1981)**
- Bogart – 65
- *The African Queen* – 65

Fannie Flagg – *I Still Dream About You* **(2010)**
- Bogart – 6 – 157-158
- *Casablanca* – 157-158

Kinky Friedman – *God Bless John Wayne* **(1995)**
- *Casablanca* – 79

Dale Furutani – *The Toyotomi Blades* **(1997)**
- Bogart – 197

William Goldman – *Control* **(1982)**
- Bogart – 163
- *Casablanca*

William Goldman – *Marathon Man* **(1974)**
- Bogart – 143, 157, 159, 161
- *Casablanca* – 143
- *The African Queen* – 143

James Grady – *Thunder* **(1994)**
- Bogart – 95
- *The Maltese Falcon* – 95
- *Casablanca* – 95
- *To Have and Have Not* – 95
- *The Big Sleep* – 95, 205

W.E.B. Griffin – *Blood and Honor* **(1996)**
- Bogart – 497

Martha Grimes – *The Case Has Altered* **(1997)**
- Bogart – 125

Martha Grimes – *Cold Flat Junction* **(2001)**
- Bogart – 59
- *Key Largo* – 59

Martha Grimes – *The Five Bells and Bladebone* **(1987)**
- *The Maltese Falcon* – 73
- *Casablanca* – 11, 236

Martha Grimes – *The Grave Maurice* **(2002)**
- Bogart – 111

Martha Grimes – *Help the Struggler* (1985)
- Bogart – 34

Martha Grimes – *The Old Wine Shades* (2006)
- Bogart – 150
- *Casablanca* – 150

John Grisham – *The Brethren* (2000)
- Bogart – 152, 163
- *Casablanca* – 164
- *Key Largo* – 163
- *The African Queen* – 164

James W. Hall – *Mean High Tide* (1994)
- *Casablanca* – 237-238, 341-342, 345, 359-360.
- *The Caine Mutiny* – 321

Pete Hamill – *The Gift* (1973)
- Bogart – 23

Pete Hamill – *The Guns of Heaven* (1983)
- Bogart – 73

Pete Hamill – *Snow in August* (1997)
- Bogart – 81, 151, 247
- *Casablanca* – 236

Pete Hamill – *Tabloid City* (2011)
- *Casablanca* – 30

Earl Hamner, Jr. – *Spencer's Mountain* (1961)
- Bogart – 170

Joanne Harris – *Chocolat* (1999)
- *Casablanca* – 305

Elizabeth Hay – *Garbo Laughs* (2003)
- Bogart – 84, 129, 150, 175, 225, 276
- *Casablanca* – 42, 129, 150, 155, 231, 273
- *The Treasure of the Sierra Madre* – 269
- *The African Queen* – 126
- *Sabrina* – 68

Elizabeth Hay – "Sayonara" (1997)
- *Casablanca* - 137

Judith Ryan Hendricks – *Bread Alone* (2001)
- *To Have and Have Not* – 187

Oscar Hijuelos – *Beautiful María of My Soul* (2010)
- Bogart – 8

Oscar Hijuelos – *The Mambo Kings Play Songs of Love* (1989)
- Bogart – 17, 105, 267, 333
- *The Barefoot Contessa* – 17

Marek Hłasko – *Sowa, córka piekarza* (*Owl, the Baker's Daughter*) (1967)
- Bogart – 21, 24

Rupert Holmes – *Where the Truth Lies* (2003)
- Bogart – 20
- *Casablanca* – 20, 238

Evan Hunter – *The Blackboard Jungle* (1955)
- Bogart – 76, 94-95
- *The Petrified Forest* – 76

Evan Hunter – *The Moment She Was Gone* (2002)
- *The Treasure of the Sierra Madre* – 67

Greg Iles – *Dead Sleep* (2001)
- Bogart – 194

Greg Iles – *The Devil's Punchbowl* (2009)
- Bogart – 505

Greg Iles – *Natchez Burning* (2014)
- Bogart – 302

Greg Iles – *Sleep No More* (2002)
- *Casablanca* – 195

Greg Iles – *Turning Angel* (2005)
- Bogart – 352

Greg Iles – *24 Hours* (2000)
- Bogart – 174, 179, 187, 188
- *To Have and Have Not* – 55
- *The Desperate Hours* – 174, 179, 187

John Irving – *A Prayer for Owen Meany* (1989)
- Bogart – 273
- *Dark Victory* – 273-274

Susan Isaacs – *After All These Years* (1993)
- *Key Largo* – 209

Susan Isaacs – *Goldberg Variations* (2012)
- *Sabrina* – 282

Susan Isaacs – *Red, White & Blue* (1998)
- *Casablanca* – 210, 398

Donald Jeffries – *The Unreals* (2007)
- Bogart – 205
- *The Maltese Falcon* – 205

Erica Jong – *Inventing Memory* (1997)
- Bogart – 189

Stuart M. Kaminsky – *Bullet for a Star* (1977)
- Bogart – 87, 88, 89, 90, 91, 92, 126
- *Bullets or Ballots* – 59
- *Dead End* – 125
- *High Sierra* – 55, 56, 86, 90-92
- *The Maltese Falcon* – 61, 87; 56, 62, 89, 143, 149

Stuart M. Kaminsky – *The Dead Don't Lie* (2007)
- *Key Largo* – 20-21

Stuart M. Kaminsky – *Denial* (2005)
- *Beat the Devil* – 191

Stuart Kaminsky – *High Midnight* (1981)
- Bogart – 167

Stuart Kaminsky – *Lieberman's Thief* (1995)
- *The Maltese Falcon* – 185
- *Casablanca* – 67

Stuart M. Kaminsky – *The Man Who Shot Lewis Vance* (1986)
- *The Maltese Falcon* – 104

Stuart M. Kaminsky – *Midnight Pass* (2003)
- *The Treasure of the Sierra Madre* – 259
- *The Barefoot Contessa* – 233

Stuart Kaminsky – *Murder on the Yellow Brick Road* (1977)
- Bogart – 66

Stuart M. Kaminsky – *Mildred Pierced* (2003)
- *The Maltese Falcon* – 115
- *Casablanca* – 208

Stuart M. Kaminsky – *Smart Moves* (1986)
- *The Petrified Forest* - 73
- *The Maltese Falcon* – 15

Stuart Kaminsky – *Think Fast, Mr. Peters* (1987)
- *The Maltese Falcon* – 26, 28, 176
- *All Through the Night* – 19

Stuart M. Kaminsky – *Vengeance* (1999)
- *The Caine Mutiny* – 165

Stuart M. Kaminsky – *To Catch a Spy* (2002)
- Bogart – 18
- *Thank Your Lucky Stars* – 18

Stuart M. Kaminsky – *Tomorrow Is Another Day* (1995)
- *Angels with Dirty Faces* – 188

Sue Kaufman – *Diary of a Mad Housewife* (1967)
- Bogart – 66
- *Casablanca* – 66

Elia Kazan – *The Assassins* (1972)
- Bogart – 195

Adam Kennedy – *Just Like Humphrey Bogart* (1978)
- Bogart – 11, 113, 160
- *To Have and Have Not* – 160
- *The Big Sleep* – 160

Jack Kerouac – *Desolation Angels* (1960)
- *The Treasure of the Sierra Madre* – 87

Jack Kerouac – *Satori in Paris* (1966)
- Bogart – 92

William X. Kienzle – *No Greater Love* (1999)
- Bogart – 68

Stephen King – *11/22/63* (2011)
- Bogart – 139
- *Casablanca* – 651

Stephen King – *Bag of Bones* (1998)
- Bogart – 84
- *Casablanca* – 383
- *Key Largo* – 84

Stephen King – *Christine* (1983)
- *The Caine Mutiny* – 126

Stephen King – *The Stand* (1978)
- Bogart – 552
- *Casablanca* – 552
- *Dark Passage* – 552

Terrill Lee Lankford – *Earthquake Weather* (2004)
- *The Maltese Falcon* – 22

Vincent Lardo – *McNally's Alibi* (2002)
- *Casablanca* – 308-309

Richard Laymon – *The Lake* (2004)
- Bogart – 186
- *Casablanca* – 186

Dennis Lehane – *A Drink Before the War* **(1994)**
- Bogart – 4, 117
- *The Maltese Falcon* – 169

Janet Leigh – *House of Destiny* **(1995)**
- Bogart – 129, 159, 165
- *To Have and Have Not* – 129

Elmore Leonard – *Be Cool* **(1999) – 156**
- *The Maltese Falcon* – 156
- *Casablanca* – 191

Elmore Leonard – "Comfort to the Enemy" (2009)
- Bogart – 104
- *To Have and Have Not* – 104

Elmore Leonard – *Djibouti* **(2010)**
- *Casablanca*

Elmore Leonard – *LaBrava* **(1983)**
- Bv – 104, 255
- *High Sierra* – 104
- *The Maltese Falcon* – 255

Elmore Leonard – *Up in Honey's Room* **(2007)**
- Bogart – 81
- *To Have and Have Not* – 81, 274

Peter Lovesey – *Diamond Solitaire* **(1992)**
- Bogart – 252

Robert Ludlum – *The Matlock Paper* **(1973)**
- *Casablanca* – 68

Michael Malone – *Dingley Falls* **(1980)**
- Bogart – 350
- *Casablanca* – 350

Michael Malone – *First Lady* **(2001)**
- *Casablanca* – 330

Michael Malone – *The Four Corners of the Sky* **(2009)**
- Bogart – 184

- *The Maltese Falcon* – 169, 397
- *Casablanca* – 185, 461, 528
- *The Treasure of the Sierra Madre* – 184-185, 315
- *The African Queen* – 120
- *The Barefoot Contessa* – 181-182

Michael Malone – "Invitation to the Ball" (1998)
- Bogart – 260
- *The Maltese Falcon* – 260

Michael Malone – *Time's Witness* **(2002)**
- Bv – 120
- *Casablanca* – 120, 531-532

Annalena McAfee – *The Spoiler* **(2011)**
- Bogart – 153

Ed McBain – *Fat Ollie's Book* **(2002)**
- Bogart – 138
- *To Have and Have Not* – 138

Ed McBain – *Gladly the Cross-Eyed Bear* **(1996)**
- *The Treasure of the Sierra Madre* – 254
- *The Caine Mutiny* – 179

Ed McBain – *Jigsaw* **(1970)**
- Bogart – 250

Mary McBride – *Say It Again, Sam* **(2004)**
- Bogart – 72

Jill McCorkle – *Life After Life* **(2013)**
- *The African Queen* – 38-39

Dermot McEvoy – *Our Lady of Greenwich Village* **(2008)**
- Bogart – 25, 45, 46
- *Angels with Dirty Faces* – 113
- *The Maltese Falcon* – 34, 46
- *Casablanca* – 25, 33, 115, 223
- *The Big Sleep* – 45
- *The Caine Mutiny* – 46

James A. Michener – "Australia" (1951)
- Bogart – 302

James A. Michener – *The Drifters* (1971)
- Bogart – 461-468, 479, 505-507, 547, 551
- *Up the River* – 463
- *The Petrified Forest* – 506
- *They Drive by Night* – 467
- *The Maltese Falcon* – 466
- *Casablanca* – 551
- *Action in the North Atlantic* – 462
- *To Have and Have Not* – 505, 506
- *In a Lonely Place* – 464-465, 465
- *The African Queen* – 479, 547
- *Deadline – U.S.A* – 463
- *Beat the Devil* – 506
- *Sabrina* – 462, 506
- *The Barefoot Contessa* – 462, 506
- *The Harder They Fall* – 462

Marcia Muller – *Coming Back* (2010)
- Bogart – 110
- *Casablanca* – 58
- *Dark Passage* – 110

Marcia Muller – *Trophies and Dead Things* (1990)
- Bogart – 12
- *All Through the Night* – 12

Marcia Muller – *Where Echoes Live* (1991)
- *They Drive by Night* – 27

Marcia Muller – *While Other People Sleep* (1998)
- Bogart – 104
- *Dark Passage* – 104

Michael P. Naughton – *Deathryde: Rebel Without a Corpse* (2008)
- Bogart – 79

- *To Have and Have Not* – 79
- *The Big Sleep* – 15
- *The Enforcer* – 79, 107-108

Tim O'Brien – *If I Die in a Combat Zone* (1975)
- Bogart – 142-144
- *Casablanca* – 142

Robert B. Parker – *Double Play* (2004)
- Bogart – 22

Robert B. Parker – *God Save the Child* (1974)
- Bogart – 223-224

Robert B. Parker – *Hush Money* (1999)
- Bogart – 162

Robert B. Parker – *The Judas Goat* (1978)
- Bogart – 43, 50, 97
- *The Maltese Falcon* – 97
- *Casablanca* – 43, 165, 169

Robert B. Parker – *Pale Kings and Princes* (1987)
- *To Have and Have Not* – 19-20

Robert B. Parker – *Playmates* (1989)
- Bogart – 11

Robert B. Parker – *Sea Change* (2006)
- Bogart – 290

Ralph Peters – *The Devil's Garden* (1998)
- Bogart – 56
- *Casablanca* – 56

Picoult, Jodi – *House Rules* (2010)
- Bogart – 273
- *Casablanca* – 273, 348

Thomas Pynchon – *Inherent Vice* (2009)
- Bogart – 97
- *Casablanca* – 360

Thomas Pynchon – *Vineland* (1990)
- *The Maltese Falcon* – 326
- *Casablanca* – 225

Robert J. Randisi – *Hey There (You with the Gun in Your Hand)* (2008)
- Bogart – 10
- *The Maltese Falcon* – 10

Ian Rankin – *Mortal Causes* (1994)
- *Casablanca* – 86

Herman Raucher – *Summer of '42* (1971)
- *Casablanca* – 129

Harold Robbins – *The Carpetbaggers* (1961)
- Bogart – 520

Elliott Roosevelt – *Murder in the Lincoln Bedroom* (2000)
- Bogart – 84-88

Lawrence Sanders – *McNally's Risk* (1993)
- Bogart – 20, 134
- *Casablanca* – 134

Lawrence Sanders – *The Sixth Commandment* (1979)
- Bogart – 29

John Sandford – *Silent Prey* (1992)
- Bogart – 325

Budd Schulberg – *The Harder They Fall* (1947)
- Bogart – 206

Stave Shagan – *City of Angels* (as *Hustle*) (1976)
- Bogart – 74
- *Casablanca* – 74

Steve Shagan – *Save the Tiger* (1972)
- Bogart – 104, 134-135, 137-138, 141, 221
- *Casablanca* – 135, 221
- *Sahara* – 134, 137-138, 141

Irwin Shaw – *Rich Man, Poor Man* (1970)
- Bogart – 152
- *The Petrified Forest* – 152

Sam Shepard – "Lost in Ruins" (1990)
- Bogart – 206, 207
- *Beat the Devil* – 206-207

Sam Shepard – *Motel Chronicles* (1982)
- *The Treasure of the Sierra Madre* – 95

Martha Sherrill – *My Last Movie Star* (2002)
- Bogart – 195, 272
- *The Maltese Falcon* – 213
- *Casablanca* – 195
- *The Treasure of the Sierra Madre* – 26

Rachel Shukert – *Love Me* (2014)
- *Angels with Dirty Faces* – 24

Rachel Shukert – *Starstruck* (2013)
- Bogart – 250

Neil Simon – *Plaza Suite* (1969)
- Bogart – 544, 547, 548

Roger L. Simon – "Summer in Idle Valley" (1999)
- Bogart – 384

Christina Skye – *Going Overboard* (2001)
- Bogart – 137
- *The Maltese Falcon* – 137
- *Casablanca* – 137, 149
- *To Have and Have Not* – 137

Nicholas Sparks – The Choice (2007)
- *Casablanca* – 134

LaVyrle Spencer – *Then Came Heaven* (1997)
- Bogart – 307
- *The Enforcer* – 307

Bernard Spiro - *The Other War: Letters from a GI in India in 1944 & 1945* **(2001)**
- Bogart – 127

William Styron – *Sophie's Choice* **(1978)**
- *The Petrified Forest* – 481

Jon Talton – *Deadline Man* **(2010)**
- Bogart – 132
- *Deadline USA* – 132

Robert K. Tanenbaum – *Betrayed* **(2010)**
- Bogart – 118-119, 293, 320
- *The Maltese Falcon* – 293
- *Casablanca* – 118-119, 320, 359

Robert K. Tanenbaum – *Enemy Within* **(2001)**
- *The Treasure of the Sierra Madre* – 56

Robert K. Tanenbaum – *Falsely Accused* **(1996)**
- *Key Largo* – 221

Robert K. Tanenbaum – *Fury* **(2005)**
- *Casablanca* – 272

Roderick Thorp – *Rainbow Drive* **(1986)**
- Bogart – 83, 350
- *The Maltese Falcon* – 350
- *The Big Sleep* – 83
- *The Treasure of the Sierra Madre* – 55-56

Margaret Truman – *Murder at the Washington Tribune* **(2005)**
- Bogart – 77

John Updike – *Bech: A Book* **(1965)**
- Bogart – 213

John Updike – "Cruise"
- *Casablanca* - 285

John Updike – "Gesturing" **(1974)**
- Bogart – 806

John Updike – *In the Beauty of the Lilies* **(1996)**

- Bogart – 277, 356
- *Casablanca* – 261, 266, 276
- *The Big Sleep* - 277

John Updike – "Morocco" (1979)
- *Casablanca* – 13

John Updike – "Packed Dirt, Churchgoing, a Dying Cat, a Traded Car" (1961)
- *Angels with Dirty Faces* – 110

John Updike – "Tristan and Iseult"
- Bogart – 149
- *Casablanca* – 149
- *Key Largo* – 149

Gore Vidal – *Myra Breckinridge* (1968)
- Bogart – 40, 62, 128-129

Michael Walsh – *As Time Goes By* (1998)
- *High Sierra* – 89
- *The Maltese Falcon* – 285
- *Casablanca* – title, 3, 7, 149-150, 222 301, 334, 406

Joseph Wambaugh – *Finnegan's Week* (1993)
- Bogart – 156
- *The Maltese Falcon* – 194
- *Casablanca* – 156

Joseph Wambaugh – *Fugitive Nights* (1992)
- *Casablanca* – 122

Joseph Wambaugh – *The Glitter Dome* (1981)
- *Casablanca* – 298

Joseph Wambaugh – *Hollywood Crows* (2008)
- *The Maltese Falcon* – 216-217

Joseph Wambaugh – *Hollywood Station* (2006)
- Bogart – 133

Joseph Wambaugh - *The Secrets of Harry Bright* (1985)
- *The Maltese Falcon* – 157, 158, 160.

Rebecca Wells – *Divine Secrets of the Ya-Ya Sisterhood* (1996)
- *Casablanca* – 290

Donald E. Westlake – *Smoke* (1995)
- *High Sierra* – 178

Donald E. Westlake – *Jimmy the Kid* (1974)
- *Casablanca* – 179

James Neel White – *I Was a P-51 Fighter Pilot in WWII* (2003)
- Bogart – 62, 177
- *Casablanca* – 177

Connie Willis – "Even the Queen" (1992)
- Bogart – 89
- *The African Queen* – 89

F. Paul Wilson – *Infernal* (2005)
- *The Maltese Falcon* – 336
- *Casablanca* – 335

Stuart Woods – *L.A. Times* (1993)
- Bogart – 188
- *Casablanca* – 15, 80, 188

Stuart Woods – *Mounting Fears* (2009)
- Bogart – 138
- *Casablanca* – 138

Stuart Woods – *Short Straw* (2006)
- *The Treasure of the Sierra Madre* – 103

Stuart Woods – *Strategic Moves* (2011)
- *Casablanca* - 104

Herman Wouk – *War and Remembrance* (1978)
- Bogart – 490

Markus Zusak – *I Am the Messenger* (2002)
- *Casablanca* – 248

IV. CREDITS OF BOGART'S FILMS REFERENCED

1. *Up the River* (Fox, 1930). Sc. Maurice Watkins. Dir. John Ford. Phot. Joseph August. Cast: Spencer Tracy (Saint Louis), Warren Hymer (Dannemora Dan), Claire Luce (Judy), HB (Steve), Joan Marie Lawes (Jean), William Collier, Sr. (Pop), George MacFarlane (Jessup).

2. *The Petrified Forest* (WB, 1936). Sc. Charles Kenyon and Delmer Daves from the play by Robert E. Sherwood. Dir. Archie Mayo. Phot. Sol Polito. Music by Bernhard Kaun. Cast: Leslie Howard (Alan Squier), Bette Davis (Gabrielle Maple), Genevieve Tobin (Mrs. Chisholm), Dick Foran (Boze Hertzlinger), HB (Duke Mantee), Joseph Sawyer (Jackie), Porter Hall (Jason Maple).

3. *Bullets or Ballots* (First National/WB, 1936). Sc. Seton I. Miller from a story by Martin Mooney and Miller. Dir. William Keighley. Phot. Hal Mohr. Music by Heinz Roemheld. Cast: Edward G. Robinson (Johnny Blake), Joan Blondell (Lee Morgan), Barton MacLane (Al Kruger), HB

(Nick "Bugs" Fenner), Frank McHugh (Herman), Joseph King (Captain Dan McLaren), Richard Purcell (Driscoll).

4. *Black Legion* (WB, 1937). Sc. Abem Finkel and William Wister Haines from a story by Robert Lord. Dir. Archie Mayo. Phot. George Barnes. Nusic by Bernhard Kaun. Cast: HB (Frank Taylor), Dick Foran (Ed Jackson), Erin O'Brien-Moore (Ruth Taylor), Ann Sheridan (Betty Grogan), Robert Barrat (Brown), Helen Flint (Pearl Davis), Joseph Sawyer (Cliff Moore).

5. *Marked Woman* (First National/WB, 1937). Sc. Robert Rossen and Abem Finkel. Dir. Lloyd Bacon. Phot. George Barnes. Music by Benhard Kaun and Heinz Roemheld. Cast: Bette Davis (Mary Dwight), HB (David Graham), Lola Lane (Gabby Marvin), Isabel Jewell (Emmy Lou Egan), Eduardo Cianelli (Johnny Vanning), Rosalind Marquis (Florrie Liggett), Mayo Methot (Estelle Porter).

6. *Kid Galahad* (WB, 1937). Sc. Seton I. Miller from the novel by Francis Wallace. Dir. Michael Curtiz. Phot. Tony Gaudio. Music by Heinz Roemheld and Max Steiner. Cast: Edward G. Robinson (Nick Donati), Bette Davis (Fluff), HB (Turkey Morgan), Wayne Morris (Ward Guisenberry), Jane Bryan (Marie Donati), Harry Carey (Silver Jackson), William Haade (Chuck McGraw).

7. *Dead End* (Goldwyn/UA, 1937). Sc. Lillian Hellman from the play Sidney Kingsley. Dir. William Wyler. Phot. Gregg Toland. Musical Dir. Alfred Newman. Cast: Sylvia Sideny (Drina), Joel McCrea (Dave Connell), HB (Baby Face Martin), Wendy Barrie (Kay Burton), Claire Trevor (Francey), Allen Jenkins (Hunk), Marjorie Main (Mrs. Martin).

8. *Swing Your Lady* (WB, 1938). Sc. Joseph Schrank and Maurice Leo from the play by Kenyon Nicholson and Charles Robinson. Dir. Ray Enright. Phot. Arthur Edeson. Music by Adolph Deutsch. Cast: HB (Ed

Hatch), Frank McHugh (Popeye Bronson), Louise Fazenda (Sadie Horn), Nat Pendleton (Joe Skopapoulos), Penny Singleton (Cookie Shannon), Allen Jenkins (Shiner Ward), Leon Weaver (Waldo Davis).

9. *Men Are Such Fools* (WB, 1938). Sc. Norman Reilly Raine and Horace Jackson from the novel by Faith Baldwin. Dir. Busby Berkeley. Phot. Sid Hickox. Music by Heinz Roemheld. Cast: Wayne Morris (Jimmy Hall), Priscilla Lane (Linda Lawrence), HB (Harry Galleon), Hugh Herbert (Harvey Bates), Penny Singleton (Nancy), Johnnie Davis (Ted), Mona Barrie (Beatrice Harris).

10. *The Amazing Dr. Clitterhouse* (First National/WB, 1938). Sc. John Wexley and John Huston from the play by Barré Lyndon. Dir. Anatole Litvak. Phot. Tony Gaudio. Music by Max Steiner. Cast: Edward G. Robinson (Dr. Clitterhouse), Claire Trevor (Jo Keller), HB (Rocks Valentine), Allen Jenkins (Okay), Donald Crisp (Inspector Lane), Gale Page (Nurse Randolph), Henry O'Neill (Judge).

11. *Angels with Dirty Faces* (First National/WB, 1938). Sc. John Wexley and Warren Duff from a story by Rowland Brown. Dir. Michael Curtiz. Phot. Sol Polito. Music by Max Steiner. Cast: James Cagney (Rocky Sullivan), Pat O'Brien (Jerry Connolly), HB (James Frazier), Ann Sheridan (Laury Ferguson), George Bancroft (Mac Keefer), Billy Halop (Soapy), Bobby Jordan (Swing).

12. *King of the Underworld* (WB, 1939). Sc. George Bricker and Vincent Sherman from the *Liberty* Magazine serial *Dr. Socrates* by W.R. Burnett. Dir. Lewis Seiler. Phot. Sid Hickox. Music by Heinz Roemheld. Cast: HB (Joe Gurney), Kay Francis (Carol Nelson), James Stephenson (Bill Forrest), John Eldredge (Niles Nelson), Jessie Busley (Aunt Margaret), Arthur Aylesworth (Dr. Sanders), Raymond Brown (Sheriff).

13. *The Oklahoma Kid* (WB, 1939). Sc. Warren Duff, Robert Buckner and Edawrd E. Paramore from a story by Paramore and Wally Klein. Dir. Lloyd Bacon. Phot. James Wong Howe. Music by Max Steiner. Cast: James Cagney (Jim Kincaid), HB (Whip McCord), Rosemary Lane (Jane Hardwick), Donald Crisp (Judge Hardwick), Harvey Stephens (Ned Kincaid), Charles Middleton (Alec Martin).

14. *Dark Victory* First National/WB, 1939). Sc. Casey Robinson from the play by George Emerson Brewer, Jr., and Bertram Bloch. Dir. Edmund Goulding. Phot. Ernest Haller. Music by Max Steiner. Cast: Bette Davis (Judith Traherne), George Brent (Dr. Frederick Steele), HB (Michael O'Leary), Geraldine Fitzgerald (Ann King), Ronald Reagan (Alex Hamm), Henry Travers (Dr. Parsons), Cora Witherspoon (Carrie Spottswood).

15. *The Roaring Twenties* (First National/WB, 1939). Sc. Jerry Wald, Richard Macaulay and Robert Rossen from a story by Mark Hellinger. Dir. Raoul Walsh. Phot. Ernest Haller. Music by Heinz Roemheld and Ray Heindorf. Cast: James Cagney (Eddie Bartlett), Priscilla Lane (Jean Sherman), HB (George Hally), Glady George (Panama Smith), Jeffrey Lynn (Lloyd Hart), Frank McHugh (Danny Green), Paul Kelly (Nick Brown).

16. *The Return of Doctor X* (First National/WB, 1939). Sc. Lee Katz from the story "The Doctor's Secret" by William J. Makin. Dir. Vincent Sherman. Phot. Sid Hickox. Music by Bernhard Kaun. Cast: Wayne Morris (Walter Barnett), Rosemary Lane (Joan Vance), HB (Marshall Quesne), Dennis Morgan (Michael Rhodes), John Litel (Dr. Francis Flegg), Lya Lys (Angela Merrova), Huntz Hall (Pink).

17. *Invisible Stripes* (First National/WB, 1939). Sc. Warren Duff from a story by Jonathan Finn, based on the book by Warden Lewis E. Lawes. Dir. Lloyd Bacon. Phot. Ernest Haller. Music by Heinz Roemheld. Cast: George Raft (Cliff Taylor), Jane Bryan (Peggy), William Holden (Tim Taylor), HB

(Chuck Martin), Flora Robson (Mrs. Taylor), Paul Kelly (Ed Kruger), Lee Patrick (Molly).

18. *Virginia City* (First National/WB, 1940). Sc. Robert Buckner. Dir. Michael Curtiz. Phot. Sol Polito. Music by Max Steiner. Cast: Errol Flynn (Kerry Bradford), Miriam Hopkins (Julia Hayne), Randolph Scott (Vance Irby), HB (John Murrell), Frank McHugh (Mr. Upjohn), Alan Hale (Olaf Swenson), Guinn "Big Boy" Williams (Marblehead).

19. *Brother Orchid* (First National/WB, 1940). Sc. Earl Baldwin from the *Collier's* Magazine story by Richard Connell. Dir. Lloyd Bacon. Phot. Tony Gaudio. Music by Heinz Roemheld. Cast: Edward G. Robinson (Little John Sarto), Ann Sothern (Flo Addams), HB (Jack Buck), Donald Crisp (Brother Superior), Ralph Bellamy (Clarence Fletcher), Allen Jenkins (Willie the Knife), Cecil Kellaway (Brother Goodwin).

20. *They Drive by Night* (First National/WB, 1940). Sc. Jerry Wald and Richard Macaulay from the novel *Long Haul* by A.I. Bezzerides. Dir. Raoul Walsh. Phot. Arthur Edeson. Music by Adolph Deutsch. Cast: George Raft (Joe Fabrini), Ann Sheridan (Cassie Hartley), Ida Lupino (Lana Carlsen), HB (Paul Fabrini), Gale Page (Pearl Fabrini), Alan Hale (Ed Carlsen), Roscoe Karns (Irish McGurn).

21. *High Sierra* (First National/WB, 1941). Sc. John Huston and W.R. Burnett from the novel by Burnett. Dir. Raoul Walsh. Phot. Tony Gaudio. Music by Adolph Deutsch. Cast: HB (Roy Earle), Ida Lupino (Marie Garson), Alan Curtis (Babe Kozak), Arthur Kennedy (Red Hattery), Joan Leslie (Velma), Henry Hull (Doc Banton), Henry Travers (Pa Goodhue).

22. *The Wagons Roll at Night* (First National/WB, 1941). Sc. Fred Niblo, Jr., and Barry Trivers from the novel *Kid Galahad* by Francis Wallace. Dir. Ray Enright. Phot. Sid Hickox. Music by Heinz Roemheld. Cast: HB (Nick Coster), Sylvia Sidney (Flo Lorraine), Eddie Albert (Matt Varney),

Joan Leslie (Mary Coster), Sig Rumann (Hoffman the Great), Cliff Clark (Doc), Frank Wilcox (Tex).

23. *The Maltese Falcon* (First National/WB, 1941). Sc. John Huston from the novel by Dashiell Hammett. Dir. John Huston. Phot. Arthur Edeson. Music by Adolph Deutsch. Cast: HB (Sam Spade), Mary Astor (Brigid O'Shaughnessy), Gladys George (Iva Archer), Peter Lorre (Joel Cairo), Barton MacLane (Lieutenant Dundy), Lee Patrick (Effie Perine), Sydney Greenstreet (Casper Gutman).

24. *All Through the Night* (First National/WB, 1942). Sc. Leonard Spigelgass and Edwin Gilbert from a story by Leonard Q. Ross (Leo Rosten) and Spigelgass. Dir. Vincent Sherman. Phot. Sid Hickox. Music by Adolph Deutsch. Cast: HB (Gloves Donahue), Conrad Veidt (Hall Ebbing), Kaaren Verne (Leda Hamilton), Jane Darwell (Ma Donahue), Frank McHugh (Barney), Peter Lorre (Pepi), Judith Anderson (Madame).

25. *The Big Shot* (First National/WB, 1942). Sc. Bertram Millhauser, Abem Finkel and Daniel Fuchs. Dir. Lewis Seiler. Phot. Sid Hickox. Music by Adolph Deutsch. Cast: HB (Duke Berne), Irene Manning (Lorna Fleming), Richard Travis (George Anderson), Susan Peters (Ruth Carter), Stanley Ridges (Martin Fleming), Minor Watson (Warden Booth), Chick Chandler (Dancer).

26. *Casablanca* (First National/WB, 1942/43). Sc. Julius J. & Philip G. Epstein and Howard Koch from the play *Everybody Comes to Rick's* by Murray Burnett and Joan Allison. Dir. Michael Curtiz. Phot. Arthur Edeson. Music by Max Steiner. Cast: HB (Rick), Ingrid Bergman (Ilsa), Paul Henreid (Victor Laszlo), Claude Rains (Captain Louis Renault), Conrad Veidt (Major Strasser), Sydney Greenstreet (Senor Ferrari), Peter Lorre (Ugarte).

27. *Action in the North Atlantic* (First National/WB, 1943). Sc. John Howard Lawson from the novel by Guy Gilpatric. Additional Dialogue by A. I. Bezzerides and W. R. Burnett. Dir. Lloyd Bacon. Phot. Ted McCord. Music by Adolph Deutsch. Cast: HB (Joe Rossi), Raymond Massey (Captain Steve Jarvis), Alan Hale (Boats O'Hara), Julie Bishop (Pearl), Ruth Gordon (Mrs. Jarvis), Sam Levene (Chips Abrams), Dane Clark (Johnny Pulaski).

28. *Thank Your Lucky Stars* (First National/WB, 1943). Sc. Norman Panama & Melvin Frank and James V. Kern from a story by Everett Freeman and Arthur Schwartz. Dir. David Butler. Phot. Arthur Edeson. Songs by Arthur Schwartz and Frank Loesser. Cast: HB (Himself), Eddie Cantor (Himself and Joe Simpson), Bette Davis (Herself), Olivia de Havilland (Herself), Errol Flynn (Himself), John Garfield (Himself), Ida Lupino (Herself).

29. *Sahara* (Columbia, 1943). Sc. John Howard Lawson and Zoltan Korda from a story by Philip MacDonald, based on an incident in the Soviet film *The Thirteen*. Adapted by James O'Hanlon. Dir. Zoltan Korda. Phot. Rudolph Maté. Music by Miklos Rozsa. Cast: HB (Sergeant Joe Gunn), Bruce Bennett (Waco Hoyt), J. Carrol Naish (Giuseppe), Lloyd Bridges (Fred Clarkson), Rex Ingram (Tambul), Richard Nugent (Captain Jason Halliday), Dan Duryea (Jim Doyle).

30. *Passage to Marseille* (First National/WB, 1944). Sc. Casey Robinson and Jack Moffitt from the novel *Men Without Country* by Charles Nordhoff and James Norman Hall. Dir. Michael Curtiz. Phot. James Wong Howe. Music by Max Steiner. Cast: HB (Matrac), Claude Rains (Captain Freycinet), Michele Morgan (Paula), Philip Dorn (Renault), Sydney Greenstreet (Major Duval), Peter Lorre (Marius), George Tobias (Petit).

31. *To Have and Have Not* (First National/WB, 1945). Sc. Jules Furthman and William Faulkner from the novel by Ernest Hemingway. Dir. Howard Hawks. Phot. Sid Hickox. Music by Franz Waxman. Cast: HB (Harry Morgan), Lauren Bacall (Marie), Walter Brennan (Eddie), Dolores Moran

(Helene de Brusac), Hoagy Carmichael (Cricket), Walter Molnar (Paul de Brusac), Marcel Dalio (Gerard).

32. *Conflict* (First National/WB, 1945). Sc. Arthur T. Horman and Dwight Taylor from a story by Robert Siodmak and Alfred Neumann. Dir. Curtis Bernhardt. Phot. Merritt Gerstad. Music by Frederick Hollander. Cast: HB (Richard Mason), Alexis Smith (Evelyn Turner), Sydney Greenstreet (Dr. Mark Hamilton), Rose Hobart (Kathryn Mason), Charles Drake (Prof. Norman Holdsworth), Grant Mitchell (Dr. Grant), Patrick O'Moore (Detective Lieutenant Rgan).

33. *The Big Sleep* (First National/WB, 1946). Sc. William Faulkner, Leigh Brackett and Jules Furthman from the novel by Raymond Chandler. Dir. Howard Hawks. Phot. Sid Hickox. Music by Max Steiner. Cast: HB (Philip Marlowe), Lauren Bacall (Vivian Rutledge), John Ridgely (Eddie Mars), Martha Vickers (Carmen Sternwood), Dorothy Malone (Bookshop Proprietress), Peggy Knudsen (Mrs. Eddie Mars), Regis Toomey (Bernie Ohls).

34. *The Two Mrs. Carrolls* (First National/WB, 1947). Sc. Thomas Job from the play by Martin Vale. Dir. Peter Godfrey. Phot. Peverell Marley. Music by Franz Waxman. Cast: HB (Geoffrey Carroll), Barbara Stanwyck (Sally Carroll), Alexis Smith (Cecily Latham), Nigel Bruce (Dr. Tuttle), Isobel Elsom (Mrs. Latham), Patrick O'Moore (Charles Pennington), Ann Carter (Beatrice Carroll).

35. *Dark Passage* (First National/WB, 1947). Sc. Delmer Daves from the novel by David Goodis. Dir. Delmer Daves. Phot. Sid Hickox. Music by Franz Waxman. Cast: HB (Vincent Parry), Lauren Bacall (Irene Jansen), Bruce Bennett (Bob Rapf), Agnes Moorehead (Madge Rapf), Tom D'Andrea (Sam), Clifton Young (Baker), Douglas Kennedy (Detective).

36. *The Treasure of the Sierra Madre* (First National/WB, 1948). Sc. John Huston from the novel by B. Traven. Dir. John Huston. Phot. Ted McCord. Music by Max Steiner. Cast: HB (Dobbs), Walter Huston (Howard), Tim Holt (Curtin), Bruce Bennett (Cody), Barton MacLane (McCormick), Alfonso Bedoya (Gold Hat), A. Soto Rangel (Presidente).

37. *Key Largo* (First National/WB, 1948). Sc. Richard Brooks and John Huston from the play Maxwell Anderson. Dir. John Huston. Phot. Karl Freund. Music by Max Steiner. Cast: HB (Frank McCloud), Edward G. Robinson (Johnny Rocco), Lauren Bacall (Nora Temple), Lionel Barrymore (James Temple), Claire Trevor (Gaye Dawn), Thomas Gomez (Curley Hoff), Marc Lawrence (Ziggy).

38. *Knock on Any Door* (Columbia, 1949). Sc. Daniel Taradash and John Monks, Jr., from the novel by Willard Motley. Dir. Nicholas Ray. Phot. Burnett Guffey. Music by George Antheil. Cast: HB (Andrew Morton), John Derek (Nick Romano), George Macready (Kerman), Allene Roberts (Emma), Susan Perry (Adele Morton), Mickey Knox (Vito), Barry Kelley (Judge Drake).

39. *Tokyo Joe* (Santana/Columbia, 1949). Sc. Cyril Hume and Bertram Millhauser from a story by Steve Fisher. Adapted by Walter Doniger. Dir. Stuart Heisler. Phot. Charles Lawton, Jr. Music by George Antheil. Cast: HB (Joe Barrett), Alexander Knox (Mark Landis), Florence Marly (Trina), Sessue Hayakawa (Baron Kimura), Jerome Courtland (Danny), Gordon Jones (Idaho), Rhys Williams (Colonel Dahlgren).

40. *Chain Lightning* (First National/WB, 1950). Sc. Liam O'Brien and Vincent Evans from a story by J. Redmond Prior. Dir. Stuart Heisler. Phot. Ernest Haller. Music by David Buttolph. Cast: HB (Matt Brennan), Eleanor Parker (Jo Holloway), Raymond Massey (Leland Willis), Richard Whorf (Carl Troxell), James Brown (Major Hinkle), Roy Roberts (General Hewitt), Morris Ankrum (Ed Botswick).

41. *In a Lonely Place* (Santana/Columbia, 1950). Sc. Andrew Solt from the novel by Dorothy B. Hughes. Adapted by Edmund H. North. Dir. Nicholas Ray. Phot. Burnett Guffey. Music by George Antheil. Cast: HB (Dixon Steele), Gloria Grahame (Laurel Gray), Frank Lovejoy (Brub Nicolai), Carl Bento Reid (Captain Lochner), Art Smith (Mel Lippman), Jeff Donnell (Sylvia Nicolai), Martha Stewart (Mildred Atkinson).

42. *The Enforcer* (United States/WB, 1951). Sc. Martin Rackin. Dir. Bretaigne Windust. Phot. Robert Burks. Music by David Buttolph. Cast: HB (Martin Ferguson), Zero Mostel (Big Babe Lazich), Ted De Corsia (Joseph Rico), Everett Sloane (Albert Mendoza), Roy Roberts (Captain Frank Nelson), Lawrence Tolan (Duke Malloy), Bob Steele (Herman).

43. *The African Queen* (Horizon-Romulus/UA, 1951). Sc. James Agee and John Huston from the novel by C.S. Forester. Dir. John Huston. Phot. Jack Cardiff. Music by Alan Gray. Cast: HB (Charlie Allnut), Katharine Hepburn (Rose Sayer), Robert Morley (Rev. Samuel Sayer), Peter Bull (Captain of the "Louisa"), Theodore Bikel (First Officer of the "Louisa"), Walter Gotell (Second Officer of the "Louisa"), Gerald Onn (Petty Officer of the "Louisa").

44. *Deadline – U.S.A.* (20th C-F, 1952). Sc. Richard Brooks. Dir. Richard Brooks. Phot. Milton Krasner. Music by Cyril Mockridge and Sol Kaplan. Cast: HB (Ed Hutchinson), Ethel Barrymore (Mrs. Garrison), Kim Hunter (Nora), Ed Begley (Frank Allen), Warren Stevens (George Burrows), Paul Stewart (Harry Thompson), Martin Gabel (Thomas Rienzi).

45. *Beat the Devil* (Santana-Romulus/UA, 1954). Sc. John Huston and Truman Capote from the novel by James Helvick. Dir. John Huston. Phot. Oswald Morris. Music by Franco Mannino. Cast: HB (Billy Dannreuther), Jennifer Jones (Gwendolen Chelm), Gina Lollobrigida (Maria Dannreuther), Robert Morley (Petersen), Peter Lorre (O"Hara), Edward Underdown (Harry Chelm), Bernard Lee (C.I.D. Inspector).

46. *The Caine Mutiny* (Stanley Kramer/Columbia, 1954). Sc. Stanley Roberts from the novel by Herman Wouk. Additional Dialogue by Michael Blankfort. Dir. Edward Dmytryk. Phot. Franz Planer. Music by Max Steiner. Cast: HB (Captain Queeg), Jose Ferrer (Lieutenant Barney Greenwald), Van Johnson (Lieutenant Steve Maryk), Fred MacMurray (Lieutenant Tom Keefer), Robert Francis (Ensign Willie Keith), May Wynn (May Wynn), Tom Tully (Captain DeVriess).

47. *Sabrina* (Paramount, 1954). Sc. Billy Wilder, Samuel Taylor and Ernest Lehman from the play *Sabrina Fair* by Samuel Taylor. Dir. Billy Wilder. Phot. Charles Lang, Jr. Music by Frederick Hollander. Cast: Audrey Hepburn (Sabrina Fairchild), HB (Linus Larrabee), William Holden (David Larrabee), Walter Hampden (Oliver Larrabee), John Williams (Thomas Fairchild), Martha Hyer (Elizabeth Tyson), Marcel Dalio (Baron).

48. *The Barefoot Contessa* (Figaro/UA, 1954). Sc. Joseph L. Mankiewicz. Dir. Joseph L. Mankiewicz. Phot. Jack Cardiff. Music by Mario Nascimbene. Cast: HB (Harry Dawes), Ava Gardner (Maria Vargas), Edmond O'Brien (Oscar Muldoon), Rossano Brazzi (Vincenzo Torlato-Favrini), Marius Goring (Alberto Bravano), Valentina Cortesa (Eleanora Torlato-Favrini), Warren Stevens (Kirk Edwards).

49. *The Left Hand of God* (20th C-F, 1955). Sc. Alfred Hayes from the novel by William E. Barrett. Dir. Edward Dmytryk. Phot. Franz Planer. Music by Victor Young. Cast: HB (Jim Carmody), Gene Tireney (Anne Scott), Lee J. Cobb (Mieh Yang), Agnes Moorehead (Beryl Sigman), E.G. Marshall (Dr. David Sigman), Jean Porter (Mary Yin), Carl Benton Reid (Rev. Cornelius).

50. *The Desperate Hours* (Paramount, 1955). Sc. Joseph Hayes from his own novel and play. Dir. William Wyler. Phot. Lee Garmes. Music by Gail Kubik. Cast: HB (Glenn Griffin), Fredric March (Dan Hilliard), Arthur

Kennedy (Jesse Bard), Martha Scott (Eleanor Hilliard), Dewey Martin (Hal Griffin), Gig Young (Chuck), Mary Murphy (Cindy Hilliard).

51. *The Harder They Fall* (Columbia, 1956). Sc. Philip Yordan from the novel by Budd Schulberg. Dir. Mark Robson. Phot. Burnett Guffey. Music by Hugo Friedhofer. Cast: HB (Eddie Willis), Rod Steiger (Nick Benko), Jan Sterling (Beth Willis), Mike Lane (Toro Moreno), Max Baer (Buddy Brannen), Edward Andrews (Jim Weyerhause), Harold J. Stone (Art Leavitt).

V. BOGART'S MONOGRAPHIC BIBLIOGRAPHY (BOOKS ONLY)

Agustí, P. *Humphrey Bogart*. Madrid: Edimat Libros: Nuevas Estructaras, 1998.

Bacall, Lauren. *By Myself*. New York: Alfred A. Knopf, 1979.

Bacall, Lauren. *By Myself and Then Some*. New York: HarperEntertainment, 2005.

Barbour, Alan G. *Humphrey Bogart*. Utica, NY: Pyramid, 1973.

Benchley, Nathaniel. *Bogart*. Boston: Little, Brown, 1975.

Benchley, Nathaniel. *Humphrey Bogart*. London: Futura, 1977.

Bogart, Stephen Humphrey, with Gary Provost. *Bogart: In Search of My Father*. New York: Dutton, 1995.

Bounoure, Gaston. *Humphrey Bogart*. Lyon: Serdoc, 1962.

Benchley, Nathaniel. *Humphrey Bogart*. Boston-Toronto: Little, Brown and Comp., 1975.

Blumberg, Hans C., and Peter Bogdanovich, Truman Capote, François Truffaut, Charles Bukowski, Yaak Karsunke, Urs Widmer, Hans Helmut Prinzler. *Humphrey Bogart: Reihe Film 8*. Munich-Vienna: Carl Hanser Velag, 1976.

Cahill, Marie. *Humphrey Bogart*. London: Bison Group, 1992.

Coe, Jonathan. *Humphrey Bogart: Take It & Like It*. New York: Grove Weidenfeld, 1991.

Cunningham, Ernest W. *The Ultimate Bogart*. Los Angeles: Renaissance Books, 1999.

Cuterland, Frank. *Humphrey Bogart*. Paris: Balland, 1981.

Duchovnay, Gerald. *Humphrey Bogart: A Bio-Biography*. Westport CT: Greenwood Press, 1999.

Eisenschitz, Bernard. *Humphrey Bogart*. Paris: Le Terrain Vague, 1967.

Eyles, Allen. *Bogart*. London: Macmillan, 1975.

Eyles, Allen. *Humphrey Bogart*. London: Sphere, 1990.

Frank, Alan G. *Bogart*. New York: Exeter Books, 1982.

Gehman, Richard. *Bogart*. Greenwich, CT: Fawcett, 1965.

Granich, Tom. *Humphrey Bogart*. Parma: Guanda, 1956.

Goodman, Ezra. *Bogey: The Good-Bad Guy*. New York: Lyle Stuart, 1965.

Halimi, Gérard. *Humphrey Bogart*. Paris: Solar, 1981.

Heinzlmeyer, Adolf, Jürgen Menningen and Berndt Schulz. *Humphrey Bogart*. Milan: Garzanti, 1988.

Hepburn, Katharine. *The Making of* The African Queen, *Or How I Went to Africa with Bogart, Bacall and Huston and Almost Lost My Mind*. New York: Alfred A. Knopf, 1987.

Hill, Jonathan, and Jonah Ruddy. *The Man and the Legend*. London: Mayflower, 1966.

Howden, Iris. *Humphrey Bogart*. London: ALBSU, 1994.

Hyams, Joe. *Bogie: The Biography of Humphrey Bogart*. New York: The New American Library, 1966.

_____. *Bogart & Bacall*. New York: McKay, 1975.

Kanfer, Stefan. *Tough Without a Gun: The Life and Extraordinary Afterlife of Humphrey Bogart*. New

York: Alfred A. Knopf, 2011.

Kőrte, Peter. *Humphrey Bogart*. Reinbek near Hamburg: Rewohlt, 1992.

Layman, Richard. *Discovering The Maltese Falcon and Sam Spade: The Evolution of Dashiell Hammett's*

Masterpiece, Including John Huston's Movie with Humphrey Bogart. San Francisco: Vince Emery, 2005.

Marinero, Manolo. *Bogart*. Madrid: Ediciones JC, 1980.

Mazeau, Jacques, and Didier Thouart. *Bogart*. Paris: Editions Pac, 1983.

McCarty, Clifford. *Bogey: The Films of Humphrey Bogart*. New York: The Citadel Press, 1965.

Michael, Paul. *Humphrey Bogart: The Man and His Films*. Indianapolis-Kansas City-New York: Bobbs-Merrill, 1965.

Pettigrew, Terence. *The Bogart File*. London: Golden Eagle Press, 1977.

Schickel, Richard, and George Perry. *Bogie: A Celebration of the Life and Films of Humphrey Bogart*. New York: Thomas Dunne Books/St. Martin's Press, 2006.

Sklar, Robert. *City Boys: Cagney, Bogart and Garfield*. Princeton: Princeton University Press, 1992.

Sperber, A.M., and Eric Lax. *Bogart*. New York: William Morrow & Co., 1997.

Tchernoff, Alexis. *Humphrey Bogart*. Paris: Pygmalion, 1985.

Thompson, David. *Humphrey Bogart* (Great Stars). New York: Faber & Faber. 2010.

Ursini, James, and Paul Duncan (Kobal Collection). *Bogart*. Köln: Taschen, 2007.

Viry-Babel, Roger. *Humphrey Bogart 1899-1957*. Paris: Avant-Scéne du Cinéma, 1973.

Part Two
GARY COOPER

Gary Cooper's publicity shot.

Born: Frank James Cooper; May 7, 1901; Helena, Montana

Died: May 13, 1961; Beverly Hills, California

Spouse: Veronica Balfe, aka Sandra Shaw (1933-his death; one child: Maria Veronica Balfe)

Academy Awards: Sergeant York (1941), *High Noon* (1952), Honorary Award (1960)

Academy Award Nominations: Mr. Deeds Goes to Town (1936), *Meet John Doe* (1941), *The Pride of the Yankees* (1942), *For Whom the Bell Tolls* (1943)

Golden Globe: *High Noon* (1952)

Golden Globe Nomination: *Friendly Persuasion* (1956)

I. REFERENCES TO COOPER'S FILMS

The organization of this part of the book is based on release dates of the films, rather than on the chronology of the literary sources. Thus, naturally, it begins with references to films that were made early in Cooper's career, and the first six that are presented below are silent productions.

***The Winning of Barbara Worth* (1926).** One of the most important westerns of the last few years of the silent period, *The Winning of Barbara Worth* is a spectacular morality tale, based upon Harold Bell Wright's popular novel. It is one of numerous films referenced in the pages of *House of Destiny* (1995), a book by Janet Leigh, who is better known as an actress than a novelist. *House of Destiny* is a drama in a Hollywood setting, where fictitious characters mingle with real-life celebrities, some of which Leigh had met in person either as a child or as an accomplished actress. One of those many names that keep appearing in her book is Gary Cooper, who is first mentioned in connection with this early western movie, in which he got sixth billing while the leading stars are Ronald Colman and Vilma Banky:

> **Henry King**, some years earlier, had directed **Gary Cooper**'s first major role in *The Winning of Barbara Worth*, and **Cooper** had become a star. The year before, **Mr. King** had directed Tyrone Power in *Lloyds of London* and Power had become a household name. Twentieth was counting this veteran director to work the same magic with Wade Colby [p. 33].

It **(1927).** Directed by Clarence Badger, *It* was a successful comedy, in which Cooper got a small part as a reporter. The film is mentioned in two literary works: John Updike's novel *In the Beauty of the Lilies* (1996) and James Neel White's nonfiction book *I Was a P-51 Fighter Pilot in WWII* (2003)—both times, interestingly, as a part of the background information about the year 1927:

> In March of 1927, **Clara Bow** created a sensation as the irresistible shop-girl Betty Lou, who wows her boss, played by Garbo's former screen lover **Antonio Moreno**, in the film adaptation of **Elinor Glyn**'s *It* [p. 182].

> Movie theaters were built in every town across America where people laughed at Charlie Chaplin and ogled at the **"It Girl."** In 1927, the first talking picture became the talk-of-the-town when Al Jolson performed in *The Jazz Singer* [p. 15].

Wings **(1927).** The first winner of the best picture Academy Award, William A. Wellman's *Wings* is a World War I aviation drama, in which Cooper has a small but memorable part as a pilot whom we briefly see prior to his fatal flight. The film is referenced in John Updike's *In the Beauty of the*

Lilies (1996) and in Max Allan Collins's *Flying Blind* (1998). In Updike's novel, the film, just like the previously mentioned *It*, constitutes a part of the background information provided by the narrator. This time, however, the year is 1929:

> In May of 1929, Charles Lindbergh, who had inspired Teddy to seize this happiness, married, at the bride's home in Englewood, New Jersey. In Hollywood, the first Academy awards went to ***Wings*** and Emil Jannings and twenty-two-year-old Janet Gaynor, who starred in three films that year [p. 222].

In *Flying Blind*, which is Collins's fictitious and suspenseful account of Amelia Earhart's last years of life, a double reference to the movie is justified by the fact that Paul Mantz, an ace pilot and "the mastermind behind Amelia's records," has multiple connections with the Los Angeles crowd. The context of the first reference is Amelia's jealous husband G. P. Putnam talking about Mantz to the book's narrator, Chicago private eye Nate Heller, whom he has hired for more than one job:

> "How sure are you that she's dallying?"
> "Fairly sure. Quite sure."
> "Which is it? There is a big difference between fairly and quite."
> "His name is Paul Mantz." He took another sip of his Manhattan; in fact, he took two sips. "He's a pilot, a stunt pilot in the movies. Cocky little pipsqueak, six years younger than A.E. Fast-talking, glib son of a bitch, full of himself."
> That latter could have been a description of Putnam.
> "I brought him into the fold myself," Putnam said, a twitch of disgust flicking in one corner of his mouth. "Met him when I was publicist on the picture ***Wings***, where he put together a small team of pilots to stage the dogfights. I thought he'd be

the ideal man to help A.E. prepare for the Honolulu-Oakland flight" [p. 46].

Another reference to the film takes place about thirty pages later, when Heller and Mantz are already acquainted, as part of the description of Mantz' office:

> The glassed-in office was in the left rear corner of the hangar, a good-size area with light tan walls that went up forever, with more signed celebrity photos than the Brown Derby—James Cagney, Joan Crawford, Pat O'Brien, Wallace Beery, **Clark Gable**, Jean Harlow, Eleanor Roosevelt. Occasionally Mantz was in the photos, and there were shots of Amy and Lindbergh and pilots I didn't recognize, as well as a sprinkling of aerial stills from movies he'd worked on, **_Wings_**, *Hell's Angels*, *Airmail* [p. 75].

Michael Malone, in his novel *The Four Corners of the Sky* (2009), names most, or all, of his chapters after movie titles. Some of them are directly related to the book's plot; others seem to be used only as lexical items, and the reason for using them usually becomes clear further in the chapter. *Wings* is used as the title of Chapter Four (p. 41), and the explanation appears a few pages later in a dramatic scene where Jack Peregrine sees his daughter Annie, now studying to be a U.S. Navy pilot, for the first time since he abandoned her as a seven-year-old girl:

> Her father stood in the yard below the Nickerson windows, yelling up at her, "Hi, Annie!"
> She didn't answer but, with slim tanned arms leaning over the sill, stared at the fields behind him.
> "You look beautiful! Come on down, say hello." He made his arms into **wings**.

She fought to ignore him.

"I hear you're a flyer. Going to Annapolis. Good for you!" [pp. 44-45].

***The Legion of the Condemned* (1928).** The title of Stuart Kaminsky's mystery *High Midnight* (1981) is in itself an allusion to *High Noon*; thus, it is extensively discussed later in the book. In the following scene, which includes a clear allusion to Wellman's *The Legion of the Condemned* (another World War I aviation drama), Cooper, as one of the main characters, is telling private eye Toby Peters about his health and fitness:

> "Toby," he went on, "I'm no fighter. I'm an actor. I've been mended and patched up, but I have more wounds than a war veteran. My pelvis was broken when I was a kid. It never mended. I can't sit on a horse straight. I have about half my hearing. A bomb went off too close to my ear one day about ten years back when I was doing a war picture with **Fay Wray** [p. 25].

***Lilac Time* (1928).** Directed by George Fitzmaurice, this outstanding aviation drama is briefly summarized in a passage of the fifth chapter (Hollywood Stunt Pilots) of James Neel White's nonfiction book *I Was a P-51 Fighter Pilot in WWII* (2003):

> In the early 1920s, dozens of movie studios produced silent movies with interested plots. In the 1928 movie ***Lilac Time***, **Gary Cooper** was a pilot in WWI France. He met a French girl played by **Colleen Moore**. She served his squadron at her family's farm by decorating dining tables with lilacs in an act of affection for the pilots. **Cooper**, engaged to an English lady of noble birth, naturally fell in love with the fair French girl. The simple plot thickens, of course, and **Cooper** is shot down

and sent to a hospital. **Colleen Moore** searches the hospitals, leaves lilacs, which **Cooper** recognizes, and the ending, as you can imagine, is nothing but a happy one [p. 25].

Betrayal **(1929).** Co-starring Emil Jannings and Esther Ralston, and directed by Lewis Milestone, *Betrayal* is a minor modern drama which is mentioned, with the title somewhat disfigured, in Mary Duffe's *The Summer Gary Cooper Won the War* (1974), a children's book using the actor's name as a part of the title. In the scene, the narrator, a teenage girl, tries to convince her mother about the appropriateness of her decision to see the film:

> "It's a **Gary Cooper** movie. I wouldn't think of missing it."
> "What's the name of it?"
> " '**Betrayed**'."
> "I should say not."
> "Why not?"
> "I don't think it's a proper show for you."
> "I have seen every **Gary Cooper** show and I don't want to break my record" [p. 30].

The Virginian **(1929).** Cooper's first talkie, *The Virginian*, directed by Victor Fleming, is also one of the actor's best westerns, one that gave him an opportunity to portray the quintessential western hero. References to this remarkable, but frequently underrated, movie have been found in six major novels. John P. Marquand, in his novel *Wickford Point* (1939), paraphrases the most famous line, derived from both Owen Wister's original novel and its 1929 (rather than any of the other existing versions—as concluded from the setting of the book: early 1930s) screen adaptation, and makes it the title of Chapter XXVII:

> *When You Call Him That—Smile* [p. 331]

A reference to the same line appears in Stuart Kaminsky's already mentioned mystery *High Midnight* (1981), in a confrontation between Cooper and mobster Lombardi, who tries to put pressure on the actor to accept a role in a cheap movie:

> "We'll see, Mr. Big Brave Cowboy Star," hissed Lombardi.
>
> There were a few seconds of silence, broken only by the sound of men in the next room grunting to install a machine.
>
> **"When you wanna call me that, smile,"** said **Cooper** with a massive, teeth-clenched grin.
>
> Lombardi was no Walter Huston. He backed away, his smile fading and the look of hate returning [p. 86].

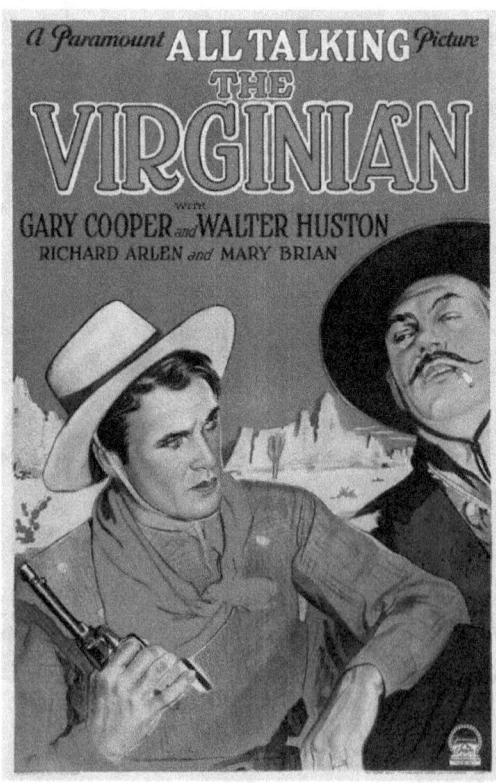

American poster for Victor Fleming's *The Virginian* (1929).

Another reference to the film comes from Ellery Queen's crime mystery *Calamity Town* (1942). The quotation is significant and interesting from the sociological point of view as Emmy, the modern female character, has expectations from men clearly different from those of Molly Wood's:

> Emmy was disappointed that Frank hadn't taken one of his deer rifles and gone stalking through the streets of Wrightsville for Jim, like **Owen Wister**'s **Virginian** (starring, however, **Gary Cooper**) [p. 40].

Still another reference to Cooper and *The Virginian* comes from Mary Duffe's already mentioned novel *The Summer Gary Cooper Won the War* (1974), and the scene is in fact a continuation of the excerpt quoted above (under *Betrayal*):

> Mother had been dead wrong about the show being improper. **Gary Cooper** wouldn't be in a show like that. All he did in this one was sort of have fun in a haystack with a girl. I was crazy about haystacks myself and I approved of adults who like them, too, especially **Gary Cooper**. He could do no wrong.
> "How was the show?"
> "I've seen **Gary Cooper** in better ones than this. There wasn't much action. I think maybe I liked **'The Virginian'** better" [p. 31].

A reference found in Elmore Leonard's *Out of Sight* (1996) mentions the title of the film plus the name of the actor who plays the villain. It is a part of a relaxed scene depicting a conversation between Karen Sisco, a U.S. Marshal, and her father, also a lawman:

> They were on the patio with Jack Daniel's over ice, the sun going down. Her dad had told her often enough it was **Walter**

Huston's favorite time of day in <u>*The Virginian*</u> and **Walter** was right. This evening he didn't mention it [p. 153].

The Texan (1930). Inspired by O. Henry's short story and directed by John Cromwell, this generally forgotten western (co-starring Fay Wray and Emma Dunn) is referenced in James D. Balestrieri's *The Ballad of Ethan Burns* (2013), a novel (or novella, about 100 pages long) almost in the form of a shooting script. What is interesting about Balestrieri's work is that despite numerous allusions to John Wayne pictures that it contains—such as *Rio Bravo*, *The Man Who Shot Liberty Valance*, *The Cowboys* and *The Shootist*— Duke himself is not mentioned even once. Instead, there are three direct references to Gary Cooper's westerns—*The Texan*, *High Noon* and *Man of the West* (in a reverse-chronological order) and each time the actor is mentioned as well. A reference to *The Texan* is evoked by a pose assumed by Quirt, one of the actors participating in the unusual western production that the book is about (Gillian Hawksworth is the director, who also replaces the leading lady, Cynthia Charles, who quit in the middle of shooting; Ethan Burns is the leading man):

> Gillian, in Cynthia's costume, gallops around the camp, waking the cast and crew. She dismounts next to Ethan. J.B., covered in paint, appears wild from lack of sleep Angelo wears his six-guns over his pajamas. Quirt is awake, fresh, already in costume, in a pose recalling Norman Rockwell's painting <u>*Gary Cooper as the Texan*</u> in which **Cooper**, in western costume, sits patiently as his lips are painted [p. 84].

Although the definite article in front of 'Texan' is not capitalized in the excerpt (which means that the noun phrase is not really a movie title), the costume that Cooper wears in that Norman Rockwell painting is definitely from (or for) this particular western film—as opposed to the one he wears in another painting by Rockwell, the one used in a poster for *Along Came Jones*.

Morocco **(1930).** Directed by Josef von Sternberg and co-starring Marlene Dietrich and Adolphe Menjou, *Morocco* was probably Gary Cooper's first film with some clearly noticeable European flavor. Ironically, the first reference to the movie was found in *The Marlene Dietrich Murder Case* (1993) by George Baxt. The book, in fact, contains multiple references to Cooper and several to the film. The following quotations, quite self-explanatory in their content, oscillate around the novel's titular character's professional and private life:

> A Hollywood star. The fantasy a reality. The dream come true. The script of her first American film, *Morocco*, on the seat next to her. Costarring with **Gary Cooper** and Adolphe Menjou. **Gary Cooper**. How she longed to sleep with **Gary Cooper**. Rudy wouldn't mind. Her husband, Rudolf Sieber, wouldn't mind at all [p. 1].
>
> This magnificent kitchen. For five days after arriving in Hollywood, accompanied by a Paramount representative, she had hunted for an appropriate house. **Josef von Sternberg** cautioned her, "Don't rent too expensive a place. Don't sign a long lease. If *Morocco* fails and you fail with it, they'll send you back to Germany."
>
> . . .
>
> Fat chance, she said to herself. . . . Fail? Me? *Morocco* was a smash hit, a sensation. Dressed in a tuxedo in a nightclub in North Africa, I dared wrap my hands around a woman's face and kiss her full on the lips. I could hear the rest of the company on the soundstage gasp. Those sharp intakes of breath. The dark look on **von Sternberg**'s face as he lit a cigarette. And my audacious query, "Didn't you like it? Shall I do it again? I can make it more suggestive." He kept the scene in the film. He knew it

would give **Marlene** her much sought after celebrity, and it did [p. 2].

Nineteen thirty-one had been a glorious year. *Morocco*, *The Blue Angel*, and *Dishonored*, in which she again scored as a German spy based on the exploits of the notorious, albeit somewhat dumpy, Mata Hari [p. 3].

Gloria was in her midtwenties and said she aspired to nothing but a husband, children, and a small house at the beach, any beach. She had been an extra in the nightclub scene in *Morocco* and caught **Dietrich**'s attention when the star saw Gloria move another extra out of the way of an arc light that made **Dietrich** look five years younger. **Dietrich** was impressed, struck up a conversation with the girl, and offered her the job as her maid [p. 17].

Dietrich wore an enigmatic smile. Everybody in the ballroom knew **she** and **Gary Cooper** had a red hot affair during the making of *Morocco*, which crazed **von Sternberg** and di Frasso, who had succeeded in stealing **Cooper** from the volatile Lupe Velez [p. 44].

An interesting reference to the film, along with a few to Cooper himself, was found in Bill Brooks's *Bonnie and Clyde* (2004). The movie is mentioned in a passage relating a conversation between Bonnie and her friend Mary, at whose place she occasionally stays:

Later, she lies in the small bed atop a crimson chenille spread and listens to "Falling in Love Again" and "Bye Bye Blues" on the radio. She listens to the soft patter of rain dripping outside the open window. She smokes and takes her notebook and in it writes a poem about a woman who has lost her sweetheart, not

Gary Cooper as Tom Brown and Marlene Dietrich as Amy Jolly in a scene from Josef von Sternberg's *Morocco* (1930).

to prison but to war. She thinks war is a much more romantic theme and imagines herself a war bride like Mary's aunt, Irma, was.

"My uncle Carl came home with gassed lungs," Mary told her one night when they came out of the movie theater after having watched **_Morocco_** with **Gary Cooper** and **Marlene Dietrich**. It was a balmy night and they stopped and got ice cream on the way home.

A war bride of a legionnaire would be romantic, Bonnie thinks as she begins to form the poem in her head.

But not a legionnaire who came home gassed and sickly. No, he would be a legionnaire that was tall and handsome and looked like **Gary Cooper** [p. 23].

In another excerpt, the reference to Cooper is connected to the news about Clyde:

The next morning she hears on the radio how Clyde Darrow and his friend have broken jail.

She waits for him to come for her.

In her mind they are just actors in a movie, like **Gary Cooper** and **Marlene Dietrich**.

It is like a movie playing in her head, she writes [p. 28].

And, in the third one, Cooper is compared to another man in Bonnie's life, Glen:

> He looks a little like **Gary Cooper**, only not as tall and with darker hair. Glen treats her swell, buys her flowers, candy, takes her to the movies [p. 33].

Fighting Caravans **(1931).** Loosely based on Zane Grey's novel of the same name, and directed by Otto Brower and David Burton, this enjoyable western is referenced in Patrick Samway's biography *Walker Percy: A Life* (1997), in a passage revealing the distinguished writer's deep interest in film (which was indirectly confirmed in his major novel, *The Moviegoer*):

> Walker looked forward to the completion of the new Greenville Country Club that was moving farther out of town. As he had in Birmingham, he played golf in Greenville; it was the one sport he would play until the end of his days. He could also spend hours at the movies; toward the end of February, the Paramount featured Al Jolson in *Big Boy*, Greta Garbo in *Inspiration*, **Gary Cooper** in ***Fighting Caravans***, and Edward G. Robinson in *Little Caesar*, followed by Bela Lugosi in *Dracula* [p. 49].

Make Me a Star **(1932).** Directed by William Beaudine, this superior comedy (starring Joan Blondell and Stuart Erwin) shows several major

Gary Cooper in costume for Otto Brower and David Burton's *Fighting Caravans* (1931).

stars, including Gary Cooper and Claudette Colbert, playing themselves in cameo appearances. The film is one of those used by Michael Malone in his novel *The Four Corners of the Sky* (2009) as chapter titles. The author's reason for using this one—as the title of Chapter Twelve (p. 79)—is the fact that Claudette Colbert's name appears on a birth certificate as the mother of protagonist Annie Peregrine Goode, and—for the same reason—most of the book's chapters are named after Colbert's movies.

The Devil and the Deep (1932). This relatively forgotten drama, directed by Marion Gering, is mentioned in George Baxt's Hollywood mystery *The Marlene Dietrich Murder Case* (1993). The following passage relates Tallulah Bankhead's opinion about her upcoming project:

> "It's really a terrific script. *The Devil and the Deep*. **Gary Cooper**'s opposite me and there's a dishy newcomer, **Cary Grant**, in the brief role of one of my lovers, which is too true to life. All of my lovers have been brief, and most of them not brief enough. And for my husband they're giving me something from England called **Charles Laughton**" [p. 144].

Gary Cooper as Jerry Day and Shirley Temple as Penelope Day in a scene from Henry Hathaway's *Now and Forever* (1934).

***Now and Forever* (1934).** This important item in the successful series of films that Shirley Temple made in the 1930s was directed by Henry Hathaway, and Miss Temple's co-stars were Gary Cooper and Carole Lombard. The film is briefly referenced in Michael Malone's novel *The Four Corners of the Sky* (2009) due to the parallel in the situations that occur in the book and in the film: a single father comes home with a baby daughter.

> More than a year passed. One day "out of the blue," Sam would say, "like **Gary Cooper** in *Now and Forever*," Jack returned home with the baby Annie and the airplane he'd named the *King of the Sky*. Grandee was in the hospital at the time, having one of her "episodes," and her son did not go to see her during his month-long stay [pp. 494-495].

***The Lives of a Bengal Lancer* (1935).** One of Cooper's greatest successes of the mid-1930s, this Indian adventure drama, directed by Henry Hathaway and co-starring Franchot Tone and Richard Cromwell, is referenced in several literary works. An allusion to the film appears in Bella and Samuel's play *Boy Meets Girl* (1936), in the somewhat extended lines by movie producer Friday (a.k.a. C.F.), who is talking about his new project:

> C.F. Something we'll be proud of. Not just another picture, but the picture of the year. A sort of **Bengal Lancer**, but as Kipling would have done it. Maybe we could wire Kipling and get him to write a few scenes. It would be darned good publicity [p. 542].

A reference to the film was also found in Alan Sillitoe's short story "The Decline and Fall of Frankie Buller" (1959), set in England before, during and after World War II. The context of the scene is Frankie Buller telling narrator Alan and the other boys he plays with (who are significantly younger) about his father's heroic deeds in World War I:

"The Sherwood Foresters. That's the regiment my dad was in. He got a medal in France for killin' sixty-three Jerries in one day. He was in a dug-out, see—" Frankie could act this with powerful realism since seeing *All Quiet on the Western Front* and ***The Lives of a Bengal Lancer***—"behind his machine gun, and the Jerries come over at dawn, and my dad seed 'em and started shootin'. They kept comin' over, but the Old Man just kept on firin' away—der-der-der-der-der-der-der—even when all his pals was dead [p. 160].

The film is mentioned by Gore Vidal in *Myra Breckinridge* (1968), in a lengthy passage narrated by the controversial protagonist:

In the Posture class I was particularly struck by one of the students, a boy with a Polish name. He is tall with a great deal of sand-colored curly hair and sideburns; he has pale blue eyes with long black lashes and a curving mouth on the order of the late **Richard Cromwell**, so satisfyingly tortured in ***Lives of a Bengal Lancer***. From a certain unevenly rounded thickness at the crotch of his blue jeans, it is safe to assume that he is marvelously hung. Unfortunately, he is hot for an extremely pretty girl with long straight blonde hair (dyed), beautiful legs and breasts, reminiscent of Lupe Velez [p. 31].

Another allusion to the film appears in Elmore Leonard's Kentucky novel *The Moonshine War* (1969), in a scene where some local guys discuss protagonist So Martin's chances in his fight against some really bad men:

Somebody asked who had seen **the Bengal Lancers** picture and they got to discussing tortures, like sticking bamboo slivers under a boy's fingernails to get him to tell where something

American poster for Henry Hathaway's *The Lives of a Bengal Lancer* (1935).

was. Maybe they'd do it to Son if they'd seen the picture [pp. 187-188].

In Loren D. Estleman's novel *The Witchfinder* (1998), the film is mentioned in a conversation between private eye Amos Walker and John Furlong, the son of world-famous architect Jay Bell Furlong, who hired

Walker to find out the name of the sender of a certain damaging photograph. Hathaway's movie serves here as an inspiration for a lucrative business:

> The dimes brightened. "You wouldn't happen to have some capital lying around you don't know what to do with, by any chance?"
>
> "I wouldn't call it capital. More like lower case."
>
> "Oh. A Shame. It's a crackerjack idea, and all mine. I borrowed against my trust fund to buy a stable of racehorses, but they all turned out to be related and there was something wrong with the bloodline. They faint when they get excited. The least little shock and they drop like laundry."
>
> "Tough break."
>
> "I thought so, too. Then I rented this old movie starring **Gary Cooper**. **The Bengal Lancer** Something."
>
> "*Lives of a Bengal Lancer*."
>
> "Have you seen it?" The dimes glowed.
>
> "I like old movies."
>
> "Well, then, you know there are a lot of battle scenes with cannons bursting and horses falling and things. The studios were terribly irresponsible about how they made horses fall back then. They used tripwires. Dozens of animals broke their legs and had to be destroyed. It was barbaric."
>
> "Now they just dump helicopter on the underage actors."
>
> "Yes." He was listening. "These days they hire trainers to teach the horses to fall on command. I started thinking about that, how I could rent these fainting horses of mine to Hollywood productions and make a fortune. I don't even remember how the movie ended, I was so full of this wonderful idea" [pp. 37-38].

Peter Ibbetson (1935). A reference to the character and the storyline of either the movie, directed by Henry Hathaway, or the original novel by

George du Maurier appears in George Baxt's *The Tallulah Bankhead Murder Case* (1987), during a conversation between Ted Valudni and his estranged wife Beth, who left him because of his friendly testimony and naming friends' names during the activities of the HUAC:

> Ted Valudni shouted into the phone, "Beth, your being unreasonable! What's so terrible about our showing up at Bankhead's together?"
> "Guilt by association." Beth was waving her left hand, drying her freshly polished nails.
> "Come off it, damn it!"
> "Ted, we are no longer a twosome. We are no longer anything. We are permanently separated, like **Peter Ibbetson** and his sweetie. We won't even meet in dreams. You go by yourself, and I'll go by myself. We'll say hello and then we'll mingle. You by yourself and me by myself" [p. 194].

Desire (1936). Frank Borzage's comedy *Desire* (co-starring Marlene Dietrich and John Halliday) is referenced in Elizabeth Hay's novel *Garbo Laughs* (2003), featuring a Canadian movie-loving family, the Golds.

> Until one day, when they were driving south on Bank Street, they saw a great yellow truck sail by with *Oh Hunger?* painted on its side, and remembered, in unison, the moment in **Desire** when **Gary Cooper** comes up with the right slogan for the new American car that **Marlene Dietrich** is going to steal from under his nose.
> The boy with the movie brain knew the scene by heart. "His boss says, I can't decide between these two: I'm *delighted* to drive a Bronson 8 or I'm *glad* to drive a Bronson 8. And **Gary Cooper** says *Delighted*. That sounds snobbish. It's too snooty. Then the boss says, So *glad* is better? And **Gary Cooper** says, If I bumped

American poster for Frank Borzage's *Desire* (1936).

into you in the street, I'd say, I'm glad to see you. No, I tell you, glad's the wrong word." Then Kenny made a grand sweep of his hand to indicate the sign on the back of **Gary Cooper**'s car, and said, " 'I'm happy to drive a Bronson 8.'"

"Is that what it was? A Bronson 8? You have an amazing memory," said his mom, and Kenny, taking advantage of this propitious moment, inquired if she wouldn't like to see *Toy Story 2*, and she said, "Does it have Cary Grant in it?" [p. 102]

The film is also alluded to over a hundred pages later, when siblings Kenny and Jane play movie trivia with their mother and family friends Dinah and Ida:

" 'All I know about you is you stole my car and I'm insane about you.'"

"I know!" cried Jane, who had pushed her way into the hallway and was standing beside Dinah. "I know! **Gary Cooper**!"

"And what's-her-name!" Kenny pounded his fist on his leg.

"Marlene –"

"**Marlene Dietrich**," yelled Jane.

"Shut up!"

"Don't say 'shut up,'" said Harriet. "Say 'be quiet.'"

"But which movie?"

"I know," yelled Jane.

"Shut up!"

"Kenny!"

"*Desire*!" he yelled triumphantly. "Give me another one!" [p. 225]

Mr. Dees Goes to Town **(1936).** Frank Capra's masterful comedy (co-starring Jean Arthur and Lionel Stander) with a strong social commentary gave Cooper, as the eccentric and reluctant millionaire, an opportunity to win the audience and earn his first Oscar nomination. The film is referenced in several narrative books. An interesting allusion to the film, one that indirectly testifies to its high quality, is the following passage from Budd Schulberg's novel *The Disenchanted* (1950), which is a disguised and fictionalized account of F. Scott Fitzgerald's last moths of life. The excerpt mentions both Manley Halliday (Fitzgerald) and Shep Stearns, a young screenwriter (most likely the author himself) assigned by the studio to collaborate with Manley on a script.

> Shep wanted to talk up—a fighting speech about a man's pride and the degradation of the marketplace. But he thought of Sara, and of his ambition to do *Informers* and **Deeds**. And then there was Manley. On the flight east he had been fascinated by the disorder of Manley's life and mind. But now he had begun to sense the dim outlines of a prolonged struggle. What sense was there in standing up to Victor Milgrim if that only further undermined the cause of Manley Halliday? [p. 203]

The pretext for a reference to the film in Elliott Roosevelt's *Murder in the Red Room* (1992) is a luncheon given to some celebrities by the First Lady (the author's mother). Though seemingly negative, Eleanor Roosevelt's comments on Cooper are in fact very favorable:

> The third was **Gary Cooper**, an actor not very well known but controversial because in some quarters his ***Mr. Deeds Goes to Town*** was perceived to have a Communist leaning.
>
> . . .
>
> **Gary Cooper** was not an actor, she concluded. He created no new persona for the screen; he only played himself. **Gary Cooper** was not **Longfellow Deeds**; **Longfellow Deeds** was **Gary Cooper**—the shy, handsome, engaging man who sat at her table.

"Americans are very hospitable people," said Edward G. Robinson.

"And tolerant," added Mrs. Roosevelt. "The little controversy about your Czech film will die down. Don't you think so, **Mr. Cooper**?"

Gary Cooper's mouth seemed to be filled with tuna salad. His eyes opened wide, and his head bobbed in an emphatic nod. "Umm-mm," he murmured [p. 41-43].

American poster for Frank Capra's *Mr. Deeds Goes to Town* (1936).

George Baxt's *The Humphrey Bogart Murder Case* (1995) is one of the author's many mysteries set in Hollywood and with real-life characters helping fictitious cop Jim Mallory with the investigation. Below is an excerpt in which the poster from Capra's masterpiece is mentioned among other clues:

> In the basement, Jim Mallory looked with interest at the wall decorations. Posters of all of **Bogart**'s films to date, including the ones in which he had minimal billing. Mallory couldn't figure out what <u>**Gary Cooper**'s *Mr. Deeds Goes to Town*</u> was doing there and asked Hazel. She told him Mayo had a small role in it, but Mallory couldn't place it [p. 63].

In John Updike's family saga *In the Beauty of the Lilies* (1996), there are several passages referring to the film industry as Alma, the heroine representing the third generation, is a Hollywood actress. The classic movie is mentioned in an excerpt which juxtaposes the style of Frank Capra with what she has to offer as a new kind of actress in the 1950s:

> Like a gambler growing desperate, the industry was making silly mistakes. Aside from the dismal English weather, Alma had found **Frank Capra**, aged twenty years since the glory days of <u>**Mr. Deeds**</u> and *Lost Horizon*, capricious and corny-minded; the kind of moral ambiguity and wary, wounded pessimism that Alma DeMott represented had no place in his sentimental concept of America [p. 432].

A reference to a funny lexical item, introduced by Capra's film (through the lines delivered in court by Longfellow Deeds's eccentric aunts) appears in Aaron Latham's mystery *Riding with John Wayne* (2006), during a conversation between screenwriter Chick Goodnight (the narrator) and film director Jamie Stone:

"Why don't you insert your scene into the script?" Jamie says.

"Sure," I say with a smile. "But there are a few differences between yours and mine. Maybe I should—?"

"No, yours is fine. Besides, there are damn few differences. I'm beginning to think you're **'pixilated.'**"

"**Pixilated**?" I scratch my memory. "That's *Harvey*, isn't it?"

"No, it's ***Mr. Deeds Goes to Town***."

Of course, I should have known. I hate getting things wrong in front of her. I feel like an idiot [p. 22].

Gary Cooper as Longfellow Deeds and Jean Arthur as Babe Bennett in a scene from Frank Capra's *Mr. Deeds Goes to Town* (1936).

Marisa de los Santos, in her novel *Belong to Me* (2008), mentions Cooper and the film as a means of simile. Tom, a man who offers the narrator/protagonist's neighbor Piper Truitt to move in with him, is compared to young Cooper:

> "It's Tom," she growled, at last.
>
> "What about Tom?"
>
> Piper put one fisted hand on one cocked hip and pointed the knife at me.
>
> "Guess," she demanded, "guess what he said to me this morning."
>
> I liked Tom. He was funny and sweet, and if you caught him in the right light, he bore a mild resemblance to **Gary Cooper** in *Mr. Deeds Goes to Town*. I tried to think of what he could have said to make Piper so furious [p. 296].

In William Bernhardt's thriller *Nemesis: The Final Case of Eliot Ness* (2009), a reference to the film takes place in a scene where Eliot Ness and his wife get ready to go to the mayor's ball:

> "The mayor wants to be reelected. We want him to be reelected, since he's the one who gave me my current job. I have to be there."
>
> "Yes, I know." Edna sighed wearily. She turned slightly and adjusted his bow tie. "And you look splendid in your tuxedo. Like **Gary Cooper** in *Mr. Deeds Goes to Town*. You're a handsome man, Eliot" [p. 225].

The Plainsman (1936). An indirect reference to this likeable and popular western, directed by Cecil B. DeMille and co-starring Jean Arthur and James Ellison, was found in Stuart M. Kaminsky's *Vengeance* (1999). Process server Lew Fonesca's good friend, Ames McKinney, is first compared to Gary

Cooper in the book's Prologue (which exemplifies the medias res narrative technique, p. 10), and then again in a passage describing the original meeting of the two men, where a reference is made to Wild Bill Hickok, the character Cooper played in *The Plainsman*:

> I spotted Ames McKinney in ten seconds, the time it took my eyes to adjust from the sun to the near darkness. The place wasn't big but the tables weren't jammed together. There was leg and elbow room and the smell of beer and something frying. The Round-Up had the universal look of a run-down bar and grill. The grizzled old man sat at a two-chair table in the corner, his back to the wall—**Wild Bill** covering himself from a sneak attack after Aces and Eights [p. 61].

Spanish poster for Cecil B. DeMille's *The Plainsman* (1936).

Gary Cooper as Michael Brandon and Claudette Colbert as Nicole de Loiselle in a scene from Ernst Lubitsch's *Bluebeard's Eighth Wife* (1938).

Bluebeard's Eighth Wife (1938). Scripted by Charles Brackett and Billy Wilder, directed by Ernst Lubitsch, and co-starring Claudette Colbert, Edward Everett Horton and David Niven, *Bluebeard's Eighth Wife* is a rather disappointing comedy considering the names involved. A reference to this and another Cooper comedy of the 1930s appears in Jacques Roubaud's *The Loop* (1993), in a passage where the narrator/protagonist unexpectedly focuses on movies:

> It wasn't until the following year, during the summer of 1945, when the choice of films finally became more abundant, that I finally saw the "American comedies" so vaunted, in nostalgic tones, by the adults I knew. I admired **Gary Cooper**

in ***Bluebeard's Eighth Wife*** or ***Mr. Deeds Goes to Town*** (less as a tuba player, in the latter, than as a fashioner of rhymes (proof of undeniable extravagance (as indicated in the French title, ***L'Extravagant Mr. Deeds***) of which I myself was guilty), and out of a natural sympathy for the two eccentric old ladies who reveal to him (as to the rest of humanity) the excellent adjective ***pixilated*** (which was translated, in the dubbing, I don't really know why, as "*pince-corné*")) [p. 323].

The Adventures of Marco Polo **(1938).** In "The Locked Room" (1986), the final part of *The New York Trilogy* by Paul Auster, the anonymous narrator (who happens to be the narrator of the other two novellas as well) briefly describes the night after a successful date with the woman he is falling in love with:

> I went straight home, realized that bed was out of the question, and then spent two hours in front of the television, watching a movie about **Marco Polo**. I finally conked out at around four, in the middle of a *Twilight Zone* rerun [p. 269].

Because the time setting of the scene is the late 1970s (most likely 1977), the Gary Cooper version of the movie, directed by Archie Mayo, is the only possibility in this context (there was no other version made until 1982).

The film is also referenced in George Baxt's *The Humphrey Bogart Murder Case* (1995). It is alluded to in a conversation columnist Hazel Dickson has with la Contessa de Marcopolo and gigolo Marcelo Amati:

> Hazel gushed, "I'll bet you photograph divinely. Now, I must interview la Contessa. Tell me, Contessa, are you truly descended from **Marco Polo**?"
>
> "Indeed I am."
>
> "But you spell the name as one word."

"It saves time."

Marcelo explained, "The names were joined over a century ago by la Contessa's grandfather.

"Did you see **Sam Goldwyn**'s movie about **Marco Polo**? It came out three years ago."

La Contessa said with distaste, "I saw it out of curiosity. Absolute nonsense" [p. 18].

The film is mentioned again when Bogart, Detective Villon and Lillian Hellman interrogate interior designer Ned Aswan about the missing treasure:

> **Bogart** told him the cornucopia story. At the finish, Ned exclaimed, "You mean we had those jewels under this roof and didn't know it?" He thought for a moment. "It was quite an interesting piece, come to think of it. **Samuel Goldwyn** bought it from us."
>
> "**Sam Goldwyn**? Maybe it was for his wife, Frances."
>
> Hellman interjected. "Nobody gives Frances Goldwyn a cornucopia. A necklace of matched pearls or a bracelet studded with star sapphires. But a cornucopia? Never."
>
> **Bogart** was laughing. "I doubt if it was intended as a gift."
>
> "It wasn't," said Ned. "It was for a movie, that awful thing **Gary Cooper** did a couple of years ago. *The Adventures of Marco Polo*. He paused. "This sudden quiet. You could hear a pin drop. Anyone got a pin?" [pp. 109-110]

Villon and Bogart continue the conversation several pages later:

> "I think if Josh suspected he had a hidden treasure, he'd have unsealed it and looked."
>
> "Maybe he did," said Villon.
>
> **Bogart** was lighting a cigarette. "Ned would have known."

"You're right. So if they had the treasure, they didn't know it and sold it to **Goldwyn** for of all crazy coincidences, *The Adventures of Marco Polo*" [p. 116].

Then, Villon and Bogart talk about the cornucopia with Samuel Goldwyn:

"There's been another murder. Maybe you haven't heard about it. Joshua Trent."

"My God. I wonder if my Frances heard. Joshua Trent? But how? Why? **Bogart** told him the how and the why.

"And I bought this cornucopia for *Marco Polo*? Maybe I did and maybe I didn't."

"You did. Ned Aswan says you did."

"If he says I did, then I did" [p. 119].

Gary Cooper as Stretch and Merle Oberon as Mary Smith in a scene from H.C. Potter's *The Cowboy and the Lady* (1938).

***The Cowboy and the Lady* (1938).** This minor modern western comedy, directed by H.C. Potter, with Merle Oberon and Walter Brennan opposite Cooper, is marginally mentioned in Stuart Kaminsky's *High Midnight* (1981). In the following scene, a fictitious director, Max Gelhorn, explains to the narrator, private eye Peters, the importance of his new project, a western in which he tries to get Cooper to play one of the leading roles:

> "You have any idea how much this picture means to me?" he said softly. "How long I've waited, planned? I've been in this town twenty-five years and never been offered anything better that second unit on **The Cowboy and the Lady**. I'm not going to miss this chance. Not you, not **Cooper**, not anybody is going to take it from me" [p. 121].

***Beau Geste* (1939).** Jack Kerouac's *Desolation Angels* (1960) includes several references to Cooper and his films. Below is an image related to *Beau Geste*, a superior adventure/morality tale directed (again) by William A. Wellman and co-starring Ray Milland and Robert Preston:

> Here the crazy Scipio came to trounce the blue eyed Carthage. Somewhere in that sand beyond the Atlas Range I saw my blue eyed **Gary Cooper** winning the **"Beau Geste."** And a night in Tangiers with Hubbard! [p. 304]

In Robert B. Parker's mystery *The Judas Goat* (1978), there is a scene set in Canada, where Hawk has an opportunity to show off to Spenser (the narrator) with his French. While the allusion may have been directed to the famous novel by Percival Christopher Wren or another movie version of the book, it is more likely that Spenser—in a conversation with his Black associate—alludes rather to the film starring Gary Cooper.

> The wife spoke to Kathie in French, showing her the

laundry and where the cookware was kept. Kathie looked blank. Hawk answered her in very polite French.

When they had gone and left us the key I said to Hawk, "Where'd you come up with the French?"

"I done some time in the Foreign Legion, babe, when things was sorta mean in Boston. You dog?"

"Hawk, you amaze me. Vietnam?"

"Yeah, and Algeria, all of them."

"**Beau Geste**," I said [p. 143].

A lobby card for William A. Wellman's *Beau Geste* (1939).

In Andrew J. Fenady's detective genre spoof *The Man with Bogart's Face* (1977), the film is mentioned—in a non-sequitur remark—during a conversation between private eye Sam Marlow, Mustafa Hakim and the latter's henchman, Wolf Zinderneuf, regarding the sought treasure, the Eyes of Alexander:

"That is merely a token payment. Bring me the Eyes –"

"Yeah, I know – one hundred thousand dollars. I'll tell you this. It's the best offer I've had so far. "

"Very good."

"I think." Sam moved to the door. "Say, Wolfie, did you know Zindeneuf was the name of the fort where everybody got killed in *Beau Geste*?"

"Yes." Zinderneuf clicked.

"Incidentally, Mr. Marlow," Mustafa Hakim asked, "just how many men have you killed?" [p. 116].

Fenady's sequel to *The Man with Bogart's Face*, entitled *The Secret of Sam Marlow* (1980), also includes a reference to the movie. This one, having only a somewhat less non-sequitur character, is a part of a friendly conversation between Sam and Lt. Marion Bumbera, a cop:

"You forget, I also know the secret of Sam Marlow." Bumbera got up, walked over to Sam and put out his right hand. "Your secret's safe, Sam. At least as far as I'm concerned. And, I'm sorry. OK?"

Sam shook Bumbera's hand and smiled. "Sure, that's a whole lot better than two in the belly. By the way, did you know that's what **Brian Donlevy** kept saying in a picture *Beau Geste*? He played **Sergeant Markoff** and went around threatening to put two or three in everybody's belly. And you didn't come up here just to shake hands."

"That was part of it" [p. 151].

Clive Cussler's adventurous mystery *Sahara* (1992) refers to the film in a couple of different places. The first excerpt relates a conversation between protagonist Dirk Pitt and his buddy, Albert Giordino:

> Giordino threw up his hands. "You're crazier than that old prospector and his cockamamy story of a Confederate ironclad with Abe Lincoln at the helm that's buried in the desert."
>
> "We have much in common," Pitt said easily. He rolled on his side and gestured toward a structure about 6 kilometers to the east a short walk from the railroad tracks. "See that old abandoned fort?"
>
> Giordino nodded. "The one with ***Beau Geste*, Gary Cooper**, and the French Foreign Legion written all over it. Yes, I see it."
>
> "Where Fort Foureau got its name," said Pitt. "No more than 100 meters separates its walls from the railroad. As soon as it's dark we'll use it for cover until we can hop an incoming train" [p. 279].

Then the film and its actors are mentioned when a group of men, including Admiral Sandecker, tries to decode a message sent by Pitt:

> "The next part reads, 'Also inform the Admiral that **Gary**, **Ray**, and **Bob** are going over to **Brian**'s house for fun and games.' Can you interpret this?"
>
> Sandecker thought a moment. "If Pitt is still coding in movies then **Gary** must be **Gary Cooper**. And I'll guess that he means **Ray Milland**."
>
> "Do you recall a picture they starred in together?"
>
> "I do indeed," Sandecker fairly beamed over the telephone. "Dirk might just as well have hung out a neon sign. They starred with **Robert Preston** and **Brian Donlevy** in a 1939 epic called ***Beau Geste***."
>
> "I saw it when I was a boy," said Bock. "The story was about three brothers who served in the French Foreign Legion."
>
> "The reference to **Brian**'s house suggests a fort."

"Certainly not the Fort Foureau hazardous waste facility. That would be the last place Levant would go" [p. 417].

Jill Barnett's World War II adventure novel *Sentimental Journey* (2002) is set in North Africa in 1942. A resemblance of its locations to the setting of *Beau Geste* is a pretext for the following reference:

> Through a perimeter of wooded crossed-stakes and entangled wire stood his objective—a bowl of Axis trouble hollowed out of an endless range of sand dunes in the Libyan desert. Dim lights downlit the corners of the buildings of the northeast side of the compound, where a convoy of trucks and tanks were lined up for fueling at first light.
>
> From here it looked like a movie set, the type of place **Gary Cooper** stormed in ***Beau Geste***. But this was 1942, a different time, a different war. This was real [p. 4].

North West Mounted Police **(1940).** This minor western (co-starring Madeleine Carroll, Paulette Goddard and Preston Foster) is significant mostly for being Cooper's first feature film shot in color. It is referenced in a couple of books. In Janet Leigh's *House of Destiny* (1995), the pretext for the reference is Cooper himself:

> On December 26, Jude continued his holiday spree and took Keane, Thelma and Matthew to the Liberty Theater to see **Cecil B. deMille**'s ***Northwest Mounted Police***. He had always enjoyed movies but he had been too busy to indulge often in the past couple of years. He didn't want to miss this one, though, because it starred his "almost" friend, **Gary Cooper** [p. 68].

In Joe Jackson's *Leavenworth Train: A Fugitive's Search for Justice in the Vanishing West* (2001), a biography on Frank Grigware, a man wronged by the law, a reference to the film is made in a passage expressing the dilemma of a Canadian Mountie:

> It was up to Corporal Coggles to do the dirty work. He was aware of what Americans thought of Mounties: tall, principled and slow to anger—an aura that Hollywood would soon attach to Nelson Eddy in the 1936 film *Rose- Marie* and to **Gary Cooper** in the 1940 ***North West Mounted Police***—lonely and vulnerable in a strong sort of way. Coggles was the farthest thing from a movie star, but he certainly felt heartsick and alone. It was his responsibility to arrest the man known in America as Frank Grigware, but here in Canada the same man, Jim Fahey, was his friend [p. 331].

Meet John Doe **(1941).** Cooper's second and last collaboration with Frank Capra, *Meet John Doe* (co-starring Barbara Stanwyck, Edward Arnold and Walter Brennan), has drawn several writers' attention. The film is mentioned in Stuart M. Kaminsky's mystery *Bullet for a Star* (1977), in a scene where private investigator Peters chases blackmail and murder suspect Harry Beaumont (a minor actor past his prime) within the Warner Brothers Studios and disturbs the set of this likable comedy-drama:

> He spotted me stepping into the light and turned to run, but his path was blocked by the extras. I started after him, and he ran right into the set.
> It was a fancy home. Edward Arnold was behind a desk wearing a tux. **Gary Cooper**, wearing a rumpled suit, was carrying on a conversation with him.
> Just as Arnold said, "Listen here, Doe" to **Cooper**, Beaumont started across the set. I went over an assistant director's back and tackled Beaumont, who thudded against the desk knocking it and Arnold over. I didn't see what happened to **Cooper**.

Beaumont had turned and had his fingers around my neck. I butted him with my head and punched him with my left hand. The right one throbbed from the earlier punch.

Somewhere behind me somebody said, "Should we cut, Mr. Capra?"

"Hell no," came a delighted voice.

I was getting tired, but Beaumont must have been in worse shape. He rolled over me. His weight was his main advantage. My head hit something, and Beaumont was off me and moving again. I could hear him puffing.

Someone helped me up. It was **Gary Cooper**.

"Thanks," I breathed.

"My pleasure," he said, lifting his eyebrow [pp. 120-121].

An allusion to the film appears in Michael Malone's mystery *Time's Witness* (2002), in a scene where the narrator/protagonist, police chief Cuddy Mangum, watches television at Christmas time:

> For an hour I lay on my wall-to-wall by the tree and clicked at the channels with my remote control. The Pope was in St. Peter's, Billy Graham was in Berlin, and the late-night comics all had reruns. And no *Chainsaw Massacres* tonight. Movie stations had gone spiritual (*Song of Bernadette*, *The Robe*), or classical (*How to Marry a Millionaire*, *The Great Caruso*), or seasonal. I sipped eggnog, which I don't much like, and flipped from old Scrooge getting terrorized by a peek at his own tombstone, to little Natalie Wood shaking down Kris Kringle for a house in the suburbs, to **Gary Cooper** just about jumping off a building so he won't let down the John Doe clubs who'd had faith in his suicide vow [p. 161].

American poster for Frank Capra's *Meet John Doe* (1941).

Another reference to the film was found in Laurence Klavan's thriller *The Cutting Room* (2004). The pretext for the reference is a striking resemblance between the situation in the book and one of the several endings of Capra's movie:

> "Something bad has to happen," she said. "Because something bad *has* happened. I just hope it won't be so bad for you."
>
> With that, she picked up her bag again. Then she tossed, as powerfully as she could, into my arms. Catching it, the force of *Ambersons* sent me stumbling back a bit, just long enough for Jeanine to make her move.
>
> Dropping the film, I ran to stop her as she scrambled up the small fence, the only guardrail the hotel had. In an early version of **Meet John Doe**, **Gary Cooper** jumps from a roof to his death. After negative previews, he is saved.
>
> Today, I was too late. Without looking back, she sprang over the edge. I watched Jeanine fly and then fall, taking with her all the movies she had seen, all the memories she had had, all the love she would never give, to other men, to children, to me [p. 265].

Marisa de los Santos offers an extremely insightful reference to the film in her novel *Love Walked In* (2005); the woman in the predicament is the book's narrator/protagonist, Cornelia Brown, the man responsible for her unhappiness – Martin Grace:

> What followed Martin's leaving the next morning—a blithe leaving on his part, as he never suspected a thing—was a miserable forty-eight hours. I wore my bathrobe and shuffled around my house crying and consuming tea and hot soup and other types of invalid food. I opened books and shut them. I

lifted the phone receiver and put it down. I remembered his voice and all the extraordinary things it had said to me. I listed on the couch, blown sideways by my own unhappiness, and tried to watch *Meet John Doe* because, despite what anyone thinks, no one does dark the way **Capra** does dark, and tried to remind myself that compared to everyone's disappointment and isolation, my disappointment and isolation were puny, not even garden variety. The movie backfired on me, though, because, as in all **Capra** films, love saves the day, and what I was pretty sure of was that it was not going to save mine, not this time [pp. 96-97].

A reference to the film in Donald Jeffries's thriller *The Unreals* (2007) is a part of a sensational document (a directory covering the period between 1985 and 1970 and listing victims ranging from President Abraham Lincoln to Pro Football Coach Vince Lombardi), which the book's protagonist, Waldo Billingsly, shares with "fredneck" Brisbane, a man he tries to impress and befriend:

> Brisbane's attention was drawn to a bulkier than average product of Old Hoss Billingsly's entitled *Political Schizophrenia*. The fredneck opened it to page 23:
>
> ### THE DEATH ROW – THE MOST RENOWNED VICTIMS OF OUR MASTERS
> The Right-Wing Lineup- Primary Suspects: The International Communist/Satanic/Globalist Empire
>
> ...
>
> 1957 – Joseph McCarthy U.S. Senator: Victim refused to give up after an unprecedented smear campaign against him, and, like **Gary Cooper** in *Meet John Doe*, came to believe in the role he was selected to play. Unlike **Frank Capra** films,

his ending at Bethesda Naval Hospital was neither happy nor explained [pp. 37-38].

Sergeant York (1941). Cooper's outstanding performance in this memorable biographical picture, directed by Howard Hawks and co-starring Joan Leslie and Walter Brennan, brought the actor his first Academy Award. Needless to say, the film is mentioned in several books. Gore Vidal's novel *Myra Breckinridge* (1968) includes numerous movie references. Below is a passage, once again (just like the one presented in the entry on *The Lives of a Bengal Lancer*) narrated by Myra/Myron Breckinridge, including a reference to this picture:

> Neither Myron nor I shared their pleasures or attitudes for we were, despite our youth, a throwback to the Forties, to the last moment in human history when it was possible to possess a total commitment to something outside oneself. I mean of course the war and the necessary elimination of Hitler, Mussolini and Tojo. And I do not exaggerate when I declare that I would give ten years of my life if I could step back in time for just one hour and visit the Stage Door Canteen in Hollywood, exactly the way that Dane Clark did in the movie of the same name, and like him, meet all the great stars at their peak and perhaps even, like Dane's buddy Bob Hutton, have a romance with **Joan Leslie**, a star I fell hopelessly in love with while watching *__Sergeant York__*. But where is **Joan** now? [p. 62]

There is one allusion to *The Pride of the Yankees* and a few to *Sergeant York* in Stuart Kaminsky's *High Midnight* (1981), an already quoted mystery narrated by private eye Peters:

> A guy I know, a writer at *Variety* who used to do publicity at Warner Brothers, told me that **Cooper** was making a baseball

picture for Goldwyn. He didn't know how far they were on shooting. He also said in passing that **Cooper** was a shoo-in for the Academy Award for <u>*Sergeant York*</u> [p. 17].

In another passage, Peters's dream combines a scene from the war movie with characters of the book's plot:

> There was no bath, just a shower stall, but the water was hot and the soap clean. The radio in the room didn't work, which was just as well. I slept and dreamed of **Sergeant York** picking off Nazis and turkeys. With each shot **Cooper** as <u>**York**</u> moistened the front sight and squinted before he shot. The Nazis turned into familiar faces—Lombardi, Costello, Marco, Tillman, Gelhorn, Fargo, Bowie and finally Lola and me. I tried to shout to **Cooper** that I was on his side, but he just lined up his sights, gobbled like a turkey and fired [pp. 124-125].

Joseph Wambaugh's *The Secrets of Harry Bright* (1985) is a mystery about two Hollywood cops, Sidney Blackpool and Otto Stringer, investigating the murder of Jack Watson, a millionaire's son. A reference to Cooper and an allusion to his first-Oscar winning role take place as the cops call back Harlan Penrod, the gay houseboy of Watson's property, who is more than willing to help them with the investigation:

> When they got back to the suite the message light on the phone was blinking, so Sidney Blackpool called the operator. The message was from Harlan Penrod.
> "Probably wants another date tonight," Otto said. "He's more ready for adoption than Oliver Twist."
> Harlan Penrod answered by saying, "Hellooooo. The Watson residence. May I help you?"
> "This is Sidney Blackpool, Harlan."

"My favorite **sergeant** since **Gary Cooper**!" Harlan twittered [p. 156].

Another reference to Cooper in the role of the famous sergeant was found in Susan Isaacs's novel *Shining Through* (1988), in a passage where narrator/protagonist Linda Voss analyzes her coworker and friend, Gladys Slade:

> Gladys was ecstatic to have all Sunday—an entire day uninterrupted by work—to talk about the office. Blair, VanderGraff and Wadley: that was the extent of her life. And I never asked for anything deeper from her, because I'd poked around and discovered her passion for the law firm was her sole passion. She liked the movies only to the degree that **Gary Cooper** in *Sergeant York* reminded her of Mr. Leland [pp. 69-70].

An unidentified player and Gary Cooper in a scene from Howard Hawks's *Sergeant York* (1941).

Gary Cooper

In Jeff Abbott's Jordan Poteet mystery *The Only Good Yankee* (1995), the film and its star are mentioned several times as the narrator/protagonist, immobile because of a broken leg, is paid three, more or less important, visits by three women, playing different roles in his life:

> She nodded and stood. "That all you wanted to tell me?"
>
> "Yeah." I eased back onto the pillow and fumbled for the remote control. I muted **Gary Cooper** in **Sergeant York** on American Movie Classics while I'd made amends with Clo. I wasn't expecting it when she leaned down, kissed my cheek, and hugged me. It was so unlike her I forgot to hug back.
>
> "Now, you keep that TV down," she snapped once my head was back on the pillow. "I'm on my break in the kitchen and I can't read the *National Enquirer* with all that jabbering [p. 239].

> She [Gretchen] toyed with one of the pillows on the couch, and I thought she'd like nothing better than to shove it over my face and watch me squirm for air for a while. Instead, she patted my cast, a little harder than necessary. "You take care, Jordy. I'm sure you'll be feeling much better about all this unpleasantness real soon."
>
> Her departure left me feeling more energized than I had in days. I sat back and watched **Gary Cooper** keep the world safe for democracy [p. 241].

> She agreed, hesitatingly, to come over. When she arrived, Clo suddenly remembered that she'd promised to take Mama over to Eula Mae's for a visit. We watched her bustle out. Candace sat down on the side of the couch, brushing her heavy brown hair over her shoulder. We made small talk about my broken leg, my messy coffee table, the merits of **Gary Cooper** as

an actor as he mutely eliminated half the Kaiser's army on the screen. If **Gary** could perform heroic deeds, maybe I could, too.

Deep breath. "Candace?"

"Yes?" He hand was buried in the bowl of popcorn, but her eyes came back to me. They looked like bits of blue heaven. I took her other hand in mine, interlocking my fingers with hers.

"I love you."

Kisses are better than painkillers for easing what ails you [p. 244].

Barbara Esstman's *Night Ride Home* (1997) is a novel set in post-World War II Missouri. It is narrated, in turn, by various characters. The reference to Cooper as York appears in a passage narrated by Maggie, a woman who returns to Missouri to her grandson's funeral and stays to take care of her daughter, Nora. In the quoted scene, she talks to Neal, her son-in-law:

> I watched his mouth move but didn't hear the words. His features, straight and regular. Good-looking enough as a boy, but better now, the way men get in their forties with just enough heft and jowl. His eyes did not waver from mine except at the moments his voice trailed off and the sentences drifted into nothing.
>
> "She's liked a ..."
>
> He shook his head.
>
> "We might have to ..."
>
> The muscles clenched as he tightened his jaw, and he looked over my shoulder at some point in the air, like **Gary Cooper** as **Sergeant York**, or Fredric March walking into the sea [p. 44].

John Weisman, in his political/military thriller *SOAR* (2003), refers to a memorable scene in *Sergeant York* as a parallel to a skillful maneuver about to be applied by the top secret unit of the Army's Delta Force:

Rowdy Yates jogged through the light ground fog the slightly less than half a kilometer to the bridge, carefully paced back, and took Ritzik and Ty Weaver aside. "Change of plans. You initiate on 'Two—just like always.' But you hit the lead truck first." Yates looked at Ritzik. "Time your countdown so Ty can shoot just as Truck One comes off the causeway. It'll bottleneck the others. They won't know what's happening in the back of the column until it's too late. I'll set the claymores off and you'll be picking 'em off from the rear like **Gary Cooper** in the old *Sergeant York* movie" [p. 183].

Barbara Stanwyck as Sugarpuss O'Shea and Gary Cooper as Professor Bertram Potts in a publicity shot for Howard Hawks's *Ball of Fire* (1941).

Ball of Fire **(1941).** The only (unfortunately) comedy that Hawks made with Cooper, and a brilliant example of the genre, is referenced in Rudy Rucker's humorous science-fiction novel *Saucer Wisdom* (1999), in two passages where there is a direct relation between the movie's two leading stars and the shape of some alien creatures:

> Tangled disk, AutoCAD city, Las Vegas, the round room. Baggy space, no clear edges. San Jose in front of me, the aliens behind me.
> "Let me see you!" Yes! I stare at them, they get closer. Inside-out starfish with spinach and fried-egg. Pukeful. **Barbara Stanwyck/Gary Cooper** from ***Ball of Fire***. Keep falling apart, globs, they laugh, I'm scared, they're like boys tormenting a frog.
> I push back: "What do you want from us?" Brain-etching agony. Donald Duck help help. Grit my teeth and push again. "How do you get here and where do you come from?" Black out from the pain. "I'm writing a book! Everyone will read it." They consult, stop etching, start talking clear channel. I'm a poking stick [p. 106].
>
> . . .
>
> Seeing Frank's distress, the aliens wriggle their stubby, starfish arms like Hindu dancers and—just like that—the smell mutates into a pleasant odor of pipe smoke and magnolia blossoms, and their bodies change shape to look like—what the hell?!—the actors in the last movie Frank happens to have watched on television, which was a 1941 **Howard Hawks** movie called ***Ball of Fire*** starring **Barbara Stanwyck** and **Gary Cooper**—yes, the three or four—or, no it's five—aliens are shaped like **Stanwyck** and **Cooper**, three **Barbara**s and two **Gary**s, all shimmery and black-and-white and moving with that slangy 1940s dynamism, dancing the rumba or something, only—oh-oh!—pieces of them coming off and floating around,

globs of shimmery humanoid film flesh drifting about the round room, **Stanwyck**'s hips here, <u>**Cooper**</u>'s head there, **Stanwyck**'s hands, <u>**Cooper**</u>'s back, a few of the pieces bump into Frank and they feel warm and real as live flesh, it's so fucking weird; Frank wants to vomit some more, but stomach is all empty now and he can only heave and retch [pp. 109-110].

The Pride of the Yankees **(1942).** One of America's most beloved pictures, especially among sports fans, *The Pride of the Yankees*, directed by Sam Wood and co-starring Teresa Wright and Walter Brennan, brought Cooper another Oscar nomination for his moving performance as baseball star Lou Gehrig. An allusion to the film appears in Herman Raucher's novel *Summer of '42* (1971), in a passage explaining fifteen-year-old Hermie's wonders about the mind of the woman he is infatuated with:

> And what dreams of Hermie inhabited her mind? What mystical instinct told her how close he was? Errol Flynn on the prowl; Tyrone Power come from Eden; <u>**Gary Cooper**</u> coming to bat with the bases loaded while **Teresa Wright** wrung her hanky in the dugout. Hermie circled her like a wolf pack. Silent, stealthy. She was the center of the universe and Hermie its panting perimeter. And because of his circling, again it was as though she were on a slow turntable, served up and presented from every angle for Hermie's delight [p. 48].

Stuart Kaminsky alludes to the picture in his mystery *High Midnight* (1981), in a scene where the book's narrator/protagonist, private eye Peters, meets Babe Ruth when trying to find Cooper:

> "We're making a movie," Ruth explained. "The Life of Lou Gehrig. <u>**Coop**</u> is Gehrig. Lot of people been trying to get in here. They find out, pester, you know." I nodded, showing that

I knew. "Some of them get unpleasant. You're not going to get unpleasant?"

"I'm not planning to be unpleasant," I said. Koenig was about fifty feet off, talking to **Cooper** and pointing in my direction.

"We're not shooting anything today, just getting some publicity shots and helping Lefty teach **Coop** how to throw a baseball," explained Dickey [p. 19].

I dropped **Cooper** at the Goldwyn Studios, where he had an appointment with the people who were doing the wardrobe for the Gehrig movie [p. 87].

Kaminsky mentions this film again (and alludes to *Sergeant York*) in his Clark Gable mystery *Tomorrow Is Another Day* (1995). The context of the scene is private eye Peters's prospect of going to the Academy Awards dinner at Coconut Grove, where he plans to stop the murders committed by a dangerous man presumably named Spelling, and his conversation with Hy, a man who runs a clothing store:

"You own the building, Hymie," I reminded him.

"I am not always easy on myself. You got a formal occasion or are you gonna dress up like a waiter again?"

"Academy Awards dinner," I said.

"Ooh, Coconut Grove. The whole schmeer. Best actor's gonna be **Gary Cooper**. ***Pride of the Yankees***. Two years in a row. First **Alvin York**. Then **Lou Gehrig**. Can't beat the combo. You can bet on it. My sister's husband delivers sandwiches to the Academy. He heard. Bet on it [p. 161].

Gary Cooper and Teresa Wright as Lou and Eleanor Gehrig in a scene from Sam Wood's *The Pride of the Yankees* (1942).

In Susan Isaacs's already mentioned novel *Shining Through* (1988), a reference to the film and its stars appears in a passage where Linda Voss describes one of the highlights in her married life with John Berringer:

> But it was still time together. And it wasn't like weekends at home, when he was editing a brief or reading the paper or listening to Mozart with his eyes closed. I had his full attention, even with my clothes on, and on Saturday night, when we saw **_The Pride of the Yankees_**, with **Gary Cooper** and **Teresa Wright**, we held hands, and he gave me his handkerchief before I even thought to ask for it [p. 246].

The film is also alluded to in George Baxt's mystery *The Greta Garbo Murder Case* (1992), in a passage relating a conversation between Samuel Goldwyn and his assistant:

"Now let's get back to business. What's next on the agenda?"

Sophie's eyes crossed and then just as quickly uncrossed. "**Gary Cooper** isn't crazy about playing **LouGehrig**."

"Goddammit!" roared Goldwyn. "That **Gary** is becoming a milestone around my neck!" He pushed his chair back from the desk and crossed to the window. He drank of his kingdom and once again felt content. "Thank God I own the studio lox stocks and barren. It's my Garden of Eden, Sophie. My paradox" [p. 47].

In Leslie Carroll's novel *Temporary Insanity* (2004), a reference to this film is made by narrator/protagonist Alice herself, in a quite self-explanatory passage that quotes a line from Lou Gehrig's famous farewell speech. The legendary baseball player's speech was delivered by Cooper first in the film, and then, repeatedly, when he, on his USO tours, entertained American troops fighting in World War II; and the line, in its complete version, ranked as #38 on the American Film Institute's List of the Top 100 Movie Quotes (2005):

> There's something nostalgic about walking through the tunnel at Yankee Stadium and emerging inside the legendary arena, inhaling the crisp evening air as you make your way to your seats. The organ music plays and you can almost hear the ghost of **Gehrig** echoing, *Today-ay-ay . . . is the happiest-est-est day-ay-ay . . .*
>
> Just thinking about it makes me cry, even though I only know the famed **"Pride of the Yankees"** as indelibly portrayed on celluloid by **Gary Cooper**. Another great Yankee was being honored at this game, as it turned out. It was Yogi Berra commemorative bobble-head doll night [p. 83].

An allusion to the protagonist of the film is made in Michael Malone's novel *The Four Corners of the Sky* (2009). Lou Gehrig is one of four real-life/literary/film characters that Dr. Clark Goode, an adoptive father of Annie Peregrine Goode, is compared to by Sam Peregrine, the lesbian companion in his life and the adoptive mother of Annie:

> There was a restless stirring here by those who feared a feminist lecture of the sort many in Emerald had heard from Sam before. She settled them with raised urgent hands. "As far as counting on men, Clark Goode is Atticus Finch. He's Virgil Tibbs. He's **the pride of the Yankees**. He's the man who shot Liberty Valance [p. 301].

***For Whom the Bell Tolls* (1943).** Ernest Hemingway's famous Spanish Civil War novel was adapted for the screen by screenwriter Dudley Nichols and director Sam Wood. In addition to Gary Cooper (Oscar nominated again), who was Hemingway's choice for the part of Robert Jordan, the international cast included Ingrid Bergman, Katina Paxinou and Akim Tamiroff. One of the first allusions to the film can be found in Steve's Shagan's satirical novel *Save the Tiger* (1972), in a passage where protagonist Harry Stoner watches television and keeps switching channels:

> Raft found out about Pearl Harbor. But too late. The Imperial Fleet sailed. He changed channels. Charlie Chan was wrapping up a complicated case on the back lot at Warner's. Harry pressed the button. **Gary Cooper** and **Akim Tamiroff** were huddled behind a snow bank in the Spanish mountains, watching a battalion of Moors cantering toward a mined bridge. **Cooper**'s hand closed over the plunger. Harry shook his head. It would never happen that way. The Moors would have sent out sappers. They'd have gone over that bridge with a vacuum cleaner. He snapped the set off [p. 35].

German poster for Sam Wood's *For Whom the Bell Tolls* (1943).

The film, along with its female star, is also referenced in William Goldman's thriller *Marathon Man* (1974). It takes place in a scene where Tom "Babe" Levy meets Elsa Opel:

She was, there was simply no room for argument, something. Probably she wasn't beautiful. Garbo was beautiful, maybe Candice Bergen might be someday. This one here was only pretty. Pretty like Jeanne Crain or Katharine Ross, no more than that. Perfectly pretty was all. This one—

Bergman in *For Whom the Bell Tolls!* That's who she reminded him of, with the short blonde hair and the eyes and . . .

. . . the eyes were really not to be believed.

So blue, dark, and deep, and—quit staring at her, don't do it too long, give it a rest—Babe admonished himself a few more times before he thought, dammit, it was too late, he had gaped too long, she had felt it [pp. 76-77].

The reference to the film in Stuart Kaminsky's *High Midnight* (1981) is a part of a chat that private detective Peters, Cooper and Hemingway have in Cooper's hunting cabin outside of Santa Barbara:

"I think I like him," Hemingway said with a friendly smile to **Cooper**.

I was hot getting irritable and I didn't give a turkey's tassel what Hemingway thought of me. No one had asked me what I thought of Hemingway.

Cooper looked out the window and moved to one of the chairs, which he sat in slowly, cocking his head with his good ear in my direction.

"Hemingstein here," he said pointing at **Hemingway**, "wanted to get away quietly. Buddy Da Silva is trying to get him to look over the screenplay of *For Whom the Bell Tolls*, and the Great White Hunter is not ready to make any decisions" [p. 128].

Four Hollywood Legends

In Stuart Woods's thriller *L.A. Times* (1993), there is paragraph describing the apartment of the main character, small-time gangster Vincente Michaele Callabrese about to become big-time film producer Michael Vincent. The description includes references to three movies from the early 1940s:

> The interior was classic New York Yuppie. Vinnie had exposed the brick on the wall with the fireplace; the furniture was soft and white, with a sprinkling of glass and leather; the art was a few good prints and a lot of original movie posters—**Casablanca, For Whom the Bell Tolls**, and *His Girl Friday* among them [p. 15].

Gary Cooper as Robert Jordan and Ingrid Bergman as Maria in a scene from Sam Wood's *For Whom the Bell Tolls* (1943), one of two Ernest Hemingway screen adaptations starring Cooper.

Elmore Leonard inserts a reference to the film in his novel *Be Cool* (1999), during a conversation between Chili and Bulkin:

> Bulkin looked past Chili and back again and said, "What can I do for you?"
>
> Chili heard **Akim Tamiroff**, that kind of accent, the tone quiet, guttural. He laid the envelope on the counter, pulled out the photo and looked up to see Bulkin's sad, damaged eyes staring at him. He said, "Did you take this picture?" And watched Bulkin look down and up again without a pause.
>
> "I don't think so."
>
> **Akim Tamiroff** in ***For Whom the Bell Tolls***. Sullen, his voice a low, grumbling sound, wine-soaked, **Pablo** drunk saying, I don't think so, *Inglés* [p. 185].

A reference to the film in Richard Laymon's horror *Endless Night* (1993) comes in a section narrated by Simon Quirt, a complex and unpredictable character who tries to outsmart the other members of the gang of rapists and murderers calling themselves "The Krulls":

> "Hi, guys. Right on time, huh? I've got Jody in the trunk. She's alive and kicking, just like you wanted. And I killed the boy. It all went great!"
>
> Okay, the gate is starting to swing open.
>
> Here we go.
>
> I don't *have* to drive through.
>
> But I'm doing it. I mean I, I'm sort of committed at this point.
>
> I should *be* committed. This is a lunatic move. Suicide.
>
> A real **Gary Cooper** move.
>
> That's **Cooper** in ***For Whom the Bell Tolls***, in case you're

wondering, where he stays behind to cover the retreat—even though he knows it'll be his ass.

"I do this for you, Maria. You go, and I will go with you."

Bullshit he goes with her. He bites the dust and turns into ant food [pp. 411-412].

Casanova Brown **(1944).** This fairly entertaining romantic comedy, directed by Sam Wood and co-starring Teresa Wright, is mentioned in Herb 'Chick' Fowle's World War II nonfiction book *Against All Odds* (1991). The actor and the film constitute a nice distraction for the author/narrator (a voluntary machine gunner)—one of the American soldiers hospitalized in Belgium who prepare a children's Christmas party, a few days before the Malmedy massacre:

> There was a show at the theater nearly every night and the night of December 13th the one advertised was **Gary Cooper** in '**Casanova Brown**'. **Gary** had always been one of my favorite actors, so I took the night off and went over to see it, since we had plenty of time to get everything ready for the kids Christmas party.
>
> The party we were planning, and working towards, would be a wonderful thing for the kids. But even more wonderful, was the time killing element it afforded these men, some of them still just boys, who were so far away from home at Christmas time, when, more than any of the year, they missed being home with their families and friends [p. 147].

Another reference to the film was found in Bernard Spiro's *The Other War: Letters from a GI in India in 1944 & 1945* (2001), in one of the three letters sent home by the author/narrator which include Gary Cooper's name:

Teresa Wright as Isabel Drury and Gary Cooper as the titular character in a publicity shot for Sam Wood's *Casanova Brown* (1944).

Dec. 16, 1944

"Why does time always pass so quickly on a soldier's afternoon off? Finished reading Bob Hope's *I Never Left Home* which was terrific, saw **Gary Cooper** in ***Casanova Brown*** which was okay but disappointing, finished writing an eight page letter to old friend Max, and here I am having to finish this letter to you by lantern light" [p. 126].

***Along Came Jones* (1945).** Based on Alan LeMay's novel *Useless Cowboy*, and directed by Stuart Heisler, this comedy western (co-starring Loretta Young and Dan Duryea) is referenced in Iris Paris's nonfiction book *Once Upon a Chariot* (2008), which is "a true story about Norma Jean Belloff, who established the USA Women's Record for Cross Country Bicycling in 1848" and which the author (Belloff's daughter) wrote as her mother's journal. The reference to Cooper in the film opens the entry dated March 8:

> I met a cowboy named Steve. Like younger **Gary Cooper** in *Along Came Jones*, he comes complete with long legs; a shy, gentle spirit; and a love of singing. Quite a captivating, country gentleman, he moves in rhythm to his fluid Texan drawl. Are all Texas men like this? He invites me to see the bull and cockfights in Ciudad Juarez, the town just across the Rio Grande. I agree to go out of curiosity and a desire to dull the ache in my heart for Neill [p. 83].

***Saratoga Trunk* (1945).** This only partially successful screen adaptation of Edna Ferber's novel, directed by Sam Wood and co-starring Ingrid Bergman, is referenced in "The Decline and Fall of Frankie Buller" (1959), one of nine short stories in Alan Sillitoe's collection *The Loneliness of the Long-Distance Runner*. Set in the author's home town, Nottingham, the story relates the relationship between the author/narrator/protagonist and a boy several years older, Frankie Buller, who—in the years before and during the war—bullies Alan and other twelve-year-olds from his street into joining his gang and leads them to war against a similar group of boys from another district. A reference to Cooper and *Saratoga Trunk* takes place in a passage toward the end of the story, when Alan meets Frankie about ten years later—now the relationship, if any, has a completely different character—and reads the content of a poster for him:

> He wanted to go. The rain was worrying him. Then,

Gary Cooper as Clint Maroon and Ingrid Bergman as Clio Dulaine in Sam Wood's *Saratoga Trunk* (1945).

remembering why he had called me over, he turned to face the broad black lettering on a yellow background. "Is that for the Savoy?" he asked, nodding at the poster.

"Yes," I said.

He explained apologetically: "I forgot me glasses, Alan. Can you read it for me, and tell me what's on tonight."

"Sure, Frankie." I read it out: **<u>Gary Cooper</u>**, in **<u>Saratoga Trunk</u>**."

"I wonder if it's any good?" he asked. "Do you think it's a cowboy picture, or a love picture?"

I was able to help him on this point. I wondered, after the shock treatment, which of these subjects he would prefer. Into what circle of his dark, devil-populated world had the jolts of electricity penetrated? "I've seen that picture before," I told him.

"It's a sort of cowboy picture. There's a terrific train smash at the end."

Then I saw. I think he was surprised that I shook his hand so firmly when we parted. My explanation of the picture's main points acted on him like a charm. Into his eyes came the same glint I had seen years ago when he stood up with a spear and shield and roared out: "CHARGE!" and flung himself against showers of sticks and flying stones [p. 175].

A reference to the film in Christopher Bram's novel *Lives of the Circus Animals* (2003) is the major focus in a scene depicting a conversation of a married couple:

> She wished they didn't feel like an old married couple.
>
> "Oh oh oh," she suddenly said. "You might know this. A line from a movie has been going through my head all day. '**I luf you like a pig lufs mud.**' Sound familiar? Is it Garbo? Dietrich?"
>
> He thought a moment. Then he broke into a smile. "Uh-uh. It's **Ingrid Bergman**. It's—what's the name?" He snapped his fingers.
>
> "*Gaslight*? **Casablanca**?"
>
> He shook his head. "No, period piece. A comedy. And she's beautiful, like always, but funny too, which makes her even more beautiful. She's a fortune hunter, and she has a great name. *Clio Dulaine!* And she's in love with **Gary Cooper**."
>
> "**Saratoga Trunk**!" cried Jessie. "It was just on AMC. How could I forget? And there's a dwarf, and a mulatto housekeeper. And you're right. She is beautiful. But not half as beautiful as **Gary Cooper**."
>
> One met so few men, or women either, who really enjoyed old movies. Gay men thought they did, but most of them knew only a few obvious title and the same tired scenes. The occasional

straight man who loved old movies was usually ashamed of knowing so much. But not Frank.

"**I luf you like a pig lufs mud,**" Frank repeated. He was staring at her [p. 155].

It is worth pointing out that the film is also briefly mentioned in Byron Janis's autobiographical book *Chopin and Beyond* (2010), in a passage which Maria Cooper Janis wrote about her familiy's visit to Pablo Picasso's villa near Cannes, when the famous artist received from Gary Cooper the white Stetson the actor had worn in the movie.

***Good Sam* (1948).** A reference to this disappointing comedy, co-starring Ann Sheridan and directed by Leo McCarey, was found only in one work. Elmore Leonard's *52 Pickup* (1974) is a mystery about a middle-aged married couple undergoing a crisis due to the man's infidelity. However, there is a moment of understanding and closeness, which includes a reference to Cooper and this picture:

> It was good to sit on the couch in the den and watch an old **Gary Cooper** movie, ***Good Sam***, and remember they had seen it together before they were married [p. 230].

***The Fountainhead* (1949).** Ayn Rand's famous novel was turned into a fairly successful movie by Rand herself as the screenwriter and director King Vidor. In addition to Cooper as Howard Roark, the leading parts are played by Patricia Neal and Raymond Massey. The film is referenced in Ira Levin's *Rosemary's Baby* (1967) and Ilene Beckerman's *What We Do for Love* (1997).

In Levin's horror the reference appears in a scene relating Rosemary's complex, stream-of-consciousness kind of thoughts while she is trying to fall asleep:

> Which didn't make sense at all, not even to Uncle Mike; so

Rosemary turned over and it was Saturday afternoon, and she and Brian and Eddie and Jean were at the candy counter in the Orpheum, going in to see **Gary Cooper** and **Patricia Neal** in *The Fountainhead*, only it was live, not a movie [p. 42].

An unidentified player, Patricia Neal (Dominique Francon) and Gary Cooper (Howard Roark) in a scene from King Vidor's *The Fountainhead* (1949).

In Beckerman's unusual little novel, the film is mentioned in a passage where narrator/protagonist Gingy (Gin) Edelstein reveals some details about her date with her first husband-to-be, the Professor (never mentioned by name), in a restaurant called the Meadows, in Framingham near Boston:

> It wasn't very crowded for a Saturday night. He ordered a martini and asked what I wanted to drink. I usually ordered a brandy alexander. But I didn't think that was a sophisticated enough drink. "A daiquiri, please," I said. **Patricia Neal** drank daiquiris in *The Fountainhead* [p. 31].

Walter Brennan (seated) as Pete Richard, John Ridgely (third from right) as Dixie Rankin, Gary Cooper (second from right) as Jonathan L. Scott and unidentified players in a lobby card for Delmer Daves's *Task Force* (1949).

***Task Force* (1949).** A possible allusion to this minor movie, directed by Delmer Daves, appears in Donald E. Westlake's (first) Dortmunder novel

The Hot Rock (1970), in a scene where two members of Dortmunder's caper gang are mentioned:

> The boards bowed the weight of the car. Murch, behind the wheel, looked like **Gary Cooper** taxiing his Grumman into position on the aircraft carrier. Nodding at Kelp the way **Coop** used to nod at the ground crew, Murch tapped the accelerator and the Mercedes-Benz went away, lights out [p. 111].

Bright Leaf **(1950).** Written by Ranald MacDougall from the novel by Foster Fitz-Simons and directed by Michael Curtiz, this fairly successful drama (co-starring Lauren Bacall and Patricia Neal) is referenced in Les Roberts's Milan Jacovich mystery *Deep Shaker* (1991), set in Cleveland. The quoted excerpt is a part of a lengthy scene in which the private eye is admitted into the house of Henry "Waco" Morgan, a successful and politically ambitious owner of a car dealership, and in the den they try to explain the mutual misunderstanding and figure out whom Morgan is being set up by:

> "Money helps you get the Ps [position, prestige, power]," he said. "And I aim to get mine in a way that should convince you I'm clean."
>
> He checked me out through the cigar smoke the way he'd scrutinize a used car or a racehorse or a new woman, weighing risks and calculating possibilities. Making a decision, he jammed the cigar between his teeth like **Gary Cooper** in ***Bright Leaf***, reached into his pocket, and produced a roll of cash the size of a tangerine. He carefully extracted five hundred-dollar bills from the middle of the roll and tossed them onto my lap.
>
> "Isn't it a little early for Christmas presents?" I said.
>
> "I'm hiring you. You want to find out who's trying to frame me, you may as well get paid for it. Unless you already got s client?" [p. 228]

Gary Cooper as Brant Royle and Patricia Neal as Margaret Jane in a publicity shot for Michael Curtiz's *Bright Leaf* (1950).

***It's a Big Country* (1951).** An anthology of eight episodes about America, each directed by someone else, the film has Gary Cooper, on horseback, introducing each story to the audience. A brief reference to the essentially forgotten movie appears in Janet Leigh's *House of Destiny* (1995). The scene setting is Idaho in 1963; Jude Abavas shows the beauty of the state to his friends:

"Idaho has so many different faces. If you go eat from Sun Valley, you go through what's called the Craters of the Moon, because of the black lava rock," Jude explained. "It's eerie! And, further east, you come to the Idaho side of the Tetons, really spectacular. Remember the movie **M-G.M** made in the early fifties about the good old U.S.A., _**It's A Big Country**_? It sure as hell is!" [p. 455]

Distant Drums (1951). The picture is not a major item in either Cooper's or director Raoul Walsh's filmography; nonetheless, its storyline inspired Larry McMurtry to create a memorable metaphor in his novel *All My Friends Are Going to Be Strangers* (1972). The book's narrator/protagonist, a published author of one novel, Danny Deck, is dissatisfied with his life and with his second book, and he manifests it in an unusually dramatic way:

> It was true. I had never felt such black, unforgiving hatred of anything as I felt for the pages in my hands. The box was soaked, but the novel was still there.... I picked off chapters and held them under. They didn't want to drown. The paper I used was too good. It wanted to float. Pages got loose and floated. I caught them and swatted them down. I shoved them under. No mercy for pages. It was a deadly battle. Part of a chapter slipped loose and floated. I splashed after it and forced it under. Finally it squished. The words gave up. I picked off another chapter, but killing the chapters was too slow. I had hundreds of pages left. Finally I grappled the novel in both hands and dove. I would carry it to the bottom. Only one of us would come up. I was **Gary Cooper**, in **_Distant Drums_**. My novel was the **Seminole chief**. We were fighting under water. The current turned me over, swirled me over. Even drunk I could swim well. The depths of the river were black. My head was pounding. I kicked and kicked, going deeper. The book in my hands was hundred-

headed, like Grendel. Parts of it nearly slipped loose in the fast current. I wadded them. My superb condition began to tell on the novel—my superior strength began to prevail. The novel got squishier and squishier, deep in the channel of the Rio Grande. Finally it got completely squishy, and I knew it was dead. I let it go and came up. My head was still pounding but the river was clear. No pages floated on it, only moonlight and the reflection of stars [pp. 284-285].

***High Noon* (1952).** A winner of four Academy Awards (including one for Cooper) and three additional nominations, this masterful western, directed by Fred Zinnemann and scored by Dimitri Tiomkin (both immigrants from Europe), remains a gem in the history of the American cinema and probably the most discussed western of all time—not only because of its contemporary political innuendoes. A number one movie on the lists of numerous famous people, *High Noon* has its own life in both fiction and nonfiction. It is also, unsurprisingly, the most frequently referenced western and one of the most extensively referenced films. Here are most of the seventy-seven references that were found.

Robert Traver's superb courtroom drama *Anatomy of a Murder* (1958), published only a few years after *High Noon*'s release, mentions the picture in a scene describing one of the minor characters, Deputy Sheriff Sulo:

> The outer jail door opened and in stalked a character straight out of ***High Noon***. His big mail-order felt hat was pushed back on his perspiring forehead; his exquisitely tailored and stitched gabardine shirt, with its cascades of pearl buttons at the shaped pockets and cuffs, was negligently open at the tanned throat, from which depended two cords held by a dollar-sized round silver clasp engraved not with Justice, not with Liberty, but with a bucking bronco. The richly tailored trousers were tucked carelessly into the tops of dusty hand-stitched laceless boots and

all he lacked, I saw, was a Bull Durham tag dangling over his heart [p. 56].

In Jack Kerouac's *Desolation Angels* (1960) Cooper in mentioned three times: once in connection with *Beau Geste*, once in a paragraph on the actor himself and on Gable (p. 268; it is presented in the part on Gable) and once in connection with *High Noon* (where, accidently, Gable is mentioned as well):

> Pregnant women who smile don't even dream about this. God Who is everything, the Already Thus, he Whom I saw on Desolation Peak, is also a smiling pregnant woman not even dreaming about this. And if I should complain about the way they manhandled **Clark Gable** in Shanghai or **Gary Cooper** in **High Noon** Town, or how I'm driven mad by old lost college roads in the moon, aye, moonlight, moonlight, moonlight me that, moonlight— Moonlight me some moonshine, adamantine you mine [p. 298].

Guillermo Cabrera Infante's *Three Trapped Tigers*, a novel set in pre-Castro Havana (originally published in Spanish in 1965), offers an unusual reference to both Gary Cooper and *High Noon*, a reference that is triggered by actor Arsenio Cué's behavior during a car ride with a group of absorbing passengers:

> He was doing an imitation of **Gary Cooper** as he drove off pulling down the brim of an imaginary stetson. He was the White Knight, the savior. Savior Cué.
> —*Un año sin verde*, I said gravely, copycatting **Katy Jurado**'s country countralto in ***High Noon***.

—See low say, said **Gary Cuéper** in Texican. The wild West dubbed in Spanish, for the audience's benefit. Self-criticism. Autocritica. He drove on and we rode together [p. 411].

An American poster for Fred Zinnemann's *High Noon* (1952) and a Polish poster for the same film (by Marian Stachurski). These two photos, just like the ones for Cooper's *Vera Cruz* (1954) and Clark Gable's *The Misfits* (1961), perfectly illustrate the significant differences between the American and Polish styles/schools of poster design.

A reference to the film in Donald Hamilton's novel *The Terminators* (1975) is part of a comment one makes about the manner American secret agent Matt Helm handled one of his many challenges:

> He had a nice, smooth, expensive tan that made his big teeth look very white when he grinned again, with a glance in the direction Erlan Torstensen had taken.
> "You really leaned on that kid," he said. "***High Noon*** stuff: *Get out of town or get dead.* Did you mean what you told him?"
> I made a face. "How the hell do I know? If he shows again, we'll see whether I meant it or not" [p. 77].

Robert B. Parker, in his novel *Mortal Stakes* (1975), quotes the lyrics of the titular song of *High Noon* to make a clear comparison between his private eye Spenser, in a moment before a deadly showdown, and Gary Cooper in his desperate predicament before and after the clock strikes twelve:

> My stomach rolled. Smooth. How come **Gary Cooper**'s stomach never rolled? **Oh, to be torn 'tween love and duty, what if I lose** ... Five forty. My fingertips tingled and the nerves along the insides of my arms tingled. The pectoral muscles, particularly near the outside of my chest, up by the shoulder, felt tight, and I flexed them, trying to loosen up ... [p. 271].

In another mystery by Parker, *Double Deuce* (1992), the same song is mentioned as it becomes the focus of an amateur, and non-sequitur, performance by Hawk, Spenser's occasional collaborator:

> Hawk began to whistle through his teeth, softly to himself, the theme from ***High Noon*** [p. 71].

Finally, in his novel *Cold Service* (2005), Parker quotes the lyrics of the film's titular song once again, and this time also mentions its original performer's name, in order to give the reader the sense of Spenser's feeling in the conclusive scene of the book, the feeling of desolateness and suspense:

> There was a thin fog lingering just over the salt marsh. The traffic on Route 1A was still desultory. Occasionally, a truck would lumber south toward Boston, but mostly it was just quiet. I felt as if **Tex Ritter** should be singing on a sound track somewhere. "**. . . look at that big hand move along, nearing high noon.**"
>
> 5:10.
>
> I took the Winchester and got out of the car and leaned on the fender. Traffic was picking up a little in 1A. Somewhere, somebody was frying something and making coffee.
>
> 5:12.
>
> One of the gulls spotted something it considered edible. It landed and grabbed it. Two other gulls landed beside it and tried to get it away. There was a fair amount of gull squawk and flutter.
>
> 5: 15.
>
> "**. . . or lie a coward, a craven coward in my grave.**"
>
> At the other end of the mall, Vinnie was out of his car, cradling the shotgun, leaning on the side of his car. The sun cleared the horizon now, lingering brightly just above the gray ocean [pp. 302-303].

Lawrence Sanders, another mystery master, uses the famous showdown cliché in a scene of *The Sixth Commandment* (1979), where The Bingham Foundation's grant investigator Samuel Todd secretly meets with a key witness, Mary Thorndecker:

But Mary Thorndecker got out of her car, too. Slammed the door: a solid *chunk* muffled in the thicker air. Maybe she didn't want to be alone with me in a closed space. Maybe she didn't trust me. I don't know. Anyway, we were both out in the open, stalking toward each other warily. **High Noon** at Crittenden [p. 274].

A reference to the film in another book by Sanders, *The Timothy Files* (1987), takes place during a conversation between Wall Street detective Timothy Cone and his boss and lover, Samantha Whatley:

"And what has Joe Washington found out?" Sam asks, looking at him narrowly.

"Oh," he says, flummoxed, "you know Joe's been working with me?"

"Will you give me credit for some brains?" she yells. "Of course I know it. Don't ever get the idea that I don't know what's going on in that office, buster, because I do. But I can't keep covering your ass if you don't play straight with me. So no more secrets—okay?"

"Okay."

"Liar," she says. "Tell me something—honestly now: Why did you try that **<u>High Noon</u>** face off with Bonadventure? He could have pounded you to a pulp. You never would have drawn your gun on him."

"Maybe, maybe not. Listen, I just don't like people who think they own the world" [p. 66].

Heinz Kohler's autobiographical novel *My Name Was Five* (1979) is set before, during and after World War II. A reference to the movie appears obviously in the section of the book where the narrator, whose father was persecuted for his anti-Nazi convictions and who himself ended up in East

Germany after the war, is freed from both the fascism and communism nightmares and enjoys life in West Berlin:

> A month later, Helga came again and this time I took her to the *Kurfürstendamm*, West Berlin's most famous avenue, where we saw a film starring **Gary Cooper**, called ***High Noon***. Then we went to the Maison de France, a West Berlin equivalent of the House of German-Soviet Friendship in we had spent so much time back I burg [p. 325].

Elmore Leonard makes a clear reference to Zinnemann's classic western in the title of his superb mystery *City Primeval: High Noon in Detroit* (1980). Though there is no other direct reference to the movie in the book, the words 'high noon' do appear without quotations marks on page 173, while there and in several other places (e.g. on pp. 132, 206-207, 333-336) the characters either refer to the idea of the quintessential Wild West showdown or make appearances of re-enacting it.

In another novel by Elmore Leonard, *Tishomingo Blues* (2002), the film is mentioned during a verbal confrontation between two factions that happen to be on the opposite sides in a Civil War battle reenactment:

> Hector smiled a little; he couldn't help it. He said, "Our general is asleep."
>
> "You his guard dogs?"
>
> "No, what you said, we getting the air."
>
> "Ask him to come out here," Arlen said, "so I can speak to him. Or I can step inside the tent."
>
> "I tole you," Hector said, "he sleeping."
>
> Arlen nodded at the table. "Those pistols loaded?"
>
> "Yes, they are," Hector said.
>
> "You know you're not suppose to put loads in your guns?"
>
> "Yes, we know it," Hector said, "the same as you know it."

Arlen said, "What're we getting to here?"

Hector turned his head to Tonto. "Fucking ***High Noon***, man."

Arlen said, "I didn't hear you."

"I tole him," Hector said, "you want to pull your guns, but you don't have the nerve" [p. 242].

Gary Cooper as Marshal Will Kane and Grace Kelly as Amy (Fowler) Kane in a scene from Fred Zinnemann's *High Noon* (1952).

A reference to the movie appears also in *Red Dragon* (1981), Thomas Harris's first book featuring Hannibal Lecter, in a scene where investigator Will Graham talks to his wife about what to do in order to catch a dangerous serial killer:

> She watched the red sun spread over the sea. High cirrus glowed above it.
> Graham loved the way she turned her head, artlessly giving him her less perfect profile. He could see the pulse in her throat, and remembered suddenly and completely the taste of salt on her skin. He swallowed and said, "What the hell can I do?"
> "What you've already decided. If you stay here and there's more killing, maybe it would sour this place for you. **_High Noon_** and all that crap. If it's that way, you weren't really asking."
> "If I *were asking*, what would you say?"
> "Stay here with me. Me. Me. Me. And Willy, I'd drag him in if it would do any good. I'm supposed to dry my eyes and wave my hanky" [p. 18].

The title of Stuart Kaminsky's mystery *High Midnight* (1981) refers to a fictitious script by a fictitious writer, Curtis Bowie, to be directed by a fictitious director, Max Gelhorn, who hopes—using the Chicago Mafia's long arm's pressure—to get Gary Cooper to play one of the leading roles. The setting of the book is 1942 and the project, never to be accomplished, antecedes *High Noon* by ten years, but the allusion, as a mere inside joke, is quite obvious. The original storyline, told to the reader (pp. 63-64) by the narrator, who happens to be private eye Toby Peters himself, does not resemble the story of *High Noon* except for the very ending when the disappointed sheriff "throws down his badge because the town has not supported him and rides wounded out of town." The resemblance gets more obvious in the variation offered by one of the protagonist's friends, dentist Sheldon P. Minck, who shares the suite with Peters:

"Doc Holliday was a dentist," said Shelly with pride. "Sheriff and the dentist are going to leave town, retire together. Town gives them a big sendoff. Then they find that a gang of guys the sheriff put in jail are free and coming to shoot it out that very day. Sheriff tries to gather the townspeople to help him. They all give excuses, except the dentist. Together the sheriff and the dentist face the gang, and in the last scene they leave town, and the sheriff, who's been wounded in the neck, throws down his badge. Huh, how about that for a story?"

"No good," I said. "Americans don't want to see stories during the war about people not wanting to help each other to fight off the bad guys."

"Maybe you're right," said Shelly. "Maybe I'm a man ahead of his time" [pp. 183-184].

Written by Ned Washington (lyrics) and Dimitri Tiomkin (music), the title song from *High Noon* (also known as "Do Not Forsake Me") was already mentioned three times due to the references found in Robert B. Parker's books. In Stuart M. Kaminsky's mystery *Retribution* (2001), its lyrics are quoted once again and the original performer named, in a scene where Lew Fonesca comes to Flo's house after somebody took a shot at her car:

> Her hands weren't steady, but steady enough. Her mouth was slightly open. **Tex Ritter** sang **"High Noon"** behind her, one of Flo's all-time favorites.
>
> . . .
>
> "He won't come back, Flo," I assured her as **Tex** sang, **"Vowed it would be my life or his'n."**
>
> . . .
>
> "You made a promise as a bride," Tex sang.
>
> . . .

"Okay, I put the bottles away," she said. "Stay sober, wait for that bastard who tried to kill me to show up, and you deliver Adele with no charges against her by Wednesday. Wednesday at high noon," she said as **Tex** sang, **"Do not forsake me, oh, my darling"** [pp. 166-168].

A town description in *Jack and the Beanstalk* (1984), a mystery by Evan Hunter (writing as Ed McBain), contains two similes which refer/allude to two classic movies—Peter Bogdanovich's *The Last Picture Show* (1971) and Fred Zinnemann's *High Noon*:

> Ananburg was only forty-four miles from downtown Calusa, but by comparison it looked like *The Last Picture Show*, a shabby, sun-burned town with a wide main street flanked by palm-lined sidewalks and wooden two-story buildings that appeared temporary, as if they were part of a movie set that would be torn down and stored as soon as the showdown gunfight was shot at **high noon** [p. 54].

In Sharyn McCrumb's Elizabeth MacPherson mystery *Lovely in Her Bones* (1985), the reference to *High Noon* is clearly used in contrast to the situation in the book:

> On the dark path to the excavation site, Deputy Coltsfoot was feeling considerably less like **Gary Cooper** in ***High Noon***. It had occurred to him that there was still a murderer at large in the area, and he had not thought to bring a gun with him. He wasn't even sure that he could have found the key to the gun case [p. 107].

In Lawrence Block's *When the Sacred Ginmill Closes* (1986), the main character is ex-New York cop Matthew Scudder, who spends a lot of time in bars and gives his friends favors for a fee. In the following passage, Skip Devoe, one of Scudder's buddies and "clients," tries not to be conspicuous when loading a big amount of cash and a gun into a car:

> He put the .45 on top of the bills, closed the case. It didn't fit right. He rearranged the bills to make a little nest for the gun and closed it again.
> "Just until we get in the car," he said. "I don't want to walk down the street like **Gary Cooper** in ***High Noon*** [p. 140].

George Baxt's mystery *The Tallulah Bankhead Murder Case* (1987) has the titular actress, operating as an amateur detective, throw up a party and invite all the suspects in order to catch a serial killer of friendly witnesses during the McCarthy era. One of the guests turns out to be Grace Kelly, who, during a conversation with Lewis Drefuss, a radio agent hiding behind an alias, mentions her collaboration with Clark Gable (in *Mogambo*) and Gary Cooper (in *High Noon*):

> "Are you co-starring?" He was running the alphabet through his mind searching for a clue to her name.
> "I'm third billed, but I don't know if it's above the title. I was below in ***High Noon*** with **Gary**."
> The name clicked now. **Grace Kelly**. He said, "**Gary Cooper** and now Clark Gable. Aren't you lucky!"
> "**Cooper** was a bore," she said, "and Gable has false teeth. What fun" [p. 206].

The protagonist of Keith Miles's novel *Double Eagle* (1987) is Alan Saxon, a British golfer and amateur detective, who is forced to solve a murder mystery during a tournament visit to California. A reference to the film is triggered by his introduction to a person having the same name as a *High Noon* character:

After closing my bedroom curtains and slipping off my trainers, I lay on the duvet with my hands behind my head. That name. **Helen Ramirez**. It rang a bell again.

A second **Katy Jurado**.

It came to me in a flash. Just before Christmas, the BBC had screened a series of <u>**Gary Cooper**</u> films. <u>*High Noon*</u> was the first and we'd watched it one night at St Albans. The film still worked superbly. What puzzled me, however, was why our hero chose the repressed **Grace Kelly** character in place of the tempestuous Mexican **Katy Jurado**. Ice instead of fire. I know which one of them I'd have taken off in a buggy.

Katy Jurado had played the part of **Helen Ramirez** [p. 32].

Jeremiah Healy's short story "In the Line of Duty," included in the collection *Raymond Chandler's Philip Marlowe: A Centennial Celebration* (1988), has a few movie references. The following passage starts with a discussion about the actresses running for the 1955 Academy Award and ends up with a laud of Gary Cooper and *High Noon*:

Mims held up a copy of the L.A. *Times* with Monday, March 28, 1955, at the top. "So, who do you like for Wednesday, Garland or Kelly?"

"I'm sorry?"

"The Oscars for last year's films. This is Hollywood, Mr. Marlowe. Movieland. The Academy's giving them out on Wednesday. Who do you think's going to win Best Actress?"

I didn't like people who called Hollywood 'Movieland.' I did, however, like to work to earn money to buy food and shelter. "Who do you like, Mr. Mims?"

"I say Garland's got it wrapped up for *A Star Is Born*. Kelly was good in *The Country Girl*, but with Judy having the baby on the way and all, you've got to lean toward her."

I hadn't seen either film. "The only thing I remember **Grace Kelly** being in was ***High Noon***."

"Boy, there was a picture, huh? But that really wasn't hers. It was **Gary Cooper**, standing alone against four bad guys. What more can you want?" [p. 269]

Robert Ludlum's *The Bourne Ultimatum* (1990) includes a reference to the western movie in a passage where the protagonist, David Webb, also known as Jason Bourne, discusses (on the phone) the options for his ultimate showdown with his long-time enemy, Carlos, or the Jackal:

"Their names ate in Swayne's Mickey Mouse loose-leaf. They had nothing to do with Carlos; they're part of Medusa. It's a mother lode of disconnected information."

"I'm not interested. Use it in good health."

"We will, and very quietly. That notebook'll be on the most wanted list in a matter of days."

"I'm happy for you, but I've got work to do."

"And you refuse any help?"

"Absolutely. This is what I've been waiting thirteen years for. It's what I said at the beginning, it's one on one."

"***High Noon***, you goddamn fool?"

"No, the logical extension of a very intelligent chess game, the player with the better trap wins, and I've got that trap because I'm using *his*. He'd smell out any deviation."

"We trained you too well, scholar."

"Thank you for that."

"Good hunting, Delta."

"Good-bye." Bourne hung up the phone and looked over at the two pathetically curious men on the couch [pp. 188-189].

In Stephen King's science-fiction thriller *The Langoliers* (1990), an allusion to the film is made in a passage relating a dream of Albert Kaussner, a young plane passenger, one of the survivors of the mysterious phenomenon experienced by the plane:

> "Okay, boys," Doc said. "Let's go cut some Dalton butt."
> They strode out together, four abreast through the batwing doors, just as the bell in the Tombstone Baptist Church began to toll **high noon.**
>
> . . .
>
> The Dalton Gang slapped leather just as the clock in the tower of Tombstone Baptist Church beat the last stroke of **noon** into the hot desert air [pp. 19-20].

In another thriller by King, *Insomnia* (1994), a reference to the masterful western takes place during a conversation between main character Ralph Roberts (suffering from insomnia) and his friend Bill McGovern:

> "It's been a bitch of a day," he said. He told McGovern about Helen's call, editing out the things he thought she might be uncomfortable with McGovern's knowing. Bill had never been one of her favorite people.
> "Glad she's okay," McGovern said. "I'll tell you something, Ralph—you impressed me today, marching up the street that way, like **Gary Cooper** in ***High Noon.*** Maybe it was insane, but it was also pretty cool." He paused. "To tell the truth, I was a little in awe of you" [p. 97].

The film is also mentioned in Robert R. McCammon's short story "I Scream Man!" (included in the collection *Blue World*, 1990), where the parallel between the situations in the film and in the book is quite clear:

Again, something rustles in the newspapers. I watch, very carefully. I have good eyes for a man my age. As Jeff ponders his tiles, I see the glint of small, greedy eyes in the corner. "He's coming out again," I tell them in a whisper, and I pick up the pistol on the floor at my side.

I've been waiting for him to make his move. I feel like **Gary Cooper** in *High Noon*. He pokes his head out, and that's all the target I need. The noise of the pistol seems to shake the house, and more blood splatters the wall in the corner. "Fixed you, you bastard!" I shout gleefully [p. 125].

Gary Cooper in a scene from Fred Zinnemann's *High Noon* (1952).

Erica Jong's novel *Any Woman's Blues* (1990) depicts a codependent relationship between Leila Sand, a talented artist (the narrator), and D.V. "Dart" Donegal, an attractive narcissist. Here is a self-explanatory passage including a reference to Cooper and his most famous film:

> From the moment I met Dart, I was sketching him. He beguiled me so. I was fascinated with him, in the archaic sense of the word—enchantment—bound to him with magic, with rapture, with invisible ropes of allure.
>
> From the sketches of him, I evolved the cowboy canvases—enormous mixed-media close-ups of Dart as the Lone Ranger, Dart as Roy Rogers, Dart as **Gary Cooper** in ***High Noon***. I took these cultural icons of my childhood and superimposed this beautiful young man upon them. I hybridized this man born in the fifties with these images from my fifties childhood, and the passion with which I did this was lost on no one [p. 66].

James Patterson's thriller *Along Came a Spider* (1992) includes two references to the film; in both cases it has something to do with the showdown between the law enforcers (Officer Mick Fescoe and Dr. Alex Cross, respectively) and villain Gary Soneji:

> Officer Mick Fescoe couldn't get his breath as he ran around the far side of the McDonald's. He stayed close to the brick wall, brushing his back against it. He'd been telling himself for months to get his ass back in shape. He was puffing already. He felt a little dizzy. That he didn't need. Dizziness, and playing ***High Noon*** with a creep, was a real bad combination [p. 215].

> Then a voice came from across the street. Gary's voice.
> He was shouting at me. It was just the two of us. Was that

what he wanted? His own **High Noon** in the middle of the capital. Live national TV coverage [p. 492].

The film is also referenced in *Sail* (2008), a novel James Patterson wrote in collaboration with Howard Roughan, where a courtroom is compared to the streets of Hadleyville:

> I WATCH as Nolan Heath slowly walks toward the witness stand as if he were **Gary Cooper** in ***High Noon***.
> This is it, isn't it?
> He knows it, I know it, the whole courtroom knows it—including the jury. *It's him against Peter.* One very determined prosecutor versus one very, *very* smart defendant. Whoever wins this ultimate showdown probably wins the trial [p. 349].

In her superior mysteries set both in the USA and England, Martha Grimes repeatedly mentions both Gary Cooper and Humphrey Bogart. The reference to Cooper and *High Noon* in her novel *The End of the Pier* (1992), illustrating the potential impact of film on a young mind, is a part of a moving scene where the female protagonist's son, Murray Chadwick, using his assumed name Chad, meets Sheriff Sam DeGheyn, soon to become a close friend of the family:

> What Chad remembered now was that they—he and Sam—had sat there in the squad car not talking for some time, enjoying, he supposed, a rather companionable silence in spite of the occasion.
> He'd been ten the first time he saw Sam. It was near the courthouse; Sam was standing looking at a Rolls parked by a fire hydrant. He had a gun on his hip and shades over his eyes; a leather jacket that barely hid the holster. He was looking at this car, shaking his head. Then he caught sight of Chad, who'd just

come out of the matinee, full of **Gary Cooper**. It was a rerun of ***High Noon***. He was thinking how he could tell his mom he'd lost the two dollars so he could go back the next Saturday and see it again. He was thinking of all this and then he'd seen Sam. To come out from seeing a sheriff, especially **Gary Cooper**, and then to see a real live sheriff standing off there in front of you with his dark glasses and his holster . . . well, that made you think [pp. 161-162].

Grimes's other references to Cooper and/or *High Noon* usually appear in her Richard Jury novels and result from the fact that Melrose Plant, a wealthy man who has voluntarily given up his titles of Earl of Caverness, fifth Viscount Ardry and some others, is fascinated with the most typical American genre. However, although it is made clear, more than once, that Plant, a character whose relationship with Scotland Yard Inspector Jury resembles that of Dr. Watson and Sherlock Holmes, likes all westerns, it is only *High Noon* that he keeps alluding to in such mysteries as *The Man with a Load of Mischief* (1981), *Jerusalem Inn* (1984), *The Five Bells and Bladebone* (1987) and *The Grave Maurice* (2002).

In John Sandford's *Winter Prey* (1993), a reference to the film appears early in the book, during a conversation between Frank and Claudia LaCourt before they are both killed by a sociopath, a fact which makes their exchange pointless and ironical:

Claudia's voice grew sharper, worried. "If you'd just shut up . . . It's *not* your responsibility, Frank. You *told* Harper about it. Jim was *his* boy. *If* it's Jim."

"It's Jim, all right. And I told you how Harper acted." Frank's mouth closed in a narrow, tight line. Claudia recognized the expression, knew he wouldn't change his mind. Like what's-his-name, in ***High Noon***. **Gary Cooper**.

"I wish I'd never seen the picture," she said, dropping her head. Her right hand went to her temple, rubbing it. Lisa had taken her back to her bedroom to give it to her. Didn't want Frank to see it [p. 5].

Another reference to the film appears in Dale Brown's military thriller *Chains of Command* (1993), in a scene set at a Turkish air base:

"Final strike report, sir," the executive officer said as he handed the teletyped report to General Petr Panchenko at his headquarters at Kayseri Air Base. Panchenko reviewed the Ukrainian-language copy as General Eyers and General Isiklar read off the English-language version.

"Pretty damn good news, I'd say," Eyers said, his hand resting on the military-issue Colt .45 holstered to his belt as if he were **Gary Cooper** in ***High Noon***. "Reconnaissance aircraft report numerous buildings, warehouses, and oil terminals destroyed at Novorossiysk, along with several docks and ... good God, they got sixty tankers, plus two destroyed in drydock. No sign of any signals from air defense radars" [p. 452].

In James Grady's thriller *Thunder* (1994), there is a long list of classic films which constitute the collection of movie buff Frank Mathews, a murder victim whose townhouse is being searched by CIA agent John Lang. The initial portion of the list is presented in Part One of the book (on Bogart); below is its continuation which includes Cooper's best film:

A boxed set of *The Best Years of Our Lives*. Six Hitchcock titles. ***High Noon*** and *The Magnificent Seven*. *Butch Cassidy and the Sundance Kid*. *The Manchurian Candidate* [p. 95].

The reference to *High Noon* in Linda Lael Miller's romance novel *The Legacy* (1994) has the same character—hey, even the identical clause (… felt like . . .)—as quotations from many other novels. Here, however, it is a woman, Jacy Tiernan, who feels like Will Kane; consequently, the showdown has a different form:

> With that, Jacy squared her shoulders and headed resolutely for the door. Hey, Jake, she said silently, if you happen to be hanging around, I could use a hand with this.
> Jacy felt like **Gary Cooper** in ***High Noon*** as she crossed the dusty street toward the Dog and Goose. The trouble was, she wasn't wearing six-guns, and Redley wasn't going to meet her out in the open. She had to seek out a man who hated her in a place she was forbidden to go [pp. 193-194].

There are two references to the film in Sara Paretsky's mystery *Tunnel Vision* (1994): one emphasizing the tension resulting from the too quickly passing time, and one making a simile between the way Marshal Will Kane and private eye V.I. Warshawski felt in different moments of the film and the book, respectively (compare it with the one above):

> "You find anything for that kid you're trying to help?" she asked.
> "Oh, Christ. My bread and butter. I'd forgotten him. And I have until five P.M. Friday. I feel like **Gary Cooper** in ***High Noon***." Ken—MacKanzie—Graham and his blasted public service [p. 147].
>
> As I passed along the bar the men on the stools eyed me narrowly, then fidgeted uneasily in their seats. I felt like **Gary Cooper** making that solitary walk down Main Street. I tried to

stand tall in my loafers, saying, "Easy, boys, and none of us will get hurt," but kept the remark under my breath [p. 333].

Scottish writer Ian Rankin is famous for his Inspector John Rebus mysteries. In his novel *Mortal Causes* (1994), the charismatic policeman is trying to recall (in an extended process) his favorite black-and-white films in order to prove to his girlfriend Patience his fondness of old movies. The last title that he comes up with is the famous western (Frank Miller's counterpart being an escaped gangster named Morris Gerald Cafferty):

> 'I'm not worried,' She took a sip of coffee. 'Yes I am. What is going on?'
> 'A bad man's coming to town.' Something struck him. 'There you are, that's another old film I like: **High Noon**' [pp. 244-245].

Pat Conroy's *Beach Music* (1995) is a contemporary novel in which the main character/narrator is Jack McCall, an American widower living in Rome. The reference to the movie, however, is triggered by another character's ridiculous behavior:

> Mike stood up dramatically and pretended he had been shot in the stomach, wheeled around, and slumped over the railing above the Grand Canal, feigning death. His performance was real enough to attract the attention of two puzzled waiters, who inquired after Mike's health.
> "Get up, Mike," said Ledare. "Try to pretend you know how to act in a good hotel."
> "I's a gut shot, *amigos*. No use to call *medicos*." Mike said. "Tell Mama I died while saying kaddish for Papa."
>
> . . .

He bowed to an elderly Italian woman who certainly had not enjoyed his performance and gave him a look of frosty annoyance. Her contempt seemed to bother Mike.

. . .

"Been to a foreign movie lately?" Mike said. . . . They just go in and out of doors or eat endless dinners. In one door and out the other. Oh, here comes the soup course. They cut their chicken up for a half-hour of screen time. That woman's face. That's all you need to know about why European movies stink."

Ledare nodded her head and said, "She criticized your acting. She didn't fall for your juvenile death scene from **_High Noon_**" [pp. 43-44].

In Reggie Nadelson's mystery *Red Hot Blues* (1995), a reference to the film appears in a scene where government man Roy Pettus asks New York police detective Artie Cohen (of Russian background) for help in the investigation of a former KGB general's murder during a live television talk show:

He said, "This was with General Ustinov's things. It was addressed to you."

"What's in it?'

Pettus smiled slowly, picked up the check, extracted a five-dollar bill from his back pocket. I saw that from time to time he allowed himself a part: he was **Gary Cooper** in **_High Noon_**.

"Fudge," he said.

"Fudge?"

"Yes. Fudge. Some photographs. You have an aunt name of Mrs. Birdie Golden?"

"Yes."

"She the type of lady asks a KGB general to carry fudge to New York City?"

I grinned. "Yes." [p. 39]

A reference to Cooper and the film appears also in Peter Lovesey's novel *The Summons* (1995), in a passage where the narrator reveals Detective Peter Diamond's feeling about the job he is asked to perform, in some ways similar to that of Will Kane's as it involves dealing with a criminal he arrested years ago:

> Something in the looks he was getting made him deeply uneasy. It was almost like admiration. It dawned on him that the entire station knew what he was being asked to take on. He was being treated like **Gary Cooper** in *High Noon* and he hadn't even agreed to the shootout.
>
> He returned upstairs to where Chief Constable was waiting. Farr-Jones definitely wasn't out of a Western. Short and dapper, with a rosebud in his lapel, he could have doubled John Mills in one of his English country gentleman roles. He shook hands as if he was applying a tourniquet [p. 55].

In John Updike's *In the Beauty of the Lilies* (1996), in a passage describing Essie Wilmot/Alma DeMott's early Hollywood career, a reference is made to one real Gary Cooper movie and one fictitious:

> This led to her first starring role, opposite **Gary Cooper** in the less successful ***High Noon***-follow-up, *Red Rock Afternoon* [p. 331].

Nora Roberts's novel *Holding the Dream* (1997, the second part of *The Dream Trilogy*) includes a reference to the film in a dialogue between the ambitious protagonist, Kate Powell, and her long-standing enemy, Candy Litchfield, in the former's store:

> She boxed and wrapped, rang up and bagged, all the while keeping a weather eye on Candy's progress. Two customers left without a purchase, but Kate refused to give Candy's viciously criticizing tongue credit for it.
> Feeling like **Gary Cooper** at the end of *High Noon*, she stepped out from behind the counter to face them alone. "What do you want, Candy?"
> "I'm browsing in a public retail facility." She smiled thinly, and exuded a not-so-subtle whiff of Opium. "I believe you're supposed to offer me a glass of rather inferior champagne. Isn't that store policy?" [p. 309]

In another book by Roberts, *Northern Lights* (2004), a mystery set in a small town in Alaska, the context triggering the reference to *High Noon* is a much more real showdown and, even, involving a woman:

> "Added to all that is the fact that he held a gun to a tourist's head, shot a state cop *and* our chief of police." She gave his biceps a quick kiss. "All of which," she added, "was caught for the record by the NBC cameraman." She stretched, one, long, sinuous move. "Great TV. Our brave and handsome hero shooting the bastard's leg out from under him, while he himself was wounded—"
> "Flesh wound."
> "Standing that bastard down like **Cooper** in *High Noon*. I'm no **Grace Kelly**, but I get hot just thinking about it".
> "Gosh, ma'am." He slapped at a sparrow-sized mosquito that got through the dope. "It wasn't nothing."

"And I looked pretty damn good myself, even when you sent me to the damn sidewalk" [p. 560].

Clearly a dedicated fan of the movie, Nora Roberts paid homage to the great western also in her novel *High Noon* (2007), where the film is referenced in three different ways. Firstly, the author does not have a problem giving its novel exactly the same title as the picture has. Secondly, in three places of her book, she quotes the lyrics of Dimitri Tiomkin's titular ballad as mottos of the three parts:

INITIAL
PHASE

Do not forsake me, oh, my darlin'.
"HIGH NOON" [p. 1]

NEGOTIATION
PHASE

Oh, to be torn 'twixt love an' duty.
"HIGH NOON" [p. 159]

TERMINATION
PHASE

I do not know what fate awaits me.
"HIGH NOON" [p. 305]

Finally, she uses the plot of the film to analyze the mental state of the villain, who, feeling harmed and sorry for himself, assumes the role of the famous fictitious lawman and tries to achieve justice through the final showdown (ignoring the fact that by doing so he places himself on the wrong side of the law). Here are the passages illustrating such a premise:

> "I am not." Amused, Phoebe shook her head. "I thought I saw a new face around, that's all. "A whistler—not wolf whistler, tune whistler. What *is* that tune? It keeps sticking in my head but I can't quite place it."
>
> As soon as she started to hum, Essie broke in. "*<u>High Noon</u>*. You know how I love my old movies. That's the theme from *<u>High Noon</u>* with <u>**Gary Cooper**</u> and **Grace Kelly**. God, what a beauty she was. And him—now that was some handsome man. **'Do not forsake, oh, my darlin',**" she sang in her light, pretty voice [p. 205].
>
> Whistling keeps the voice disguised, anonymous. What does the song mean? **Do not forsake me.** Who was forsaken? Who did or might do the forsaking?
>
> *<u>High Noon</u>*. One man standing up against corruption and cowardice (rabbit as cowardice?) Rat as desertion of townspeople. Snake as corruption. <u>**Cooper**</u> as sheriff (wasn't he? Rent the damn movie), standing alone in the final showdown.
>
> Was it about the movie or just the song? she wondered. She did a search, found the lyrics and printed them out for the file she would make.
>
> **High noon** was a kind of deadline, wasn't it? Do this by this time or pay the price.
>
> She sat back. And if it was Arnie Meeks harassing her, he wouldn't be thinking about symbols and hidden meanings. It just wasn't his style.
>
> Still, she'd make up the file. And on the way home, she'd hunt up a copy of *<u>High Noon</u>* [pp. 302-303].
>
> "I feel sick. I feel . . . No! No! Don't! Please, don't! Roy's eyes wheeled as he strained against the shackles. "Please, God .

..Okay...Okay. I...I'm—I'm tired of listening to you whine, you worthless piece of shit. Keep it up and—and I'll blow you to hell and be done with it."

"If you do that, I won't know why you wanted me out here tonight. Why you're angry. Will you give me a name to call you?"

"He—" Roy's teeth chattered. "S-sure, Phoebe. You can call me **Cooper**."

Though her throat tightened, she wrote the name clearly on the pad, followed it up with *High Noon*. "All right, **Cooper**. Since I can't talk to you directly, I can't hear how you feel. Can you tell me how you feel?"

"Powerful. In fucking charge" [p. 318].

When she closed her eyes, pressed her fingers against her lids, all she could see was Roy. She dropped her hands into her lap. "A failure, a professional failure that was personal to him. Who did I lose, Dave? When? How? I need to go back over my case files, all the way back. Any hostage or hostage-takers, any cop or bystander, anyone who was injured or killed during an incident where I was negotiator.

"I think it's going to be a woman," she added.

"Why?"

"Because he's **Gary Cooper**. Because Roy was chained to a woman's grave" [p. 324].

It could be other law enforcement, it could be military, even paramilitary," Phoebe said. "But everything points to cop to me. **Gary Cooper**—sheriff. He doesn't lose, not **Grace Kelly** or his honor. That's the way it was supposed to be. But on what could symbolize a wedding day, the day Angela Brentine was reclaiming her independence, taking the next step toward becoming her lover's wife, she's killed in a gun battle. Killed by the bad guys, sure, but also—in the subject's mind—because I stood by—the townspeople—and didn't take action, or didn't allow action to be taken. Guilt by cowardice is part of the theme of the movie" [p. 392].

She turned back to the laptop. "We have to get in there, find the files, find the ones he took with him. That's the target." As it churned, she pressed a hand to her stomach. "I think he gave himself the go, the green light. Today. I think it has to be today."

She looked at her watch and felt the chill as she noted it was ten fifty-five. "**High Noon**. We've got an hour to find him" [pp. 430-431].

In Dale Furutani's mystery *The Toyotomi Blades* (1997), a reference to the film is made by Japanese-American detective Ken Tanaka, who—when threatened by the Japanese mafia during his first visit to Tokyo—refuses to fight single-handedly:

"I'm going to do what they used to do in the old West. I'm leaving town. I'll return on the day of the show."

"I thought the frontier marshal always stayed in town to fight out with the tough guys." Hirota picked up his cup to sip the hot tea.

"That was **Gary Cooper** in ***High Noon***. This is Ken Tanaka in Tokyo. I don't feel I have a responsibility to protect the capital city of Japan from a couple of Yakuza. The Tokyo police don't seem too interested in pursuing the case, so I'm going to do what's best to protect me" [p. 87].

There are two references to Cooper (the other one, not quoted here, on page 258) and one to *High Noon* in Randy Alcorn's science-fiction thriller *Edge of Eternity* (1998). The context of the following excerpt is narrator/protagonist Nick Seagrave trying, in a moment of a challenging situation, to compare himself to the Wild West hero of the silver screen:

The claustrophobia plagued me worse than anything. I stopped and picked stony grit out of my raw elbows, trying to control my breathing.

"You okay, Nick?" Gordy asked.

"Sure," I said. "Why wouldn't I be?"

"Why was I so concerned about maintaining my **Gary Cooper-*High-Noon*** image? Nick the loner, brave, self-reliant, powerful, incredibly competent. Who was I kidding? [p. 234]

In Ralph Peters's thriller *The Devil's Garden* (1998), a reference to the film takes place in a scene where Bob Felsher, a man of Oak Leaf Oil, comes home after a long day at work to his wife, a reheated supper and a movie on the television screen. The reference to *High Noon* has a clearly ironical overtone as the comment about the film is made by Felsher, a greedy and unscrupulous man, so ambitious and power-hungry that he would not hesitate to order kidnapping or even murder:

When he finished eating, Felsher rinsed off his plate and put it in the dishwasher while his wife went into the den to turn on the big-screen TV and load the VCR. It was a pleasant routine, and he considered that he led a very pleasant life.

They watched ***High Noon***, a favorite of his, and as it was rewinding, he put his arm around his wife and said:

"That's the problem with this country today. Nobody's willing to stand up for what's right. Nobody cares about doing the right thing. It's all me, me, me" [p. 87].

In Susan Isaacs's epic mystery *Red, White and Blue* (1998), a reference to the great western is a part of a passage in which the narrator reveals the feelings of the female protagonist related to the prospects of saving her relationship with the hero:

What do you do for a living, Mr. Blair? Nothing much. I fix cars, hang out with psychopaths and risk my life for my country every day. Charlie couldn't see himself in New York, and right now, wherever he was, Lauren had to be—at least to his mind. Well, she thought, from Odysseus to the marshal in **High Noon**, the hero had a good woman waiting. Was that what Charlie's "I love you" had meant to ensure? [p. 347]

Andrew Neiderman's mystery *Curse* (2000) is set in Sandburg, a hamlet in the Catskills, and the duel between public defender Del Pearson and ambitious prosecutor Paula Richards does resemble the conflict between Will Kane and Frank Miller. Here are some lines from the book emphasizing these similarities:

"I will issue the gag order immediately," he said.

"Thank you, Your Honor."

The judge sat back and nodded, almost smiling.

"I was expecting you to ask me to relieve you," he said with a twinkle in his cool, gray eyes.

"I guess I'm like **Gary Cooper** in **High Noon**," Del said. "It seems to me I've got to stay."

The judge did smile.

"One of my favorite movies." He glanced at the clock and then at Del. "Paula Richards is coming on the noon train."

"I'll be here," Del said, smiling, and left, somehow a little buoyed [pp. 226-227].

"All right, Anna," he said, shaking his head, "If I don't end up in the hospital getting my stomach pumped, I'll be back tomorrow."

She nodded.

"I know you will be back," she said.

When he stepped out of the shop, he took a deep breath and gazed around the village. He smiled to himself, recalling his conversation with Judge Landers and the comparison he had made between himself and **Gary Cooper** in *High Noon*, claiming he had this deep sense of responsibility. With the reporters gone, the village looked like the village in *High Noon* just before the big gunfight. It had returned to its look of hibernation, vacant and deserted, but perhaps it was only each building, each telephone pole, every door frozen, waiting, its population holding its communal breath [p. 285].

In another novel by Neiderman, *The Hunted* (2005), Centerville (in the Catskills, again) is the equivalent of Hadleyville of *High Noon*, and Sheriff Willie Brand is the counterpart of Will Kane—even though the plot of Neiderman's thriller, action-packed and full of surprises, is much more complex. The passage below includes a simile based on a memorable scene from Zinnemann's movie, which is hardly referred to in other literary works:

"You look ambitious this morning," Willie quipped.

"Sat up watchin' a late show with my father," Jerry said. "Bruce told me to tell you he'll meet you at Sam's, He's havin' breakfast there."

"All right. Mind the store," Willi said. "If Flo Jones calls, raise me on the two-way."

"Right, Chief."

Willie grunted and hurried out. When he stepped through the doorway of Sam's Luncheonette, he felt like **Gary Cooper** in *High Noon* going to the bar to ask for volunteers to help fight the Miller gang [36].

Gary Cooper's performance in the film is praised in Christina Skye's novel *Going Overboard* (2001), in a scene where the book's protagonists, photographer Carly Sullivan and Navy SEAL Ford McKay, carry on a relatively serious discussion about movies. The quoted excerpt is Ford's response to Carly's praise of Humphrey Bogart's performances in a couple of films:

> "Competent, but I'll still take Brando or Pacino in *The Godfather* or John Wayne in *The Searchers*." McKay stood up and stretched. "I almost forgot **Gary Cooper** in ***High Noon***" [p. 138].

A novel published in the same year by another female author, Elizabeth Hay's *A Student of Weather* (2001), alludes to the film once again by quoting the song's lyrics, in a beautiful narrative/descriptive passage that comes after the novel's climax:

> Standing close to the car, she makes a rapid sketch of this fiercely guarded place. Then, working quickly and gingerly, she gathers grasses to take home to Mrs. Gallot. Prairie wool, they call it, because it's so coarse and matted.
>
> Behind the wheel again, and out on the main road, she rolls her window all the way down and drives for a time, zooming up to the crest of a low hill, then dropping down into a valley full of wolf willow, its smell so intoxicating that she breaks into a song – **"Do Not Forsake Me Oh My Darlin'"** – and there is no one, absolutely no one on this patched and bumpy road in this nearly empty province, to say hush [p. 360].

In another novel by Hay, *Garbo Laughs* (2003), *High Noon* is mentioned three times. The context of the first passage is Dinah Bloom's effort to meet Harriet and Lew Gold after she learned about the family's movie interests from their son Kenny:

> Harriet and Lew were wearing shirts and shorts faded from

countless summers; the books in their laps were library books. They didn't look like Frank Sinatra types, thought Dinah, they looked like professors who would never get tenure. And she liked them immediately and without reservation.

To Lew she said, "You're the man who sings the song from *High Noon*."

About a month ago, when she was peeling a late-night peach on the back steps and it was too dark and leafy to make out the source, she'd heard a voice in the alley on the other side of the big oak, just past Bill Bender's garage, a man speaking to a dog in a tone so natural and easy that she'd known everything about him she needed to know. Then he began to sing softly, " **'Do Not Forsake Me,'** " and that was it: her heart said uncle [p. 22].

The second excerpt shows Harriet admiring her son at a time when she takes him to visit Dinah after Kenny reveals the trouble he got into on a school trip to the Aviation Museum:

> He cheered up. They'd gone to see Dinah and he told her the whole story. He sat at the foot of her bed and rattled on, full of gestures, his hands as long and beautiful as **Gary Cooper**'s when he held the reins in *High Noon*, his thin, young back curved, the muscles in his neck strained. Then, as suddenly, he ran out of steam [p. 116].

One more reference to the film—alluding to some of its famous assets, such as suspense and brevity resulting from the unity of time—takes place during a discussion about *Titanic*, and the people that offer their opinions are Dinah, Harriet and Jack Frame (aunt Leah's stepson):

> Then everyone else descended upon her. Jane starry-eyed

and peevish, as she tended to be after seeing a movie; Kenny impressed and eager to talk about the enormous queue (they had to step over fallen electrical wires to get to it) and the size of the sinking ship; smart Dinah quick to point out the missed opportunity. *Titanic* should have taken a leaf from **_High Noon_**, she said, and been made in real time. How long did it take the ship to sink? Two hours? The perfect movie length. They could have focused on a **Gary Cooper** hero, some courageous man on a ship of fools. Then the suspense would have been real.

"You're talking documentary," said Harriet, looking up from the soup and thinking about Grierson.

Jack Frame, clean-shaven, but still padding about in bare feet, said, "**_High Noon_** wasn't documentary. The crop-dusting scene in *North by Northwest* wasn't documentary. They were real time" [p. 166].

Patricia Sprinkle's novel *Who Left That Body in the Rain?* (2002) is a Southern mystery, and its narrator/protagonist is Judge MacLaren Yarbrough, who, along with her husband Joe, is involved in a murder investigation, but the reference to the film appears in a domestic scene:

"Why don't you let Skell handle his own mess for a change? He's twenty-three years old. You come back in the dining room and let your mother properly admire your hair."

I felt so sick, though, that I could hardly walk behind her to the dining room. Gwen Ellen and even Laura wanted Skell home, but my stomach felt like it does whenever Joe Riddley watches **_High Noon_** and **Gary Cooper** starts walking down that seemingly deserted street" [p. 171].

In Isabel Wolff's novel *Out of the Blue* (2003), a reference to the film is a part of a conversation clearly revealing serious marital problems. Not unlike in some other novels, the stereotypical statement "I feel/felt like . . ." is uttered by a woman:

> "Faith," Peter went on quietly. "I realize you're angry, and I deserve it. And I know I've got myself in a…mess. But that doesn't mean we have to make an immediate decision to get divorced. Can't we just cool off?"
> "I have cooled off," I replied. "I'm deep frozen." Peter was staring at me incredulously. I felt like **<u>Gary Cooper</u>** in **<u>High Noon</u>** [p. 144].

Hap Cawood's novel *The Miler* (2003) in set in Kentucky in the 1950s. A reference to the film appears in a scene where a young runner, nicknamed JJ, is challenged by a guy who is compared to a *High Noon* villain:

> One time Mother hired Mr. Craxton to cut the grass, giving him free access to our basement where the lawn tools were stored. The next day our grass clippers and a wrench set were missing.
> "Hey, Jaybird," Birdseed called out, standing like a gunslinger who might be looking for **<u>Gary Cooper</u>** in **<u>High Noon</u>**, except he was smaller and scruffier than the man in the movie. "I read in the *Enterprise* how you were a fast runner." Pokey stood aside, keeping his eyes on me as Birdseed went on. "I'm fast. Let's race."
> I'm in the scene. "I don't want to race you. You don't run what I run" [pp. 120-121].

In S. A. Griffin's "America Poem" (2003, about 120 verses long), Cooper, along with Gable's prime movie, is mentioned in lines focused on selected pop-culture symbols:

. . .
    it was Monroe Garbo Harpo Chico Groucho
Presley
Gone With The Wind
The Babe and baseball
hearts filled with hotdogs and homeruns
jazz pouring out of speakeasies like
hot pepper sauce over flat tongues
F.D.R.
J.F.K.
<u>**Gary Cooper**</u> and <u>**High Noon**</u>
Hank Williams Pete Seeger Huddie Ledbetter and
America
was an eager young debutante
in sift white and pink crinoline and taffeta dresses . . .
[pp. 129-130]

David Cole's mystery *Shadow Play* (2004) contains numerous references to western films, especially to John Ford's trilogy, but also to a couple of Gary Cooper movies, *High Noon* and *Man of the West*. The reference to *High Noon* is triggered by narrator/protagonist Laura Winslow's mention of another movie, *Outland*, which many film critics tie to *High Noon* due to the resemblance in the plot (regardless of the extremely different genres), while she talks to Marvin Katz, a Hollywood agent past his prime.

    "There's a Sean Connery movie," I said.
    "Miss Winslow, enough already with movies."
    "*Outland*."
    "<u>*High Noon*</u>, right? On some planet?"
    "One scene where he sees one of the meth pushers on a video monitor, he takes after the guy, chases him all over the space station and into the kitchen, the guy has this reddish

plastic bag, looks like a silicon breast implant, except it's red. They fight, the guy throws the implant into a bubbling cauldron and without hesitating Connery sticks an arm into the cauldron and pulls out the package."

"Ever hear of a log line?"

"No."

"The complete Hollywood concept. Pitch a movie in one sentence. *Outland*? Perfect log line. **_High Noon_** on a space station. So. You're a dog with a bone," Katz said. "Did I give you the right bone?" [p. 232]

Mary McBride's mystery *Say It Again, Sam* (2004) contains three references to Cooper, the first one of which is combined with *High Noon*. While all of it is about Sheriff Sam Mendenhall, the context of the first excerpt is the interrogation of Sam by a son of his childhood friend, Joe Dolan, and the woman mentioned in the third passage is Sam's former sweetheart, Beth Simon:

> Sam shrugged. He wasn't going to argue with an elf in a striped T-shirt and ref canvas Keds.
>
> The elf sneered. "I bet you don't even wear a gun."
>
> "Don't need one," Sam said in a voice faintly reminiscent of **Gary Cooper** in **_High Noon_**.
>
> "How tall are you?" Joe's offspring demanded.
>
> "Six-two. How tall are you?"
>
> The boy lifted his shoulders, then let them drop. He probably didn't even know how tall he was, or maybe he figured it wasn't cool to proclaim he was all of four-foot-two or –three. "What do you weigh?"
>
> "Depends," Sam said.
>
> "Oh, yeah? On what?"
>
> "On whether or not I've eaten a little boy for breakfast."

> The kid's eyes bulged like little green crabapples, and it was all Sam could do not to laugh [p. 8].

> It took about two minutes—and two miles—down the road for Sam to feel less like **Gary Cooper** and more like one of the Keystone Kops [p. 9].

> "Oh, and Sam?" Blanche said. "I guess you heard about Beth Simon coming back."
> "Yep."
> "Wonder how long she plans to stay out there at the lake?"
> "Dunno."
> He was sounding like **Gary Cooper** again, he thought [p. 22].

Mary Daheim's mystery *The Alpine Pursuit* (2004) has several references to the films, movie stars and singers of the 1950s due to the Fifties Celebrity Night at the Bourgettes' diner, where some of the characters are planning to go. The book's narrator, publisher Emma Lord, entertains quite an original idea:

> We left the diner a little after seven, just as Lucy and Desi arrived along with Buddy Holly and a couple of Elvises. I'd been tempted to stay, but I didn't want to sit alone. I wished I'd had the nerve to call Milo and tell him I'd dress up like **Grace Kelly** if he'd come as **Gary Cooper** from *High Noon*. Tom would have done it. Milo would think I was nuts [p. 231].

In Bruce Davis's nonfiction book *We're Dead, Come on In* (2005), the pretext for the reference to the film is the description of a real-life lawman, Sheriff Marcell C. Hendrix of Greene County Sheriff's Department, Missouri, who was shot and killed in 1932:

If chasing the likes of Harry Young and the Jackson Jellies had hardened Marcell Hendrix, you'd never know it from this picture. He is a man of straight posture, head held high. Casting an actor to play the sheriff's life on film, the first thought might be **Gary Cooper** in his *High Noon* years [p. 105].

The reference to Cooper in Thomas O'Callaghan's thriller *Bone Thief* (2006) is related to the description of the book's protagonist, New York policeman Detective Lt. John Driscoll:

> Driscoll carried his height with a forceful stride that made his 6'2" stature seem intimidating. There was a swagger to his walk, not unlike that of **Gary Cooper**'s in *High Noon*. Precinct women found him irresistible, but Driscoll was impervious to feminine adulation [p. 28].

Marvin Olasky's novel *Scimitar's Edge* (2006) is a political thriller about four Americans in Turkey facing a deadly threat from terrorists. Zinnemann's western is mentioned repeatedly as the drama develops:

> Malcolm approached the podium and peered out at the crowd. At six feet two inches with his wheat-colored complexion and wavy blond bangs, he looked like a handsome, beefy Roman senator.
> He spoke about the US power and the Middle East: "The era of hit-back foreign policy is over. Some Americans are trapped in old Western movies, eager to channel **Gary Cooper** in *High Noon*. But shooting is the last refuge of those not brave enough to fight for peace" [p. 18].
>
> Pheobe smiled apologetically. "I don't how much of that I can take just now. Perhaps we could touch on lighter topics. I

was thinking of my favorite movie, *It's a Wonderful Life*. What film has stuck with you?"

Malcolm though for a moment and said, "I like *The Godfather* and *Miller's Crossing*. Crime, violence, and the American way."

Sally said, "I'm embarrassed, but my mom watched *The Sound of Music* again and again."

Hal jumped in: "Nothing to be embarrassed about. I'll confess to my low-class favorite: the old Western, **High Noon**. Comes from my granddad; I guess he wasn't only a ghost with macabre stories. He taught me to love Westerns: 'Clean pictures with red blood,' he called them" [pp. 114-115].

Sally said she didn't want to be alone, so Hal went into her room. She went into the bathroom while he turned on the television and was surprised to see **High Noon** dubbed into Turkish.

It all came back to Hal as he watched **Gary Cooper** talking with Kemal gutturals: the Miller gang coming to town on **Cooper**'s wedding day to shoot him and shoot up the town as well. The citizens saying it wasn't their job to fight. The pastor saying right and wrong were clear, but he didn't want people to get killed. The just-married hero, faced with bad choices but knowing he has to act.

Sally came out of the bathroom carrying a small piece of paper. "Did you ever see **High Noon**?" Hal asked. "It's great."

She shook her head, sat on the bed, and picked up her knitting needles as he quickly turned back to the movie. But he soon heard a sound that stabbed him. Sally was quietly crying. He moved to her side.

Wordlessly, Sally handed him a note: "Suleyman says, take off your clothes. Your breasts—smooth, firm and insolent—will fill my hands. Do not forget. I will take you at my house."

"I wish you would go back to the US," Hal said, hugging her and rubbing her neck.

Sally bit her upper lip. "I can't. We're bait." They watched some more as **Grace Kelly**, playing the sheriff's wife, prepared to leave town, but then came back to help her husband defeat the gang.

"Odds were four to one against him, but he won with her help," Hal said. "That's Hollywood, but our odds are a lot better." He turned off the television.

"I feel better now, but"—she smiled and quoted <u>*High Noon*</u>'s theme song—"**do not forsake me, oh my darling**" [p. 238].

Lionel R. Saporta's *Gifts* (2006) is a collection of poems and short stories. The short story "Gifts," revealing the views of Greek refugees, contains a passage that can be considered a feast for western aficionados:

My eyes would roam from the screen to my dad's face and back again, as we sat together watching *Red River* over and over, and as we watched Gregory Peck in *Yellow Sky*, **Gary Cooper** in <u>*High Noon*</u>, Henry Fonda in *My Darling Clementine*, and every other western film Hollywood would produce. I was watching him learn, as I learned myself, what it was to be an American: how to act and feel, even how to live and die, in these newly discovered wide open spaces on the screen and in our minds. He was acquiring the stoicism of this new frontier. A man didn't speak of his feelings here, or cry here; he just took life by the throat and shook it, and when his dyin' time came, well, he just up and died [p. 48].

William Bernhardt's novel *Capitol Murder* (2006) includes a reference to

Cooper as Will Kane in the description of Judge Herndon, as perceived by the book's protagonist, Oklahoma defense attorney Ben Kincaid:

> Ben did rather like the way the judge conducted the jury questioning. Judge Herndon was a tall man, lean, with a slow, studied expression reminiscent of **Gary Cooper** in *High Noon*. He knew Glancy was concerned that the judge would show partisan bias, but as conducted his measured, careful jury questioning, Ben saw few indications of favoritism. Maybe because he knew the press was watching, but appeared determined to observe each and every punctilio of federal criminal procedure [pp. 78-79].

In Harry Mark Petrakis's novella "Legends of Glory" (2007), a reference to Cooper in *High Noon* was found in an excerpt from a letter that soldier Noah (a.k.a. Achilles), stationed in Iraq, writes to his parents and grandparents. As often, the pretext is a resemblance between Cooper and one of the characters; here it is Noah's good friend:

> When we're not on patrol, we stay in our compound, playing cards and telling stories. I have met a fellow Hoosier, Larry Dobson, who is a farm boy from Kouts, and we have become great friends. He is tall and lanky (kind of how **Gary Cooper** looked in *High Noon*) and has red hair and a wonderful sense of humor and he makes us laugh a lot. We are the only two Indiana boys in our unit and we have hit it off really well. We spend as much time together as we can [p. 148].

In James Scott Bell's mystery *Try Darkness* (2008), narrator/protagonist Ty Buchanan goes to see his opponent, billionaire land developer Sam DeCosse, and, having taking out the left knee of bodyguard Devlin with a putter, continues the final negotiation. The allusion to the famous showdown is made by DeCosse:

> He [DeCosse] shook his hand. "The world is changing. Now, what do you want?"
> "I'm ready to settle with you," I said. "But we have to do it my way."
> "With putters at **high noon**."
> Devlin was still on the floor. Probably wondering why nobody was paying attention to him [p. 274].

Another unusual showdown between the hero and a bunch of bad men triggers a comparison to Fred Zinnemann's classic in William Forstchen's apocalyptic novel *One Second After* (2009):

> Some local good old boys had taken a distinct dislike to "long-haired faggots" living nearby and one night did a "drive-by," blowing out the kitchen door with a load of buckshot, yelling for the faggots to come out and get what they deserved.
> His roommates were freaked, one of them cried that they were in the middle of *Deliverance*. But their attackers had not counted on one of the "faggots" being from New Jersey, already into Civil War reenacting, and someone who knew guns. He had come out, Dragoon revolver in hand, leveled it, and fired off two rounds of his cannon. Not aiming to kill, just to make them duck a bit. After pumping out the two rounds, he lowered his aim straight at the chest of the redneck with the shotgun.
> "Next shot's for real," John said calmly.
> The rednecks piled into their truck and disappeared in one helluva hurry, his buddies standing on the porch, in awe as he walked back, feeling more than a little like **Gary Cooper** in ***High Noon***.

"Peace through superior firepower," he said calmly, then went inside and poured himself one helluva vodka to calm down while his roommates chattered away, reenacting the drama for half the night [pp. 48-49].

Sophie Littlefield's debut novel *A Bad Day for Sorry* (2009) contains a reference to the film in a passage describing narrator/protagonist Stella Hardesty's little weakness, in which she indulges in her sewing shop in a small Missouri town:

Stella lowered her gun hand to her side and let the Raven hang there casually. She could go from full dangle to aimed and ready to shoot in about a tenth of a second. That was a trick she'd worked on most of last winter when business was slow at the shop—sitting on her stool behind the cash register and practicing her draw, tucking the gun into the drawer when the bell at the door signaled a customer's arrival.

She's also taught herself to spin the thing on her finger just like **Gary Cooper** in *High Noon*, but that trick was strictly for her own enjoyment. She didn't mind having a little flair, but she wasn't an idiot: guns, after all, were serious business [pp. 11-12].

Robert K. Tanenbaum refers to the film in at least two of his mysteries. In his novel *Depraved Indifference* (1989), the reference takes place when New York Assistant District Attorney Roger "Butch" Karp is being scolded by his wife, Marlene Ciampi, for not being enough flexible in his work:

"What did you want me do? Lean over and yank his crank?"

"Yes! Yes, I did!" she cried out. "I expected you to lean a little, compromise, stroke the bastard, for chrissakes. There are a million ways you could wriggle out of any deal you made. What the fuck does it mean? Here's a flash, baby—you're not going to save the world in this job. You're not **Gary Cooper, high noon** has come and gone, and I'm sick of it. This crap about 'a man's go t' do whut a man's go t' do—it's exhausting. It's murdering me—" [p. 231]

In Tanenbaum's *Betrayed* (2010), there are two references to *High Noon*. First, the author uses the example of the film, along with another western classic, to explain the reasons for District Attorney "Butch" Karp's attraction to the western genre:

> Karp had learned his moral values from his parents. But their values were reinforced and magnified by his heroes on the silver screen, such as **Gary Cooper** in ***High Noon*** and Alan Ladd in *Shane*. At the top of the list of heroes was John Wayne as he appeared in westerns and World War II movies. Karp had lived for the Saturday matinees at the Avalon and King's Way theaters on King's Highway in Brooklyn, just a few blocks east of Ocean Parkway, where he grew up.
>
> . . .
>
> Such morality tales were not lost on Karp as a boy, nor was their deeper meaning ignored by the man. Many years later, as an adult, he'd recognize these themes as allegories for the potential for evil that resides within every human. While most resisted their baser impulses, those who didn't were the sorts of criminals he prosecuted on behalf of the People.
>
> Karp's appreciation for the romanticized hero of the Old West wasn't the result of his belief that such a man had existed. It was what that hero represented. An ideal of living up to principles. A role model to aspire to. And if you failed at first, then, like one of Karp's screen idols, you picked yourself up, dusted yourself off, and climbed back into the saddle again [p. 31].

Then, a few lines from the movie are quoted in the exchange between Karp and Dirty Warren, a Manhattan newsstand vendor:

> Karp shook his head. He'd been playing the movie-trivia game with Dirty Warren since they'd met years before. The little man had yet to win a round, but he was up against years of experience. When he was a boy, Karp and his mother had loved going to shows and discussing films and theater, and movie trivia remained an avocation in adulthood.
>
> "You forgot the rest of the quote," he said, " '**The public doesn't give a damn about integrity. A town that won't defend itself deserves no help.**' Way too easy, Warren, the cold weather must be slowing you down. It's ***High Noon*** with **Lon Chaney Jr.** playing the character of **Martin Howe**. And the year was 1952."
>
> "Ah, crap," Dirty Warren swore. "I didn't expect to see you today, so I just came up with that one off the top of my head when I heard ... oh boy whoop asshole ... Kenny talking about integrity."
>
> "Well, a great film, one of my favorites," Karp replied. "Okay, you finish the quote: '**And in the end you wind up dyin' all alone on some dusty street. For what?**' "
>
> Dirty Warren grinned and, hooking his thumbs in an imaginary vest, said, " '**For a tin star. It's all for ...** whoop whoop screwed your sister ... **nothin', Will. It's all for nothin'**.'" [p. 76]

A. D. (Ann Deborah) Scott's *A Small Death in the Great Glen* (2010), a novel set in the Scottish Highlands of the 1950s, is a thriller focused on a mysterious death of a boy. The reason why *High Noon* is referenced here is an imminent showdown between the lonely protagonist, Jimmy McPhee, and three opponents, the Gordon brothers:

> The other drinkers, agog, watched the protagonists in the

wall mirrors where they were half obscured by the advertisements etched into the glass for beers and whiskies. Joanne watched the two Jimmies face up to each other, trying not to make a move nor breathe too loudly.

Gary Cooper, *High Noon*, popped into my head, except Jimmy McPhee was facing down three instead of four. She had trouble suppressing a nervous giggle [p. 288].

Laurie Stevens's serial-killer mystery *The Dark Before Dawn* (2011) is set in California, and its protagonist is L.A. Sheriff's detective Gabriel McRay. The following passage, including a reference to the film, reveals his discouragement by the challenges of the investigation:

Gabriel leaned heavily against the scratchy bark of a tree trunk, unable to do anything until things cooled down. Nothing had turned out like he had thought. He should be like **Gary Cooper** in *High Noon*, facing the bad guy and bringing him home to face the music. Ming should be on his arm and together they should all be living happily ever after [p. 289].

Ace Atkins's novel *Robert B. Parker's Lullaby* (2012) has two clear allusions to *High Noon*, both resulting from the predicament that Spenser finds himself in when he tries to rescue a fourteen-year-old girl from the Boston gangsters:

"You want her, you meet me at the Sully Square Station in thirty minutes," Flynn said. "No cops. No Hawk. You go to the inbound ramp. Mattie will be on the train. You get on. I get off. But if something goes wrong between now and then with the Donovan girl, all bets are off."

"I'm starting to feel like **Will Kane**," I said [p. 292].

> I watched the boys. They rested their elbows on their knees and studied the ground between their feet like a couple ballplayers at the ready.
>
> Mattie shook her head as the T rambled on. My heart kept a steady beat. I could hear Tex Ritter singing as we approached Haymarket Station [p. 297].

A portion of Stuart Nadler's novel *Wise Men* (2013) is set in 1952; thus, the reference to the poster for *High Noon* has a contemporary flavor. The narrator/protagonist's name is Hilly (Hilton) Wise, which explains the title.

> My father was the one to fetch me that day. When he found me standing in the cold on Elm Street, shivering in my car coat, searching for a familiar face, he laughed. He was proud of my gumption. I'd been standing on the corner by the Triumph Theater, staring at the movie bill for **_High Noon_, Gary Cooper** brandishing his pistol. Apparently, I'd been sold out by the guy I'd clobbered, and my father had come to get me not even a half hour after I'd gotten off the train [p. 10].

The reference to *High Noon* in James D. Balestrieri's *The Ballad of Ethan Burns* (2013) appears in a conversation between the book's protagonist, Ethan Burns, a middle-aged TV (game show) personality and the son of a famous silent-period western star, and B.J., a member of Ethan's TV crew trying to discourage him from producing his own western (needless to say, B.J. will eventually change his mind and voluntarily join the team of Ethan's controversial project):

> Ethan does a caged lion bit, pacing in an office. Movie and TV posters and autographed pictures of tars line the walls. Piles of scripts sit on shelves.
>
> Behind a desk sits a well-kept man, a bit older than Ethan,

who has managed to keep a full head of his salt and pepper hair. "All that stunt on 'Kathy Anne' did was trash what was left of your reputation," he explains. "So your contract was with a mindless game show. You painted yourself as a guy who walks out. Now you're **_Gary Cooper_** in **_High Noon_**, wandering around town champing at the bit, trying to drum up support for a project no one cares about. Ethan, it's long past noon. The bad guys aren't coming. They're here. They run the whole town" [p. 28].

In Michael Palmer's novel *Political Suicide* (2013), a reference to the film is used to illustrate the manner in which one soldier manages to execute an extremely courageous act:

> From the accounts Lou had read, Mark Colson strode into the line of fire with the calmness of **_Gary Cooper_** in **_High Noon_**. He shot and killed all but one of the Taliban militiamen. The one he did not kill, he mortally wounded. However, before he died, that Taliban fighter was able to toss a grenade at the fallen U.S. soldiers. Mark immediately fell on the grenade, saving the lives of five men, while sacrificing his own. He was posthumously awarded the Medal of Honor for bravery above and beyond the call of duty [p. 63].

***Vera Cruz* (1954).** An undeniably entertaining western, Robert Aldrich's *Vera Cruz* has two great actors of diametrically different personalities, Gary Cooper and Burt Lancaster. Their superior performances, along with the tension caused by their characters' unusual relationship, elevate the film to something much more than just a series of stunts and action sequences. Consequently, the references to the movie found in literature include the names of both of the actors.

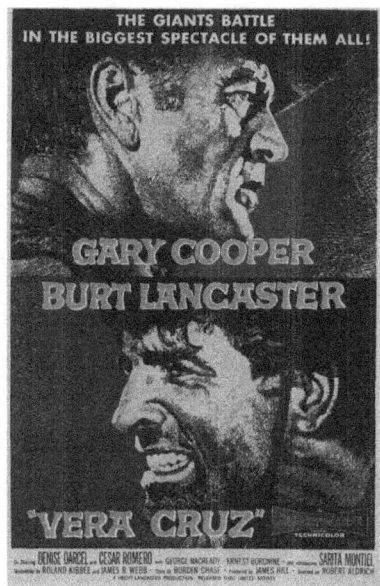 

An American poster for Robert Aldrich's *Vera Cruz* (1954) and the Polish poster for the same movie (by Waldemar Świerzy).

The first excerpt from Larry McMurtry's novel *Moving On* (1970) catches Patsy Carpenter and her husband Jim in a cozy moment at home:

> Jim was reading, alternating between *The Rise of the Novel* and a fat Eric Ambler omnibus that she had found him secondhand. "What's the late movie?" he asked. "I'm tired of reading. Want to watch TV awhile?"
>
> "Not desperately," she said, but she went to the TV and wheeled it over where he could see it better. The guide was lost—it was always lost. She went to the kitchen and found the day's paper and looked up the late movie.
>
> "It's something called **_Vera Cruz_**," she said. "**Burt Lancaster, Gary Cooper, Denise Darcel**, and others."
>
> "Let's watch a little. Come and sit with me awhile."
>
> She turned the TV on and went to the bed, but instead

of sitting with him she lay on her stomach, her face on her arms. There was the sound of gunfire from behind her. "**Burt Lancaster** seems to be the bad guy," Jim said, stroking her hair. "It's about Maximilian."

...

She sat up and let him hold her hand; they watched the movie awhile. She wished the feeling of dullness would leave her. Jim was too cheerful even to notice that she was dull. "**Gary Cooper** looks kind of sick," he said. "How long was this before he died?"

...

"Don't ask me?" she said, idly picking the Eric Ambler book and looking into it.

She shut her eyes, though it was not a bad movie. **Burt Lancaster** was bad with flair. He had a great smile [pp. 540-541].

In the same book, about a hundred pages later, we find a passage referring to Cooper himself and his specific manner of speaking:

Her spirits rose, and while they were high the phone rang. She was prepared for Jim—for his nicest apologetic voice. Instead she got the voice of Sonny Shanks.

"Mornin'," he said.

"Oh, mornin' yourself," she said. "You sound like **Gary Cooper**."

"Wish I did. How's Texas?"

"Fine. Where are you?"

"I'm one block from the famous Sunset Strip, in Los Angeles. Far enough to suit you?" [pp. 649-650]

Gary Cooper (Benjamin Trane), Denise Darcel (Countess Marie Duvarre) and Burt Lancaster (Joe Erin) in a scene from Robert Aldrich's *Vera Cruz* (1954).

Sam Shepard's *Motel Chronicles* (1982) is a unique and unusually personal book, an illustrated diary whose dated entries constitute a collection of unrelated impressions and reflections (sometimes delayed by many years) in the form of poems and tales. One of those entries contains a funny reference to this western:

> I remember trying to imitate **Burt Lancaster**'s smile after I saw him and **Gary Cooper** in *Vera Cruz*. For days I practiced in the back yard. Weaving through the tomato plants. Sneering. Grinning that grin. Sliding my upper lip up over my teeth. After a few days of practice I tried it out on the girls at school. They didn't seem to notice. I broadened my interpretation until I started getting strange reactions from the other kids. They would look straight at my teeth and a fear would creep into their eyes. I'd forgotten how bad my teeth were. How one of the front ones was dead and brown and overlapped the broken one

right next to it. I'd actually come to believe I was in possession of a full head of perfect pearly **Burt Lancaster**-type of teeth. I didn't want to scare anyone so I stopped grinning after that. I only did it in private. Pretty soon even that faded. I returned to my empty face.

4/25/81 Homestead Valley, Ca. [p. 14]

The Great American (1997), a novel by Alex Abella (an American writer born in Cuba), tells a story about a U.S. Marine, William Morgan, who ends up fighting against Batista, and, as shown in the following excerpt, has ample opportunities to act like a real hero:

"Who are these guys?" said Morgan, angered by the sudden violence.

"Let it be," cautioned Max.

Morgan, with the strength of the righteous, jerked Max aside and in a few strides was next to the girl, who lay sprawled on the sidewalk, whimpering, as the little man in the brown suit beat her with a blackjack. People around the scene pretended to go on with their business, shining shoes, wiping tables, buying groceries, staring fixedly into space, refusing to get involved even though every muscle in their bodies strained to jump in.

Morgan shoved the little man headfirst into a torn poster on the wall of the movie ***Vera Cruz***, **Burt Lancaster** and Kirk Douglas facing off in a manly duel.

"Leave her alone!" [p. 32]

There is an obvious error in the description of the poster: while Lancaster and Douglas co-starred in several movies, including one western, it was obviously Gary Cooper, not Douglas, who faced Lancaster in the final duel in *Vera Cruz*.

Gary Cooper as Jess Birdwell in William Wyler's *Friendly Persuasion* (1956).

***Friendly Persuasion* (1956).** William Wyler's screen adaptation of Jessamyn West's novel gave Cooper one more opportunity to give a remarkable performance in an outstanding movie. His co-stars include Dorothy McGuire, as his wife, and Anthony Perkins, as their son. The only reference to the film was found in Kathy Hogan Trocheck's mystery *Every Crooked Nanny* (1992), in a scene where the narrator, ex-policewoman Callahan Garrity, now working as a cleaning lady, tries to find out something about Beechy Creek, Arizona, where, according to the rumor, people still practice polygamy:

> "A few years ago, Uncle Something wanted to have this young girl sealed to him, like for his fourteenth or fifteenth wife. But the girl's father wouldn't let her, and this man killed the father and the girl in some kind of ritual thing. Are you sure you didn't see the movie? *Blood Atonement*, it was called."
>
> I'd never seen any movie about Mormons that I could recall, unless it was that old **Gary Cooper** film *__Friendly Persuasion__*. No, wait, that was about the Quakers, I think.
>
> "Patti Jo," I said. "Do you mean that Whit Collier was a polygamist or a member of this weird sect? He seemed pretty normal when I met him" [pp. 280-281].

Love in the Afternoon **(1957).** The only romantic comedy that Cooper made in the 1950s, Billy Wilder's *Love in the Afternoon* (co-starring Audrey Hepburn and Maurice Chevalier), is a truly rewarding film with numerous unforgettable scenes. It is mentioned is several novels, albeit by relatively unknown writers.

A reference to the film appears in Ilene Beckerman's *What We Do for Love* (1997), in a passage relating the movies that protagonist Gingy saw when dating the Professor, her future husband:

> We went to the movies a lot, too. We had an agreement. For every film he chose, I could choose the next.
>
> For his Ingmar Bergman's *Wild Strawberries*, I chose **Audrey Hepburn** and **Gary Cooper** in *__Love in the Afternoon__*.
>
> For his Akira Kurosawa's *Seven Samurai*, I chose Leslie Caron and Fred Astaire in *Daddy Long Legs* [p. 44].

American poster for Billy Wilder's *Love in the Afternoon* (1957).

The film is also referenced in Lynn Ruth Miller's novel *Starving Hearts* (2000), in a passage focused on the marital problems, mostly related to sex frustrations, revealed by narrator/protagonist Susan Talberg:

> I hated to get up in the morning because of Michael's insatiable desire to ejaculate inside me; I loathed going to bed at night. I began to hope he really <u>was</u> schtupping Elaine Bloom. She'd have to be quicker than mercury to manage any pleasure from my husband's brand of instant intercourse.
>
> I had finally stopped dreaming about food. I dreamed of good sex, instead. Every night after I endured my husband's

dry thrusts inside me, I closed my eyes and opened my arms to **Gary Cooper**. He clasped me in his arms just the way he had embraced **Audrey Hepburn in *Love in the Afternoon***. We walked through daffodils in the park, I in my flowing white dress, my straw hat in my hand and he in an open shirt and soft gray slacks. We smiled at a little bird twittering in a dogwood tree and had sex in the grass behind a sheltered copse.

My dreams were so real that I was sure Michael would see my bruised mouth and the love bites on my neck. But as soon as I opened my eyes, I was jolted into cold reality as my husband mounted me for his morning calisthenics [p. 141].

A poignant reference to the film was found in Judith Ryan Hendricks's novel *Bread Alone* (2001). The quotation is concluded with a punchline whose bitterness results from the narrator/protagonist's own recent experience:

I open the window a crack, stretch out on top of the bedcovers. Without thinking, I reach for the remote, turn on the TV. An old black-and-white movie flickers soundlessly. ***Love in the Afternoon***. **Audrey Hepburn** and **Gary Cooper** cavorting through Paris. I've seen it so many times I know it by heart. I love the ending, where he's going away and she's walking along beside the train, giving him this line of bullshit about all the lovers she's going to have when he's gone. The train picks up speed and she's talking faster, and then she's running alongside until suddenly **Coop** realizes that he can't live without her and he reaches out and sweeps her off the platform onto the train, beside him. Kiss and fade to black.

Pretty soon she'll be coming home to their gorgeous apartment in New York to find the locks changed and all her clothes in the hall. I hit the remote control and the screen goes blank with an electrical pop [p. 68].

Gary Cooper (Frank Flanagan), Audrey Hepburn (Ariane Chavasse) and Maurice Chevalier (Claude Chavasse) on the set of Billy Wilder's *Love in the Afternoon* (1957).

While Elizabeth Hay's novel *Garbo Laughs* (2003) brims with movie references—due to the presented family's fascination with classic films—*Love in the Afternoon* is mentioned during a discussion about Greta Garbo and *Ninotchka*:

> "She's good at being in love," Harriet said. "But she's not in love with Melvyn Douglas. That's easy to tell."
>
> "They wanted Cary Grant for the part," Dinah said.
>
> "Ah! That would have been a different story." And Harriet imagined Cary in the part, and in other parts he had turned down. How different **_Love in the Afternoon_** would have been had Cary said yes, and **_Sabrina_** too [p. 68].

While Harriet Gold, the mother, is right about the hypothesis that all the three films—*Ninotchka*, *Sabrina* and *Love in the Afternoon*—would have been different movies had Cary Grant accepted the roles played by Douglas, Bogart and Cooper, respectively, it does not necessarily mean that all of the films would have been better. Although Bogart and Cooper were considered by some to be miscast in the Billy Wilder pictures, both the actors offered some special angles to their portrayals—angles that Cary Grant might not have been able to provide.

A reference to the film appears also in Stephen King's political fantasy *11/22/63* (2011), in a passage referring to an intimate scene involving the book's protagonist, Jake Epping, also known as George Amberson, and Sadie, the woman he falls in love with:

> When we made love in Sadie's bedroom, she always kept a pair of slacks, a sweater, and a pair of moccasins on her side of the bed. She called it her emergency outfit. The one time the doorbell bonged while we were naked (a state she had taken to calling *in flagrante delicious*), she got into those threads in ten seconds flat. She came back, giggling and waving a copy of *The Watchtower*. "Jehova's Witnesses. I told them I was saved and they went away."
>
> Once, as we ate ham-steaks and okra in her kitchen afterward, she said our courtship reminded her of that movie with **Audrey Hepburn** and <u>**Gary Cooper**—*Love in the Afternoon*</u>. "Sometimes I wonder if it would be better at night." She said this a little wistfully. "When regular people do it."
>
> "You'll get a chance to find out," I said [p. 387].

Man of the West (1958). Based on Will C. Brown's novel *The Border Jumpers* and directed by Anthony Mann, this controversial—in some ways—western (co-starring Julie London and Lee J. Cobb) is referenced in a few relatively obscure books.

Thomas H. Cook's *Peril* (2004) is a suspense novel with several intriguing characters. Abe, one of them, deliberates about what path to choose after a mysterious woman appears in his life. His dilemma is illustrated in the following passage, which includes a reference to the famous western:

He didn't know how long she'd have to live this way. He knew only that it was part of the package, something you signed on for if you signed on for her.

And that's what he'd done, he knew, he'd signed on. But for what exactly? He shook his head at his helplessness. If it were a movie, he'd know what to do. If it were a guy bothering her, he'd be like **Gary Cooper** or somebody like that. ***Man of the West**,* that was the movie he thought of. He'd be like **Gary Cooper** in *Man of the West*. The problem was that in the movies it always ended with that final showdown. No cops came around later to investigate. No guys in lab coats examining fibers. No grand jury mulling it over. No fourteen-page indictment, no lengthy trial, no heart-stopping conviction . . . no consequences at all. In the movies, a bad guy was dead, and, quite rightly, nobody gave a fuck [p. 176].

One of the main characters and, as it eventually turns out, the major villain in David Cole's Southwestern mystery *Shadow Play* (2004) is Vincent Basaraba, an Indian who changed his name from Begay after he got interested in movie acting and in fact played in some western films, first as a child extra, then as a supporting actor and occasionally as a lead. Now a casino owner, he is collecting funds to produce a remake of *Man of the West*, with himself playing Gary Cooper's role. Consequently, there are numerous references in the book to both Cooper (whose name is even used as the title of a major part of the book) and his classic western. Following are four excerpts from the book; the first three relate a conversation between Basaraba and Laura Winslow (the book's narrator/protagonist, a private investigator), in the fourth one, Laura talks to Marvin Katz, Basaraba's agent:

And the other poster. I had to walk over there, reached out, realized I shouldn't touch it before I saw it was under glass.

"*Man of the West*."

"It's one of the few remaining original posters."

Gary Cooper upright, almost the entire right side of the poster, knees flexed, six-guns in each hand. Wide-brimmed hat, red bandanna flowing out, as though blown by winds ahead of the reddish cloud banks across near the bottom of the poster.

GARY COOPER
AS THE
MAN OF THE WEST

"The role that fits him like a gun fits a holster," Vincent read.

On the left side, the dark outline of another six-gun, a still from the movie inset showing **Jack Lord** holding a knife to **Cooper**'s throat as **Julie London** looks on.

"**Take those clothes off, girl,**" I said, not even bothering to read the print, it was one of the best-known lines from the movie. "**Real slow like.** Great movie."

"You really liked it?"

"One of my favorite Westerns." [p. 135]

"*Man of the West*," I said. Unable to take my eyes off the poster. "One of my all-time favorite Westerns. **Julie London** was great in that movie, right?" [p. 137]

"And this model, this three-dimensional landscape. What is this?"

"Where I'm going to make my next movie."

"What's the movie about?"

"A remake of *Man of the West*. I play the **Gary Cooper** part."

"And this landscape model?"

"Where I'm building my sets, where we'll shoot the entire movie."

"And where is that?"

"Here. Right here." He swirled his hands over the valleys of the landscape. "In the Palm of God" [p. 139].

"If this movie gets made, would Vincent be cast?"
"**Dock Tobin**."
"The **Lee J. Cobb** part? He's a crazy old man."
"So now you got it," Katz said [pp. 232-233].

The film is also referenced in in James D. Balestrieri's *The Ballad of Ethan Burns* (2013). The context of the quoted excerpt is Octavio 'Tavi' Rivera, young screenwriter, presenting his script to Ethan Burns, a discouraged TV personality hoping to do something great for a change:

"My name is Octavio Rivera. Tavi . . . I think you'd be right for it . . . My script."

"I told you, I'm fresh out of connections. That's what being the host of *Who Can Tell?* means. Nobody knows me. Nobody wants to."

"I have nothing, Mr. Burns. No contract, no agent. Just a pile of student loans and a hundred twenty pages of words. Will you read it?"

"I haven't seen a script in years . . . Send it—"

"I have a copy right here."

Tavi takes a screenplay from his backpack, hands it to Ethan.

"A writer after all . . . ***Man of the West*** . . . Sorry, Tavi, that title's taken."

"I know. **Gary Cooper**. Julie London. Lee J. Cobb. 1958. **Anthony Mann**. I'm bad at titles. The rest is all mine."

"Well, at least you steal from the best. Maybe one'll come to me..." [p. 18]

Since the book is a comedy, there is a happy ending: the script will be filmed—against all odds—and the title changed to *Paintbrush Valley*.

***They Came to Cordura* (1959).** This ambitious, if only partially successful, adaptation of the novel by Glendon Swarthout, was directed by Robert Rossen, who also wrote the script in collaboration with Ivan Moffat. The impressive cast—besides Cooper, who gave a great performance despite being miscast—includes Rita Hayworth, Van Heflin and Richard Conte.

In Stephen King's *Dolores Claiborne* (1993), there is no reference to any specific Gary Cooper movie. The narrator/protagonist of the novel, Dorothy Claiborne, does mention the actor's name in one of the flashback scenes where she gives up trying to make it clear to her abusive and jealous husband that she is not paying attention to anyone and anything around them:

> I ask him if he saw anything green.
>
> "No," he says, but I seen a man down there in that restaurant lookin up your dress, Dolores. His eyes were just about hangin out on springs. And you *knew* he was lookin, didn't you?"
>
> I almost told him **Gary Cooper** coulda been sittin in the corner with **Rita Hayworth** and I wouldn't have known it, and then thought, Why bother? It didn't do any good to argue with Joe when he'd been drinking; I didn't go into that marriage with my eyes entirely shut, and I'm not gonna try to kid you that I did.
>
> "If there was a man lookin up my dress, why didn't you go over and tell him to shut his eyes, Joe?" I asked [p. 86].

The combination of the two names referred to in this passage—Cooper and Hayworth—may be viewed as an indirect allusion to Robert Rossen's western *They Came to Cordura*, the only film in which the two stars ever appeared together. Such a hypothesis is also supported by the fact that the quoted scene is set in either 1960 or 1961.

Gary Cooper (George Radcliffe), Deborah Kerr (Martha Radcliffe) and Eric Portman (Jeremy Clay) in a scene from Michael Anderson's *The Naked Edge* (1961).

***The Naked Edge* (1961).** Cooper's last film, directed—just like the actor's penultimate project, *The Wreck of the Mary Deare*—by Michael Anderson, was similar in its storyline to Alfred Hitchcock's *Suspicion*, a movie released twenty years earlier. The actor's co-star here is Deborah Kerr.

The only reference to the film was found in "Drumcondra," a poem by Michael Feeney Callan (an Irish novelist, poet, biographer, filmmaker and painter), which is included in his collection *An Argument for Sin: A Poetry Excursion* (2013). The actor and the movie are mentioned in the opening part of the poem; the film itself is mentioned again in the middle:

From my own Ravello, perambulating with mine own Giraldus,

    the astounding befell: my feet connected with my Muybridge shadow.

    Outside the Drummer on Palatine Hill, opposite dour St. Pat's,

    with the diamond marquee advertising **<u>Gary Cooper</u>** in **<u>The Naked Edge</u>**.

    O woe life's procession.

    . . .

    The shed my father built, the jumper, the bridge in Griffith Park (the old

        dairy farm),

    Ray McAnally – who knew? – in **<u>The Naked Edge</u>**; all bridges swept away

        with stretch and hair and time. [pp. 124-125].

Gary Cooper's screen career spanned thirty-seven years. Excluding his work as an extra, he appeared in about ninety feature films. He collaborated with fifty-nine directors, most frequently with Henry Hathaway, with whom he shares credits of seven pictures. He made four movies with Cecil B. DeMille and Sam Wood, and three with William A. Wellman, Victor Fleming and Howard Hawks. The major directors that made two films with Cooper include Frank Borzage, King Vidor, Lewis Milestone, Ernst Lubitsch, Frank Capra, William Wyler, Delmer Daves and Michael Anderson. Cooper made four pictures with Fay Wray, but his most successful onscreen relationship was with Barbara Stanwyck, with whom he appeared in three films, including two superior productions directed by Capra and Hawks, respectively. His major two-time co-stars include Marlene Dietrich, Carole Lombard, Jean Arthur, Ingrid Bergman, Susan Hayward, Teresa Wright and Patricia Neal. His significant one-time female co-stars were Merle Oberon, Lauren Bacall, Grace Kelly, Audrey Hepburn, Dorothy

McGuire, Rita Hayworth and Deborah Kerr. Cooper's close friend, Walter Brennan, provided strong support in as many as eight of his movies. What needs to be mentioned once again is that Cooper's name is rightly associated with the western genre, as not only did he appear in a large number of cowboy films (about twenty-five), but he is also the second and one of only four actors that won an Academy Award for a leading role in a western picture.

American poster for Rouben Mamoulian's *City Streets* (1931).

Gary Cooper as Cole Harden and Doris Davenport as Jane Ellen Mathews in a scene from William Wyler's *The Westerner* (1940).

Out of the total number of Cooper's films, forty-four (about half) are discussed in this publication due to the references that have been found. The ones referenced in the largest number of works are *High Noon* (eighty-one), *Beau Geste* (ten), *Mr. Deeds Goes to Town* and *Sergeant York* (eight each), *The Pride of the Yankees* (seven), *The Virginian* and *For Whom the Bell Tolls* (six each) and *The Lives of a Bengal Lancer*, *Meet John Doe* and *Love in the Afternoon* (five each). Thus, the list includes all the six films for which Cooper was nominated for an Oscar as well as the actor's other major artistic and box-office successes. The few important items in Cooper's filmography that are neither on the list nor even included in the book due to no known literary references are Rouben Mamoulian's *City Streets* (1931), Frank Borzage's *A Farewell to Arms* (1932, from the novel by Ernest Hemingway), William Wyler's *The Westerner* (1940), Fritz Lang's *Cloak and Dagger* (1946), Otto Preminger's *The Court-Martial of Billy Mitchell* (1955), Philip Dunne's *Ten North Frederick* (1958, based upon the novel by John O'Hara) and Delmer

Daves's *The Hanging Tree* (1959, from Dorothy M. Johnson's novella). *The Westerner*, where Cooper, as drifter Cole Harden, gives a suitably and consciously underacted performance opening the stage for Walter Brennan's outstanding characterization as Judge Roy Bean, is probably the most definite oversight. Thus, accepting those seven films as inevitable exceptions, we can safely state that literary references represent Cooper's work on the screen in an extensive and fairly valid manner.

An unidentified player, Geraldine Fitzgerald (Edith Chapin), Gary Cooper (Joe Chapin), Diane Varsi (Ann Chapin) and John Emery (Paul Donaldson) in a lobby card for Philip Dunne's *10 North Frederick* (1958).

II. REFERENCES TO COOPER: THE MAN, THE ACTOR, THE CELEBRITY

References to Cooper began to appear in literature as soon as in the mid-1930s, when the actor had already established his position as a major star, but before he received any prestigious awards—his first Academy Award nomination was soon to be announced. Ironically, the very first novel that includes a reference to Cooper's name is Horace McCoy's *They Shoot Horses, Don't They?* (1935), a book set in Los Angeles during the Depression Era and focused on the infamous dance marathons. In the quoted scene the female protagonist, Gloria, is advised by Vincent (Socks) Donald, one of the marathon promoters, to marry her dancing partner (the narrator) for the sake of publicity:

> "Yeah," Socks said. I want you two kids to get married. A public wedding."
>
> "Married?" I said.
>
> "Now, wait a minute," Socks said. "It's not that bad. I'll give you fifty dollars apiece and after the marathon is over you can

get divorced if you want to. It don't have to be permanent. It's just a showmanship angle. What do you say?"

"I say you're nuts," Gloria said.

"She doesn't mean that, Mr. Donald—" I said.

"The hell I don't," she said. "I've got no objections to getting married," she said to Socks, "but why don't you pick out **Gary Cooper** or some big-shot producer or director? I don't want to marry this guy. I got enough trouble looking for myself—" [p. 77]

Gary Cooper in a publicity shot.

In a popular play by Bella and Samuel Spewack, *Boy Meets Girl* (1936), Cooper and Gable are mentioned in the same sentence as potential candidates to replace the adult leading actor in a western series involving a baby star, Happy:

> ROSETTI. Larry, I don't want to hurt your feelings, but I can't get you a new contract the way things are now. B.K. is dickering to borrow **Clark Gable** or **Gary Cooper** for Happy's next picture [p. 562].

Arthur Kober's *"Having Wonderful Time"* (1937), a play included in the same collection as *Boy Meets Girl*, has several movie references. Cooper is mentioned in the opening setting description of Act One, Scene III, as part of "ad lib conversation from the groups as they come on":

> "Your **Gary Cooper** is nothing but a string bean. Go love a string bean!" "I suppose your Nelson Eddy is better?" "At least my Nelson Eddy can sing" [p. 701].

Cooper, or rather his car, is mentioned in Clifford Odets's play *Golden Play*, in a dialogue between Joe Bonaparte and Lorna Moon:

> JOE: Go home, Lorna. If you stay, I'll know something about you....
> LORNA: You don't know anything.
> JOE: Now's your chance—go home!
> LORNA: Tom loves me.
> JOE (*after a long silence, looking ahead*): I'm going to buy a car.
> LORNA: They make wonderful cars today. Even the lizzies—

JOE: **Gary Cooper**'s got the kind I want. I saw it in the paper, but it costs too much—fourteen thousand. If
I found one second-hand— [p. 266]

The self-explanatory reference to Cooper in John Dickson Carr's mystery *The Crooked Hinge* (1938), included in the conclusions of Inspector Elliot's interrogation, is probably the first indication of the actor's megastar status in literature:

> From the housekeeper, the cook, and the other maids he learned little except domestic details; about Betty he learned little except that she liked apples and wrote letters to **Gary Cooper** [p. 417].

The second indication of Cooper's well-established fame was found in Nathanael West's *The Day of the Locust* (1939), an imaginative novel by the legendary author, who was killed in an automobile accident at age thirty-seven. The mere mention of the actor's name is one of the sparks leading to the tragic, uncontrolled events of the conclusive scene of the book:

> In this part of the mob no one was hysterical. In fact, most of the people seemed to be enjoying themselves. Near him was a stout woman with a man pressing hard against her from in front. His chin was on her shoulder, and his arms were around her. He paid no attention to him and went on talking to the woman at her side.
>
> "The first thing I knew," Tod heard her say, "there was a rush and I was in the middle."
>
> "Yeah. Somebody hollered, 'Here comes **Gary Cooper**,' and then wham!" [p. 164]

Another important book about Hollywood by another major writer of that period is F. Scott Fitzgerald's unfinished novel *The Last Tycoon* (1940/41). The book includes two references to Cooper. In the following quotation, depicting a discussion between a movie producer (Stahr) and an English writer (Boxley), the reason for mentioning Cooper is once again his status as a megastar:

> "I keep wishing you could start over," Boxley said. "It's this mass production."
> "That's the condition," said Stahr. There's always some lousy condition. We're making a life of Rubens—suppose I asked you to do portraits of rich dopes like Bill Brady and me and **Gary Cooper** and Marcus when you wanted to paint Jesus Christ! Wouldn't you feel you had a condition? Our condition is that we have to take people's own favorite folklore and dress it up and give it back to them. Anything beyond that is sugar. So won't you give us some sugar, Mr. Boxley?" [p. 137]

The second reference appears in Chapter Six, which was only started by Fitzgerald; thus, the passage may or may not have been written by the great author himself. The actor is mentioned in a scene that takes place in a restaurant where studio boss Monroe Stahr and Cecilia Brady (the book's narrator) take Brimmer, a man whose mission is to defend the rights of Hollywood writers:

> **Gary Cooper** came in and sat down in a corner with a bunch of men who breathed whenever he did and looked as if they lived off him and weren't budging. A woman across the room looked around and turned out to be Carole Lombard—I was glad that Brimmer was at least getting an eyeful [p. 162].

The beginning of the 1950s brought about a couple of novels with extensive and essential references to Cooper, both unambiguously cashing on the actor's fame and grandeur. In J. D. Salinger's *The Catcher in the Rye* (1951), the actor's name is used as a trick by protagonist/narrator Holden Caulfield during a dance he does not enjoy:

> I danced with them all—the whole three of them—one at a time. The one ugly one, Laverne, wasn't too bad a dancer, but the other one, old Marty, was murder. Old Marty was like dragging the Statue of Liberty around the floor. The only way I could even half enjoy myself dragging her around was if I amused myself a little. So I told her I just saw **Gary Cooper**, the movie star, on the other side of the floor.
>
> . . .
>
> Here's what was very funny, though. When we got back to the table, old Marty told the other two that
>
> **Gary Cooper** had just gone out. Boy, old Laverne and Bernice nearly committed suicide when they heard
>
> that. They got all excited and asked Marty if she'd seen him and all. Old Marty said she'd only caught a
>
> glimpse of him. That killed me [pp. 73-74].

Set in Hawaii before and during World War II, James Jones's lengthy novel *From Here to Eternity* (1951) offers an excellent drama and character study. Early in the book there is a captivating, though action-free, scene in which the soldiers chat about some early western movie stars in the barracks. The animated discussion is concluded with an exchange about Cooper. (In order to save space, Jones's narrative prose is replaced with brief announcements of the speakers.)

Treawdwell: "John Wayne was another good one."

Maggio: "Not any more. He's graduated into Adventure. Give him five more years he'll move up into Drama."

Treadwell: "That's the same way **Gary Cooper** started. "He really use to be a real cowboy once."

Maggio: "You cant compare **Gary Cooper** to John Wayne."

Treadwell: "I aint comparing them. All I said was that they both started out in Westerns. You cant compare none of them to **Gary Cooper**."

Maggio: "I guess not. I hope not. **Gary Cooper** goes deeper than just plain adventure. If theys anybody shows all the things this country stands for its **Gary Cooper**."

Treadwell: "That's what Hedda Hopper says."

Maggio: "Hedda Hopper, my ass. If I like **Gary Cooper** its my business. And its in spite of Hedda Hopper, not because of Hedda Hopper. Even my old daddy likes **Gary Cooper**. He go to see him every time he's on, even if its raining, and he cant speak ten words a English" [p. 182].

Later in the book, Cooper is mentioned again, along with several other actors, in a passage clarifying protagonist Robert E. Lee Prewitt's motivation for joining he army:

When he joined the Army he had visions of coming home bronzed by southern seas like Errol Flynn, a world traveler like Ronald Colman, an adventurer like Douglas Fairbanks Jr., a man to be reckoned with like **Gary Cooper**, a man of the world like Warner Baxter, a man people would listen to respectfully like President Roosevelt—not as much as President Roosevelt, but the same idea [p. 518].

In his next novel, *Some Came Running* (1957), James Jones uses Cooper's name again—this time to make a comment about the resemblance between gambler "Bama" Dillert, one of the book's two protagonists, and Cooper's well-known image as a Westerner:

> The small petite cherry-headed Doris was looking up at 'Bama with a demure child's expression. And 'Bama, with his semi-western hat, tall and with that tiny hanging belly, a reserved wry expression on his usually sneering face, suddenly looked a lot, Wally thought, like **Gary Cooper** [pp. 244-245].

William Gibson's *The Cobweb* (1954) is a psychological novel commenting on morality within the medical profession. Cooper's name is mentioned—in the context of an unlikely movie description—during a conversation of two young patients of an exclusive psychiatric clinic, in which the girl is pretending to interview the boy:

> Sue lifted a fold of paper out of her blouse pocket, and thrusting forth one leg, dug in her jeans for a pencil. Stevie stood over her watching, she had chestnut hair which was cut short, a pretty ear and cheek, plump white arms, and even seemed to have something like breasts under the blouse; though his taste was for blondes in ankle-strap shoes, none was available, and he was wondering should he, would she, could he, when she pinched up a pencil stub to write.
> "The first thing I'm supposed—"
> Steve said in a rush. "Sue, there's a movie downtown in which **Gary Cooper** plays an eleven-year-old boy scout, which ought to be interesting to see. Would you, I—" [pp. 159-160]

In Herman Wouk's *Marjorie Morningstar* (1955), the actor is referenced in a lengthy passage describing Marjorie's experience and first impressions with her job in a clothing store:

She was placed in the women's underwear section, substituting for a girl who had mumps. For the first hour or so of the first day she worked at Gorman's, Marjorie really enjoyed it. There was an exciting novelty about standing at her ease in the black dress of a salesgirl on the wrong side of the counter, while women in hats and coats thronged by noisily, looking preoccupied and mean. It was gay to make change, to chirp brightly about nightgowns and panties to customers, to crouch and search around in the stacks of boxes, to fill out sales slips with a sharp fresh-smelling pencil. She was, in fact, Katharine Hepburn playing a store clerk in the first reel of a smart comedy. The trouble was that the young millionaire played by **Gary Cooper** didn't show up [p. 362].

An interesting, or even ironic, fact about the quotation is that Gary Cooper and Katharine Hepburn have never been co-stars in any movie.

Herman Wouk's World War II epic novel *The Winds of War* (1971) contains several references to Cooper, all related to the radio career of Madeline Henry, the daughter of Navy Commander Victor "Pug" Henry:

He flourished a brown envelope at her. "Now then. **Gary Cooper** is at the St. Regis, Room 641. This is a sample of *Who's in Town* script. Take to him. We may get him for Thursday."

"**GARY COOPER**? You mean the MOVIE STAR?" Madeline in astonishment zoomed words like her mother.

"Who else? He may ask you questions about the show and about me. So listen and get this rundown in your head. We work without an audience in a little studio, very relaxed. It's a room with armchairs, books, and a rug, really nice, like a library in a home. It's the same room Mrs. Roosevelt uses for her show. . . . The whole show runs an hour and a half."

. . .

A maid opened the door of the hotel suite where **Gary Cooper**, in a gray suit, sat eating lunch at a wheeled table. The star rose, immensely tall and slim, smiling down at Madeline. He put on black-rimmed glasses, glanced over the script as he drank coffee, and asked questions. He was all business, the farthest thing from a bashful cowboy; he had the manner of an admiral. When she mentioned the *Over the Coffee* show he brightened. "Yes, I remember that." Almost at once, it seemed, she was out on the sunny street again, overwrought, thrilled to her bones. *"England mobilizes! Hitler smashes into Poland!"* the news vendor at the corner hoarsely chanted.

"Bless your little heart," Cleveland said as she came into the office. He was banging rapidly at a typewriter. "**Cooper** just called. He likes the idea and he's in." Ripping the yellow sheet out of the machine, he clipped it with others. "He remarked on what a nice girl you were. What did you say to him?"

"Hardly anything."

. . .

He paused at the door. "Do you mind working nights? You'll get paid overtime. If you come back here around eight-thirty tonight, you'll find Thursday's rough on my desk, with **Cooper**'s spot."

"Mr. Cleveland, I haven't been hired yet."

"You have been."

. . .

On Cleveland's desk the interview with **Gary Cooper** now lay, a mass of crude typing, quick scrawls and red crayon cuts. The note clipped to it said: *Try to copy it all over tonight. See you around ten.* Madeline groaned; she was terribly tired [p. 133-135].

Cleveland glanced at his watch and at the beauty, who drooped her eyelids contemptuously at Madeline. Madeline felt like a worm. Cleveland rumpled his hair and shook his head. "Look, you know these Navy characters. Write him a letter, that's all. Invite him to come on the Thursday morning show. Mention **Gary Cooper**, if you want to. Sign my name, and take it over to the Warwick. Can you do that?"

"Certainly" [p. 137].

"That man may not amuse you, Dad, but millions of people are mad for him. He makes fifteen thousand dollars a week."

"That's kind of obscene right there. It's more than a rear admiral makes in a year."

"Dad, in two weeks I've met the most marvelous people. I met **Gary Cooper**. Just today I spent two hours with Miss Pelham. Do you know that I had lunch with the Chief of Naval Operations? Me?"

"So I heard. What's this fellow Cleveland like?"

"He's brilliant" [p. 183].

Most of the books by Jack Kerouac are abundant in film references. Cooper's name is mentioned three times in *Desolation Angels* (1960), twice in the context of films *Beau Geste* and *High Noon* and once in a passage (pp. 267-268) quoted in Part Three (on Clark Gable). In the author's earlier novel, *On the Road* (1955), the actor becomes instrumental in a simile used to describe a new character:

Okay, it was agreed, Stan was coming with me. He was rangy, bashful, shock-haired Denver boy with a big con-man smile and slow, easy-going **Gary Cooper** movements [p. 262].

Four Hollywood Legends

In Jean Kerr's satirical novel *Please Don't Eat the Daisies* (1957), the actor and his western films get promoted to the level of being topics of intellectual conversations at a certain kind of parties:

> I can remember when I was a girl—way back in Truman's administration—and No-Cal was only a gleam in the eye of the Hirsch Bottling Company. In those days it was fun to go to parties. The conversation used to crackle with wit and intelligence because we talked about *ideas*—the esthetic continuum in western culture, **Gary Cooper** in western movies, the superiority of beer over lotion as a wave-set, and the best way to use leftover veal [p. 127].

Probably the first foreign-language narrative work including a reference to Cooper is Julio Cortázar's novel *The Winners* (1960). At the same time the book offers probably the first example of something that can be described as indirect praise by mistake: even though Cooper did not star in the film being referred to, his name comes to the lady's mind first.

> "I heard that breakfasts on these ships are very complete," said Nelly's mother peevishly. "I read that they even serve orange juice. Do you remember that movie, honey? The one where the young girl was working . . . and the father was something in a newspaper and didn't want her to go out with **Gary Cooper**?"
> "But no, Mam, it wasn't in that movie."
> "Yes, don't you remember it was in technicolor and she sang that bolero in English at night . . . But you're right, it wasn't with **Gary Cooper**. It was the one with the train accident, do you remember?"
> "No, Mama," Nelly said. "It's really something how she always mixes them up."

"But they were serving orange juice, all the same," Doña Pepa insisted [pp. 89-90].

John O'Hara referenced Gary Cooper in at least two of his works. In the novel *From the Terrace* (1958), the actor is one of several celebrities participating in a dinner party at Romanoff's. The first of the two quotations involving Cooper and Spencer Tracy (from p. 957) is presented in Part Four (on Tracy). Here is the second one:

> Sadie quickly looked about her and said: "When I heard **Spencer Tracy** and **Gary Cooper** were going to be here, I said to Annabella, for God's sake not to put me next to them. They're my favorites, and Charles Boyer, and I wouldn't know what on earth to talk about."
>
> "We haven't met Charles Boyer, but **Cooper** and **Tracy** are easy to talk to," said Alfred. "As a matter of fact, **Tracy** has a very good sense of humor, dryly sarcastic."
>
> "What about **Mr. Cooper**?"
>
> "Polite. Very good manners, and *interested*," said Sadie [p. 959].

Cooper plays the role of celebrity again in O'Hara's short story "Can I Stay Here?" (1964). However, he appears only in a picture that becomes a pretext for a famous stage/movie actress past her prime, Theresa (Terry) Livingston, to reminisce about the good old times in front of her maid Irene as they get ready for the first visit by Evelyn Blackwell, a daughter of the actress's old lover:

> "That's a wonderful picture of **Gary Cooper** and I. I must remember to have that enlarged. **Gary**. Dolores Del Rio. A writer, his name I forget. Fay Wray. That's Cedric Gibbons. He was married to Dolores Del Rio. Frances Goldwyn. Mrs. Samuel.

Dear Bill Powell and Carole Lombard. There we are all, my first year in Hollywood. My second, actually, but I have no pictures of the first time. That was a Sunday luncheon party at Malibu. Look at **Gary**, isn't he darling? He wasn't a bit interested in me, actually. That was when he and the little Mexican girl, Lupe Velez, they were quite a thing at that time. You know, I haven't really looked at that picture in ages. Certainly dates me, doesn't it? And this one. Do you know who that is? I must have told you" [p. 288].

In the novel *The Ski Bum* (1964) by Lithuanian-French writer Romain Gary, Gary Cooper is mentioned only in one sentence, but that was apparently enough to change the title of the book to *Adieu Gary Cooper* when it was translated into French in 1969. Here is the excerpt where the reference occurs; Lenny, a young American in Switzerland, accepts a loan of 50 francs which is unexpectedly offered to him by an extremely attractive young American woman, almost a perfect stranger named Jess, from the 500 francs she has just borrowed from someone else, and this is how it all begins:

> But she was walking away now and it was getting him nowhere, he could feel Angel getting nervous behind his back, scratching his lighter, nervous bastards those Arabs, not like their camels at all. She was now fifteen yards away, good shooting distance, like a **Gary Cooper** movie, pity old **Coop** was dead now, he'd kind of like him. He liked all sorts of people he had never met.
> – Hey!
> He walked up toward her. Play it on your looks, close range, you can't miss there.
> – I'll pay it back, if you give me half a chance.
> – Forget it.
> – Well, I mean it. Where can I find you?

Some of those American kids are really terribly good-looking it's got something to do with the way they're fed when they're babies. She had learned a few things about child care and she had even done some volunteer work in a nursery in Ghana, when they were stationed there.

– You don't have to pay it back. I'm so rich it hurts. Anyway, I'll be around. I'm usually feeding the birds by the bridge over there [pp. 41-42].

In James Leo Herlihy's novel *Midnight Cowboy* (1965), Cooper and Ronald Colman, an actor he resembles in some respects, are mentioned as role models for the book's protagonist, confused and misplaced young Westerner Joe Buck:

This one seemed to have to do with the identity of Joe Buck, for even though the conversation had little to do with him, it proceeded on the assumption that Locke's guest was a kind of ideal and perfect being, composed of all the manliness and heroism of an early **Gary Cooper** with the culture and sensibility and compassion of a Ronald Colman [p. 220].

William P. McGivern's novel *The Caper of the Golden Bulls* (1966) is a crime comedy set in several places of Gibraltar and Spain, including the streets of Pamplona during the annual real-life running of the bulls. While describing the life at Gibraltar, the author mentions the names of two American screen cowboys, one being the king of the B western and one specializing in A westerns among other prestigious genres:

For tourists and seamen there were Swiss watches, Toledo blades, watered perfumes, cuckoo clocks, banderillas in red and white streamers, figures of the Virgin and the Buddha, jade necklaces and bracelets, tambourines, castanets, guitars, and gaudy scarves emblazoned with the images of Roy Rogers and **Gary Cooper**, of stallions muzzling mares in front of Canadian sunsets, of the peerless Manolete gazing sorrowfully at idealized bulls and senoritas [p. 101].

In Philip Roth's satirical novel *Portnoy's Complaint* (1967), Gary Cooper is mentioned—as part of a metaphor—in a long passage in which the protagonist/narrator describes his family:

My Aunt Clara at that time—or was it all the time?—was going through one of her "nervous seizures"—in comparison to Aunt Clara, my own vivid momma is a **Gary Cooper**—and when Heshie came home at the end of the day with his arm in a cast, she dropped in a faint to the kitchen floor. Heshie's cast was later referred to as "the straw that broke the camel's back," whatever that meant [pp. 58-59].

Sue Kaufman's *Diary of a Mad Housewife* (1967), a bestselling novel about the problems of a New York married couple, has a scene in which the narrator/protagonist, Bettina Balser, meets an attractive man who reminds her of Cooper:

Then one hot September night I attended a meeting of ardent Adlai supporters like myself, and a tall sandy-haired young man took the floor. He stood up in front of us, loosened his tie, gave a **Gary Cooper** sort of "shucks" shrug, and, apologizing, took off his seersucker jacket. He had on brilliant red suspenders [p. 26].

In James A. Michener's *Iberia* (1968), a nonfiction book about the author's travels in Portugal and Spain, Cooper (along with another great western star) is mentioned in a passage describing the habits, the taste and the family of one Señor Don Pedro Pérez Montilla, a member of the Casino de Badajoz (an old and honorable club) and an owner of two big plantations, one growing cork trees and one growing wheat, pigs and sheep:

> 'Don Pedro reads the *ABC* each morning, but nothing else. He goes to the movies only when they show **Gary Cooper** or John Wayne. He has two fine daughters who went for a while to the convent school, but now they're waiting for someone to marry them. Don Pedro would probably not allow them to marry a man whose family did not belong to our club. Otherwise where would the new family fit in?' [p. 56]

In Michael Crichton's science-fiction thriller *The Andromeda Strain* (1969), there is a situation of a serious crisis, in which a hero like the characters portrayed by Cooper—in both his western and non-western movies—is prayed for:

> A quavering, irritable voice spoke to them.
> "You took your sweet time coming, didn't you? Still I am glad you have arrived at last. We are in need of reinforcements. I tell you, it's been one hell of a battle against the Hun. Lost 40 per cent last night, going over the top, and two of our officers are out with the rot. Not going well, not at all. If only **Gary Cooper** was here. We need men like that, the men who made America strong. I can't tell you how much it means to me, with those giants out there in the flying saucers" [pp. 79-80].

Joe David Brown's novel *Addie Pray* (1971), the basis for Peter Bogdanovich's movie *Paper Moon* (1973), has a scene in which the eleven-year-old heroine/narrator compares one of the minor characters, a man she suspects might be her father, to Cooper:

> Another one of the men was Mr. Thad Bledsoe, who worked down at Burchfield's drugstore for the longest sort of time. I always thought he bore a strong resemblance to **Gary Cooper**, because he was tall and quiet and had a long sad face [p. 13].

In Brian Garfield's *Death Wish* (1972), the actor is mentioned, along with a few others, in a passage describing protagonist Paul Benjamin's nostalgic mood:

> He bought another deink and sat listening to the sad simple tunes. They made the past a troubled reality; he drank quickly and bought a third, and sat twirling the glass in his fingers. Remembering the times when everything existed in its ordered place, when you could tell right from wrong. Days of black telephones, two-decker buses on Park Avenue, ticker-tape parades for heroes you didn't laugh at, a pad of check blanks at every cash register, Grable and **Gable** and Hayworth and **Cooper**, an amiable cop on the beat, a fish wrapped in a newspaper, clandestine dreams in plain brown wrappers, Uncle Irwin in the Depression wearing white shirts to prove to the world he could afford the laundry bill, the importance of chastity and the evils of alcohol and the goodness of Our American Boys, Pat O'Brien and apple pies and motherhood and tell-it-to-the-Marines and the *Darktown Strutters' Ball* and Glenn Miller's *Stardust. Jesus I remember Glenn Miller. By crap yes I remember Glenn Miller—very important to remember Glenn Miller* [p. 142].

In Kurt Vonnegut, Jr.'s *Breakfast of Champions* (1973), a random reference to the actor is made during a conversation between Kilgore Trout and a truck driver who gives him a ride on his way to an arts festival:

"Um," said Trout. Up ahead was a white man hitchhiking with his pregnant wife and nine children.

"Looks like **Gary Cooper**, don't he?" said the truck driver of the hitchhiking man.

"Yes, he does," said Trout. **Gary Cooper** was a movie star [pp. 127-128].

A reference to the actor appears in Richard Condon's political thriller *Winter Kills* (1974), in a scene where a government man on a secret mission, Keifetz, tries to decide what name he should use in his fake passport. The joke intended by Daisy, a woman Keifetz is planning to marry, testifies to the actor's popularity even in 1974, the time at which the book was written and is set:

"Hong Kong is out too, sir. If it isn't Singapore, they'll think of Hong Kong."

"If it's more than one airport, they'll have to check passenger manifests, so I can't travel with this passport. What name should I use?"

"**Gary Cooper**!"

He fell about with laughter. She laughed so hard she had to lean against the wall [pp. 192-193].

Robert B. Parker's baseball mystery *Mortal Stakes* (1975) has already been mentioned due an allusion to *High Noon*, which takes place later in the book. Below is a reference to the actor himself, which appears in a scene relating the conversation between private eye Spenser and Bucky Maynard, a Red Sox media man, about the latter's driver and errand boy, Lester Floyd:

"Nice kid, though," I said. Lester had hooked both elbows over the railings and was standing with one booted foot against the wall and one foot flat on the ground. **Gary Cooper**. He spit a large amount of brown saliva toward the batter's cage, and I realized he was chewing tobacco. When he got into an outfit, he went all the way [p. 88].

John Gregory Dunne's *True Confessions* (1977) is a mystery set in Los Angeles, and its characters include celebrities from the movie industry and the Church. A reference to Cooper appears in a passage describing the social connections between representatives of the two worlds:

> Think croquet. A sedentary game. He played it once a week with Samuel Goldwyn. A quiet game, just the two of them. The big games, the money games with David Niven and **Gary Cooper**, Goldwyn held on Sunday, but the Cardinal usually had an ordination on Sunday, or a confirmation. In any case, he was never quite sure who David Niven was. "*The Scarlet Pimpernel*, Danaher, *The Scarlet Pimpernel*," Samuel Goldwyn said, "four million domestic, that's who David Niven is." It amused the Cardinal that the two men called each other Goldwyn and Danaher. No one had called him Danaher to his face in nearly sixty years, and he was damned if he was going to put a Mister in before Goldwyn's name [p. 269].

A reference to Cooper in Larry McMurtry's novel *Somebody's Darling* (1978) is a part of a passage where screenwriter Joe Percy, the narrator of the first part of the book, depicts himself in his usual sarcastic tone:

> No artist was likely to paint my picture, standing with my drink, on the rich red carpet, but I was the last of 15,000 nonetheless—maybe even the last of 16,000. My companions had been slaughtered in passes, too—the passes of Benedict Canyon, Laurel Canyon, Topanga Canyon, and all the other canyons. They had not fallen to Afghan hordes exactly, but they

had all fallen, one way or another. One couldn't even blame Goldwyn or Mondschiem or Harry Cohn or any of the other moguls—not really. We had been our own Afghan hordes, cutting ourselves down ruthlessly out of childish disappointment at our own inadequacies and the stubborn intractability of life. It was just not like the movies—life, I mean: not **Gary Cooper**'s grin, not **Paulette Goddard**, not dancing in the rain. The direction was poor, the staging hasty, and there was no one competent in the editing room. Life was like pictures only in that it hardly ever managed to be as exciting as its previews [p. 88].

Cooper is mentioned twice in Michael B. Druxman's *Gable: A One-Person Play in Two Acts* (1984), both references rather self-explanatory—Gable himself is speaking, of course:

> Back in those days, **Gary Cooper** had the reputation of being Hollywood's leading cocksman. He drove a Duesenberg and it's said that he was "hung like a horse."
> I ordered my own custom-built Duesenberg. Insisted it be a foot longer than Coop's [p. 29].
>
> . . .
>
> The first director of ***Gone with the Wind*** was George Cukor.
> *(Carefully chooses words.)*
> George is . . . an intelligent . . . gifted man . . . He was not my kind of director.
> *(Crosses* DC; *plays scene with Selznick)*
> David, I can't work with Cukor. Maybe **Gary Cooper**'s still available, but. . . . [p. 38]

Cooper's mannerisms, especially the ones associated with his western image, are referred to in Loren D. Estleman's mystery *Downriver* (1988). The following passage is a part of a scene in which private eye Amos Walker (the narrator) and ex-convict DeVries are interrogated by county sheriff R. E. Axhorn after an unfortunate event:

> For a minute Axhorn sat without speaking, bent forward with his elbows on his thighs, circling the brim of his Stetson through his fingers **Gary Cooper** fashion. Then he looked up at me from under his brows. "You told Corporal Hale you were run off the road?" [p. 20]

Another thriller by Estleman, *Something Borrowed, Something Black* (2002), includes a reference to the actor in a passage describing Laurie's reaction when she is handed a note (as it turns out later, written by her husband) by a young man dressed up as a cowboy, who is supposed "to keep her company" while her husband is away:

> She stared at it. She'd suspected a pickup: someone who'd seen *Midnight Cowboy* a time too many but hadn't watched long enough to learn the **Gary Cooper** routine was a bust. Maybe he was a bit player moonlighting as a messenger, and hadn't time to change out of his costume between jobs [p. 56].

In Barbara Kingsolver's novel *The Bean Trees* (1988), there is a description that mistakenly refers to Gregory Peck instead of to Gary Cooper, as Peck never played in Foreign Legion films, but Cooper did, e.g. *Morocco* and *Beau Geste*:

> The hail turned to rain and kept up for half an hour. A guy came out of the little boarded-up building and leaned against one of the orange poles near us. I wondered if he lived there, or what. (If he did live there, did he paint the sperms?) He had on a camouflage army pants and a black baseball cap with cloth flaps hanging down in the back, such as Gregory Peck **or whoever** it was always wore in those Foreign Legion movies [p. 38].

Gary Cooper

Tim O'Brien's short story collection *The Things They Carried* was published in 1990, but the two stories quoted below must have been written several years earlier. In "On the Rainy River" (originally published in *Playboy*), where the author explains the circumstances leading to his decision to join the army (and the Vietnam War), there is a lengthy passage depicting his complex vision:

> The crowd swayed left and right. A marching band played fight songs. All my aunts and uncles were there, and Abraham Lincoln, and Saint George, and a nine-year-old girl named Linda who had died of a brain tumor back in fifth grade, and several members of the United States Senate, and a blind poet scribbling notes, and LBJ, and Huck Finn, and Abbie Hoffman, and all the dead soldiers back from the grave, and the many thousands who were later to die—villagers with terrible burns, little kids without arms or legs—yes, and the Joint Chiefs of Staff were there, and a couple of popes, and a first lieutenant named Jimmy Cross, and the last surviving veteran of the American Civil War, and Jane Fonda dressed up as Barbarella, and an old man sprawled beside a pigpen, and my grandfather, and **Gary Cooper**, and a kind-faced woman carrying an umbrella and a copy of Plato's *Republic*, and a million ferocious citizens waving flags of all shapes and colors—people in hard hats, people in headbands—they were all whooping and chanting and urging me toward one shore or the other [p. 56].

In "The Ghost Soldiers" (which originally appeared in *Prize Stories: The O. Henry Awards* in 1982), a reference to Cooper appears in a passage describing the complex feelings the narrator experiences not during or before a battle, but during the execution of a silly and cruel prank:

There was a light feeling in my head, fluttery and taut at the same time. I remembered it from the boonies. Giddiness and doubt and awe, all those things and a million more. It's as if you're in a movie. There's a camera on you, so you begin acting, you're somebody else. You think of all the films you've seen, Audie Murphy and **Gary Cooper** and the Cisco Kid, all those heroes, and you can't help falling back on them as models of proper comportment. On ambush, curled in the dark, you fight for control. Not too much fidgeting [p. 197].

Stephen King's *The Langoliers* (1990), already mentioned under *High Noon*, also contains a reference to Cooper himself—as a simile within a description of Bob Jenkins, a mystery writer flying from Los Angeles to Boston and realizing, along with others, that some of the fellow passengers of the Boeing 767 have mysteriously disappeared from their seats:

"Shucks, ma'am—t'warn't nothin'," Bob Jenkins said, doing a very passable **Gary Cooper** imitation, and Albert burst out laughing [p. 79].

In John Updike's novel *Rabbit at Rest* (1990), Cooper and three other Hollywood stars are mentioned in a passage revealing Harry "Rabbit" Angstrom's perception of *Working Girl*, the movie he went to see with his wife, daughter and grandson:

Harry likes it, in the movie, when you see that Melanie Griffith in her whorehouse underwear has a bit of honest fat to her, not like most of these Hollywood anorectics, and when she bursts in upon her boyfriend with the totally naked girl, like herself supposed to be Italian but not like her aspiring to be a Wall Street wheeler-dealer, riding the guy in the astride position, her long bare side sleek as the skin of a top shell and her dark-nippled boobs right on screen for a good five seconds. But the plot, and the farce of the hero and heroine worming their way into the upper-crust wedding, he feels he saw some forty years ago with Cary Grant or **Gary Cooper** and Irene Dunne or Jean Arthur. When Roy loudly asks, "*Why* don't we go now?" he is willing to go out into the lobby with him, so Janice and Judy can see the picture to the end in peace [pp. 106-107].

An unusual reference to Cooper appears in Updike's novel *Brazil* (1994), in a scene where upper-class young woman Isabel Leme, separated by force from her poor black boyfriend by her father, a world-famous ambassador, chat two years later with her university friends (in Brasilia) about politics just moments before her unexpected reunion with Tristão Raposo:

"Marx himself is a romantic fool," Nestor scoffed. "He thinks the proletariat is one big superman when in fact it is a collection of sniveling, petty-minded connivers and free-loaders. Like the capitalists, the Communists seek to paper over the oppressions and cruelties of their societies with glamorous myths. What are Castro and Mao and Ho Chi Minh but our movie stars, Mickey Mouses and **Gary Cooper**s on their posters? All governments seek to hide from us the truths about ourselves. Only in a state of anarchy does the truth about men emerge. We are beasts, killers, savages, whores" [p. 101].

In another novel by Updike, *In the Beauty of the Lilies* (1996), the narrator describes Cooper's acting as Alma's co-star in a fictitious movie made in the early 1950s:

As it happened, Alma would play opposite, within the next few years, both **Gary Cooper** and (in new wide-screen CinemaScope) **Clark Gable**. . . . There was a quiet about

Cooper, and a taciturn passivity in the hands of the director, that approached stupidity. Alma, even as a novice, established herself as a resister on the set, an actress with her own ideas and her own image to foster. As ardent on the seventh take as on the first, she felt in **Cooper**'s arms the full edge of her much greater youth and energy and desire. Yet, seeing the first rough cut of the film (they would never let an ingénue see the rushes) and then the final product at the premiere, she was astonished at how **Cooper** dominated the screen—at how his leathery face, with its baleful Nordic eyes and slightly frozen mouth, so inert-seeming in the cluttered glare of the sound stage, possessed a steady inner life beside which her own apparition was flickering, nervous, discontinuous [p. 318-319].

A reference to Cooper in Scott Turow's *The Burden of Proof* (1990) is a part of the description of Chicago through the eyes of Alejandro Stern, then a thirteen-year-old immigrant from Argentina:

When Stern stepped off the train in Chicago, he believed his life had started. They went on to Kindle County, where cousins of his father's were waiting, but Chicago would always be what he thought of a America, with its massive, soot-smeared buildings of brick and stone and granite, full of smokestack arms and sullen, teeming throngs, the land of **Gary Cooper**, of steel, skyscrapers, automobiles. He recognized in every face that day the striving children of immigrants [pp. 103-104].

In Mario Puzo's novel *The Fourth K* (1990), another movie star, a fictitious character described as "one of the most famous actors in Hollywood" (p. 260), is compared to Cooper, and—admittedly—the resemblance is there in many respects:

> Gibson Grange was a "bankable" star in the movie business. That is, if he agreed to do a movie, that movie was financed immediately by any studio. Which was why Rosemary was so anxiously pursuing him. He also looked exactly right. He was in the old American **Gary Cooper** style, lanky, with open features; he looked as Lincoln would have looked if Lincoln had been handsome. His smile was friendly, and he listened to everyone intently when he or she spoke. He told a few good-humored anecdotes about himself that were funny. This was especially endearing. Also, he dressed in a style that was more homespun than Hollywood, baggy trousers and a ratty yet obviously expensive sweater with an old suit jacket over a plain woolen shirt. And yet he magnetized everyone in the garden. Was it because his face had been seen by so many millions and shown so intimately by the camera? Were these mysterious ozone layers where his face remained forever? Was it some physical manifestation not yet solved by science? The man was intelligent, David could see that. His eyes as he listened to Rosemary were amused but not condescending, and though he seemed to always agree with what she was saying, he never committed himself to anything. He was the man David dreamed of being [p. 261].

In Michael Malone's novel *Foolscap or, The Stages of Love* (1991), a reference to Cooper is a result of the physical resemblance between the actor and a college professor:

> Theo, on the other hand, was no clotheshorse, although he was considered the best looking of the three. In fact, a group of female graduate students had once commented together on Professor Ryan's close resemblance to the young **Gary Cooper**; but then **Cooper** hadn't been much of a clotheshorse either. At home, Theo wore jeans and sweatshirts; his teaching wardrobe

consisted of three corduroy suits—Old, Not So Old, and Pretty New—though Jonas Marsh had told him that one corduroy suit was one too damnable many. Steve had often offered to drive him to a "great discount mall" only fifty miles away, but Theo wasn't interested [p. 621].

Theo reminded himself that she owed him two chapters of her dissertation. She was very pretty.

She smiled up at him. "There you are! Hi! I just wanted to—" She slapped his hands together in hers, then hers flew away. "You were *fantastic*! Really! Did you sing professionally? I bet you did. Wait'll the class sees you in this!"

"Oh, hi, Jenny. Thanks." He ran his hand through his wavy hair, a gesture that increased his resemblance to the young **Gary Cooper**. "I just did it, you know, on the spur of the moment" [pp. 74-75].

...

Theo made him a present of the Day-Glo sunglasses. "Hey, totally super," said the future earl. "Anyone ever tell you you look a bit like **Gary Cooper** in the early stuff?"

"Well, actually, people do," Theo admitted. "Actually the playwright Ford Rexford told me that, and he knew **Cooper**."

This information won Willie over completely. "Ford Rexford wrote *Preacher's Boy*. It's one of my favorite movies" [p. 212].

One may strongly argue with the part of the first excerpt referring to Cooper's dressing habits. The statement may be true about some of the actor's characters—John Doe, for example—but privately Cooper had been known for dressing meticulously and in good taste. This is documented by the book *Gary Cooper: Enduring Style*, written by G. Bruce Boyer and the actor's daughter, Maria Cooper Janis.

Gary Cooper

In Oscar Hijuelos's novel *The Fourteen Sisters of Emilio Montez O'Brien* (1993), Cooper, in the context of his prime genre, is mentioned in a passage describing the Hollywood career of the titular Irish-Cuban protagonist. This particular section of the book is set in 1955:

> Despite the success of his first priest movie and the occasional good notice, he was never given a chance to act for a first-rate director, and the B-picture scripts he received—for now he was considered a good B actor—he read with a mixture of pity and contempt both for himself and for the poor writers who'd been forced to sit and produce such material. Not that he always felt dissatisfied, but as he moved from one film to the next, he had the feeling that he was on some kind of forced march, that it was his unpleasant destiny to linger in B land. He tried to test for some really classy movies—he'd played a small part that year in a **Gary Cooper** Western—and yet, as his days became clouded with work, romantic escapades, and weekend drunks, he sometimes felt that things were hopeless [pp. 323-324].

In another novel by Hijuelos, *A Simple Habana Melody* (2002), there are several, and indisputably favorable, references to the actor. The first excerpt includes a quotation from one of the letters the book's protagonist, Cuban composer Israel Levis (which name turns out responsible for his European misfortunes), receives from Rita Valladares, the love of his life:

> And what were those letters often about but the occasional discomforts and exaltations of her life: "Hollywood is crazy, but certain stars like **Gary Cooper** are very nice"; or: "My last tour was barbaric—my promoters are working me like a slave, my dear boy; my throat is hoarse and I think, on top of it all, I've caught a cold. I'm tired of living out of a suitcase. . . . I miss

my children, and Habana. I can't wait until I get home.—Love, Chiquita...."

Why did he treasure those letters so? [p. 9]

The second passage, which gives some background information about Europe circa 1936, mentions Cooper in two different contexts: as Hitler's favorite actor (a fact contradictory to other sources, pointing out at Clark Gable to be the one) and the narrator's reflection on fame:

> According to Israel's friend Ernesto Lecuona, who often played Berlin with his band, the Lecuona Cuban Boys, Adolf Hitler himself, master of the Third Reich, whose favorite movie star was **Gary Cooper**, was said to have secretly attended several of their performances, in disguise; and because Lecuona performed his own arrangement of *"Rosas Puras"* during his concerts, it could be said, much to Levis's later bemusement, that Hitler was familiar with—and possibly liked—that winsome tune.) So frequently was Levis introduced and applauded as he sat in a Paris club that he came to expect it, and felt a near disappointment if for some reason he had not been noticed. On certain occasions, movie stars like Johnny Weissmuller, **Gary Cooper** and Marlene Dietrich drew attention away from him, and while he did not mind it, at times, he eventually developed the disease that comes with fame—even a composer's fame—a desire to be noticed [p. 232].

The last two excerpts offer an opinion on the actor himself and Paris of 1939, respectively:

> Passing the time, however briefly, with an actor whose films had much entertained Levis back in Habana was but one of many such brushes with the famous. **Gary Cooper**, he would

remember, was a gentleman. The writer Hemingway was a bit bombastic, but generous about buying people drinks—he liked that [p. 233].

And what of those fanciful American films that one saw from time to time?

And how could one feel comfortable in the city that played host to Charlie Chaplin and **Gary Cooper**? [p. 255]

George Baxt's *The Marlene Dietrich Murder Case* (1993) has already been quoted several times in this publication. It includes references to two of Cooper's films, *Morocco* and *The Devil and the Deep*, and numerous to the actor himself. Below is just one of them, a part of a conversation the actor has with William A. Wellman at a Hollywood party, in which he reveals his proverbial taciturnity and restraint:

William Wellman, the director, said to **Gary Cooper**, "I phoned Lindberg ostensibly to wish him and his wife a happy New Year. O sort of matter-of-factly let drop Madam Chu's premonition about the possible kidnapping of a national hero's baby, and you know what that modest bastard said?"

"Nope."

"There are a lot of other national heroes around. Can you believe that?"

"Yup" [p. 40].

In another novel by Baxt, *The Mae West Murder Case* (1993), Cooper is referenced in a passage relating a dialogue between Mae West and her unusual "witch" friend, Agnes Darwin, which takes place in front of other visitors, detectives Herb Villon and Jim Malory and Rabbi Morris Rothfeld:

"Mae," Agnes said dryly, "you can't screw around with history."

"Agnes, I can do anythin' I damn well please. Hmmm." She was back floating on her cloud. "Now for the dauphin what's my husband, I think I'll insist on **Gary Cooper**."

"He is physically all wrong," advised Agnes.

"Get your eyes examined, honey. He is physically all right, and how, ummmmm!"

"Mae, I've got to be going," said the rabbi [pp. 33-34].

Baxt's mystery *The Humphrey Bogart Murder Case* (1995) was also already quoted in this part of the book because of the references it contains to *Mr. Deeds Goes to Town* and *The Adventures of Marco Polo*. A reference to Cooper, without any attachment to a specific film, appears in a passage where the narrator praises the accomplishments of Samuel Goldwyn:

> Sam Goldwyn had been presiding over his kingdom for almost two decades, when he broke away from Metro-Goldwyn-Mayer to go it as an independent. He let them keep his name and they let him keep his integrity. . . . His major asset was Ronald Colman who he nursed successfully from silent into talkies. He developed **Gary Cooper** into a major star. His only serious misjudgment was the Russian actress Anna Sten [p. 117].

Cooper's name appears both in the title and within Sam Shepard's tale "Gary Cooper, Or the Landscape" (1994). This short narrative is an account of a dialogue between the narrator (most likely the author himself) and a Swedish female:

> Since I was a little girl I've dreamed about the West.
> In Sweden?
> Yes! Oh, yes. I used to have visions about it.
>
> . . .

Where did you hear about the West in Sweden?

Movies. American movies. We see that great landscape in our dreams. It haunts us.

...

So in Sweden, when you're watching an American western, you're all staring at the background? Is that it?

I suppose. It's so evocative to us. All that space. Sweden is very close.

So it doesn't matter who's in the western—it could be John Wayne or Jerry Lewis—because everyone's really captured by the landscape?

Well, we love the actors too, of course.

Who's your favorite?

Mine, personally?

Yes. Do you have a favorite?

I guess I would have to say **Gary Cooper**.

The Coop!

Oh, yes. He personified something, I think.

What was that?

Excuse me?

That he "personified."

Oh, I don't know. That wonderful mixture of shyness—how do you say it?—vulnerability, I suppose, and yet strong at the same time. It's very western. Women love that.

...

But when you get right down to brass tacks, which is more important—**Gary Cooper** or the landscape?

Oh, I would hate to have to choose between them.

Say you had to. Say it was a question of life or death.

I would have to say the landscape.

There you go.

But I love them both [pp. 178-180].

Four Hollywood Legends

In her Hollywood novel *House of Destiny* (1995), Janet Leigh refers to three Cooper movies (*The Winning of Barbara Worth*, *North West Mounted Police* and *It's a Big Country*), and she mentions the actor outside of a specific movie context in a couple of places. Here is a passage relating a stage in Jude Abavas' life outside of Hollywood:

> Jude was promoted to mountain manager at Sun Valley. At the invitation to the Union Pacific Railroad, Ernest Hemingway and wife-to-be, Marty, had arrived for the first time at Sun Valley the previous fall. It was the start of the writer's love affair with Wood River Valley. Now in the fall of 1940, Hemingway and "Ol Podner," movie legend **Gary Cooper**, planned their annual hunting expedition. Jude desperately wanted to be their scout, but the established ranchers and his supervisors prevailed. He did, however, have brief encounters with these two giants creating yet more treasured memories [pp. 67-68].

The actor's name is mentioned a few pages later, once again in connection with Sun Valley:

> Despite the war, Sun Valley operated in a relatively normal manner. Both the lodge and inn were at capacity, complete with a full quota of celebrities: Claudette Colbert, Norma Shearer, Ann Sothern, the **Gary Cooper**s, the Ray Millands, the Henry Hathaways, the Darryl Zanucks and, briefly, Wade Colby. There was one change to the usual agenda. Instead of just taking afternoon tea and socializing in the Redwood Room, guests and employees gathered together to knit for the troops. Thelma joined this endeavor to do her part and received an unexpected bonus [p. 78].

Gary Cooper

In Richard Ford's novel *Independence Day* (1995), there is a scene in which father (Frank Bascombe/the narrator) and his young adult son (Paul) have a serious conversation, in which the latter is compared to Cooper:

> "There's this place in California, okay? You go to college and work on a ranch and get to brand cows and learn to rope horses."
> "Sounds good," I say, nodding, wanting to keep our spirit level high.
> "Yep, it is," he says, a young **Gary Cooper**.
> "You think you can study astrophysics on a cayuse?"
> "What's a cayuse?" He's forgotten about being a cartoonist [p. 343].

Kinky Friedman's mystery *God Bless John Wayne* (1995) has, in fact, nothing to do with Duke, but it does include several movie references. The author, clearly a fan of Cooper's most famous picture, came up with quite an original epithet which he repeatedly uses instead of a digital description of that particular time of day:

> By **Gary Cooper time** I was beginning to experience a rather abnormal emotional state, the psychological term for which is the Swiss cheese effect [p. 115].
>
> When I'd finally become a homo erectus, fed the cat, made some coffee, lit my first cigar of the morning, and tried to decide whether or not to change the cat litter, it was half past **Gary Cooper time** and way past time to sit down at my desk and do some cold, deductive, Sherlockian thinking [p. 125].
>
> By **Gary Cooper time**, with our cover still holding nicely, we were able to swim around on the grounds and inside much of the castle in the blithe, practiced manner of the deadly candiru fish [p. 230].

Stuart M. Kaminsky makes references to Cooper and his films in several books. In *Tomorrow Is Another Day* (1995), in addition to alluding to *Sergeant York* and *The Pride of the Yankees*, he mentions the actor by name in two places. The following excerpt is a scene where police captain Phil Pevsner loses control in a bar and his younger brother, private eye Toby Peters, tries to appease the bartender by giving him money he received from client Clark Gable:

> The bartender threw the bat in the general direction of my brother, but it was so wide and to the right that it had to be a pickoff play or a wild pitch to save face.
>
> "He really a cop?" the woman in red screamed at me.
>
> "Yep," I said.
>
> "Let's get out of here," Phil said. "Before I do something I won't regret."
>
> I dropped another one of **Clark Gable**'s five-spots. When the bartender glared at me, I dropped another five to ease his pain.
>
> "Get out of here," the bartender said softly through clenched teeth, in a not-bad **Gary Cooper** [p. 135].

The other passage is a part of a long scene where Peters, dressed up as a waiter, tries to catch a serial killer at the Academy Awards dinner, with the help from his friends, Shelly and Gunther:

> Shelly went out, Gunther followed, and I was last. Bob Hope was at the podium making jokes about William Bendix and pretending to be hurt because he wasn't nominated for *The Road to Morocco*. I found my table and put the water pitcher down next to Ronald Reagan. I knew some people sitting at the tables, worked on cases for them. **Gary Cooper**, **Bette Davis**,

but I didn't figure they'd recognize me or even take a good look [p. 189].

In Kaminsky's other mystery, *Vengeance* (1999), the name of the actor emerges as a part of a simile in the description of Lew Fonesca's old friend, Ames McKinney, who resembles Gary Cooper in more than one way:

> I wasn't alone in the car. Ames McKinney sat erect, seat-belted next to me, riding shotgun. Literally. He had an old Remington M-10 twelve gauge pump-action shotgun lying across the lap of his yellow slicker. Ames seldom spoke. He had said almost all he had to say in his seventy-four years of life. Ames looked like an aged **Gary Cooper** with long white hair and a face of sunned leather.
>
> He knew how to use a gun, though he was not supposed to have one. Ames had come to Sarasota three years earlier in search of his business partner, who had run off with all the money from the sale of their business back in Arizona. Ames and his partner had gone out to the white sand behind the trees on South Lido Beach and had an old-fashioned shoot-out [p. 10].

The above passage comes from the book's Prologue, which puts us in the middle of the story, in medias res, but the original meeting of Fonesca and Ames comes later, on pp. 60-61, and the passage is discussed earlier in the book, under *The Plainsman* (1936).

Pete Hamill's *Snow in August* (1997) is a moving and insightful novel, set in the post-World War II New York, about the friendship and mutual education that develop between a fatherless Irish boy (his father was killed in the Battle of the Bulge) and a rabbi from Prague. A reference to Cooper is a part of a passage where the narrator reveals the boy's pondering about what he should believe regarding the two conflicting opinions about Jews:

But that couldn't be. This was an *encyclopedia*; if it was full of lies, someone would write to a newspaper or the mayor or some other big shot; they'd expose the lies. If they were lies. Maybe the stuff he heard on the street was the real lie. He would have to ask his mother about it. Or Father Heaney. Father Heaney was tough, but he wasn't mean. He didn't say much, but shit, neither did **Gary Cooper**. Father Heaney would tell Michael the truth. The boy didn't completely trust what he heard on the street [pp. 43-44].

In Max Allan Collins's political mystery *Majic Man* (1999), set in the late 1940s, there is a scene where private investigator Nate Heller tries to obtain information from Mac Brazel about a UFO that landed around Roswell, New Mexico, a while ago. The reference to Cooper makes a sarcastic allusion to the actor's characteristic manner of delivery:

He turned away, but I caught him looking at me in the mirror behind the bar; I looked back at him in it, and said, "I'd like to talk to you about what happened out at your ranch July before last."

His bottle of beer arrived, with a glass. "I don't talk about that."

"You know, you're an American citizen, Mr. Brazel. The military can't tell you what to do and what to say, or what not to say."

Brazel was pouring the beer. "I'm not sure about that."

"What did you find, Mr. Brazel, out in that field?"

He sipped the beer, savored it, then—speaking so slowly it would have irritated **Gary Cooper**—said, "I'll tell you one thing, mister. It sure as hell wasn't a weather balloon" [p. 177].

John Dunning's mystery *Two O'Clock, Eastern Wartime* (2001) is set in

1942; thus, when a minor character of the book is compared to Cooper, the actor is in his prime:

> "Didn't I see that name Hartford on a building downtown?"
> "Now you've got it." Said beauty. "Hartford runs the world."
> "And Hartford is a man, right?"
> "That's what they tell me." She cocked her head slightly. "Did anyone ever tell you you look like a workingman's **Gary Cooper**? ... A nice homely plainsman, long and lanky and quiet. My name's Rue Nicholas."
> "Jordan Ten Eyck" [p. 59].

An excerpt from one of the three letters including Gary Cooper's name from Bernard Spiro's *The Other War: Letters from a GI in India in 1944 & 1945* (2001) is quoted under *Casanova Brown*. Below are excerpts from the other two letters (the first one also mentioning Gable and Bogart):

> December 16 through 31, 1944
>
> And for the rest of the month, through Christmas and New Years Eve—not a blessed piece of news for the folks that I could sink my teeth into or poise my pen onto. A couple of more major meals than usual, a couple of gifts for us from our officers—like tobacco, butts and one cigar each. (No, I'm sure they didn't know then about that stuff causing cancer. Don't you all remember Bette Davis, **Clark Gable**, **Gary Cooper** and **Bogie** always puffing away for all they were worth?) And a little extra time off ... [p. 127].

> Miscellany through Jan. 15, 1945
>
> After bringing Mom and Dad up to date on the latter tale of intrigue, I fearlessly detailed for them in a ten page letter, my experience is a Jimmy Stewart/**Gary Cooper** type of do-

gooder, honest to the point of nausea, in attempting to right a few wrongs I'd discovered at work involving false entries in the records (for profit) committed by one of Lt. Harris' cohorts [p. 180].

Adriana Trigiani makes a nice reference to Cooper in her novel *Big Cherry Holler* (2001). Pete Rutledge learns that he is only the second fiddle in narrator/protagonist Ave Maria's life, a part of her "European vacation fantasy," and he is being dropped by her in front of the motel where he is staying—after a family dinner in her home:

> "Okay, babe. I know when I'm licked." Pete opens the door of the Jeep and swings his long legs out to the ground. He swivels and looks at me. "Thanks for dinner. And Etta. And Jack. I really like Jack." Pete leans over and kisses me on the cheek. Then he gets out of the Jeep.
> "Pete?" I call after him. "Good luck."
> "Thanks." He smiles and waves.
> I watch him walk into the lobby of the Trail Motel. He has to drop his head under the walkway awning. And he looks to me a little like the great **Gary Cooper**—Pete sort of rode into town, set things straight, and gone [p. 258].

In Bill Crider's novel *We'll Always Have Murder: A Humphrey Bogart Mystery* (2001), the actor's name is mentioned in the very first paragraph; thus, no explanation is necessary:

Jack Warner's plan had been to make Buck Sterling (real name, Seymour Grape) the new **Gary Cooper**. Buck had the look of a westerner, even though he'd been born in Pittsburgh and lived there most of his life, but when he made his first oater, a little problem cropped up: Buck developed an unfortunate interest in horses, especially palominos [p. 1].

The actor is also mentioned, in a relatively insignificant reference, in

Martha Sherrill's *My Last Movie Star* (2002), in a scene relating a meeting between Clementine James (the narrator) and Myrna Loy in front of LAX:

> She was waiting at the curb, behind the wheel of an incredibly long lemon-yellow Duesenberg convertible with whitewall tires. The interior was green—the same color as Tom Swimmer's Woody—and Myrna was wearing a powder-blue suit with a plunging neckline. A gardenia was pinned at the plunge.
> "Where'd this come from?" I asked, crouching down to look at her.
> "Borrowed it from **Gary Cooper**," she yelled against the traffic noise. "Come on, get in" [pp. 248-249].

Thomas McGuane's family morality tale *The Cadence of Grass* (2002) includes a reference to Cooper, which, in fact, is part of the family's poignant description:

> Paul would deliver this load and take his reward down there to Evelyn and save the ranch, just as Whitelaw delivered all the bottles for half a million square miles and saved the ranch. Old Bill was heading into his last snowstorm to save the ranch. It's as if, Paul thought, we're all in the same **Gary Cooper** movie and can't get out. He hung on the oars and let his most genuine smile warm his face. Thank God I still have my sense of humor, he thought, then threw his old clothes into the river.
> He was a new man [p. 230].

Elizabeth Hay's novel *Garbo Laughs* (2003)—in addition to containing references to *Desire*, *High Noon* and *Love in the Afternoon*—mentions Cooper by name, both in the context of those films and, once, outside of the context.

The excerpt (p. 255), relating the Golds' vacation in Havana, is presented in Part Four (on Tracy).

Nora Roberts's novel *Northern Lights* (2004) was already mentioned due to its reference to *High Noon*. Below is a passage mentioning Gary Cooper (along with another big western star), which relates a conversation between the book's protagonists, Meg Galloway and Nate Burke, two romantically involved fighters for law and order in Lunacy, Alaska:

> "An enterprising little town," Meg commented as they drove through.
> "It is that."
> "And after today, a safer one. Thank you. Otto nailed that. It's thanks to you, chief."
> "Aw shucks, ma'am."
> She rubbed a hand over his. "You say that like **Gary Cooper**, but you've got Clint Eastwood—Dirty Harry years—in your eyes" [p. 550].

Aaron Latham's mystery *Riding with John Wayne* (2006) was already mentioned in the entry on *Mr. Deeds Goes to Town*. Below is another reference from that book, this time to the actor himself as part of the name of a relatively famous place in Los Angeles:

> At 3 p.m. the next day, we all gather in Paramount's full-sized **Gary Cooper** Theater to look at the screen tests [p. 45].

There are several references to Gary Cooper in Donald Jeffries's thriller *The Unreals* (2007). In three of them, including one presented under *Meet John Doe*, a major character is compared to a Frank Capra hero. Below are two excerpts, one in which the resemblance is worn by the book's protagonist, Waldo Billingsly, and one where the simile refers to Jeanne, the woman in love with him:

Waldo set his features in that classic James Stewart-**Gary Cooper** look of determination he wore whenever the situation merited it. "Of course, that's a real possibility. But. . . . I just know he's alive somewhere- I can feel it in my heart" [p. 37].

"Have you seen our Security staff? Even if I thought they *would* help us, I doubt if they could. Look, if you don't want to come with me, I'll go alone." The expression on Jeanne's pretty face was not unlike the **Gary Cooper**-James Stewart look of determination that all **Frank Capra** heroes, as well as her true love Waldo Billingsly, were noted for. "After all, Janie, I love Waldo. If I don't try and save him, who will?" [p. 331].

In James Scott Bell's crime drama *Try Fear* (2009), the narrator/protagonist is independent defense lawyer Ty Buchanan, who appears in court in two different cases. The judge in the second case happens to remind him of the famous actor:

As soon as I walked in, the clerk motioned for me and said Judge Hughes wanted to see me in chambers.
Radavich was already there when I came in.
"Sit down," Hughes said. He was a tall, sinewy man. Sort of a **Gary Cooper** quality about him. He was sixty-six years old and had been on the bench longer than I'd been alive [p. 151].

Byron Janis wrote some warm words about Gary Cooper in his captivating, not only autobiographical, book *Chopin and Beyond: My Extraordinary Life in Music and the Paranormal* (2010). The world-famous pianist was asked by his wife, Cooper's daughter, to compose a special theme song for a documentary called *Gary Cooper: American Life, American Legend*, and his reaction is described in the following passage:

I muttered something like, "I can't do that . . . well, I'll try," and went back to bed. But the idea intrigued me, and I had such love and respect for her father, both as I have come to know him through his daughter and through the roles he portrayed on the screen. I agreed to give it a try [pp. 173-174].

Cooper, along with many other movie stars (including Gable and Tracy), is also mentioned in Rachel Shukert's Hollywood novel *Love Me* (2014). The context of the quoted passage is actress Margo Preston's unwelcome encounter with columnist Perdita Pendleton:

"Perdita," Margo said. "Hello."
"Don't tell me I saw the divine Dane dash out on you? Not a lovers' quarrel, I hope?" Her beady eyes glittered in anticipation of a scoop.
"Not at all," Margo cooed. "He simply had to run. He's playing cards with **Clark Gable** tonight at the Clover Club."
"Without you? The beast."
"Not really. I'm relieved, honestly." Margo tried to laugh gaily. "You know what those boys can get up to."
"I certainly do." Perdita nodded sagely. Well, I'm here dining with **Gary Cooper**. William Powell is supposed to meet us. Still licking his wounds over the **Gable**-Lombard union, poor thing." Her lipsticked mouth stretched in the customary wide smile that somehow never seemed to reach her eyes. "You're welcome to join us."
"That's ever so sweet of you," Margo said, "but I've just finished, and anyway, I really must go" [p. 199].

References to Gary Cooper and his films have been found in more than 220 works by over 160 authors. The writers who—based on the discovered data—showed the biggest interest in him include Stuart (M.) Kaminsky (eight sources/references to ten films), Elmore Leonard (seven/six), Martha Grimes (six/one), George Baxt (five/seven), Stephen King (five/three), Robert B. Parker (four/two), Michael Malone (three/five), John Updike (three/four), Larry McMurtry (three/two), Loren D. Estleman (three/two), Nora Roberts (three/one), Susan Isaacs (two/three), Elizabeth Hay (two/three), Marisa de los Santos (two/two) and William Bernhardt (two/two). The literary works where the references appear were published in a time span of eighty years, from 1935 till now (how many generations of authors?), with more than half (125) between 1990 and 2009, and as many as nine in the current decade, which, of course, is far from being ended. The above statistics clearly indicate that the number of works mentioning the actor or his films keeps consistently growing, and, thus, prove unambiguously that Cooper's legend is far from fading; in fact, it is more alive now than ever.

Gary Cooper as Longfellow Deeds in a scene from Frank Capra's *Mr. Deeds Goes to Town* (1936).

Gary Cooper as Robert Jordan in a publicity shot for Sam Wood's *For Whom the Bell Tolls* (1943).

It is worth noting that among the literary works which include references to Cooper there are six items that use (or allude to) the actor's name or one of his movies. They are *The Summer Gary Cooper Won the War* (1974) by Mary Duffe, *City Primeval: High Noon in Detroit* (1980) by Elmore Leonard, *High Midnight* (1981) by Stuart Kaminsky, "Gary Cooper, Or the Landscape" (1994) by Sam Shepard, *My Name Is Gary Cooper* by Victor Rodger and *High Noon* (2007) by Nora Roberts. Furthermore, the French version of Romain

Gary's novel *Ski Bum* (1964) is entitled *Adieu Gary Cooper*. The actor's name is also used as a title of a major part (covering Chapters 26 through 32) in David Cole's mystery *Shadow Play* (2004).

Regardless of the genre—and it needs to be emphasized that Cooper appeared in a remarkable variety of films set in many different periods and in numerous places of the world, consequently wearing a wide range of modern and historical costumes and looking great in all—the actor successfully and convincingly combined heroic characteristics with unexpected sensitivity, which—with his tall and lean silhouette, unquestioned charm, engaging personality, love for the outdoor life and unusually economical acting style—guaranteed for him a special position among the American movie stars and recognition from both film critics and movie fans all over the world.

Gary Cooper's moral nobility was carved on his face.

His acting versatility cannot be questioned, and regardless of the quality of his films his performances were consistently at least good, most frequently remarkable. However, the greatest performances in Cooper's career are clearly those which resulted from the perfect or absolute fusion of the man he was with the man he played on the screen—The Virginian, Frederick Henry and Robert Jordan, Longfellow Deeds and John Doe, Lieutenant McGregor and Beau Geste, Wild Bill Hickok and Cole Harden, Alvin C. York, Lou Gehrig (despite the fact the Cooper was not much of a baseball fan), Jess Birdwell and, above all, Marshal Will Kane—portrayals that deserve the highest praise for the actor's unique achievement on both the intellectual and emotional level. Consequently, Gary Cooper is not only the man that we respect for his outstanding talent; Gary Cooper is also the man that we will never stop loving for the deepest and unforgettable emotions that he evoked and keeps evoking in us, the devoted audience, by endowing his understanding and sensitive-looking face and his own deeply humane traits to the distinguished real-life men and fictitious characters that he was deservedly fortunate to portray.

On the other hand, several directors probably made the mistake of casting Cooper against type. It took place especially toward the end of the actor's career, with movies such as *Man of the West*, *They Came to Cordura*, *The Wreck of the Mary Deare* and *The Naked Edge*. Because of Cooper's nobility being carved on his face, with uprightness, honesty and compassion emanating especially from his eyes, it is hard for a thoughtful viewer to believe that Link Jones could ever have been a member of Dock Tobin's band of ruthless outlaws, just like it is hard to believe in Thomas Thorn's act of cowardice or the crimes that the characters in Coop's last two films, both directed by Michael Anderson, are accused or suspected of. Consequently, the act of redemption in the first two films, as spectacular as it is, appears to be redundant or anticlimactic; and the final scenes where Cooper is cleared of the charges in the last two movies do not offer any surprise. Does it mean that Cooper should have turned those roles down because of their questionable plausibility? The answer is obviously negative. It is always a pleasure to watch

Cooper, and those four movies gave him a rare opportunity to tackle a new challenge, a challenge to cope with material that required of him to stretch, or even expand by force, his morally crystal and so well defined screen persona. A professional of the highest caliber that he was, Cooper, just like the characters he played in those pictures, accepted the challenge against all odds, and, just like those characters, turned out victorious once again.

Two significant aspects of Cooper's persona, traits that largely enhance the realism of the actor's roles and films, are modesty and vulnerability. They have been dominant and rather obvious almost since his first major picture, *The Winning of Barbara Worth*, and remained important throughout his impressive career. In the 1950s, when Cooper and John Wayne emerged as the top two western stars, the contrast between Cooper's unassuming persona and Wayne's self-assurance bordering with arrogance and physical immunity bordering with immortality (despite his characters' death in some later movies) may have not been conspicuous to many viewers and critics. Later on, however, when the screen heroes portrayed by such actors as Clint Eastwood, Sylvester Stallone and Arnold Schwarzenegger were endowed with supernatural powers, typically outnumbered in confrontations and effortlessly victorious without even a scratch, the comics provenience of such characterizations, juvenile and clichéd, choosing cheap excitement over realism, became the antithesis to Cooper's adult and plausible offer. Thus, there is no exaggeration in the statement that the Gary Cooper hero is the last of the heroes of human proportions to be found in American culture or Western culture in general—a hero whose existence was indirectly prolonged for a decade or so by such actors as Henry Fonda, James Stewart and Gregory Peck through some of their western and nonwestern roles.

By a strange coincidence I got exposed to Cooper for the first time the year he died, and the two films that I saw at that time, within a period of just a few weeks, were *Mr. Deed Goes to Town* and *High Noon*. Without a doubt, two of the foremost accomplishments in the actor's career, the movies influenced my life in a degree that I am not able to describe. Not only did Cooper become my favorite actor, never to lose that honor, but also he, or, more correctly, the sum of his major characters, became my role model that I have tried to live up to not only in my younger years but, literally, throughout my life. At different stages of my personal and professional existence, especially at difficult moments, I frequently found myself thinking of what Gary Cooper would do in such or such a situation, and, regardless of the consequences, I usually did not regret having followed this kind of guidance. (Admittedly, however, there has been nothing in my ordinary life even remotely comparable to the spectacular and astounding deeds of my collective idol.) Thus, Cooper's idealistic and heroic but, at the same time, complex and enormously human persona, manifested in numerous captivating screen portrayals, has successfully served as a precious moral "lighthouse"—certainly for me, but possibly also for many boys and men all over the world.

Polish "Solidarity" poster for the first election after the major political changes of 1989 (by Tomasz Sarnecki).

Gary Cooper

As a man who spent forty years living in Poland under the communist regime, I have two more very personal reasons to show gratitude to Gary Cooper and his work. First, the movie *Friendly Persuasion*, in which the actor plays the father of a Quaker family during the Civil War, was used as a meaningful gift from President Reagan to President Gorbachev during a summit meeting in the USA (the two leaders, in addition to Pope John Paul II and Lech Wałęsa, turned out to be instrumental in the collapse of communism—first in Poland and then in the rest of the Soviet Bloc). Second, the image of the actor walking alone in *High Noon* (the same as the one used on the side of the Gary Cooper stamp sheet) appeared on the political poster designed (by Tomasz Sarnecki, anonymously at that time) for the first free election in Poland—with Will Kane wearing the "Solidarity" badge on his chest and holding a ballot with the word 'WYBORY' (election) in his hand. Thus, this and the penultimate paragraph strongly suggest that evidence of the Gary Cooper impact can be also found in some other, clearly unexpected, areas—in a scale of an individual and in a scale of a nation.

III. LIST OF REFERENCES (FOUND) TO COOPER AND HIS FILMS

While the year after the book title refers to the copyright/publication date (to provide an accurate sense of chronology), the page numbers are taken from the specific editions in which the references were found—as described in the Overall Bibliography (Reference Sources).

Jeff Abbott – *The Only Good Yankee* **(1995)**
- Cooper – 239, 241, 244
- *Sergeant York* – 239, 241, 244

Alex Abella – *The Great American* **(1997)**
- *Vera Cruz* – 32

Randy Alcorn – *Edge of Eternity* **(1998)**
- Cooper – 234, 258
- *High Noon* – 234

Ace Atkins – *Robert B. Parker's Lullaby* **(2012)**
- *High Noon* – 292, 297

Paul Auster – "The Locked Room" **(1986)**
- *The Adventures of Marco Polo* – 269

James D. Balestrieri – *The Ballad of Ethan Burns* (2013)
- Cooper – 18, 28, 84
- *The Texan* – 84
- *High Noon* – 28
- *Man of the West* – 18

Jill Barnett – *Sentimental Journey* (2002)
- Cooper – 4
- *Beau Geste* – 4

George Baxt – *The Greta Garbo Murder Case* (1992)
- Cooper – 47
- *The Pride of the Yankees* - 47

George Baxt – *The Humphrey Bogart Murder Case* (1995)
- Cooper – 63, 110, 117
- *Mr. Deeds Goes to Town* - 63
- *The Adventures of Marco Polo* - 18, 110, 116 119

George Baxt – *The Mae West Murder Case* (1993)
- Cooper – 33

George Baxt – *The Marlene Dietrich Murder Case* (1993)
- Cooper – 1, 5, 40, 42, 44, 70, 144, 192
- *Morocco* – 1, 2, 3, 17, 44
- *The Devil and the Deep* – 144

George Baxt – *The Tallulah Bankhead Murder Case* (1987)
- Cooper – 206
- *Peter Ibbetson* – 194
- *High Noon* – 206

Ilene Beckerman – *What We Do for Love* (1997)
- Cooper – 44
- *The Fountainhead* – 31
- *Love in the Afternoon* – 44

James Scott Bell – *Try Darkness* (2008)
- *High Noon* – 274

James Scott Bell – *Try Fear* (2009)
- Cooper – 151

William Bernhardt – *Capitol Murder* (2006)
- Cooper – 78-79
- *High Noon* 78-79

William Bernhardt – *Nemesis: The Final Case of Eliot Ness* (2009)
- Cooper – 225
- *Mr. Deeds Goes to Town* – 225

Lawrence Block – *When the Sacred Ginmill Closes* (1986)
- Cooper – 140
- *High Noon* – 140

Christopher Bram – *Lives of the Circus Animals* (2003)
- Cooper – 155
- *Saratoga Trunk* – 155

Gene Breaznell – *Deadly Divots* (2003)
- Cooper – 11
- *High Noon* – 11

Bill Brooks – *Bonnie and Clyde: A Love Story* (2004)
- Cooper – 23, 28, 33
- *Morocco* – 23

Dale Brown – *Chains of Command* (1993)
- Cooper – 452
- *High Noon* – 452

Joe David Brown – *Addie Pray* (1971)
- Cooper – 13

Michael Feeney Callan – "Drumcondra" (2013)
- Cooper – 124
- *The Naked Edge* – 124-125

John Dickson Carr – *The Crooked Hinge* (1938)
- Cooper – 417

Leslie Carroll – *Temporary Insanity* (2004)
- Cooper – 83

- *The Pride of the Yankees* – 83

Hap Cawood – *The Miler* (2003)
- Cooper – 121
- *High Noon* – 121

David Cole – *Shadow Play* (2004)
- Cooper – 135, 139, 167, 171, 174, 191, 221, 229, 231
- *High Noon* – 232
- *Man of the West* – 135, 137, 139, 171, 191, 192, 221, 222, 228, 231, 233

Max Allan Collins – *Flying Blind* (1998)
- *Wings* – 46, 75

Max Allan Collins – *Majic Man* (1999)
- Cooper – 177

Richard Condon – *Winter Kills* (1974)
- Cooper – 193

Pat Conroy – *Beach Music* (1995)
- *High Noon* – 44

Thomas H. Cook – *Peril* (2004)
- Cooper – 176
- *Man of the West* – 176

Julio Cortázar – *The Winners* (1960)
- Cooper – 89-90

Michael Crichton – *The Andromeda Strain* (1969)
- Cooper – 79-80

Bill Crider – *We'll Always Have Murder* (2001)
- Cooper – 1

Clive Cussler – *Sahara* (1992)
- Cooper – 279, 417
- *Beau Geste* – 279, 417

Mary Daheim – *The Alpine Pursuit* (2004)
- Cooper – 231
- *High Noon* – 231
-

Bruce Davis – *We're Dead, Come on in* (2005)
- Cooper – 105
- *High Noon* – 105

Marisa de los Santos – *Belong to Me* (2008)
- Cooper – 296
- *Mr. Deeds Goes to Town* – 296

Marisa de los Santos – *Love Walked In* (2005)
- *Meet John Doe* – 96-97

Michael B. Druxman – *Gable: A One-Person Play in Two Acts* (1984)
- Cooper – 29, 38

Michael B. Druxman – *Tracy: A One-Person Play in Two Acts* (1984)
- Cooper – 68

Mary Duffe – *The Summer Gary Cooper Won the War* (1974)
- Cooper – title, 30-31, 40
- *Betrayal* (as *Betrayed*) – 30
- *The Virginian* – 30-31

John Gregory Dunne – *True Confessions* (1977)
- Cooper – 269

John Dunning – *Two O'Clock, Eastern Time* (2001)
- Cooper – 59

James Ellroy – *L.A. Confidential* (1990)
- Cooper – 181

Loren D. Estleman – *Downriver* (1988)
- Cooper – 20

Loren D. Estleman – *Something Borrowed, Something Black* (2002)
- Cooper – 56

Loren D. Estleman – *The Witchfinder* (1998)
- Cooper – 38
- *Beau Geste* – 30
- *The Lives of a Bengal Lancer* – 38

Barbara Esstman – *Night Ride Home* (1997)
- Cooper – 44

- *Sergeant York* – 44

Howard Fast – *The Dinner Party* (1987)
- Cooper – 294-295
- *The Virginian* – 294-295

Andrew J. Fenady – *The Man with Bogart's Face* (1977)
- *Beau Geste* – 116

Andrew J. Fenady – *The Secret of Sam Marlow* (1980)
- *Beau Geste* – 151

F. Scott Fitzgerald – *The Last Tycoon* (1940/41)
- Cooper – 137, 162

Richard Ford – *Independence Day* (1995)
- Cooper – 343

William R. Forstchen – *One Second After* (2009)
- Cooper – 49
- *High Noon* – 49

Herb 'Chick' Fowle – *Against All Odds* (1991)
- Cooper – 147
- *Casanova Brown* – 147

Kinky Friedman – *God Bless John Wayne* (1995)
- Cooper – 115, 125, 230
- *High Noon* – 115, 125, 230

Dale Furutani – *The Toyotomi Blades* (1997)
- Cooper – 87
- *High Noon* – 87

Brian Garfield – *Death Wish* (1972)
- Cooper – 142

Romain Gary – *The Ski Bum* (1964)
- Cooper – 42

William Gibson – *The Cobweb* (1954)
- Cooper – 160

William Goldman – *Marathon Man* (1974)
- *For Whom the Bell Tolls* – 76-77

James Grady – *Thunder* (1994)
- *High Noon* – 95

S. A. Griffin – "America Poem" (2003)
- Cooper – 130
- *High Noon* – 130

Martha Grimes – *Belle Ruin* (2005)
- Cooper – 20

Martha Grimes – *The End of the Pier* (1992)
- Cooper – 161-162
- *High Noon* – 161-162

Martha Grimes – *The Five Bells and Bladebone* (1987)
- Cooper – 236
- *High Noon* – 236

Martha Grimes – *The Grave Maurice* (2002)
- Cooper – 45, 146
- *High Noon* – 45, 146

Martha Grimes – *Jerusalem Inn* (1984)
- Cooper – 294
- *High Noon* – 294

Martha Grimes – *The Man with a Load Mischief* (1981)
- Cooper – 37
- *High Noon* – 37

Pete Hamill – *Snow in August* (1997)
- Cooper – 44

Donald Hamilton – *The Terminators* (1975)
- *High Noon* – 77

Thomas Harris – *Red Dragon* (1981)
- *High Noon* – 18

Elizabeth Hay – *Garbo Laughs* (2003)
- Cooper – 102, 116, 166, 225, 255
- *Desire* – 102, 225
- *High Noon* – 22, 116, 166

- *Love in the Afternoon* – 68

Elizabeth Hay – *A Student of Weather* (2001)
- *High Noon* – 360

Jeremiah Healy – "In the Line of Duty" (1988)
- Cooper – 269
- *High Noon* – 269

Jeremiah Healy – *Yesterday's News* (1989)
- Cooper – 141

Judith Ryan Hendricks – *Bread Alone* (2001)
- Cooper – 68
- *Love in the Afternoon* – 68

James Leo Herlihy – *Midnight Cowboy* (1965)
- Cooper – 220

Oscar Hijuelos – *The Fourteen Sisters of Emilio Montez O'Brien* (1993)
- Cooper – 323

Oscar Hijuelos – *A Simple Habana Melody* (2002)
- Cooper – 9, 232, 233, 255

Evan Hunter – *Jack and the Beanstalk* (1984)
- *High Noon* – 54

Greg Iles – *Blood Memory* (2005)
- Cooper – 263

Greg Iles – *Mortal Fear* (1997)
- Cooper – 211

Guillermo Cabrera Infante – *Three Trapped Tigers* (2015)
- Cooper – 411
- *High Noon* – 411

Susan Isaacs – *Red, White & Blue* (1998)
- *High Noon* – 347

Susan Isaacs – *Shining Through* (1988)
- Cooper – 69-70, 246
- *Sergeant York* – 70
- *The Pride of the Yankees* – 246

Joe Jackson – *Leavenworth Train: A Fugitive's Search for Justice in the Vanishing West* **(2001)**
- Cooper – 331
- *Northwest Mounted Police* – 331

Byron Janis, with Maria Cooper Janis. *Chopin and Beyond* **(2010)**
- Cooper – 133, 149, 173-174, 219-220
- *Saratoga Trunk* – 220

Donald Jeffries – *The Unreals* **(2007)**
- Cooper – 37, 38, 51, 55, 331
- *Meet John Doe* – 38

James Jones – *From Here to Eternity* **(1951)**
- Cooper – 518

James Jones – *Some Came Running* **(1957)**
- Cooper – 244-245

Erica Jong – *Any Woman's Blues* **(1990)**
- Cooper – 66
- *High Noon* – 66

Stuart M. Kaminsky – *Bullet for a Star* **(1977)**
- Cooper – 120, 121
- *Meet John Doe* – 120-121

Stuart Kaminsky – *High Midnight* **(1981)**
- Cooper – 11, 14, 16-28, 33-36, 41, 46, 47, 50- 54, 57, 58, 61, 64, 76, 81-87, 90, 92-94, 101, 102, 115, 116, 118-122, 124-143, 145, 150, 160, 174, 176-179
- *Legion of the Condemned* – 25
- *The Virginian* – 86
- *The Cowboy and the Lady* – 121
- *Sergeant York* – 17, 125
- *The Pride of the Yankees* – 17, 19, 24, 87
- *For Whom the Bell Tolls* – 128
- *High Noon* – 63-64, 183-184

Stuart M. Kaminsky – *The Man Who Shot Lewis Vance* (1986)
- *Beau Geste* – 193

Stuart M. Kaminsky – *Retribution* (2001)
- *High Noon* – 166-168

Stuart Kaminsky – *Think Fast, Mr. Peters* (1987)
- Cooper – 18

Stuart M. Kaminsky – *Vengeance* (1999)
- Cooper – 10
- *The Plainsman* – 61

Stuart M. Kaminsky – *Tomorrow Is Another Day* (1995)
- Cooper – 135, 161, 189
- *Sergeant York* – 161
- *The Pride of the Yankees* – 161

Sue Kaufman – *Diary of a Mad Housewife* (1967)
- Cooper – 26

Adam Kennedy – *Just Like Humphrey Bogart* (1978)
- Cooper – 108

Jack Kerouac – *Desolation Angels* (1960)
- Cooper – 268, 298, 304
- *Beau Geste* – 304
- *High Noon* – 298

Jack Kerouac – *On the Road* (1955)
- Cooper – 262

Jean Kerr – *Please Don't Eat the Daisies* (1954)
- Cooper – 127

Stephen King – *Dolores Claiborne* (1993)
- Cooper – 86
- *They Came to Cordura* – 86

Stephen King – *11/22/63* (2011)
- Cooper – 387
- *Love in the Afternoon* – 387

Stephen King – *Insomnia* **(1994)**
- *High Noon* – 97

Stephen King – *The Langoliers* **(1990)**
- Cooper – 79
- *High Noon* – 19-20

Stephen King – *The Regulators* **(1996)**
- Cooper – 256

Barbara Kingsolver – *The Bean Trees* **(1988)**
- *Morocco* – 38
- *Beau Geste* – 38

Laurence Klavan – *The Cutting Room* **(2004)**
- Cooper – 265
- *Meet John Doe* – 265

Arthur Kober – *"Having Wonderful Time"* **(1937)**
- Cooper – 701

Heinz Kohler – *My Name Was Five* **(1979)**
- Cooper – 325
- *High Noon* – 325

Aaron Latham – *Riding with John Wayne* **(2006)**
- Cooper – 45
- *Mr. Deeds Goes to Town* – 22

Richard Laymon – *Endless Night* **(1993)**
- Cooper – 412
- *For Whom the Bell Tolls* – 412

Janet Leigh – *House of Destiny* **(1995)**
- Cooper – 33, 67, 68, 78
- *The Winning of Barbara Worth* – 33,
- *North West Mounted Police* – 68
- *It's a Big Country* – 455

Elmore Leonard – *Be Cool* **(1999)**
- *For Whom the Bell Tolls* – 185

Elmore Leonard – *City Primeval: High Noon in Detroit* **(1980)**
- *High Noon* – 132, 206-207, 333-336

Elmore Leonard – *52 Pick Up* **(1974)**
- Cooper – 230
- *Good Sam* – 230

Elmore Leonard – *The Moonshine War* **(1969)**
- *The Lives of a Bengal Lancer* – 187

Elmore Leonard – *Out of Sight* **(1996)**
- *The Virginian* – 153

Elmore Leonard – *Pronto* **(1993)**
- *Beau Geste* – 169

Elmore Leonard – *Tishomingo Blues* **(2002)**
- *High Noon* – 242

Ira Levin – *Rosemary's Baby* **(1967)**
- Cooper – 42
- *The Fountainhead* – 42

Sophie Littlefield – *A Bad Day for Sorry* **(2009)**
- Cooper – 12
- *High Noon* – 12

Peter Lovesey – *The Summons* **(1995)**
- Cooper – 55
- *High Noon* – 55

Robert Ludlum – *The Bourne Ultimatum* **(1990)**
- *High Noon* – 189

Michael Malone – *Foolscap or, The Stages of Love* **(1991)**
- Cooper – 19, 75, 212

Michael Malone – *The Four Corners of the Sky* **(2009)**
- *Wings* – 41,
- *Make Me a Star* – 97
- *Now and Forever* – 494
- *The Pride of the Yankees* – 301

Michael Malone – *Time's Witness* (2002)
- Cooper – 161
- *Meet John Doe* – 161

John P. Marquand – *Wickford Point* (1939)
- *The Virginian* – 331

Mary McBride – *Say It Again, Sam* (2004)
- Cooper – 8, 9, 22
- *High Noon* – 8

Robert McCammon – "I Scream Man!" (1990)
- Cooper – 125
- *High Noon* – 125

Robert McCammon – *Swan Song* (1987)
- *High Noon* – 43, 923

Horace McCoy – *They Shoot Horses Don't They* (1935)
- Cooper – 77

Sharyn McCrumb – *Lovely in Her Bones* (1985)
- Cooper – 107
- *High Noon* – 107

William P. McGivern – *The Caper of the Golden Bulls* (1966)
- Cooper – 101

Thomas McGuane – *The Cadence of Grass* (2002)
- Cooper – 230

Larry McMurtry – *All My Friends Are Going to Be Strangers* (1972)
- Cooper – 284
- *Distant Drums* – 284-285

Larry McMurtry – *Moving On* (1970)
- Cooper – 540-541, 649-650
- *Vera Cruz* – 540-541

Lartry McMurtry – *Somebody's Darling* (1978)
- Cooper – 88

James A. Michener – *Iberia* (1968)
- Cooper – 56

Keith Miles – *Double Eagle* **(1987)**
- Cooper – 32
- *High Noon* – 32

Linda Lael Miller – *The Legacy* **(1994)**
- Cooper – 193
- *High Noon* – 193

Lynn Ruth Miller – *Starving Hearts* **(2000)**
- Cooper – 141
- *Love in the Afternoon* – 141

Reggie Nadelson – *Red Hot Blues* **(1995)**
- Cooper – 39
- *High Noon* – 39

Stuart Nadler – *Wise Men* **(2013)**
- Cooper – 10
- *High Noon* – 10

Andrew Neiderman – *Curse* **(2000)**
- Cooper – 227, 285
- *High Noon* – 227, 285

Andrew Neiderman – *The Hunted* **(2005)**
- Cooper – 36
- *High Noon* – 36

Tim O'Brien – "The Ghost Soldiers" **(1990)**
- Cooper – 197

Tim O'Brien – "On the Rainy River" **(1990)**
- Cooper – 56

Thomas O'Callaghan – *Bone Thief* **(2006)**
- Cooper – 28
- *High Noon* – 28

Clifford Odets – *Golden Boy* **(1937)**
- Cooper – 266

John O'Hara – "Can I Stay Here?" **(1964)**
- Cooper – 288

John O'Hara – *From the Terrace* (1958)
- Cooper – 957, 959

Marvin Olasky – *Scimitar's Edge* (2006)
- Cooper – 18, 238
- *High Noon* – 18, 238

Michael Palmer – *Political Suicide* (2013)
- Cooper – 63
- *High Noon* – 63

Sara Paretsky – *Tunnel Vision* (1994)
- *High Noon* – 147, 333

Iris Paris – *Once Upon a Chariot* (2008)
- Cooper – 83
- *Along Came Jones* – 83

Robert B. Parker – *Cold Service* (2005)
- *High Noon* – 302

Robert B. Parker – *Double Deuce* (1992)
- *High Noon* – 71

Robert B. Parker – *The Judas Goat* (1978)
- *Beau Geste* – 143

Robert B. Parker – *Mortal Stakes* (1975)
- Cooper – 88
- *High Noon* – 271

James Patterson – *Along Came a Spider* (1992)
- *High Noon* – 215, 492

James Patterson and Howard Roughan – *Sail* (2008)
- Cooper – 349
- *High Noon* – 349

Ralph Peters – *The Devil's Garden* (1998)
- *High Noon* – 87

Harry Mark Petrakis – "Legends of Glory" (2007)
- Cooper – 148
- *High Noon* – 148

Mario Puzo – *The Fourth K* (1990)
- Cooper – 261

Ellery Queen – *Calamity Town* (1942)
- *The Virginian* – 40

Ian Rankin – *Mortal Causes* (1994)
- *High Noon* – 245

Herman Raucher – *Summer of '42* (1971)
- Cooper – 48
- *Pride of the Yankees* – 48

Les Roberts – *Deep Shaker* (1991)
- Cooper – 228
- *Bright Leaf* – 228

Nora Roberts – *High Noon* (2007)
- Cooper – 205, 302-303, 318, 324, 392
- *High Noon* – 1, 159, 205, 302-303, 305, 318, 431

Nora Roberts – *Holding the Dream* (1997)
- Cooper – 309
- *High Noon* – 309

Nora Roberts – *Northern Lights* (2004)
- Cooper – 550, 560
- *High Noon* – 560

Elliott Roosevelt – *Murder in the Red Room* (1992)
- Cooper – 41-44
- *Mr. Deeds Goes to Town* – 41-42

Philip Roth – *Portnoy's Complaint* (1967)
- Cooper – 58

Jacques Roubaud – *The Loop* (1993)
- Cooper – 323
- *Mr. Deeds Goes to Town* – 323
- *Bluebeard's Eighth Wife* – 323
-
-

Rudy Rucker – *Saucer Wisdom* (1999)
- Cooper – 106, 110
- *Ball of Fire* – 106, 110

J. D. Salinger – *The Catcher in the Rye* (1951)
- Cooper – 74

Patrick Samway – *Walker Percy: A Life* (1997)
- Cooper – 49
- *Fighting Caravans* – 49

Lawrence Sanders – *The Sixth Commandment* (1979)
- *High Noon* – 274

Lawrence Sanders – *The Timothy Files* (1987)
- *High Noon* – 66

John Sandford – *Winter Prey* (1993)
- Cooper – 5
- *High Noon* – 5

Lionel R. Saporta – "Gifts" (2006)
- Cooper – 48
- *High Noon* – 48

Budd Schulberg – *The Disenchanted* (1950)
- *Mr. Deeds Goes to Town* – 203

A.D. Scott – *A Small Death in the Great Glen* (2010)
- Cooper – 288
- *High Noon* – 288

Steve Shagan – *Save the Tiger* (1972)
- Cooper – 35
- *For Whom the Bell Tolls* – 35

Sam Shepard – "Gary Cooper, Or the Landscape" (1994)
- Cooper – 178-180

Sam Shepard – *Motel Chronicles* (1982)
- Cooper – 14
- *Vera Cruz* – 14, 86

Martha Sherrill – *My Last Movie Star* (2002)
- Cooper – 249

Rachel Shukert – *Love Me* (2014)
- Cooper – 199

Alan Sillitoe – "The Decline and Fall of Frankie Buller" (1959)
- Cooper – 175
- *The Lives of a Bengal Lancer* – 160
- *Saratoga Trunk* – 175

Christina Skye – *Going Overboard* (2001)
- Cooper – 138
- *High Noon* – 138

Bella & Samuel Spewack – *Boy Meets Girl* (1936)
- Cooper – 562
- *The Lives of a Bengal Lancer* – 542

Bernard Spiro – *The Other War: Letters from a GI in India in 1944 & 1945* (2001)
- Cooper – 126, 127, 180
- *Casanova Brown* – 126

Patricia Sprinkle – *Who Left That Body in the Rain?* (2002)
- Cooper – 171
- *High Noon* – 171

Laurie Stevens – *The Dark Before Dawn* (2011)
- Cooper – 289
- *High Noon* – 289

Robert K. Tanenbaum – *Absolute Rage* (2002)
- Cooper – 206, 310

Robert K. Tanenbaum – *Betrayed* (2010)
- Cooper – 31
- *High Noon* – 31, 76

Robert K. Tanenbaum – *Depraved Indifference* (1989)
- Cooper – 231
- *High Noon* – 231

Robert Traver – *Anatomy of a Murder* (1958)
- *High Noon* – 56

Adriana Trigiani – *Big Cherry Holler* (2001)
- Cooper – 258

Kathy Hogan Trocheck – *Every Crooked Nanny* (1992)
- Cooper – 280
- *Friendly Persuasion* – 280

Scott Turow – *The Burden of Proof* (1990)
- Cooper – 104

John Updike – *Brazil* (1994)
- Cooper – 101

John Updike – *In the Beauty of the Lilies* (1996)
- Cooper – 318, 319, 320, 321, 331
- *It* – 182
- *Mr. Deeds Goes to Town* – 342
- *Wings* – 222
- *High Noon* – 331

John Updike – *Rabbit at Rest* (1990)
- Cooper – 106

Gore Vidal – *Myra Breckinridge* (1968)
- Cooper – 62, 86
- *Lives of a Bengal Lancer* – 31
- *Sergeant York* – 62

Elaine Viets – *Murder Between the Covers* (2003)
- Cooper – 237-238
- *High Noon* – 237

Kurt Vonnegut, Jr. – *Breakfast of Champions* (1973)
- Cooper – 128

Joseph Wambaugh – *The Secrets of Harry Bright* (1985)
- Cooper – 156
- *Sergeant York* – 156

John Weisman – *SOAR* (2003)
- Cooper – 183
- *Sergeant York* – 183

Nathanael West – *The Day of the Locust* (1939)
- Cooper – 164

Donald E. Westlake – *The Hot Rock* (1970)
- Cooper – 111
- *Task Force* – 111

James Neel White – *I Was a P-51 Fighter Pilot in WWII* (2003)
- Cooper
- *It* – 15
- *Lilac Time* – 25

Isabel Wolff – *Out of the Blue* (2003)
- Cooper – 144
- *High Noon* – 144

Stuart Woods – *L.A. Times* (1993)
- *For Whom the Bell Tolls* – 15

Herman Wouk – *Marjorie Morningstar* (1955)
- Cooper – 362

Herman Wouk – *The Winds of War* (1971)
- Cooper – 133, 135, 137, 183

IV. CREDITS OF COOPER'S FILMS <u>REFERENCED</u>

1. *The Winning of Barbara Worth* (Goldwyn/UA, 1926). Sc. Frances Marion from the novel by Harold Bell Wright. Dir. Henry King. Phot. George Barnes and Gregg Toland. Music by Ted Henkel. Cast: Ronald Colman (Willard Holmes), Vilma Banky (Barbara Worth), Charles Lane (Jefferson Worth), GC (Abe Lee), Paul McAllister (The Seer), E.J. Ratcliffe (James Greenfield), Clyde Cooke (Tex).

2. *It* (Paramount, 1927). Sc. Hope Loring and Louis D. Lighton from Elinor Glyn's adaptation of her own novel. Dir. Clarence Barger. Phot. H. Kinley Martin. Cast: Clara Bow (Betty Lou), Antonio Moreno (Cyrus Waltham), William Austin (Monty), Jacqueline Gadsdon (Adele Van Norman), Julia Swayne Gordon (Mrs. Van Norman), Priscilla Bonner (Molly), GC (Reporter).

3. *Wings* (Paramount, 1927). Sc. Hope Loring and Louis D. Lighton from a story by John Monk Saunders. Dir. William A. Wellman. Phot. Harry

Perry. Music by John S. Zamecnik. Cast: Clara Bow (Mary Preston), Charles "Buddy" Rogers (Jack Powell), Richard Arlen (David Armstrong), Jobyna Ralston (Sylvia Lewis), El Brendel (Herman Schwimpf), Henry B. Walthall (Mr. Armstrong), GC (Pilot).

4. *The Legion of the Condemned* (Paramount, 1928). Sc. John Monk Saunders and Jean De Limur from a story by Saunders. Dir. William A. Wellman. Phot. Henry Gerrard. Cast: GC (Gale Price), Fay Wray (Christine Charteris), Barry Norton (Byron Dashwood), Lane Chandler (Charles Holabird), Francis McDonald (Gouzalo Vasques), Albert Conti (Von Hohendorff), Charlotte Bird (Tart in Café).

5. *Lilac Time* (First National, 1928). Sc. Carey Wilson from Willis Goldbeck and Adela Rogers St. Johns' adaptation of the play by Jane Cowl and Jane Murfin and the book by Guy Fowler. Dir, George Fitzmaurice. Phot. Sid Hickox. Music by Nathaniel Shilkret. Cast: Colleen Moore (Jeannine Berthelot), GC (Captain Philip Blythe), Burr McIntosh (General Blythe), Eugenie Besserer (Madame Berthelot), Kathryn McGuire (Lady Iris Rankin), Cleve Moore (Flight Commander), George Cooper (Sergeant Hawkins).

6. *Betrayal* (Paramount, 1929), Sc. Hans Kraly and Leo Birinsky from a story by Victor Schertzinger and Nicholas Soussanin. Dir. Lewis Milestone. Phot. Henry Gerrard. Music by John S. Zamecnik. Cast: Emil Jannings (Poldi Moser), Esther Ralston (Vroni), GC (André Frey), Jada Welles (Hans), Douglas Haig (Peter), Bodil Rosing (André's mother).

7. *The Virginian* (Paramount, 1929). Sc. Howard Estabrook from the novel by Owen Wister and the play by Owen Wister and Kirk LaShelle. Dir. Victor Fleming. Phot. J. Roy Hunt and Edward Cronjager. Cast: GC (The Virginian), Walter Huston (Trampas), Richard Arlen (Steve), Mary Brian (Molly Wood), Chester Conklin (Uncle Hughey), Eugene Pallette (Honey Wiggin), E.H. Calvert (Judge Henry).

8. *The Texan* (Paramount, 1930). Sc. Daniel L. Rubin from the short story "A Double-Dyed Deceiver" by O. Henry. Dir. John Cromwell. Phot. Victor Milner. Cast: GC (Enrique "Quico," the Llano Kid), Fay Wray (Consuelo), Emma Dunn (Señora Ibarra), Oscar Apfel (Thacker), James Marcus (John Brown), Donald Reed (Nick Ibarra), Soledad Jimenez (The Duenna).

9. *Morocco* (Paramount, 1930). Sc. Jules Furthman from the novel *Amy Jolly* by Benno Vigny. Dir. Josef von Sternberg. Phot. Lee Garmes. Music by Karl Hajos. Cast: GC (Tom Brown), Marlene Dietrich (Amy Jolly), Adolphe Menjou (Kennington), Ullrich Haupt (Adjutant Caesar), Juliette Compton (Anna Dolores), Francis McDonald (Corporal Tatoche), Albert Conti (Colonel Quinneveries).

10. *Fighting Caravans* (Paramount, 1931). Sc. Edward G. Paramore, Jr., Keene Thompson and Agnes Brand Leahy from the novel by Zane Grey. Dir. Otto Brower and David Burton. Phot. Lee Garmes and Henry Gerrard. Cast: GC (Clint Belmet), Lily Damita (Felice), Ernest Torrence (Bill Jackson), Fred Kohler (Lee Murdock), Tully Marshall (Jim Bridger), Eugene Pallette (Seth Higgins), Roy Stewart (Couch).

11. *Make Me a Star* (Paramount, 1932). Sc. Sam Wintz and Walter De Leon (adaptation by Arthur Kober) from the book *Merton of the Movies* by Harry Leon Wilson and the play by George S. Kaufman and Moss Hart. Dir. William Beaudine. Phot. Allen Siegler. Cast: Stuart Erwin (Merton Gill), Joan Blondell ("Flips" Montague), ZaSu Pitts (Mrs. Scudder), Ben Turpin (Ben), Charles Sellon (Mr. Gashwiler), Florence Roberts (Mrs. Gashwiler), GC (himself).

12. *The Devil and the Deep* (Paramount, 1932). Sc. Benn Levy from a story by Harry Hervey. Dir. Marion Gering. Phot. Charles Lang. Cast: GC (Lieutenant Sempter), Tallulah Bankhead (Pauline Sturm), Charles Laughton (Commander Charles Sturm), Cary Grant (Lieutenant Jaeckel), Paul Porcasi ((Hassan), Juliette Compton (Mrs. Planet), Henry Kolker (Hutton).

13. *Now and Forever* (Paramount, 1934). Sc. Vincent Lawrence and Sylvia Thalberg from an original story, "Honor Bright," by Jack Kirkland and Melville Baker. Dir. Henry Hathaway. Phot. Harry Fischbeck. Cast: GC (Jerry Day), Carole Lombard (Toni Carstairs), Shirley Temple (Penelope Day), Sir Guy Standing (Felix Evans), Charlotte Granville (Mrs. J. H. P. Crane), Henry Kolker (Mr. Clark).

14. *The Lives of a Bengal Lancer* (Paramount, 1935). Sc. John L. Balderston, Waldemar Young and Achmed Abdullah from a novel by Major Francis Yeats-Brown. Dir. Henry Hathaway. Phot. Charles Lang, Jr. Music by Milan Roder. Cast: GC (Lieutenant McGregor), Franchot Tone (Lieutenant Fortesque), Richard Cromwell (Lieutenant Stone), Sir Guy Standing (Colonel Stone), Douglass Dumbrille (Mohammed Khan), C. Aubrey Smith (Major Hamilton), Kathleen Burke (Tania Volkanskaya).

15. *Peter Ibbetson* (Paramount, 1935). Sc. Vincent Lawrence and Waldemar Young from the novel by George DuMaurier and the play by John Nathaniel Raphael. Dir. Henry Hathaway. Phot. Charles Lang, Jr. Music by Ernst Toch. Cast: GC (Peter Ibbetson), Ann Harding (Mary, Duchess of Towers), John Halliday (Duke of Towers), Ida Lupino (Agnes), Virginia Weidler (Mimsey), Douglass Dumbrille (Colonel Forsythe), Dickie Moore (Gogo).

16. *Desire* (Paramount, 1936). Sc. Edwin Justus Mayer, Waldemar Young and Samuel Hoffenstein from a comedy by Hans Szekely and R. A. Stemmle. Dir. Frank Borzage. Phot. Charles Lang, Jr. Music by Frederick Hollander. Cast: Marlene Dietrich (Madeleine de Beaupré), GC (Tom Bradley), John Halliday (Carlos Margoli), William Frawley (Mr. Gibson), Ernest Cossart (Aristide Duval), Akim Tamiroff (Police Official), Alan Mowbray (Dr. Edouard Pauquet).

17. *Mr. Deeds Goes to Town* (Columbia, 1936). Sc. Robert Riskin from the story "Opera Hat" by Clarence Budington Kelland. Dir. Frank Capra.

Phot. Joseph Walker. Music by Howard Jackson. Cast: GC (Longfellow Deeds), Jean Arthur (Babe Bennett), Lionel Stander (Cornelius Cobb), George Bancroft (McWade), Douglass Dumbrille (John Cedar), Raymond Walburn (Walter), H.B. Warner (Judge Walker).

18. *The Plainsman* (Paramount, 1936). Sc. Waldemar Young, Harold Lamb and Lynn Riggs based on data from the stories "Wild Bill Hickok" by Frank J. Wilstach and "The Prince of the Pistoleers" by Courtney Ryley Cooper and Grover Jones (adaptation by Jeanie MacPherson). Dir. Cecil B. DeMille. Phot. Victo Milner and George Robinson. Music by George Antheil. Cast: GC (Wild Bill Hickok), Jean Arthur (Calamity Jane), James Ellison (Buffalo Bill Cody), Helen Burgess (Louisa Cody), Porter Hall (Jack McCall), Charles Bickford (John Latimer), Anthony Quinn (Indian Warrior).

19. *Bluebeard's Eighth Wife* (Paramount, 1938). Sc. Charles Brackett and Billy Wilder from a play by Alfred Savoir (adaptation by Charlton Andrews). Dir. Ernst Lubitsch. Phot. Leo Tover. Music by Frederick Hollander and Werner R. Heymann. Cast: Claudette Colbert (Nicole de Loiselle), GC (Michael Brandon), Edward Everett Horton (The Marquis de Loiselle), David Niven (Albert de Regnier), Elizabeth Patterson (Aunt Hedwige), Herman Bing (Monsieur Pepinard), Warren Hymer (Kid Mulligan).

20. *The Adventures of Marco Polo* (Goldwyn/UA, 1938). Sc. Robert E. Sherwood from a story by N.A. Pogson. Dir. Archie L. Mayo. Phot. Rudolph Mate. Music by Hugo Friedhofer. Cast: GC (Marco Polo), Sigrid Gurie (Princess Kukachin), Ernest Truex (Binguccio), Binnie Barnes (Nazama), Alan Hale (Kaidu), Basil Rathbone (Ahmed), Lana Turner (Nazama's maid).

21. *The Cowboy and the Lady* (Goldwyn/UA, 1938). Sc. S.N. Behrman and Sonya Levien from a story by Leo McCarey and Frank R. Adams. Dir. H.C. Potter. Phot. Gregg Toland. Music by Alfred Newman. Cast: GC (Stretch), Merle Oberon (Mary Smith), Walter Brennan (Sugar), Patsy Kelly

(Katie Callahan), Harry Davenport (Uncle Hannibal Smith), Mabel Todd (Elly), Fuzzy Knight (Buzz).

22. *Beau Geste* (Paramount, 1939). Sc. Robert Carson from the novel by Percival Christopher Wren. Dir. William A. Wellman. Phot. Theodor Sparkuhl and Archie Stout. Music by Alfred Newman. Cast: GC (Beau Geste), Ray Milland (John Geste), Robert Preston (Digby Geste), Brian Donlevy (Sergeant Markoff), Susan Hayward (Isobel Rivers), J. Carrol Naish (Rasinoff), Donald O'Connor (Beau at twelve).

23. *North West Mounted Police* (Paramount, 1940). Sc. Alan LeMay, Jesse Lasky, Jr., and C. Gardner Sullivan based on "Royal Canadian Mounted Police" by R.C. Fetherston-Haugh. Dir. Cecil B. DeMille. Phot. Victor Milner and W. Howard Greene. Music by Victor Young. Cast: GC (Dusty Rivers), Madeleine Carroll (April Logan), Paulette Goddard (Louvette Corbeau), Preston Foster (Sergeant Jim Brett), Robert Preston (Constable Ronnie Logan), George Bancroft (Jacques Corbeau), Akim Tamiroff (Don Duroc).

24. *Meet John Doe* (WB, 1941). Sc. Robert Riskin from a story by Robert Presnell and Richard Connell. Dir. Frank Capra. Phot. George Barnes. Music by Dimitri Tiomkin. Cast: GC (Long John Willoughby/John Doe), Barbara Stanwyck (Ann Mitchell), Edward Arnold (D.B. Norton), Walter Brennan (Colonel), James Gleason (Henry Connell), Spring Byington (Mrs. Mitchell), Gene Lockhart (Mayor Lovett).

25. *Sergeant York* (WB, 1941). Sc. Harry Chandlee, Howard Koch, Abem Finkel and John Huston from the diary of Sergeant York as edited by Tom Skeyhill. Dir. Howard Hawks. Phot. Sol Polito and Arthur Edeson. Music by Max Steiner. Cast: GC (Alvin C. York), Joan Leslie (Gracie Williams), Walter Brennan (Pastor Rosier Pile), Margaret Wycherly (Mother York), George Tobias (Michael T. "Pusher" Ross), Ward Bond (Ike Botkin), Stanley Ridges (Major Buxton).

26. *Ball of Fire* (Goldwyn/RKO, 1941). Sc. Charles Brackett and Billy Wilder from an original story, "From A to Z," by Thomas Monroe and Billy Wilder. Dir. Howard Hawks. Phot. Gregg Toland. Music by Alfred Newman. Cast: GC (Professor Bertram Potts), Barbara Stanwyck (Sugarpuss O'Shea), Oscar Homolka (Professor Gurkakoff), Henry Travers (Professor Jerome), S. Z. Sakall (Professor Magenbruch), Tully Marshall (Professor Robinson), Leonid Kinskey (Professor Quintana).

27. *The Pride of the Yankees* (RKO, 1942). Sc. Jo Swerling and Herman J. Mankiewicz from a story by Paul Gallico. Dir. Sam Wood. Phot. Rudolph Mate. Music by Leigh Harline. Cast: GC (Lou Gehrig), Teresa Wright (Eleanor Gehrig), Walter Brennan (Sam Blake0, Dan Duryea (Hank Hanneman), Esla Janssen (Mom Gehrig), Ludwig Stossel (Pop Gehrig), Babe Ruth (Himself).

28. *For Whom the Bell Tolls* (Paramount, 1943). Sc. Dudley Nichols from the novel by Ernest Hemingway. Dir. Sam Wood. Phot. Ray Rennahan. Music by Victor Young. Cast: GC (Robert Jordan), Ingrid Bergman (Maria), Katina Paxinou (Pilar), Akim Tamiroff (Pablo), Arturo de Cordova (Agustin), Vladimir Sokoloff (Anselmo), Fortunio Bonanova (Fernando).

29. *Casanova Brown* (Christie/International Pictures/RKO, 1944). Sc. Nunnally Johnson from the play *The Little Accident* by Floyd Dell and Thomas Mitchell. Dir. Sam Wood. Phot. John Seitz. Music by Arthur Lange. Cast: GC (Casanova Brown), Teresa Wright (Isabel Drury), Frank Morgan (Mr. Ferris), Anita Louise (Madge Ferris), Patricia Collinge (Mrs. Drury), Jill Esmond (Dr. Zernerke), Emory Parnell (Frank).

30. *Saratoga Trunk* (WB, 1945). Sc. Casey Robinson from the novel by Edna Ferber. Dir. Sam Wood. Phot. Ernest Haller. Music by Max Steiner. Cast: GC (Colonel Clint Maroon), Ingrid Bergman (Clio Dulaine), Flora Robson (Angelique Buiton), Jerry Austin (Cupidon), John Warburton

(Bartholomew Van Steed), Florence Bates (Mrs. Coventry Bellop), Curt Bois (Augustin Haussy).

31. *Along Came Jones* (Cinema Artists/International Pictures/RKO, 1945). Sc. Nunnally Johnson from the novel by Alan LeMay. Dir. Stuart Heisler. Phot. Milton Krasner. Music by Arthur Lange, Hugo Friedhofer and Charles Maxwell. Cast: GC (Melody Jones), Loretta Young (Cherry de Longpre), William Demarest (George Fury), Dan Duryea (Monte Jarrad), Frank Sully (Cherry's Brother), Russell Simpson (Pop de Longpre), Arthur Loft (Sheriff).

32. *Good Sam* (RKO, 1948). Sc. Ken Englund from a story by Leo McCarey and John Klorer. Dir. Leo McCarey. Phot. George Barnes. Music by Robert Emmett Dolan. Cast: GC (Sam Clayton), Ann Sheridan (Lu Clayton), Ray Collins (Reverend Daniels), Joan Lorring (Shirley Mae), Edmund Lowe (H.C. Borden), Louise Beavers (Chloe), Ruth Roman (Ruthie).

33. *The Fountainhead* (WB, 1948). Sc. Ayn Rand from her novel. Dir. King Vidor. Phot. Robert Burks. Music by Max Steiner. Cast: GC (Howard Roark), Patricia Neal (Dominique), Raymond Massey (Gail Wynand), Kent Smith (Peter Keating), Henry Hull (Henry Cameron), Ray Collins (Enright), Moroni Olsen (Chairman).

34. *Task Force* (WB, 1948). Sc. Delmer Daves. Dir. Delmer Daves. Phot. Robert Burks and Wilfrid M. Cline. Music by Franz Wazman. Cast: GC (Jonathan L. Scott), Jane Wyatt (Mary Morgan), Wayne Morris (McKinney), Walter Brennan (Pete Richard), Julie London (Barbara McKinney), Bruce Bennett (McCluskey), Jack Holt (Reeves).

35. *Bright Leaf* (WB, 1950). Sc. Ranald MacDougall from the novel by Foster Fitz-Simons. Dir. Michael Curtiz. Phot. Karl Freund. Music by Victor Young. Cast: GC (Brant Royle), Lauren Bacall (Sonia Kovac),

Patricia Neal (Margaret Jane), Jack Carson (Chris Malley), Donald Crisp (Major Singleton), Gladys George (Rose), Jeff Corey (John Barton).

36. *It's a Big Country* (MGM, 1951). Sc. Dorothy Kingsley, William Ludwig, Helen Deutsch, George Wells, Allen Rivkin, Dore Schary and Isobel Lennart. Dir. Clarence Brown, Richard Thorpe, John Sturges, Charles Vidor, Don Weis, William A. Wellman and Don Hartman. Phot. John Alton, Ray June, William Mellor and Joseph Ruttenberg. Musical Supervision by Johnny Green. Cast: GC (Texas), Fredric March (Papa Esposito), Gene Kelly (Icarus Xenophon), Ethel Barrymore (Mrs. Brian Patrick Riordan), William Powell (Professor), Janet Leigh (Rosa Szabo), Van Johnson (Adam Burch).

37. *Distant Drums* (WB, 1951). Sc. Niven Busch and Martin Rackin from a story by Busch. Dir. Raoul Walsh. Phot. Sid Hickox. Music by Max Steiner. Cast: GC (Captain Quincy Wyatt), Mari Aldon (Judy Beckett), Richard Webb (Lieutenant Richard Tufts), Arthur Hunnicutt (Monk), Ray Teal (Private Mohair), Robert Barrat (General Zachary Taylor), Clancy Cooper (Sergeant Shane).

38. *High Noon* (Stanley Kramer/UA, 1952). Sc. Carl Foreman from the short story "The Tin Star" by John M. Cunningham. Phot. Floyd Crosby. Music by Dimitri Tiomkin. Cast: GC (Marshal Will Kane), Grace Kelly (Amy Fowler Kane), Katy Jurado (Helen Ramirez), Lloyd Bridges (Harvey Pell), Thomas Mitchell (Jonas Henderson), Otto Kruger (Percy Mettrick), Lon Chaney, Jr. (Martin Howe).

39. *Vera Cruz* (Hecht-Lancaster/UA, 1954). Sc. James R. Webb and Roland Kibbee from a story by Borden Chase. Dir. Robert Aldrich. Phot. Ernest Laszlo. Music by Hugo Friedhofer. Cast: GC (Benjamin Trane), Burt Lancaster (Joe Erin), Sarita Montiel (Nina), Denise Darcel (Countess Marie Duvarre), Cesar Romero (Marquis de Labordere), Ernest Borgnine (Donnegan), George Macready (Emperor Maximilian).

40. *Friendly Persuasion* (Wyler/Allied Artists, 1956). Sc. From the novel by Jessamyn West. Dir. William Wyler. Phot. Ellsworth Fredricks. Music by Dimitri Tiomkin. Cast: GC (Jess Birdwell), Dorothy McGuire (Eliza Birdwell), Marjorie Main (Widow Hudspeth), Anthony Perkins (Josh Birdwell), Richard Eyer (Little Jess), Phyllis Love (Mattie Birdwell), Robert Middleton (Sam Jordan).

41. *Love in the Afternoon* (AA, 1957). Sc. Billy Wilder and I.A.L. Diamond from the novel *Ariane* by Claude Anet. Dir. Billy Wilder. Phot. William Mellor. Musical Adaptation by Franz Waxman. Cast: GC (Frank Flannagan), Audrey Hepburn (Ariane Chavasse), Maurice Chevalier (Claude Chavasse), John McGiver (Monsieur X), Lise Bourdin (Madame X), Bonifas (Commissioner of Police), Audrey Wilder (Brunette).

42. *Man of the West* (Ashton/Mirisch/UA, 1958). Sc. Reginald Rose from the novel by Will C. Brown. Dir. Anthony Mann. Phot. Ernest Haller. Music by Leigh Harline. Cast: GC (Link Jones), Julie London (Billie Ellis), Lee J. Cobb (Dock Tobin), Arthur O'Connell (Sam Beasley), Jack Lord (Coaley), John Dehner (Claude), Royal Dano (Trout).

43. *They Came to Cordura* (Goetz-Baroda/Columbia, 1959). Sc. Ivan Moffat and Robert Rossen from the novel by Glendon Swarthout. Dir. Robert Rossen. Phot. Burnett Guffey. Music by Elie Siegmeister. Cast: GC (Major Thomas Thorn), Rita Hayworth (Adelaide Geary), Van Heflin (Sergeant John Chawk), Tab Hunter (Lieutenant William Fowler), Richard Conte (Corporal Milo Trubee), Michael Callan (Private Aubrey Hetherington), Dick York (Private Renziehausen).

44. *The Naked Edge* (Pennebaker-Baroda/UA, 1961). Sc. Joseph Stefano from the novel *First Train to Babylon* by Max Ehrlich. Dir. Michael Anderson. Phot. Edwin Hillier. Music by William Alwyn. Cast: GC (George Radcliffe), Deborah Kerr (Martha Radcliffe), Eric Portman (Jeremy Clay),

Diane Cilento (Mrs. Heath), Hermione Gingold (Lilly Harris), Peter Cushing (Mr. Wrack), Michael Wilding (Morris Brooke).

V. COOPER'S MONOGRAPHIC BIBLIOGRAPHY (BOOKS ONLY)

Arce, Hector. *Gary Cooper: An Intimate Biography*. New York: Bantam, 1980.

Barahona, Fernando Alonso. *Gary Cooper*. Barcelona: Royal Books, 1994.

Bertet, Paloma, et al. *Gary Cooper*. Madrid: Rueda J.M., 2003.

Boyer, G. Bruce, and Maria Cooper Janis. *Gary Cooper: Enduring Style*. Brooklyn, NY: PowerHouse Books, 2011.

Carpozi, Jr., George. *The Gary Cooper Story*. New Rochelle, N.Y.: Arlington House, 1970.

Chardair, Nichols. *Gary Cooper*. Paris: Balland, 1981.

Dickens, Homer. *The Films of Gary Cooper*. New York: The Citadel Press, 1970.

Escoube, Lucienne. *Gary Cooper, le cavalier de l'ouest*. Paris: Éditions du Cerf, 1965.

Ford, Charles. *Gary Cooper*. Paris: Jean-Jacques Pauvert, 1963.

Gehman, Richard. *The Tall American: The Story of Gary Cooper*. New York: Hawthorn Books, 1963.

Hamann, G. D. *Gary Cooper in the 30s*. Hollywood, CA: Filming Today Press, 1996.

Janis, Maria Cooper. *Gary Cooper Off Camera: A Daughter Remembers*. New York: Harry N. Abrams, 1999.

Jordan, René. *Gary Cooper*. New York: Pyramid Communications, 1974.

Kaminsky, Stuart M. *Coop: The Life and Legend of Gary Cooper*. New York: St. Martin's Press, 1980.

Kobal, John, ed. *Legends: Gary Cooper*. Boston: Little, Brown, 1985.

Meyers, Jeffrey. *Gary Cooper: American Hero*. New York: William Morrow, 1998.

Rivère, Isabelle, Pierre H. Verlhac. *Gary Cooper: Bilder eines Lebens*. Leipzig: Henschel, 2010.

Schickel, Richard (Kobal Collection). *Gary Cooper*. Boston: Little, Brown, 1985.

Swindell, Larry. *The Last Hero: A Biography of Gary Cooper*. Garden City, N.Y.: Doubleday, 1980.

Thomson, David. *Gary Cooper*. New York: Faber and Faber. 2010.

Part Three
CLARK GABLE

Clark Gable in a publicity shot.

Born: William Clark Gable; February 1, 1901; Cadiz, Ohio

Died: November 16, 1960; Los Angeles, California

Spouses: Josephine Dillon (1924-1930, divorced); Maria Franklin Gable (1931-1939, divorced); Carole Lombard (1939-1942, her death); Sylvia Ashley (1949-1952, divorced); Kay Williams (1955-his death; one child: John Clark)

Academy Awards: It Happened One Night (1934)

Academy Award Nominations: Mutiny on the Bounty (1935), *Gone with the Wind* (1939)

Golden Globe Nominations: Teacher's Pet (1958), *But Not for Me* (1959)

I. REFERENCES TO GABLE'S FILMS

Just like in the other parts of the book, this section is arranged according to the chronology of the films, and—within the film entries—according to the chronology of the references, with all quotations by one author presented in an uninterrupted sequence. The only exception is the entry on *Gone with the Wind*, where the references are arranged first according to the quoted lines that they include, and then according to the chronology of the references.

The Painted Desert **(1931).** This absolutely forgotten western, directed by Howard Higgin and starring William Boyd, Helen Twelvetrees and William Farnum, is referenced in Michael B. Druxman's *Gable: A One-Person Play in Two Acts* (1984). This is what the only character of the play, Clark Gable himself, has to say about the film:

I didn't know the first thing about riding. She sent me out to the Griffith Park Riding Academy for three weeks of lessons. I learned fast.

The picture was ***The Painted Desert*** with **William Boyd** in his pre-Hopalong Cassidy days. I was the lead heavy.

You didn't see it?

Thank God! [pp. 25-26]

A Free Soul **(1931).** Directed by Clarence Brown and co-starring Norma Shearer and Lionel Barrymore, this romantic crime drama is referenced in several works. In Michael B. Druxman's *Gable* (1984), a commentary on the film is naturally provided by Gable himself, the only character of the play:

> **Norman Shearer,** being married to Irving Thalberg, was the "queen" of the Metro lot. All the best scripts went to her first. In 1931, I was chosen to appear with her, **Lionel Barrymore** and **Leslie Howard** in an exciting little picture called *A Freel Soul*. I played a rather unsavory character . . . **Ace Wilfong**.
> (*Crosses R: takes 1020s style dinner jacket and bow tie from rack and puts them on.*)
> Nobody in the movie liked poor **Ace**. **Barrymore** said to him:
> (*Imitates* **Barrymore**.)
> "**The only time I hate democracy is when one of you mongrels forget where you belong.**"
>
> Norma even had a better line. "**I found out that swine should travel with swine.**"

True, **Ace** was a gangster . . . mixed up into everything from opium to white slavery. But, is that any reason for those high society folk not to invite me over to dinner?

Norma's character sure as hell spent a lot of time . . . "visiting my rooms."
(*Plays scene with Shearer.*)
"You gotta get over this idea you're doing me a big favor. You're crazy about me and you know it. You came here because you liked it. Same as me."

Then, **Thalberg** had me shove her. Not too hard. Just enough to plop her down on the sofa.

Irving figured that move would turn the audience totally against me, and give her all the sympathy.
(*Pantomimes shoving Shearer onto sofa.*)
"You take it and like it! You're through! You're mine and I want you. From now on, you listen to me. We get married in the morning. . . . You look good to me."

Next scene, **Leslie Howard** walks in and shoots me.

I may have been dead, but my fan mail skyrocketed. The women loved the way I roughed-up Shearer. John Barrymore compared me to Valentino . . . but with Jack Dempsey's body [pp. 27-28].

An informative reference to the film, and a couple of names behind the story, can be found in George Baxt's novel *The Marlene Dietrich Murder Case* (1993):

Marlene turned and was happy to see her good friend Adela Rogers St. John. Adela was just about the best chronicler of life in Hollywood, and magazines across the world paid handsomely for her services. Her father had been the notorious and sadly alcoholic criminal lawyer Earl Rogers. But when sober, he was a genius in the courtroom. *A Freel Soul*, which starred **Norma Shearer** and **Lionel Barrymore,** was based on Adela and her father and made a star of **Clark Gable** as the sadistic gangster who slapped **Miss Shearer** around [p. 141].

Clark Gable as Ace Wilfong and Norma Shearer as Jan Ashe in a scene from Clarence Brown's *A Free Soul* (1931).

The same information, in a somewhat different manner, is provided by Baxt in another of his Hollywood novels, *The Humphrey Bogart Murder Case* (1995):

> "That figures," said Bogart. Miss St. Johns was Hollywood's most respected, most prolific dispenser of news and gossip. Even the major columnists deferred to her. Her father had been the notorious, hard drinking criminal lawyer Earl St. John. Adela fashioned a story about herself and her father into ***A Free Soul****,* starring **Norma Shearer** and **Lionel Barrymore** and a young **Clark Gable** whose impact as a sadistic gangster made him an "overnight" success after seven years of struggles [pp. 56-57].

An extensive reference to the film and its stars appears in Adriana Trigiani's *The Queen of the Big Time* (2004), an epic novel set in Pennsylvania, in a scene which turns out to be much more than just a movie date. The characters are Nella Castelluca (the narrator) and Franco Zollerano:

> On the way to Easton to see the new **Norma Shearer** picture, ***A Freel Soul***, I tell Franco Chettie's news. He is happy for them, but doesn't say much. I think his reaction is odd. Maybe he's angry with me for talking about him with Chettie, and maybe my mention of Steckel's embarrassed him. He probably *was* getting his watch fixed [p. 177].
>
> The story of ***A Freel Soul*** is dark and complex. **Clark Gable** plays a gangster. **Lionel Barrymore** is the lawyer who gets him off a rap. **Norma Shearer** plays **Lionel**'s daughter, a flapper who falls for **Clark Gable**. The father, who's a lush, is bereft when his daughter goes for a gangster.
>
> "Get ready. This is the best scene," Franco whispers.
>
> "Have you already seen it?" I whisper back.

He nods that he has. That's odd. He came all the way to Easton to see the show and now he's back? Who did he see it with the first time, and why would he see it again?

Clark Gable is telling **Norma Shearer** in no uncertain terms that she is a woman; she resists him but then tells him that she loves him and that nothing will keep them apart. Franco reaches to hold my hand. He threads his fingers through mine. Then I feel something cold on my ring finger. He has slid an engagement ring onto my hand! I look down at the emerald-cut diamond and a squeal with delight [p. 178].

***Susan Lenox: Her Rise and Fall* (1931).** In this relatively rewarding melodrama directed by Robert Z. Leonard, Clark Gable is cast as Rodney Spencer, opposite Greta Garbo as the titular protagonist and Jean Hersholt as Karl Ohlin. The film is briefly mentioned in George Baxt's mystery *The Greta Garbo Murder Case* (1992), in a conversation between Garbo, Peter Lorre and screenwriter Salka Viertel about the cast of the star's possibly new (fictitious) project, *Joan the Magnificent*, to be directed by Erich von Stroheim:

> "There's a wonderful bunch lined up for the Inquisitors." Lorre had regained their attention.
> "Boris Karloff is playing the chief inquisitor."
> "Oh good, good, that is very good." Salka nodded her approval as Garbo continued to speak. "The industry has never given him a chance to show what a truly fine actor he really is. Who else?"
> **"Jean Hersholt."**
> "Also good. We were together in **Susan Lenox**. He's good to work with. He isn't selfish. He gives."
> "Victor Jory."

"Another one misused by the industry. It's all very impressive. Still..."

Lorre said gravely, "Greta, sit on your doubts" [p. 17].

Hell Divers **(1931).** Directed by George W. Hill and starring Gable, Wallace Beery, Conrad Nagel, Marjorie Rambeau and Dorothy Jordan, this fairly successful aviation drama is referenced (with an incorrect title), along with two other Gable films, in George Baxt's *The Clark Gable & Carole Lombard Murder Case* (1997), in a narrator's passage describing the current political situation in the world:

> Poland had fallen to the Nazis, and France, it was predicted, was next in line despite their supposedly impenetrable Maginot Line, which one American general likened to a tinker toy construction. Carole worried about **Clark**. Though he was almost forty, she knew he wouldn't resist the lure of the air force and would enlist at the earliest possible moment should America be forced into the war. He had already been involved in several wars, the Civil War in ***Gone with the Wind***, the World War in ***Hell Below***, Chinese pirates in ***China Seas***, to name the more prominent ones. She'd think by now he'd had enough of war. She looked at **Gable** with an expression reflecting a powerful love. **Bogart** saw the look and envied **Gable** [p. 134].

Red Dust **(1932).** A reference to this memorable drama, directed by Victor Fleming and co-starring Jean Harlow and Mary Astor, was found in a few books. An allusion to the film appears at the beginning of Chapter 33 of Jack Kerouac's *Desolation Angels* (1960):

> Then it's time for the late show on TV so me and Nessa make more ryes and Cokes in the kitchen, bring them out tinkly by the fire, and we all draw our chairs before the TV screen

to watch **Clark Gable** and **Jean Harlow** in a picture about rubber plantations in the 1930's, the parrot cage, **Jean Harlow** is cleaning it out, says to the Parrot: "What *you* ben eatin, *cement?*" and we all roar with laughter.

"Boy they don't make pictures like *that* anymore" says Julien sipping his drink, tweaking his mustache [p. 272].

Jean Harlow as Vantine and Clark Gable as Dennis Carson in a scene from Victor Fleming's *Red Dust* 1932).

In Stuart Kaminsky's mystery *High Midnight* (1981), the movie is mentioned in a scene where private investigator Peters, worried about Gary Cooper's safety, surprises the actor and his guests at the hunting cabin outside of Santa Barbara:

> The wooden door unlatched and opened, and **Cooper** stood before me wearing a hunting jacket that looked like a cleaned-up version of the one **Gable** wore in **Red Dust** [p. 126].

In Michael B. Druxman's play *Gable* (1984), the King of Hollywood reminds the audience that the film was one of the reasons why he would like Victor Fleming to replace George Cukor for *Gone with the Wind*:

> **Victor Fleming** was a gutsy man's director. We'd worked together on **Red Dust** and **Test Pilot**, and at that time, he was just finishing up *The Wizard of Oz* [p. 39].

***No Man of Her Own* (1932).** A brief reference to the film, directed by Wesley Ruggles, also appears in Michael B. Druxman's play *Gable* (1984). This is what the actor says there about the picture and his future wife:

> I guess it's time to talk about Carole.
> I first met her in 1932. I went over to **Paramount** to co-star with her in **No Man of Her Own**. She was married to Bill Powell at the time, and I was still with Rhea.
> We didn't get along. At the end of filming, she gave me a present... a large ham... with my picture on the label [p. 34].
> [Photo 78. Caption: Clark Gable (Babe Stewart), Carole Lombard (Connie Randall) and Dorothy Mackaill (Kay Everly) in Wesley Ruggles's *No Man of Her Own* (1932).]

The film is referenced a few times in George Baxt's *The Clark Gable & Carole Lombard Murder Case* (1997), first in a conversation between the two titular characters (the third character mentioned here, Lydia Austin, is a young actress, Lombard's protégé, who later turns out to be a murder victim):

> **Carole** had gone back to Lydia Austin. If **Carole** was anything, thought **Clark**, she's tenacious. Why didn't he fall in love with her back in 1932 when they made *No Man of Her Own*? He gave voice to the question and **Carole** put Lydia Austin to one side, albeit reluctantly.
>
> I was still in love with Bill Powell and you were making believe you were in love with Ria. Anyway, I thought you were having it off with **Dorothy Mackaill**." **Mackaill**, a former star at Warner Brothers, was on the skids, but she had saved her money and invested wisely and now occupied the penthouse of a hotel in Honolulu. She gladly accepted the second lead to **Lombard** in *No Man of Her Own*, thinking it would lead her to better roles in secondary films—a very wise decision that kept her in the spotlight until 1935 when she went to England for some films there [pp. 63-64].

It is mentioned again in a lengthy passage the narrator gives to his female protagonist:

> Behave yourself is what **Carole** had done in her many years in the limelight. Her mother was a loving and very moral woman and she inspired **Carole**, who was a good little girl and remained a good little girl until she found out why boys were different from girls, clapped her hands with joy, and began what in her high-minded way she considered scientific experiments. By the time she became a working actress and exposed to all forms of sexual aberrations about which she was tolerant but

largely uninterested, **Carole** had only one objective, **a man of her own**. For a long time the title of the 1932 movie she did with **Clark**, *No Man of Her Own*, was right on the nose. She would look back on that movie and wonder why she and **Clark** never cottoned to each other despite the fact that each was married to other people [p. 163].

The White Sister **(1933).** The only reference to this unremarkable drama, which was directed by Victor Fleming and co-starring Helen Hayes, was found in George Baxt's mystery *The Greta Garbo Murder Case* (1992), in a scene where the titular protagonist of the novel is visited by screenwriter Salka Viertel:

> "I have never played a nun. **Mayer** wanted me to do *The White Sister* years ago but I said no, Lillian Gish had already done it beautifully as a silent. So Helen Hayes played the nun" [p. 11].

Night Flight **(1933).** Based on the novel by Antoine de Saint-Exupéry and directed by Clarence Brown, this above-average aviation drama, set in South America, is referenced in James Neel White's *I Was a P-51 Fighter Pilot in WWII* (2003), a personal and autobiographical account of the first forty years of aviation. The film and its male stars are mentioned at the end of the fifth chapter, Hollywood Stunt Pilots. Incidentally, the movie's all-star cast includes William Gargan, who is also mentioned in the same nonfiction book by White, in a passage presented in Part Four (on Spencer Tracy):

> Action movies in 1933 became more popular as the Depression took hold, as in *Parachute Jumper* with Bette Davis and Douglas Fairbanks and in *Night Flight* with **John Barrymore** and **Clark Gable** [p. 26].

Clark Gable as Patch Gallagher and Joan Crawford as Janie Barlow in a scene from Robert Z. Leonard's *Dancing Lady* (1933).

Dancing Lady **(1933).** Written by Allen Rivkin and P. J. Wolfson from a book by James Warner Bellah (John Ford's western trilogy!), and directed by Robert Z. Leonard, this musical co-starring Joan Crawford and Franchot Tone is referenced, along with many superior films (including another one with Gable), in Adriana Trigiani's novel *Big Cherry Holler* (2001). Below is just the first batch of a long list of the titles that Spec Broadwater reads to movie theater owner Jim Roy Honeycutt from the canisters that have been saved from a fire:

> "Let's see what we got, buddy," Spec says to Jim Roy. Then he reads the tape on the sides as I hold the flashlight: "*The Thin Man*, **Dancing Lady**, *My Man Godfrey*, *Stagecoach*, *The Heiress*, *Midnight* with Don Ameche and Claudette Colbert. That would've been a tragedy right there if they burned up." Spec shuffles through the reels: "There's *Bachelor Mother*, yeah, Ginger Rogers was sexy in that one; *The Barretts of Wimpole Street*, *Topaz*, *Pride and Prejudice*, *Jezebel*, **It Happened One Night** . . ."
> "**Clark Gable**!" I shriek. Spec gives a look [p. 122].

It Happened One Night **(1934).** A winner of five major Academy Awards—for best picture, script (Robert Riskin), direction (Frank Capra) and two leading players (Gable and Claudette Colbert)—this unforgettable classic is referenced in numerous books. One of the first references to the film was found in Walker Percy's novel *The Moviegoer* (1960), in a passage where narrator/protagonist Binx Bolling shares his personal thoughts and philosophical experiences with the reader:

> The greatest success of this enterprise, which I call my vertical search, came one night when I sat in a hotel room in Birmingham and read a book called *The Chemistry of Life*. When I finished it, it seemed to me that the main goals of my search were reached or were in principle reachable, whereupon I went out and saw a movie called ***It Happened One Night*** which was itself very good. A memorable night. The only difficulty was that though the universe had been disposed of, I myself was left over [p. 60].

American poster for Frank Capra's *It Happened One Night* (1934).

A nice allusion to the film appears in Herman Raucher's novel *A Glimpse of Tiger* (1971), in a scene where the female protagonist (the titular Tiger) looks out her window in the Manhattan apartment which she shares with Luther and contemplates:

> She looked out the window at the cars going by five floors below. What if she could *be* in one of them? That one. No, that one. Where would it take her? How many cars would stop and pick her up if she did the **Claudette Colbert** bit with the skirt

raising? One out of four? Five? If she yanked her skirt higher, how many? If she put her skirt so high over her head that she couldn't see at all—and if she just stood there as a pair of legs—how many people? She had good legs [p. 26].

An allusion to another scene in the film was found in another novel by Raucher, *There Should Have Been Castles* (1978). In the following excerpt, the female protagonist, Ginnie, makes an important decision to go back to her true love:

> Though I could believe anything about Maggie, I couldn't think the smallest evil of Ben. Yes, I'd speak with him, of course I would. Yes, I'd see him, you bet your ass I would. And, yes, it would have to be soon because I just wasn't making it without him. Sleeping with Richie was to have someone to hang onto when the world was falling away, and after that one time, I slept single-o. In the spare bed. **Claudette Colbert** to Richie's **Clark Gable** [p. 448].

In Stuart Kaminsky's *Think Fast, Mr. Peters* (1987), the context of the reference is private investigator Peters being confronted by his landlady, Mrs. Plaut, who comes to tell him about a telephone call for him:

> Mrs. Plaut stood, her vision perfect, scanning the mess in my room with disapproval. She wasn't leaving. I was wearing wrinkled boxer shorts and an undershirt just like the one **Clark Gable** had worn in ***It Happened One Night***.
>
> . . .
>
> "The telephone waits," she reminded me as I crossed the room in search of a shirt. I paused, shrugged, felt the stubble on my face, tasted the tin on my cratered tongue, and shuffled toward the door scratching my stomach and not feeling much

like **Clark Gable**. Mrs. Plaut two-stepped out of my path, mop held high [pp. 5-6].

A funny reference to one of the memorable scenes of the film was found in Connie Willis's short story "At the Rialto" (1989):

> "I wanted a donut," I said pitifully.
> He took my menu away from me, laid it on the table, and stood up. "There's a great place next door that's got the donut **Clark Gable** taught **Claudette Colbert** how to dunk in *It Happened One Night*."
> The great place was probably out in Long Beach someplace, but I was too weak with hunger to resist him. I stood up. Stephanie hurried over [pp. 451-452].

There are several references to Gable and his films in Kirk Douglas's novel *Dance with the Devil* (1990). The one to *It Happened One Night* comes late in the book when director Danny Dennison is anxiously waiting outside of the theater for the premiere of his film *Everyman* to be over:

> He got up; he just couldn't sit there waiting. He had to return to the studio. There was such a heavy turnout to see his film it was difficult to find a parking spot. He shut off the ignition and sat quietly. Then, on impulse, he left the car and entered a side door, walking slowly down the deserted hallway to the projection room. He glanced at the posters on the wall depicting scenes from important movies: *It Happened One Night*, *Lawrence of Arabia*, *On the Waterfront*, *The Bridge on the River Kwai*. How nice it would be, he thought, to have a scene from *Everyman* join this elite collection [p. 288].

A reference to the movie in George Baxt's *The William Powell and Myrna Loy Murder Case* (1996) is made by Ida Koverman, Louis B. Mayer's assistant and "hatchet woman," while she discusses with her boss the possibility of punishing William Powell and Myrna Loy for their involvement in a murder investigation:

> Ida reminded him, "The last time you punished a star, you loaned **Clark Gable** to Columbia Pictures for *It Happened One Night* and he won an Academy Award and now Columbia is almost as powerful as we are" [pp. 139-140].

In another novel by Baxt, *The Clark Gable & Carole Lombard Murder Case* (1997), a reference to the movie is made by the narrator in a passage where Lombard and Gable talk to bodyguards Sammy and Roy:

> Roy remonstrated, "But, Mrs. Gable, we don't plan to go swimming. We're bodyguards!"
> Carole patted his cheek. "You dear sweet thing. This is Hollywood, the Gomorrah of the West Coast. Just about everybody will be shedding their outer garments and plunging into the Pacific." The blood drained from Roy's face and Carole could see he was trembling slightly. "My God!" said Carole. "You've got nothing to be ashamed of. I can tell you're both built beautifully. Aren't they, **Pappy**?" **Gable** ignored her, taking the stairs in his ascent two at a time. He didn't like being reminded that he was almost forty and a bit flabby to boot. He'd never had a spectacular physique, even when he shed his shirt in *It Happened One Night* and single-handedly destroyed the underwear industry because he was barechested. Lately, when he had to bare his chest in a film his skin was tightly taped back to give an illusion of masculinity [p. 69].

Max Allan Collins's *Flying Blind* (1998) is a superior example of historical (and suspenseful) fiction, focused on the mystery surrounding Amelia Earhart's tragic flight. A reference to the film appears in a passage where narrator/private eye Nate Heller reflects on his predicament after he manages to prevent pilot Paul Mantz from being shot by his jealous wife and before he is paid a visit by Amelia in his hotel room:

> Bare-chested like **Gable** in ***It Happened One Night*** (and Mantz in what happened tonight), I lay atop the nubby pink bedspread, reading *Film Fun* magazine, which was mostly jokes and pictures of pretty girls; I never claimed to go in for Proust [p. 86].

In Elizabeth Hay's *A Student of Weather* (2001), an original novel set in the 1930s, the film is referenced in two places; first in a scene revealing the fantasy of Norma Joyce, one of the two sisters:

> Soon she'll go downstairs and say good morning Lucinda through nearly closed lips so that her sister will not smell her breath, but in the meantime she pictures herself running away to the apple-strewn east like **Claudette Colbert** running lickety-split to **Clark Gable** [p. 2].

Then, the movie plays a somewhat bigger role in a conversation between Norma Joyce and Maurice Dove, a botany student changing the sisters' lives:

> He outlines their tough, light, flexible existence. The stems, or culms, are usually hollow with a series of solid joints from which a leaf branches out. The leaf's lower part is a split sheath wrapped tightly round the stem so it won't tear in the wind, and the stem itself slips easily out of the wind's grasp. The undersides of the leaves have very few pores; in dry weather they roll up like

waterproof tubes to hold in every precious drop of water vapour. As beautifully engineered, he says with a wink, as **Claudette Colbert**'s nifty legs. Slender-tipped, smooth, loose and open, lax at flowering time, puberulent.

"What's that?"

"From the same root as puberty. Covered with fine hairs or down."

The soft hair of the world. And here was his measured, even-grass-writing going across the page. Quaking grass, orchard grass, love grass. From the Greek *eragrostis* for *Eros*, god of love, and *agrostis*, a grass. "Often persistent after their fall," the book said prophetically, "old-world species have long been known as love grass."

"You've seen the movie?" she asks.

Maurice smiles. He likes this about her, the way her mind leaps from one thing to another, in this case back to those nifty legs.

"*It Happened One Night*? I've seen it twice."

"You liked it?"

"Sure. Have you seen it?"

"My mother took me. For my fifth birthday" [pp. 33-34].

The film is also mentioned in Adriana Trigani's novel *Lucia, Lucia* (2003), in a scene where the protagonist, Lucia Sartori, about to marry John Talbot, slowly begins to realize that she is going to be jilted (a fact which makes the reference ironic):

> Rosemary paces back and forth, trying to see out the crack in the window to the street. I stand patiently, holding my bouquet of calla lilies (modeled on **Claudette Colbert**'s *It Happened One Night*). I put the flowers in the front and fluff my skirt. There is an ornate gold cross on the wall, the center of

Clark Gable as Peter Warne and Claudette Colbert as Ellie Andrews in a scene from Frank Capra's *It Happened One Night* (1934).

which is a mirror with the sacred heart of Jesus painted on it. I catch the reflection of my eyes in the mirror. Then I lean in and look closely. My eyes are blue, like my father's, and they are clear, since I slept well last night, but something is wrong. I can feel it, and I can see it in my own eyes [p. 201].

Three Gable films are mentioned in Marisa de los Santos's novel *Love Walked In* (2005). The reference to *It Happened One Night* is unusually brief, but quite meaningful—one more example proving that seven is a lucky number:

> Six dates. I had to admit she had a point.
> And then came date seven. A little date I like to call *Date Seven* or ***It Happened One Night*** [p. 47].

In James Scott Bell's novel *Try Dying* (2007), lawyer Ty Buchanan tries to find the killer of his fiancée and to clear himself of the charges of murdering another woman. He meets with the latter's coworker, Greg Beck, to look at her notes, and reminisces about his deceased fiancée:

> I scanned the rest of the notes. Beck waited patiently, softly drumming the steering wheel. Made me think about going back in time, playing drums for Jacqueline. Going back and telling her not to get on the freeway that day. Getting in a car with her and driving someplace together, anyplace, and getting married, like they used to do in those old movies on the thirties. **Clark Gable** and **Claudette Colbert**. Us. Alive [p. 243].

An obvious paraphrase of and an allusion to the film is the mere title of Jeffrey Cohen's humorous mystery *It Happened One Knife* (2008). While the titular knife is a murder weapon in the book, Capra's movie is mentioned briefly and only twice— first as part of the movie theater program announcement:

> **Friday**
> ***It Happened One Night*** (1934) and *Screwball* (this week) [p. 248];

then in a dialogue between narrator/protagonist Elliot Freed (the owner of the theater) and the chief of police, Barry Dutton:

> Dutton's eyebrows started to orbit his head. "You're going on with the showing tonight?" he asked.
> "I let Leo in for free. He'd kill me if I didn't show the movie. But just ***It Happened One Night***. After all the police activity, there won't be time for the new one."
> Dutton shook his head. "Movie people are crazy," he said. Then a thought occurred to him, and he smiled at me. "You know, C. Francis Jenkins was one of the men credited, along with Thomas Edison, with inventing the motion picture projector" [p. 278].

William Bernhardt's novel *Nemesis: The Final Case of Eliot Ness* (2009) contains references to two films directed by Frank Capra—*It Happened One Night* and *Mr. Deeds Goes to Town*—both taking place during a domestic scene involving Mr. and Mrs. Ness. The latter is obviously presented in the part on Gary Cooper; below is the former:

> Ness tiptoed as he stepped through the front door of their bungalow. It was late—it always was—and he didn't want to wake Edna if he could avoid it. Unfortunately, he was so loaded down with files and paperwork it was difficult to walk, much less creep.
> A light came on. Edna was sitting in an armchair in the living room, wide awake. She was wearing her best dress, a lovely red satin number that he thought made her look like **Claudette Colbert** in ***It Happened One Night***.
>
> . . .
>
> "We missed the Petersons' party."

The words hung in the air like a dirigible, suspended between them but going nowhere.

Ness racked his brain but couldn't think of anything to say, nothing intelligent, nothing witty, certainly nothing conciliatory. "Was that tonight?"

"Yes of course it was. Why do you think I'm dressed this way? Just so you could indulge your **Claudette Colbert** fantasy when you finally stumbled through the door?" [173-174]

One of the major plots in Michael Malone's novel *The Four Corners of the Sky* (2009) is protagonist Annie Peregrine Goode's attempt to find out the name of her mother as, according to her birth certificate, it is Claudette Colbert. Consequently, just like many other Colbert films, Frank Capra's classic is used a chapter title (Chapter 41, p. 375), and, furthermore, it is referenced in several parts of the book.

When a child, of course, Annie hadn't recognized the famous name of the dead movie star and so had believed when she'd first seen her birth certificate that **Claudette Colbert** really was her mother's name. Aunt Sam, the film lover, had tried to break the news to her gently and had eventually introduced her to the actress by playing her a tape of ***It Happened One Night***.

From the moment Annie watched **Claudette Colbert** dive off her father's yacht in the beginning of that film, then hop on a night bus in Miami and wisecrack her way north with **Clark Gable**—the man for whom Clark Goode had been named—she had liked the small unflappable woman with her chic French bangs, throaty voice, and civilized laughter, with her new moon of an eyebrow raised at the folly of men [p. 246].

Annie's memories raced through snippets of all the **Claudette Colbert** films she'd studied so earnestly as a child. It was easy to imagine the star in the setting. "The movie star

Claudette Colbert? *It Happened One Night*, *Palm Beach Story*, that **Claudette**?" [p. 290]

The next three excerpts involve two men in Annie's life: Brad Hopper, the man she is about to divorce (mentioned in the middle excerpt only), and Dan Hart, the man she will end up marrying (in all three):

Dan threw an imaginary lasso at the sky. "'**I'm going to reach up and grab stars for her,**' You know that line? **Clark Gable**? *It Happened One Night*?"

At the surf's edge, she called back over her shoulder, "Of course I know that line. Didn't my dad tell me my mother was **Claudette Colbert**?" [p. 386]

She came to the abrupt decision that she would simply tell Brad the truth about Dan. And that decision stopped her cold because she had to ask herself what the truth was. Bizarrely enough, what popped into her mind was the line that **Claudette Colbert** said near the end of *It Happened One Night* when she was about to marry a man she didn't even like and her father asked her to tell him about the **Clark Gable** character, the one she'd ridden with the bus all the way from Miami. And **Claudette Colbert** had told her father, "**I don't know very much about him ... Except that I love him**" [p. 446].

Touching the skin of his hand, his wrist, his arm, as if to memorize the unfamiliar, she thought again, oddly, of *It Happened One Night*, of a moment when **Clark Gable** was cooking breakfast for **Claudette Colbert** in their roadside motel cabin, how delicious the simple egg had tasted to the spoiled heiress [p. 452].

Irene Bennett Brown's mystery *Where Gable Slept* (2010) contains—naturally—a large number of references to Gable himself. *It Happened One*

Night is one of four Gable films referenced there. In fact, it appears in a series of titles mentioned by the book's protagonist, Celia Landrey—a local historian, walking-tour guide, inn owner and amateur detective in Pass Creek, Oregon—when she speaks about the famous actor's relationship with his father and about the actor's Academy Awards (which, nota bene, she confuses with Oscar nominations):

> "He was so angry and disappointed that he didn't speak to his son for nearly ten years," she told them. "Poor Dad, how could he guess that **Clark** would eventually win three Academy Awards for Best Actor?" When one of her tourists asked, she happily told them, "He won for the films ***It Happened One Night*** in 1934, ***Mutiny on the Bounty*** in 1935, and ***Gone with the Wind*** in 1939" [pp. 92-93].

In Jill McCorkle's novel *Life After Life* (2013), focused on the lives—past and present—of the residents and employees (and volunteers) of Pine Haven Retirement Facility in Fulton, North Carolina, there is a passage in which Rachel Silverman, a retired Boston lawyer, expresses her discontent and impatience with some volunteering young visitors:

> "The real Christian thing would be if you children just came and visited and listened to what we could teach you. Come because you like us and want to spend time with us, not to get your stupid points for school that you'll talk about in your college-entry essay. Don't bullshit me—I know what this is all about. I have lost some of my physical abilities but none of my mental ones, okay? If I were the real reason you were coming, then we would be doing something I am interested in. Maybe we would read and discuss current events or we might decide to buy a lottery ticket and be creative with our number selection. Maybe we would watch something like ***It Happened One Night***

or read something like *The Scarlet Letter* or *The Awakening* and discuss the ever-evoking roles of womanhood in film and literature" [pp. 128-129].

Men in White **(1934).** A reference to this rather disappointing drama, based on a play by Sidney Kingsley and co-starring Myrna Loy, was found in George Baxt's *The William Powell and Myrna Loy Murder Case* (1996). In the following excerpt, Powell, Loy and Detective Herb Villon talk about a murder weapon:

> Powell said, "Minnie, you never cease to amaze me. What the hell is it and how the hell do you know what it is? You know nothing about surgical tools."
>
> "I most certainly do," said Myrna, eyes ablaze. "Two years or so back when **Clark** and I co-starred in ***Men in White***. He was a physician and had to learn medical terminology and how to identify certain instruments and you know how hungry I get when there's a chance at gaining some knowledge, so I studied with **Clark**. He was grateful for my company because he's so dumb and knew I'd help him with the tough parts. Herb, that thing you're holding is called a xyster" [p. 186].

Manhattan Melodrama **(1934).** W. S. Van Dyke's superior crime drama, co-starring Myrna Loy and William Powell, is referenced in several works. Thomas Pynchon's complex novel *Gravity's Rainbow* (1973) contains a plentiful of movie references. The following passage includes an unambiguous allusion to the film through the description of the circumstances of John Dillinger's demise:

> John Dillinger, at the end, found a few seconds' strange mercy in the movie images that hadn't quite yet faded from his eyeballs—**Clark Gable** going off unregenerate to fry

in the chair, voices gentle out of the deathrow steel *so long, Blackie* . . turning down a reprieve from his longtime friend now Governor of New York William Powell, skinny chinless condescending jerk, **Gable** just wanting to get it over with, "Die like ya live—all of a sudden, don't drag it out—" even as bitchy little Melvin Purvis, staked outside the Biograph Theatre, lit up the fatal cigar and felt already between his lips the penis of official commendation—and federal cowards at the signal took Dillinger with their faggots' precision . . . there was still for the doomed man some shift of personality in effect—the way you've felt for a little while afterward in the real muscles of your face and voice, that you *were* **Gable**, the ironic eyebrows, the proud, shining, snakelike head—to help Dillinger through the bushwhacking, and a little easier into death [p. 516].

Myrna Loy as Eleanor and Clark Gable as Blackie Gallagher in a scene from W. S. Van Dyke's *Manhattan Melodrama* (1934).

Don DeLillo's political novel *Libra* (1988) is focused on the events surrounding and leading to the assassination of JFK. Guy Bannister, a retired FBI agent, reminisces about the Bureau's work in the 1930s in front of a bartender in the Katz & Jammer Bar:

> He knocked back the last bourbon and watched the man come forward.
> "We got him coming out of the Biograph in Chicago, July of '34, shot him dead in an alleyway three doors down from the theater."
> "This is who are we talking about," says the jug-eared barman.
> "Mr. John Dillinger. This is who. Fill the fucking glass."
> "Rocks or not?"
> "Famous finish. Old Dillinger buffs could tell you what was playing at the movie house when we gunned him down."
> "All right I'll bite."
> "*Manhattan Melodrama* with **Clark Gable**."
> The barman poured the drink, oblivious.
> "Whenever there's a famous finish in the vicinity of a movie house, it behooves you to know what's playing" [p. 140].

The context of the reference in George Baxt's *The William Powell and Myrna Loy Murder Case* (1996) is the narrator expressing Myrna Loy's thoughts about her frequent co-star, William Powell:

> Powell yanked her away from the table and led the way to theirs. "Well, Minnie, it's been too long a time since we've lunched."
> "Three days, for God's sake."
> "That's much too long a time." Myrna smiled. She adored her friend. Not once since their first film together in 1934,

Manhattan Melodrama, had he ever made a pass at her. Unlike **Spencer Tracy** and **Clark Gable** and Victor Fleming, who never ceased to try to force their attention on her. Her marriage to Arthur Hornblow hadn't dampened their enthusiasm, it just heightened the challenge [p. 7].

The protagonist of Elmore Leonard's novel *The Hot Kid* (2005) is Deputy U.S. Marshal Carl Webster, whose many accomplishments include the demise of John Dillinger. Thus, here is one more account of the famous event which, once again, includes a reference to one of Gable's early films:

Manhattan Melodrama.

Clark Gable is **Blackie**. **William Powell** is **Jim**. **Myrna Loy** is Eleanor. They said **Myrna Loy** was one of Dillinger's favorites. **Muriel Evans** is **Tootsie**, the platinum blonde, and she ain't bad. **Blackie** loses **Eleanor** to **Jim**, because **Jim**'s such a swell guy. But it's okay with **Blackie** because he and **Jim** were boyhood pals and are still close friends, even though they're on opposite sides of the law, **Blackie** a gangster and **Jim** a prosecuting attorney and finally the governor. **Blackie** bumps off **Jim**'s assistant, a snake who has evidence that would keep **Jim** from winning the governor's seat. **Blackie** is tried and convicted, sentenced to die in the electric chair. **Jim**, now the governor, could commute his sentence to life, but won't because he lives by the letter of the law. **Eleanor** tells **Jim** if **Blackie** hadn't plugged his assistant in the men's room at Madison Square Garden, witnessed by a blind beggar, he wouldn't of been elected governor. **Jim** still won't budge. **Eleanor** can't believe he won't help his friend. She leaves **Jim**, unable to continue being his wife. At the last moment **Jim** gives in, commutes **Blackie**'s sentence to life. But **Blackie** won't accept it. If he doesn't go to the chair, **Jim** will have to resign his office. **Blackie** goes to the chair, Carl thinking during the scene, They're going to muss his slick hair with the metal skullcap, that part that looks like it was cut into his scalp. Carl only used a little water. He'd lost interest knowing what was going to happen. There was a good scene of **Jim** and **Eleanor** getting back together, out in the hall. Carl felt his eyes dew-up just a little. That **Myrna Loy** was all right [pp. 364-366].

One more reference to the film in connection with the death of John Dillinger appears in James Lee Burke's Dave Robicheaux mystery *Creole Bell* (2012). The context is a conversation between Gretchen Horowitz and Alafair—not accidently, after they leave a movie theater and after seeing a film starring Johnny Depp:

> Alafair had never seen anyone watch a film with such intensity. Even when the credits had finishing rolling, Gretchen waited until the trademark of the studio and the date of production had trailed off the screen before she allowed herself to detach. The film was *Pirates of the Caribbean*.
> "Do you know what John Dillinger's last words were?" she asked.
> "No," Alafair replied.
> "It was in Chicago, at the Biograph Theater. He had just come out of seeing **<u>Manhattan Melodrama</u>** with the two prostitutes who sold him out to the feds. You've heard about the lady in red, right? Actually, she was wearing orange. Anyway, John Dillinger said, 'Now, that's what I call a movie.' Did you see *Public Enemies*? Johnny Depp played Dillinger. God, he was great. The critics didn't understand what the film was about, though. That's because a lot of them are stupid" [p. 212].

***Forsaking All Others* (1934).** A reference to this mediocre comedy-drama, directed by W. S. Van Dyke and co-starring Joan Crawford and Robert Montgomery, was, surprisingly, found in three books. George Baxt, in his mystery *The Tallulah Bankhead Murder Case* (1987), makes a reference to the film in a dialogue between Tallulah Bankhead and police detective Jacob Singer, whom the famous movie star befriends:

> "Of course, dahling, I was starring on Broadway in <u>*Forsaking All Others*</u>. A disaster, but I kept it running for over one hundred performances. Not bad in those depression days, and anyway it was my own money." She laughed. "All that gorgeous cash I earned at Paramount Pictures went into that very bad play. Actually it became a rather amusing film with Miss Crawford and **Mr. Gable**. But that's useless trivia [p. 72].

Joan Crawford as Mary Clay and Clark Gable as Jeff Williams in a scene from W. S. Van Dyke's *Forsaking All Others* (1934).

In another mystery by Baxt, *The William Powell and Myrna Loy Murder Case* (1996), the context of the reference is Powell and Loy talking about other movie stars:

> "We can't have Franchot Tone thinking that. Heaven forbid. He might complain to his wife and she might get Mr. Mayer to put me on suspension."
> "Miss Crawford wouldn't do that to you."
> "Why not? She elbowed me out of ***Forsaking All Others*** and got the part for herself. There!" She snapped the compact shut and sought Franchot Tone [p. 89].

A reference to the movie in Marisa de los Santos's novel *Love Walked In* (2005) is a part of an insightful passage about important signs, deep thoughts that narrator/protagonist Cornelia Brown shares with the reader:

> What surprisingly few people know is that before **Joan Crawford** was terrifying with eyebrows like two shrieking crows, she was adorable and sylphlike and funny. At the end of ***Forsaking All Others***, a film that will charm you but will not alter the warp and woof of your life's fabric, **Joan** finds out it was old pal **Clark Gable** not, as she had supposed, lifelong love **Robert Montgomery** who, on what was supposed to be her wedding day, filled her room with cornflowers, her favorite of all flowers. When a friend informs her of this, her pretty face fills with light, the scales fall from her eyes. The flowers are a sign! She is transfigured! **Clark** is her man! Put aside the fact that, despite **Robert Montgomery**'s goofy cuddliness and nice posture, a choice between him and **Clark Gable** is no choice at all; put aside the fact that **RM** got drunk and married a floozy with an appallingly artificial speaking voice the night before he was supposed to marry **Joan**. It's the flowers that send **Joan**

out the door, stranding **RM** on their would-be second wedding day, and onto the ship that's about to carry **Clark** away forever [pp. 27-27].

The Call of the Wild **(1935).** William A. Wellman's *The Call of the Wild* is one of the most successful screen adaptations of Jack London's fiction. Below are some of the references found to this quasi-western and its stars. In Lorenzo Carcaterra's *Sleepers* (1995), the author/narrator of this captivating memoir describes the life of his own group of 1960s' "dead end boys" in Kitchen's Hell, New York, and mentions the film, in the context of a few others, as the major resource in the boys' spiritual and intellectual education:

> We lived inside every book we read, every movie we saw. We were Cagney in *Angels with Dirty Faces* and **Gable** in <u>*The Call of the Wild*</u>. We were *Ivanhoe* on our own streets and Knights of the Round Table in our clubhouse [p. 85].

A reference to the private lives of this movie's stars is made in George Baxt's mystery *The Clark Gable and Carole Lombard Murder Case* (1997):

> **Clark** pulled her away and when he felt they were safely out of Ria's earshot, he burst out laughing. "Okay, baby, score one for you. That was beautiful!"
> "Hee hee hee hee. She left herself open for that one. You're not mad at me?"
> He kissed her cheek. "I'm mad about you."
> "Uh-oh," said Carole.
> "What?"
> "**Loretta Young**."
> "She's here?"
> "Heading straight for us. Haven't you seen her since <u>*Call of the Wild*</u>?"

...

It was an open secret in Hollywood that when co-starring in the movie version of Jack London's *The Call of the Wild*, **Young** and **Gable** had a torrid affair while on location, which resulted in a daughter, Judy [p. 101].

American poster for William A. Wellman's *The Call of the Wild* (1935).

Adriana Trigiani makes a reference to the movie in several of her books. She mentions the film and its leading lady briefly in her novel *Big Stone Gap* (2000), in a scene where Jack Mac shows Ave Marie his house:

> While we're in the attic room, he shows me some photographs in the family album. There are pictures of his mother when she was a girl. I think she looked like **Loretta Young** in ***Call of the Wild***; Jack tells me his father always thought so, too. He tells me his parents had a real love affair, and how sad she was for so long after he died [p. 241].

The picture is also one of five Gable films mentioned in Trigiani's novel *Big Cherry Holler* (2001). The context of the passage is Ave Maria catching sight of Pete Rutledge, a man she got infatuated with during her European trip, who unexpectedly visits her in her American home where she lives as a wife and mother. Ironically, but understandably, later in the book, narrator Ave Maria compares Pete to Gary Cooper:

> Through the door from the living room, which connects to the kitchen, I see Pete Rutledge in a yellow rain slicker, standing in the doorway. He is so tall, he has to duck his head down; his shoulders barely fit in the frame. His blue eyes stand out against the bright yellow collar of the slicker. His hair is wet, and he hasn't shaved. He reminds me of **Clark Gable** in ***Call of the Wild***, just a little. I wish I didn't think this man looked like all my favorite movie idols, but in certain ways, and in certain lights, he does [p. 181].

The film is referenced twice in Trigiani's novel *Very Valentine* (2009). The context of the first passage is a conversation between the book's narrator/protagonist, Valentine Roncalli, and the family's seasoned employee, June.

The topic is triggered by a question about Teodora Angelini, Valentine's grandmother:

> "Where's Teodora?" June asks.
> "She's not up yet," I tell her.
> "Hmm." June opens a cabinet, pulls out a red corduroy work smock and puts it on. "You think she's okay?"
> "Yeah, sure." I look at June. "Why do you ask?"
> "I don't know. She seems tired lately."
> "We've been staying up late watching the **Clark Gable** DVD boxed set."
> "That'd do it."
> "Last night it was *__The Call of the Wild__*."
> June whistles low. "**Gable** was sex on a stick in that one."
> "**Loretta Young** was pretty great, too."
> "Oh, she was a true beauty. And it was all real. Those were her lips and her bones. She fell in love with **Gable** when they were making that picture, you know. She got pregnant, kept it secret, had the baby, and gave her up for adoption. Then guess what she did? She adopted her own baby back, named her Judy, and pretended for years that the girl wasn't biologically hers."
> "Seriously?"
> "Back then you couldn't have a child out of wedlock. It would have ruined her. These stars today? Even bad acting can't ruin them." June pours herself a cup of coffee [p. 60].

The second excerpt constitutes a perfect example of juxtaposition: the imagined and the real versions of Valentine and Roman's love life:

> I turn over and put my arm around Roman, who has fallen into a deep sleep. I imagined so much more for us with the full run of the house. I dreamed of romantic nights drinking

wine on the roof while I point out the hues and shifts of the Hudson River; I imagined Roman making me dinner in the old kitchen downstairs, then making love in this bed in my room. Other nights, where we just relax, he with his feet up on the old ottoman, me next to him while we watch **_The Call of the Wild_** so I might teach him everything I know about **Clark Gable**. Instead, he is gone all day, works through supper and into the night, comes home near dawn, bone tired, and crashes. As soon as the sun is up, after a quick cup of coffee, he is gone again [p. 312].

The film is alluded to in John Douglas Miller's novel *The Greek Summer* (2003), in a scene where a group of young people discusses philosophy and literature:

> "What do you talk about?"
> "Well. We've been talking about Plato's *Republic*. And we talk about **Jack London**."
> "About **Buck** the sled dog?"
> "There was more to **London** than that."
> "I've never actually read it. But I saw the **Clark Gable** movie."
> "If I asked you to do me a favor, would you do it?" I looked at her. She looked back.
> "I guess it would depend on what the favor was."
> "It's nothing crazy. Would you get **London**'s book *Martin Eden* and read it?"
> "*Martin Eden?*"
> "Would you? And then tell me what you think of it. Maybe your sister would read it too" [p. 75].

***Mutiny on the Bounty* (1935).** Based on the famous book by Charles Nordhoff and James Norman Hall, Frank Lloyd's *Mutiny on the Bounty* (co-starring Charles Laughton and Franchot Tome) is definitely one of Gable's best pictures as well as his foremost acting achievements. Possibly the first reference to the film was found in James A. Michener's tale "Polynesia" (1951), in a passage relating the brief movie career of a local man:

> The William astonished the family by becoming a movie star! He played in many Hollywood productions, including *Tabu* and ***Mutiny on the Bounty***. A relative says, "He usually played the native chief but he was also very good as village constable." At one period of film shortage the local movie played ***Mutiny*** two or three times a week. "We all kept going to see Roustabout Willie say to **Captain Bligh**, 'No, thanks. No rum. It makes me dizzy.'" He returned home rich and is still a famous figure about town [p. 46].

Charles Laughton as Captain Bligh and Clark Gable as Fletcher Christian in a scene from Frank Lloyd's *Mutiny on the Bounty* (1935).

A reference to the movie, and to Gable and his private life, appears in John Gregory Dunne's mystery *True Confessions* (1977), in a passage where cop Tom Spellacy goes to MacArthur Park in order to obtain information from Brenda, a woman he knows has a lot of secrets:

> Tom Spellacy knew enough not to rush her. She would say what she had to say when she wanted to say it. No sooner. He checked the other benches around the lake. No one there but old people feeding birds. He knew the type. They would strike up a conversation with the mother of a child and say the baby was the picture of Ginger Rogers or the image of **Clark Gable**. And then almost without pausing for breath they would begin talking about *Kitty Foyle* or **Mutiny on the Bounty** and after that Carole Lombard and *Nothing Sacred* and wasn't it a shame the way poor Carole went, what it must have done to **Clark**, but at least he knew she died selling war bonds for her country, that must have been a comfort [pp. 226-227].

The film is even referenced in a science-fiction book, Arthur C. Clarke's *2010: Second Odyssey* (1982). Although the movie show that takes place in the space involves a fourth screen version of the famous story (hence, the title is not underlined), clearly nonexistent when the novel was written, the narrator's commentary includes a comparison to an actor, Gable's co-star, of the 1935 picture:

> It did not last long, for Tanya quickly ordered all those not on essential duty to get some rest—if possible, some sleep—in preparation for the Jupiter swing-by only nine hours ahead. When those addressed were slow to move, Sasha cleared the decks by shouting, "You'll hang for this, you mutinous dogs!" Only two nights before, as a rare relaxation, they had all enjoyed the fourth version of **Mutiny on the Bounty**, generally agreed by movie historians to have the best **Captain Bligh** since the

fabled **Charles Laughton**. There was some feeling onboard that Tanya should not have seen it, lest it give her ideas [pp. 238-239].

George Baxt's *The Clark Gable & Carole Lombard Murder Case* (1997) contains references to several Gable films, including a brief one to *Mutiny*, which, once again, appears in a conversation between the two titular protagonists and their bodyguards. The scene takes place in a car driven on Sunset Boulevard in the direction of Malibu Beach:

"How delicious! Boys! Roll down your windows and smell the Pacific Ocean." They obeyed immediately. "**Pappy**!" Her voice commanded attention. "Inhale, **Pappy**, inhale! Smell the Pacific Ocean! It's clean, so virginal, so out of this world."

Unexcited by the prospect of what the Pacific aroma promised, **Clark** said, "When I was making **Mutiny on the Bounty** I had my fill of the Pacific Ocean. Give me the smell of horseflesh and bay—"

"And manure," Carole interjected swiftly. She said to the boys, "**Pappy** dotes on manure. He can't get enough of it" [p. 83].

***San Francisco* (1936).** Another milestone in Gable's filmography, W. S. Van Dyke's *San Francisco* (co-starring Spencer Tracy and Jeanette MacDonald), was, nonetheless, a project that Gable did reluctantly. Most of the references are presented in Part Four (on Tracy); below is one found in Thomas Pynchon's *Vineland* (1990), a novel set mostly in California in 1984 and, in the flashbacks, in the Nixon era and far beyond, and focused on a large group of people in their personal and political struggles tying the current days with the 1960s. A reference to Gable and an allusion to one of his early films appear in a flashback passage in which Sasha is telling her daughter Frenesi about the World War II times in San Francisco:

"Platters spinning, mellow reed sections," Frenesi would speculate, "I love it! Tell me more!"

"Oh, the joints were jumping those nights. Uniforms all over the place. Wild and rowdy like in the **Clark Gable** movie. Bars that would stay open all day and night, trumpet and saxophone music blasting at you out of doorways, big crowds at the hotel ballrooms . . ." [p. 78]

Clark Gable as Blackie Norton and Jeanette MacDonald as Mary Blake in W. S. Van Dyke's *San Francisco* (1936).

***Cain and Mabel* (1936).** Directed by Lloyd Bacon, this successful musical romance (co-starring Marion Davies), is referenced in several books. The main character in James Jones's *From Here to Eternity* (1951) is Robert E. Lee Prewitt, but the scene below refers to another soldier, Bloom, also a boxer, before his first bout as a middleweight:

> Finally, early in the afternoon, he had to give up. He went off to the matinee at Theater # 1. He was terribly upset and very nervous, and they were showing **Clark Gable** in *The Prizefighter and the Lady*, and he needed badly to rest up and relax, for tonight [p. 445].

Jones makes an error in the above reference, as Gable did not star in the mentioned movie; he did play in *Cain and Mabel* whose story perfectly fits the other title, but in *The Prizefighter and the Lady* the boxer is played by Max Baer, and the lady by Myrna Loy. An indirect indicator that Jones meant the Gable boxing movie rather than the one he mentions by title is the fact that the actor is mentioned to again some forty pages later, this time in a humorous scene:

> Nobody argued with him. Prew tried on one of the hats, farcically. If you can only laugh, if you can only turn it into a joke. Then you'll be all right. For a while. The hat came clear down onto his ears and the brim stood out sharp all around and the crown was tight to his head, a pot, but still wrinkled.
> "Look just like **Clark Gable**, bud," the trustee grinned. "Specially you keep it down on the ears" [p. 484].

In Martha Sherrill's novel *My Last Movie Star* (2002), the film is mentioned in the extensive passage focused on the career of Marion Davies:

Just a few pictures left to make, perhaps ... ***Cain and Mabel*** or *Ever Since Eve*. Not long ago in the span of things, really, she'd sung and danced on a stage about six blocks away. On Forty-second Street in the New Amsterdam Theatre, she'd been a Ziegfeld girl at just sixteen or seventeen—lying about her age and saying she was older—while William Randolph Hearst sat in the second-row orchestra staring up her short dress [pp. 188-189].

Parnell **(1937).** John M. Stahl's biographical drama, co-starring Myrna Loy and Edna May Oliver, turned out to be a major artistic and box-office disappointment, and a serious mistake on Gable's part. Clark Gable (the character) talks about the film, just like about many of his other movies, in Michael B. Druxman's play *Gable* (1984):

> **Metro** looked for a suitable subject. They came up with ***Parnell***.
>
> Joan Crawford was smart. She read the script, and turned it down. **Myrna Loy** wasn't so smart.
> (*Takes long **Parnell** coat from costume rack, puts it on.*)
> I guess my ego had gotten out of hand at that point. I wanted to compete with Muni. I'd just been crowned "King of Hollywood," so I figured I'd be the logical choice to play the "underground King of Ireland."
>
> The only thing I had in common with **Charles Stewart Parnell** was a mustache. And, even he had a pair of mutton chop side-whiskers.
>
> I had "great" love scenes with **Myrna**.
> (*Goes into scene with **Loy**, attempting a disastrous Irish accent.*)

"Katie, have you never felt there might be someone, somewhere ... who, if you could meet them, was the person that you'd been always meant to meet? Have you never felt that?"

(*Chuckles.*)

The critics murdered me. One of them said I looked like "a steel organizer gone Park Avenue," and that I walked through my part "with the heavy tread of the Golem."

(*Hangs coat on costume rack.*)

For years after that, whenever my head got a bit swelled, Carole would whisper into my ear: "Remember **_Parnell_**" [pp. 33-34].

Saratoga (1937). A reference to this mediocre film directed by Jack Conway, well-known mostly because of the circumstances surrounding its production (Jean Harlow's tragic death), was found in John Dandola's mystery *West of Orange* (1990). The context is a phone conversation between MGM publicist Edie Koslow and her boss, Howard Dietz, about the possibility of canceling Ann Rutherford's participation in the premiere of *Edison, the Man* due to the danger to her life:

But we can't go underground just because a percentage of the public is a little screwy. We're in a business."

"That's more cold than necessary."

"Yeah, it is. I'm sorry."

"Keeps things in perspective. We're the studio who couldn't let Harlow die in peace. We had to finish **_Saratoga_** with a double so we could reap the profits" [p. 100].

Test Pilot (1938). This relatively successful drama, directed by Victor Fleming and co-starring Myrna Loy and Spencer Tracy, is referenced in a few books. In Adriana Trigiani's *Big Stone Gap* (2000), a novel set in the Blue

Ridge Mountains of Virginia, it is mentioned in a scene where the book's protagonist, Ave Maria Mulligan, experiences an unexpected kiss:

> And then we stop. Theodore kisses me. It's not the usual friendly kiss I have become accustomed to all of these years. So at first I don't lock in. I'm confused. Then his lips, wordless and soft, persist. My spine turns from rivets of bone into a velvet ribbon spinning off its wheel and pooling into the floor. I hold on to him like **Myrna Loy** did **Clark Gable** when they jumped out of a two-seater plane in *__Test Pilot__*. My waist is on a swivel as he dips me. But the kiss doesn't end. Moments later, when it does, my body feels like it is full of goose feathers. Theodore holds my face while everyone dances around us, offering looks of approval [p. 39].

An extensive reference to the film appears in Martha Sherrill's *My Last Movie Star* (2002), in a passage relating a telephone conversation between the book's narrator, journalist Clementine James, and her new assistant, photographer Franklin Warner, about Myrna Loy's autobiographical book:

> "Don't tell me," I said. "Don't tell me anything else."
> "She lies too. There's something skirting around the issue of William Powell and whether she ever slept with him. And she spends an entire paragraph discussing why she never cries in any of her movies. I just saw *__Test Pilot__* again. And she cries twice."
> "*__Test Pilot__*?"
> "Big studio release. With **Spencer Tracy** and **Clark Gable**. Actually, I think both of them were in love with her in real life. Isn't there something in her book about showing **Gable** into the bushes when he tries to kiss her one night? Anyway, **Victor Fleming** directed *__Test Pilot__* when he was on a roll—

immediately after ***Captains Courageous*** and before *The Wizard of Oz* and **Gone with the Wind**."

"**Gable** is a test pilot? How did I miss that one?"

"It's dark—and much less mythic and hokey than *The Right Stuff*. **Gable** is a tortured guy who needs to chase death and drink. On a coast-to-coast flight, his plane crashes into a Kansas cornfield. It's **Myrna**'s cornfield—psychologically symbolic, I suppose. Anyway, she's terribly regal and full of delightful put-downs, considering she's a farm girl."

"What did you expect?"

"Then she and **Gable** fall in love. Lots of superb verbal banter. He loves her. He hates her. He loves her again—and that's only the first twenty minutes. Once he gets his plane fixed, there's a terrific scene where he flies off into the sky and leaves her behind to marry some young Kansas dweeb—is that the word? **Gable**'s plane is in the air just a few minutes before he turns around and comes back for her. She's wearing a sweater set and nice skirt when she climbs his airplane and they fly off together" [pp. 246-247].

Too Hot to Handle (1938). Jack Conway's adventure comedy, co-starring Myrna Loy and Walter Pidgeon, is referenced in at least two works: Michael B. Druxman's *Gable: A One-Person Play in Two Acts* (1984) and Martha Sherrill's novel *My Last Movie Star* (2002). In Druxman's play, the context is Gable talking about his participation in World War II and his personal threat posed by Adolf Hitler:

> What really scared me was being captured. Hitler'd put a five thousand dollar price on my head.
>
> I swore I'd never bail out. If I'd ever fallen into enemy

hands, they'd've put me in a cage like a big gorilla, and exhibited me all over Germany.

That little asshole with the funny mustache liked my movies. They tell me that ***Too Hot to Handle*** was one of his favorites [pp. 47-48].

In Sherrill's novel, the reference to the film, just like to some others, is related to the extended visit by Myrna Loy's ghost:

"Fans are so loyal. They're always there, wherever you go, wherever you turn," Myrna said. She chuckled, then uncrossed her jodhpurs and paddock boots, the aviator's costume she wore into ***Too Hot to Handle***." But you get used to it. And you even start to miss them—when they go away" [p. 224].

***Gone with the Wind* (1939).** Margaret Mitchell's National Book Award and Pulitzer Prize-winning novel (1936) was turned into a movie that became one of the greatest hits in film history. One of the eight Academy Awards went to the picture itself, while the other major winners included Sidney Howard (best script), Victor Fleming (best director), Vivien Leigh (best actress), Hattie McDaniel (best supporting actress) and Ernest Haller and Ray Rennahan (best color cinematography). Clark Gable was nominated for the Best Actor Oscar, but he lost to Robert Donat for *Goodbye, Mr. Chips*.

The immense popularity of the movie is indirectly confirmed by the fact that three lines from it are included on the American Film Institute's List of the Top 100 Movie Quotes (2005). All three also happen to be quoted in one or more literary works. The #1 item on the list ("Frankly, my dear, I don't give a damn.") is mentioned in several books. Joseph Wambaugh, in his novel *The Glitter Dome* (1981), makes the line a part of the cops' exchange in the squadroom:

All the detectives and Gladys Bruckmeyer stopped doing business and listened as the captain cackled hysterically at a joke the nonexistent visitor just told.

"Something's wrong with the captain!" Gladys Bruckmeyer cried out.

"**Frankly, my dear, I don't give a damn!**" said the Weasel, sounding just like **Clark Gable** [p. 298].

There are two allusions to *Gone with the Wind* in Denis Hamill's *Fork in the Road* (2000), of which the second one is worth quoting. The reference, including a paraphrase of the line, appears in a scene where a beautiful Irish woman of a questionable background, Gina Furey, is the only person criticizing a movie screened at a Malibu Colony house, where she is taken by the book's protagonist, young filmmaker Colin Coyne:

"Tell me why you think it's a load of shit," Thompson said.

"Everything was goin' great guns until the malarkey endin'," she said. "There's just no way that fella would take her back after she cheated on him like that."

"But the film is about forgiveness," Thompson said. "About how love is more powerful than anger."

"Hollywood shite," she said. "No woman in the audience will ever fantasize about a fella who would take back a cheater. Say what you want about the old pictures, but when **Clark Gable** tells **Scarlett O'Hara** that **he doesn't give a damn**, every woman in the picture house wanted him. No one wants a jellyfish for a man. Not where I come from, anyway. You asked, so there yeh are, now, the endin; is a load of shite" [p. 315].

Aaron Latham's mystery *Riding with John Wayne* (2006) abounds with movie allusions, four of them focused on *Gone with the Wind*, and two of those referring to the famous line. The first allusion appears as a part of a conversation between the book's narrator, young screenwriter Chick Goodnight, and female film director Jamie Stone, who is making a movie from his script:

> Jamie and I walk side by side to the parking lot behind the Galley. We are so close to the ocean, I can smell it. My rented Chevy is parked a couple of slots over from her baby-blue vintage Mercedes ragtop. Her ride is bout fifty years old, dating from a time when Hollywood made more westerns than anything else.
> "See you tomorrow," I say.
> "If you think you're up to it," she says.
> "I'll be better tomorrow."
> "You sound like **Scarlett O'Hara**."
> "Yeah, and **frankly I don't give a damn**" [p. 73].

The second reference takes place during an animated exchange between Jamie, Buddy Dale, the film's repulsive producer, and true Texan Clyde Goodnight, Chick's father:

> "I didn't give you permission to hire a dialogue coach," he says angrily. "You can't spend money unless I authorize it."
> "We need a dialogue coach," she says.
> "No you don't. **Clark Gable** didn't bother with one in <u>**Gone with the Wind**</u>. Besides, this is just some dodge to slip Chick's down-on-his-luck daddy some money. He is Chick's dad, isn't he?"
> "Yes, I am," my father says, getting up slowly. "And proud to be so. What's it to you, if'n I may inquire?" [p. 292]

The film, along with its legendary producer, is mentioned again some thirty pages later in a narrative passage:

We are almost ready to shoot the death of Jimmy Goodnight. What we are about to stage reminds me a little of the Atlanta-is-burning scene in ***Gone with the Wind***. To film that sequence, **David O. Selznick** burned down some old sets on his back lot It was a great night in movie history [p. 325].

The final allusion, through a paraphrase of the line, takes place at the end of the book when the movie is already finished. The dialogue, needless to say, involves Chick and Jamie:

"*I love you!*" I SCREAM.

"Frankly, mister," she says breathlessly, "**I do**—really, absolutely, eternally do—**give a damn.**" She pauses. "Wait, rewrite, strike eternally. We'll see" [p. 373].

Clark Gable as Rhett Butler and Vivien Leigh as Scarlett O'Hara in a scene from Victor Fleming's *Gone with the Wind* (1939).

The title of Stuart M. Kaminsky's novel *Tomorrow Is Another Day* (1995) is an allusion to the #31 item of the list, the complete version of which is "After all, tomorrow is another day!" The book's narrator/protagonist, private eye Toby Peters, works on a case for Clark Gable, who is one of the men threatened to be killed by a mysterious murderer. Consequently, the novel contains numerous references to both Gable and *Gone with the Wind*, the filming of a scene of which constitutes the prologue of the book. And two paragraphs from that part of the book are probably among those that are most worthy of quoting:

> The wagon was off to the right, in the darkness. Wally and I had been there when **Dorothy Fargo** and **Yakima Canutt**, dressed like **Scarlett O'Hara** and **Rhett Butler**, had gone over the action with **Menzies** and his assistant. **Yak** had been around forever, a lean, board-hard man with a dark Indian face, as much the king of stunt men as <u>**Clark Gable**</u> was the king of Hollywood.
>
> . . .
>
> I grunted in understanding. Wally had gotten me on this job and assigned me to work with him on the detail guarding **Selznick** and the crew. Easy work. And I needed the money. I also wanted to meet <u>**Clark Gable**</u>. I'd only seen him once before from a distance when I tried to keep fans from Mickey Rooney at an M-G-M premiere at Grauman's Chinese.
>
> I've been around Hollywood for all of my almost fifty years. Stars didn't impress me, except for Jimmy Stewart, Buck Jones, and <u>**Gable**</u>. I'd heard a lot about <u>**Gable**</u>, some good, some bad, and I wanted to know how much of it was true. But more important, I was getting paid [pp. 3-4].

A paraphrase of the #1 line appears at the end of the book. After Gable helps Peters catch the killer, the two men talk about what needs to be done, and then there is a brief exchange between the actor and the killer:

> "Why don't you take off? I'll take Spelling in. He may rant about seeing **Clark Gable**, but I'll remind the police that you're in England flying missions over Germany."
>
> "Maybe that'd be best," he said.
>
> "So damn close," Spelling cursed, trying to sit up. "Now, what's going to happen to me?"
>
> "**Frankly, mister**," said **Gable**, touching the bill of his cap in mock salute, "**I just don't give a damn**" [p. 200].

The #59 item on the list ("As God is my witness, I'll never be hungry again.") appears in one of the three allusions found in Jill McCorkle's novel *Life After Life* (2013), which was already mentioned in the entry on *It Happened One Night*. The first passage, pertaining to Scarlett's estate and her famous promise (to herself), emerges in the discussion among the elderly residents of Pine Haven Retirement Facility about different names people choose for their suites:

> "Toby is one of the smartest people living here," Sadie told Rachel, and before she could say that this was quite obvious, one resident had named her suite Shangri-La and another named hers Camp David. Then one pounced on **Tara** and another Twelve Oaks, leaving several other unimaginative ones disappointed. The one who got **Tara** now spends her time striking a pose and saying things like "**I'll never be hungry again!**" only to have Stanley Stone reply with "That's because you eat all the goddamn time. And not even good stuff. I see you eating old mess like Twinkies" [p. 126].

The second one is part of a description of Kendra Palmer, a vain and selfish wife of Ben the magician and an uncaring mother of Abby, the sensitive girl who lost her dog:

> Kendra has never liked the other girls but learned early to pretend that she did so she could get closer to the boys she was interested in. She has always thought of herself as a **Scarlett O'Hara** type and does believe that the end always justifies the means [p. 150].

The final reference takes place in a passage involving three characters—beautician C.J. Loomis, Hospice volunteer Joanna Lamb and Luke Whisnant (Joanna's fourth husband, deceased):

> One of the many therapy sessions Luke insisted she take involved unpacking the heart. You close your eyes and take every person and every thing taking up space in your heart out and set them on your make-believe lawn. Every grievance and relationship and project. And then when the space inside is empty and clean, you survey the goods and decide what to put back. It was Luke's favorite exercise and one that she and C.J. have talked about many times since, laughing over the notion of whole corpses exhumed and expunged, exorcised. Joanna had told Luke that her imagined yard looked like Gettysburg or like that scene in ***Gone with the Wind*** when the camera pulls back and there are wounded and dead bodies as far as the eye can see—enough emotional carnage to keep the buzzards feasting for centuries [p. 266].

The remaining references to *Gone with the Wind*, some including other lines from the picture, are presented in a chronological order, with quotations by the same author kept in an uninterrupted sequence. Stuart Kaminsky has already been mentioned and will be mentioned a few more times. There are a few allusions to his *Murder on the Yellow Brick Road* (1977). The first passage has private investigator Peters analyzing the situation on the way to see the suspect of the murder committed at the MGM studio on the set of *The Wizard of Oz*:

> On the way down to try to get a word with Wherthman, I realized that Mayer had a few reasons to worry about publicity. The primary witnesses for the case against Wherthman seemed to be the studio's top star and top director. Coming off of *The Wizard of Oz* and **Gone With the Wind**, Fleming was almost as great publicity material as **Gable** [p. 36].

In the second excerpt, Peters gets information from Fleming, one of the witnesses of the murder:

> "I like what we did on that picture," he continued patting down his hair. "I came in on it late after a couple of other directors, and I was pulled off it early to take over **Gone With the Wind**. Still, I spent more than a year on *Oz* and it was the toughest damn thing I've ever done. Those two pictures have been damn good for me, but I wouldn't want to make either one of them again. Even if no one remembers *Oz*, I will and with mixed memories" [p. 49].

The longest excerpt is a part of a scene where Peters meets with Gable at the swimming pool of William Randolph Hearst's castle in San Simeon to talk about the murder:

> It was **Clark Gable**. He picked up a towel and dried his hands as he stepped forward and smiled. He took my hand.
> "Toby Peters, isn't it?" Good to meet you."

"Good to meet you," I said. He went to a bench against the wall, and I followed him as he continued to dry himself.

"Want to take a swim before we talk?" he asked. I said I didn't swim.

"I don't either," he said running the towel over his hair. "Not more than a few strokes. And this damn pool is over my head. There's no shallow end. There's an outdoor pool with a shallow end on the other side of the house, but it's too cold tonight to go out."

. . .

"Shoot," said **Gable** with a wave of his hand.

"You saw two midgets arguing at the studio?"

"Right," he said looking at me the way he looked at **Thomas Mitchell** in *Gone With the Wind*. "One of them is dead, murdered I hear."

. . .

He stood with me, shook my hand and patted me on the back.

"Happy I could help, Peters," he said. The towel was around his neck and he was gripping it in both hands. His dark hair fell over his brow. All he needed was **Victor Fleming** and a camera crew [pp. 70-72].

An allusion to a musical piece from the film appears in Kaminsky's mystery *Smart Moves* (1986), in a scene that takes place in a bar where private eye Toby Peters talks with Pauline Santiago after she announces to him that she is pregnant with his child:

> Charlie at the piano was playing **"Tara's Theme"** from *Gone with the Wind*. The bartender was reading his book in the amber darkness, and the other couple was sitting silently [p. 146].

In Kaminsky's *Retribution* (2001), a mystery set in Florida, unlike the ones mentioned above, process server Lew Fonesca drives a car with his friend Ames, thinking about the woman he lost, his wife which was killed in a hit-and-run accident:

> She liked her coffee black, her tea unsweetened, herbal, but not mint. Her favorite food was grilled seafood. She wore solids, purples, greens, and grays. Old jewelry. She had a necklace that looked like the one **Scarlett O'Hara** wore at the ball before the war [pp. 128-129].

In another Florida mystery by Kaminsky, *Bright Futures* (2008), Fonesca talks on the phone with a guy who threatens to kill him if he does not quit the murder investigation. The conversation turns into a pop-culture exchange:

> "What can I do to convince you?"
> "Stop shooting at me, that would make a nice start," I said.
> "Lewis," Ames said firmly.
> "What's your favorite movie?" I asked
> "What?"
> "Your favorite movie. Mine's *The Third Man*, or *Mildred Pierce*, or *The List of Adrian Messenger*, or *On the Waterfront*, or *The Seven Samurai*, or *Once Upon a Time in America*, or *Comanche Station* . . .
> "You're crazy," he said.
> "Deeply neurotic," I corrected. "You have a favoriye movie?"
> "***Gone with the Wind***."
> "And?'
> "*Wuthering Heights. From Here to Eternity*" [p. 60].

Sidney Sheldon's *A Stranger in the Mirror* (1976) is a Hollywood novel, where Gable is mentioned with several other major movie stars in a passage illustrating one of the shades of aspiring actor Toby Temple's personality as he is interviewed by Mrs. Tanner of Actors West:

> "You don't judge talents by rules, lady! Okay—so I haven't acted. And why? Because people like you won't give me a chance. You see what I mean?" It was W. C. Fields' voice.
>
> Alice Tanner opened her mouth to interrupt him, but Toby never gave her the opportunity. He was Jimmy Cagney telling her to give the poor kid a break, and James Stewart agreeing with him, and **Clark Gable** saying he was dying to work with the kid and Cary Grant adding that he thought the boy was brilliant. A host of Hollywood stars was in that room, and they were all saying funny things, things that Toby Temple had never thought of before [p. 70].

An interesting reference to the film, including a few quoted lines, appears in John Gregory Dunne's mystery *True Confessions* (1977), in a passage where Corinne, cop Tom Spellacy's pregnant girlfriend, tries to fall asleep after they have sex:

> She was wide awake now and in her mind she began to make a list. Corinne always made lists when she couldn't sleep. It was her way of counting sheep. Somewhere in the apartment, there was a list of lines from ***Gone with the Wind***. She was always adding to it. **"I believe in Rhett Butler—that's the only cause I know." "Some little town in Pennsylvania—called Gettysburg." "If you have enough courage, you can do without a reputation." "She's a pale-faced mealy mouthed ninny and I hate her."** Corinne thought: **"Fiddledeedee. I get so bored I could scream."** She must remember to write that down. What else? [p. 199]

In Adam Kennedy's *Just Like Humphrey Bogart* (1978), the film is mentioned in a passage describing Paul Lincoln, the rich husband of Helen, a good friend of the narrator/protagonist, young actor Duffy Odin, whom she is trying to help:

> She hated his body, had from the beginning, couldn't stand to look at him. "But he thinks he's divine," she said. "Loves to parade around naked and show himself off. Room service waiters, chambermaids, they all get to look at him whether they want to or not. He holds press conferences in the bathtub, sitting there in the suds and bubbles, smoking a cigar and explaining why **Gone with the Wind** should have a different title. He wants to rename everything. Movies, cities, people" [pp. 106-107].

A reference to the film was found in Iris Rainer Dart's novel *Beaches* (1985), in a scene where actress-singer Cee Cee Bloom brings her friend Bertie Barron, who appears to be in hard labor, to the hospital:

> Cee Cee emerged from the guest room. By some miracle she was fully made up and dressed in a darling powder blue pants outfit, much more Sarasota-style than Hollywood.
> "Ready?" she asked, grabbing the keys from the coffee table.
> Bertie wanted to lie down in the back seat of the Cadillac but she couldn't, because she had to direct Cee Cee to the hospital. Cee Cee blabbed endlessly, said she felt like **Butterfly McQueen** in **Gone with the Wind** because she didn't know nothin' about birthin' no babies, and laughed, and said that maybe someday she'd have a baby herself, so she wanted to observe very carefully how all this maternity ward shit looked, and then she started to cry and told Bertie that Allan Jackson had left her again—but it didn't matter—that she was dating some very nice

new men, and one of them was a successful movie producer and they had a lot in common [p. 236].

In Barbara Taylor Bradford's *Act of Will* (1986), a drama of three generations of talented women, there is a scene in which Audra, Laurette (her husband's sister) and Christina (her daughter) talk about movies before going to see *Goodbye Mr. Chips*:

> Laurette, who was a real fan and read a lot about films and film stars, had been telling them about the movie, relating something of the story.
>
> "Don't tell us any more," Audra exclaimed. "Otherwise you'll spoil it for us."
>
> "Oh sorry," Laurette apologized, and, changing the subject, she went on, "What *I* can't wait to see is **_Gone with the Wind_**. I've been reading about it in *Picturegoer Magazine* and it sounds wonderful. Vivien Leigh looked so beautiful in last week's issue, and **Clark Gable**! *He's* just gorgeous" [p. 209].

In another novel by Bradford, *Her Own Rules* (1996), the movie is mentioned due to a character's (Amelia Silvers) resemblance to Vivien Leigh (in the eyes of protagonist Meredith Stratton):

> The woman slowly turned, and Meredith realized immediately that she was sitting in a wheelchair. Her breath caught in her throat as she returned the woman's steady gaze. Meredith was startled by her beauty. Dark hair, parted in the middle, tumbled around a pale, heart-shaped face. Wonderful high cheekbones, a dimpled chin, and a sensual mouth were nothing in comparison to the amazing vivid green eyes below perfectly arched black brows. It's the woman from **_Gone with the Wind_**, she thought.

Amelia said, "You're looking rather strange. Are you feeling all right?"

Meredith realized she was staring and exclaimed, "Oh yes, I'm fine. *Sorry*. I'm sorry to stare at you, it's very rude." The words tumbled out, and then because of her youth and ingenuousness, she rushed on unthinkingly. "You're so beautiful. You look like **Vivien Leigh** in ***Gone with the Wind***. Doesn't everybody tell you that?"

"Not everyone. And thank you for your lovely compliment," Amelia answered with a smile and exchanged an amused look with Jack [pp. 84-85].

In her novel *Where You Belong* (1999), Bradford creates an extremely cozy situation in which American journalists Valentine Denning (the narrator) and Jake Newberg, following a traumatic experience in Kosovo, enjoy the luxurious villa called Les Roches Fleuries in Saint-Jean-Cap-Ferrat, southeastern France, which Jake was allowed to use whenever he wished by his close friend Peter Guiseborn, who inherited the villa from his great-aunt. In a scene where they are about to watch a movie from Peter's collection, their conversation inevitably leads to two films that are clearly among the author's true favorites:

Now he was saying, "Don't you think that's a great idea, Val? We'll watch some old movies tonight. Peter has stacks of them, there's quite a wide video selection in his library and there are lots of choices."

"I wonder if he has *Love Affair*?" I said, thinking out loud.

"He might. I know he's got ***Casablanca*** and many of the other classics from the thirties, forties, and fifties. He's even got ***Gone with the Wind***. I wouldn't mind watching *that* again."

I started to laugh.

"What's the matter?" he asked, raising a brow quizzically.

Continuing to laugh, I said, "Are you feeling homesick for Atlanta, Jake?"

Laughing with me, he nodded. "I'm always homesick for Georgia in one way or another, but it just happens to be a really fabulous movie. Let's watch it, okay?"

"Anything you want," I answered [p. 83].

In still another book by Bradford, *Breaking the Rules* (2009), it is someone's resemblance to Leslie Howard that becomes a pretext to mention the movie. It takes place during a supper to which protagonist M invites her friend Derek Alan Kenneth Small, known as Dax:

"I guess so. But you know, I like it. Dax, I mean. It sort of suits you, and your personality. Not to mention your blond good looks. Matinee-idol looks, I might add."

"My mother always told me I resembled **Leslie Howard**." Placing the mug on the table, he murmured, "If you know who he was."

"Do you think I'm an ignoramus, for heaven's sake! Of course I know who he was. He played Ashley Wilkes in ***Gone with the Wind***. And guess what? Since I'm Marie Marsden, they called me M and M at school. How about that?" [p. 19]

In Saul Bellow's novel *More Die of Heartbreak* (1987), a reference to Gable and the film appears in a scene where narrator/protagonist Kenneth offers some of his unique ideas to Dita, his devoted listener:

"Ladies are very accepting nowadays, they've learned it's the spirit that counts, and if they care for you it doesn't matter all that much to them. On the other hand, Vilitzer's son Fishl told me that it was a common feminine fantasy to put together an ideal man. No real person has everything they dream of, so they assemble parts and elements from here and there—a large cock, a sparkling personality, millions of dollars, a bold brilliant spirit like Malraux, the masculine attraction of **Clark Gable** in *Gone with the Wind*, the manners of a French aristocrat, the brain of a superman in physics" [p. 255].

Susan Isaacs's novel *Shining Through* (1988) contains three allusions to the film. A minor reference to the film appears in a passage where the narrator/protagonist, a law firm secretary named Linda Rose Voss, describes one of her coworkers:

> I'd always been intrigued by Wilma. Her entire life was dedicated to men and to getting them. She made no pretense that she cared about who the mayor was, or what Gladys had thought of *Gone with the Wind*. She never looked beyond her own cleavage [p. 13].

Then, an allusion to the movie takes place when the narrator tries to come up with an excuse for standing up another of her coworkers and a friend, Gladys Slade, and compares her to Scarlett O'Hara:

> I sat in the subway as it hurtled into Queens, and I tried to think up a good excuse for Gladys. But I couldn't concentrate. I looked up at an ad for Prince Albert Crimp Cut Pipe Tobacco, with its picture of a boringly handsome middle-aged man who looked the way lawyers were supposed to but never did (except John, who looked better), and worked on feeling bad that I was behaving so rottenly to a friend. But the only thought that came to mind was that an hour in the sun would do Gladys good. Her skin was so white: not **Scarlett O'Hara**, southern magnolia white, but bloodless, like typing paper [p. 118].

When Linda marries her boss, John Berringer, they socialize with members of the upper class, including Henry and Florence Avenel. The description of the Avenels' house is a pretext for another allusion to the film:

> Henry and Florence Avenel lived somewhere in Westchester, in an important-looking white house with pillars that would have been perfect for Thomas Jefferson or **Scarlett O'Hara** but seemed a little much for a bulgy-eyed corporate lawyer who looked like a toad in a striped tie. . . . Just as you drove up and were about to go Ooh! you saw another, newer, smaller, semi-**Tara** on the left and an English Tudor squeezing in on the right [p. 152].

A funny reference to a memorable scene in the film was found in Robert B. Parker's *Crimson Joy* (1988). After psychologist Susan Silverman confronts a patient about knowing that he is a serial killer, she has five martinis in the early afternoon and her boyfriend, private eye Spenser, is forced to stop cooking and carry her to her bedroom:

> With my arms still around her I detached my left arm and shut off the flame under the chicken. Then I slid my left arm down her backside and scooped her into my arms. She pushed her head against my shoulder and locked her arms around my neck. I carried her through the living room and down the hall to her bedroom.
> It's not as easy as it looked in ***Gone With the Wind*** [p. 171].

In another mystery by Parker, *Blue Screen* (2006), the narrator, Boston private investigator Sunny Randall, talks on the phone with Hollywood agent Tony Gault about Hollywood Investment Team, a company arranging financing, and a poignant reference to the box-office success of *Gone with the Wind* is made:

Olivia de Havilland (Melanie Hamilton Wilkes), Ward Bond (Tom, a Yankee Captain), Clark Gable (Rhett Butler) and Leslie Howard (Ashley Wilkes) in a scene from Victor Fleming's *Gone with the Wind* (1939).

"Find a film project that's floundering," Tony said. "Put it together with an investor who wants to be a movie mogul."

"What does the investor get out of it?"

"Depends," Tony said, "on how good his lawyer was when they made the deal. If he gets a percentage of the profits, he gets nothing. I know accountants who could prove that **_Gone with the Wind_** showed no profit" [p. 160].

The film, along with the unusual opinion about it, is mentioned again some twenty pages later when Randall relates the conversation to Jesse Stone, chief of police in Paradise, Massachusetts, with whom he joins forces to track a murderer of a rising star's sister:

"Tony Gault told me," I said to Jesse, "That if you sign onto a movie deal and don't know much, you could end up with a percentage of the profit."

"Uh-huh."

Jesse had put a bowl of water on his office floor for Rosie, and she was drinking from it and making a lot of noise.

"And he told me that there were accountants out there who could make it look like *Gone with the Wind* didn't make a profit."

"Which is why you're better off," Jesse said, "with a piece of the gross" [p. 183].

The focal event in John Dandola's mystery *West of Orange* (1990) is the premiere of *Edison, the Man*, a movie produced by MGM. Consequently, several MGM-related celebrities are mentioned in the following excerpts. (Capitalization of the words in the title is inconsistent in the original text.)

Parades had become Strickling's forte. He was responsible for both this one and the one in Atlanta for *Gone With The Wind* [p. 93].

Dietz laughed and explained to Tony and Mulvey, "Estelle and Donald, there next to her, were with me down in Atlanta for the *Gone With the Wind* premiere."

"Yeah?" Mulvey perked up. "I saw that. Good picture" [p. 141].

After they had pieced only that much together, Dietz had phoned Estelle in New York at one in the morning and summoned her to a breakfast meeting at eight-thirty. She seemed the closest to Donald in longevity at Metro and working relationship and they'd put in time together in Atlanta on the *Gone With the Wind* premiere" [p. 198].

"Estelle, what'd'ya think of *Gone With the Wind*?" Dietz broke the ice.

"That **Selznick**'s batty and for my money Robert Young should've played **Ashley Wilkes**. He's the most underrated actor the studio's got."

"Hear, hear!" Tracy cheered on with a mouthful of toast.

Estelle took a drag on her cigarette. "**Leslie Howard** amounted to the Charlie McCarthy of the Confederacy. The picture's only weak link . . ."

Tracy hooted. "You sure you're not **Victor Fleming** in drag?" he asked her.

"He's better looking," Estelle rocketed back.

Dietz said, "Now that we've heard your fine taste in film casting, I meant what'd you think about working on *__Gone With the Wind__*'s premiere" [p. 199-200].

An allusion to the movie appears also in Kirk Douglas's *Dance with the Devil* (1990). The context is a scene where the author lets the reader know about director Danny Dennison's nostalgic thoughts on the back lot of the studio:

> Danny had to get away; he headed for the back lot, a graveyard of abandoned and dismembered sets. As he passed a row of staircases, he wondered how many different scenes had been played on those steps and all the steps like them in the deserted back lots of the studios of the world. Errol Flynn dueling his way down a staircase; Douglas Fairbanks leaping with sword in hand from balustrade to chandelier; **Clark Gable** carrying **Vivien Leigh** up the steps at **Tara**. He had those memories from his childhood, when he went to the Rialto with Margaret Dennison and thought how exciting it would be to make movies [p. 164].

An allusion to a memorable scene in the film was found in John Grisham's *The Firm* (1991), even though the situation calling for such a comparison, being a part of a set-up arranged by the 'good guys,' is absolutely fake:

> She rolled to face the balcony, and when he finished she felt him sit on her side of the bed. He gently touched her shoulder. "Libby, wake up." He shook her, and she bolted stiff.
> "Wake up, dear," he said. A gentleman.
> She gave him her best sleepy smile. The morning-after smile of fulfillment and commitment. The **Scarlett O'Hara** smile the morning after **Rhett** nailed her. "You were great, big boy," she cooed with her eyes closed.
> In spite of the pain and nausea, in spite of the lead boots and bowling-ball head, he was proud of himself. The woman was impressed. Suddenly, he remembered that he was great last night [p. 350].

A minor reference to the film and one of its supporting actresses appears in Elmore Leonard's *Maximum Bob* (1991), in a passage where young policeman Gary Hammond (a sergeant in the Detective Bureau) and two deputies try to solve the problem of a transgressing alligator:

> Gary turned toward the porch, see what the gator was doing, and just then heard a voice that sounded like a young black girl.
> "You bes' hurry up get that car."
> The one in ***Gone With the Wind***, **Butterfly McQueen**.
> That was who he thought of and turned back expecting to see the deputies grinning, one of them way out of line trying to be funny [p. 68].

The protagonist of Elmore Leonard's World War II-time mystery *Up in Honey's Room* (2007) is U.S. Marshal Carl Webster, here hunting two escaped German POWs. A reference to Gable appears in a passage focused on the "Jewish problem" as seen through the eyes of Walter Schoen, a German-born butcher of a questionable allegiance:

> Walter, meanwhile squinting at his destiny, knew he would not be dealing with the Jewish problem. The press here portrayed Himmler as the most hated man in the world. Even people Walter knew who were vocally anti-Semitic said it would give them an incredible sense of relief if the Jews would go someplace else. There was talk about sending them all to live on the island of Madagascar. You don't exterminate an entire race of people. We're Christians, the Jews are a cross we must bear. They're pushy, insolent, think they're smart, they double-park in front of their delicatessens on Twelfth Street—also on Linwood—and what do we do? Nothing. We make fun of them. Someone says, But they do make movies we go to see. Well, not Walter. The last movie he saw was **_Gone with the Wind_**. He thought **Clark Gable** the blockade runner was good, but the rest of the movie a waste of time. Walter had better things to do, work toward becoming as well known as Himmler, perhaps even a Nazi saint [pp. 70-71].

In John Updike's novel *In the Beauty of the Lilies* (1996), a tragic scene of the film is referred to by Essie, who is reminiscing about her early boyfriend:

> Benjy had a very interesting mouth in profile, fitted together so precisely, and a little angrily, like **Vivien Leigh**'s in **_Gone with the Wind_**. That had been such a tremendous movie, though she didn't like it when the little girl fell off the horse and died, and

preferred *The Wizard of Oz*, where nobody got hurt except the witches [p. 264].

Numerous references to the film, frequently including Gable and other stars, appear in Rebecca Wells's *Divine Secrets of the Ya-Ya Sisterhood* (1996), as the Walker belles, at one point or another, discuss the movie and a variety of issues related to this most important picture for the South:

> Teensy brought the latest *Modern Screen* with her, so we're reading all about **Gone With the Wind**. Miss Yankee **Vivien Leigh**'s picture is all over it, which just breaks our hearts. We have still not forgiven them for not casting Tallulah. **Vivien** is not only a Southerner, she isn't even an American! [p. 110]

A clipping from *The Atlanta Journal* dated December 15, 1939, found by Sidda in her scrapbook, is presented below as a quotation within a quotation:

> Social brilliance without compare in Atlanta's romantic history wrote a glorious chapter of accomplishment for the Junior League's **Gone With the Wind** costume ball at City Auditorium Thursday night....
>
> **Clark Gable**, **Vivien Leigh**, **Olivia De Havilland**, Claudette Colbert, Carole Lombard, and dozens of governors, capitalists, socialites from Maine to California, and magnates whose genius has created a mighty industry in motion pictures, statesmen, and writers and actors, all richly garbed, were serenaded with spirituals by a group of Negroes in plantation costume from the Ebenezer Baptist Church. Fifty members of the Junior League then promenaded through the curtain one by one, each attired in a gorgeous party frock of **Scarlett O'Hara**'s day [pp. 111-112].

The following excerpts from two letters sent by Viviane to Necie are rather self-explanatory:

> So then old William drives us to Peachtree Street and he finds us a good place and we sit on the roof of the car to watch the parade. Oh, it was so crowded, I mean people were eight and ten deep. And then the parade started. Necie, there must have been fifty or sixty cars, with stars sitting in the back of convertibles, looking like royalty. **Clark Gable** himself was there! Honey, I am not kidding! I saw him with my own two eyes. And he is just as wonderful as I thought he would be. Carole Lombard was with him and they waved and smiled at us, and I swear to you, Necie, *he looked right at me*. Teensy and Caro are still trying to act like this did not happen, but they are just jealous. I'm telling you the truth: **Clark Gable** *looked at me and smiled* [pp. 120-121].

> I forgot to tell about the theater! The Hollywood people made it so the front of the Loew's Grand looks exactly like the front of **Tara**. And there somehow was a whole lawn they grew across Peachtree Street for all the stars to walk on. They walked on this new grass the whole way. **Mr. Gable** was so chivalrous, Necie. He said exactly what I would have wanted him to say. He said that the night wasn't his night but that the night *belonged to **Miss Mitchell***. Oh, that really showed me what **Mr. Gable** is made of. That made me fall in love with him to the point that I will just never get over it [p. 128].

Jill McCorkle's novel *Carolina Moon* (1996) is an engaging character study, set in Fulton, North Carolina. The passage below, which includes an original reference to Fleming's classic, mentions three major characters: Queen Mary Strutts Purdy, also known as Quee, a 69-year-old owner of a smokers' clinic called "Smoke-Out Signals," Tom Lowe, a thirty-nine- year-old-man she employs as a carpenter (who also happens to be the son of her deceased lover), and Mary Denise Parks (Denny), a thirty-five-year-old woman soon to join the staff of the clinic and become romantically involved with Tom:

> Tom turns from the window where he has watched Quee oversee the trash pickup, and he drives the final nail into the molding at the top of the closet space. Quee didn't want a door on the closet. Said she preferred the curtain look. She had supplied him with the curtain already on a heavy brass rod and asked that he hang it in place once the closet was finished. The curtain was green, velvet she'd bought from that crazy old junk man she supports. She told Tom when she saw it she knew it was perfect, kind of a ***Gone with the Wind*** look to welcome Mary Denise. He figures a ***Gone with the Wind*** look means that if Mary Denise ever finds herself with nothing to wear she could snatch down the curtain over her closet and put it around her [p. 61].

The Clark Gable and Carole Lombard Murder Case (1997) by George Baxt brims with references to the film. Below is probably the most informative one, a narrative passage inserted among the exciting events which take place during a party at Miriam Hopkins':

> The beach was swarming with photographers and reporters having a field day. For them, Miriam's guests were a banquet and they couldn't be happier feasting. **David O. Selznick**, never one to let an opportunity for publicity to slip by, took command of the press. He reminded them that **Clark Gable** and Carole would be departing for Atlanta for the world premiere of ***Gone with the Wind*** along with himself, his wife, and **Clark**'s co-stars

in the movie. No, **Leslie Howard** wouldn't be with them; the British patriot was back in England helping with the war effort. He deftly sidestepped questions about why the Negro actresses **Hattie McDaniel** and **Butterfly McQueen** had been exempted from the junket.

"They're not going to be with us," said Carole pointedly, "because the mayor of Atlanta couldn't come up with decent accommodations for them." **Selznick** started to turn red purple and his wife rummaged in her handbag for his glycerin capsules. **Selznick**'s heart was in the right place but it occasionally malfunctioned. **Gable** chuckled at Carole's bluntness. He would miss the two actresses. They had been great fun on the set, filming a movie he loathed participating in [pp. 120-121].

Another excerpt worth quoting is a brief passage related, thematically, to the one above:

In the plane flying to Atlanta for the world premiere of *Gone with the Wind*, Carole held tightly to **Clark**'s arm. She was terrified of flying. Irene Selznick had plied her with sedatives, which didn't seem to have helped, and now she tried applied psychology. "Carole, tell us again how you captured Oscar Levant and stood by while the Jap committed suicide."

Carole came alive. "You really want to hear it *again*?" [p. 182]

Tom Wolfe's reference to the film (or the book) in *A Man in Full* (1998), a novel set in Atlanta, Goergia, in a part of a passage that offers an interesting lesson in history, politics and business:

It was no use walking up any farther, because there was no office of Colonial Real Properties to be found. But there wasn't one for First Gould Guaranty, either. For the biggest—First Gould—as well as the smallest—Colonial Real Properties—this was merely a dummy address that enabled one to carry out so-called overseas financial operations. The banks, for example, could use the Bahamas to set up Eurodollar accounts for their customers. Individuals could hide money here, in Bahamian banks, with a secrecy that was tightly protected by Bahamian banking laws. Not for nothing did Nassau call itself Little Switzerland. Ever since the Civil War, when blockade runners—such as **Rhett Butler** in *Gone with the Wind*—used the Bahamas as a safe harbor from which to do business with the Confederacy, American had been using the Bahamas to get around American laws [p. 497].

The narrator of Max Allan Collins's political thriller *Majic Man* (1999) is Chicago private investigator Nate Heller, who goes to New Mexico in order to obtain information about a mysterious landing of a UFO two years before. One of the people he talks to is Air Force Nurse Maria Selff, who—in the narrator's perception—ends up being treated just like the heroine of *Gone with the Wind* once was:

> I went to her, gathered her in my arms—she was trembling all over, bawling like a baby, and I cradled her in my arms, patted her back, rocking her, saying, "It'll be all tight . . . it'll be fine . . don't you cry . . . shush . . . shush." She whimpered and sobbed for quite a while, as I held her, and finally it abated, and she relaxed, face against my shoulder, as I kept rocking her.
>
> She was feather-light, when I carried her up the stairs like **Rhett Butler** whisking **Scarlett O'Hara** away, only my **Scarlett** was sleeping, snoring even, a very unfeminine snore that made me smile [p. 156].

In another mystery by Collins, *Quarry in the Middle* (2009), a reference to the film takes place during a conversation between the narrator, a hit man using an alias Jack Gibson, and a waitress of the Paddlewheel casino in Haydee's Port, Illinois:

"So," I asked her, "you don't live in Haydee's Port?"
"No!" she said, eyes so wide you'd think I goosed her. "*Nobody* lives in Haydee's Port!"
"What about your boss?"
She got coy. "What boss is that?"
"Mr. Cornell. Does he live across the river, too?"
My knowing the boss's name was enough for her to replace coy with chatty. "He lives close. A regular mansion. Ever see **Gone with the Wind**?"
"Sure."
"Like that. White pillars and everything."
"He lives in **Tara** and you're a wage slave, huh?" [p. 54]

In Muriel Barbery's unusual novel *Gourmet Rhapsody* (2000), the reasons for a couple of references to the movie are a dog's name and an interior description, respectively:

He was a Dalmatian, and I'd baptized him Rhett, in honor of **Gone with the Wind**, my favorite film, because if I had been a woman, I would have been **Scarlett**—the one who survives in a world that is dying [p. 103].

But when I went into the main room, I was carried away. This was just as I had dreamt America would be, and despite all my expectations, flouting my certainty that once I was there I would revise all my clichés, it was exactly as I had imagined: a large rectangular room with wooden tables and booths covered in red leatherette; on the walls were photos of actors, a poster from ***Gone with the Wind*** with **Scarlett** and **Rhett** on the boat taking them to New Orleans; a vast, well-polished wooden counter cluttered with butter, maple-syrup dispensers, and ketchup bottles [pp. 115-116].

In addition to three relatively insignificant allusions to the film (all mentioning Rhett Butler) in Elizabeth Hay's novel *Garbo Laughs* (2003), the book references the movie in an interesting passage where young Kenny shares with his mother the top-five lists. Here are his favorite films:

> "And your top five movies?" she asked, her voice quite sharp.
> "*The Godfather, West Side Story, Some Like It Hot, The Wizard of Oz*, ***Gone with the Wind***."
> "Kenny," she said broken-heartedly, 'you've been reading too many top-one hundred lists. You've been corrupted. Be truthful' [p. 276].

Clark Gable is a minor character in Stuart Woods's mystery *The Prince of Beverly Hills* (2004), where, consequently, he is mentioned frequently in various contexts. The reference to *Gone with the Wind* in the book is not, however, related to his name:

> Rick spent the afternoon reading ***Gone with the Wind*** in his office. He had somehow not gotten around to it when the book had been published three years before, but it was being filmed at Metro, and he wanted to read it before seeing the movie [p. 82].

In another mystery by Woods, *Beverly Hills Dead* (2008), there are numerous references to Clark Gable and one to the location of his most famous movie:

"Thanks," Tom turned around and drove out of the "forty acres," as it was known, the back lot where many films had been shot, including a lot of the exteriors for ***Gone with the Wind*** [p. 183].

A memorable scene from the film is evoked in Marisa de los Santos's novel *Love Walked In* (2005) as the book's narrator, Cornelia Brown, quotes her mother in the context of reminiscing about a family tragedy (her own mother's untimely death):

> "I swore nothing like that would ever touch this family," and her whole body tilted forward when she said it, so great was her ferocity. It was the scene in ***Gone with the Wind***, **Scarlett** raising her fist into the air, Georgia in ashes around her, the morning sun turning the world red [p. 271].

A reference to Gable in *Gone with the Wind* appears also in Stieg Larsson's mystery *The Girl with the Dragon Tattoo* (2005), in a passage where the titular female protagonist, Lisbeth Salander, analyzes her recent discoveries in the research she carries out for investigative reporter Mikael Blomkvist:

> Three hours later, getting on for 8:30, Salander had concluded that Gottfried Vanger had been close to where at least five of the eight murders were committed, either during the days before or after the event. She was still missing information about the murders in 1949 and 1954. She studied a newspaper photograph of him. A slim, handsome man with dark blond hair; he looked like **Clark Gable** in ***Gone with the Wind*** [pp. 476-477].

In Joseph Wambaugh's *Hollywood Station* (2006), the film and its female protagonist are mentioned in a conversation between minor criminal Farley Ramsdale and his girlfriend Olive Oyle:

> "We'll get by, Farley. You should eat something. And you should not get discouraged, and try to always remember that tomorrow's another day."
>
> "Jesus Christ," Farley said, staring at her. "**_Gone with the Fucking Wind_**!"
>
> "What, Farley?"
>
> Farley, who, like most tweakers, stayed up for days watching movie after movie on the tube, said, "You're what woulda happened to **Scarlett O'Hara** in later life if she'd smoked a chuck wagon load of Maui ice. She'd have turned into you! 'Tomorrow is another fucking day'!" [p. 121]

Two references to the film were found in James Lee Burke's *The Tin Roof Blowdown* (2007), a Dave Robicheaux novel depicting post-Katrina life in New Orleans. The first excerpt is triggered by some unusual pieces of furniture that Eddy and Bertrand Melancon come across during their plundering operation:

> Now they were going house-to-house on a flooded street where every live oak was broken in half on top of the yards, only one house with lights working in it, choppers flying overhead to the hospital roof, not a police boat in sight, Bertrand and Eddy both working the upstairs of a mansion that had beds in it with canopies over them, like the kind in **_Gone with the Wind_**, Eddy stuffing a woman's fur coat into a drawstring laundry bag along with a handful of necklaces he found buried at the bottom of her panty drawer [p. 59].

The second reference is part of a passage describing Sidney Kovick, a character introduced by the narrator/protagonist as "an enigmatic man whose personality was that of either a sociopath or a master thespian":

> He owned a flower shop, loved movies, and always wore a carnation in his lapel. His favorite quote was a paraphrase of a line spoken by **Rhett Butler** in *Gone with the Wind*: "**Great fortunes are made during the rise and fall of nations.**" Sidney was invited to the governor's inauguration ball, rode on the floats during Mardi Gras, and performed once on the wing of a biplane at an aerial show over Lake Pontchartrain [p. 93].

In Marcia Muller's *The Ever-Running Man* (2007), Sharon McCone asks Kendra Williams, the assistant office manager, about the whereabouts of Kendra's gay boss, Ted Smalley, and a reference is made to a supporting actress in the movie:

> "He go home early?" I asked.
> "No, the dentist. Between his twitchiness over having his teeth cleaned and you flying, he's been wringing his hands like **Butterfly McQueen**. He said to tell you that all's on an even keel here. And I can testify to that." She handed me a few message slips. "Nothing important, I don't think."
> "Thanks." I went along the catwalk to my office, amused by the reference to the *Gone with the Wind* character who had performed her histrionics long before Kendra—or even her mother—was born [p. 234].

Another reference to the film, related to the name of the famous estate, appears in James Patterson's *Maximum Ride: School's Out Forever* (2006):

"What's your house like?" Nudge asked. "Is it all white with big columns? Like **Tara**? Did you see that movie?"

"***Gone with the Wind***," Anne said. "No, I'm afraid my house isn't anything like **Tara**. It's an old farmhouse. But I do have fifty acres of land around it. Plenty of room for you guys to run around. We're almost there" [p. 59].

In Eileen Favorite's imaginative novel *The Heroines* (2008), the two protagonists, Penny and her mother, experience unusual relationships with some famous literary characters of the past. Chapter 14 of the book is called 'What would Scarlett do?' and, as expected, it refers mostly to the popular novel by Margaret Mitchell. However, the movie version is inevitably mentioned in some sections. Here is the evidence:

As if I had some gift for conjuring (which I didn't), the door banged open and a woman staggered into the foyer. Her black hair was wild, her face as white as the snowy birch trees outside. She had mauve circles beneath her eyes, but one glimpse at their jade color and her tiny waist told me instantly who she was, though she wasn't quite as beautiful as **Vivien Leigh**. She reached a shaky hand to the desk for support, then collapsed on the cold tile with a sickening thud [p. 112].

Whenever Mother and Gretta referred to Heroines I didn't remember, I always felt left out, and though I'd often tried, I could never get Mother to tell me about that particular Heroine's visit. I sensed that Gretta knew not to speak of it either. There were many things she wouldn't speak about, especially the war. I was somewhat surprised that Gretta knew Scarlett's story, but I realized later that ***Gone with the Wind***had been a big hit in Germany [p. 114].

"**Ashley**!"

Mother and I locked eyes, and she shook her head gravely

as if she knew that I wanted to rush to the bed to talk **Scarlett** out of loving him. Mother gave me too much credit. This was a few months before Emma Bovary arrived, before my rebellious hormones kicked into high gear. I'd seen *Gone with the Wind* enough times to know that nobody could talk **Scarlett** out of anything [p. 115].

A reference to the film, and to one of its leading actresses, was found in Rebecca Miller's novel *The Private Lives of Pippa Lee* (2008). In the following excerpt, Grace, Pippa Lee's daughter, analyzes the character of her twin-brother's girlfriend:

So off he went to Europe with Stephanie, that loyal hound. Grace knew that Ben loved Stephanie for what she wasn't (neurotic, blunt, alluring, hilarious) as much as for what she was (constant, sweet, accommodating yet intelligent—a sort of modern-day **Olivia de Havilland** in *Gone with the Wind*). In essence, she knew her brother had chosen a girl as unlike herself as possible [p. 37].

A somewhat amusing reference to the film and its female protagonist appears in Larry McMurtry's novel *Rhino Ranch* (2009), which is the final part of the author's "Thalia" series (with Duane Moore as the focal character in all five). The quoted scene has Dal, a Cambodian woman employed by Moore Drilling, entertaining both Duane and Bobby Lee:

"I went to the Colorado School of Mines," Dal said. "I wanted to know what was in the earth, and now I do know. How was curry?"
She was giving dinner to Duane and Bobby Lee at the tiny table in her room.

"It was the second hottest meal I ever ate," Bobby said. "And I lapped up every bite of it, ma'am."

"You don't have to call me ma'am," she said, with a mischievous look at Duane. He had never seen her look mischievous before.

"I am not **Scarlett O'Hara**," she added.

Neither Duane nor Bobby could immediately place **Scarlett O'Hara**.

"***Gone with the Wind***," Dal said. "Very popular in Asia. What have eaten that is hotter than my curry?" [p. 159]

A *Gone with the Wind*-related anecdote about accents is told in Adriana Trigiani's novel *Home to Big Stone Gap* (2006) by narrator/protagonist Ave Maria MacChesney, who is helming the town musical:

> As we read, some actors actually attempt Austrian accents: they fail miserably, falling into the **Vivien Leigh**-Door Ford problem. The story goes that when England's **Vivien Leigh** auditioned for the role of **Scarlett O'Hara** in ***Gone with the Wind***, they brought in a dialogue coach to help take her accent from the British highbrow to Southern fried. She'd say "Four-door Ford" as "fo-ah do-ah fo-ah," over and over again, hoping to capture out twang. Evidently, I'm not the only one familiar with the ***GWTW*** dialogue-coach story [p. 94].

A reference to the film in another novel by Trigiani, *Very Valentine* (2009), is a part of a humorous goodbye scene where narrator/protagonist Valentine witnesses her grandmother being more than chivalrously treated by a local man on the Isle of Capri:

> Gram goes out the front door, takes the banister, and goes

down the stairs. Dominic waits for her on the last step. I quickly skip around Gram to give them a private moment.

I go to the car, which is parked at the side of the inn, load her suitcase into the trunk, and wait. Through the thick boxwood hedge, I can see the two of them embrace. Then he dips her, gives her a kiss, backbend style, the likes of which I have not seen since **Clark Gable** kissed **Vivien Leigh**, in the commemorative DVD of ***Gone with the Wind*** [p. 274].

Irene Bennett Brown's mystery *Where Gable Slept* (2010) includes several references to *Gone with the Wind*. First, it is one of the tourists visiting Pass Creek, Oregon, that talks about the actor and his most famous movie:

> The lady's friend, holding her own red hat to allow a warm breeze to riffle her gray hair, asked, "My goodness, can we see the bed where **Clark Gable** *slept*? When I was a lot younger, he was my favorite actor. I don't know how many times I saw ***Gone With The Wind***, but my husband, bless his soul, claimed it was too many." She grinned. "Jealous, I guess, of that good-looking **Clark Gable**"[p. 3]

The second passage containing an allusion to the film pertains to the appearance of the book's protagonist, Celia Landrey, here in the role of the small town's tour guide:

> It was hard to keep her mind on the job and fulfill her promise to the dozen tourists she'd grouped in front of the library a short while later. Today she wore an emerald green formal, probably made for a high school prom, but the closest she could come to Scarlet O'Hara in ***Gone With The Wind*** [p. 47].

A couple of objects related to the film are mentioned in a passage describing Celia's search of the famous house, which she carries out as part of her investigation:

> Not here, though. She moved on, completing a search of other tables in the room, including a tall curio cabinet, finding interesting odd and ends, among them a blue glass boot holding a lot of very old pennies, a little souvenir railroad mug, three or four ancient and empty liquor decanters, a pair of **Rhett Butler** and **Scarlet O'Hara** figurines, which Celia instantly fell in love with [p. 188].

Fannie Flagg references *Gone with the Wind* in a few of her novels, notably in *The All-Girl Filling Station's Last Reunion* (2013), where a couple of major movies are mentioned within the narrator's background description of the period:

> Poland has fallen, but life in America carried on as usual. Kids still played baseball, and the 1939 World's Fair in New York was being mobbed by people thrilled about seeing all the marvelous inventions that were in the works. The World of Tomorrow exhibit promised nothing but an exciting future. Elsewhere, across the country, women and girls sat in movie houses, swooning over **Clark Gable** in ***Gone with the Wind***, while men and boys were enthralled watching John Wayne ride shotgun across the West in *Stagecoach* [p. 98].

Boom Town **(1940).** The third and last item in the onscreen partnership of Gable and Tracy, this relatively rewarding picture, directed by Jack Conway, is referenced in a few books, including Michael Malone's novel *The Four Corners of the Sky* (2009). It is also one of many Claudette Colbert films used by the author as chapter titles (this one of Chapter 38, p. 329).

In the book, however, the epithet refers to Miami, which is made clear by Cuban con artist Raffy Rook in his conversation with U.S. Navy pilot Annie Peregrine Goode:

> "Unfortunately. But that was later. So I start to see him and Diaz everywhere. Your dad was on a roll, treating large crowds to dinner at the best places. Taking twenty, thirty people, a la carte. Annie, fast forward five, six years, here in Miami we have condos and clubs, night lights, Marlins, Dolphins, SoBe, the Grove, it's a **boomtown**, an American Riviera" [p. 335].

Clark Gable as Big John McMasters and Hedy Lamarr as Karen Vanmeer in a scene from Jack Conway's *Boom Town* (1940).

***Honky Tonk* (1941).** This typical (meaning unremarkable) MGM western, directed by Jack Conway and co-starring Lana Turner, is briefly and vaguely alluded to by Gable himself in Michael B. Druxman's play *Gable* (1984), in a passage combining history with the actor's personal life:

> The Japanese bombed Pearl Harbor on December 7, 1941. In January, Carole was asked to go on a tour to promote the sale of War Bonds. I'd have gone with her, but I was scheduled to start a picture with **Lana Turner** [p. 41].

Lana Turner as Elizabeth Cotton and Clark Gable as 'Candy' Johnson in a scene from Jack Conway's *Honky Tonk* (1941).

***Somewhere I'll Find You* (1942).** Wesley Ruggles's mediocre war drama, co-starring Lana Turner and Robert Sterling, was Gable's last movie before he joined the military forces fighting in World War II. The film is referenced in two books. In Barbara Taylor Bradford's novel *Remember* (1991), there is a scene in which war correspondent Nicky Wells and photographer Cleeland

Donovan, having finished their job in Beijing, discover their love for each other and enjoy their new relationship having lunch and watching a movie:

Stepping over to the bookcase, he continued, "Which movie did you choose in the end?"

"It's called **_Somewhere I'll Find You_**, with **Clark Gable** and Lana Turner playing foreign correspondents who . . . get involved with each other on a foreign assignment."

"Aha!" he exclaimed. A wide grin spread across his face. "How appropriate. I couldn't have chosen better myself."

The minute the film started rolling, Clee sat down on the cushions, leaned over and kissed the tip of her nose, then picked up a tuna-salad sandwich and settled back to watch.

They laughed a lot during the film. It had been made in 1942 and was somewhat unrealistic. It had a sweetness, an innocence about it, and this made it seem dated to the two tough news veterans accustomed to difficult, often harrowing foreign assignments.

"Hey, Nick, this is really sappy," Clee muttered at one moment, looking at her from the corner of his eye.

"I know. A lot of old movies are."

. . .

"You're right, but occasionally this one does have a ring of truth to it, especially when **Gable**'s on the screen." The legendary star was Nicky's favorite, and a few seconds later, when **Gable** said, 'I don't print anything until I've heard it twice and seen it three times,' Nicky said, " That's going to be *my* motto from now on!"

He rolled his eyes to the ceiling in mock horror.

"Wait a minute," Nicky said swiftly, "you've got to admit **Gable** plays a terrific newspaperman, with just the right amount of dash and panache. And he *is* gorgeous."

"True, true." Clee turned her face to his and kissed her lightly on the mouth. "And so are you," he said softly [pp. 130-131].

Another reference to *Somewhere I'll Find You* appears in Jeffrey Cohen's already quoted mystery *It Happened One Knife* (2008). Below is a passage in which narrator Elliot Freed analyzes some past events in the lives and careers of a legendary team of comedians, Harry Lillis & Les Townes, whom he suspects of committing a recent crime:

The official record listed the fire as electrical in nature, and did not classify it as suspicious. Townes, at least outwardly inconsolable, didn't return to the set of *Step This Way* for eight weeks, a very long time during the reign of the studio system (**Clark Gable**, for example, was back on the set of ***Somewhere I'll Find You*** only thirty-eight days after Carole Lombard's death in a plane crash). It was up to Harry Lillis, who was also grieving for a lost love, to shoot around his partner and eventually to cover Townes's absence by claiming that he, Lillis, had pneumonia and couldn't film [p. 58].

Adventure **(1945).** Gable's comeback after his military service, directed by Victor Fleming, turned out to be a rather disappointing film despite two talented female co-stars, Greer Garson and Joan Bennett. The movie is referenced in Michael B. Druxman's play *Gable* (1984), in a scene where Gable talks about his situation after World War II:

Metro took its time finding me a picture to do, after I came back. I wasn't in a hurry to get back in front of the cameras either.

Finally, they decided to pair me with the new "queen" of the lot ... **Greer Garson** ... "sweet Mrs. Miniver."

(*He takes seaman's cap off costume rack; puts it on.*)

That was the bad part. On the positive side of the ledger, **Vic Fleming** was directing. **Joan Blondell** and **Thomas Mitchell** had supporting roles.

It was called *__Adventure__*, and it was lousy [p. 52].

The Hucksters **(1947).** Under the guidance of another frequent collaborator, Jack Conway, Gable appeared in another disappointing picture, though clearly superior to *Adventure*, two years later, and, again, the female co-stars—Deborah Kerr and Ava Gardner—did not help. The movie is mentioned in Janet Leigh's *House of Destiny* (1995), in a passage where Jude fills in Wade about how he spent the previous night, how he was forced to leave the movie theater before the show began due to an incident with a pervert:

"I don't know and I don't care! I just got the hell out of there. I know one thing, no more solo movies for me!"

Wade was now gasping for breath between spasms of laughter. "But other than that, how did you like the film?"

"How do I know? I really wanted to see ***The Hucksters***, too, damn it!"

"Maybe you and I can go back—to your favorite theater," Wade kidded.

"Cut it out! Fine cast—**Clark Gable**, Ava Gardner . . ."

"What a body on that one! Wade sighed, his attention mercifully diverted.

"You can say that again! But don't! Anyway, **Ava Gardner, Deborah Kerr**—classy lady—**Gloria Holden, Adolphe Menjou**—"

"Please—please don't mention his name!" Wade pleaded. "He is one of the reasons I have this splitting headache!"

"You have a splitting headache because you got plastered!" Jude reported. "Don't blame poor **Adolphe Menjou**. Somehow, I doubt he was even there" [pp. 157-158].

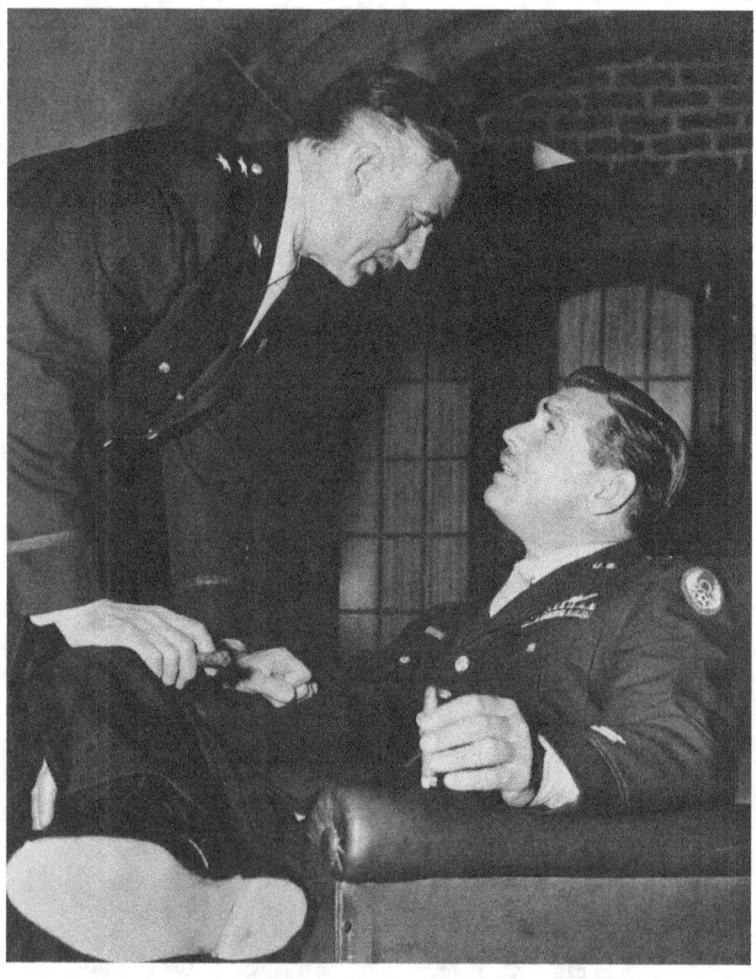

Walter Pidgeon as General Kane and Clark Gable as General Dennis in a scene from Sam Wood's *Command Decision* (1948).

Command Decision (1948). Directed by Sam Wood and featuring Clark Gable, Walter Pidgeon, Van Johnson and Brian Donlevy, *Command Decision* is a successful World War II picture, one of Gable's best from that period. A brief, self-explanatory reference to the film was found in Joseph Wambaugh's book *The Choirboys* (1975):

> Deputy Chief Lynch was a man to reckon with because he had thought of the most printable slogan in the history of the department. It was the slogan for a simple plan to spread out the staff officers geographically, giving them line control over everything in a given area. But if the plan were to be newsworthy, it needed a word or words to make it sound sophisticated, military and *dramatic*.
> It came to Deputy Chief Lynch in a dream one night after he saw **Command Decision** on "The Late Show."
> "Territorial Imperative!" he screamed in his sleep, terrifying his wife.
> "But what's it mean, sir?" his adjutant asked the next day.
> "That's the beauty of it, stupid. It means whatever you want it to mean," Chief Lynch answered testily [p. 14].

The movie, along with a few other war/aviation films, is also referenced in Andrew J. Fenady's humorous mystery *The Secret of Sam Marlow* (1980):

> Once again Sam was one of Hell's Angels; he was Errol Flynn in *Dive Bomber*. Dana Andrews coming in on *A Wing and a Prayer*. Tyrone Power in *A Yank in the RAF*. John Garfield in *Air Force*. Gregory Peck in *Twelve O'Clock High*. **Clark Gable** in **Command Decision** [p. 121].

And the film is mentioned by Gable himself, the only character in Michael B. Druxman's play *Gable* (1984), in his comments about another of his movies, *Adventure*:

> But, it made money, and ... though I hate to admit it ...

it was probably no worse than most of the pictures I made for **Metro** afterwards.

An exception: *__Command Decision__*. I was proud of that one.

Any Number Can Play **(1949).** A brief reference to this forgettable, if not completely flawed, film, directed by Mervyn LeRoy and co-starring Alexis Smith and Wendell Corey, appears in Michael B. Druxman's play *Gable* (1984):

> *__Any Number Can Play__*. It wasn't much of a picture, but I'll never forget it. I was doing a love scene with **Alexis Smith**, and she got her goddamn tooth caught in my mustache [p. 53.]

Across the Wide Missouri **(1951).** Directed by William A. Wellman, this relatively rewarding picture is also one of Gable's better westerns, but it does not mean a lot since westerns were not Gable's forte despite his unquestioned masculinity. An original reference to the film, and to the song related to the movie, offering some insight about film and music correlation, was found in John Edgar Wideman's short story "Across the Wide Missouri" (1981):

> "Here's a good one. Meant to look at the paper before now, but we been real busy. Wanted to be sure there was a good one but it's alright, got a Western at the Stanley and it's just down a couple blocks past Gimbels. **Clark Gable**'s in it. *__Across the Wide Missouri__*."
>
> The song goes something like this: *A white man loved an Indian Maiden* and la de da-/-la de da. And: *A-way, you've gone away . . . Across the wide Mis-sour-i*. Or at least those words are in it, I think. I think I don't know the words on purpose. For the same reason I don't have it on record. Maybe fifteen or twenty times in the thirty years since I saw the movie I've heard the song or pieces of the song again. Each time I want to cry. Or do

cry silently to myself. A flood of tears the iron color of the wide Missouri I remember from the movie [p. 139].

Jack Holt as Bear Ghost and Clark Gable as Flint Mitchell in a scene from William A. Wellman's *Across the Wide Missouri* (1951).

A brief reference to the film was also found in Michael B. Druxman's play *Gable* (1984). In the quoted excerpt, Gable speaks about his fourth wife, Sylvia Ashley:

> She was a lady of refinement. Society background. She didn't like hunting. She didn't like fishing.
>
> She went on location with me for **_Across the Wide Missouri_**. We shot that in the wilds of Colorado, and there weren't many modern luxuries.
>
> She was out of place. Didn't fit in. We both knew it.
>
> A few months later, she went on a trip by herself to Nassau. I changed the locks while she was gone.
>
> It was easier that way [p. 55].

Lone Star (1952). Directed by Vincent Sherman and co-starring Ava Gardner and Broderick Crawford, *Lone Star* is also a minor item in Gable's filmography even though it was co-scripted by Borden Chase (the author of *Red River*). This unexpired western is briefly mentioned in Michael B. Druxman's play *Gable* (1984):

> What's my latest? **_Lone Star_**, filmed in glorious black-and-white on the Culver City backlot [p. 56].

Never Let Me Go (1953). This political melodrama based on Andrew Garve's (real name: Paul Winterton) novel and directed by Delmer Daves was referenced in Andrew J. Fenady's *The Man with Bogart's Face* (1977). The context is a telephone conversation between the protagonist, private detective Sam Marlow, and his attractive client, Gena Anastas, followed by Sam's afterthoughts which are triggered by Gena's resemblance to Gene Tierney:

> It was only 7:30 when he got home and called Gena.
>
> "Would you like to go to a little party tonight?" she asked.

"I thought we were having one of our own."

"That comes later." He voice was driving him nuts.

He could see her face, pure and plaintive the way she looked in **_Never Let Me Go_** when she was a Russian ballerina in love with **Gable** and **Gable** had to get her out from behind the Iron Curtain [pp. 137-138].

Mogambo **(1953).** Directed by John Ford, this African adventure/romance drama, in which Gable again has two major female co-stars, Ava Gardner and Grace Kelly, is a remake of Gable's earlier movie, a fact which is mentioned in one of the discovered references. An allusion to the film, in Gable's own words (as imagined by the author), appears in Michael B. Druxman's play *Gable* (1984):

> The first picture we did was in glorious black-and-white, but for the second one, they offered Technicolor and Africa.
>
> I guess **MGM** figured that if they could afford to send Stewart Granger there, they could afford to send me, too.
> (*Puts on safari shirt and hat.*)
> John Mahin did the script.
> (*To unseen Mahin:*)
> Yeah, John, I read it.
> (*Not too sincerely.*)
> It's okay.
>
> Turning **_Red Dust_** into a safari picture is a great idea. It probably works better here than in the original.
>
> Kenya sounds like fun. That's where the Mau Maus are on the warpath, isn't it?

Nothing's bothering me.

Sure, I think **Ava Gardner**'s a good choice for **Harlow**'s old role.

I don't know **Grace Kelly**. Who is she?

She can't be that "up and coming" if I've never heard of her.

I told you that nothing's bothering me. . . .

Okay. There is something.

It stinks.

My part is lousy.

Gardner's got all the funny lines. . . .

It's not funny, you son-of-a-bitch!

What?
(*Repeating Mahin's comment.*)
"The audience won't laugh until they see my reaction."
(*Nods.*)
Yeah, I am a reactor.

You're right, John. That will work.
(*To audience:*)
And, it did. <u>**Mogambo**</u> was one of the most successful pictures I ever made for **Metro**.

Grace Kelly as Linda Nordley and Clark Gable as Vic Marswell in John Ford's *Mogambo* (1953).

Remember that climactic scene? **Grace** and I'd been fooling around together in the jungle. She comes to my tent to tell me she's going to leave her husband. I decide to be gallant and dump her.... And she finds **Ava** in my arms.

(*Goes into scene.*)

"What're you surprised about? You always sort of guessed that **'Kel'** and I were old friends, didn't you? It's okay for old friends to have a drink, isn't it?

"Listen, **Mrs. N.**, you're not going to tell me that you've taken this all seriously, are you?

"You know how it is on safari. It's in all the books. The woman always falls for the white hunter, and we guys make the most of it. Do you blame us?"
(*To audience:*)
Don't I make a great son-of-a-bitch?
(*Removes hat; starts to unbutton shirt.*)
About **Grace Kelly**?

She's quite a girl [pp. 57-58].

George Baxt's *The Tallulah Bankhead Murder Case* (1987) makes a reference to both *Mogambo* and its original version, *Red Dust*, also starring Gable, during a conversation between Grace Kelly and another guest invited to Tallulah Bankhead's 'rounding-up all the suspects' party. Nota bene: Kelly (or Baxt) is wrong about the release date of *Red Dust*; the movie was made in 1932, i.e. twenty years earlier.

The actress told him, "I'm leaving for Africa to do a picture with **Clark Gable** and Ava Gardner. I just found out it's a remake of one he did ten years ago with Jean Harlow, ***Red Dust***. Now it's called ***Mogambo***. **John Ford**'s directing and I've been warned that means there'll be a lot of whiskey consumed" [p. 206].

***Soldier of Fortune* (1955).** Written by Ernest K. Gann from his own novel and directed by Edward Dmytryk, this mediocre adventure drama (co-starring Susan Hayward) is alluded to in William Goldman's novel *Father's Day* (1971). The book's protagonist, Amos, going through a horrible time, sneaks into a movie theater, but not because he is interested in the film:

Gene Barry as Louis Hoyt and Clark Gable as Hank Lee in Edward Dmytryk's *Soldier of Fortune* (1955).

Amos stared dead ahead and was confronted by **Clark Gable** in living color trying to find **Susan Hayward**. **Gable** was oldish kind of, too weary for his role, but he still had style and Chubbycheeks and the usher were moving very slowly down, still many rows behind him.

. . .

Gable was fighting now, but clearly a winner even though the enemy had size and youth. **Gable** worked inside the other guy's reach, tore his guts up with a left, crashed him a right to the mush and it was over. I saw this picture, Amos remembered. It was a best seller, I think, what the hell's the name of it, the background's the Orient and **Clark** baby was a **soldier of fortune** and **Susan** was what, she was an American but why was she visiting Hong Kong and what exactly was her occupation, think now think—

. . .

Amos turned front again, staring at **Gable** and a great plan B, he fantasized, would have been maybe a stink bomb, yeah, he had a stink bomb and he lobbed it across to the far aisle and when it starting spreading the usher would head over there, Chubbycheeks with him, and in the commotion, whammo, he was up and out and gone and back to Forty-eighth Street and probably Betsy had the kid healed by now, hadn't Betsy once said something about wanting to be a nurse when she was a kid?

. . .

On the screen, **Gable** was talking to an untrustworthy-looking Oriental man. The Oriental raised his inscrutable eyes, looked up at **Gable**, nodded, and in the next cut **Gable** was driving his car along a Hong Kong road and the fat woman next to Amos said, "You'll tell 'em, you been to college!" very loud and very clear.

Amos glanced at her. Her eyes were glued on **Gable** as she said, "That's right, you tell 'em, you been to college!"

. . .

"You're so goddam smart," the fat woman said, as **Gable** continued his lonely drive, "you just tell 'em, tell 'em all you want, they pay to hear you tell 'em, you been to college!"

. . .

Completely unaware, the woman watched **Gable** drive. "Why the hell shouldn't they listen to you, you been to college."

Amos was about to scrunch down deeper into his seat when, from directly across the aisle, the old bum was awake. **Gable** had transferred onto a motor launch now, and as he roared off, the bum said, "You don't expect me to believe that I hope," to no one in particular.

It's another one, Amos realized, seeing the blank look on the old bum's face. **Gable** opened the throttle on the motor launch full, and the motor sound built in the theater.

. . .

In the darkness, Amos dared to turn in time to the see the cop moving roughly across a row toward a trench-coated figure and the usher was supplying light and Amos took off then, because all the time he hadn't needed a plan, no, he was never any whiz at derring-do, what he'd needed was a break and this was it and when you got it, when you had Chybbycheeks triumphant over the wrong man, you didn't wait around, you went, so Amis did, to the front of the theater where **Gable** loomed gigantic and dotted and left from there to the exit sign and then with some power Amos forced the door open and then he was on Forty-second Street and free and careful not to make a spectacle, careful not to bolt, Amos walked his legs off to the corner and across [pp. 157-161].

Run Silent, Run Deep **(1958).** Robert Wise's memorable World War II submarine drama *Run Silent, Run Deep* (co-starring Burt Lancaster) is referenced in Dermot McEvoy's novel *Our Lady of Greenwich Village* (2008). The pretext for the reference is actor Jack Warden, who is mentioned in the description of protagonist Wolfe Tone O'Rourke's old neighborhood in New York City:

> Still waiting for the light to change, O'Rourke thought back forty years to how the Square used to be. The Starbucks on Grove Street used to be Jack Delaney's, a saloon housed in a wonderful nineteenth-century brownstone. Delaney's was an old speakeasy, and its most distinctive oddity was the sulky cart

hanging from the ceiling in the main dining room. The great character actor, **Jack Warden**, had lived in an apartment above. Everybody knew **Jack**'s face, but no one knew his name. He was the trusty enlisted man who protected sub captain **Clark Gable** in ***Run Silent, Run Deep***, and Paul Newman's mentor in *The Verdict*. Most famously, he was Juror Number Seven in *Twelve Angry Men*, the guy who wants to get out of there but fast because he has tickets to the Yankee game. **Jack**, too, used to drink at the Moat [p. 3].

American poster for Robert Wise's *Run Silent, Run Deep* (1958).

***Teacher's Pet* (1958).** Written by Fay and Michael Kanin, and directed by George Seaton, *Teacher's Pet* (co-starring Doris Day and Gig Young) is a nice, deep and entertaining comedy, if generally underrated. An extensive and rather insightful reference to the film appears in Michael B. Druxman's play *Gable* (1984):

> Did you see ***Teacher's Pet***? The picture I did with **Doris Day**?

Clark Gable as Commander 'Rich' Richardson and Burt Lancaster as Lieutenant Jim Bledsoe in a scene from Robert Wise's *Run Silent, Run Deep* (1958).

Moves SR into the "playing area," as LIGHTS ADJUST *accordingly.*

I played a newspaper editor....

(***Gable*** *takes off shirt to reveal bare chest. Tosses shirt into costume rack; gets white shirt with loosened tie around collar from rack. Winks at audience.*)

We'll talk about undershirts later.

(*Puts on shirt. Keeps collar unbuttoned, tie loose.*)

There was a scene where I fired this young copy boy. Told him to go back to school. He wanted to learn the newspaper game the "hard" way, like I had.

(*Goes into scene.*)

"The hard way isn't always the best way," I said. "I'm not sure if it ever is.

"Experience is the jockey. Education is the horse. You'll find out there are a lot of other places in the world besides the City Room. You only spend eight hours a day here. If you're lucky, you sleep eight. That leaves eight hours to talk to other people about other things. And, if all you know is newspapers, you'll always be excusing yourself and leaving the table. I've spent one-third of my life going to, staying in and coming back from Men's Rooms. And, that's not going to happen to you. You're fired!"

(*Ponders.*)

That scene played from the heart [pp. 14-15].

The picture is also alluded to in Wolf Arnold's short story "Farm Work," or Chapter One of *Interlude in Ravenna* (2007). The scene is a conversation between two young people in East Germany who meet at a summer work camp in the late 1950s:

"Christina," I said, collecting myself. "Why don't you leave it alone? The organization, you know? You're too young for politics."

"It's not politics," she replied and removed my hand from her thigh. "It's for peace. For world peace. We have to struggle for it. All the peace-loving forces must unite, you see?"

"No, I don't." I feared that my attitude will put me in a position of losing her.

"I'll teach you. You are in the *Freie Deutsche Jugend*, are you not?" She looked at me like a math teacher at her student who finally had mastered a complex problem.

"Yes," I said. "I am."

"Then I'll teach you."

"All right," I said.

"You guys . . ." She bit her lips. The teacher showed her human side. I was a **teacher's pet**. **Clark Gable** couldn't be happier [p. 12].

It Started in Naples **(1960).** The last comedy and the penultimate movie in Gable's career was written (in collaboration with Jack Rose, Suso Cecchi D'Amico, Michael Pertwee and Jack Davies) and directed by Melville Shavelson. It is set in Italy, and, thus, the co-stars are Sophia Loren and Vittorio De Sica. This relatively charming picture is referenced in Adriana Trigiani's novel *Very Valentine* (2009), which is also, at least partially, set in Italy. The reason why the book's narrator/protagonist, Valentine Roncalli, goes back to the country of her ancestors is to learn more about shoe-making techniques for the company she runs. There, on the Isle of Capri, she meets a seventy-year-old master of the old profession, Costanzo Ruocco:

> The walls behind Costanzo's work space are cluttered with a collage of photographs. There are plenty of pictures of people I've never seen before wedged between Italian icons **Sophia Loren**, on holiday and wearing flat gold leather sandals, and Silvio Berlusconi, wearing Costanzo's loafers in navy blue. I point out to a picture of **Clark Gable**.
> "My favorite actor," I tell him.
> "Not me. I like John Wayne."
> We laugh.
> "I made **Clark Gable**'s shoes for ***It Started in Naples***," he says as he picks up *il martello* and hammers the edge of the strap."
> "What was he like?"
> "Tall. Nice. Very nice." He shrugs [p. 302].

The Misfits **(1961).** A major item in the history of the cinema, this Arthur Miller (script) and John Huston (direction) film is often discussed in the context of the tragic and untimely death of its three stars: Gable, Marilyn Monroe and Montgomery Clift. One of the best contemporary westerns of all time, the picture is referenced in several books.

Michael B. Druxman's play *Gable* (1984) is set on *The Misfits* location.

Gable, the sole character of the play, says a lot about the project. Here are his probably quintessential comments:

> *The Misfits*?
> (*Again, he ponders.*)
> It's about people who sell their work, but not their lives [p. 9].
>
> I was in Italy when they sent me the script of *The Misfits*. It intrigued me, but I didn't really understand it.
> I liked the character of Gay Langland ... the rugged action ... and the money they offered was hard to refuse.
> If we ever get finished, I think I'll have two things in my career to be proud of: *Gone with the Wind* and this [pp. 63-64].

 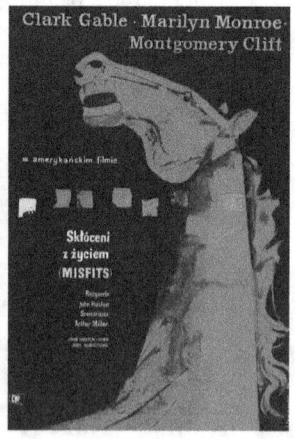

American poster for John Huston's *The Misfits* (1961) and the Polish poster for the same film (by Jerzy Jaworowski).

Elizabeth Evans's novel *The Blue Hour* (1994) is a family mystery drama set in 1959. Consequently, the reference to the film by the young narrator has a realistic, contemporary flavor, even though Yves Montand—mentioned in the passage—had nothing to do with *The Misfits*; he was Marilyn Monroe's co-star in her previous project, *Let's Make Love*.

> The movie magazines were ballast. While I gazed at *Star Town*, I remained in Lake Bascomb. I ran my fingernails over the fine wale of my bedspread, and the bedspread said, "Shh." The cover story featured a ring of photographs: **Marilyn Monroe**, **Clark Gable**, **Arthur Miller**, **Montgomery Clift**, and Yves Montand, all of them working on a movie called *The Misfits*. Underneath the ring of photos was the question, in hot red, "WHO'S SORRY NOW?" [p. 265].

In John Updike's epic novel *In the Beauty of the Lilies* (1996), the narrator refers once again to Essie/Alma's relationship with Clark Gable, her one-time co-star and namesake for her son:

> Her only child, a son, was born in April of 1959, the same year her career entered its second, triumphant, platinum-blonde phase with the (considering that this was still the Eisenhower era) daring and somewhat feminist sex-comedy *Cream Cheese and Caviar*, opposite Paul Newman. Calling her solemn-faced infant Clark was not, in view of **Gable**'s sudden death in the following year, auspicious. As **Gable** had lived by acting, so he died by it: it was said that doing his own stunts and putting up with the drug-addled **Marilyn Monroe** while shooting *The Misfits* in desert heat killed him [p. 359].

A nice reference to the film appears in David Cole's Southwestern mystery *Butterfly Lost* (1999), in a scene where the book's narrator/protagonist, half-Hopi private investigator and hacker Laura Winslow, experiences a warm, nearly romantic moment with Kimo Biakeddy, a Navajo man she befriends in the course of her investigation:

> "I don't know you well enough yet," I said. "I don't trust you. Yet."
>
> He bristled at that. I snuggled over next to him and leaned my head against his shoulder, and he put his arm around me like **Clark Gable** and **Marilyn Monroe** in *The Misfits*, where **Marilyn** asks how he knows the way home at night in the desert and he says, Just follow that star and it'll lead us right back home [p. 174].

A triple and extensive reference to the film appears in *Hey There (You with the Gun in Your Hand)* (2008), a Rat Pack mystery by Robert J. Randisi. It is worth quoting in its entirety, even though it is focused primarily on Marilyn Monroe and marginally on Gable. The narrator is Las Vegas pit boss Eddie Gianelli; Frank Sinatra is his interlocutor in the first excerpt, New York gunman Jerry Epstein in the third one.

> "How do you like the cabin?"
>
> "It's great. Kind of like a rustic suite."
>
> "Exactly," Frank said. "It's got a huge bedroom. Three, four and five never get rented out."
>
> "Never?"
>
> "Five is mine," Frank explained, spreading his arms. "Three is for broads—like when **Marilyn** comes out. She's in **Reno** now, making *The Misfits* with **Clark Gable**. I asked her to come out here, but they're givin' her a hard time bein' late to the set."
>
> I nodded. I'd read about that in the papers. [p. 10]
>
> I was walking through Harrah's casino when I saw her. You couldn't miss her. The blond hair, pale skin, red mouth, all

those curves—and the crowd she was drawing. It was **Marilyn Monroe**, all right, wearing a long-sleeved checkered shirt tucked into tight jeans. She was alone, trying to clear a path for herself to walk as people crowded in around her, trying to talk to her or touch her. I thought the look in her eyes was confused, or ... kind of vacant. She also looked scared. I remembered what Frank said about the movie company having trouble with her being on time for the scenes of *The Misfits*.

But right now she was just trying to walk, and having a tough time of it. I could see she was on the verge of panic, so I did the only thing I could think of.

"Okay, okay, clear the way," I shouted, wading in with my arms waving like a windmill.

Everybody turned to look at me, wondering who the hell I was. They shrunk back from me, because I looked like a madman.

"Outta the way, outta the way!" I yelled.

Marilyn looked at me, too, as I reached her and put my arm around her. Good God, but she felt good, a beautiful, solid girl who really filled out her clothes.

"Wha—who are you?" she asked. I could feel her breath on my face.

"My name's Eddie," I said. "I'm a friend of Frank's. Come on!"

I pulled her along, still waving my free arm. People pulled back from my perceived authority, and I knew I had to get her out of there before she realized I was nobody.'

"Are you staying here?" I asked her.

"Yes, but ... I couldn't find the elevators."

"Stay close," I said, and felt one of her arms go around me.

I took her to the elevators as some of the crowd started to follow us.

"... the hell is ..."

"... he think he's doin'?"

I heard the words behind us as I pressed the button for the elevator. Luckily, the car was already on the ground floor, so the doors opened.

"In you go," I said, giving her a gentle push. "Got your room key?"

"Oh, yes, but ..."

"What floor?"

"Four."

I leaned in and pressed four, then started to step out. She reached for me as the doors closed. Her hand caught the front of my shirt and she kissed me quickly on the cheek. I admit it, my head swam.

"Eddie ... thanks, honey."

"Any time," I said, and she was gone.

As the doors closed I looked around the casino to see if **Clark Gable** or **Montgomery Clift** were anywhere. I wondered if they were staying in the hotel, too.

Once **Marilyn** was gone, people started gambling again and continued on to the hotel lobby. Things were back to normal for everyone but me. I had **Marilyn**'s kiss on my cheek, her scent in my nose and still had the feel of her weight against me.

Oh boy ... [p. 179].

We were walking through the casino in Harrah's when I said, "I saw **Marilyn Monroe** in here earlier tonight."

"Yer shittin' me."

"I shit you not."

"What was she doin' here?"

"She's shootin' a movie with **Clark Gable**," I said. "*The Misfits*."

"Wow. She look good?"

I thought of the handkerchief in my pocket with her lipstick on it.

"She looked great" [p. 189].

Marilyn Monroe (Roslyn Tabor), Clark Gable (Gay Langland) and Montgomery Clift (Perce Howland) in a scene from John Huston's *The Misfits*.

In another Rat Pack mystery by Randisi, *You're Nobody 'Til Somebody Kills You* (2009), the episode of the improbable encounter of Eddie and Marilyn has its continuation as the depressed movie star needs Eddie's help in more than one way. Following are some of the passages relating the two protagonists' conversations; Dean Martin is also mentioned a couple of times; Eddie's interlocutor in the third excerpt is Jerry Epstein.

> Blond hair, red mouth, flawless, pale skin. To the public at large that's what **Marilyn Monroe** was. But they had never seen the **Marilyn** who was standing in front of me at that moment.
> "Eddie," she said, in that breathy voice of hers. "Come on in."
> I entered the cottage, speechless, and closed the door behind me. She was wearing a pair of capri pants that hugged her assets, and a sweater that listed to one side, leaving a single shoulder bare. A single smooth, creamy shoulder, I might add.
> "**Miss Monroe** –" I started, but she turned quickly, her hair swinging into her eyes. She tossed it back with a quick jerk.
> "Please, Eddie," she said, "call me **Marilyn**. Is Dean outside?"
> "Yeah—yes, he said you wanted to see me alone. **Marilyn**, I don't understand. We've only met once, and that was for about three minutes."
> She laughed, her beautiful face brightening at the memory of that moment. "I remember very well. It was last year in Harrah's in Reno. You rescued me from a crowd of people and helped me get to the elevator."
> "And that was it," I said. "We haven't seen each other or spoken since then."
> "Oh, but Eddie," she said, "I have to tell you, the way you took control? I don't think I've ever felt safer. And I feel safe with you now."

"Well, I wasn't all that smart that time," I said. "I was so involved in what I was doing I thought you were in town shooting *The Misfits* with **Gable**."

"B-but . . . **Clark** had died months before that, like twelve days after we finished shooting."

"Sure, I knew that. I felt real stupid later when I thought back on it."

"I was in town doing some publicity."

Suddenly, her eyes got sad—the way they'd been when she opened the door—and her mouth quivered. And it wasn't the famous **Marilyn** mouth I was looking at.

"Eddie—" she said, reaching a hand out to me blindly as tears filled her eyes.

"Hey, hey," I said, taking her hand and leading her to a chair. She sat down and I crouched down in front of her.

Marilyn couldn't help herself. Even in that moment she was radiating not only sex, but sadness. I knew what Dean had meant when he said I'd see for myself how fragile she was. Of course I'd heard stories of her moods. Also, her tumultuous love life, marriage and divorce from famous men like Joe DiMaggio and playwright Arthur Miller, a love affair with Frank that ended when he got engaged to Juliet Prowse [pp. 15-16].

"**Marilyn**, tell me whatever you can."

"Well . . . after **Clark** died the newspapers were saying it was shooting *The Misfits* that killed him."

"Was it a tough shoot?" The film had been out almost a year, but I hadn't seen it yet.

"Very tough. He insisted on doing his own stunts, even though he was sick."

"Did everyone on the movie know he was sick?"

"No," she said, "he kept it to himself. Even **John Huston**, the director, didn't know."

"So?"

"He suffered two heart attacks, and the second one killed him," she said. Then she released my hands and covered her face. "They said it was all the stress on the set that killed him . . . that because I made him wait and wait . . . that I was responsible."

Jesus, I thought, what a thing for her to have to live with.

I crouched in front of her again, took her in my arms to soothe her. There I was with everybody's sex symbol and I felt like I was holding a child. If someone had told me even yesterday that I could hold **Marilyn Monroe** in my arms and not be aroused I'd have called them a liar. But all I could think was, this poor kid . . .

"**Marilyn**, come on . . . you just told me how hard a shoot it was."

"Yes," she said, "but the newspapers didn't talk about that, didn't talk about what **John Huston** had put him through . . . didn't mention that he smoked three packs a day . . . or that he'd lost forty pounds in a hurry to do the movie. Not, it was all about me. . . ."

"But you know that wasn't true" [p. 19-20].

"I'm sorry to disappoint you, Jerry," I said, "but she didn't jump me. She's more of a scared kid than a nympho."

"What's got her scared?"

"Well, for one thing, folks are sayin' she caused the death of **Clark Gable** while they were makin' *The Misfits*."

"That's crazy," he said. "**Gable** was an old guy doin' his own stunts. I read about all that stuff. Sure, she kept 'em waitin' a lot in the desert—but how could that kill him? Don't they have fancy, air-conditioned dressing rooms?"

"That's just what I told her, Jerry" [pp. 57-58].

She took her face in both hands. "I must look awful. My hair, my face."

"You shine, **Marilyn**," I said, "with or without makeup."

She got a funny look on her face. "Did you see *The Misfits*?"

"No," I said, "I never had the chance. I'm sorry."

"Don't be, only... what you just said, it was like a line **Clark** said to me in the movie. Not word, for word, but he said 'Roslyn, you shine,'..."

"I'm sorry if I brought back a bad memory."

"There was a lot about that shoot that was bad," she said, "but some of it was good. **Arthur** and me, we were like cats and dogs. That was near the end. But **Clark**... I loved him" [pp. 240-241].

Irene Bennett Brown's mystery *Where Gable Slept* (2010) is set in a small Oregon town, Pass Creek, in which the Gable House, a tourist attraction because of an alleged visit of the famous movie star, is a murder scene. While both Gable and some of his movies are repeatedly mentioned in the book, there is only one, but relatively poignant, reference to the actor's last picture. John Wayne Stewart, an old man who used to be a stuntman in some of Gable's films, is a new tenant in the inn run by narrator Celia Landrey. While in the quoted scene the man entertains the protagonist (who is also a local historian, a walking tour guide and an amateur detective) with his stories, he would end up saving Celia's life and helping her catch a dangerous murderer.

That evening, at John Wayne Stewart's invitation, Celia had dinner with him at the Mellow Mushroom. Remembering Myrna's work there, the many friendships the woman had made and how matters had ended made it difficult to enjoy the old fellow's constant chatter, stories of his time "in the movie business."

"**Clark Gable** played the part of an aging cowboy in *The Misfits*," he was telling her, "but I don't think the ladies liked seeing him old. At the time, I was so lolly-gagged over **Marilyn**

Monroe in *The Misfits*, I wasn't hardly myself. Nowadays," he said, chuckling, "I'd be more apt to feel that way over **Thelma Ritter**—she was in the movie, too" [p. 205].

Clark Gable appeared in over seventy pictures, collaborating with numerous talented directors. He made as many as nine films with Clarence Brown, six with Jack Conway, five with Victor Fleming, four with Robert Z. Leonard and three with William A. Wellman and Raoul Walsh. In the 1930s, the actor's regular female co-stars were Joan Crawford and Myrna Loy (in seven movies each), Jean Harlow (five) and Norma Shearer (three). Later on, Lana Turner appeared opposite Gable in four pictures and Ava Gardner in three. Other major actresses that shared credits with Gabe include Greta Garbo, Carole Lombard, Helen Hayes, Claudette Colbert, Vivien Leigh, Greer Garson, Barbara Stanwyck, Gene Tierney, Susan Hayward, Doris Day, Sophia Loren and Marilyn Monroe. Among male stars it is Spencer Tracy who holds the record of co-starring in three Gable films.

Never complaining about the lack of acting offers, Gable achieved longevity as the King of Hollywood despite the fact that the number of prestigious films in his career is rather modest when compared with the heritage of some other great actors—such as Bogart, Cooper and Tracy, but also James Stewart, Henry Fonda, Cary Grant and Burt Lancaster. Moreover, Gable was not the greatest actor in the narrow sense of the word. Playing, incessantly and consistently, nobody but himself in a variety of genres and settings, Gable was nonetheless flawless and often fascinating, winning the adoration of many women and the friendship of millions of men in movie theaters all over the world.

The number of Gable's pictures that are represented in this publication is thirty-nine, which is more than half of his overall filmography. Unsurprisingly, the largest number of references (115) was found to *Gone with the Wind* (some of which, however, may have been meant for the book rather than the film), and the second best record is far away, with *It Happened One Night* referenced only in twenty-one works. The other runners-up include *The Call of the*

Polish poster (by Wiktor Górka) for Raoul Walsh's *The Tall Men* (1955), one of Gable's several films not recognized in fiction and possibly his most rewarding standard Western.

Wild (eight references), *Mutiny on the Bounty*, *Test Pilot* and *The Misfits* (seven each), *Manhattan Melodrama*, *San Francisco* and *Boom Town* (five each), and *A Free Soul* and *Red Dust* (four each). Thus, it seems that most, or even all—with the exception of *Teacher's Pet* (mentioned only in two books)—of Gable's major films are mentioned in the above ranking. However, it is worth pointing out that his two foremost artistic achievements, such as *It Happened One Night* and *The Misfits*, possibly along with *Mutiny on the Bounty*, should have ended up much closer to *Gone with the Wind* than they did. Furthermore, possibly four of Gable's other pictures, certainly not masterpieces but notable for one reason or another, should have been found among those referenced. They are Robert Z. Leonard's *Strange Interlude* (1932; from the play by Eugene O'Neill), Clarence Brown's *Idiot's Delight* (1939; from Robert E. Sherwood's play), Raoul Walsh's *The Tall Men* (1955; based on a novel by Clay Fisher, aka Will Henry, probably Gable's most rewarding standard western) and Walsh's *Band of Angels* (1957; inspired by Robert Penn Warren's novel).

II. REFERENCES TO GABLE: THE MAN, THE ACTOR, THE CELEBRITY

Just like Gary Cooper's, Clark Gable's name began to appear in narrative literature in the mid-1930s when, as an Academy Award winner for *It Happened One Night*, the actor was already in his prime, enjoying fame, mostly good reviews and ample cash flow. One of the first references to the actor was found in Clifford Odets's play *Waiting for Lefty* (1935). It takes place in a scene where Joe comes home after negotiating a strike at his work and asks his wife about the missing furniture:

>JOE: Where's all the furniture, honey?
>EDNA: They took it away. No installments paid.
>JOE: When?
>EDNA: Three o'clock.
>JOE: They can't do that.
>EDNA: Can't? They did it.
>JOE: Why, the palookas, we paid three-quarters.
>EDNA: The man said read the contract.
>JOE: We must have signed a phoney....
>EDNA: It's a regular contract and you signed it.

JOE: Don't be so sour, Edna.... *(Tries to embrace her.)*

EDNA: Do it in the movies, Joe—they pay **Clark Gable** big money for it.

JOE: This is a helluva house to come to. Take my word! [pp. 7-8]

Clark Gable in a publicity shot.

In Bella and Samuel Spewack's play *Boy Meets Girl* (1936), the actor is mentioned there three times. The context of the first reference is cowboy star Larry Toms' comparing his status with that of the famous star:

> LARRY. Just because I don't get **Gable**'s fan mail don't mean I ain't got his following. A lot of those that want to write me ain't never learned how [p. 539].

Then, both Gable and Gary Cooper are mentioned by his agent as a potential threat to his contract:

> ROSETTI. Larry, I don't want to hurt your feelings, but I can't get you a new contract the way things are now. B.K. is dickering to borrow **Clark Gable** or **Gary Cooper** for Happy's next picture [p. 562].

Finally, another flattering comment is made by Susie, a waitress-turned-actress, who ended up getting to play the mother of serial baby character Happy:

> SUSIE. All the girls are crazy about **Clark Gable** [p. 564].

The actor is also referenced in another play, *The Women* (1937) by Clare Boothe, included in the same collection as *Boy Meets Girl*, called Sixteen Famous American Plays. The interesting thing about Boothe's play is that it has no male characters. Men are only, but extensively, talked about. Here is the quotation of the lines spoken by Maggie, one of the minor characters:

> MAGGIE. She's indulging a pride she ain't entitled to. Marriage is a business of talking care of a man and rearing his children. It ain't meant to be no perpetual honeymoon. How long would any husband last if he was supposed to go on acting

forever like a red-hot **Clark Gable**? What's the difference if he don't love her? [p. 639]

James M. Cain's mystery *Double Indemnity* (1936) is one of the quintessential examples of novel noir. The narrator of the book is Walter Huff of the General Fidelity of California, an insurance salesman who becomes a victim of his own greedy racket. In the following passage, which is a part of a scene where Huff gets home from work and is served dinner by his Filipino servant, he makes a statement about the current fashion:

> I was so nervous I could hardly chew, but I got it all down somehow. I had hardly finished my coffee when he had everything washed up, and had changed to cream-colored pants, white shoes and stockings, a brown coat, a white shirt open at the neck ready to go out with the girl. It used to be that what a Hollywood actor wore on Monday a Filipino house boy wore on Tuesday, but now, if you ask me, it's the other way around, and the boy from Manila beats **Clark Gable** to it [p. 46].

In another novel by Cain, *Serenade* (1937), the actor is referenced in a lengthy passage expressing the narrator/protagonist's negative opinion about Hollywood:

> The only thing they think is good for its own sake is a producer that couldn't tell Brahms from Irving Berlin on a bet, that wouldn't know a singer from a crooner until he heard twenty thousand people yelling for him one night, that can't read a book until the scenario department has had a synopsis made, that can't even speak English, but that is a self-elected expert on music, singing, literature, dialogue, and photography, and generally has a hit because somebody lent him **Clark Gable** to play in it [p. 99].

Budd Schulberg, in his novel *What Makes Sammy Run?* (1941), uses Gable as a prestige factor in a passage where unscrupulous and overambitious screenwriter Sammy Glick offers uneven collaboration to narrator Al Manheim, a man for whom he worked as an office boy before he started climbing up in his career:

> "Well, now that you're using your head for something besides butting against a stone wall," Sammy said, "I think I can put you onto a good thing. Julian was beginning to get too much dough to work with me anyway. I need somebody in the lower brackets—to balance what I'm getting. So, while I was getting my message this morning, it hit me like a ton of scripts. Why the hell don't I get Al? He needs a break and he's just what I need. So you're being transferred to our unit tomorrow. We're going to have a helluva picture—we just got word this morning that we can get **Gable** from Metro for the lead. It'll mean an A credit right off the bat. And, if you click, I'm liable to let you in on something really big that I'm not able to break yet."
>
> "It's very nice of you to rearrange my life for me this way," I said, "but what about Masaryk?" [pp. 184-185]

In another novel by Schulberg, *The Disenchanted* (1950), the actor is mentioned in an interesting passage where the narrator reveals the preparations and thoughts of a young screenwriter, Shep Stearns, who was just asked to collaborate on a screenplay with a veteran writer, Manley Halliday (F. Scott Fitzgerald):

> Shep sank into an easy chair to scan *The Hollywood Reporter*. In a few minutes he knew almost everything there was to know about what had happened in Hollywood in the past twenty-four hours. He knew whose preview was SMASH B.Q. and whose was just OKAY. He knew who had been penciled in for the

lead opposite **Gable** and who had been planted at Warners'. He guessed the name of the *what* director whose car was reported to have been parked all night outside the Bel Air home of *what g.g.* (the abbreviation automatically recognized for glamour girl) and he knew what famous couple it was, mistakenly reputed *phtting* by a rival columnist, who were actually more *that way* than ever [p. 46].

A reference to Gable in Tennessee Williams's play *The Glass Menagerie* (1945) becomes a part of Tom's lengthy and poignant commentary on the role of movies in the modern American society:

> TOM: Yes, movies! Look at them— [a wave toward the marvels of Grand Avenue] All of those glamorous people—having adventures—hogging it all, gobbling the whole thing up! You know what happens? People go to the *movies* instead of *moving!* Hollywood characters are supposed to have all the adventures for everybody in America, while everybody in America sits in a dark room and watches them have them! Yes, until there's a war. That's when adventure becomes available to the masses! *Everyone's* dish, not only **Gable**'s! Then the people in the dark room come out of the dark room to have some adventures themselves—goody, goody! It's our turn now, to go to the South Sea Island—to make a safari—to be exotic, far-off! But I'm not patient. I don't want to wait till then. I'm tired of the *movies* and I am *about to move!* [p. 59]

There are two references to Gable in Herman Wouk's *Marjorie Morningstar* (1955). The first one is used in a simile expressing the distance between the titular female protagonist and Noel Airman, a man she is falling in love with:

It occurred to her, as she stood there in the blizzard with her breath smoking, that she was hardly better than the squealing simpletons who gathered in fan clubs to worship an actor. Noel Airman was as remote from her as **Clark Gable**, and as unaware of her existence. But though surprised at herself, and ironically amused, she somehow was not really ashamed. She went home half frozen but obscurely satisfied, and she did not do it again [pp. 142-143].

Then, a reference to Gable is made by Marjorie's friend, Marsha, in a conversation between the two of them:

"Why should you cry, of all people?" Marjorie said. "You've got the world by the tail. I'm awfully happy for you."
Marsha said, laughing, "Just my luck, you know, that you'd practically trip over Lou in my living room. I was going to tease you. Tell you he was six feet tall and looked like **Clark Gable** and owned a yacht and so forth. Not but what there isn't plenty to brag about Lou, but still—you know, now that you've seen him, it's like you'd peeked at the end of a mystery story [pp. 385-386].

In Gerald Green's novel *The Last Angry Man* (1956), a reference to Gable appears in a scene relating a meeting of an important advertising agency on the subject of a new TV show called *Americans USA*. The company's vice president, Woody Thrasher, realizes the resemblance between the actor and Kev Lord, a big figure in the agency:

Lord nodded his magnificent head. He saved his words for airtime: a man who was paid four thousand dollars a week for talk didn't go around wasting the stuff. Thrasher wondered what went on inside that great square head with its white crew haircut. He was an elderly **Clark Gable** with overtones of a headmaster—the kind who was always ready to clasp two masculine hands around the trembling mitt of the new boy's mother [p. 285].

John D. MacDonald's horror *The Executioners* (1957), subsequently filmed twice and published as *Cape Fear*, is a novel about unfair revenge. However, the passage where a reference to Gable takes place relates a relaxed scene in which Carol Bowden tells her husband Sam about her fantasy when she was fifteen years old, the age of their daughter:

> "No, it isn't. I was desperately unhappy when I was fifteen. Every mirror broke my heart. I was a mess. And so I wasn't going to be able to marry him."
> "Who was he?"
> "Don't snicker at me now. **Clark Gable**. I had it all arranged. He was going to come to Texas to make a movie, and it was going to be a movie about oil wells. And I was going to go out to where they were making the movie and one day he would turn and he would look right at me, and smile in that funny quizzical way, with one eyebrow up and one down, and he'd stop the cameras and come over and look at me. Then he would signal to somebody, who would come running to him and he would say, pointing at me as I stood proud and haughty in my beauty, 'She is my next leading lady. Fix up the contracts.' But, oh dear, I was such a mess" [p. 137].

The actor is also mentioned in one of the first novels by William Goldman, *Your Turn to Curtsy, My Turn to Bow* (1958), in a lunch conversation between two young people, Peter Bell and Tillie Keck, who met at a summer camp:

> She shook her head. "I can't. I got to watch my figure. I

count calories very carefully. I know how many calories are in almost anything you can name. It's a knack I have." She started nibbling on another cookie.

"That must come very handy," Peter said.

"It does. Calories and movie stars. They're my two best subjects. I know everything about Greta Garbo, for instance. Everything. And **Clark Gable**. I know all about him too." She waved her hand. "It's just a knack." She finished eating and they got up, Peter paying for lunch, opening the door for her. She brushed against him as she walked past, her green skirt swirling her long tanned legs [p. 29].

Evan Hunter's *Strangers When We Meet* (1958) is a main stream novel containing several cinematic references, all of which pertain to famous leading men of the screen. Used as similes, they do not require any commentary. Here is the one pertaining to Gable:

His eyes were bright and brown, and his hands were thick builder's hands curling with thick builder's hair, but the fingernails were manicured. Altar studied him and wondered whom he was playing. He decided it was a young **Clark Gable** in an old movie. He even had **Gable**'s trick of quirking mouth and eyebrows simultaneously, as if he were secretly amused by a cosmic joke too rarefied for the rat pack to appreciate [p. 173].

In addition to being a part of the allusion to *Red Dust*, the actor himself is referenced several times in Jack Kerouac's *Desolation Angels* (1960). Here is a passage which uses his and other celebrities' names to define a certain time period:

Me'n Sliv stand bouncing to the beat and finally the girl in the skirt comes to us, it's Gia Valencia, the daughter of the mad

Spanish anthropologist sage who'd lived with the Pomo and Pit River Indians of California, famous old man, whom I'd read and revered only three years ago while working the railroad outa San Luis Obispo—"Bug, give me back my shadow!" he yelled on a recorded tape before he died, showing how the Indians made it at brooks in old California pre-history before San Fran and **Clark Gable** and Al Jolson and Rose Wise Lazuli and the jazz of the mixed generations—[pp. 124-125]

There are also two paragraphs mentioning him together with Gary Cooper; one is quoted below and one (from p. 298) in Part Two (on Cooper).

Tho she is beautiful, and gifted, 't were better for all of you to fall into a Tiger's mouth than to fall into her net of plans." *Oyes?* Meaning by that, for every **Clark Gable** or **Gary Cooper** born, with all the so called glory (or Hemingway) that goes with it, comes disease, decay, sorrow, lamentation, old age, death, decomposition— meaning, for every little sweet lump of baby born that women croon over, is one vast rotten meat burning slow worms in graves of this earth [pp. 267-268].

A reference to the actor appears also in Jack Kerouac's novel *Satori in Paris* (1966), in a passage describing one of the narrator/protagonist's adventures in France, this one taking place at Paris Orly Airport:

I go back at one.
"Half hour delay."
I decide to sit out, but suddenly I have to go to the toilet at 1:20—I ask a Spanish-looking Brest-bound passenger: "Think I got time to go to the toilet back at the terminal?"
"O sure, plenty time."

I look, the mechanics out there are still worriedly fiddling, so I hurry that quartermile back, to the toilet, lay another franc for fun on La Française, and suddenly I hear "Ma – Thil – Daa" singsong with the word "Brest" so I like **Clark Gable**'s best fast walk hike on back almost as fast as a jogging trackman, if you know what I mean, but by the time I get there the plane is out taxiing to the runway, the ramp's been rolled back which all those traitors just crept up, and off they go to Brittany with my suitcase [p. 57].

In John Nichols's novel *The Sterile Cuckoo* (1965), Gable, along with a few other male movie stars, is mentioned in a passage describing the sexual fantasies of the book's protagonist, Pookie Adams:

Her way of saving me was to explain how she had grappled with puberty and come out of it reasonably sane and at least capable of slinking into a drug store and asking for Kotex or Tampax or what have you without going through the entire color scale. She told me how she used to make up pornographic daydreams about herself and men, how she had been kissed, fondled, and raped time and time again by the likes of **Clark Gable**, Errol Flynn, Cary Grant . . . even Jimmy Stewart, who was by far the shyest of the lot and always got her out in an apple orchard or on the swinging couch suspended from the back porch ceiling of a ranch house in Wyoming, or New Mexico, or Colorado [pp. 30-31].

There are two passages in John O'Hara's novella "James Francis and the Star" (from the mid-1960s) including references to Gable. The first one is presented in Part Four (on Tracy); below is the second one, focused on movie stars' participation in World War II:

Then in 1942 the alert Public Relations men of the Air Force beat the Marine Corps to it with a firm offer of a captaincy to Red Fulton. The Navy ran a poor third. There was a certain amount of apprehensive discussion among the Air Force brass. Jimmy Stewart was a fully qualified peacetime pilot and properly belonged in the Air Force. **Clark Gable** was not a pilot and had no better education than Rod Fulton, but was given a commission. What then if all three big movie stars got killed? What would be the effect on military and civilian morale? It was decided that the chance was worth taking on the theory that as far as service personnel were concerned, movie stars were expendable, and that if all three men got killed, the civilian population would know that we were in a war. Public Relations hoped that if anyone got killed it would not be Stewart or **Gable** [p. 187].

A reference to Gable and a few other Hollywood stars appears in O'Hara's novella "Natica Jackson" (1966), in an exchange between a rising star and her agent:

> "But what the hell, I had a different name then myself, and Natica Jackson used to be Anna Jacobs if I'm not mistaken."
> "Getting me off the subject of Jay Chase, Morris," she said.
> "Yeah, I was. But I'll get you back on the subject I wanted to talk about. You and pictures. Natica, I see you—do you know what I see you as? I see you as like Garbo. **Gable**. Lionel Barrymore. Crawford. I see you as much a part of the **Metro** organization as **Mr. Schenck**. **L. B. Mayer**. The lion. Wally Beery. Them [p. 374].

In his novel *Go to the Widow-Maker* (1967), James Jones writes about the relationship between Ron Grant, a playwright, and his wife, Lucky. On page 44, Lucky compares the two of them to the famous Hollywood couple, saying: "I've always thought of us as **Clark Gable** and Carole Lombard." The names of the two celebrities are subsequently used several more times by the narrator himself to give the reader more input about the characters' relationship:

> Up to the age of thirty-seven, which was now, Ron Grant had never had what he considered a true love affair. As a result, he had come to believe no such thing existed—except in the movies of **Clark Gable** and **Carole Lombard**.
>
> . . .
>
> All he [Grant] wanted was to have just once in his life one love affair that was like those accursed **Clark Gable**-**Carole Lombard** films of youth, that was all.
>
> . . .
>
> He [Grant] supposed he had to count that one, since it had lasted so long. But it had certainly never been a true one, a **Clark Gable**-Carole Lombard one [pp. 54-55].
>
> The delighted clerk handed Grant a handkerchief for the lipstick on his face the second time he came back. "Compliments of the house, Madam," he said to Lucky. It was a scene from a **Clark Gable**-Carole Lombard movie of a happier time if there ever was one in life, and everybody was participating [p. 78].
>
> She did not know if he had already been doing it before. But she herself had only caught him and become aware of it after they returned to New York from Grand Bank. She herself had married him in all good faith, and had been true to him—at least until she had found out for sure he was stepping out, she added with a sour smile—and while they perhaps had not loved each other like **Clark Gable** and **Carole Lombard** had, she had felt they had a serious and honorable marriage [p. 532].

The fact that Jones refers to Gable and Lombard as many as six times in one novel, each time using them as a model of a married couple, must suggest that the writer held the stars in exceptionally high esteem. Whether it is true or not, he skillfully uses the reference as an image-drawing short cut, a concise simile or metaphor; consequently, the sentences with the stars' names—even when taken out of context—poignantly narrate the story of the Grants' married life, with the echoes of the stars' names emphatically pointing out the unattainable.

Gable is mentioned by Gore Vidal in *Myra Breckinridge* (1968) in four places. Some of them are quoted in the parts on Bogart and Tracy; below is one worth quoting here:

> "Talent is not what Uncle Buck and I deal in, Miss Van Allen," I said, lightly resting on my hand on Buck's clenched fist. "We deal in *myths*. At any given moment the world requires one full-bodied blonde Aphrodite (Jean Harlow), one dark siren of flawless beauty (Hedy Lamarr), one powerful inarticulate brute of a man (John Wayne), one smooth debonair charmer (Melvyn Douglas), one world-weary corrupt lover past his prime (**Humphrey Bogart**), one eternal good-sex woman-wife (Myrna Loy), one wide-eyed chicken boy (Lon McCallister), one gentle girl singer (Susanna Foster), one winning stud (**Clark Gable**), one losing stud outside the law (James Cagney), and so on [pp. 128-129].

In Herman Raucher's novel *A Glipse of Tiger* (1971), there is an allusion to *It Happened One Night*. The image from that scene appears to be resumed or continued over 100 pages later, this time with a reference to Gable:

> Tiger could not believe how ridiculous he was in that Aquascutum trench coat surrounded by Dunhill pipe smoke.

And damned if he didn't nudge her with his elbow and wink and say, "Always get into cabs with strangers?"

Actually it was a good question. Why *had* she gotten into the cab? Did she think he was Luther? Or poor expiring Tom Dietrich? Or **Clark Gable**? Did she think it was her father come from Indianapolis on a white horse? Or did she think it was a total stranger and did that idea tickle her? Or did she not think at all, which was more apt to be the case, judging from her behavior over the last few days [p. 132].

A minor reference to the actor appears also in Larry McMurtry's novel *All My Friends Are Going to Be Strangers* (1972). In the quoted excerpt, the book's narrator/protagonist, writer Danny Deck, has a chat and a drink with a gas station operator who used to be in the movies:

He folded up his newspaper, which was the St. Louis *Post-Dispatch*. Then he reached inside the door and flipped a switch. All the filling station lights went off.

"I'd rather drink by moonlight," he said.

We drank by moonlight. The man's name was Peter Paul Neville. He talked while we drank. He had quit the movies in 1933. He had known **Clark Gable**, and many other stars. When he quit the movies he went in the oil business. He quit the oil business in 1945. He had enough money to last him [p. 276].

In Thomas Pynchon's already mentioned novel *Gravity's Rainbow* (1973), set during World War II, Gable is mentioned again—this time in reference to his unusual voice, here compared to that of General Eisenhower's:

Pökler does manage to tell a little about Laszlo Jamf, but keeps getting sidetracked off into talking about the movies, German movies Slothrop has never heard of, much less seen . .

. yes here's some kind of fanatical movie hound all right—"On D-Day," he confesses, "when I heard General Eisenhower on the radio announcing the invasion of Normandy, I thought it was **Clark Gable**, have you ever noticed? the voices are *identical*. . . ." [p. 577]

A double reference to Gable appears in Robert B. Parker's novel *Mortal Stakes* (1975), in a scene where Spenser, feeling lonely and sorry for himself, sits at the desk in his office, drinking bourbon:

> I held the bottle up toward the window and looked at how much was left. Half. Good. Even if I finished it, there was another in the file cabinet. Warm feeling having another one in the file cabinet. I winked at the file cabinet and grinned with one side of my mouth like **Clark Gable** used to. He never did it at file cabinets, though, far as I could remember. I drank some more and rinsed it around in my mouth. Maybe my teeth will get drunk. I giggled. Goddamned sure **Clark Gable** never giggled. Drink up, teeth [p. 208].

Michael Malone, in his novel *The Delectable Mountains or, Entertaining Stranger* (1976), uses a reference to the famous Judy Garland song as a way to describe a woman's affection:

> But perhaps it was all a matter of envy with Suzanne, for she did not deceive me by pretending to be contemptuous of Calhoun Grange, even if his "Method" was wrong. Of course, she wasn't as infatuated as Sabby Norah, who followed Calhoun around looking like Judy Garland mooning, **"You made Me Love You"** to **Clark Gable**. Grange was as close as Sabby had come yet to the world she worshiped, and she was memorizing him like a poem [p. 153].

Malone's "Love and Other Crimes" (2000) is a short story about Patty Raiford, a southern belle getting married for the fifth time. The groom is Joe Raulett, also known as the Seafood King. Here is the description of the groom, using a comparison to the famous actor, or rather—like in many other literary similes—to his trade-mark mustache:

> The Seafood King was a good-looking man—sort of like Ted Turner with the prematurely gray hair and the **Clark Gable** mustache. But he was an awful dancer [p. 135].

In addition to multiple references to *It Happened One Night* and one non-sequitur allusion to *Boom Town*, Michael Malone's novel *The Four Corners of the Sky* (2009) contains one reference to Gable that is not related to any specific movie:

> At Pilgrim's Rest, the two "singles" took up watching classic movies after supper almost every night. Clark had never been the film buff that Sam was, although he'd been named **Clark** by a Southern mother infatuated by **Clark Gable**. But under Sam's influence, he became a fan [p. 184].

Andrew J. Fenady's *The Man with Bogart's Face* (1977) contains several references to Gable, in addition to the one to his film *Never Let Me Go*, presented earlier in the book. The actor's name (usually an item on a list of celebrities) is mentioned, for instance, as one of the figures at the Wax Museum, where Sam takes Gena and they meet the place's proprietor, Spoony Singh:

> "Quite a showman," said Sam.
> "Is he actually an Indian?"
> "Bona fide. Born in Punjab."
> "And you really were here this morning?"

"Would *I* lie? Come on." They walked past several wax figures, including **Gable**, Monroe, Wayne, and Crosby, and came to the House of Mirrors. In front of it was a wax figure of **Bogart** [pp. 80-81].

In Fenady's sequel to *The Man with Bogart's Face*, *The Secret of Sam Marlow* (1980), Gable is mentioned several times, most often together with Spencer Tracy and/or some other movie stars. Below is an excerpt in which the actor appears alone, or, rather, in connection with two fictitious movie stars, Sandra Kent and Biff Brock:

> On Stage 7 Sam stood in the shadows and watched Sandra Kent, in a bikini, kissing her leading man, who was in a beach robe. His name was Biff Brock and everybody in town knew he was acey-deucey, but most of America and the rest of the free world considered him mighty macho. It didn't seem to matter to Sandra one way or the other. She was gobbling him up like he was **Gable** [p. 63].

In William Styron's novel *Sophie's Choice* (1978), the actor is one of several movie references that are made in a passage describing Sophie's life in Poland before World War II:

> Then there were the movies. During the war she had missed them with almost the same longing as she had missed music. In Cracow before the war there had been a period when she had drenched herself in American movies—the bland innocent romances of the thirties, with stars like Errol Flynn and Merle Oberon and **Gable** and Lombard. She had also adored Disney, especially Mickey Mouse and *Snow White*. And—oh God!—Fred Astaire and Ginger Rogers in *Top Hat*! And so in New York's paradise of theatres she and Nathan sometimes went on

weekend binges—staring themselves red-eyed through five, six, seven films between Friday night and the last show on Sunday [pp. 313-314].

Clark Gable is mentioned in Fannie Flagg's novel *Coming Attractions* (1981), in a passage where narrator Daisy Fay talks about her father's experiences in California:

> After daddy left Louisiana, he was stationed in California and got Margaret O'Brien to sign the back of one of my pictures. He said she has false teeth just like Grandma. He also said that Red Skelton was a wonderful guy and told the boys dirty jokes to cheer them up. All of my Hollywood true-life stories come as a result of Daddy having been there during the war. **Clark Gable** is the best-looking man Daddy has ever seen, even though his mustache is uneven [pp. 16-17].

Gable is the second, next to Bogart, most frequently referenced movie star in the unusual prose by Charles Bukowski. For the passage from the short story "The Murder of Ramon Vasquez," see Part One (on Bogart). Below is an excerpt from "The Gut-Wringing Machine," a short story about two strange individuals, Danforth and Bagley, who run the Satisfactory Help Agency, specializing in putting bodies through the wringer. Here is the dialogue between the agency owners and one of their clients, Barney Anderson, after the treatment:

> "Barney?" asked Bagley.
> "yes sir!"
> "who are your heroes?"
> "George Washington, Bob Hope, Mae West, Richard Nixon, the bones of **Clark Gable** and all the nice people I've seen at Disneyland. Joe Louis, Dinah Shore, Frank Sinatra, Babe

Ruth, the Green Berets, hell the whole United States Army and Navy and especially the Marine Corps, and even the Treasury Dept., the CIA, the FBI, United Fruit, the highway Patrol, the whole god damned L.A. Police Dept., and the County Cops too [p. 53].

It is worth mentioning here that Barney's list of heroes before the treatment consisted of Cleaver, Dillinger, Che, Malcolm X, Gandhi, Jersey Walcott, Grandma Barker, Castro, Van Gogh, Villon and Hemingway (p. 52).

In Bukowski's novel *Hollywood* (1989), which is a fictionalized account of the making of *Barfly* (a movie based on Bukowski's autobiographical screenplay), the narrator (Henry Chinaski) makes an allusion to the old times in the movie capital by referring to a variety of its symbols:

> I followed Jon through Hollywood, the light and the shadows of Alfred Hitchcock, Laurel and Hardy, **Clark Gable**, Gloria Swanson, Mickey Mouse and **Humphrey Bogart**, falling all around us [p. 132].

The actor's name is mentioned in Stuart M. Kaminsky's *Bullet for a Star* (1977), in a scene where Brenda Stallings Beaumont, an attractive movie star, is trying to seduce narrator/private eye Peters:

> She shook her head no and unbuttoned her white blouse. The bra matched the slip and her skin was tan and smooth. It was happening, but I couldn't figure out why and didn't want to ask. Brenda Stallings, the beautiful blonde who had appeared in front of me in theaters ten times her own size in love scenes with **Gable** and Freddie March, was looking at me as if I were Flynn [p. 41].

In another mystery by Kaminsky, *Think Fast, Mr. Peters* (1987), there is a passage where Peters talks to Sal Lutrzma, a talent agent, about his need of a Peter Lorre imitator, and Gable is mentioned as one of the celebritiws most frequently imitated:

> "You making a joke?" he asked. He then informed the pictures on one wall. "He's making a joke." Then back to me. "This town is up to its ass in Peter Lorre imitators. Everyone does Peter Lorre and Jimmy Durante, and Jean Sablon. Hell, I should have asked Edgar if the damn bird could do Jean Sablon. I've got Jimmy Stewarts, **Clark Gable**s and more Bette Davises than you'd need in a lifetime" [p. 41].

The actor's name pops up again in the final paragraph of Kaminsky's *The Devil Met a Lady* (1993), where the author announces his next book:

> All this took place a few months after I got a call from **Clark Gable**, who wanted me . . . but that's another story [p. 194].

In Kaminsky's mystery *Mildred Pierced* (2003), the star is mentioned once again when Peters talks about Joan Crawford, a major character in the novel:

> Crawford had been linked to almost every male star she had ever acted with, which made the list stretch all the way back to Lon Chaney, Sr., in the silent days, and on up to Robert Montgomery and **Clark Gable** in the more recent past [p. 17].

Gable becomes a part of a sarcastic simile in Lawrence Sanders's mystery *The Sixth Commandment* (1979). The context of the scene is the narrator, foundation's grant investigator Samuel Todd, talking about one of the dislikeable characters:

> I started my second cup of black coffee, and looked up to see Constable Ronnie Goodfellow standing opposite. From where I sat, he looked like he was on stilts. Did I tell you what a handsome guy he was? A young **Clark Gable**, before he grew a mustache [p. 263].

Michael B. Druxman's play *Gable* (1984) contains references to as many as twenty-one of Gable's pictures. Here are conclusive words of the play that are said after the actor exits the stage for the first and last time:

> His widow blamed his insistence on performing his own strenuous stunts for the film as part of the cause of his death.
>
> On March 20, 1961, Kay Williams Gable gave birth to a son. The child was named John Clark Gable.
>
> In an interview several years later, Joan Crawford said, "**Clark Gable** was the King of an empire called Hollywood. The empire is not what it once was – but the King has not been dethroned, even after death" [p. 66].

In Druxman's play *Tracy* (1984), on the other hand, we get a chance to find out what Tracy, in the author's opinion, thought about Gable:

> I liked **Gable**. Had some good times . . . on and off the set. We were drinking buddies.
>
> He could handle it better than me.

I'm the one who named him "The King."

That's right.

I got to the studio one morning, and couldn't get through the gate. A bunch of fans had surrounded **Gable**'s car.

Nobody noticed me.

I stood up in my convertible, and shouted, "Long live the King! And now, for Christ's sake, let's get inside and get to work."

Howard Strickling, Metro's publicity chief, heard about it . . . passed the remark on to Ed Sullivan . . . and that's how it all started [p. 48].

In Don DeLillo's satirical novel *White Noise* (1984/5), Gable is mentioned as one of several movie stars that died young in a seemingly non-sequitur exchange between college professors, colleagues of narrator/protagonist Jack Gladney:

"Ask me Joan Crawford."
"September thirty, nineteen fifty-five. James Dean dies. Where is Nicholas Grappa and what is he doing?"
"Ask me **Gable**, ask me Monroe" [p. 68].

George Baxt references Gable in several of his famous Hollywood-based mysteries. In *The Alfred Hitchcock Murder Case* (1986), the actor is mentioned in a passage describing a costume ball:

He saw several Adolf Hitlers and the Marx Brothers,

and there were at least three Noel Cowards. A Mussolini was dancing crazily on the grass with Joan of Arc, and through the open French windows leading to the villa's ballroom, Hitchcock saw the orchestra led by a cadaverous young man sporting an ill-fitting toupee that looked like a golf mound. As Hitchcock mingled with the cleverly masked and costumed crowd, he marveled at the ingenuity of some of the guests in the ballroom. There were Greta Garbo and Marlene Dietrich and Winston Churchill and **Clark Gable**. Beyond them at the sumptuous buffet was a hopeful but inadequate Tarzan in a loincloth revealing a body sadly in need of muscles, with a Jane sadly in need of a bosom [p. 259].

In Baxt's *The Marlene Dietrich Murder Case* (1993), Gable is referencned in several conversations; the first two times, during a Rolls-Royce ride to Dietrich's New Year's Eve party—the interlocutors include film producer Monte Trevor, businessman Ivar Tensha and the countess Dorothy di Frasso:

"Marlene deserves better than a silly expression. Don't you agree, Monte?"

"I wish I could get her for a movie," said Trevor, "I dream of casting her as *Salome*."

"*Salome*," whispered Tensha, "the dance of the seven veils." Di Frasso expected drool to seep from his mouth, but none was forthcoming.

"And as Herod," continued Trevor, "I see this young actor Paramount has brought over from London, Charles Laughton."

Di Frasso agreed. "That would be very interesting. You'll need someone sexy for John the Baptist. How about **Gable**?"

"Dietrich and **Gable**. Now wouldn't that be a fascinating combination." Tensha licked his lips. If he wasn't so damned rich, thought di Frasso, he'd be repulsive. She wondered if there was a Mrs. Tensha, and if so, how to get rid of her.

Said Monte Trevor, "Louis B. Mayer doesn't lend his stars without driving a hard bargain."

"Whatever the money," said di Frasso, "it would be worth it for **Gable**. He's hot box office" [pp. 12-13].

The actor's name is mentioned again in a passage which reveals the chauffeur's thoughts:

> Trevor glared at her. She was busy renewing her face. They were almost at their destination. The cigar smoke was causing her eyes to tear. She asked Trevor to lower a window. While carefully rouging her lips, she eyed the chauffeur, who was staring at her in the rearview mirror. Not that young, thought the chauffeur, but what the hell. If she could be a ticket to a screen test. **Gable** got to where he is by using older women, Pauline Frederick, Alice Brady, Jane Cowl. His first wife who taught him all he'd ever know about acting, Josephine Dillon, was twenty years older. And his current wife, Rhea, she's at least fifteen years older and rich to boot. His eyes sent di Frasso an unsubtle signal. She rewarded him with a raised eyebrow, which she hoped he recognized meant she was lowering her guard [pp. 14-15].

In addition to an allusion to *Gone with the Wind*—the book more than the film (as the movie is talked about only as a possible project)—Baxt's mystery *The Mae West Murder Case* (1993) contains also a reference to Gable. The actor is mentioned as a part of the gossip information provided by Mae West to her detective friends, Herb Villon and Jim Mallory, while she complains about her supporting players:

She watched them leave, then returned her attention to the detectives. "You know, it's not as though I don't have enough to worry about these days. My supportin' players are a bunch of prima donnas. I got Alice Brady from the Broadways Bradys—her father William is a great producer and married to a terrific actress, Grace George. Alice is pretty good herself, but now she's doin' supports and she still can't live with it. To think she once had an affair with **Clark Gable**. Then there's Elizabeth Patterson. Now she's been around since the year one [p. 22].

In George Baxt's *The Humphrey Bogart Murder Case* (1995), Gable is mentioned during a dinner including Dashiell Hammett, Lillian Hellman, Humphrey Bogart and his wife, Mayo Methot:

The grin disappeared from **Bogart**'s face. Mayo said to Hellman, "I never seem to have enough shoes. Are you as crazy about shoes as I am?"

"I am crazy about money and **Clark Gable** in no particular order," replied Hellman.

"**Gable** has false teeth," said Mayo.

"So did George Washington," said Hellman [pp. 47-48].

A Gable-related gossip appears in Baxt's *The William Powell and Myrna Loy Murder Case* (1996), in a scene where the novel's titular stars talk about Hollywood's illegitimate children:

"And they didn't leave them on anybody's doorstep either. They just continued to live the lie. I must ask **Clark** if he still insists Loretta's daughter isn't his. The child's protruding ears are a dead giveaway."

"Perhaps the child's protruding ears are simply protruding ears" [p. 164].

Ed Gorman's short story "The Alibi" (1988), included in *Raymond Chandler's Philip Marlowe: A Centennial Celebration*, is set in 1956. A reference to Gable appears as part of the description of a fancy hotel off Hollywood Boulevard, where a murder case brings private eye Raymond Chandler:

> Wandering over to the window, I looked down on the April afternoon. They didn't let you into this section of the city if you drove anything less than a Packard and then it had better have been waxed and buffed and polished within the past twenty-four hours. I glanced over the suite once more. In the vast marble lobby, an area that suggested a set from *Quo Vadis* gone slightly to seed, there were photographs of the stars who'd stayed over the years—the young Douglas Fairbanks, Jr., **Clark Gable**, and Garbo herself. I tried to imagine them sitting in this staid, icy room laughing their silver Hollywood laughs, but somehow the stiff worked against my sense of nostalgia [p. 289].

Susan Isaacs's novel *Shining Through* (1988) has been mentioned before due to its allusions to *Gone with the Wind*. The actor himself is mentioned in the book twice. First, he becomes a part of a brief and sarcastic exchange between Linda Voss and Gladys Slade regarding their earnest boss, Mr. Edward Leland:

> "How was Mr. Leland today?" Gladys insisted.
> "The usual. He wanted to gossip about Carole Lombard and **Clark Gable** and—"
> "Come on. Didn't he seem at all funny?"
> "Yeah, Gladys. He told me three jokes. *Very* dirty. About filthy things you never even heard of" [p. 22].

Nearly a hundred pages later the actor is mentioned again, this time by Linda Voss in a heated discussion with John Berringer, her boss and lover, regarding Nan, a woman who broke the engagement with John and whom he still loves:

> "So every upper-class person commits adultery?"
>
> "Conventional rules don't apply to Nan," he said sharply.
>
> I took a couple of sips of the juice. It was bitter, like drinking liquid tin. No wonder little Nannie preferred mimosas. I said, "Conventional rules don't apply to Adolf, either."
>
> John gave me his first real smile. "That's really not an apt comparison."
>
> "Why not? Everybody has to obey the rules."
>
> "That's too simplistic."
>
> "I don't think so. Because if you say Edward Leland's daughter or Adolf Hitler has special rules, then why not Henry Morgenthau and **Clark Gable**? And who decides who gets special treatment? The person who wants special treatment? Me? You?" [p. 116]

A minor reference to Gable, or rather to his famous mustache, appears, as part of an epithet, in Susan Isaacs's mystery *After All These Years* (1993). The man wearing such a mustache is Theodore Higbee, who tries to stop his wife Cass from helping narrator/protagonist Ruthie Myers in her private investigation which would clear her of murder charges:

> "Time to go," I said to Cass.
>
> "What are we doing?"
>
> "We have to find out what Stephanie knows about Mandy and Richie."
>
> "And after she tells us, we must ask her to introduce us to the lady."
>
> Theodore's smile evaporated. He disengaged his arm from his wife's and stroked his **Clark Gable** mustache with his

thumb and index finger. Whatever you do, Rosie, Cass in not going with you" [p. 255].

A random reference to Gable, as a part of an unoriginal metaphor, appears in Susan Isaacs's epic *Red, White and Blue* (1998), in a passage where the narrator addresses the dreams of a young woman, one of the ancestors of the book's heroine, investigative journalist Lauren Miller:

> What eighteen-year-old girl doesn't have time for a best friend, or even a good friend, what with two jobs and a mother who never had time for a friend either? What eighteen-year-old girl has never been kissed, except by Selwyn Klein, the Party's foremost recruiter in all five boroughs, the Communist **Clark Gable** without the mustache—who, when she finally told him she wouldn't join the Party, acted as if he wanted to snatch the kiss back? What eighteen-old-old girl who'd pulled straight A's in high school wasn't finally ready for some fun? [pp. 74-75]

Gable is referenced twice in John Dandola's mystery *West of Orange* (1990). The context of the first one is MGM publicist Edie Koslow speculating about the local barber, the man whose son found the body of the first victim, because of his precautions taken to avoid leaks:

> Maybe the barber was a former politico or a fallen politico. Maybe he was an ex-bootlegger or an ex-gunrunner or even an ex-cop. Edie played the game with herself all the way down to the lobby in the elevator. She trued casting the barber, putting every mask on him her mind could conjure up. Brian Donlevy, Barton MacLane, **Gable**, **Spence**. Maybe he sang with a quartet—Nelson Eddy [p. 24].

In the second passage, MGM publicity boss and Tracy express their differences referring to the idea of exchanging Ann Rutherford for Edie, who was kidnapped by the murderer (coworker Donald Jarvis):

> "But I *do like* Edie Koslow! I'm the reason she's here and nothing better goddamn happen to her!" **Tracy**'s finger was poking into Strickling's chest.
>
> Strickling stood his ground. "Stop the Irish Mafia crap, **Spence**, You can't go 'round making physical threats, you're a star for Chrissake."
>
> "Oh, does that mean that if I get kidnapped, you'll ransom me back? Unless it's in exchange for **Gable**?" **Tracy** was now nose to nose with Strickling [p. 203].

In addition to allusions to *It Happened One Night*, *San Francisco* and *Gone with the Wind*, Kirk Douglas's novel *Dance with the Devil* (1990) contains a direct reference to Gable. It takes place in a dialogue between the book's protagonist, film director Danny Dennison, and his agent and friend Milton Schultz, who asks Danny to hire his lover:

> "Give Darlene a part."
>
> "But it's set. All I haven't cast yet is the herd of buffalo."
>
> "Write something in—unless you want to keep flying with me to Las Vegas."
>
> Danny laughed. "And I thought you were worried about *my* quota."
>
> "Listen—" Milt's voice was unusually serious. "These girls don't go after me for looks. As Sarah always reminds me, **Clark Gable** I'm not—so, *boychik*, I gotta deliver" [p. 105].

Oscar Hijuelos's novel *The Fourteen Sisters of Emilio Montez O'Brien* (1993) contains a reference to Gable in a passage describing the protagonist as seen by his sister Gloria:

Perhaps one of those sporty tennis-types in town—for when they walked along the main street of Cobbleton, she was always aware of the way the young women looked at her brother, and she had seen them making eyes at him when he in his usher's outfit would lead some of the ladies to their seats, and when they went into the ice-cream parlor there was always a little group of girls to start giggling, as if he were (and this would be funny enough) some movie star like **Clark Gable** or Joel McCrea, whom people always said Emilio resembled [pp. 225-226].

In Barbara Taylor Bradford's drama *Angel* (1993), a flattering reference to Gable is made in a scene when costume designer Rosie Madigan identifies people in a framed photograph to singer Johnny Fortune:

"When somebody wants to stay lost, they usually manage to stay lost," Johnny remarked, and looked down at the photograph he was still holding. "And who's the handsome guy with the wonderful **Clark Gable** smile?"

"That's my brother."

"Isn't he Nell's boyfriend?" Johnny said.

"Yes, he is."

"He's a good-looking son of a gun. He oughta be in pictures too" [p. 281].

The actor is also mentioned in Barbara Burnett Smith's mystery *Writers of the Purple Sage* (1994), in a passage where the narrator/protagonist, aspiring writer Jolie Wyatt, tries to console her teenaged son, Jeremy, about their undesired prospects to move from Purple Sage to Austin:

"Hey, maybe we can at least figure a way to keep Diablo," I said, as if his horse were the reason for his upset. "They have stables around Austin." Jeremy wasn't buying it for a second. I tried to sound even more optimistic—my pitch was nearing the lunatic range. "Maybe I'll win the lottery. Maybe I'll sell a book."

One of Jeremy's eyebrows went up in a gesture that would have done **Clark Gable** proud. "I don't believe in fairy tales anymore," he said [p. 18].

In addition to including a reference to *The Misfits*, Elizabeth Evans's novel *The Blue Hour* (1994) mentions Gable outside of a film context, in a passage relating two girls' dialogue prompted by a movie magazine:

> She [Penny] laughed, and came to sit on the edge of my bed. "Let me see." Reluctantly, I handed over the magazine. She flipped through it, then studied the cover. "Did I ever tell you, once I sent away for a picture of **Clark Gable**, and when I got it, it was signed, 'Best wishes, Errol Flynn'?" [p. 266]

A non-sequitur reference to the actor appears in Richard Ford's novel *Independence Day* (1995), in a scene where protagonist Frank Bascombe visits the Basketball Hall of Fame with his son Paul:

> Paul is staring at me down the length of the conveyor. Conceivably he's been barking his approval while I've been shooting but doesn't want it known. I have in fact enjoyed the whole thing thoroughly.
>
> "Take your best shot!" I shout through the loud crowd noise. The ball boy, off to one side now, is chatting up his chunky, ponytailed blond sweetheart, laying his two meaty hands on her two firm shoulders and goo-gooing in her eyes like **Clark Gable**. For some reason, having I'm sure to do with queuing theory, no one is on the conveyor at the moment [pp. 278-279].

Philip Roth's Pulitzer Prize-winning novel *American Pastoral* (1997) makes a reference to the actor in the passage describing the reaction to Jerry Levov's romantic idea. The excerpt is presented here, rather than under a specific movie, because Lana Turner made more than one film with Gable:

> Atop the coat he placed a heart that he cut out of cardboard and painted his name on in Gothic letters, and the package was sent parcel post. It had taken him three months to transform an improbable idea into nutty reality. Brief by human standards.
>
> She screamed when she opened the box. "She had a fit," her girlfriends said. Jerry's father also had a fit. "This is what you do with the parachute your brother sent you? You cut it up? You cut up a parachute?" Jerry was too humiliated to tell him that it was to get the girl to fall into his arms and kiss him the way Lana Turner kissed **Clark Gable**. I happened to be there when his father went after him for curing the skins in the midday sun [pp. 32-33].

In John Updike's novel *In the Beauty of the Lilies* (1996), the narrator compares Gable's and Cooper's acting styles and personalities in the context of their work as Alma's co-stars in some fictitious movies from the early 1950s:

> **Gable** was more engageable—a woman's man who had climbed up from Ohio's oil fields on a ladder of female sponsors, beginning with his stepmother. He flirted with Alma, turning on that slowly spreading smile like a ruthless squeeze of superior strength. A few times, in the thirsty, dusty weeks of the Nevada location shoot, he slept with her, like a sleepy lion obliging a female cub. But the times didn't add up to anything more; there was in **Gable** a loneliness too big for Alma to begin to fill. Where **Cooper** was a sublime accident, who had cartooned

and ranched and bummed about before backing into acting as a crowd extra, **Gable** had never been anything but an aspiring actor, He thought in billboard terms. He had loved Lombard; in Hollywood that had matched him with every giantess from Jean Harlow to Ava Gardner, Lombard, all soft gay golden toughness, a foul-mouthed publicity hound and frenetic practical joker, had been in his heart's match, and she had smashed herself against a mountain while trying to sell war bonds [p. 320].

In Dominick Dunne's *Another City, Not My Own* (1997), writer/journalist Gus Bailey talks to his ex-wife Peach about the O.J. Simpson trial, which he is currently covering, and an analogy is made between the relationship of a couple of lawyers and the frequent situation between two movie co-stars:

> People want to know if Marcia Clark and Chris Darden are having an affair. I don't know if they are or not, and I wouldn't tell if I did know.... They've become very close. It's only natural when you spend that many hours a day together, working as tandem, passionately believing in the same thing, as they do, that O.J. killed these people. It's like when you're on location for a movie. The two leads usually fall in love, at least for the length of the picture. Like **Loretta Young** and **Clark Gable**. Ali McGraw and Steve McQueen. On and on. When the picture's over, so's the romance [p. 238].

Loren D. Estleman, in his Detroit novel *Edsel* (1995), mentions Gable in three places, each time giving narrator/protagonist Connie Minor a different topic to comment upon—the changes brought about by the passing of time, the negative effects of television on the business in movie theaters and the questionable merits of convertibles:

Now we had to go to war again, first with cavalry, then with rockets. If nothing much changed between FDR's snooty profile on a newsreel screen and Frankie Orr's humble face on the box in the living room, from that point forward nothing stayed put. **Clark Gable**'s cocky grin dissolved into Marlon Brando's Neanderthal pout. Buicks sprouted holes that had no function [p. 20].

"Movies are in trouble because for the price of ten Saturday nights anyone can put a box in his living room that spews out **Clark Gable**, Sugar Ray Robinson, and Gorgeous George week long. That's why the people who still go to tem dress like bums and talk all the way through the feature. They think they're still home" [pp. 68-69]

"Ragtops are for kids." In fact I'd been planning to ask for one almost until the time I placed the order. All my life, the open car had represented a world of hand-rolled cigars, easily rolled women, winters in Miami, and hundred-dollar tips. Tom Mix had driven a white Auburn with carved horns on the radiator and the top down to make room for his ten-gallon hat, **Clark Gable** and Carole Lombard had roared off to their honeymoon in a red Bentley convertible, and James dean had hurtled a black Porsche bareheaded off a desert road into the Milky Way of immortality, two years dead now and still climbing [p. 273].

A reference to Gable's physiognomy, or rather his hairdo, appears also in Estleman's thriller *Jitterbug* (1998), in a passage describing a young farmer's preparations to go to the big city with his girlfriend after he gets permission from his strict father:

Gunther thanked him and went inside to clean up. He

put on his suit, brushed his hair straight back, and teased forth a lock to form an apostrophe above his right eye, like **Clark Gable**. He couldn't do much about his square jaw and beefy neck, which had German farm boy all over them, and wished he had the confidence to carry off a silk scarf tucked into an open shirt collar, Ronald Colman style [p. 158].

Estleman's mystery *Retro* (2004) contains three references to the actor. While two of them—on pp. 32 and 174 (his mustache again) are rather insignificant—the last one is worth quoting. A reporter from the past, Ms. Eyck, offers some facts and her opinion to the book's narrator/protagonist, Detroit private detective Amos Walker:

> She let that one sail past. She'd already taken her swipe at the postmodern press. "So I took in some sun, met Lana Turner and **Clark Gable**, and took the train back home with enough feature stuff to fill the section. **Gable** had false teeth and bad breath, and he was still sexier than the milk-babies who fill theaters today. Or I'm told they do. I haven't seen a picture on the big screen since they turned the Michigan into a parking garage" [p. 229].

Max Allan Collins's *Flying Blind* (1998) was already mentioned in the entry on *It Happened One Night*. The actor himself is mentioned several more times in the book. The following description of a minor character is a part of a scene in which private detective Nate Heller rescues Amelia Earhart form an overly enthusiastic crowd of fans in Detroit:

"We got a problem here!" I said to the Hudson rep who was Amelia's official escort. Arms outstretched like an umpire, I was doing my best to keep the clawing crowd away from an increasingly spooked Amelia; she was behind me, and we were backed up to a Hudson Eight on display there.

The Hudson rep was a little guy with George Raft's hair, **Clark Gable**'s mustache and Stan Laurel's face [p. 43].

A physical description of a major character of the book, ace pilot Paul Mantz, in a scene just prior to his introduction to the protagonist, offers a good pretext to mention Gable again:

> A fourth man, who brought up the rear in the confident manner of a commanding officer who allows his troops to lead the charge, wore a gray suit and a lighter gray shirt with a gray and black tie and looked as dapper as a movie star, or anyway a movie executive. Small but with a solid, square-shouldered build, he was almost handsome, with bright dark brown eyes, a jutting nose, and a jaunty jutting chin; his slicked-back black hair and slip of a mustache were apparently on loan from **Clark Gable** [pp. 63-64].

And, in another scene (a dialogue between Heller and one of Mantz's mechanics), the actor is mentioned as one of numerous Hollywood customers of Mantz's charter service, *Honeymoon Express*:

> "Nate Heller," he said. He gave me half a smile; something odd lingered in his expression. "If you're looking for the boss, he's on a charter, sort of."
> "What do you mean, 'sort of'?"
> The half-smile continued and seemed strained. "Well, him and Terry and **Clark** and Carole went off to La Gulla."
> **Gable** and Lombard. I was not impressed. I had met actors before. And Terry was Mantz's new wife, or soon to be, anyway [p. 146].

Later in the book, there is another simile connecting Mantz's mustache with Gable:

> The first person in Hollywood I recognized was in the movies all right, but most tourists wouldn't have known his name any more than his **Gable**-mustached, nearly handsome face: Paul Mantz—in a single-breasted hunter green sport jacket with gathered waist and double-patch pockets, a yellow open-neck shirt, and light green slacks—sauntered into the Cine-Gril, put his hand on my shoulder, ordered a martini in a frosted glass from the black-jacketed bartender and then said hello [p. 216].

The actor is mentioned once again as a celebrity in a scene where Margot DeCarrie (Amelia's secretary) takes Heller to Earl Carroll's, an exclusive restaurant on Hollywood Boulevard:

> Actually, quite a few famous people were seated around us: Mantz's charter customers **Gable** and Lombard, Tyrone Power and Sonja Henie, Jack Benny and his wife Mary Livingston, Edgar Bergen without Charlie McCarthy (but with a lovely blonde), all seated at various tables of larger parties otherwise consisting of people I didn't recognize [p. 229].

The last reference to Gable in the book is related to his military service during World War II:

> Paul Mantz's military service was stellar, and not just because the movie actors serving under him included **Clark Gable**, Ronald Reagan and Alan Ladd. His unit shot over thirty thousand feet of aerial combat footage and hundreds of training films, and while most of his duty was stateside, as he operated

out of so-called Fort Roach (at Hal Roach Studios), Lt. Colonel Mantz shot stunning combat footage over the North Atlantic and in Africa [p. 320].

In Max Allan Collins's political thriller *Majic Man* (1999), the actor's name appears again; here he is mentioned in a conversation between the book's narrator, private eye Nate Heller, and the assistant manager of the Lodge hotel in Cloudcroft, New Mexico:

> "Listen, Mac, you got any suites available?"
> "Just one; we're underbooked, and even off-season, the suites get snapped up."
> "But you do have one?"
> "Yes," he said, but shook his head, no. "The Governor's Suite. It's pretty expensive—it's where Pancho Villa, Judy Garland, Conrad Hilton and **Clark Gable**'ve stayed."
> "Together?"
> That made him chuckle; he looked like he hadn't chuckled in a while [p. 135].

Stuart Woods must be Gable's dedicated fan because the actor is referenced in many of his books. In L.A. mystery *Dead Eyes* (1994), Gable is mentioned in a passage referring to the Racket Club in Pam Springs, where a movie star (Chris Calloway) and a cop protecting her and romantically interested in her (Jon Larsen) have lunch:

> The Racket Club was not busy, but it was cool and dark, and Larsen wasn't looking for a crowd. From behind the bar movie stars of another day smiled down on them—**Clark Gable**, Lana Turner, and Rita Hayworth mugged for the camera beside the pool [p. 117].

Four Hollywood Legends

Woods's *The Prince of Beverly Hills* (2004) is a story of a young man, Rick Barron, who—due to some favorable circumstances—is elevated from a patrol cop to an executive position at one of Hollywood's top studios. He befriends the fictitious Centurion's number one male star, Clete Barrow, who—in turn—is a good friend of Gable. Thus, Gable and David Niven appear in numerous passages describing their encounters with those two fictitious characters. In the first passage, Eddie Harris, the general manager of the studio, enlightens Rick about the studio prior to offering him the position of the chief of security:

> "We're hot, and the whole town knows it. Being new, we've had to borrow a lot of stars for productions, which puts our costs up, but we're building a stable, and since we stole Clete Barrow from Metro, 'it's getting easier. What **Clark Gable** is to Metro, Clete Barrow is to us" [pp. 16-17].

When Rick is invited to his first party at the Harrises', he meets a few celebrities there:

> A waiter appeared at Rick's elbow with a tray of martinis, and he took one. As he did, two other couples were being shown in, and Rick found himself being introduced to Sam Goldwyn and William Wyler and their wives. The party was completed when **Clark Gable** and Carole Lombard arrived, accompanied by an attractive older woman, who turned out to be Sol Weinman's sister, Adele Mannheim [p. 29].

> "**Clark**," Wyler said, "would you act on television?"
>
> "In what?" **Gable** replied, "a baseball game or a puppet show? And you can say I didn't say so."
>
> Goldwyn wrinkled his brow. "That didn't sound right, **Clark**."
>
> Everybody laughed except Goldwyn, who seemed surprised to find himself funny [p. 30].

Both Gable and Niven become significant characters in the part of the book when they join Rick and Clete for a fly-fishing trip to Oregon, and, while being there, they discuss the development of the political situation in Europe. Rick flies his father's plane both ways.

Clark Gable got out of the driver's seat of the pickup, followed by a tall, slender young man with a mustache.

"You've met **Clark**, I think," Clete said.

"Sure I have," Rick replied, offering **Gable** his hand.

"How are you, Rick? Looking forward to some trout fishing?"

"I'm looking forward to learning about it, **Clark**. It's my first time."

"This is David Niven," **Gable** said, introducing the young man. "Another limey."

. . .

He put **Gable** and Niven in the rear seat, Clete in the front, then climbed into the pilot's seat.

. . .

"We're going to follow the coast to the mouth of the Rogue River, then follow the river up to the camp," Rick said. "Clete, will you recognize it from the air?"

"I will," **Gable** said. "There's a big red barn and a farmhouse, and the strip runs parallel to the river along the north bank. There's a windsock near the barn."

. . .

Gable produce some thick ham sandwiches. "Ma made 'em for us," he shouted. He gave everybody but Rick a beer, and gave him a Coca-Cola.

. . .

After half an hour, **Gable** tapped him on the shoulder. "It's up ahead there. See the barn?"

Rick put the nose down slightly and retarded the throttle. "Got it."

"The windsock is to the left of the barn," **Gable** yelled. "Usually, you land to the west."

. . .

"Pull up right there," **Gable** said, pointing to the spot beside the barn.

. . .

They loaded everything into Jake's pickup, and he handed the key to **Gable**. "Everything's ready down at the cabin," he said. "I'll see you when I see you."

"Three or four days," **Gable** said. . . . Twenty minutes later, they were unloaded and had opened two bottles of whiskey, scotch for Clete and David, bourbon for Rick and **Clark**.

"Man," **Gable** said, "I can't tell you how good it feels to get out of the city and up here." . . .

"Well," Niven said, "it's pretty, but it isn't Scotland, and trout aren't salmon."

Gable grinned at him. "I can tell we're going to have to shoot you before the weekend's over."

. . .

Clete snapped off the radio. "Well, it seems that even Chamberlain has finally faced facts."

"We'll be at war within a week," Niven said.

"Ah, don't worry about it, David," **Gable** said. "You Limeys will kick Hitler's ass back to the Rhine in no time."

"I hope you're right, **Clark**," Clete said.

Later, **Gable** grilled some steaks, and they had a subdued dinner, washed down with quantities of whiskey. There were two bedrooms in the cabin: Clete and Niven took one, Rick and **Gable** the other. There were two single beds with lots of blankets, and Rick settled in. He was astonished to see **Gable** take out his teeth, brush them thoroughly in the sink, then put them in a glass of water beside the bed.

...

He found **Gable** in the kitchen making pancakes.

"Morning, Rick."

"Morning, **Clark**. Are Clete and David up yet?"

"Those crazy Limeys are having a dip in the river," **Gable** said.

...

"You're both insane," **Gable** said. "Get some clothes on. Breakfast is ready and I don't want to look at your dicks while I'm eating."

...

For the rest of the day, Rick was given an intense course of instruction in fly-fishing by **Gable**, who was clearly a master of the sport.

...

"I fell for you and your country, pal," **Gable** said, "but thank God we're not in it."

"Not yet," Niven said.

"Roosevelt will do everything he can to keep us out of it," Rick said.

"Yes," Clete said, "and it won't be enough."

"I'm afraid you might be right," **Gable** said. "If things go badly for England, Roosevelt will try to get us into it." He turned to Rick. "And you know what that means."

For the first time, Rick gave thought to the idea that he, personally, might have to go to war. "I guess I'll have to go," he said. "How about you, **Clark**?"

"Not me. I'm past draft age, and Ma and I are trying like hell to get pregnant. The combination of those two things will keep me out, I guess. If I were younger and single, I'd go, though.

I wouldn't like it much, but I'd go. I talked to Jimmy Stewart last week, and he's been taking flying lessons for a long time, to get a leg up."

...

They continued eating breakfast in silence, then Clete put his fork down. "I've got to get back to LA," he said. "I've got things to do."

"So have I," Niven said.

Gable spoke up. "Well, why don't we wrap it up here and go home. Weather okay to fly, Rick?"

...

Rick went back and helped unload the airplane. When they were done, he said his goodbyes to **Gable** and Niven, then turned to Clete [pp. 200-209].

Soon after they get back from their fishing trip in Oregon, Clete Barrow and David Niven join their military units in England, and Rick receives letter from both of them:

> Clete exhibited a boyish enthusiasm for everything he was learning in the Royal Marines, and especially for commando tactics, which had yet to be used in the war. **Clark Gable** passed on a couple of letters from David Niven, too, which were hilariously funny [p. 270].

During Rick's stay in San Diego with his military unit, Eddie Harris comes down from Los Angeles, and they have dinner together at the Hotel del Coronado. Gable becomes an important part of their conversation:

> "You're getting into television?"
>
> "Well, not until after the war, but I think there'll be an explosion of sets as soon as they can start making them again, so

there'll be money to be made. You heard about Carole Lombard, of course."

"Yes, I wrote **Clark** a letter but didn't hear back from him. He must have been inundated with mail after she died."

"He took it very hard. He volunteered for the draft, you know; got a commission and trained as a gunner in bombers."

"I read something about it."

"They'll never let him fly missions, you know. If he got killed, it wouldn't be good for morale, but he's in England" [pp. 297-298].

In the sequel to *The Prince of Beverly Hills* called *Beverly Hills Dead* (2008), there is one reference to *Gone with the Wind* and five to Gable himself. The first one takes place when Eddie Harris, the chairman of Centurion, and Rick Barron, now a producer/director, discuss the future of their new star, Vance Calder:

"Don't worry; he's happy, and he's going to stay that way."

"He's going to be our **Clark Gable** and our Clete Barrow, all wrapped up in one" [p. 35].

A few days later Rick and Vance talk at the party at the Harrises', and there is a brief reference to the fly-fishing trip described in detail in *The Prince of Beverly Hills*:

"How did you like Adele?"

"She's lovely. I enjoyed her company."

"Good. I didn't want to mention it before, but she's a large stockholder in Centurion. You know, the first time I came to this house I wore a tuxedo borrowed from wardrobe, and I was seated next to Adele. The other guests were the Goldwyns and the **Clark Gable**s."

Four Hollywood Legends

. . .

"David and I once went trout fishing in Oregon with **Clark Gable** and Clete Barrow," Rick said to Vance [p. 50].

After the shooting of *Bitter Creek*, Vance's first movie, is completed, Rick and Eddie discuss a new contract for the rising star:

> Eddie laughed. "You're not kidding, pal, but Sol never ran into anything like this. When **Gable** came along around, what, 1930, they paid him a weekly salary, and although he's making, what, five grand a week now, it's still a weekly salary. But not Cary Grant; he went independent, and he's going to make a lot more money in his career than **Gable** will in his. That's what Hy is going for, and it's exactly what I would be doing if I were Vance's agent [p. 158].

In another novel by Stuart Woods, *Bel-Air Dead* (2011), which is a sort of sequel to *Beverly Hills Dead*, the future of Centurion Studios is discussed during a gathering of some major shareholders in a house of the widow of Vance Calder. Rick Barron, a veteran producer/director now in his nineties, talks about the past and makes an extensive reference to an important event that dates back to 1939 (originally narrated in *The Prince of Beverly Hills*):

> "That's right, he did. In September of 1939 I flew Clete, David Niven, and **Clark Gable** up to Oregon for some steelhead fishing on the Rogue River. We were up there when we heard Neville Chamberlain on the shortwave radio, announcing that a state of war existed between Britain and Germany. We returned to L.A. immediately, and before you knew it, Clete and Niven had left for England, where they joined their old regiments. Niven had a splendid war record, and Clete died at Dunkirk, getting his men onto boats. After **Clark**'s wife, Carole Lombard,

was killed in an airplane crash while returning from a bond tour, **Clark** enlisted, too. So did I, but for a different reason [p. 19].

In yet another book by Woods, a Stone Barrington novel entitled *Son of Stone* (2011), a reference to Gable is once again related to a comparison between him and Vance Calder, the fictitious megastar and main character of several earlier books by the author. The quoted excerpt is a part of a conversation between Kelli Keane of the *New York Post* with Jess, a young film buff from the Arts section from whom she tries to get some information about Calder:

> "Bachelor for most of his life, lived quietly, didn't give interviews—print or TV, except once for a *New Yorker* profile. The old-timers like Calder didn't do the publicity thing much."
> "How come?"
> "They didn't need to. The studios handled publicity but kept the press off their backs. I mean, you never saw **Clark Gable** on *The Tonight Show*, did you?" [pp. 118-119]

The actor is mentioned in Elliott Roosevelt's mystery *Murder in the Lincoln Bedroom* (2000) as one of those who missed the War Bond rally (with an auction of items belonging to celebrity donors), organized by the First Lady in the White House:

> Some of the donors would not be present. **Clark Gable**, for example, who was serving in the armed forces, had sent a white silk scarf he had worn in a picture featuring him as a suave playboy type [p. 83].

Elizabeth Hay's novel *A Student of Weather* (2001) was already quoted in the entry on *It Happened One Night*. A reference to Gable is made in an excerpt where Norma Joyce bombards her sister with a series of unrelated questions:

> Have you written to Maurice? she asked her sister. When do you think he'll come back? What was his sister's name? Did he say? Did Maurice say?
>
> Who do you think is more handsome? Maurice or Joel McCrea? Lucinda? Who's more handsome? Maurice or **Clark Gable**?
>
> Who's richer? Lucinda, who's richer? Maurice or Uncle Dennis? [p. 37]

In Bill Crider's novel *We'll Always Have Murder* (2001), there are two references to Gable, in addition to two insignificant ones to *Gone with the Wind*. They appear in a brief passage describing the appearance of movie studio owner Thomas Wayne:

> Thomas Wayne was behind it, and he stood up as we came through the door. He was tall and thin, with a pinched face and ears that stuck out like **Gable**'s. He wasn't as handsome as **Gable**, though, and he didn't have that winning smile. He didn't have any smile at all [p. 66].

A reference to Gable appears also in Garrison Keillor's novel *Lake Wobegon Summer 1956* (2001), in a passage where narrator/protagonist Gary makes a funny observation about the lawn he has been taking care of:

> And I was surprised myself at how verdant and thick and green it got by the end of May. I cut it close and soak it regularly and the result is a lawn worthy of millionaires and Hollywood stars—if **Clark Gable** had our lawn, he'd sit on it every day and grin for the photographers. Every day Daddy looks at this

perfection, and once, prompted by Mother, he said, "It's looking pretty good," but mostly he searches for flaws, a ragged edge, a few brown blades, a lone clump of skunk cabbage, and he delights in pointing these out [pp. 10-11].

Gable is clearly Adriana Trigiani's favorite actor, as his name and films appear in several of her books. His prestigious position as an unquestioned celebrity is emphasized in her novel *Milk Glass Moon* (2002), in a passage describing the Villa d'Este on Lake Como, Italy, where the protagonists, Ave Maria and her husband Jack Mac, are invited by hotel manager Battista Barbari to spend a couple of days:

> As in all fairy tales, the road leads to a castle, known on this lake as the Cardinal's Palace. The Queen's Pavilion, a burnt-umber-faced villa with a boat launch at its base, faces the main building, where Battista has booked us. Jack says nothing, as he has never seen anything like this either. Only the most glamorous and elegantly dressed, coiffed, and perfumed belong here. No wonder Ava Gardner and Frank Sinatra honeymooned here; Caroline of Brunswick, Princess of Wales, was kept in exile here; **Clark Gable** roamed these grounds; and Ginger Rogers swam in the pool that floats on the lake. This is heavenly, and stars belong here. Jack and me? We'll do our best not to gape our two days away in awe of all we see [p. 175].

The fact that the author and her protagonists (both male and female), interior decorator Bartolomeo di Crespi in this one, know everything about Gable is emphasized once again in Trigiani's novel *Rococo* (2005), in a passage where the narrator makes a simile related to Gable's private life:

> I haven't been introduced to his current wife, Doris Falcone, née Cassidy. She doesn't look like Lonnie's type at all. First of

all, she's not younger than Lonnie, seeming to be in her upper fifties. She's tall and willowy. At this party, she's a good foot taller than any of the other guests. Her shoulder-length hair is a soft dove gray, offset perfectly by a shirtwaist party dress in a mild pink Pucci print, which she wears with pink Pappagallo flats. "She's a dead ringer for **Lady Sylvia Ashley**." I say to no one in particular, thinking of **Clark Gable**'s fourth wife, the zipper-thin British royal-by marriage who came to the States and charmed Hollywood and its leading men after the war [pp. 82-83].

In Trigiani's *Home to Big Stone Gap* (2006), the actor is mentioned at a Christmas gathering, as a part of Fleeta's digression during a general discussion about Burt Reynolds:

"Let me finish," Fleeta continues. "It was like when I was a girl and I was in love with **Clark Gable**. I felt like if I got on a train and went to Hollywood, that if I met him, he might give me a tumble. That's how I feel about Burt. He seemed like he'd give every girl an equal shot to get in his drawers. That's all I'm saying" [p. 188].

In another novel by Trigiani, *Very Valentine* (2009), the assets of Gable as a man are made obvious in an exchange between three ladies: narrator Valentine, her grandmother (Teodora Angelini, Gram), and June, the latter's old friend and the family business's employee:

"We've got everything under control," I tell her.
"Besides that, you were hardly wasting time up there. Weren't you dreaming of **Gable**?" June says, smiling.
"How do you know?" Gram asks her.
"Who doesn't dream of **Gable**?" June shrugs [p. 62].

We are reminded of Gable's war experience once again in James Neel White's *I Was a P-51 Fighter Pilot in WWII* (2003), a nonfiction book that also mentions his movie *Night Flight*. The following excerpt is a part of Chapter 88, Bodney Entertainment:

> USO performances brought amateur and professional entertainers to the ETO. Stars from Hollywood especially were welcome. **Clark Gable** visited Bodney in 1943. He was a photographer's delight, handsome and debonair. It was reported that he acted in real life like he acted in the movies. He flew B-17 missions over Germany as a news gathering photographer. Observers claimed that 487th Squadron Commander, Lt Col Bill Halton, was a shade better looking than **Gable**, mustache and all [p. 319].

The actor's name is mentioned numerous times in Martha Sherrill's *My Last Movie Star* (2002)—both in connection with his movies and independently. Below is a brief part of a conversation between journalist Clementine James and *Flame* magazine editor Ed Nostrum, who tries to make her reveal who is her favorite actor. After a number of wrong guesses, including Lee Marvin, Clint Eastwood and John Wayne, he gets close to the truth:

> "I'm not into this game."
> "I have it," he said. "**Rhett Butler**." And then he leaned across the small café table and put his hands on either side of my face. "'**Scarlett, I want to take your head between my hands . . .**'"
> "You're close," I said.
> "**Gable**."
> I didn't say anything.

"I knew it was **Gable**. That explains why you like me so much" [p. 205].

Gable's name pops up several times in Paula Marantz Cohen's novel *Jane Austen in Boca* (2002), in a conversation between three women who try do decide what to do on a Saturday night:

> "Okay," said Flo, relenting as she always did after teasing Lila. "I'll tell you what we'll do: I'll rent a **Clark Gable** movie and make some popcorn. You can both come over and watch."
>
> "Sitting home and watching television is not my idea of Saturday-night entertainment," declared Lila. "I like human company."
>
> "**Clark Gable** is better than human company."
>
> "Well, you can stay home," said Lila huffily. "I'm going to go out. May, will you join me? The JCC has a talk by one of those guru doctors on lowering your blood pressure through stress management. They say it will be very well attended."
>
> "Well . . ." said May. "I was feeling a little tired—"
>
> "May wants to watch **Clark Gable**, interrupted Flo. "He does more for stress management than a guru doctor."
>
> "Flo, mind your own business. Just because you have no interest in meeting anyone doesn't mean you have to influence May."
>
> "Please," interceded May. "I wouldn't mind going to hear the guru doctor, Lila, only I'm feeling a little tired. Flo isn't influencing me. I do like **Clark Gable**."
>
> "All right," said Lila. "I like **Clark Gable**, too. We'll watch the movie tonight, but you have to promise to do something tomorrow, even if it's only going to the clubhouse to hear Pinkus Lotman on parking violations in the pods. If we don't do things, we might as well be dead" [pp. 8-9].

Lilian Jackson Braun's mystery *The Cat Who Brought Down the House* (2003) contains two references to Gable. The first one appears in a passage where the actor is mentioned as one of the celebrities whose autographed photographs are loaned by the collection's owner, Thelma Thackeray, who has just returned to her hometown Pickax after a long career in Hollywood, for an animal-welfare fund-raising initiative:

> "Well, Thelma has a collection of autographed photos of old movie stars that she'll lend us for an exhibit. I assured her that we have a locked case for such exhibits. **Clark Gable**, Mae West, John Wayne, Joan Crawford, etc.—isn't that exciting?" [p. 64]

In the second reference, Gable is also accompanied by other movie stars; this time, however, he is mentioned by Thelma herself in a conversation with local columnist James Mackintosh Qwilleran:

> Qwilleran asked, "When did movies come to Pickax?"
> "Bud and I turned twelve, and Pop gave us the Pickax Movie Palace for a birthday present. It had been the old opera house—closed for ages—and he said he got it cheap. That's when we started seeing Garbo, John Barrymore, **Gable**, and the Marx Brothers. We saw *Duck Soup* three times. When I saw *The Gay Divorcee* with Ginger Rogers and Fred Astaire, that's when I knew I had to go to Hollywood" [p. 127].

The protagonist of Valerie Block's novel *Don't Make a Scene* (2007) is Diane Kurasik, a middle-aged single woman who runs a movie theater in Greenwich Village. Consequently, the book brims with movie references, mostly from the golden period. Below is a passage focusing on a legendary actress and her two husbands:

During the day, Diane was on edge from the demolition; at night, she walked through the hyped-up, overemphatic entertainment district to her private eye's lair and turned on the TV. Even if you have a lot in common with someone, it doesn't always work. During her brief marriage to older man-about-town William Powell, party-girl Carole Lombard suffered toxic poisoning, malaria, pneumonia, influenza, pleurisy and chronic anemia. She famously said that George Raft was the sexiest man in Hollywood, but she remodeled herself as one of the guys in order to go fishing and play poker with her second husband, **Clark Gable**, "the King of Hollywood" at the time. Still: **Gable** was uncultured, limited and legendarily cheap with waitresses and cab drivers. Lombard had the shock of her life when she saw his false teeth grinning up at her from the nightstand on their honeymoon night. She died in a plane crash two years later, at the height of her fame and his. Who knows what might have happened? [p. 168]

In James Scott Bell's mystery *Try Dying* (2007), the main villain, corrupt public figure named Rudy Barocas, owns a seemingly well-meaning organization called Triunfo. A description of its location leads to a reference to a couple of screen legends:

Triunfo was headquartered in one of those renovated office buildings in Hollywood, this one on Vine. The Pantages was around the corner, one of the last reminders of old Hollywood. I could see the stack of flying saucers that made up the Capitol Records building. Outside of Musso & Frank, and the Egyptian and Chinese theaters, there wasn't much recognizable from the days when Garbo and **Gable** went out among 'em. The local city powers were trying to make Hollywood a respectable place again, and a lot of building was going on. They were trying to stir up a good nightlife [p. 96].

Bell's *Try Darkness* (2008), a sequel to *Try Dying*, has protagonist/narrator Ty Buchanan experience a nightmare while staying in a trailer at a Benedictine monastery, St. Monica's:

> It felt like I was running with an ankle weights on. I ran down an alley that ended at a wall about a hundred feet high. The wall had caricatures on it of old movie stars. They were grotesque caricatures. Charlie Chaplin looked like a serial killer. **Gable** had a wicked smile [p. 27].

Clark Gable is also mentioned in Michael P. Naughton's mystery *Deathryde: Rebel Without a Corpse* (2008), but the reference is more about Carole Lombard and plane crashes, in general, than him:

> "Sometimes death is just a coin toss," Coffin Joe said. It was the day before *Harold & Maude* and he was giving tourists their money's worth of celebrity death trivia
>
> The Big Sleep hearse had just left Westwood Memorial Mortuary and was now heading south on Beverly Glen towards Santa Monica Boulevard and Hollywood Forever.
>
> "Carole Lombard, who was married to **Clark Gable**, could not make up her mind," he said, "whether to take a plane or a train in 1942. She tossed a coin and opted for the plane."
>
> . . .
>
> "Needless to say the coin toss cost her her life and she perished in the plane crash at just 33 years old. A coin toss also killed Richie Valens when he persuaded this cat named Tommy Allsup—" [p. 92]

In addition to containing a reference to *Run Silent, Run Deep*, Dermot McEvoy's *Our Lady of Greenwich Village* (2008) mentions Gable outside of any movie context, in a passage offering a biography and physical description of narrator/protagonist Jude Wolfe Tone O'Rourke's deceased uncle, Myles Francis Kavanagh:

> Frank Kavanagh, after his IRA troubles, somehow got to America in the early 1920s, probably illegally, probably as a seaman. He had Hollywood good looks that would put **Clark Gable** to shame [p. 269].

Clyde Edgerton's novel *The Bible Salesman* (2008) contains a reference to Gable in four different places, each time resulting from the resemblance car thief Preston Clearwater bears to the actor:

> "Nice car," said the boy. "Fifty Chrysler." He reached out his hand. "I'm Henry Dampier. Henry was surprised at the man's big hand. And he had big ears. He looked a little bit like **Clark Gable**, but without a mustache.
> "Preston Clearwater," said the man [p. 4].
> Caroline, sitting on the quilt she'd brought from home, saw Henry, Carson, and the man approaching. She pulled the towel over her legs. The man wore pleated pants, suspenders, a blue tie and white shirt. He reminded her of somebody, but she couldn't place who. **Clark Gable**? [pp. 140-141].
> He seemed kind and asked her question after question about her teaching, and while he asked, it came to her that Glenn never asked those kinds of questions. It also came to her that he looked like **Clark Gable**, for sure. Henry had mentioned him in his letters, but not how handsome he was [p. 147].
> "Oh yeah. That was a bad time. Mr. Clearwater. Do you

remember having any thoughts about what he was up to that one time you saw him?"

"I thought he looked businesslike. Handsome. Nice. Kind of big ears, but not too big, I guess."

"He did look a little like **Clark Gable**" [p. 234].

Jeffrey Cohen's humorous mystery *It Happened One Knife* (2008) has been mentioned twice before—in the entries on *It Happened One Night* and *Somewhere I'll Find You*. Below is a passage including a reference to Gable himself, in a dialogue between Elliot Freed and Sharon, his ex-wife:

> On my way to the doors, I noticed Sharon walking out of my office. "I really need to remember to lock that door." I said. "Everybody's walking in and out of there lately."
>
> "I'm just leaving," she said. "Came to say good night, and you weren't there."
>
> "You're not staying for **Claudette Colbert** and **Clark Gable**?" I asked. "Mostly **Clark Gable**?"
>
> "He never did that much for me, I'm sorry to say," my ex-wife told me. "I prefer less oily hair. Something curlier." She put her hand on top of my unruly mop.
>
> "**Clark** couldn't help it that it was the 1930s," I said.
>
> "I guess, but he could have cut back on the Vitalis" [p. 280].

A brief reference to Gable appears in E. Duke Vincent's suspenseful novel *The $trip* (2009), in a passage describing a famous place in Beverly Hills:

> Nick's flight back to Vegas didn't leave until three, so he decided to lunch at the Polo Lounge. A valet took his rental when he arrived at the Beverly Hills Hotel and he strolled into a lobby awash in history and wallpapered in banana leaves.

The legendary lodgings were a stop for everyone from Duke Wayne to the Duke of Windsor. **Gable** and Lombard, Burton and Taylor, Montand and Monroe had all cavorted between its storied sheets. Howard Hughes used to rent twenty-five rooms at a clip and lived in one set of bungalows for almost thirty years [p. 30].

Irene Bennett Brown's mystery *Where Gable Slept* (2010) has been quoted several times before in this book due to the references to such films as *It Happened One Night*, *Mutiny on the Bounty*, *Gone with the Wind* and *The Misfits*. Gable himself, in addition to the title, is mentioned on many pages of Brown's novel (starting with p. 1 and finishing with p. 218). Below is the passage which introduces/explains the multiple references to the star:

> The rest of Celia's group of five tourists waited on the sidewalk before the green Victorian house where actor **Clark Gable** once lived [p. 1].
>
> Celia struggled for composure, not easy in a mothball-smelly 1920's peach chiffon and pointy toed shoes from Goodwill, her period costume for the day. She continued her presentation, convinced that Pass Creek's 2,100 citizens wouldn't stand for anyone destroying **Gable** House. Her smile warmed as she said, "**Clark Gable** was in his early twenties when he used a small inheritance from his grandfather to come west. He worked in the timber industry in more than one Oregon town. In fact, he worked in a lumber mill here in Pass Creek for two years, a mill that no longer exists. At the time, this home was operated as a small hotel by an elderly widow, Mrs. Hannah Blake" [p. 2].
>
> "There's a story told," Celia began as they circled to see a blooming orchard in back, "that after **Clark Gable** became famous, he slipped into Oregon with his wife, Carole Lombard, to show her this place. They were here for only a couple of days,

but they slept in the master bedroom and breakfasted on the side porch behind the rose trellis you see there. He picked roses for her in the rose gardens that were planted by the original owner, Hannah Blake, decades ago" [p. 4].

There are two references to Gable in Stephen King's *11/22/63* (2011), both related to a young man interested in acting, who is mistreated by both his coach and other players, and consoled by the book's protagonist, Jake Epping, using the name George Amberson:

> I thought about him handing him some Kleenex and decided they weren't up to the job. I fetched a dish wiper from the kitchen drawer instead. He scrubbed his face with it, got himself under some kind of control, then looked at me desolately. His eyes were red and raw. He hadn't started crying as he approached my door; this looked like it had been going on all afternoon.
> "Okay, Mike. Make me understand."
> "Everybody on the team's makin fun of me, Mr. Amberson. Coach started callin me **Clark Gable**—this was at the Lion Pride Spring Picnic—and now *everybody's* doing it. Even Jimmy's doing it" [p. 320].
>
> And of course Coach Borman didn't like it. The Coach Bormans of the world never do. In this case, however, there wasn't much he could do about it, especially with Mimi Corcoran on my side. He certainly couldn't claim he needed Mike for football practice in April and May. So he was reduced to calling his best lineman **Clark Gable**. There are guys who can't rid themselves of the idea that acting is for girls and queers who sort of *wish* they were girls. Gavin Borman was that kind of guy [p. 322].

There are several references to Gable in Rachel Shukert's *Starstruck* (2013) and several in its sequel *Love Me* (2014). A few of those excerpts are presented in Part Four (on Tracy). Here are two more quotations, both from *Starstruck*: one relating an exchange between Margo Sterling and her thoughtful housekeeper, and one revealing Margo's hopes about her rival marrying someone other than Dane Forrest.

> "Emmeline." Margaret's eyes filled with tears. "I . . . How did you . . . How can I ever thank you?"
> Emmeline made a harrumphing noise as she gathered up the tray. "Miss Margo, I'm sure I don't know what you're talking about." She paused at the door, looking over her shoulder. "But I'll tell you what: you get me **Clark Gable**'s autograph, we'll call it even" [p. 54].
> They'd get to talking and he'd tell her how he and Diana, whatever the rumors, had only ever been just good friends, and in fact, Diana was getting married to someone else, someone possibly glamorous . . . who would it be? **Clark Gable**. Diana was getting married to **Clark Gable** and the wedding was top-secret, naturally, and that was the reason she hadn't been seen in public for almost two months [p. 107].

The Gable references presented in Sections I and II of this part of the book are derived from over 230 works by more than 140 authors. The writers most frequently mentioning Gable and/or his films include Stuart (M.) Kaminsky (with twelve works, where references were found to a total of four films), George Baxt (eight/sixteen), Adriana Trigiani (eight/seven), Joseph Wambaugh (eight/two), Barbara Taylor Bradford (six/two), Michael Malone (five/two), Stephen King, Greg Iles and Stuart Woods (five/one each), Elmore Leonard (four/two), and Robert B. Parker, Loren D. Estleman and Susan Isaacs (four/one). Another writer worth mentioning in this context is Michael B. Druxman, who referenced Gable in two of his plays, with twenty-

Clark Gable

Clark Gable as Rhett Butler in Victor Fleming's *Gone with the Wind* (1939), the part and the movie being his unquestionably greatest achievements.

one films evoked in the one-person play on Gable and five (including one not mentioned before) in the play on Tracy.

Gable is also one of those movie stars whose name or films are either mentioned or alluded to in the titles of several literary works, or the actor himself becomes one of the main characters in an otherwise fictitious narrative. Here is the complete list of such works that were discovered in the research: *Murder on the Yellow Brick Road* (1977) by Stuart Kaminsky, *Gable: A One-Person Play in Two Acts* (1984) by Michael B. Druxman, *Tomorrow Is Another Day* (1995) by Stuart M. Kaminsky, *The Clark Gable & Carole Lombard Murder Case* (1997) by George Baxt, *It Happened One Knife* (2008) by Jeffrey Cohen and *Where Gable Slept* (2010) by Irene Bennett Brown.

Spanish poster for John Huston's *The Misfits* (1961), the last film in the careers of both Clark Gable and Marilyn Monroe.

Clark Gable's screen persona is defined by such traits as irresistible charm, tolerable insolence and unpredictable bravado; hence, many of his movies are focused on professions or undertakings involving danger and risk, and many are remembered for their action-packed sequences and remarkable stunts. Ironically, this kind of tendency is also illustrated by the actor's last film, *The Misfits*, where, according to numerous and reliable sources, Gable insisted on performing some of the stunts with the wild stallions himself, a decision that may have been responsible for his untimely death.

In his top artistic achievements—*It Happened One Night*, *Gone with the Wind* and *The Misfits*—not only does Gable seem to be irreplaceable, but he appears to have been born to play the parts of reporter Peter Warne, adventurer Rhett Butler and aging cowboy Gay Langland, or—to put it in a reverse way—those parts appear to have been written with Gable in the authors' minds. The same, however, cannot be said about Gable's other major film, *Mutiny on the Bounty*, where Fletcher Christian is limned in such a way that a lot of space is left out for the actor's interpretation. Consequently, in the other screen versions of the book by Charles Nordhoff and James Norman Hall the rebellious officer is portrayed by actors of significantly different personae, such as Errol Flynn (in the 1933 film), Marlon Brando (1962) and Mel Gibson (1984).

The temporal distribution of Gable references shows an unusual tendency. The number of works written in the 1930s and 1940s that mention Gable and/or his films is only around five in each of the decades. In the next two decades, 1950s and 1960s, the respective numbers are between ten and fifteen. Then they about double, reaching mid-twenties in both the 1970s and the 1980s, and then double again to exceed fifty in the 1990s. The growth continues in the twenty-first century, with references found in over eighty works published between 2000 and 2009, and in fourteen books copyrighted in 2010 or later. These statistics lead to a rather obvious conclusion—the actor's legend among writers grows proportionately to the number of years that have passed since his death—and the prediction that it will still keep growing for some time is also quite well grounded.

III. LIST OF REFERENCES (FOUND) TO GABLE AND HIS FILMS

While the year after the book title refers to the copyright/publication date (to provide the accurate sense of chronology), the page numbers are taken from the specific editions in which the references were found—as described in the Overall Bibliography (Reference Sources).

Randy Alcorn – *Edge of Eternity* **(1998)**
- Gable – 24

Wolf Arnold – "Farm Work" (2007)
- Gable – 12
- *Teacher's Pet* – 12

Muriel Barbery – *Gourmet Rhapsody* **(2000)**
- *Gone with the Wind* – 103, 115

George Baxt – *The Alfred Hitchcock Murder Case* **(1986)**
- Gable – 259

George Baxt – *The Clark Gable and Carole Lombard Murder Case* **(1997)**
- Gable – 1, 5-16, 18-26, 29-35, 49-58, 61-64, 68-70, 76, 83, 88-93, 96-97, 99-103, 105-107, 112-115, 121-131, 134, 135, 141-144, 146-153,

155-164, 166-168, 170-183
- *Hell Divers* (as *Hell Below*) – 134
- *No Man of Her Own* – 63, 64, 163
- *It Happened One Night* – 69
- *The Call of the Wild* – 101
- *China Seas* – 134
- *Mutiny on the Bounty* – 83
- *San Francisco* – 102
- *Gone with the Wind* – 1-5, 9, 79, 82, 107, 121, 131, 134, 157, 182

George Baxt – *The Greta Garbo Murder Case* (1992)
- Gable – 60
- *The White Sister* – 11
- *Gone with the Wind* – 15

George Baxt – *The Humphrey Bogart Murder Case* (1995)
- Gable – 48, 57
- *A Free Soul* – 56, 57

George Baxt – *The Mae West Murder Case* (1993)
- Gable – 22
- *Gone with the Wind* – 111, 112

George Baxt – *The Marlene Dietrich Murder Case* (1993)
- Gable – 13, 14, 141
- *A Free Soul* – 141

George Baxt – *The Tallulah Bankhead Murder Case* (1987)
- Gable – 72, 206
- *Red Dust* – 206
- *Forsaking All Others* – 72
- *Gone with the Wind* – 19, 41
- *Mogambo* – 206

George Baxt – *The William Powell and Myrna Loy Murder Case* (1996)
- Gable – 7, 29, 34, 90, 94, 140, 164, 186
- *It Happened One Night* – 140
- *Manhattan Melodrama* – 7

- *Men in White* – 186
- *Forsaking All Others* – 89

James Scott Bell – *Try Darkness* (2008)
- Gable – 27

James Scott Bell – *Try Dying* (2007)
- Gable – 96, 243
- *It Happened One Night* – 243

Saul Bellow – *More Die of Heartbreak* (1987)
- Gable – 255
- *Gone with the Wind* – 255

William Bernhardt – *Nemesis: The Final Case of Eliot Ness* (2009)
- *It Happened One Night* – 173, 174

Valerie Block – *Don't Make a Scene* (2007)
- Gable – 168

Steven Bochco – *Death by Hollywood* (2003)
- *Gone with the Wind* – 55

Clare Boothe – *The Women* (1937)
- Gable – 639

Barbara Taylor Bradford – *Act of Will* (1986)
- Gable – 209
- *Gone with the Wind* – 209

Barbara Taylor Bradford – *Angel* (1993)
- Gable – 281

Barbara Taylor Bradford – *Breaking the Rules* (2009)
- *Gone with the Wind* – 19

Barbara Taylor Bradford – *Her Own Rules* (1996)
- *Gone with the Wind* – 84, 85

Barbara Taylor Bradford – *Remember* (1991)
- Gable – 130, 131
- *Somewhere I'll Find You* – 130, 131

Barbara Taylor Bradford – *Where You Belong* (1999)
- *Gone with the Wind* - 83

Lilian Jackson Braun – *The Cat Who Brought Down the House* (2003)
- Gable – 64, 127

Irene Bennett Brown – *Where Gable Slept* (2010)
- Gable – 1-4, 9, 10, 17, 25, 27, 43, 51, 52, 92, 93, 115, 186, 188, 192, 203, 208, 215, 217, 218
- *It Happened One Night* – 93
- *Mutiny on the Bounty* – 93
- *Gone with the Wind* – 3, 47, 93, 188
- *The Misfits* - 205

Charles Bukowski – "The Gut-Wringing Machine"
- Gable – 53

Charles Bukowski – *Hollywood* (1989)
- Gable – 132

Charles Bukowski – "The Murder of Ramon Vasquez"
- Gable – 215

James Lee Burke – *Creole Belle* (2012)
- *Manhattan Melodrama* – 212

James Lee Burke – *The Glass Rainbow* (2010)
- *Gone with the Wind* – 9, 421

James Lee Burke – *The Tin Roof Blowdown* (2007)
- *Gone with the Wind* – 59, 93

Barbara Burnett – *Writers of the Purple Sage* (1994)
- Gable – 18

James M. Cain – *Double Indemnity* (1936)
- Gable – 46

James M. Cain – *Serenade* (1937)
- Gable – 99

Colin Campbell – *Montecito Heights: A Resurrection Man Novel* (2014)
- *Gone with the Wind* – 10

Lorenzo Carcaterra – *Sleepers* (1995)
- Gable – 85
- *The Call of the Wild* – 85

Arthur C. Clarke – *2010: Odyssey Two* (1982)
- *Mutiny on the Bounty* – 238, 239

Jeffrey Cohen – *It Happened One Knife* (2008)
- Gable – 58, 280
- *It Happened One Night* – 248, 278

Paula Marantz Cohen – *Jane Austen in Boca* (2002)
- Gable – 8, 9

David Cole – *Butterfly Lost* (1999)
- Gable – 174
- *The Misfits* – 174

Max Allan Collins – *Flying Blind* (1998)
- Gable – 43, 64, 75, 86, 146, 216, 229, 320
- *It Happened One Night* – 86

Max Allan Collins – *Majic Man* (1999)
- Gable – 135
- *Gone with the Wind* – 156

Max Allan Collins – *Quarry in the Middle* (2009)
- *Gone with the Wind* – 54

Richard Condon – *Winter Kills* (1974)
- *Gone with the Wind* – 148

Pat Conroy – *The Lords of Discipline* (1980)
- *Gone with the Wind* – 83

Thomas H. Cook – *Breakheart Hill* (1995)
- *Gone with the Wind* – 169

Patricia Cornwell – *Isle of Dogs* (2001)
- *Gone with the Wind* – 23

Julio Cortázar – *The Winners* (1960)
- *Gone with the Wind* – 246, 247

Bill Crider – *We'll Always Have Murder: A Humphrey Bogart Mystery* (2001)
- Gable – 66
- *Gone with the Wind* – 64, 126

John Dandola – *West of Orange* (1990)
- Gable – 18, 24, 203
- *Saratoga* - 100
- *Gone with the Wind* – 17, 23, 93, 141, 183, 198-200, 202
- *Boom Town* – 17, 18

Iris Rainer Dart – *Beaches* (1985)
- *Gone with the Wind* – 236

Bruce Davis – *We're Dead, Come on in* (2005)
- Gable – 174

Don DeLillo – *Libra* (1988)
- Gable – 140
- *Manhattan Melodrama* – 140

Don DeLillo – *White Noise* (1984/5)
- Gable – 68

Marisa de los Santos – *Love Walked In* (2005)
- Gable – 27, 28
- *It Happened One Night* – 47
- *Forsaking All Others* – 27
- *Gone with the Wind* – 271

Kirk Douglas – *Dance with the Devil* (1990)
- Gable – 105, 164
- *It Happened One Night* – 288
- *San Francisco* – 48, 56
- *Gone with the Wind* – 164

Michael B. Druxman – *Gable: A One-Person Play in Two Acts* (1984)
- Gable – all pages, especially 10, 33, 46, 49-51, 56, 66
- *The Painted Desert* – 26
- *A Free Soul* – 27

- *Red Dust* – 39, 57
- *No Man of Her Own* – 34
- *It Happened One Night* – 32
- *Mutiny on the Bounty* – 31
- *San Francisco* – 31
- *Parnell* – 33, 34, 53
- *Test Pilot* – 24, 39
- *Too Hot to Handle* – 48
- *Gone with the Wind* – 37-40, 61, 64
- *Boom Town* – 10
- *Honky Tonk* – 41
- *Adventure* – 52
- *Command Decision* – 53
- *Any Number Can Play* – 53
- *Across the Wide Missouri* – 55
- *Lone Star* – 56
- *Mogambo* – 57-59
- *Teacher's Pet* – 14, 15
- *The Misfits* – 7, 9, 43, 44, 63-65

Michael B. Druxman – *Tracy: A One-Person Play in Two Acts* (1984)
- Gable – 46-49, 51, 53-55, 68
- *Call of the Wild* – 51
- *San Francisco* – 47, 54
- *Parnell* – 48, 49
- *Test Pilot* – 54
- *Boom Town* – 53

Dominick Dunne – *Another City, Not My Own* (1997)
- Gable – 38, 238
- *The Call of the Wild* – 238
- *Gone with the Wind* – 213

John Gregory Dunne – *True Confessions* (1977)
- Gable – 227

- *Mutiny on the Bounty* – 227
- *Gone with the Wind* – 199

Umberto Eco – *Foucault's Pendulum* (1988)
- *Gone with the Wind* – 24, 495

Clyde Edgerton – *The Bible Salesman* (2008)
- Gable – 4, 141, 147, 234

James Ellroy – *L.A. Confidential* (1990)
- Gable – 181

Loren D. Estleman – *Edsel* (1995)
- Gable – 20, 68, 273

Loren D. Estleman – *Jitterbug* (1998)
- Gable – 158

Loren D. Estleman – *Retro* (2004)
- Gable – 32, 174, 229

Loren D. Estleman – *Something Borrowed, Something Black* (2002)
- *Gone with the Wind* – 172

Elizabeth Evans – *The Blue Hour* (1994)
- Gable – 265, 266
- *The Misfits* – 265

Eileen Favorite – *The Heroines* (2008)
- *Gone with the Wind* – 112-115

Andrew J. Fenady – *The Man with Bogart's Face* (1977)
- Gable – 20, 81, 92, 138
- *Never Let Me Go* – 138

Andrew J. Fenady – *The Secret of Sam Marlow: The Further Adventures of the Man with Bogart's Face* (1980)
- Gable – 17, 63, 118, 121
- *Test Pilot* – 118
- *Boom Town* (as *Boomtown*) – 118
- *Command Decision* – 121

Fannie Flag – *The All-Girl Filling Station's Last Reunion* (2013)
- *Gone with the Wind* – 98

Fannie Flagg – *Coming Attractions* (1981)
- Gable – 17, 76
- *Test Pilot* – 76
- *Gone with the Wind* – 307

Fannie Flagg – *Standing in the Rainbow* (2002)
- Gable – 527
- *Gone with the Wind* – 244

Isabel Fonseca – *Attachment* (2008)
- *Gone with the Wind* – 33

Richard Ford – *Independence Day* (1995)
- Gable – 279

Ernest K. Gann – *The High and the Mighty* (1953)
- Gable – 125

Brian Garfield – *Death Wish* (1972)
- Gable – 142

William Goldman – *Father's Day* (1971)
- Gable – 157-161
- *Soldier of Fortune* – 157-161

William Goldman – *Your Turn to Curtsy, My Turn to Bow* (1958)
- Gable – 29

Ed Gorman – "The Alibi" (1988)
- Gable – 289

Gerald Green – *The Last Angry Man* (1956)
- Gable – 285

S. A. Griffin – "America Poem" (2003)
- *Gone with the Wind* – 130

Martha Grimes – *Belle Ruin* (2005)
- *Gone with the Wind* – 334

Martha Grimes – *Cold Flat Junction* (2001)
- *Gone with the Wind* – 273

John Grisham – *The Firm* (1991)
- *Gone with the Wind* – 350

Denis Hamill – *Fork in the Road* (2000)
- Gable – 315
- *Gone with the Wind* – 14, 315

Elizabeth Hay – *Garbo Laughs* (2003)
- *Gone with the Wind* – 75, 250, 266, 276

Elizabeth Hay – *A Student of Weather* (2001)
- Gable – 2, 37, 87
- *It Happened One Night* – 2, 34

Judith Ryan Hendricks – *Bread Alone* (2001)
- *Gone with the Wind* – 200

Oscar Hijuelos – *The Fourteen Sisters of Emilio Montez O'Brien* (1993)
- Gable – 226

Tony Hillerman – *Skeleton Man* (2004)
- Gable – 73, 76

Khaled Hosseini – *The Kite Runner* (2003)
- Gable – 251, 256, 258

Evan Hunter – *Strangers When We Meet* (1958)
- Gable – 173

Greg Iles – *Black Cross* (1995)
- Gable – 320
- *Gone with the Wind* – 67, 149, 320

Greg Iles – *Blood Memory* (2005)
- *Gone with the Wind* – 79

Greg Iles – *The Devil's Punchbowl* – (2009)
- *Gone with the Wind* – 57

Greg Iles – *The Quiet Game* (1999)
- *Gone with the Wind* – 17

Greg Iles – *Turning Angel* (2005)
- *Gone with the Wind* – 297

Guillermo Cabrera Infante – *Three Trapped Tigers* (1965)
- Gable – 487

Susan Isaacs – *After All These Years* (1993)
- Gable – 255

Susan Isaacs – *Any Place I Hang My Hat* (2004)
- *Gone with the Wind* – 258, 348

Susan Isaacs – *Red, White & Blue* – (1998)
- Gable – 75

Susan Isaacs – *Shining Through* (1988)
- Gable – 22, 116
- *Gone with the Wind* – 13, 118, 152

Byron Janis, with Maria Cooper Janis. *Chopin and Beyond* (2010)
- *Gone with the Wind* – 36

Maureen Johnson – *Suite Scarlett* (2008)
- *Gone with the Wind* – 77

James Jones – *From Here to Eternity* (1951)
- Gable – 445, 484
- *Cain and Mabel* – 445

James Jones – *Go to the Widow-Maker* (1967)
- Gable – 54, 55, 78, 532

James Jones – *Some Came Running* (1957)
- *Gone with the Wind* – 307

Erica Jong – *Any Woman's Blues* (1990)
- *Gone with the Wind* – 53

Stuart M. Kaminsky – *Bright Futures* (2008)
- *Gone with the Wind* – 60

Stuart M. Kaminsky – *Bullet for a Star* (1977)
- Gable – 41

Stuart M. Kaminsky – *The Devil Met a Lady* (1993)
- Gable – 194

Stuart Kaminsky – *High Midnight* (1981)
- Gable – 126

Stuart Kaminsky – *Lieberman's Thief* (1995)
- *Gone with the Wind* – 67

Stuart M. Kaminsky – *Mildred Pierced* (2003)
- Gable – 17
- *Gone with the Wind* – 81

Stuart Kaminsky – *Murder on the Yellow Brick Road* (1977)
- Gable – 35, 36, 42, 47, 48, 50, 60, 62, 64, 65, 69, 70-72, 79, 80, 101, 118, 119, 142
- *Gone with the Wind* – 36, 49, 71

Stuart M. Kaminsky – *Poor Butterfly* (1990)
- *San Francisco* – 16

Stuart M. Kaminsky – *Retribution* (2001)
- *Gone with the Wind* – 129

Stuart M. Kaminsky – *Smart Moves* (1986)
- *Gone with the Wind* – 146

Stuart Kaminsky – *Think Fast, Mr. Peters* (1987)
- Gable – 5, 6, 41
- *It Happened One Night* – 5

Stuart M. Kaminsky - *Tomorrow Is Another Day* (1995)
- Gable – 3-5, 7, 8, 17-24, 26, 36, 40, 41, 44, 48, 62, 65-72, 74, 75, 93, 100, 103, 104, 109, 112, 113, 118, 127, 135, 140, 147-157, 165, 166, 170, 176, 185, 196-200
- *Gone with the Wind* – 1, 4, 17, 19, 62, 64, 70, 73, 75, 76, 78-80, 85, 91, 93, 99, 104, 176, 195-200

Garrison Keillor – *Lake Wobegon Summer 1956* (2001)
- Gable – 11

Adam Kennedy – *Just Like Humphrey Bogart* (1978)
- *Gone with the Wind* – 107

Jack Kerouac – *Desolation Angels* (1960)
- Gable – 125, 267, 268, 272, 298
- *Red Dust* – 272

Jack Kerouac – *Satori in Paris* (1966)
- Gable – 57

Stephen King – *11/12/63* (2011)
- Gable – 320, 322

Stephen King – *Duma Key* (2008)
- *Gone with the Wind* – 141

Stephen King – *The Green Mile* (1996)
- *Gone with the Wind* – 339

Stephen King – *Lisey's Story* (2006)
- *Gone with the Wind* – 149

Stephen King – "What Is It in French?" (2002)
- *Gone with the Wind* – 436

Laurence Klavan – *The Cutting Room* (2004)
- Gable – 5
- *Gone with the Wind* – 5

Laurence Klavan – *The Shooting Script* (2005)
- Gable – 215
- *Gone with the Wind* – 215

Stieg Larsson – *The Girl with the Dragon Tattoo* (2005)
- Gable – 477
- *Gone with the Wind* – 477

Aaron Latham – *Riding with John Wayne* (2006)
- Gable – 292
- *Gone with the Wind* – 73, 292, 325, 373

E. Duke Lawrence – *The $trip* (2009)
- Gable – 30

Janet Leigh – *House of Destiny* (1995)
- Gable – 158
- *The Hucksters* – 158

Elmore Leonard – *The Hot Kid* (2005)
- Gable – 364, 365
- *Manhattan Melodrama* – 364, 365, 375

Elmore Leonard – *Maximum Bob* (1991)
- *Gone with the Wind* – 68

Elmore Leonard – "Tenkiller" (2002)
- *Gone with the Wind* – 204

Elmore Leonard – *Up in Honey's Room* (2007)
- Gable – 71
- *Gone with the Wind* – 71

Sinclair Lewis – *Kingsblood Royal* (1947)
- *Gone with the Wind* – 77

Laura Lippman – *In a Strange City* (2001)
- *Gone with the Wind* – 185

John D. MacDonald – *The Executioners* (1957)
- Gable – 132

Michael Malone – *The Delectable Mountains or, Entertaining Stranger* (1976)
- Gable – 153

Michael Malone – *The Four Corners of the Sky* (2009)
- Gable – 184, 246, 386, 446, 452
- *It Happened One Night* – 246, 290, 375, 386, 446, 452
- *Boom Town* – 329, 335

Michael Malone – *Handling Sin* (1983)
- Gable – 424

Michael Malone – "Love and Other Crimes" (2000)
- Gable – 135

Michael Malone – *Time's Witness* (2002)
- Gable – 27

Charles Martin – *Maggie* (2006)
- *Gone with the Wind* – 364, 601

Ed McBain – *Jack and the Beanstalk* (1984)
- *Gone with the Wind* – 115

Jill McCorkle – *Life After Life* (2013)
- *It Happened One Night* – 129
- *Gone with the Wind* – 126, 150, 266

Jill McCorkle – *Carolina Moon* (1996)
- *Gone with the Wind* – 61

Dermot McEvoy – *Our Lady of Greenwich Village* (2008)
- Gable – 3, 269
- *Run Silent, Run Deep* – 3

Larry McMurtry – *All My Friends Are Going to Be Strangers* (1972)
- Gable – 276

Larry McMurtry – *Rhino Ranch* (2009)
- *Gone with the Wind* – 159

James A. Michener – "Polynesia" (1951)
- *Mutiny on the Bounty* – 46

John Douglas Miller – *The Greek Summer* (2003)
- Gable – 75
- *The Call of the Wild* – 75

Rebecca Miller – *The Private Lives of Pippa Lee* (2008)
- *Gone with the Wind* – 37

Marcia Muller – *The Ever-Running Man* (2007)
- *Gone with the Wind* – 234

Stuart Nadler – *Wise Men* (2013)
- Gable – 103

Michael P. Naughton – *Deathryde: Rebel Without a Corpse* (2008)
- Gable – 92

John Nichols – *The Sterile Cuckoo* (1965)
- Gable – 30

Flannery O'Connor – "A Good Man Is Hard to Find" (1953)
- *Gone with the Wind* – 131

Clifford Odets – *Waiting for Lefty* (1935)
- Gable – 8

John O'Hara – "James Francis and the Star"
- Gable – 183, 187

John O'Hara – "Natica Jackson" (1966)
- Gable – 374

John O'Hara – *Pal Joey* **(1939)**
- *It Happened One Night* – 77

Iris Paris – *Once Upon a Chariot* **(2008)**
- *Gone with the Wind* – 124

Robert B. Parker – *Bad Business* **(2004)**
- *Gone with the Wind* – 246

Robert B. Parker – *Blue Screen* **(2006)**
- *Gone with the Wind* – 160, 183

Robert B. Parker – *Crimson Joy* **(1988)**
- *Gone with the Wind* – 171

Robert B. Parker – *Mortal Stakes* **(1975)**
- Gable – 208

James Patterson – *Maximum Ride: School's Out Forever* **(2006)**
- *Gone with the Wind* – 59

Walker Percy – *Love in the Ruins* **(1971)**
- *Gone with the Wind* – 151, 339

Walker Percy – *The Moviegoer* **(1960)**
- Gable – 82, 83
- *It Happened One Night* – 60
- *Gone with the Wind* – 175

Ralph Peters – *The Devil's Garden* **(1998)**
- *Gone with the Wind* – 268, 269

Jayne Anne Phillips – *Machine Dreams* **(1984)**
- *Gone with the Wind* – 70

Jodi Picoult – *Picture Perfect* **(1995)**
- *Gone with the Wind* – 198

Jodi Picoult – *Songs of the Humpback Whale* **(1992)**
- *Gone with the Wind* – 57

Bill Pronzini – *Shackles* (1988)
- *Gone with the Wind* – 76

Mario Puzo – *The Fourth K* (1990)
- *Gone with the Wind* – 330

Thomas Pynchon – *Gravity's Rainbow* (1973)
- Gable – 516, 577
- *Manhattan Melodrama* – 516

Thomas Pynchon – *Vineland* (1990)
- Gable – 78
- *San Francisco* – 78

Robert J. Randisi – *Hey There (You with the Gun in Your Hand)* (2008)
- Gable – 10, 179, 189
- *The Misfits* – 10, 179, 189

Robert J. Randisi – *You're Nobody 'Til Somebody Kills You* (2009)
- Gable – 19, 33, 57, 99, 167, 240, 241, 265
- *The Misfits* – 19-20, 57, 240, 241

Herman Raucher – *A Glimpse of Tiger* (1971)
- Gable – 132
- *It Happened One Night* – 26

Herman Raucher – *Ode to Billy Joe* (1976)
- *Gone with the Wind* – 37

Herman Raucher – *There Should Have Been Castles* (1978)
- *It Happened One Night* – 448
- *Gone with the Wind* – 583

Harold Robbins – *The Carpetbaggers* (1961)
- Gable – 483, 520
- *Gone with the Wind* – 476

Harold Robbins – *Never Leave Me* (1954)
- Gable – 125

Harold Robbins – *Where Love Has Gone* (1962)
- Gable – 251, 252

Elliott Roosevelt – *Murder in Georgetown* (1999)
- Gable – 178
- *Mutiny on the Bounty* – 177, 178

Elliott Roosevelt – *Murder in the Lincoln Bedroom* (2000)
- Gable – 83

Judith Rossner – *Looking for Mr. Goodbar* (1975)
- *Gone with the Wind* – 36

Philip Roth – *American Pastoral* (1997)
- Gable – 33

Philip Roth – *Our Gang* (1971)
- *Gone with the Wind* – 90

Lawrence Sanders – *The Case of Lucy Bending* (1982)
- *Gone with the Wind* – 21

Lawrence Sanders – *The Sixth Commandment* (1979)
- Gable – 263

Budd Schulberg – *The Disenchanted* (1950)
- Gable – 46
- *Gone with the Wind* – 341

Budd Schulberg – *The Harder They Fall* (1947)
- Gable – 188

Budd Schulberg – *What Makes Sammy Run?* (1941)
- Gable – 185

Alice Sebold – *The Almost Moon* (2007)
- *Gone with the Wind* – 159

Sidney Sheldon – *A Stranger in the Mirror* (1976)
- Gable – 70

Martha Sherrill – *My Last Movie Star* (2002)
- Gable – 119, 205, 246-248, 272, 306
- *Cain and Mabel* – 188
- *Test Pilot* – 246-248, 251
- *Too Hot To Handle* – 224
- *Gone with the Wind* – 246

Rachel Shukert – *Love Me* (2014)
- Gable – 6, 79, 196, 199, 222
- *Gone with the Wind* – 49, 65, 196

Rachel Shukert – *Starstruck* (2013)
- Gable – 54, 107, 289, 290, 295, 336

Barbara Burnett Smith – *Writers of the Purple Sage* (1994)
- Gable – 18

Bella & Samuel Spewack – *Boy Meets Girl* (1936)
- Gable – 539, 562, 564

Bernard Spiro - *The Other War: Letters from a GI in India in 1944& 1945* (2001)
- Gable – 127

Kathryn Stockett – *The Help* (2009)
- *Gone with the Wind* – 58, 172, 185

William Styron – *Sophie's Choice* (1978)
- Gable – 313

Paul Theroux – *Saint Jack* (1973)
- *Gone with the Wind* – 145

Janet Thornburg – "Lucky Lady" (2005)
- Gable – 46
- *Gone with the Wind* – 46

Adriana Trigiani – *Big Cherry Holler* (2001)
- Gable – 122, 181
- *Dancing Lady* – 122
- *It Happened One Night* – 122
- *The Call of the Wild* – 181
- *Test Pilot* – 122
- *Gone with the Wind* – 121

Adriana Trigiani – *Big Stone Gap* (2000)
- Gable – 39, 73
- *Call of the Wild* – 241
- *Test Pilot* – 39

Adriana Trigiani – *Home to Big Stone Gap* (2006)
- Gable – 188
- *Gone with the Wind* – 94

Adriana Trigani – *Lucia, Lucia* (2003)
- *It Happened One Night* – 201

Adriana Trigiani – *Milk Glass Moon* (2002)
- Gable – 175

Adriana Trigiani – *The Queen of the Big Time* (2004)
- Gable – 178
- *A Free Soul* – 177, 178

Adriana Trigiani – *Rococo* (2005)
- Gable – 82

Adriana Trigiani – *Very Valentine* (2009)
- Gable – 60, 62, 213, 274, 302
- *The Call of the Wild* – 60, 213
- *Gone with the Wind* – 274
- *It Started in Naples* – 302

Kathy Hogan Trocheck – *Every Crooked Nanny* (1992)
- *Gone with the Wind* – 296

John Updike – *Bech: A Book* (1965)
- *Gone with the Wind* – 121

John Updike – *In the Beauty of the Lilies* (1996)
- Gable – 273, 318, 320, 332, 359
- *Gone with the Wind* – 264
- *The Misfits* – 359

Gore Vidal – *Myra Breckinridge* (1968)
- Gable – 34, 40, 62, 129
- *Boom Town* – 36

E. Duke Vincent – *The $trip* (2009)
- Gable – 30

Joseph Wambaugh – *The Choirboys* (1975)
- *Command Decision* – 14

Joseph Wambaugh – *Finnegan's Week* (1993)
- *Gone with the Wind* – 12

Joseph Wambaugh – *Floaters* (1996)
- Gable – 88
- *Gone with the Wind* – 88

Joseph Wambaugh – *Fugitive Nights* (1992)
- Gable – 168

Joseph Wambaugh – *The Glitter Dome* (1981)
- Gable – 298

-*Gone with the Wind* – 298

Joseph Wambaugh – *Hollywood Hills* (2010)
- *Gone with the Wind* – 58

Joseph Wambaugh – *Hollywood Station* (2006)
- Gable – 242
- *Gone with the Wind* – 121

Joseph Wambaugh – *The Secrets of Harry Bright* (1985)
- Gable – 1985

Rebecca Wells – *Divine Secrets of the Ya-Ya Sisterhood* (1996)
- Gable – 112-114, 120, 121, 123, 128, 140, 141
- *Gone with the Wind* – 110-114, 118, 123, 127-130, 136, 139-141, 162

Donald E. Westlake – *The Road to Ruin* (2004)
- *Gone with the Wind* – 61

James Neel White – *I Was a P-51 Fighter Pilot in WWII* (2003)
- Gable – 26, 319
- *Night Flight* – 26

John Edgar Wideman – "Across the Wide Missouri" (1981)
- Gable – 133, 139
- *Gone with the Wind* – 133
- *Across the Wide Missouri* – 139

Tennessee Williams – *The Glass Menagerie* (1945)
- Gable – 59

Connie Willis – "At the Rialto" (1989)
- Gable – 452
- *It Happened One Night* – 452

F. Paul Wilson – *Infernal* **(2005)**
- *Gone with the Wind* – 336

Tom Wolfe – *A Man in Full* **(1998)**
- *Gone with the Wind* – 497

Stuart Woods – *Bel-Air Dead* **(2011)**
- Gable – 19

Stuart Woods – *Beverly Hills Dead* **(2008)**
- Gable – 35, 50, 158
- *Gone with the Wind* – 183

Stuart Woods – *Dead Eyes* **(1994)**
- Gable – 117

Stuart Woods – *The Prince of Beverly Hills* **(2004)**
- Gable – 16, 17, 29, 30, 200-209, 270, 297, 298
- *Gone with the Wind* – 82

Stuart Woods – *Son of Stone* **(2011)**
- Gable – 119

Herman Wouk – *Marjorie Morningstar* **(1955)**
- Gable – 143, 386

Herman Wouk – *Youngblood Hawke* **(1962)**
- *Gone with the Wind* – 78

IV. CREDITS OF GABLE'S FILMS <u>REFERENCED</u>

1. *The Painted Desert* (Pathé, 1931). Sc. Howard Higgin and Tom Buckingham. Dir. Howard Higgin. Phot. Ed Snyder. Cast: William Boyd (Bill Holbrook), Helen Twelvetrees (Mary Ellen Cameron), William Farnum (Cash Holbrook), J. Farrell MacDonald (Jeff Cameron), CG (Rance Brett), Charles Sellon (Tonopah), Hugh Adams ('Dynamite').

2. *A Free Soul* (MGM, 1931). Sc. John Meehan from the novel by Adela Rogers St. John. Dir. Clarence Brown. Phot. William Daniels. Cast: Norma Shearer (Jan Ashe), Leslie Howard (Dwight Winthrop), Lionel Barrymore (Stephen Ashe), CG (Ace Wilfong), James Gleason (Eddie), Lucy Beaumont (Grandma Ashe), Edward Brophy (Slouch).

3. *Hell Divers* (MGM, 1931). Sc. Harvey Gates and Malcolm Stuart Boylan from a story by Frank Wead. Dir. George Hill. Phot. Harold Wenstrom. Cast: Wallace Beery (Windy), CG (Steve), Conrad Nagel (Duke), Dorothy Jordan (Ann), Marjorie Rambeau (Mame Kelsey), Marie Prevost (Lulu), Cliff Edwards (Baldy).

4. *Susan Lenox – Her Fall and Rise* (MGM, 1931). Wanda Tuchock, Leon Gordon and Zelda Sears from the novel by David Graham Phillips. Dir. Robert Z. Leonard. Phot. William H. Daniels. Music by William Axt. Cast: Greta Garbo (Susan Lenox), CG (Rodney Spencer), Jean Hersholt (Karl Ohlin), John Miljan (Burlingham), Alan Hale (Jeb Mondstrum), Hale Hamilton (Mike Kelly), Hilda Vaughn (Mrs. Astrid Ohlin).

5. *Red Dust* (MGM, 1932). John Lee Mahin from the play by Wilson Collison. Dir. Victor Fleming. Phot. Harold Rosson. Cast: CG (Dennis Carson), Jean Harlow (Vantine), Gene Raymond (Gary Willis), Mary Astor (Barbara), Donald Crisp (Guidon), Tully Marshall (McHarg), Forrester Harvey (Limey).

6. *No Man of Her Own* (Paramount, 1932). Sc. Maurine Watkins and Milton H. Gropper from a story by Edmund Goulding and Benjamin Glazer. Dir. Wesley Ruggles. Phot. Leo Tover. Cast: CG (Babe Stewart), Carole Lombard (Connie Randall), Dorothy Mackaill (Kay Everly), Grant Mitchell (Charlie Vane), George Barbier (Mr. Randall), Elizabeth Patterson (Mrs. Randall), J. Farrell MacDonald ('Dickie' Collins).

7. *The White Sister* (MGM, 1933). Sc. Donald Ogden Stewart from the novel by F. Marion Crawford and Walter Hackett. Dir. Victor Fleming. Phot. William Daniels. Music by Herbert Stothart. Cast: Helen Hayes (Angela Chiaromonte), CG (Giovanni Severa), Lewis Stone (Prince Guido Chiaromonte), Louise Closser Hale (Mina), May Robson (Mother Superior), Edward Arnold (Father Saracinesca), Alan Edwards (Ernesto Traversi).

8. *Night Flight* (MGM, 1933). Sc. Oliver H. P. Garrett from the novel by Antoine de Saint-Exupéry. Dir. Clarence Brown. Phot. Oliver T. Marsh. Music by Herbert Stothart. Cast: John Barrymore (Riviere), Helen Hayes (Simone Fabian), CG (Jules Fabian), Lionel Barrymore (Inspector Robineau), Robert Montgomery (Auguste Pellerin), Myrna Loy (Wife of Brazilian Pilot), William Gargan (Brazilian Pilot).

9. *Dancing Lady* (MGM, 1933). Sc. Allen Rivkin and P. J. Wolfson from the novel by James Warner Bellah. Dir. Robert Z. Leonard. Phot. Oliver T. Marsh. Music by Burton Lane, Harold Adamson, Richard Rodgers, Lorenz Hart, Jimmy McHugh and Dorothy Fields. Cast: Joan Crawford (Janie Barlow), CG (Patch Gallagher), Franchot Tone (Tod Newton), May Robson (Dolly Todhunter), Winnie Lightner (Rosette LaRue), Fred Astaire (Himself), Robert Benchley (Ward King).

10. *It Happened One Night* (Columbia, 1934). Sc. Robert Riskin from a story by Samuel Hopkins Adams. Dir. Frank Capra. Phot. Joseph Walker. Music by Howard Jackson (uncredited). Cast: CG (Peter Warne), Claudette Colbert (Ellie Andrews), Walter Connolly (Alexander Andrews), Roscoe Karns (Shapeley), Jameson Thomas (Westley), Alan Hale (Danker), Arthur Hoyt (Zeke).

11. *Men in White* (MGM, 1934). Sc. Waldemar Young from the play by Sidney Kingsley. Dir. Richard Boleslavsky. Phot. George Folsey. Music by William Axt. Cast: CG (Dr. George Ferguson), Myrna Loy (Laura Hudson), Jean Hersholt (Dr. Hochberg), Elizabeth Allan (Barbara Dennin), Otto Kruger (Dr. Levine), C. Henry Gordon (Dr. Cunningham), Wallace Ford (Shorty).

12. *Manhattan Melodrama* (MGM, 1934). Sc. Oliver T. Marsh, H.P. Garrett and Joseph L. Mankiewicz from a story by Arthur Caesar. Dir. W. S. Van Dyke. Phot. James Wong Howe. Music by Willam Axt (uncredited). Cast: CG (Blackie Gallagher), William Powell (Jim Wade), Myrna Loy (Eleanor), Leo Carrillo (Father Joe), Nat Pendleton (Spud), George Sidney (Poppa Rosen), Isabel Jewell (Annabelle).

13. *Forsaking All Others* (MGM, 1934). Sc. Joseph L. Mankiewicz from the play by Edward Barry. Dir. W.S. Van Dyke. Phot. Gregg Toland and George Folsey. Music by William Axt Cast: Joan Crawford (Mary Clay), CG (Jeff Williams), Robert Montgomery (Dillon Todd), Charles Butterworth (Shemp), Billie Burke (Aunt Paula), Frances Drake (Connie Barnes Todd), Rosalind Russell (Eleanor).

14. *The Call of the Wild* (20th C-F, 1935). Sc. Gene Fowler and Leonard Praskins from the novel by Jack London. Dir. William A. Wellman. Phot. Charles Rosher. Music by Alfred Newman (uncredited). Cast: CG (Jack Thornton), Loretta Young (Claire Blake), Jack Oakie ('Shorty' Hoolihan), Reginald Owen (Smith), Frank Conroy (John Blake), Katherine DeMille (Marie), Sidney Toler (Joe Groggins).

15. *China Seas* (MGM, 1935). Sc. Jules Furthman and James Kevin McGuiness from the novel by Crosbie Garstin. Dir. Tay Garnett. Phot. Ray June. Music by Herbert Stothart. Cast: CG (Captain Alan Gaskell), Jean Harlow (China Doll), Wallace Beery (James MacArdle), Lewis Stone (Davids), Rosalind Russell (Sybil Barclay), Dudley Digges (Dawson), C. Aubrey Smith (Sir Guy).

16. *Mutiny on the Bounty* (MGM, 1935). Sc. Talbot Jennings, Jules Furthman and Carey Wilson from the book by Charles Nordhoff and James Norman Hall. Dir. Frank Lloyd. Phot. Arthur Edeson. Music by Herbert Stothart. Cast: Charles Laughton (Captain Bligh), CG (Fletcher Christian), Franchot Tone (Roger Byam), Herbert Mundin (Smith), Eddie Quillan (Ellison), Dudley Digges (Bacchus), Donald Crisp (Burkitt).

17. *San Francisco* (MGM, 1936). Sc. Anita Loos from a story by Robert Hopkins. Dir. W. S. Van Dyke. Phot. Oliver T. Marsh. Music by Edward Ward. Cast: CG (Blackie Norton), Jeanette MacDonald (Mary Blake), ST (Father Mullin), Jack Holt (Jack Burley), Jessie Ralph (Mrs. Burley), Ted Healy (Mat), Shirley Ross (Trixie).

18. *Cain and Mabel* (MGM, 1936). Sc. Laird Doyle from a short story by H.C. Witwer. Dir. Lloyd Bacon. Phot. George Barnes. Music by Heinz Roemheld (uncredited). Cast: Marion Davies (Mabel O'Dare), CG (Larry

Cain), Allen Jenkins (Dodo), Roscoe Karns (Reilly), Walter Catlett (Jake Sherman), Robert Paige (as David Carlyle, Ronny Cauldwell), Hobart Cavanaugh (Milo).

19. *Parnell* (MGM, 1937). Sc. John Van Druten and S. N. Behrman from the play by Elsie T. Schauffler. Dir. John M. Stahl. Phot. Karl Freund. Music by William Axt. Cast: CG (Charles Parnell), Myrna Loy (Katie), Edna May Oliver (Aunt Ben), Edmund Gwenn (Campbell), Alan Marshal (Willie), Donald Crisp (Davitt), Billie Burke (Clara).

20. *Saratoga* (MGM, 1937). Sc. Anita loos and Robert Hopkins. Dir. Jack Conway. Phot. Ray June. Music by Edward Ward. Cast: CG (Duke Bradley), Jean Harlow (Carol Clayton), Lionel Barrymore (Grandpa Clayton), Frank Morgan (Jesse Kiffmeyer), Walter Pidgeon (Hartley Madison), Una Merkel (Fritzi Kiffmeyer), Cliff Edwards (Tip).

21. *Test Pilot* (MGM, 1938). Sc. Vincent Lawrence and Waldemar Young from a story by Frank Wead. Dir. Victor Fleming. Phot. Ray June. Music by Franz Waxman. Cast: CG (Jim), Myrna Loy (Ann), ST (Gunner), Lionel Barrymore Drake), Samuel S. Hinds (General Ross), Marjorie Main (Landlady), Ted Pearson (Joe).

22. *Too Hot to Handle* (MGM, 1938). Sc. Laurence Stallings and John Lee Mahin from a story by Len Hammond. Dir. Jack Conway. Phot. Harold Rosson. Cast: CG (Chris Hunter), Myrna Loy (Alma Harding), Walter Pidgeon (Bill Dennis), Leo Carrillo (Chris's assistant), Johnny Hines (Parsons), Virginia Weidler (Hulda), Henry Kolker ('Pearly' Todd).

23. *Gone with the Wind* (MGM, 1939). Sc. Sidney Howard from the novel by Margaret Mitchell. Dir. Victor Fleming. Phot. Ernest Haller. Music by Max Steiner. Cast: CG (Rhett Butler), Vivien Leigh (Scarlett O'Hara), Leslie Howard (Ashley Wilkes), Olivia de Havilland (Melanie Hamilton),

Evelyn Keyes (Suellen O'Hara), Thomas Mitchell (Gerald O'Hara), Hattie McDaniel (Mammy).

24. *Boom Town* (MGM, 1940). Sc. John Lee Mahin from a story by James Edward Grant. Dir. Jack Conway. Phot. Harold Rosson. Music by Franz Waxman. Cast: CG (Big John McMasters), ST (Square John Sand), Claudette Colbert (Betsy Bartlett), Hedy Lamarr (Karen Vanmeer), Frank Morgan (Luther Aldrich), Lionel Atwill (Harry Compton), Chill Wills (Harmony Jones).

25. *Honky Tonk* (MGM, 1941). Sc. Marguerite Roberts and John Sanford. Dir. Jack Conway. Phot. Harold Rosson. Music by Franz Waxman. Cast: CG ('Candy' Johnson), Lana Turner (Elizabeth Cotton), Frank Morgan (Judge Cotton), Claire Trevor ('Gold Dust' Nelson), Marjorie Main (Mrs. Varner), Albert Dekker (Brazos Hearn), Henry O'Neill (Daniel Wells).

26. *Somewhere I'll Find You* (MGM, 1942). Sc. Marguerite Roberts from a story by Charles Hoffman. Dir. Wesley Ruggles. Phot. Harold Rosson. Music by Bronislau Kaper. Cast: CG (Jonathan 'Johnny' Davis), Lana Turner (Paula Lane), Robert Sterling (Kirk 'Junior' Davis), Patricia Dane (Crystal McRegan), Reginald Owen (Willie Manning), Lee Patrick (Eve Manning), Charles Dingle (George L. Stafford).

27. *Adventure* (MGM, 1945). Sc. Frederick Hazlitt Brennan and Vincent Lawrence from the novel by Clyde Brion Davis (adaptation by Anthony Veiller and William H. Wright). Dir. Victor Fleming. Phot. Joseph Ruttenberg. Music by Herbert Stothart. Cast: CG (Harry Patterson), Greer Garson (Emily Sears), Joan Blondell (Helen Melohn), Thomas Mitchell (Mudgin), Tom Tully (Gus), John Qualen (Model T), Richard Haydn (Limo).

28. *The Hucksters* (MGM, 1947). Sc. Luther Davis from the novel by Frederic Wakeman (adaptation by Edward Chodorov and George Wells). Dir. Jack Conway. Phot. Harold Rosson. Music by Lennie Hayton. Cast: CG

(Vic Norman), Deborah Kerr (Mrs. Dorrence), Sydney Greenstreet (Evan Llewellyn Evans), Adolphe Menjou (Mr. Kimberly), Ava Gardner (Jean Ogilvie), Keenan Wynn (Buddy Hare), Edward Arnold (David Lash).

29. *Command Decision* (MGM, 1948). Sc. William R. Laidlaw and George Froeschel from the play by William Wister Haines. Dir. Sam Wood. Phot. Harol Rosson. Music by Miklos Rozsa. Cast: CG (General Dennis), Walter Pidgeon (General Kane), Van Johnson (Tech. Sergeant Evans), Brian Donlevy (General Garnet), Charles Bickford (Elmer Brockhurst), John Hodiak (Colonel Ted Martin), Edward Arnold (Congressman Arthur Malcolm).

30. *Any Number Can Play* (MGM, 1949). Sc. Richard Brooks from the book by Edward Harris Heth. Dir. Mervyn LeRoy. Phot. Harold Rosson. Music by Lennie Hayton. Cast: CG (Charley Enley Kyng), Alexis Smith (Lon Kyng), Wendell Corey (Robbin Elcott), Audrey Totter (Alice Elcott), Frank Morgan (Jim Kurstyn), Mary Astor (Ada), Lewis Stone (Ben Sneller).

31. *Across the Wide Missouri* (MGM, 1951). Sc. Talbot Jennings from a story by Talbot Jennings and Frank Cavett, loosely inspired by the book by Bernard DeVoto (uncredited). Dir. William A. Wellman. Phot. William Mellor. Music by David Racksin. Cast: CG (Flint Mitchell), Ricardo Montalban (Ironshirt), John Hodiak (Brecan), Adolphe Menjou (Pierre), J. Carrol Naish (Looking Glass), Jack Holt (Bear Ghost), María Elena Marqués (Kamiah).

32. *Lone Star* (MGM, 1952). Sc. Borden Chase and Howard Estabrook from a magazine story by Borden Chase. Dir. Vincent Sherman. Phot. Harold Rosson. Music by David Buttolph. Cast: CG (Devereaux Burke), Ava Gardner (Martha Ronda), Broderick Crawford (Thomas Craden), Lionel Barrymore (Andrew Jackson), Beulah Bondi (Minniver Bryan), Ed Begley (Anthony Demmet), William Farnum (Tom Crockett).

33. *Never Let Me Go* (MGM, 1953). Sc. Roland Millar and George Froeschel from the novel *Come the Dawn* by Roger Bax (Paul Winterton). Dir. Delmer Daves. Phot. Robert Krasker. Music by Hans May. Cast: CG (Philip Sutherland), Gene Tierney (Marya Lamarkina), Richard Haydn (Christopher St. John Denny), Bernard Miles (Joe Brooks), Belita (Valentina Alexandrova), Kenneth More (Steve Quillan), Theodore Bikel (Lieutenant).

34. *Mogambo* (MGM, 1953). Sc. John Lee Mahin from the play by Wilson Collison. Dir. John Ford. Phot. Robert Surtees and F.A. Young. Music by A. N. Watkins. Cast: CG (Vic Marswell), Ava Gardner (Eloise "Honey Bear" Kelly), Grace Kelly (Linda Nordley), Donald Sinden (Donald Nordley), Philip Stainton (John Brown-Pryce), Laurence Naismith (Skipper), Dennis O'Dea (Father Josef).

35. *Soldier of Fortune* (20th C-F, 1955). Sc. Ernest K. Gann from his novel. Dir. Edward Dmytryk. Phot. Leo Tover. Music by Hugo Friedhofer. Cast: CG (Hank Lee), Susan Hayward (Jane Hoyt), Michael Rennie (Inspector Merryweather), Gene Barry (Louis Hoyt), Alex D'Arcy (Rene Dupont Chevalier), Tom Tully (Tweedie), Anna Sten (Madame Dupree).

36. *Run Silent, Run Deep* (UA, 1958). Sc. John Gay from the novel by Commander Edward L. Beach. Dir. Robert Wise. Phot. Russell Harlan. Music by Franz Waxman. Cast: CG (Commander 'Rich' Richardson), Burt Lancaster (Lieutenant Jim Bledsoe), Jack Warden (Yeoman 1st Class Mueller), Brad Dexter (Ensign Gerald Cartwright), Don Rickles (Quartermaster 1st Class Ruby), Nick Cravat (Russo), Joe Moross (Chief Kohler).

37. *Teacher's Pet* (Paramount, 1958). Sc. Fay and Michael Kanin. Dir. George Seaton. Phot. Haskell B. Boggs. Music by Roy Webb. Cast: CG (James Gannon/James Gallangher), Doris Day (Erica Stone), Gig Young (Dr. Hugo Pine), Mamie Van Doren (Peggy DeFore), Nick Adams (Barney Kovac), Peter Baldwin (Harold Miller), Marios Ross (Katy Fuller).

38. *It Started in Naples* (Paramount, 1960). Sc. Melville Shavelson, Jack Rose and Suso Cecchi d'Amico from a story by Michael Pertwee and Jack Davies. Dir. Jack Rose. Phot. Robert L. Surtees. Music by Alessandro Cicognini and Carlo Savina. Cast: CG (Michael Hamilton), Sophia Loren (Lucia Curcio), Vittorio De Sica (Mario Vitale), Marietto (Nando Hamilton), Paolo Carlini (Renzo), Giovanni Filidoro (Gennariello), Claudio Ermelli (Luigi).

39. *The Misfits* (UA, 1961). Sc. Arthur Miller from his novella. Dir. John Huston. Phot. Russell Metty. Music by Alex North. Cast: CG (Gay Langland), Marilyn Monroe (Roslyn Tabor), Montgomery Clift (Perce Howland), Thelma Ritter (Isabelle Steers), Eli Wallach (Guido), Kevin McCarthy (Raymond Tabor), Estelle Winwood (Church Lady).

V. GABLE'S MONOGRAPHIC BIBLIOGRAPHY (BOOKS ONLY)

Bret, David. *Clark Gable: Tormented Star*. London: JR Books Ltd, 2007.

Cahill, Marie: *Clark Gable: A Hollywood Portrait*. New York: Smithmark, 1992.

Carpozi, Jr., George. *Clark Gable*. New York: Pyramid, 1961.

Essoe, Gabe. *The Films of Clark Gable*. Secaucus, N.J.: The Citadel Press, 1970.

Fearfar, Ronald. *Clark Gable*. Paris: Balland, 1981.

Gable, Kathleen Williams. *Gable: A Personal Portrait*. Englewood Cliff, NJ: Prentice-Hall, 1961.

Garceau, Jean, and Inez Cocke. *Dear Mr. G--: The Biography of Clark Gable*. Boston: Little, Brown, 1961.

Grant, Neil (and Clark Gable). *Gable in His Own Words*. London: Hamlyn, 1992.

Harris, Warren G. *Clark Gable: A Biography*. New York: Harmony Books, 2002.

_____. *Gable and Lombard*. New York: Simon & Schuster, 1974.

Jordan, René. *Clark Gable*. New York: Galahad Books, 1973.

Morella, Joe, and Edward Z. Epstein. *Gable & Lombard & Powell & Harlow*. New York: Dell, 1976.

Samuels, Charles. *The King, a Biography of Clark Gable*. New York: Coward-McCann, 1962.

Scagnetti, Jack. *The Life and Loves of Gable*. Middle Village, NY: J. David, 1976.

Spicer, Chrystopher J. *Clark Gable: Biography, Filmography, Bibliography*. Jefferson, NC: McFarland, 2002.

_____. *Clark Gable, in Pictures: Candid Images of the Actor's Life*. Jefferson, NC: McFarland, 2011.

Tornabene, Lyn. *Long Live the King: A Biography of Clark Gable*. New York: G. P. Putnam's Sons, 1976.

Wayne, Jane Ellen. *Clark Gable: Portrait of a Misfit*. New York: St. Martin's Press, 1993.

Williams, Chester. *Gable*. New York: Fleet Press Corp., 1968.

Part Four
SPENCER TRACY

Spencer Tracy in a publicity shot.

Four Hollywood Legends

Born: Spencer Bonaventure Tracy; April 5, 1900; Milwaukee, Wisconsin

Died: June 10, 1967, Beverly Hills, California

Spouse: Louise Treadwell (1923-his death, two children: son John Ten Broeck and daughter Louise Treadwell 'Susie')

Academy Awards: Captains Courageous (1937), *Boys Town* (1938)

Academy Award Nominations: San Francisco (1936), *Father of the Bride* (1950), *Bad Day at Black Rock* (1955), *The Old Man and the Sea* (1958), *Inherit the Wind* (1960), *Judgment at Nuremberg* (1961), *Guess Who's Coming to Dinner* (1967)

Golden Globe: The Actress (1953)

Golden Globe Nominations: The Old Man and the Sea (1958), *Inherit the Wind* (1960), *Guess Who's Coming to Dinner* (1967)

I. REFERENCES TO TRACY'S FILMS

Once again, just like in the case of the other three actors, the discussion of the film references is organized here chronologically, according to the release date of the pictures. Thus, in Tracy's case, it begins with a movie released in 1930, when the talking pictures were already the norm and the silent cinema was pushed toward history.

***Up the River* (1930).** By an astonishing coincidence, two of the greatest Hollywood stars, Bogart and Tracy, made their film debut in the same picture. It is also astonishing that the movie was directed by John Ford, a director who specialized in westerns but never hired Gary Cooper, another great star of that period and one of the very top screen Westerners. For Bogey it was the only collaboration with Ford; Tracy would work with the legendary director one more time: on *The Last Hurrah* (1958). But, in 1930, both Tracy and Bogart were absolutely new to the public. Nevertheless, both actors are included in the interesting excerpt found in George Baxt's novel *The Humphrey Bogart Murder Case* (1995), which is presented in Part One of the book (on Bogart).

An allusion to the film appears also in James A. Michener's novel *The Drifters* (1971), along with numerous references to other Tracy's and Bogart's films. Here is the passage which explains some of the circumstances triggering those references:

> I said that Holt remembered almost every film made by his heroes, but when he told me they had never worked on the same picture, I was bothered, for I seemed to remember a still photograph showing them together in a movie about a prison riot. When I asked about this, Holt growled, 'Impossible. They'd destroy each other,' but I could not get that old photo out of my mind, so I wrote to a film magazine and received confirmation: they had played together in **Tracy**'s first film but never thereafter. I forwarded the letter to Holt in Burma, and he wrote back: 'Must have been a terrible picture. I'd like to see it someday' [p. 463]

Michener, or his narrator, a man named Fairbanks, is right about one thing: *Up the River* is a prison movie; however, there is no riot in the film, and all the characters, including those played by Tracy and Bogart (in fact, befriending and helping each other) are rather mild in their behavior. Still, the artistic qualities of that picture are clearly inferior to those of both actors' major achievements in their subsequent careers.

Michael B. Druxman's *Tracy: A One-Person Play in Two Acts* (1984) contains references to as many as thirty Tracy pictures. *Up the River* is one of them; it is mentioned by the great actor, the sole character of the play, when he describes the beginning of his movie career:

> But the play took me to Hollywood. **John Ford** had seen *The Last Mile* and, in 1930, cast me in a picture for **Fox** . . . *Up the River*. A prison film, naturally.
>
> They paid me a thousand dollars a week. That was a fortune to me then. I felt guilty about taking it.
>
> When I arrived at the studio. . . . This, by the way, was the old **Fox** studio prior to the coming of 20th Century and Darryl Zanuck. . . . I was informed that there was no script.
> (*Chuckles.*)
> That's what studios did back then. They'd announce a title . . . a cast. . . . Then, if enough theaters wanted to book the picture, they'd think up a story.
>
> We finally made *Up the River* as a prison comedy. I was the funny guy, and my straight man was **Humphrey Bogart** [p. 34].

Quick Millions **(1931).** Tracy's second feature film, a rewarding crime drama directed by Rowland Brown, is also referenced in Michael B. Druxman's play *Tracy* (1984):

> **Winnie Sheehan**, the studio boss, decided I should be **Fox**'s resident "tough guy." I liked that idea. They cast me as "Bugs" Raymond in *Quick*

Millions. **Sally Eilers** was my leading lady, and **George Raft** had a small part [p. 35].

Society Girl **(1931).** In this rather disappointing boxing drama directed by Sidney Lanfield, Tracy plays the second lead, opposite James Dunn and Peggy Shannon. In Druxman's play *Tracy* (1984), the movie is mentioned in a passage where Tracy addresses Winnie Sheehan:

> When something good comes up, you give it to **Jimmy Dunn**.
> I know you think he's up-and-coming. I played second fiddle to him in *Society Girl* [p. 36-37].

20,000 Years in Sing Sing **(1932).** Michael Curtiz's superior prison drama (co-starring Bette Davis and Arthur Byron) was based on the nonfiction book by Warden Lewis E. Lawes. Allusions to the film were found in three works. It is first mentioned in Tracy's continuation of the monologue addressed to Winnie Sheehan in Michael B. Druxman's *Tracy* (1984):

> I used to be up-and-coming. What am I now? Down-and-going?
> Yes, you did let me do *20,000 Years in Sing Sing*.
> It was a damn good picture. **Bette Davis** is sensational.
> What're you beaming about, **Winnie**? It was made on loan-out to **Warner Brothers**.
> Why can't you give me something good like that here [p. 37].

George Baxt's *The Tallulah Bankhead Murder Case* (1987) makes a reference to Warden Lewis Lawes's book that inspired the famous movie. The book is mentioned by Tallulah Bankhead in a conversation with her agent, Lewis Drefuss, and her good friend, police detective Jacob Singer.

Even though the charismatic actress brags about having performed in the famous prison, it is more likely that she knows about the book because of the film than that she has read the books itself.

> Over her shoulder to Lewis, who had finally closed his mouth, she said, "Jacob is a genius and much too modest. Jacob, I'm sure one day you'll write your book and stagger all of us. The way Lewis Lawes did with his **_Twenty Thousand Years in Sing Sing_**. You've heard of Lawes, haven't you, Lewis dahling?" Lewis hadn't. "He was the warden at Sing Sing. I did a Sunday-night performance there once, dahling, and they didn't want me to leave!" [pp. 110-111].

In Thomas Pynchon's novel *Vineland* (1990), two famous films are mentioned in an unusual exchange between Zoyd Wheeler and Hector Zuñiga, a policeman who was sent by federal prosecutor Brock Vond to take Zoyd's daughter Prairie, whose mother, Frenesi, is having an extended affair with Vond:

> Finger to his lips, Zoyd went and put his daughter, who'd nodded out in the salt breezes, down on the bed in the other room, and her bottle and her duck nearby, and came back in eyeballing the oversize brick, getting nervous.
> "Let me guess – *2001: A Space Odyssey* [1968]."
> "Try **_20,000 Years in Sing Sing_** [1933]."
> Zoyd lounged against the giant slab, needing the support. "Wa'n't even your idea, was it?" [p. 294]

Shanghai Madness **(1933).** Directed by John G. Blystone and co-starring Far Wray and Ralph Morgan, this adventure drama is not as bad as it sounds in the actor's own words, as imagined by Druxman in his play *Tracy* (1984):

> Ever hear of **_Shanghai Madness_**? I did that with **Fay Wray**.

How about *Marie Galante*? **Winnie** produced that one himself.
(*Shouts.*)
I needed their goddamn money [p. 40].

Man's Castle **(1933)**. In this superior melodrama directed by Frank Borzage, Tracy's co-stars are Loretta Young, Marjorie Rambeau and Glenda Farrell. The movie is referenced in two works: Michael B. Druxman's play *Tracy* (1984) and George Baxt's *The Clark Gable & Carole Lombard Murder Case* (1997). In Druxman's *Tracy* (1984), the actor describes his private relationship with his co-star:

> **Loretta Young** was twenty when we did *Man's Castle* at **Columbia**.
> One night, I asked her to have dinner with me. I was tired of eating alone. It was just one of those things . . . off-hand, unpremeditated.
> We did dine together, and the next day it cracked in the papers.
> Our dates continued to hit the papers, and I continued to hit the photographers. Paid for a lot of smashed cameras.
> I left home. Louise and I separated [pp. 38-39].

The quoted excerpt from Baxt's mystery relates a conversation between Gable and Lombard, who were just joined by Loretta Young:

> Carole admired Loretta's beach pajamas. "They're so *you*," said Carole. "I bet they cost a bundle."
> "I like to pamper myself every now and then. **Clark**, I see Ria's here."
> **Clark** said nothing. Carole said vivaciously, "Why, it's just like old home week."
> There was a beatific expression on Loretta Young's face.

Saint Loretta, thought **Clark**. He and **Spencer Tracy** had traded notes on her one drunken night at a saloon near the Metro lot. They had finished a rough day's shoot on *San Francisco* with **Jeanette MacDonald**, who both agreed should have been a nun. **Spencer** and Loretta had an affair back in 1933 when they were filming *A Man's Castle* and **Spencer**'s drinking was truly getting out of hand [p. 102].

Whipsaw **(1935).** Co-starring Myrna Loy, this relatively rewarding picture directed by Sam Wood is referenced in George Baxt's *The William Powell and Myrna Loy Murder Case* (1996), in a passage where Myrna Loy talks to Detective Jim Mallory at the scene of murder:

> "I was wondering if you'd say anything," said Myrna. "You have to be a detective. No reporters permitted on the premises." Jim reminded her they had met when she came to the precinct for some instruction on police procedure for *Whipsaw*. Myrna didn't remember him but sweetly said she did. Mallory wondered if it made sense to fall in love with her despite the fact she was married, albeit, from what he discerned, at the present somewhat shakily [p. 124].

Fury **(1936).** Directed by Fritz Lang and co-starring Sylvia Sidney, this masterful crime drama is probably Tracy's best picture of the 1930s. Unfortunately, the reference in Michael B. Druxman's play *Tracy* (1984) is the only one that has been found. The actor compares his work at MGM with that of Paul Muni at Warner Brothers:

> Maybe **Thalberg** felt I could handle a more serious kind of material ... like Paul Muni was doing over at Warner Brothers.

Spencer Tracy as Joe Wilson (first from left) and Bruce Cabot as Kirby Dawson (second from right) in Fritz Lang's *Fury* (1936).

> Muni had made *I Am a Fugitive from a Chain Gang*, so **Metro** gave me ***Fury***.
> It was a real shocker. Dealt with mob rule ... lynch law. Best thing I'd ever done on film [p. 46].

San Francisco **(1936).** Allusions to this memorable musical melodrama, directed by W. S. Van Dyke and co-starring Clark Gable and Jeanette MacDonald, were found in several sources. A relatively lengthy reference appears in Michael B. Druxman's play *Tracy* (1984), where the actor quotes his own lines from a scene with the leading lady:

> Gave to **Jeanette MacDonald** a "typical **Tracy** speech" in that picture.
> LIGHTS ADJUST to the past, as he goes into scene with **MacDonald**.

"You're in probably the wickedest, most corrupt, most Godless city in America. Sometimes it frightens me and I wonder what the end is going to be. But nothing can harm you if you don't allow it to. Because nothing in the world . . . no one in the world is all bad [p. 47].

A reference to the film and Tracy in Stuart M. Kaminsky's mystery *Poor Butterfly* (1990) is a part of a scene where private eye Toby Peters talks to his eccentric landlady, Mrs. Plaut:

"I'm going to San Francisco on business," I said. "I'll be gone for a while."
She tilted her head toward me and adjusted her hearing aid.
"To San Francisco," she repeated. "I was in San Francisco during the great earthquake. **Mr. Spencer Tracy** and **Miss Jeanette MacDonald** did not have the facts straight in their film. It was not Mrs. O'Leary's cow that started the earthquake. Mrs. O'Leary's cow started the fire in Chicago at an earlier time" [p. 16].

In Kirk Douglas's novel *Dance with the Devil* (1990), *San Francisco* is not referenced directly, but the lyrics of Gus Kahn and Bronislau Kaper's titular song are quoted twice. The first time it is a part of the conversation that takes place in Kraków between the book's Polish protagonist, Luba Woda, and her close friend from the circus, Valentine:

Luba hesitated, afraid to interrupt. "What do you dream about?" she asked timidly.
"San Francisco."
"San Francisco? Where's that?"
"California. In America. That's where I want to go."
"Why there?"

Spencer Tracy as Father Mullin and Clark Gable as Blackie Norton in a scene from W. S. Van Dyke's *San Francisco* (1936).

"I heard a song." And he sang, "***San Francisco, open your golden gates!*** Did you ever hear it?"

She shook her head and Valentine continued, "I want to get away from this shitty place—it's a goddamn Communist prison! And these useless Solidarity strikes only make things worse." He leaped up on the parapet. "I want to march through those golden gates!" And in a loud voice that echoed against the castle walls, he sang: "*San Francisco, open your golden gates . . . la la la, lal la la . . .*" Those were the only words he knew [p. 48].

The second time the lyrics are quoted when Luba is in her house, thinking about Valentine:

> Together? thought Luba. She wanted to be together with Valentine, not her mother. She didn't want to be a little girl. She wanted to be a woman—Valentine's woman. She jumped up from the bed and went over to the small barred window. She looked across the silent courtyard, and in a loud voice, she sang out: "*San Francisco, open your golden gates!*"
> Magda bolted up in bed. "What's the matter with you?!"
> Like an echo, Valentine's voice answered: "*San Francisco, open your golden gates!*"
> "What's that" said Magda.
> "Just a song," Luba said, bouncing back on her cot [pp. 56-57].

Libeled Lady (1936). Directed by Jack Conway and co-starring Jean Harlow, William Powell and Myrna Loy, this superior comedy is mentioned in Michael B. Druxman's play *Tracy* (1984) and Marisa de los Santos's novel *Love Walked In* (2005). Tracy, as the only character of Druxman's play, mentions the film rather too briefly, considering its unquestioned assets:

> That same year, I did a cute farce with **Harlow** and **Bill Powell** . . . *Libeled Lady* . . . [p. 46].

While in *Love Walked In* the woman infatuated with the debonair movie star is narrator Cornelia Brown, the reference is quite self-explanatory:

Spencer Tracy (Haggerty), Jean Harlow (Gladys) and William Powell (Bill Chandler) in a scene from Jack Conway's *Libeled Lady* (1936).

Truth be told, I'm a little superstitious about names. Back in college, I dated an enormous, blond, dumb fraternity boy from Boston Rouge with a voice like a foghorn purely on the strength of his being named **William Powell**, whom everyone knows from the *Thin Man* movies, but who is even better in <u>Libeled Lady</u> and is one of those men whose handsomeness you believe in completely even though you know it doesn't exist [p. 9].

***Captains Courageous* (1937).** Rudyard Kipling's novel was turned by Victor Fleming into a remarkable movie, which was possible due to the excellent performances by the whole cast, especially Tracy (who won his first Academy Award), Freddie Bartholomew, Lionel Barrymore, Michael Douglas and Mickey Rooney. Needless to say, references to the film were found in numerous sources.

A triple allusion to the film, clearly resulting from tech rep Harvey Holt's fascination with Tracy and his movies, was found in James A. Michener's novel *The Drifters* (1971), either as a tool of analogy or an example of artistic greatness:

> The son of the Pan American agent in New Delhi cringes before a bully at the international school: 'You remember how **Spencer Tracy** made **Freddy** [misspelled] **Bartholomew** face up to life on that ship' [p. 462].

> It was obvious that Holt was trying to control himself, and he asked, 'You don't really know any of the great pictures, do you? Like when **Spencer Tracy** was teaching **Freddy Bartholomew** to be a man?' [p. 506]

> 'Goddammit!' Holt cried, banging the table. 'You're a bunch of illiterates. You really know nothing. How do you suppose a man gets character? By seeing the great plays and movies and reading the great books. Every one of you young punks would have had more character if you'd seen **Spencer Tracy** as the Portuguese fisherman . . .' [p. 507]

The film is referenced in Robert B. Parker's mystery *Early Autumn* (1981); the context is a typical argument between private investigator Spenser and his girlfriend Susan about the negative consequences of his job:

> "It wouldn't be that way all the time."
> "Really? Who would guard him when we were being a twosome? Do you plan to employ Hawk as a baby-sitter?"
> I ate a doughnut, I drank coffee. "I don't know," I said.
> "Wonderful," Susan said. "That's really wonderful. So what do I do while you're playing *Captains Courageous*? Should I

A cover for the publicity brochure used during the original distribution of Victor Fleming's *Captains Courageous* (1937).

maybe join a bridge club? Take dancing lessons? Thumb through *The Total Woman?*"

"I don't know. I don't know what you should do, or I should do. I know only what I won't do. I won't turn the kid back to them and let them play marital Ping-Pong with him some more. That's what I know. The rest has to be figured out. That's what I wanted to talk with you about."

"Oh, lucky me," Susan said [p. 154].

Here is what Tracy himself thought about his role in the film according to Michael B. Druxman's play *Tracy* (1984):

> My favorite **MGM** picture? **Captains Courageous**.
>
> I played Manuel, the Portuguese fisherman.
>
> It was embarrassing when the make-up department curled my hair. Joan Crawford saw me, and thought I was Harpo Marx.
>
> I worked hard on developing an authentic Portuguese accent. They hired a real Portuguese fisherman to coach me.
>
> I had the script in front of me and came to this certain line. I said, "Now here, for example, would you say 'leetle fish'?"
>
> And the man said: "No, I would say 'little fish'."
>
> That ended that [p. 50].

Kurt Vonnegut's *Bluebeard* (1987) is a fictional autobiography of Rabo Karabekian (1916-1988), a one-eyed painter born in California to Armenian immigrants. A reference to Tracy and his first-Oscar winning film is made in a passage in which the narrator relates to Circe Berman, the woman who encouraged him to write his autobiography, the circumstances of his father's death:

> "And how did your father die?" she said.
>
> "In the Bijou Theater in San Ignacio in 1938," I said. "He

went to the movie alone. He never even considered remarrying."

He still lived over the little store in California where he had got his first foothold in the economy of the United States of America. I had been living in Manhattan for five years then—and was working as an artist for an advertising agency. When the movie was over, the lights came on, and everybody went home but Father.

"What was the movie?" she asked.

And I said, "***Captains Courageous***, starring **Spencer Tracy** and **Freddie Bartholomew**" [p. 16].

The narrator refers to the film once again a few pages later in order to illustrate a hypothetical situation:

> If my father had managed to survive ***Captains Courageous***, starring **Spencer Tracy** and **Freddie Bartholomew**, and had lived to see the paintings I did after the war, several of which drew serious critical attention, and a few of which I sold for what was quite a bit of money back then, he surely would have been among the great American majority which snorted and jeered at them [pp. 19-20].

In Sharyn McCrumb's mystery *The Hangman's Beautiful Daughter* (1992), a reference to the film and its star appears in a scene that takes place in the sheriff's office and relates a conversation between Sheriff Spencer Arrowood, Deputy Joe LeDonne and dispatcher Martha Ayers:

> Joe LeDonne strolled in, flipping through the mail, and glanced out at the curtain of rain. "Is that supposed to be a costume or not?" He pointed to Vernon Woolwine, who was hurrying toward the café for his morning doughnut. He was slouched low against the onslaught of rain, hands thrust deep

in his pockets. He was wearing a yellow plastic raincoat and matching rubber boots.

"Could be Paddington Bear," called Martha, who had been observing Vernon from her own window.

"Or **Spencer Tracy** in *Captains Courageous*," Spencer suggested.

LeDonne turned away. "Maybe he just doesn't want to get wet" [p. 203].

In Richard Price's crime novel *Freedomland* (1998), the picture is mentioned within two women's discussion about their respective sons' (one of them invented) favorite movies:

> "Do you know how hard it is to get a kid to sit through a black-and-white movie?" Brenda asked. "Well, you should know."
>
> "Me?" Jesse was thrown, then remembered her cover story—another surge of adrenaline.
>
> "What movies does Michael like?"
>
> "*Rocky*," Jesse said. "*Four. Rocky Four.*"
>
> "How old is he?"
>
> "How old?" Jesse scrambled, unable to remember what she had said before. "You know, same as yours."
>
> "You know what I bet he'd like?" Brenda was growing desperately animated again. "*Big*. What else . . . *A League of Their Own, Fried Green Tomatoes, The Secret Garden, Harvey*. You ever see that? With the six-foot rabbit? What else . . . **Captains Courageous**. Actually, that was too sad, plus it's black-and-white."
>
> "That's a lot of movies," Jesse said, wanting to move out of this dogleg in the conversation [p. 191].

An allusion to the film, through two versions of a paraphrase of its title, in Lawrence Sanders's novel *McNally's Dilemma* (1999) is a result of the unusual outfit narrator/protagonist Archy McNally decides to put on for an excursion to Palm Beach:

> I resurrected my bell-bottom jeans with the button fly, purchased during my stay in New Haven at an Army/Navy surplus store. At the time, this outlet was giving fierce competition to J. Press and Chipp for the Eli trade. I topped a blue and white boat-neck pullover with a yachting cap and shod my feet in a pair of Topsiders. My role model for this outfit was Cary Grant aboard the *True Love*, in the film *The Philadelphia Story*, but my mirror told me I had somehow managed to clone a cross between Gene Kelly and Rudy Vallee.
> "*Anchors Aweigh*," Veronica said.
> "How did you ever guess?"
> "Archy, we're not—"
> "Never anticipate," I broke in. "All that's required is that you put your trust in **Captain Courageous**."
> She stepped back and surveyed her leader. "**Captain Gorgeous**, I would say" [p. 85].

Test Pilot **(1938).** Victor Fleming's solid aviation melodrama, co-starring Clark Gable and Myrna Loy, is mentioned in several works. A reference to Tracy and Gable, along with two (out of three) films that they co-starred in, appears Andrew J. Fenady's *The Secret of Sam Marlow* (1980). The interlocutors of the quoted dialogue are private investigator Sam Marlow and cop Tim Foley:

> Foley stood back and looked at the plane. "Where the hell did you ever dig this up?"

"In a graveyard. She's a Republic P-47 Thunderbolt right out of WW II—completely restored with a converted two-man cockpit and ready for WW III."

" 'Beautiful Darlin' Betsy.' " Tim read the inscription on the front of the fuselage. "Who's that?"

"That, my young fugitive from the kindergarten, is the name of McMasters and Sands' first oil well."

"McMasters and Sands—never heard of 'em."

"**Gable** and <u>Tracy</u> in *<u>Boomtown</u>*—named their first well after Claudette Colbert."

"Yeah?" Tim grinned. "You look more like something out of *<u>Test Pilot</u>*."

"Ah, you saw that one, huh?"

"On television. That was **Gable** and <u>Tracy</u>, too, wasn't it?"

"Yeah, <u>Tracy</u> died in the end and **Gable** cried. So did I" [pp. 117-118].

Clark Gable as Jim and Spencer Tracy as Gunner in a scene from Victor Fleming's *Test Pilot* (1938).

The film is also mentioned in Fannie Flagg's novel *Coming Attractions* (1981), in a passage where the narrator, young Daisy Fay (here about eleven years old), shares her impressions after going to the movies with her friend Michael:

> Michael and I went up there yesterday and saw an old movie, *Test Pilot*, with **Clark Gable** and **Spencer Tracy**. I hated it. **Clark Gable** and **Spencer Tracy** were friends and they went everywhere and flew planes. **Myrna Loy, Clark Gable**'s wife, sat at home and waited and didn't do anything except at the end of the movie when she had a little boy. Every time they have somebody born in the movies, it is a little boy. They never have little girls being born. What makes boys so great and wooooonnnderfullll? I can do anything a boy can do. I can even beat up Michael. It must be terrible to be born a girl and know that your daddy really wanted a little boy [p. 76].

In Michael B. Druxman's play *Gable* (1984), the only character, Gable himself, uses the film as an example to describe his collaboration with Tracy:

> When I did a scene with him, I had to get it right by the second take. Otherwise, he'd run right over me.
> Steal the whole scene. I'd just stand there with my mouth open . . . looking like an idiot.
>
> Remember his death scene in *Test Pilot*?
> (*Kneels; pantomimes cradling Tracy in his arms.*)
> I was holding him. His life was slipping away. He said his last line . . . very poignant. His eyes closed. His head fell to one side.
>
> I started to react. His face twitched. I started to react again.

He let out a final gasp of breath. The beginning of a smile appeared at the corner of his mouth.

> I started to laugh.
> (*Drops body; stand up.*)
> Damn it, **Spence**! Will you die already?
> (*To audience:*)
> We worked well together. Too bad it'll never happen again.

Somebody would have to take second billing [p. 24].

There is an interesting and extensive movie reference in Adriana Trigiani's novel *Big Cherry Holler* (2001). While *Test Pilot* is mentioned in the second batch of movies saved from the fire of a movie theater (owned by Jim Roy Honeycutt) by a young fireman, Tracy's name is used in the subsequent paragraph to illustrate the likely ignorance of the accidental benefactor:

> "Let's see, there's *The Ghost of Mrs. Muir*, *Song of Bernadette*, **Test Pilot**, *Wuthering Heights*, *Dinner at Eight*, *Goodbye, Mr. Chips*, *The Women*, *Sullivan's Travels*; there's Claudette agin with *The Palm Beach Story*, the Duke in *The Quiet Man*, *How Green Was My Valley*, thank you Jesus, it looks like we saved most of Maureen O'Hara. And lookee. Henry Fonda in *The Trail of the Lonesome Pine*. It's here, Jim Roy!"
>
> . . .
>
> Jim Roy breathes deeply. Most of his treasure has been saved, and saved by a kid who probably wouldn't know **Spencer Tracy** from Joel McCrea. Seats and screens and popcorn machines can be replaced, but prints that Jim Roy has collected all these years cannot [p. 122].

In Martha Sherrill's novel *My Last Movie Star* (2002), there is an extensive scene in which the film, along with *Captains Courageous* and a few other movies, is mentioned within a discussion of an autobiographical book by Myrna Loy. The first half of the passage is presented in the part on Clark Gable; below is the other half where Tracy is also mentioned:

> "It gets very grown-up after that. **Gable** goes on binges and disappears for days on end. His test-pilot buddies are being roasted alive in their exploding planes. **Spencer Tracy** is a sidekick, and he's in love with **Myrna** too. Anyway, the movie becomes a tortured triangle, and obviously somebody has to die."
>
> "**Tracy**. He's the sidekick, so he has to. **Myrna** cries once for **Gable**, when his plane crashes and she's afraid he's dead. And again when **Tracy** goes down. Not a flood of tears, but there's liquid, actual fluid—a bit more than brimming. Doesn't that constitute crying in a movie? Or does one have to wipe one's face?"
>
> "Franklin, I have to get going."
>
> "Wait. She has the best line when she meets **Gable** for the first time. Unforgettably delivered, perfectly timed, and on the edge between earnestness and incredible irony—which is hard to pull off. She watches his plane crash, and she sees him getting out alive. He's wearing a leather flight jacket and a long white scarf. His face is so amazing—his mouth is always loaded with emotion. And she looks at him, completely unimpressed or trying to be completely unimpressed, and she says, 'Oh. I know you. You're the prince. A nice charming prince right out of the sky. A young girl's dream. And I've been waiting for you all my life'" [pp. 247-248].

***Boys Town* (1938).** Another milestone in Tracy's career, *Boys Town*, directed by Tay Garnett and co-starring Mickey Rooney, won two Academy

Awards: one for the original screenplay and one for Tracy as best actor. A lot of information about the picture is offered by the allusions, which were found in numerous resources.

One of the first references to the movie appears in James A. Michener's novel *The Drifters* (1971); it is a part of a lengthy scene in which Harvey Holt is trying to convince the international group of young people about the assets of Bogart's and Tracy's films:

> Holt bit his lip, then asked, 'You never saw **Mr. Tracy** when he fought for the soul . . . the future of **Mickey Rooney**? That time when **Tracy** was a priest?' [pp. 506-507]

In Andrew Potok's autobiographical book *Ordinary Daylight: Portrait of an Artist Going Blind* (1980), both the movie and its leading star are mentioned in a passage describing the author's expectations and impressions of a rehabilitation center:

> St. Paul's Rehabilitation Center for Newly Blinded Adults had in its name the most revolting connotations. I imagined **Spencer Tracy** in *Boys' Town*, silent busy nuns in bare-bulbed corridors, forlorn clinics with nailed-down, fluorescent green offices stacked with caseloads. But as difficult as the word *rehabilitation* was to handle, the word *blind* was worse. It was fraught with archetypal nightmares: beggars with tin cups, the useless, helpless, hopeless dregs of humanity. It was a word I still couldn't say, not to my friend or my family, and when Dr. Lubkin first said it to me, *speaking of me*, I wanted to scream [p. 139].

Robert R. McCammon's futuristic novel *Swan Song* (1987) offers a poignant reference to the film in the course of a philosophical and theological

Mickey Rooney as Whitey Marsh and Spencer Tracy as Father E. Flanagan in a scene from Norman Taurog's *Boys Town* (1938).

discussion between Father Doyle Halland and a nun—after they witness a true tragedy:

> "I'm very good at judging which way the wind blows—and I'd have to say that now I judge God, or the power that we know as God, to be very, very weak. A dying candle, if you like,

surrounded by darkness. And the darkness is closing in." He sat without moving, just watching the fire burn.

"You don't sound much like a priest."

"I don't feel like one, either. I just feel . . . like a worn-out man in a black suit with a stupid, dirty one collar. Does that shock you?"

"No. I don't think I can be shocked anymore."

"Good. Then that means you're becoming less of an optimist too, doesn't it?" He grunted. "I'm sorry. I guess I don't sound like **Spencer Tracy** in *Boys Town*, do I? But those last rites I gave . . . they fell out of my mouth like ashes, and I can't get that damned taste out of my mouth." His gaze slipped down to the bag at Sister's side [p. 235].

In Thomas Pynchon's *Vineland* (1990), an allusion to the main character of the movie is made by Sister Rochelle in a conversation with DL (Darryl Louise Chastain), who is in a lamentable predicament as a result of her serious mistake—applying the Vibrating Palm, an assassination technique, to the wrong man:

"Why tell me?"

"What? Who else can I tell that'll understand?"

"Just what I wanted today, just when the cash flow's starting to turn around, just as I'm finding my life's true meaning as a businessperson, I might've known it, in you waltz and suddenly I've got to be **Father Flanagan**." She shook her head, pursed her lips like a nun, but sat and heard out DL's confession [pp. 153-154].

Both Tracy and the film are mentioned in Lorenzo Carcaterra's *Sleepers* (1995); the reference appears in the book's second motto:

BOOK ONE
"This much I do know—
there's no such thing as a bad
boy."
—**Spencer Tracy** as
Father Eddie Flanagan
in *Boys'Town* [p. 5]

In W.E.B. Griffin's World War II novel *Blood and Honor* (1996), the movie and its two leading actors come out in American officers' conversation about a German one:

" 'My friend von Wachtstein'?"
Christ, I'm supposed to meet Peter tonight at The Fish. I'll be on my way to Santo Tomé instead.
"He was a guest of honor at your father's requiem mass at your estancia.'
"You must have friends all over," Clete said. "Von Wachtstein was there for good manners. He's running around with one of the Carzino-Cormano girls."
"So I heard. You ever think of trying to make friends with him?"
"He's a German officer, for Christ's sake."
"You see *Boys Town*? **Spencer Tracy** said 'there's no such thing as a bad boy,' meaning **Mickey Rooney**. I figure maybe that *all* Germans aren't bad. As a matter of fact, I know a couple of good ones. Maybe von Wachtstein's one of the good ones. You ever hear the phrase 'turning an agent'?"
"No. But I guess what it means."
"Think about it, Tex," Leibermann said. "And think about telling me why the Germans, the bad ones, they call them 'Nazis,' want Ettinger dead" [pp. 443-444].

Mike Sager's collection *Scary Monsters and Super Freaks* includes a short story "The Temple of Doom" (2003), where both Tracy and *Boys Town* are referenced in a passage comparing a distinguished monk to Father Flanagan:

> The monks were pampered and beloved figures, led by their abbot, Phra Maha Pairat Kanthong. Phra means something like Father or Reverend. Maha is a title denoting rank. Pairat, as he was called, was 36 years old. He'd been in Phoenix since the beginning of the Wat. To an American mind, he conjured the image of **Spencer Tracy** in *Boys Town*, known for his enthusiasm, his strength, his devotion to boxing, gardening and TV news.
>
> . . .
>
> Though he liked to tease and laugh, some say Pairat was troubled. The congregation was thin, the coffers were low. The children, almost all of them half-American, didn't attend very often. Sometimes, on Sundays, the congregation sparse, he almost despaired. He knew his concerns were earthly, unworthy for a monk. Yet still he worried—a human with responsibilities, a holy man, still a man [p. 295].

Philip Roth's novel *The Plot Against America* (2004), which is a political fantasy about what could have happened in the early 1940s if Charles A. Lindbergh had been elected President, includes a lengthy passage related to the film, but—even more—to the real Boys Town:

> I needed a note, and I needed clothes. I had to look to Mr. Kuenze like a kid he could trust, and I couldn't turn up without clothes. And this time I needed a plan, what my father called "a long-range plan." It came to me immediately: my long-range plan would be to save enough of the money I earned at the pretzel factory to buy a one-way train ticket to

Omaha, Nebraska, where **Father Flanagan** ran **Boys Town**. I knew about **Boys Town** and **Father Flanagan**—as did every boy in America—from the movie with <u>Spencer Tracy</u>, who won an Academy Award for playing the famous priest and then donated his Oscar to the real **Boys Town**. I was five when I saw it at the Roosevelt with Sandy on a Saturday afternoon. **Father Flanagan** took in boys from the street, some of them already thieves and little gangsters, and brought them out to his farm, where they were fed and clothed and received an education and where they played baseball and sang in a choir and learned to become good citizens. **Father Flanagan** was father to all of them, regardless of race or creed. Most of the boys were Catholic, some Protestant, but a few needy Jewish boys lived on the farm as well—this I knew from my parents, who, like thousands of other American families who'd seen the movie and wept, made an annual ecumenical contribution to **Boys Town**. Not that I'd identify myself as Jewish once I reached Omaha. I'd say—speaking aloud at long last—that I didn't know what I was or who. That I was nothing and nobody—just a boy and nothing more, and hardly the person responsible for the death of Mrs. Wishnow and the orphaning of her son. Let my family raise her son as their son from here on out. He could have my bed. He could have my brother. He could have my future. I'd make my life with **Father Flanagan** in Nebraska, which was even farther from Newark than Kentucky [p. 349].

A reference to Tracy and the film was also found in June Harman Betts's memoir *Father Was a Caveman* (2007), in a passage summarizing the cultural highlights of 1938:

That year, of 1938, in the entertainment world Kate Smith introduced a new song called God Bless America, Orson Welles and the Mercury Radio Theater frightened Americans with War of The World, a newscast style presentation of an invasion by little green men from Mars. Bette Davis won an Oscar for the movie Jezebel, **Spencer Tracy** won for *Boys Town*. Of far more importance to the Harman family, Smoke Hole Caverns was opened to the public [p. 203].

In James Scott Bell's mystery *Try Darkness* (2008), Father Bob tells a story about his childhood to the protagonist/narrator, lawyer Ty Buchanan:

> "He was sixteen now, ripe for the picking, living out in Compton. He had to learn to survive on the street, and he did."
> I tried to imagine Father Bob as a gangbanger. Couldn't do it.
> "And then one day he met a black priest, which he never knew existed. This priest saw something in the kid, took him under his wing. It was a real **Spencer Tracy** moment."
> "What's that mean?"
> "The movie. *Boys Town*. **Tracy** played the priest who thought you could always get through to the boys if you showed empathy and kindness and a little love [p. 183].

In Rachel Shukert's novel *Love Me* (2014), Tracy in the film is mentioned in the radio broadcast as Frank Capra, the president of the Academy of Motion Picture Arts and Sciences, announces the nominees for the 1938 Best Actor Academy Award. In the group there is one fictitious nominee, Dane Forrest, a gorgeous young actor with whom protagonist Margo Sterling, his co-star, is living.

> "And now, for the acting nominations."
> Mr. Capra's voice was ebullient as usual, but it hit Margo

like a splash of icy water to the face. She drew her breath in sharply.

"For the Academy Award for Best Actor the nominees are as follows," he continued. "**Spencer Tracy** for ***Boys Town***. Charles Boyer for *Algiers*. James Cagney for ***Angels with Dirty Faces***. Dane Forrest for *The Nine Days' Queen*."

"Mr. Forrest!" George jumped about three feet in the air. "My God! We have to celebrate! I'll make a special breakfast; we'll open a bottle of champagne—" [p. 24]

One more reference to the film was found in Murray H. Edwards's short story "With a Lot of Help from My Friends" (2009), in a scene where a woman tells a man that she is pregnant with his baby:

I break the silence. "Come on, Meryl. What's up?"

In a voice not much above a whisper, she says, "You're going to be a father."

"Beg your pardon?" I hear the words "be a father" and for some reason think of the Catholic priest **Spencer Tracy** played in **"Boys Town."** But I don't think that's what she means.

"You're going to be a father. A daddy."

"You sure?"

She says, "I suspected something a few weeks ago, but didn't think it was possible. I mean, well, you know. But I had this funny feeling, so I went by the doctor's office and they called me this morning with the test results" [pp. 84-85].

Stanley and Livingstone **(1939).** In this fairly rewarding adventure drama directed by Henry King, Tracy is cast as newspaperman Henry M. Stanley, while Dr. David Livingstone is played by Cedric Hardwicke. The only reference to the film was found in John Dandola's mystery *West of Orange* (1990), where movie stars Tracy, Rita Johnson and Ann Rutherford, along with MGM Publicity Chiefs Howard Strickling and Howard Dietz, are the special guests at the world premiere of *Edison, the Man* in Orange towns, New Jersey. MGM publicist Donald Jarvis talks to a local lady:

> Over coffee someone was relaying a conversation he'd had yesterday, "So this reporter calls 'cause his paper was going to reprint one of its Sunday supplements from the 1880's—when Edison first moved to town—and the reporter had noticed that there was an article in the paper back then that **Stanley**, who had discovered **Livingstone**, had himself gotten lost on a second trip to Africa and they were sending someone to look for *him*."
>
> "You just can't make this stuff up," one of the women shook her head as she lit a cigarette.
>
> "So the reporter thought it was a great tie-in, seeing that **Spencer Tracy** had played **Stanley** only last year and could we get him a movie still from that picture?"
>
> "C'mon, Donald, you gotta give the guy credit," the woman with the cigarette said. "He may be a breath of local talent."
>
> "Agreed," Donald answered. "But it took me forever to explain that **Tracy** had done that picture on loan-out and it wasn't our studio's production and he just couldn't understand it" [pp. 51-52].

I Take This Woman (1940). This mediocre drama, directed by W. S. Van Dyke and co-starring Hedy Lamarr, is referenced in Stuart Kaminsky's mystery *High Midnight* (1981), in a scene where Peters is planning a date with Carmen, a cashier at Levy's restaurant:

> I invited her to go to the Hitching Post on Hollywood and Vine to see Johnny Mack Brown in *West of Carson City*. She said she wanted to go to the Olympic and see ***I Take This***

Woman with **Spencer Tracy**. For some reason Ginger Rogers and George Brent were going to be there in person [p. 27].

Edison, the Man **(1940)**. Clarence Brown's solid biography of America's famous scientist and entrepreneur becomes the focal event in John Dandola's already cited mystery *West of Orange* (1990), where, understandably, there are several references to the film. The first reference is related to Edie, the MGM publicist in charge of the premiere of the film in Orange towns, New Jersey:

> The doorman directed her the few blocks over to Orange Park. The main avenue was lined with exclusive stores and shops. On the way she passed another of the six area movie houses where *Edison, the Man* would premiere. The "Coming Soon" displays said as much [p. 37].
>
> **Spence** was responsible for this, her being taken back into the fold. He never cared for the public relations chicanery but he had spotted Edie one noontime in the commissary with Laraine Day and the gorgeous *goy* and stopped by the table. **Spence** went to Strickling and said if someone had to be assigned to him for *Edison, the Man*, he wanted Edie Koslow because she was "efficient, not pushy, and an all-round good broad" [pp. 45-46].

Then, Policeman Mulvey, barber Tony and MGM publicist Edie go the scene of the third murder:

> The police managed to keep the public at bay across the street and on adjacent corners. Mulvey used his badge to get him and Edie into the inner circle. Tony waved them to the porch of a big rambling Victorian house where he and Degnan had a view into the alley through a chain-like fence. The alleyway

belonged to the Windsor Theatre. Thursday night, ***Edison, the Man*** would premiere here [p. 111].

The last allusion is made by a radio broadcast announcer:

> "Yes, these people are gathered here to partake in kicking off the two-day world Pageant of Progress which will include the official world premiere of MGM Studio's production of ***Edison, the Man*** here on Thursday. Yes, here, ladies and gentlemen, here in West Orange, New Jersey, which beginning tonight will become The Brightest Spot in the World?" [pp. 163-164]

Another reference to this movie was found in Fannie Flagg's philosophical novel *Can't Wait to Get to Heaven* (2006), in a passage relating Elner Shimfissle's incredible encounter with Thomas Alva Edison himself:

> "Yes, but if it makes you feel any better, I think they are going to have to go right back to your idea anyway." She suddenly thought of something. "Hey, did you know they made a lot of movies about you?"
> "Oh, yes?"
> "Yes, good ones too. I saw two of them at the Elmwood Theater, Mickey Rooney was in one, then **Spencer Tracy** played you as a grown man. I liked both of them, really."
> "So, Elner," asked Tom, "how do you like it here? Are you enjoying yourself so far?"
> "Oh, am I! Even more, now that I know I'm not in any trouble. I was just getting ready to tell Raymond, this is the grandest place I've ever been, it's even better than I thought it would be" [pp. 150-151].

***Northwest Passage* (1940).** Based on the famous novel by Kenneth Roberts, directed by King Vidor and beautifully photographed in color by William V. Skall and Sidney Wagner, *Northwest Passage* (featuring Robert Young, Walter Brennan and Ruth Hussey) is referenced briefly in Michael B. Druxman's play *Tracy* (1984):

> <u>*Northwest Passage*</u> was no picnic. Almost drowned crossing a river on that one . . . [p. 53].

***Boom Town* (1940).** Directed by Jack Conway, this memorable adventure drama co-starring Clark Gable, Claudette Colbert and Hedy Lamarr is mentioned in a few sources. The one reference which deserves to be quoted here comes from John Dandola's mystery *West of Orange* (1990). The context of the scene is MGM executive China (originally Chinaman, due to his permanently slanting eyes) Mannix giving pointers to publicist Edie Koslow, the girl in charge of the upcoming world premiere of *Edison the Man*:

> Strickling headed to his office and Mannix said in his fatherly tone, "Edie, I want you to keep an eye on **Spence** when he gets there. He's hittin' the sauce. Hates working on ***Boom Town***. Two Oscars and he says we still keep plopping him back in **Gable**'s shadow. He liked playing Edison. Let him soak up some spotlight again" [pp. 17-18].

***Dr. Jekyll and Mr. Hyde* (1941).** Robert Louis Stevenson's famous novel was turned, fairly successfully, into another screen version by Victor Fleming, who hired Tracy to play the dual titular role and Ingrid Bergman as his female co-star. The film is referenced in four works.

Thomas Pynchon's excellent novel *Gravity's Rainbow* (1973) is set during World War II and is abundant in cultural references from that period. The following passage mentions both the movie itself and the title of George Grossmith's song which plays a significant role in it:

They don't want you listening to too much of that stuff—at least not the way Haydn presents it (a strange lapse in the revered composer's behavior): cello, violin, alto and treble kazoos all rollicking along in a tune sounds like a song from the movie **Dr. Jekyll and Mr. Hyde**, "You Should See Me Dance the Polka," when suddenly in the middle of an odd bar the kazoos *just stop completely*, and the Outer Voices fall to plucking a non-melody that tradition sez represents two 18th-century Village Idiots vibrating their lower lips. At each other [p. 712].

Spencer Tracy as the titular character of Victor Fleming's *Dr. Jekyll and Mr. Hyde* (1941).

In Stuart Kaminsky's *Murder on the Yellow Brick Road* (1977) the picture is mentioned in a scene where private eye Peters talks with Victor Fleming, an important witness at a crime scene, and psychiatrist Dr. Roloff:

> "Dr. Roloff has been kind enough to give me some ideas for my next picture," **Fleming** explained, "a version of **Dr. Jekyll and Mr. Hyde**."

I must have looked surprised because **Fleming** added, "I know it's been done with Freddie March. A good film, but I have some ideas and **Spencer Tracy** is interested. But that's another game. What can I do for you, Peters? Can we get you something to eat?" [p. 47]

Tracy's attitude toward the film, as imagined by Michael B. Druxman, is made clear in his play *Tracy* (1984):

> **Metro** may have given me a new contract, but they sure as hell gave a miserable assignment to go along with it . . . ***Dr. Jekyll and Mr. Hyde***.
>
> Did I fight to get out of that one. I mean, how could anybody compete with the memory of Fredric March?
> They flattered me into doing it. Said I'd win a third Oscar.
>
> Somerset Maugham visited our set one day. He watched me in a scene for a few minutes, then turned to the director and asked: "Which one is he now?" [p. 55]

An allusion to Tracy in the costume and makeup for the film appears in Susan Snively's Key West poem "Spencer Tracy" (included in her 1997 poetry collection, *The Undertow*). Since the poem is 25 verses long, below is approximately a half of this original work:

> Later, when the clouds have moved to Cuba,
> Hemingway's cats come out to be fed—
> Marilyn Monroe, blonde, sumptuous, toothless;
> mean, grizzled **Spencer Tracy**; Jennifer Jones,
> a wayward opportunist; and Gertrude Stein,

who is just as I imagined,
solid, repetitive, a picky feeder.

...

It will take time to unload
its suspicious cargo. **Spencer Tracy**, in his **Hyde**-suit,
shows Jennifer his teeth. He's old and put-upon.
There's a lot about the world he doesn't like
but he claims it anyway,
his property, littered with felled fruit [p. 6].

Woman of the Year **(1942).** Written by Ring Lardner, Jr. and Michael Kanin, and directed by George Stevens, this remarkable comedy was the first film in the fruitful, for consisting of nine items, and long-lasting acting collaboration of Spencer Tracy and Katharine Hepburn. The movie is referenced in several resources.

A memorable quotation from the film is offered by Tracy himself as the sole character of Michael B. Druxman's play *Tracy* (1984):

> *Woman of the Year*:
> (*Goes into scene.*)
> **"You know, it's too bad I'm not covering this dinner of yours tonight, because I've got an angle that would really be sensational: the outstanding woman of the year isn't a woman at all"** [pp. 56-57].

The movie and its stars are mentioned in two separate passages of Connie Willis's science-fiction short story "At the Rialto" (1989): in both cases a reference is made to the same scene in the movie:

> "You want to go get some breakfast?" David whispered.
> "I already ate," I whispered back, and waited for my stomach to growl and give me away. It did.

Spencer Tracy as Sam Craig and Katharine Hepburn as Tess Harding in a scene from George Stevens's *Woman of the Year* (1942).

"There's a great place down near Hollywood and Vine that has the waffles **Katharine Hepburn** made for **Spencer Tracy** in *Woman of the Year*."

"Ssh," I said.

"And after breakfast we could go to Frederick's of Hollywood and see the bra museum."

"Will you please be quiet? I can't hear."

"Or see," he said, but he subsided more or less for the remaining ninety-two black, gray, and polka-dotted slides [446].

The air conditioning still wasn't fixed. I fanned myself with a Hollywood brochure and then opened it up and read it. There was a map of the courtyard of Grauman's Chinese on the back cover. Deborah Kerr and Yul Brynner didn't have a square together either, and **Katharine Hepburn** and **Spencer Tracy** weren't even on the map. She made him waffles in **_Woman of the Year_**, and they hadn't even given them a square. I wondered if Tiffany the model-slash-actress had been in charge of assigning the cement. I could see her looking blankly at **Spencer Tracy** and saying, "I don't show a reservation for you" [p. 456].

There are two references to the film in Elizabeth Hay's novel *Garbo Laughs* (2003). The first one takes place during a movie discussion between teenage siblings Jane and Kenny:

> "Romance," yelled Kenny.
> Jane came into the kitchen, furrowing her brow and asking herself, "Which movies had a lot of chemistry in them?"
> Kenny said, "**Katharine Hepburn** and **Spencer Tracy** in **_Woman of the Year_**."
> "You think **Katharine Hepburn** and **Spencer Tracy** had chemistry?" Utter disbelief from the big sister.
> "Oh yeah. Sparks flew. *Casablanca*'s pretty romantic too" [p. 42].

The second quotation, less positive and including a reference also to another Tracy movie, relates a discussion between adults, Harriet (Jane and Kenny's mother), Bill Bender (their neighbor) and Harriet's aunt Leah, about the blacklisted screenwriters:

> "I knew Grierson more in the last years of his life," said Bill Bender. "But he was still sharp, sharp, sharp. Opinionated, opinionated, opinionated. More a talker than a listener. A splendid writer too. Like all those Scots. Well, he got cut down in the Red scare."
> "He wasn't a Red," said Leah.

"I'm not saying he was. I'm saying he got cut down in the Red scare."

"What would you say he was?" asked Harriet.

But before he could speak, "A *liberal*," said Leah with contempt. It would always be the ultimate insult. *You liberals*.

Harriet raised her spear and attacked. "They weren't the best screenwriters in the world, you know, the ones who were blacklisted. I've seen some of their movies and they were pretty bad. ***Woman of the Year***, for instance. It was awful."

"**Ring Lardner, Jr.**," said Bill Bender.

"***Thirty Seconds Over Tokyo*** was even worse."

"**Dalton Trumbo**," said Bill Bender.

Leah drew air sharply through her teeth, rubbed the fingers of her right hand against her thumb, and said levelly, "Faulkner could write any old shit for the screen, nobody held him accountable. But a radical writes a bad screenplay and he's no good, never was, never will be. Liberals use any excuse to dismiss the Left" [p. 165].

The film is briefly, but poignantly, referenced in Valerie Block's novel *Don't Make a Scene* (2007), after a scene relating a telephone conversation between Diane Kurasik, a Greenwich Village movie theater director, and her parents:

"Let's meet this guy," Diane's father said. "If you like him, I bet we'll like him. He's how old?"

Diane agreed in theory to this meeting, but continued to avoid scheduling it.

Sometimes a movie can survive a terrible ending because the rest of it hangs together so beautifully. Take ***Woman of the Year*** (**George Stevens, 1942**), with an ending tacked on by the studio in spite of furious protest from screenwriters **Ring**

Lardner, Jr. and **Michael Kanin**. The film is remembered in spite of the vindictive ending, which puts **Katharine Hepburn** "in her place" in the kitchen, thereby undercutting the spirit and premise of the strong-willed-career-woman picture.

Endings were not on Diane's mind, however [pp. 313-314].

Stephen King, in his novel *Duma Key* (2008), mentions the movie twice, both times as a result of a comparison between the book's major character, Elizabeth Eastlake, and Katharine Hepburn. The first excerpt is presented under *Adam's Rib*; below is the second one:

> I had ordered her a suite, and the living room was big. There had apparently been a before-show party, because there were two room-service tables and lots of plates with the remains of canapés on them. I spotted two—no, three champagne buckets. Two of the bottles were sticking bottoms-up, dead soldiers. The third appeared to still be alive, although on life support.
>
> That made me think of Elizabeth again. I saw her sitting beside her China Village, looking like **Katharine Hepburn** in <u>**Woman of the Year**</u>, saying *See how I've put the children outside the schoolhouse! Do come see!* [p. 404]

Keeper of the Flame **(1944).** Tracy and Hepburn again, this time directed by George Cukor, who work with the couple repeatedly, were not as effective in this drama as they usually were in comedies. The film is one of Tracy's ten pictures referenced in James A. Michener's novel *The Drifters* (1971). Just like in most of the other allusions, the movie is mentioned in an analogy:

> A Japanese politician with a notable reputation proves to be a fraud: 'It's exactly like <u>**Spencer Tracy**</u> proving the facts about **Miss Hepburn**'s husband.' Invariably he referred to lean and lovely **Katharine Hepburn** in the formal style, and once when

an embassy wife in Indonesia gossiped about her, Holt rose and left the room [p. 462].

Spencer Tracy as Steven O'Malley and Katharine Hepburn as Christine Forrest in George Cukor's *Keeper of the Flame* (1944).

***The Seventh Cross* (1944).** Based upon the well-known novel by Anna Seghers, this superior political drama directed by Fred Zinnemann is one of the most prestigious, if not very successful at the box-office, items in Tracy's filmography. A reference to the film was found in two major books.

Gore Vidal's shocking novel *Myra Breckinridge* (1968) has a passage in which narrator/protagonist laments about the changes brought about by television, especially the changes affecting the film industry. The following excerpt includes references to two of Tracy's movies:

> Now television executives and technicians occupy all the tables and order what used to be Louis B. Mayer Chicken Soup, only the name of Mayer has been, my guide told me, stricken

from the menu. So much for greatness! Even more poignant as reminders of human transiency are the empty offices on the second floor of the Thalberg Building. I was particularly upset to see that the adjoining suites of **Pandro S. Berman** and the late Sam Zimbalist were both vacant. Zimbalist (immortal because of *__Boom Town__*) died in Rome while producing *Ben Hur* which saved the studio's bacon, and **Pandro S. Berman** (*Dragon Seed, The Picture of Dorian Gray, __The Seventh Cross__*) has gone into what the local trade papers refer to as "indie production." How tragic! **MGM** without **Pandro S. Berman** is like the American flag without its stars [p. 36].

The film is also referenced in James A. Michener's novel *The Drifters* (1971). It is mentioned at the end of the chapter on Pamplona, after Harvey Holt, seriously wounded by a bull on the Bastille Day while heroically saving other runners, recuperates in a hospital and is offered a marriage by Britta, a Norwegian girl over twenty years younger:

> She came to the bed and kissed him. 'Get well soon,' she said and left the room.
>
> Holt looked at me in bewilderment, then wiped his cheek and said, 'Seems all you have to do to get kissed by a pretty girl is to take a horn six inches in your gut.'
>
> Trying to get into focus what Britta had said, he made his usual comment. 'It's like the time **Signe Hasso** watched over **__Spencer Tracy__**. She was Scandinavian too.' I didn't get this at all, and he growled, 'When they were hiding from the Nazis' [p. 572].

Thirty Seconds Over Tokyo **(1944).** Mervyn LeRoy's superior World War II drama is memorable for, among other things, its remarkable cast, including

American poster for Mervyn LeRoy's *Thirty Seconds Over Tokyo* (1944).

Tracy, Van Johnson, Robert Walker, Phyllis Thaxter and Robert Mitchum. It is mentioned in a few, relatively significant, books.

In Gore Vidal's already mentioned *Myra Breckinridge* (1968), there is a reference to this film, even though it has nothing to do with the war or the movie's plot in any essential way:

> Though I cannot say that the pleasure of others has ever had any effect upon me except to produce a profound melancholy, I was *almost* pleased at Mary-Ann's delight. "You must be very happy," I whispered like **Phyllis Thaxter** in <u>*Thirty Seconds over Tokyo*</u>, with wonderful **Van Johnson** [p. 147].

A brief reference to the picture was found in Loren D. Estleman's mystery *Downriver* (1988), narrated by private eye Amos Walker:

> I brought myself a wary second drink and warily flipped the record on the turntable. When that side was finished I tried some wary TV. It was getting thin by that time.

I caught the last twenty minutes of a colorized version of ***Thirty Second Over Tokyo*—Spencer Tracy** had blue eyes and a complexion of Deanna Durbin's—and then the newsbreak came on just before sign-off. Someone had blown up a restaurant in Beirut and so far three groups had claimed credit for the explosion [p. 51].

Another reference to both Tracy and the film appears in Robert B. Parker's mystery *Double Play* (2004), in a lengthy passage being one of several chapters narrated by a young character named Bobby, who happens to be the author himself, which are distinguished from the rest of the book by italics:

At the movies we saw Bataan, Flying Tigers, Guadalcanal Diary, ***Thirty Seconds over Tokyo***, *Wake Island. The Japs were unremittingly wrong. We were brave. Even the misfits learned before the end of the movie that the war had to be won. All of the bomber crews and rifle squads were a melting pot of American ethnicity, Murphy, Martinelli, Shapiro, Swenson and DeLisle. On the screen the war was fought by **Spencer Tracy** and Cary Grant, John Garfield, John Wayne, Robert Mitchum, **Humphrey Bogart**, Robert Taylor. Of course, we would win* [p. 22].

***Adam's Rib* (1949).** Written by Ruth Gordon and Garson Kanin, this enormously entertaining picture is the artistic and commercial peak of the Tracy-Hepburn-Cukor collaboration. Unsurprisingly, the film is referenced in several literary works, which constitute quite a variety of genres.

In Michael B. Druxman's play *Tracy* (1984), an extensive quotation is offered by the actor himself as he speaks about the great onscreen fights he and Katharine Hepburn used to have:

Adam's Rib . . . We're married attorneys, and she's just beaten me in court, using a shoddy trick. I've just threatened her and **David Wayne** with a pistol . . . a licorice pistol.

(*Goes into scene, using his finger to represent the unseen pistol.*)

"I'll never forget this neither. I'll never forget that no matter what you think you think . . . you really think the same as I do. That I've no right. That no one has a right . . . to break the law. That your client has no right. That I'm right. That you're wrong."

(*Takes bite from pistol; to audience:*)

All through that speech, **Kate**'s muttering:

(*Mimics*)

"Despicable . . . vile . . . dirty . . . low . . . worthless . . . corrupt . . ." [p. 57]

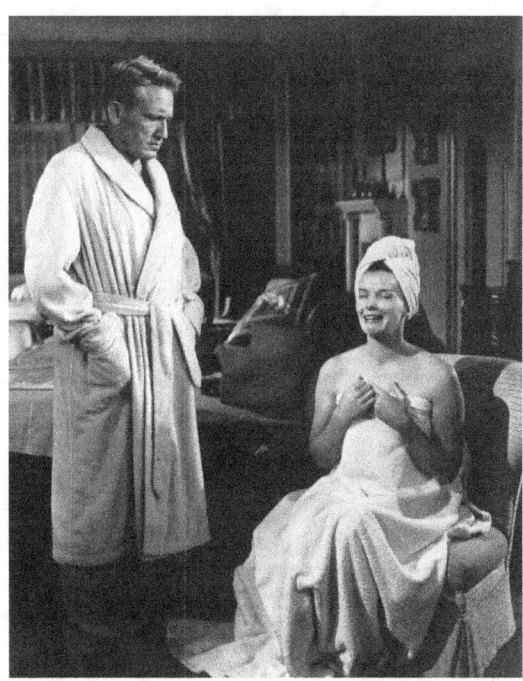

Spencer Tracy and Katharine Hepburn as Adam and Amanda Bonner in a scene from George Cukor's *Adam's Rib* (1949).

In Roderick Thorp's crime novel *Rainbow Drive* (1986), set in Los Angeles, it is mentioned as a part of a publicity slogan:

> Galaxy International was a giant whorehouse and Norman Birnbaum its boss pimp, which made Gretchen Heidl one of the whores, she said—one of the *lesser* whores. The fact was that Dick Albert's role in her film was perhaps the juiciest for an established star since Dustin Hoffman's in *Tootsie*, a classic case of playing against type. But the Birnbaum-Galaxy party line—a rehearsal for the publicity campaign that would accompany the film—was that the story was unimaginably clever, the best man-woman brawl since **_Adam's Rib_**, and that its stars would be elevated to screen immortality [p. 84].

John Updike, in his epic novel *In the Beauty of the Lilies* (1996), includes this and a few other pictures within the narrator's commentary on the movie situation in the period following World War II:

> The big Hollywood movies at the end of the Forties were *Easter Parade* and *The Treasure of the Sierra Madre*, *Rope* and *Johnny Belinda*, *Red River* and *On the Town*, **_Adams' Rib_** and *Samson and Delilah*. Attendance was down from the peak of 1946, but only industry insiders noticed, or grasped the significance of the anti-monopolistic legal rulings which would separate the great studios from their theatre chains [p. 311].

A brief reference to the film and its stars appears in LaVyrle Spencer's *Then Came Heaven* (1997), a spiritual novel set in the author's hometown, Browerville, Minnesota, in the 1950s. The quoted passage describes an interior of a bar:

> Clothespinned to a long drooping wire along the deep left

wall were dance bills advertising New Year's Eve bands at all the dance halls around the area, as well as an advertisement showing Ralph Bellamy smoking a Camel. An outdated campaign poster had a picture of Slip Walter, who'd run for Sheriff. At the Clarissa Theater, **Spencer Tracy** and **Katharine Hepburn** were playing in *Adam's Rib* and at Long Prairie it was *Ma and Pa Kettle Go to Town*. But in the municipal liquor store it was the same depressing business as usual [pp. 196-197].

An allusion to the film appears in Scott Turow's novel *Personal Injuries* (1999), in a passage where two lawyers (one, Robbie Feaver, working secretly for the FBI) are compared to Spencer Tracy and Katharine Hepburn in—judging by the context—their roles in *Adam's Rib*:

> From the start, Sennett and McManis had known that there was a finite number of complaints they could file in a short period. Tuohey's cohort would feel put upon and suspicious if there were too many 'specials'; Mort could become curious about the extraordinary volume of referrals coming upstairs from me; and the judges might grow wary if Robbie and McManis kept showing up as matched opponents, like **Tracy** and **Hepburn** [pp. 106].

A famous line from the movie is quoted by the narrator/protagonist in Laurence Klavan's thriller *The Cutting Room* (2004), soon after he is told by a couple of his friends that they are going to have another baby:

> I smiled uneasily as the two proceeded to lecture me on the ups and downs of relationships, the back and the forth, the give and the take, how friendship becomes more important than sex, and how men and women are different, but *"vive la difference,"* as **Spencer Tracy** said in *Adam's Rib* [p. 55].

Four Hollywood Legends

The movie, along with *Woman of the Year*, is mentioned in Stephen King's novel *Duma Key* (2008), and the pretext is the resemblance which narrator/protagonist Edgar Freemantle sees between Elizabeth Eastlake, an old woman he meets in Florida, and Katharine Hepburn:

> In the center of the room was the woman Ilse and I had seen on the day we tried exploring Duma Key Road. Then she'd been in a wheelchair, her feet clad in blue Hi-Tops. Today she was standing with her hands planted on the grips of a walker, and her feet—large and very pale—were bare. She was dressed in a high-waisted pair of beige slacks and a dark brown silk blouse with amusingly wide shoulders and full sleeves. It was an outfit that made me think of **Katharine Hepburn** in those old movies they sometimes show on Turner Classic Movies: *Adam's Rib*, or, *Woman of the Year*. Only I couldn't remember **Katharine Hepburn** looking this old, even when she was old [pp. 140-141].

In Jeffrey Cohen's *It Happened One Knife* (2008), there is a scene in which narrator Elliot Freed invites his ex-wife, whom he is still in love with, to his home to watch a movie together:

> I sat down on the foam rubber futon that was pretending to be a sofa. I should have considered that move more carefully, because if Sharon ever did manage to choose a movie for us to watch, I'd need a spotter to get me back to my feet. The futon is a little low to the floor. Ants have been known to look down on it.
>
> "Here," she said, and handed me *Adam's Rib*. A good choice, and appropriate to the company. Now if I could just get to a standing position . . .
>
> . . .

Naturally with a video collection that vast and important, I'd had to replace the twenty-two-inch television I'd been using with a flat-screen, high-definition beauty that had an audio system far superior to the one in my theatre, which I charged people money to hear. So ***Adam's Rib*** had never looked nor sounded better [pp. 150-151].

In Daphne Uviller's novel *Super in the City* (2009), narrator/protagonist Zephyr Zuckerman's imagination leads to a simile involving a situation from the classic film:

> On our first day of deliberations (we'd tell our kids), we would vehemently disagree, practically spitting venom across the copper-colored water pitchers. In the ensuing days, though, I'd be so articulate that he'd come to see my point of view and be in such awe of my verbal acrobatics that he would fall madly, helplessly in love with me. We'd me like **Katharine Hepburn** and **Spencer Tracy** in ***Adam's Rib***, but jurors instead of lawyers. Was there a paying position whose requirements included exceptional execution of jury service? [162-163]

Father of the Bride (1950). Written by Frances Goodrich and Albert Hackett and directed by Vincente Minnelli, this memorable family comedy (co-starring Joan Bennett and Elizabeth Taylor) is referenced in at least three novels—James A. Michener's *The Drifters* (1971), Adriana Trigani's *Lucia, Lucia* (2003) and Michael Malone's *The Four Corners of the Sky* (2009)—and one play, Druxman's *Tracy*.

Here is the excerpt from *The Drifters*, which offers a funny, self-explanatory allusion:

> An installation runs considerably over the budget: 'Exactly

what **Spencer Tracy** faced when he was trying to get **Elizabeth Taylor** married' [p. 462].

A brief reference to the film in Adriana Trigani's *Lucia, Lucia*, a novel set in New York City in the early 1950s, is triggered by the upcoming Valentine's Day wedding, for which the book's protagonist, Lucia Sartori, helps the bride to be, her best friend Ruth Kaspian, design a dress:

> Ruth is built a lot like **Elizabeth Taylor**, so we took ideas from the actress's gown in ***Father of the Bride*** and merged them with a design by Vincent Monte-Sano, who recently had a trunk show at Bonwit Teller's [p. 82].

In *The Four Corners of the Sky*, the allusion takes place in a scene where Annie's aunt/adoptive mother, Sam Peregrine, makes comments about Annie's mother-in-law's expectations regarding Annie's father:

> Nevertheless, as Sam remarked to Clark and Georgette when, a few months after the wedding, they sat at Pilgrim's Rest, looking through the wedding photos, it was as if Brad's mother could never recover from Jack's absence, as if she had always imagined him some rumpled grumpy **Spencer Tracy**, who should have been grousing in his armchair about losing the teenaged **Elizabeth Taylor** to a younger man and having to pay for it, whereas Annie's father had failed even to show up, proving himself, Sam had to admit, no **Spencer Tracy** [p. 91].

Pat and Mike **(1952).** Directed by George Cukor, this seventh picture of the remarkable and extensive Tracy-Hepburn collaboration is alluded to in Lawrence Sanders's mystery *The Second Deadly Sin* (1977), through a line that has become quite famous over the years:

She began reaching high overhead, then bending deeply from the hips to touch the floor. But not with her fingertips; her palms. He could see then what a slender, whippy body she had. No excess anywhere. He recalled with pleasure a line from an old movie he had enjoyed. **Spencer Tracy** looking at **Katharine Hepburn**: "**Not much meat on her, but what there is, is cherce**" [p. 113].

Charles (Bronson) Buchinski (Henry 'Hank' Tasling), Spencer Tracy (Mike Conovan), Katharine Hepburn (Pat Pemberton) and an unidentified player in a scene from George Cukor's *Pat and Mike* (1952).

The same line is quoted by Tracy himself, the sole character of Druxman's play *Tracy* (1984):

> Then, there was that marvelous comment I made in ***Pat and Mike***:
> (*In character:*)
> "**Not much meat on her, but what's there is cherce**" [p. 57].

Plymouth Adventure **(1952).** The director of this rather disappointing costume adventure drama was Clarence Brown, who had at his disposal, in addition to Tracy, such great names as Gene Tirney, Van Johnson and Leo Genn. Tracy's critical comments about some of his films from the early 1950s, including this one, are presented in the following passage from Michael B. Druxman's play *Tracy* (1984):

> Management had changed at **Metro**. **Mayer** was out . . . **Schary** was in. With the exception of ***Father of the Bride*** and ***Black Rock***, the only pictures of mine that had done well were those with **Kate**.
> They'd thrown things like ***Malaya*** and ***Plymouth Adventure*** at me. I started to feel like I was reliving the days at **Fox** all over again [p. 62].

Bad Day at Black Rock **(1955).** Written by Millard Kaufman and Don McGuire from a suspenseful short story by Howard Breslin, directed by John Sturges, and featuring, in addition to Tracy, Robert Ryan, Anne Francis, Lee Marvin, Ernest Borgnine, Dean Jagger and Walter Brennan, this unforgettable contemporary western drama is probably Tracy's foremost achievement of the 1950s. It is suitably referenced in several sources.

One of the first references to the film appears in Sam Shepard's *Motel Chronicles* (1982), in a short entry dated nearly seventeen years after the two movies, one starring Tracy and one starring Gary Cooper, were originally released:

> I keep praying
> for a double bill
> of
> ***BAD DAY AT BLACK ROCK***
> and

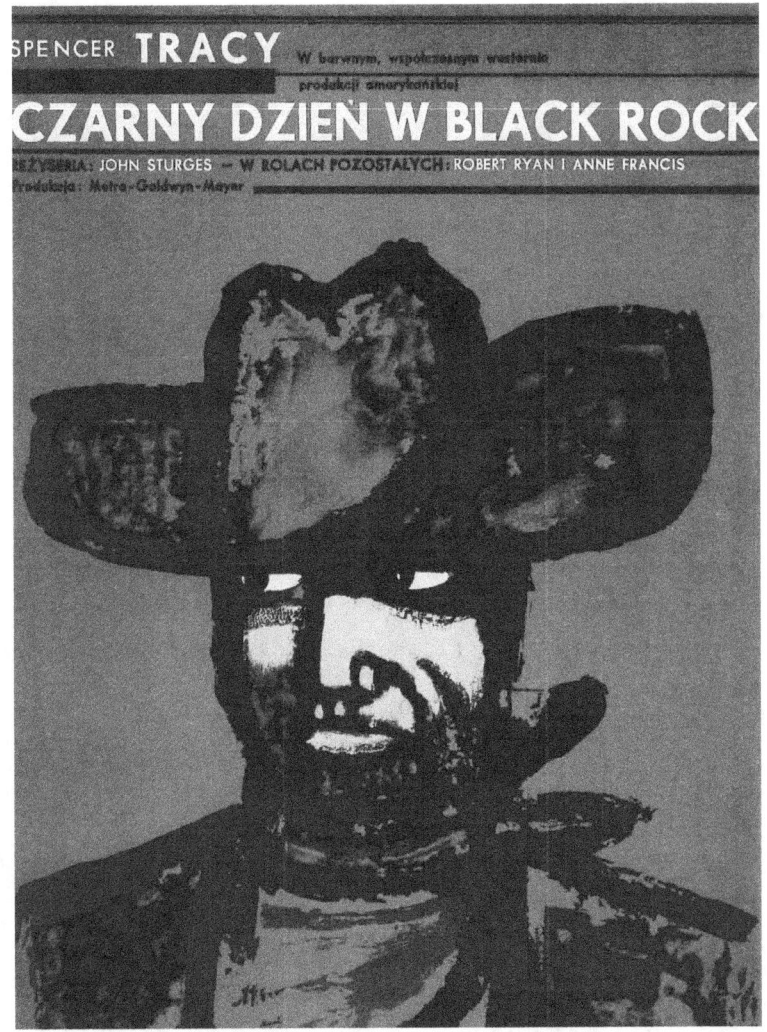

Polish poster (by Maciej Hibner) for John Sturges's *Bad Day at Black Rock* (1955).

VERA CRUZ
4/28/81Santa Rosa, Ca. [p. 86]

A lengthy passage containing a reference to Tracy and *Bad Day at Black Rock* appears in Loren D. Estleman's Detroit novel *Edsel* (1995). The narrator, journalist Connie Minor, takes his girlfriend, Agnes DeFilippo, to the Bel-Air Drive-In. During the show, they express their different opinions about the actor and the film:

> The feature was **Bad Day at Black Rock**.
>
> . . .
>
> "What are you grumbling about?" she asked.
>
> "I thought it was a western. It sounded like a western. That's what I was in the mood for."
>
> "It *is* a western."
>
> "The hero wears a fedora and the villain drives a pickup truck."
>
> "There are horses."
>
> "There were neckties in *Earth vs. the Flying Saucers*, but that didn't make it a gangster picture."
>
> "Well, I like it. **Spencer Tracy** is looking old, though. It's kind of sad."
>
> "We're the same age."
>
> "We're grumpy because there ought to be a law against advertising a movie as a western that isn't a western."
>
> . . .
>
> "And every time **Spencer Tracy** turns his back I can see the outline of his arm tied behind to make it look like he has only one. He didn't lose it at all; he just misplaced it. Meanwhile I'm out sixty cents and it's been so long since I've seen a real western I'm about to break out in little red saddles all over my body."
>
> . . .
>
> "**Ernest Borgnine**'s about to beat the hell out of **Tracy**. I don't want to miss any of it while I'm waiting for the kid to make change."

"I though you hated this picture."
"I didn't say that. I said it wasn't a western."

...

On the surfaces of his [private detective J. W. Pierpont's] eyeglasses, **Spencer Tracy** grasped **Anne Francis** by the wrist [pp. 181-184].

In Barbara Taylor Bradford's drama *Angel* (1993), there is an extremely positive reference to Tracy and his performance in this contemporary western, when the narrator describes the fascinations of one of the main characters, movie star Gavin Ambrose:

> But it was these men of historical greatness who had been *his* heroes, not football players, baseball stars or rock musicians, whom his friends had constantly put on pedestals. He *had* admired a few actors, of course, being an aspiring actor himself. Paul Newman and **Spencer Tracy** were a couple of the very special ones who were in a league of their own.
> **Tracy** in ***Bad Day at Black Rock*** was hard to top; so was Newman in *Fort Apache, the Bronx* [p. 217].

Bradford refers to the movie once again in her novel *Where You Belong* (1999), but this time the title is not italicized as it serves as a simile used to describe protagonist/narrator Valentine Denning's time of bad news following an extended moment of ecstasy:

> A week after our remarkable dinner with Fiona and David, my newfound inner peace and contentment suddenly shattered, blown to smithereens by several unexpected and unwelcome phone calls.
> The bad news came filtering into the Beekman Place apartment on a cold but sunny Wednesday morning, thereafter

etched in my mind as **Bad Day at Black Rock**, to remind me that the good things didn't last very long for little old Val [p. 206].

And, the author uses the film once again as part of a simile in her novel *Just Rewards* (2006), but this time it is a male character, Shane O'Neill, that makes the reference (no italics again, quotation marks instead):

> On the short drive to Robin's house, Paula ran the events of yesterday through her mind. It had turned out to be Black Friday in a sense or, as Shane had said at dinner, "**Bad Day at Black Rck**," quoting the title of one of his favorite movies [p. 555].

A similar allusion to the film, just by using the title to describe a situation, appears also in Larry McMurtry's novel *Loop Group* (2004), in an exchange between protagonist Maggie and a minor character, Diego Jones, about Dr. Tom (a shrink):

> "It's a **bad day at Black Rock**," Diego said, when Maggie approached.
> "Why, what's wrong?" Maggie asked.
> "That cunt bodybuilder beat him up again," Diego informed her.
> Actually what Maggie found when Dr. Tom let her into the office wasn't as bad as Diego had let her expect. Dr. Tom just had a small band Band-Aid on one cheek, and a cast on his left hand [p. 71].

In *Montecito Heights: A Resurrection Man Novel* (2014) by Colin Campbell, there are two references to the film, both related to the experiences of the book's protagonist, John Grant, quite similar to the ones that Tracy's

John J. Macreedy faced in John Sturges's classic picture. The destination of Grant's trip is Absolution, Texas:

> Steam didn't rise up from the engine as the rain pulled in at the one-stop bug hutch of a town. This wasn'tthat kind of train. This wasn't the iconic steam engine of the Old West with its cowcatcher grill and enormous chimney. It was the squat, bulky diesel of the Southern Pacific that hadn't changed since the '50s. Grant felt like **Spencer Tracy** stepping down from the streamliner at **Black Rock**. That was another place trains never stopped at [p. 362].

> The elephant in the room was the keys hanging from each pigeonhole.
> "Got a lot of keys though."
> "That I do. But each one's taken."
> Grant felt like he should fold one arm up his sleeve. This was playing like an homage to **Spencer Tracy** in ***Bad Day at Black Rock***. He wondered briefly if the clerk was having him on—a little gentle humor—then he dismissed the thought. The lines etched into the clerk's face were more from grimaces and frowns than smiles and laughter. His voice was gravel dry [p. 369].

***The Mountain* (1956).** Directed by Edward Dmytryk, this mountain-climbing adventure drama (co-starring Robert Wagner and Claire Trevor) is mentioned in Michael B. Druxman's play *Tracy* (1984) and in Jeff Long's novel *The Wall* (2006). The reference in Druxman's play is very brief:

> With all my complaining about the altitude, I'm embarrassed to tell you the title of my next picture.
> *The Mountain*. It was shot in France on Mont Blanc [p. 66].

Four Hollywood Legends

Long's *The Wall* is a thriller about two legendary mountaineers, Hugh and Lewis, determined—after many years—to try to climb El Cap again. The quoted passage reveals some bygone ideas, or unfulfilled dreams, of one of them:

> They swiveled the machinery around. White light hosed the meadow and trees like a Flash Gordon death ray. In the really old days, rangers would push flaming logs off Yosemite Falls to entertain the tourists. Lewis had toyed with the idea of using the walls for a giant drive-in movie screen. He wanted to show climbing movies, what else. That was in the pre-*Eiger Sanction* era, when the pickings were slim: Walt Disney's *Third Man on the Mountain*, and the **Spencer Tracy** movie *The Mountain*, and a sci-fi flick about the yeti. On slack nights, he said they could do slide shows about El Cap on El Cap [p. 58-59].

Desk Set **(1957)**. Tracy and Hepburn were joined by Gig Young in this successful comedy directed by Walter Lang. This is what Tracy says about the film according to Michael B. Druxman's play *Tracy* (1984):

> **Kate** came home, and we did another picture together . . . ***Desk Set*** at **Fox**. **Walter Lang**, the director, asked me to come in for a pre-production conference.
>
> "If you want to see how I act," I said, "you can do that on the first day of shooting. I'm gray and I'm fat."
> (*To unseen* ***Kate***:)
> You're right, **Kate**. I really am an old grouch [p. 66].

Katharine Hepburn as Bunny Watson and Spencer Tracy as Richard Sumner in a scene from Walter Lang's *Desk Set* (1957).

The film is also referenced in Janet Thornburg's short story "Chosen" (2005). The passage makes a comparison between the situation of Marilyn, a not-so-young aspiring actress, and a role Katharine Hepburn played opposite Tracy in one of their nine movies:

> In her thirty years as an office temp, she's had hundreds of offers to go permanent. Just this morning, the Dean of Students Services at the private university where she's working practically begged her to accept a permanent position as his Administrative Aide. He mentioned health insurance, vacation pay, a retirement package. No interview—no audition. Just twenty years of playing **Kathryn** [misspelled] **Hepburn** to the Dean of Students' **Spencer Tracy** in **_Desk Set_**. A role to last a lifetime. Never another audition.
>
> Of course, Marilyn admits, the dean is not at all like **Spencer Tracy**. He's dull and pompous, and the job is tedious. But that's all to the good. If even a fraction of her brain remains

functional, she'll be able to maintain and she'll never ever think of doing another play [p. 82].

The Old Man and the Sea (1958). Not easy to be filmed, Ernest Hemingway's novella (quoted as one of the reasons for the author's 1954 Nobel Prize) has essentially one character, if we do not treat the sea, or the big fish, as the other one. The little book, however, was turned into a digestible final product through the efforts of both Tracy and three directors, out of which John Sturges ended up receiving the credit. References to this important picture were found in several works.

Two allusions to the movie appear in James A. Michener's novel *The Drifters* (1971). The first excerpt is one more example of Harvey Holt's film-related analogies; the second one is a product of misunderstanding: Gretchen corrects Holt who refers to Tracy as the Portuguese fisherman, having in mind his role in *Captains Courageous*.

> A difficult job can be completed only by the exercise of indomitable will: 'Your problem is the same one **Spencer Tracy** faced when he was determined to catch that fish' [p. 462].

> 'It was a Cuban fisherman,' Gretchen corrected, 'and he was trying to catch a big fish ... and it was a perfectly dreadful picture' [p. 507].

In Michael B. Druxman's play *Tracy* (1984), the film is briefly talked about by the actor himself:

> **The Old Man and the Sea** almost became my life's work. It took forever to film ... first in Cuba, and then in a studio tank.
>
> **Hemingway** hated the picture ... my performance. He must've been surprised when I got an Oscar nomination for it.
> So was I.

Spencer Tracy as the hero challenging the big fish in a scene from John Sturges's *The Old Man and the Sea* (1958).

"The old man was dreaming about the lions."
I liked that line [p. 66].

The movie and its star are mentioned in Leigh Riker's novel *Acts of Passion* (1985), in a passage where playwright Conor Ramsey and young actress Gillian Shepard discuss the condition of an aging actor:

> "He was probably crying for himself," Conor observed when Gill posed the question to him. He went on fixing salad

for their dinner, the first night in the new house. "I've seen him pull the stops oh his tearducts a thousand times—it's just easier these days, I'm sure."

"Because he's failed?"

"Why else?"

"But he isn't failing now, he's marvelous in his part as Solomon; he could be another wonderful character like **Spencer Tracy** in *The Old Man and the Sea*. Pitting himself against nature.

"And losing," Conor said [p. 247].

Another reference to this film appears in the prologue of Oscar Hijuelos's novel *The Mambo Kings Play Songs of Love* (1989), where the author, only here and in the epilogue relating the story in the first person singular (as, in reality, he is the son of one of the two main characters), tries to wake up his uncle Cesar because of the episode of *I Love Lucy* in which his uncle and his father (now dead) were special guests performing their greatest hit, "Beautiful María of My Soul," is being rerun on television:

> A commercial was running on the television, and so, as I knew I wouldn't have much time, I began to slap his face, pull on his burning red-hot ears, tugging on them until he finally opened one eye, because he asked," Nestor, what are you doing here?"
>
> "It's me, Uncle, it's Eugenio."
>
> I said this in a really earnest tone of voice, just like that kid who hangs out with **Spencer Tracy** in the movie *The Old Man and the Sea*, really believing in my uncle and clinging on to his every word in life, his every touch like nourishment from a realm of great beauty, far beyond me, his heart. I tugged at him again, and he opened his eyes. This time he recognized me [p. 5].

In Annalena McAfee's novel *The Spoiler* (2011), the film is alluded to, via Ernest Hemingway, as legendary war correspondent Honor Tait is interviewed by gossip columnist Tamara Sim:

> Tamara pulled back. She had to be more cautious. Play the old woman at her own game. Appeal to her intellectual snobbery and then, when she was relaxed and singing like a linnet, go in for the kill. Sinatra. Picasso. Liz Taylor. Marilyn. She looked over at the photograph of the young Honor with Castro. Or was it Franco?
>
> "What about Spain?" she asked suddenly. There had been a module on the Spanish civil war at Brighton Poly. Though Tamara had chosen the Hollywood option instead, she had looked at the syllabus, seen the photographs.
>
> "What about it?"
>
> Tamara chewed her pencil as she reached for an answer. Then she remembered, and her voice had a bright ring of certainty.
>
> "Your time as a war correspondent with **Ernest Hemingway**, for instance!"
>
> Tamara congratulated herself. Yes. The boozy, bearded big-game hunter, who wrote the screenplay for the **Spencer Tracy** vehicle, ***The Old Man and the Sea***. They must have made quite a couple, **Hemingway** and Tait.
>
> Honor screwed up her eyes as if in pain. She did not know how much more of this she could stand [pp. 58-59].

The Last Hurrah **(1958).** This superior adaptation of the famous novel by Edwin O'Connor, scripted by Frank Nugent, directed by John Ford and co-starring Jeffrey Hunter, Dianne Foster and Pat O'Brien, is referenced in Dermot McEvoy's novel *Our Lady of Greenwich Village* (2008). The quoted excerpt describes the habits of Congressman Swift, a New York politician whose other habits have caused his heart attack and a big-time scandal:

> He had hands softer than an archbishop's, with beautiful sculptured cuticles and fingernails that gleamed from their careful biweekly shellacking. Not a Thursday or a Monday went by without Jackie Swift getting a manicure. And he was a master of the two-handed handshake. The right for the shake, and the left for the top of the other man's hand. Jackie, as he liked to say, could "cup-it with the best of them." He had learned it by watching **John Ford**'s *The Last Hurrah*. He loved the scene where **Spencer Tracy** worked the wake, "cupping" hands left and right [p. 51].

***Inherit the Wind* (1960).** The first item of the fruitful and remarkable collaboration of Tracy and director Stanley Kramer was a screen version of the famous play by Jerome Lawrence and Robert E. Lee. Co-starring Fredric March, Gene Kelly, Dick York and Donna Anderson, this captivating drama is referenced in numerous works.

One of the first allusions to the film appears in James A. Michener's novel *The Drifters* (1971). A representative of the old generation, patriotic tech rep Harvey Holt, tries to convince the young characters of the book about the assets of the American cinema:

> They were discussing the flicks, as they called them, and their enthusiasms were quite different from Holt's. They went for directors, for the provocative, half-formed statement, and they were very high on Ingmar Bergman and Antonioni. They agreed that Hollywood had never made a decent movie, whereupon Holt asked, 'What about **Spencer Tracy** and **Fredric March** when they had that duel over science?'

None of the young people knew what he was talking about, so they ignored the question [p. 551].

Spencer Tracy (Henry Drummond), Harry Morgan (The Judge) and Fredric March (Matthew Harrison Brady) in a scene from Stanley Kramer's *Inherit the Wind* (1960).

The film is also mentioned in two one-person plays by Michael B. Druxman: *Gable* (1984) and *Tracy* (1984). The quoted passage in the former reveals an interesting hypothesis of what Gable might have thought of his three-time co-star and friend:

> I don't think I ever envied **Tracy** more than I do at this minute. He's back in Hollywood doing ***Inherit the Wind*** with pros like **Freddie March, Gene Kelly** and **Stanley Kramer**. And, I'm up here in the desert trying to get a picture done with a bunch of screwballs.
>
> **Spence** and I have a lot of respect for each other. We're both envious of what the other has. He wishes like hell he had my fan adulation. And, I wish like hell I had his talent [p. 23].

The excerpt from the latter reveals Tracy's opinion about the film:

> First picture I did for **Stanley Kramer** was <u>*Inherit the Wind*</u>. It was based on the Broadway play by **Lawrence** and **Lee** about the Scopes "Monkey" trial.
> (*Takes off turtleneck and tosses it into chest. Underneath, he wears an off-white shirt, tie and very old suspenders.*)
> I played **Clarence Darrow** and **Fredric March** was **William Jennings Bryan.**
> (*Crosses* DC.)
> It was quite an experience working with **Freddie**. He's one of our great actors. Also Wisconsin born ... Racine.
>
> I think we spent half our time on the set figuring out ways to upstage the other. He'd sit there during my speeches, wagging that oversized straw fan of his, and when he was center stage, I'd sit behind him, listening ... picking my nose.
> (*Chuckles*)
> It was a hell of a show [pp. 15-16].

A reference to Tracy and the film appears also in Archer Mayor's *Scent of Evil* (1992), a mystery set in Brattleboro, Vermont. In the quoted passage, Lt. Joe Gunther, who investigates the murder of stockbroker Charlie Jardine, goes to see the victim's partner in his office:

> That hunch was confirmed when the receptionist returned to usher me into Clyde's office. The room, with two large windows overlooking Main, was quintessential transplanted old Bostonian—lots of burnished wood, padded leather, and glass-paneled bookcases—as incongruous in this building as if it had been on a shipboard.
> Behind a massive antique partner's desk was a large, white-

haired man in a seersucker suit and a red bow tie, looking vaguely like **Spencer Tracy** in ***Inherit the Wind***, except for the face, which was square, florid, and utterly without expression [p. 72].

British columnist Beryl Bainbridge mentions the film, along with its star, as she opens her essay "Citizen's arrest," published within her memoir *It Happened Yesterday* (1998):

> *I'm not going to go into this one. I like my bank manager, and I daresay it's not his fault that times have changed and banks are not what they were. Also, I'm solvent, which makes one feel less critical.*
>
> I feel rather like Perry Mason at the moment, or Ironside – they may be one and the same – or even **Spencer Tracy** in ***Inherit the Wind***. Perhaps the latter is going a bit far. At any rate, I've become very involved in the law. Let me explain [p. 123].

Another relatively interesting reference to the film appears in Michael Malone's short story "Blue Cadillac" (2002), in which the narrator/protagonist, high-tech sales rep Braxton Cox, meets a sexy girl named Marie (driving a blue Cadillac to Graceland to fulfill her deceased mother's wish), and later finds out that she comes from the town of the infamous trial:

> Her name was Marie. She was nineteen and had lived her whole life in Dayton, Tennessee. Braxton told her, "You live right where ***Inherit the Wind*** happened. I know somebody's mother was an extra in the movie. With **Spencer Tracy**?" She hadn't known about it. It was before her time and she'd never heard of **Clarence Darrow** and **William Jennings Bryan** fighting the famous monkey trial over teaching evolution [pp. 29-30].

The film is also mentioned in Paula Marantz Cohen's novel *Jane Austen in Boca* (2002), in a scene where a club board in Boca Raton, Florida, is deciding about a controversial project:

> The board listened to the case politely.
>
> "What," someone asked, "is the story the film is going to tell?"
>
> Amy responded that this was a difficult question to answer. "We'll try to capture the daily life of the club: how you spend your day, what you like to do and talk about, that sort of thing." A number of members nodded their heads as if rehearsing their day as she spoke. Amy continued, "In time, what happens is that a story emerges; it kind of finds its way into the film—like a lost child." There were further nods and murmurs as they tried to take this image in. "But you have to understand," she concluded, smiling her most ingratiating smile, "with a documentary we can't entirely predict what the story will be in advance. It has to take shape on its own. It's fishing for diamonds, so to speak." There was another murmur and rustle among the audience as they considered this metaphor.
>
> "Personally"—it was Pinkus Lotman, rising slowly with the mannered deliberation of **Spencer Tracy** in *Inherit the Wind*, a film that had much impressed him—"I'm against it. It's a powder keg. She says she's fishing, and fishing is not what we want here [p. 184].

A reference to Tracy and his great performance is also made in Stephen J. Cannell's novel *Runaway Heart* (2003), in a scene where Attorney Herman Strockmire pleads his case to Judge Melissa King:

> "Your Honor, if I might, I'd like to please try to convince you that a fine of a million dollars is excessive, and I really think

this problem with the amended complaint doesn't deserve a Rule Eleven penalty. It's not about the validity of the lawsuit." She was scowling angrily and he was beginning to sweat. His forehead felt damp, so he took out his handkerchief and wiped his face, folding it afterwards, then putting it carefully away, trying to look like **Spencer Tracy** in *Inherit the Wind*, instead of a fat, sweating mouthpiece about to get reamed [p. 107].

In Lawrence Block's mystery *Small Town* (2003), a reference to the film appears in a scene where writer John Creighton, accused of strangling a woman, is analyzing the appearance of his attorney:

John Blair Creighton looked at his attorney, standing there with his thumbs hooked under his suspenders and his stomach pushing forcefully against his shirtfront, and decided the man looked like **Clarence Darrow**—or, more accurately, like the actor playing **Darrow** in *Inherit the Wind*. Well, he thought, if the man had to intimidate someone, he could do worse. **Darrow**, as he recalled, generally won [p. 67].

A reference to the film was also found in John Douglas Miller's novel *The Greek Summer* (2003). Two guys, Miller (the narrator) and Bowman, analyze the possible consequences after they write an anonymous letter:

"Try to remember," I said. "Think real hard. It hasn't been thirty minutes ago that we heard him breathing out threats and slaughter. I don't know what he has in mind, but as of this moment he thinks the Amazon wrote the letter and tried to sting him on the deal."

"So what's the worst he could do?" Bowman asked. "He's gonna go around complaining for a few days, and when he realized no one is listening, he'll finally shut up."

"Yeah. As **Spencer Tracy** said in *Inherit the Wind*, 'We can dare to hope.'"

"Okay, mister movie man. As **Harry Morgan** said in *Inherit the Wind*, 'I can do more than that.'"

"What are you gonna do, Judge Bowman?" I asked. "Find the Earthquake in contempt of court?"

"I don't know," he said, and we sat there in silence for another ten minutes or so [p. 141].

A reference to the film in C. J. Box's Joe Pickett novel *In Plain Sight* (2006) is a part of a long descriptive paragraph about Governor Spencer Rulon:

> Loud and profane, Rulon campaigned for governor by crisscrossing the state endlessly in his own pickup and buying rounds for the house in every bar from Yoder to Wright, and challenging anyone who didn't plan to vote for him to an arm-wrestling, sports-trivia, or shooting contest. The word most used to describe the new governor seemed to be "energetic." He could turn from a good old boy pounding beers and slapping backs into an orator capable of delivering the twelve-minute closing argument by **Spencer Tracy** in *Inherit the Wind* from memory. His favorite breakfast was reportedly biscuits and sausage gravy and a glass of Pinot Noir [p. 7].

In Ron McCoy's article "It Ain't Me, Babe: Working for Richard Nixon," published in *Time It Was: American Stories from the Sixties* (2007) by Karen Manners Smith and Tim Koster, the film and its star are mentioned poignantly as a part of the author's own biographical sketch:

> I graduated from high school in 1966 and enrolled at Arizona State University, where I majored in political science

in the naïve belief that "poli-sci" as taught in the classroom is directly related to its practice in the real world. I wanted to become a lawyer and enter politics. I the movies, I'd seen the kind of lawyer I wanted to be: **Spencer Tracy** in *Inherit the Wind* and Gregory Peck in *To Kill a Mockingbird*.

Such was the state of affairs one morning in February 1967, when Don Johnson, a former head of the American Legion, whom I had met at the Legion's national convention in 1965, rang me on the phone in my dorm room [p. 292].

In Caitlín R. Kiernan's novel *The Drowning Girl* (2012), a reference to the film becomes a digression as narrator/protagonist India Morgan Phelps tells Abalyn about her unusual encounter with four strange-looking people:

"I saw that they weren't wearing habits, but long black cloaks, with hoods that covered their heads. Suddenly, I wasn't even sure they were women. They might just as well have been men, from all I could make out of them. And then—and yeah, I know how this sounds—and then I fancied they weren't even people."

"You *fancied*? No one actually says they *fancied*."

"Language is a poor enough means of communication as it is," I told her. "So we should use all the words we have." It wasn't really an original thought; I was paraphrasing **Spencer Tracy** from *Inherit the Wind*.

She shrugged, said, "So the nuns who weren't nuns might not even have been people. Go on," and took another bite of her apple [p. 52].

***The Devil at 4 O'Clock* (1961).** Based on Max Catto's novel, this memorable adventure drama, directed by Mervyn LeRoy and co-starring

Frank Sinatra, is referenced in Hank Klimitas's *Twice a Survivor: A Katrina Journal* (2006), in an excerpt that is quite self-explanatory:

> When the hurricane was at its peak, I thought I smelled gas in the laundry room. I turned off the heater. The other one is located in the attic to my east. If the first heater goes, I'm sitting right over it. That could be the ball game. This whole thing is turning into a mind game. I think about miners trapped in coalmines (my grandfather was a miner). The news also mention a siege and dead school children in Russia (yesterday was the one-year anniversary); I think of **Spencer Tracy** in *Devil at 4 O'Clock*. All of these miseries—what is going to happen to me? What is going to happen? Once again, I am grateful that my family and the dogs are safe [p. 38].

Judgment at Nuremberg **(1961).** One of best achievements in the careers of both Tracy and Kramer, the film (co-starring Burt Lancaster, Maximilian Schell, Richard Widmark and Marlene Dietrich) is referenced in Michael B. Druxman's play *Tracy* (1984) and in Nelson DeMille's novel *Word of Honor* (1985). This is what Tracy, the sole character of Druxman's play, says about the movie:

> I signed for *Judgment at Nuremberg* because I wanted to work with Laurence Olivier. He's the best actor today.
> Then, he got sick ... quit ... and **Burt Lancaster** took over for him.
> **Max Schell** won the Oscar for that one.
> I hated his acceptance speech. Who did he think he was? Thanking "that grand old man" [p. 67].

The reference to the film in DeMille's book appears in a passage presenting the political and legal discussion between General Van Arken and Colonel Horton:

> Horton reflected a moment before continuing. "There were only a handful of voices raised against the Allied tribunals. I was not among those who had the wisdom or foresight to see that what we were meting out was not justice but revenge. And even if I had understood that, I would not have had the moral courage to raise my voice." He looked at Van Arken. "I mean, my God, Hollywood blessed us with **Spencer Tracy** and *Judgment at Nuremberg*. There was not even the slightest doubt that we were not wholly on the side of the angels." They continued on in silence awhile, then Colonel Horton said, "General, when you were a young captain working on the prosecution side in the My Lai cases, you were operating in a different world, a different moral climate [pp. 415-416].

***It's a Mad, Mad, Mad, Mad World* (1963).** An unusual and rather controversial item in the Tracy-Kramer collaboration, this crazy comedy (co-starring Milton Berle, Cid Caesar, Phil Silvers, Mickey Rooney, Jimmy Durante and other comedians) is referenced in four works.

The allusion to the film found in James A. Michener's novel *The Drifters* (1971) has an ironic flavor. The girl mentions the film hoping to appease Harvey Holt, who is insulted by the young characters' incapability to appreciate Tracy's pictures, and she makes it even worse by choosing the wrong item:

> Gretchen flushed and for a moment it looked as if she would lash back at him, but her natural good manners stopped her, and she said with conciliatory warmth, 'I'm sorry. Mr. Holt. I did see **Mr. Tracy** once when he was excellent. As a corrupt

cop in ***It's a Mad, Mad, Mad, Mad World***. He showed a true sense of comedy' [p. 507].

The film is briefly mentioned in Michael B. Druxman's play *Tracy* (1984):

> They said I looked eighty in my last picture, ***It's a Mad, Mad, Mad, Mad World***. I was only sixty-three.
> I felt like a hundred.
> But, I'm like Archie Moore. We refuse to play dead. How can a man retire when the phone keeps ringing and he keeps getting good offers?
> That's the spirit, **Tracy**. You can do it [p. 9].

In addition to being dedicated to Stanley Kramer (among other celebrities), Michael P. Naughton's humorous crime novel *Deathryde: Rebel Without a Corpse* (2008) includes two references to the film—first as James DeRossa, a.k.a. James Dean, gives a signal on the phone to start the operation that is supposed to avenge his father's death, then as a part of Detective Hank Gladwin's deliberations:

> A woman's voice answered.
> "It's time to roll *Harold & Maude*," Dean said.
> The voice on the other end laughed.
> He grinned and continued with the instructions. "The procession has been set up and it's payback time. We'll meet at the Y tomorrow."
> "***It's a Mad, Mad, Mad, Mad World***," the voice on the end said.
> Dean joked, "Baby, Baby, It's a Wild World," quoting Cat Stevens.
> "At least with *Harold & Maude* in it," she said.
> "See you tomorrow," Dead said [p. 123].

On the drive back Gladwin thought about **Spencer Tracy** in *It's a Mad, Mad, Mad, Mad World*, and how old those crazy people were chasing the Smilers' money that was buried under the elusive "W" in Santa Rosita Park. **Jimmy Durante**'s voice echoed in his mind saying it's under the big "Dubya."

The big Dubya . . .

Where the hell is it?

Gladwin began to wonder if the *Operation Grim Reaper* tapes were just a ruse [p. 145].

Two references to the film appear in Kathryn Stockett's novel *The Help* (2009), both during a conversation between the narrator/protagonist, Skeeter Phelan, and her friend, Hilly Holbrook:

"We'll make it a double date, then."

I don't answer. I don't want Hilly and William coming along. I just want to sit with Stuart, have him look at me and only me. Twice, when we were alone, he brushed my hair back when it fell in my eyes. He might not brush my hair back if they're around.

"William'll telephone Stuart tonight. Let's go to the picture show."

"Alright," I sigh.

"I'm just dying to see *It's a Mad, Mad, Mad, Mad World*. Won't this be fun," Hilly says. You and me and William and Stuart."

It strikes me as suspicious, the way she's arranged the names. As if the point were for William and Stuart to be together instead of me and Stuart. I know I'm being paranoid. But everything makes me wary now [p. 206].

I stare at her, my best friend, trying to see just what she's read in my things. But her smile is professional if not sparkling. The telling moments are gone.

"Can I get you something to sip on?"

"No, I'm fine." Then I add, "Want to hit balls at the club later? It's so gorgeous out."

"William's got a campaign meeting and then we're going to see **It's a Mad, Mad, Mad, Mad World**."

I study her. Didn't she ask me, just two hours ago, to double-date to this movie tomorrow night? Slowly I move down to the end of the dining table, like she might pounce on me if I move too fast. She picks up a sterling fork from the sideboard, thrums her index finger along the tines.

"Yes, um, I heard **Spencer Tracy**'s supposed to be divine." I say. Casually, I tick through the papers in my satchel [p. 212].

Guess Who's Coming to Dinner (1967). A winner of two Academy Awards, one for Katharine Hepburn and one for William Rose (script), and eight additional nominations, including two for Stanley Kramer (as producer and director) and one for Tracy, this was the great actor's last film. The picture also remains to be an important item in film history, even though it is quite controversial in terms of its message, which was probably well intended but rather missed. A reference to the film was found in several sources.

The film is mentioned, only a few years after its release, in James A. Michener's novel *The Drifters* (1971) as one more example of the juxtaposition in the perception of the American cinema by Holt and the group of young people:

> 'His pictures were mostly corn,' Cato said. 'Some of my white friends took me to see **Guess Who's Coming to Dinner?** What crap.'
>
> Suddenly Holt shot his hand out and grabbed Cato by the arm. 'Don't ridicule what you don't understand,' he said grimly;

then, seeming ashamed of himself for having lost his temper, he stomped upstairs and a few minutes later we heard streaming from his tape recorder "The Stars and Stripes Forever" and "From the Halls of Montezuma" [p. 507-508].

Katharine Hepburn and Spencer Tracy as Christina and Matt Drayton in Stanley Kramer's *Guess Who's Coming to Dinner* (1967).

It should not be surprising that it is also one of the thirty Tracy films mentioned in Michael B. Druxman's play *Tracy* (1984). Here is what Druxman says about the movie through Tracy's mouth:

> Thank you **Stanley Kramer** for <u>**Gues Who's Coming to Dinner**</u>. The Old Bucko needed this "last hurrah," if that's what it's to be.
> (*Rises*)
> The script's about a liberal, well-to-do couple, **Kate** and myself, whose daughter plans to marry a prominent black doctor. **Kate**'s niece, **Katherine Houghton**, is the daughter and **Sidney Poitier** plays the doctor.

There's a spot during my seven page speech ... after I've been lectured by the prospective groom's mother ...

Most of the moment is played by **Kate**.

LIGHTS ADJUST, *as he goes into scene.*

"Mrs. Prentiss says that like her husband, I'm a burnt-out old shell of a man who cannot even remember what it's like to love a woman the way her son loves my daughter. And, strange as it seems, that's the first statement made to me all day with which I'm prepared to take issue, because I think you're wrong. You're as wrong as can be.

"I admit that I hadn't considered it ... hadn't even thought about ... but I know exactly how he feels about her, and there is nothing ... absolutely nothing ... that your son feels for my daughter that I didn't feel for Christina.

"Old, yes. Burnt-out, certainly. But, I can tell you. The memories are still there ... clear, intact, indestructible ... and they'll be there if I live to be 110" [p. 69].

A reference to the film in William X. Kienzle's mystery *No Greater Love* (1999) is a part of a passage revealing the thoughts of Andrea Zawalich, a woman deeply hurt by the fact that her gender prevents her from becoming a priest:

Sometimes after she had been unilaterally rejected, someone told her the story of Branch Rickey and how he had integrated professional baseball by signing the uniquely talented Jackie Robinson to play for the Brooklyn Dodgers. Robinson was baseball's version of **Sidney Poitier** in <u>*Guess Who's Coming to Dinner*</u>. It helps the cause if one integrates with the very best of any race, color, or creed [p. 170].

Stuart M. Kaminsky includes a reference to the film in his novel *Midnight Pass* (2003). It takes place in a scene where John Gutcheon, a receptionist at the building where Sally Porovsky works, tells Fonesca about his parents:

> "My parents are very understanding people," he explained. "Very liberal. They walked out on **_Guess Who's Coming to Dinner?_** when they first saw it. Couldn't accept that a beautiful man like **Sidney Poitier**, who played a world-famous, wealthy and brilliant surgeon, would be in love with that dolt of a white girl" [p. 75].

In Jeffrey Cohen's already mentioned novel *It Happened One Knife* (2008), narrator/movie theater proprietor Elliot Freed shares his views on the assets and weaknesses of certain films:

> I'd already limited myself to comedy films, and half the time to those made at least a quarter century ago. To further limit myself to comedy films from at least a quarter century ago that contained no material offensive to a Midland Heights audience would be to ensure constant showings of **_Guess Who's Coming to Dinner_** for the rest of my life, which wouldn't be long, since I would soon commit suicide. The movie's heart is in the right place, but, oh boy, is it dull! [p. 184]

An extensive and possibly most insightful reference to the film appears in Herman Koch's novel *The Dinner* (2009), as a side discussion between two married couples—Paul (the narrator, a retired, or rather "nonactive," history teacher) and Claire Lohman and Serge (Paul's older brother, a politician) and Babette Lohman—as they meet in an exclusive restaurant for dinner to address some serious problems of their children:

> After that, we went back to films for a little bit. Claire

said that **_Guess Who's Coming to Dinner?_** was "the most racist movie ever." Everyone knows the story, set in the late 1960s. The daughter of a wealthy white couple (played by **Spencer Tracy** and **Katharine Hepburn**) brings her new fiancé home to meet her parents. To their great dismay, the fiancé (played by **Sidney Poitier**) turns out to be black. During dinner, the truth gradually becomes clear: the black man is a good black man, an intelligent black man in a nice suit, a university professor. In intellectual terms, he is far superior to the white parents of his fiancé, who are mediocre, upper-middle-class types chock-full of prejudices concerning Negroes.

"And that's precisely where the racist hook comes in, in those prejudices," Claire had said. "The black people the parents know about, from TV and the neighborhoods where they're afraid to go, are poor and lazy and violent criminals. But their future son-in-law, fortunately, is a well-adapted Negro, who has put on the white man's neat three-piece suit. In order to look as much like the white man as he can."

Serge looked at my wife with the look of an interested listener, but his body language betrayed the fact that he found it hard to listen to any woman he couldn't immediately place in simple categories like "tits," "nice ass," or "wouldn't kick her out of bed for eating crackers."

"It wasn't until much later that the first unadapted blacks appeared in movies," Claire said. "Blacks who wore baseball caps and drove flashy cars: violent blacks from the worst neighborhoods. But at least they were themselves. They were no longer some watered-down version of a white man."

...

"And what's bad about adapted black people, Claire?" he [Serge] said. "I mean, to hear you tell it, you'd rather have them remain themselves, even if that means they go on killing each other in their ghettos over a few grams of crack. With no prospect of improvement."

...

"I'm not talking about improvement, Serge," Claire said. "I'm talking about the way we—Dutch people, white people, Europeans—look at other cultures. The things we're afraid of. If a group of dark-skinned men was coming toward you down the sidewalk, wouldn't you feel a stronger urge to cross the street if they were wearing baseball caps, rather than neat clothing? Like yours and mine? Or like diplomats? Or office clerks?"

...

"In order to understand what this lady was saying about her upstairs neighbors," I went on, because no one else was saying anything, "you have to turn the situation around. If the two sweet homosexuals hadn't fed the cats at all but instead had pelted them with stones or tossed poisoned pork chops down to them from their balcony, then they would have been just plain dirty faggots. I think that's what Claire meant about ***Guess Who's Coming to Dinner?*** That the friendly **Sidney Poitier** was a sweet boy too. That the person who made that movie was absolutely no better than the lady in that program. In fact, **Sidney Poitier** was supposed to serve as a role model. An example for all those nasty Negroes, the uppity Negroes. The dangerous Negroes, the muggers and the rapists and the crack dealers. When you people put on a good-looking suit like **Sidney**'s and start behaving like the perfect son-in-law, we white folks will be your friends" [pp. 77-80].

In Barbara Kingsolver's novel *Flight Behavior* (2012), a reference to the film is made during a telephone conversation between two close friends, in which one informs the other about inviting a total stranger to supper:

"You're the one with the international man of mystery coming to supper. Possibly the leader of the free world."

"Yeah, I better get cracking," Dellarobia said. "My house looks like the toxic waste dump of the free world."

"Hey," Dovey said. "You all are just like ***Guess Who's Coming to Dinner!***"

"What do you mean?"

"You know, that old movie. Where the white girl brings home her boyfriend and her parents freak out because he turns out to be **Sidney Poitier**."

"Gosh, that rings a bell. **Sidney Poitier**." Dellarobia felt deranged, losing familiar names and movie titles. She used to check out movies from the library by the half dozen, along with every book that wasn't nailed down. . . .

Dovey wouldn't give up on her theatrical revelation. "You have to have seen ***Guess Who's Coming to Dinner***. They do these, like **Hepburn**athons on Turner [p. 109].

During a career that spanned nearly four decades, Tracy appeared in about seventy-five pictures, a number very similar to that of both Bogart and Gable. He collaborated with numerous directors of the highest caliber, most frequently with George Cukor and Victor Fleming (five films with each), Frank Borzage and Stanley Kramer (four times with each), and John G. Blystone, W. S. Van Dyke and John Sturges (three movies with each). His most notable two-time collaborators include John Ford (not counting *How the West Was Won*, in which Tracy was the narrator only and Ford directed one of five episodes), Jack Conway, Mervyn LeRoy, Vincente Minnelli and Edward Dmytryk. While Katharine Hepburn holds the absolute record of starring with Tracy in as many as nine films, there are some other major actresses that appeared opposite him more than once—Joan Bennett (in four pictures), Claire Trevor and Hedy Lamarr (in three each), and Sally Eilers, Jean Harlow, Myrna Loy, Lana Turner and Elizabeth Taylor (in two each).

It is also worth pointing out that Van Johnson, just like Clark Gable, appeared opposite Tracy in three pictures, and so did Mickey Rooney, with the number not including *Young Tom Edison*, a film in which Tracy appeared in an uncredited cameo as a man admiring a portrait of Thomas A. Edison. By a strange coincidence, Tracy and Rooney played the famous scientist in two biographical movies which were released the same year (1940). Another interesting trivia is related to Tracy and Fredric March. March won an Oscar for his titular role in the 1932 version of *Dr. Jekyll and Mr. Hyde*, and Tracy appeared in the 1941 version of the classic Robert Louis Stevenson story. In 1960, they met on the set of *Inherit the Wind*—not only to compete professionally as actors, but also to compete as lawyers in their respective characterizations as Defense Attorney Henry Drummond and Prosecutor Matthew Harrison Brady in the famous monkey trial.

Spencer Tracy and Katharine Hepburn as Grant and Mary Matthews in a scene from Frank Capra's *State of the Union* (1948), one of Tracy's several relatively significant films with no references found.

There are as many as thirty-nine Tracy films, more than a half of his total number, referenced in this publication. The largest numbers of allusions were found to *Boys Town* and *Inherit the Wind*—fourteen to each; the runners-up in this respect include *Adam's Rib* (nine), *Captains Courageous* and *Bad Day at Black Rock* (eight each), *Guess Who's Coming to Dinner* (seven), *Test Pilot* (six), *San Francisco*, *Boom Town*, *Woman of the Year* and *The Old Man and the Sea* (five each), and *Thirty Seconds Over Tokyo*, *Father of the Bride* and *It's a Mad, Mad, Mad, Mad World* (four each). Thus, the two films that brought Tracy his Academy Awards are among those at the top of the list, which also covers all the movies for which the actor won the additional Oscar nominations. Tracy's other important pictures are also represented here; however, two of his unquestioned masterpieces, *Fury* and *Judgment at Nuremberg*, deserve much more attention from writers than they got, with a reference to the former found in one source only and to the latter in two. Besides, it is rather disappointing that no reference was found to such relatively significant pictures as Victor Fleming's *Tortilla Flat* (1942, from John Steinbeck's remarkable novel), Elia Kazan's *The Sea of Grass* (1947, from a superior novel by Conrad Richter), Frank Capra's *State of the Union* (1948, Tracy's only Capra film, with Hepburn co-starring), John Sturges's *The People Against O'Hara* (1951, a memorable crime drama from a novel by Eleazar Lipsky) and Edward Dmytryk's *Broken Lance* (1954, a western version of *The Brothers Karamazov*).

II. REFERENCES TO TRACY: THE MAN, THE ACTOR, THE CELEBRITY

Despite being a two-time Academy Award winner by the end of the 1930s, Tracy did not seem to be recognized by fiction authors until the early 1940s. One of the very first references to the actor was found in F. Scott Fitzgerald's unfinished novel *The Last Tycoon* (1940/41). In the quoted excerpt, Cecilia Brady (the book's narrator, a daughter of a big movie producer) relates the meeting between production manager Monroe Stahr (on whom she has a crush) and a rather unwelcome guest, Brimmer:

> Brimmer, the Party Member, was announced, and going to meet him I slid over to the door on one of those gossamer throw-rugs and practically into his arms.
>
> He was a nicer-looking man, this Brimmer—a little on the order of **Spencer Tracy**, but with a stronger face and a wider range of reactions written up in it. I couldn't help thinking as he and Stahr smiled and shook hands and squared off, that they were two of the most alert men I had ever seen [p. 156].

Based on such a description of Brimmer, it is not surprising that it took an actor of Jack Nicholson's talent and versatility to be able to portray him in the movie version of the book.

Spencer Tracy in a publicity shot.

In another novel concerned with Hollywood, Budd Schulberg's *What Makes Sammy Run?* (1941), Tracy and Marlene Dietrich are repeatedly mentioned in an extensive passage explaining the skillful manipulation behind a certain project:

> The story of how he did it was so intriguing that we both forgot to order. Sammy would walk up to a director and say, "**Spencer Tracy** and Marlene Dietrich in *Titanic*. Do I have to say any more?"
>
> Then he would just walk away from the guy, significantly, and leave it in his lap. The director has been desperate for a socko story all year. **Tracy** and Dietrich in *Titanic*. Jesus, it sounds like something. Natural suspense. And two great characters. Maybe **Spence** is a good two-fisted minister who tries to straighten Marlene out. Marlene is a tramp, of course. He's real. She's anything for a laugh. Then, even though the boat is going down you bring the audience up with a hell of a lift because Marlene suddenly sees the light.
>
> Meanwhile Sammy bumps into a supervisor. "I was just telling Chick Tyler my new story," he says. "He went off nut about it. **Spencer Tracy** and Marlene Dietrich in *Titanic*. Do I have to say any more?"
>
> . . .
>
> Now Sammy manages to cross the path of the General Manager in Charge of Production. Sammy has heard that he's been a little burned lately because people are saying he is losing touch with studio activities.
>
> "How do you do, sir," Sammy says. "I suppose Tyler and Hoyt have told you my story for Dietrich and **Tracy**. *Titanic*? Everybody who's heard it seems very excited about it."
>
> He has heard about Glick, of course, and he never likes to appear ignorant of anything. "Yes, I have, Glick," he says.

"Sounds very interesting. I'm going to call you all in for a conference on it some time this week" [pp. 162-163].

Tracy, along with Gable and Mickey Rooney, is also mentioned in another novel by Schulberg, *The Harder They Fall* (1947), in a passage describing Eddie Lewis's boxing-match publicity efforts in California:

> The pictures we knocked off were right down the old Graflex groove. There must be something about the chemistry of a press agent and a still camera that makes it impossible for them to produce any other kinds of pictures except the ones I set up at Metro—Toro squaring off with Mickey Rooney standing on a box; Toro with a couple of pretty stock-girls in bathing suits feeling his muscles; Toro on the set with **Clark Gable** and **Spencer Tracy** showing off the size of his fist. "Two stars see fist that will make Coombs see more stars," I captioned that one [p. 188].

A brief reference to the actor appears in James M. Cain's mystery *Love's Lovely Counterfeit* (1942), in a passage describing the reaction of Ben Grace, mafia boss Sol Caspar's chauffeur, after listening in his hotel room to the radio announcement in which June Lyons, the Mayor's close associate, discloses a hook-up, the alliance between the crime, the Mayor and the police:

> An exultant light in his eye, Ben snapped off the radio. Then, moving with catlike silence, he went to the door, jerked it open. The hall was empty. Then he put on his coat, picked up his hat, and went out to the **Tracy** picture at the Rialto [p. 220].

The actor is also mentioned in William Bradford Huie's novel *Mud on the Stars* (1942), the basis for Elia Kazan's movie *Wild River* (1960), in a passage that includes a sarcastic comment about the prospects of an aspiring actor:

> I met Chick and Bob in Margaret's place. They liked to place bets, but they were "slow pay" and Margaret never encouraged them to play. Chick was from Syracuse—he had finished at Cornell—and Bob was from South Dakota and the University of Illinois. They shared an apartment. Chick worked intermittently at something-or-other, and he had a girl who worked for Postal Telegraph who gave him money. Bob was an actor-in-waiting. In three years he had been rewarded with two routine movie tests, so his future was assured. He had only to wait around and pick up a few bit parts at Pasadena Playhouse. **Spencer Tracy** couldn't live forever [p. 188].

John O'Hara mentions Tracy in at least two of his works. In the novel *From the Terrace* (1958), the actor is one of several celebrities participating in a dinner party at Romanoff's. The second of the two quotations involving Tracy and Gary Cooper (from p. 959) is presented in Part Two (on Cooper); the first one is presented below:

> Fritz and Annabella Warren's dinner party was at Romanoff's, in a small diningroom off the front room. **Gary Cooper, Spencer Tracy,** Antonio Moreno, Irene Dunne, Loretta Young, and Constance Bennett were there to give Sadie Warren some movie names to remember. Robert Benchley, a Harvard classmate of Fritz Warren's, and James Malloy, a novelist whom Sadie admired, were there. The others were naturalized or first-generation Southern Californians whose Somerset-Chilton connections were as active as though they had only moved to Albany [p. 957].

O'Hara's "James Francis and the Star" (probably written in the mid-1960s) is a novella set mostly in Los Angeles before, during and after World War II. It relates the ups and downs of a relationship between writer John Francis Hatter and his protégé, movie star Rod Fulton. Here is a part of their dialogue at the time before the young actor hit it big:

> "I wish *I* thought so," Rod had said. "I'm about ready to go back and start hitting the managers' offices in New York."
> "Not till you click here," said James Francis. "I won't let you. These muzzlers out here gave **Gable** the same kind of a run-around. **Tracy**. Astaire. I could name you a dozen. With a dame it's different. A dame can make it on her back, whereas there aren't many producers that are fairies. So be patient a little while longer" [p. 183].

Tracy and a few other famous actors from Hollywood's golden period are recurrent names in Harold Robbins's novel *The Carpetbaggers* (1961). Set in the executive and artistic circles of the movie industry, the book is a fictionalized epic about one of the greatest moguls. Here are some excerpts of passages utilizing the real names from the dream factory and, indirectly, pointing out at the ambiguity of fame:

> "Only because he never gave me a chance." Dan grinned mirthlessly. "Now it's his turn to sweat a little. I'm waiting to see how he likes it." He walked angrily to the door but by the time he turned back to David, his anger seemed to have disappeared. "Keep in touch, David. There's an outside chance I could spring **Tracy** and **Gable** from **Metro** on loan if you came up with the right property" [p. 483].
> I could see the quick look of confidence come into his eyes. "Get a couple of big names," he said. "Use the girl if you want

but back her up. **Bogart**. <u>**Tracy**</u>. Colman. **Gable**. Flynn. Any one of them insures it for you."

"I suppose you can get them for me?"

He missed the sarcasm. "I think I could help," he said cautiously.

...

I shook my head. "Stars are great, I'm not fighting them. But not this time. We're doing a story based on the Bible. When somebody looks up at that screen at John or Peter, I want them to see John or Peter, not **Gable**, <u>**Tracy**</u> or **Bogart**. Besides, the girl is the important thing" [p. 520].

In Gore Vidal's novel *Myra Breckinridge* (1968), in addition to the references to *Boom Town*, *The Seventh Cross* and *Thirty Second Over Tokyo*, Tracy himself is mentioned, once again, among other movie stars of the golden period:

If only Myron could have seen this! Of course he would have been saddened by the signs of decay. The spirit of what used to be has fled. Most dreadful of all, NO FILM is currently being made on the lot; and that means that the twenty-seven huge sound stages which saw the creation of many miracles: **Gable**, Garbo, Hepburn (Katharine), Powell, Loy, Garland, <u>**Tracy**</u> and James Craig are now empty except for a few crews making television commercials [p. 34].

James A. Michener's novel *The Drifters* (1971) contains an abundance of references to both Tracy and Bogart. Quoted below are two passages (out of a few—the others are presented in Part One, on Bogart) that explain the reasons for the series of references, followed by an excerpt related to the overall Tracy-Hepburn collaboration:

There was another subject for which Holt used a specialized vocabulary: the general area of life itself, the passions, triumphs and despairs that overtake the average man. For here he related all value judgments to **Spencer Tracy** and **Humphrey Bogart** [p. 461].

Because **Tracy** and **Bogart** summarized the best that America was producing in those middle decades, Holt remembered almost every picture they had made and considered it appropriate that they had never appeared in the same film. 'They wouldn't have fitted,' he said when I asked him about this. 'Completely different men.' He did not say, 'Their styles were different.' He said that as men they would have clashed, for he saw them not as actors but as living men who happened to be thrust into evocative situations [p. 463].

Holt turned completely around in his chair so that he could stare at Gretchen. 'It's just dawned on me. Sometimes you're stupid. You got fine marks in college, I'm sure, but you're stupid. You know, if you had seen those great pictures in which **Mr. Tracy** and **Miss Hepburn** tried to adjust to each other—good man, good woman, but all man and all woman . . .' He hesitated, then said quietly, 'Maybe, Miss Gretchen, you would now know how to get along with men better than you do' [p. 507].

The mistake in Harvey Holt's conviction that Tracy and Bogart had never been in the same picture is addressed in the entry on *Up the River*.

In Larry McMurtry's novel *All My Friends Are Going to Be Strangers* (1972), Tracy is mentioned at the end of a scene where the book's narrator/protagonist, young novelist Danny Deck, meets with Hollywood producer Leon O'Reilly to discuss a project based on his first novel and is flabbergasted by the enormous changes that O'Reilly suggests to be put in the storyline:

Then he decided it might be even more dramatic if the bad

son had a wife who was secretly in love with the good son but was too good a woman to break her marriage vows. "There's conflict for you," Leon said. "You're wonderful to work with, you know." When five o'clock came I was exhausted, not from talking or even from thinking, but just from listening. Leon had not so much as loosened his tie all day, and his eyes were as bright as they had been when he was hacking at the raw fish.

"I think we're solid," he said, when he shook my hand. I'll have Juney type this up in outline form and send it right off to you. It's not to be considered restrictive, of course. Feel free to invent and embroider. I want Brando and Burton for the two sons, maybe **Spencer Tracy** for the old man. Think what a picture that would make [p. 137].

William Goldman's *Magic* (1976) is a psychological thriller about the unusual life and career of an unusual entertainer named Corky Withers. In the following scene, which depicts a conversation between Corky and a woman he meets in the Garden Court of the Frick Museum in the middle of Manhattan, where Corky unexpectedly begins to weep, Miss Flanagan, because this is her name, compares the protagonist to the famous actor:

> She sat down alongside him on the bench. "I'm Miss Flanagan, what's your name?"
> "Corky people call me."
> "Why really were you crying—I'm a terrible snoop."
> "You'll laugh."
> "Never at tears."
> "I got a piece of wonderful news yesterday."
> "I'm not laughing," Miss Flanagan said. "But that's not to say I don't see the humor."
> "Why are you looking at me like that?" Corky said.
> "Before I've noticed you before and you've always reminded

me of somebody and I just realized who. You look like a young **Spencer Tracy**."

"Big ears and big nose you mean?"

She shook her head. "It's in the eyes. I believe you. You should run for president. I always thought that **Spencer Tracy** would have made a wonderful president."

...

"I go that way. Let me taxi you home."

"I'm not in the habit of traveling with strange men."

"I only drink blood on Tuesdays," Corky told her.

She studied his eyes. "Just like **Spencer Tracy**," she said, she held out her arm [p. 16].

In Andrew J. Fenady's *The Man with Bogart's Face* (1977), Tracy is mentioned twice. The first reference is a part of the passage where the narrator reveals private eye Sam Marlow's thoughts to the reader at the turning point of his life (when—through plastic surgery—he has assumed Bogart's heroes' persona along with the actor's physical appearance):

> Well, this is it, Sam thought to himself. Clients. Cases. Danger. Dough. Just like the old days. The Saturday matinees. When there were good guys and bad guys. When there were **Gable**s and **Tracy**s – Garfields and Powells (Dick and William) – yes, and **Bogart**. The real article. There was never anybody else like **Bogart** – up to now [p. 20].

Then, Tracy's name, along with several others, appears in a scene describing the beginning of an erotic feast offered to Sam by his irresistible client, Gena Anastas:

> The prelude was over; the cymbals clashed and the symphony started. It was all the music ever played – all the love

songs ever written – birds on the wing – the beat beat beat of the tom-toms – till the end of time – something to remember you by – Sunday, Monday, or always – dancing in the dark – I've got you under my skin. It was Gilbert and Garbo, **Gable** and Garson, **Tracy** and Hepburn, Ladd and Lake, **Bogart** and Bacall [p. 92].

In the sequel, *The Secret of Sam Marlow* (1980), Fenady also includes references to all four of the stars, and two of them are mentioned in the following passage reminiscing about the good old years in Hollywood:

In the salad days of cinema—the thirties and forties—every studio had a personality. An aura, almost an aroma. MGM was the biggest, most star-splattered. And it knew how to show its stars to best advantage. Huge, glowing close-ups that were practically portraits. Under Louis B. Mayer it was the most American of studios. Mom's apple pie. Upbeat. **Gable**, Garbo, Garson, **Tracy**, Hepburn, and Turner. With a couple of Taylors—Robert and Elizabeth. Glamour [p. 17].

Adam Kennedy's novel *Just Like Humphrey Bogart* (1978) is also one of quite a large number of books including references to all four great movie stars that are the subject matter of this publication. The names of Tracy and Cooper appear together in a passage where Paul Lincoln, a rich and well-connected man, offers advice and help to the narrator/protagonist, aspiring young actor Duffy Odin:

"I know you're not. And neither am I. In the business everybody will know what your real name is. We'll see to that. I'll help you. But the public is something else. Between Newark and Pasadena they don't care if you're Jewish but they'd rather you didn't have a Jewish name. **Tracy**. **Cooper**. McQueen.

Those are the names the public likes. The best thing for you is to call yourself Duffy Ryan. I've thought about it. It's a good Irish name. Robert Ryan's dead now so you won't be confused with him. Fine man, Robert Ryan. Serious actor and a terrific athlete. Did you know that?" [p. 108].

In Sam Shepard's play *Fool for Love* (1983), a reference to Tracy is made in a long monologue by Eddie, as he tells a story to Martin and the Old Man:

> We could barely see a foot in front of us, it was so dark. And these white owls kept swooping down out of nowhere, hunting for jackrabbits. Diving right past our heads, then disappearing. And we just kept walking silent like that for miles until we got to town. I could see the drive-in movie way off in the distance. That was the first thing I saw. Just square patches of color shifting. Then vague faces began to appear. And, as we got closer, I could recognize one of the faces. It was **Spencer Tracy**. **Spencer Tracy** moving his mouth. Speaking without words. Speaking to a woman in a red dress. Then we stopped at a liquor store and he made me wait outside in the parking lot while he bought a bottle [p. 49].

Tracy's name appears in the title of Sam Shepard's tale "Spencer Tracy Is Not Dead" (1990) and then is used several times by the narrator, an actor who has problems trying to cross the American-Mexican border due to preposterous formalities:

> His hands, clasped in front of his belt, hold the forms that he's carried from the border control. He seems completely bewildered by this shift of attitude and out of his depth. "What's your name?" she persists.
>
> "My name is **Spencer Tracy**," I tell her.

"**Spencer Tracy**? It's **Spencer Tracy**, Maria!" she screams across the room, then catches herself and looks hard at my face, as though studying one of her immigration forms. "**Spencer Tracy** the actor? No."

"Yes, ma'am. The very one."

"No, but you're famous, I know that. I've seen you. What's your real name? **Spencer Tracy** is dead."

"Nope. He's very much alive."

At this point, all the secretaries and women officials, led by Maria, are prowling toward me like people who've heard there's a car wreck. "Maria! **Spencer Tracy** is dead, isn't he? Isn't he dead?" Maria is totally stumped, but she's clutching a little scrap of notepaper and a pen, just in case I'm somebody [pp. 192-193].

"Don't you recognize him?" They all shake their heads, but some of them shyly hold out their little slips of paper and ballpoint pens.

"Why do you want my autograph when you don't even recognize me?" I ask them.

"Because you're famous. You're **Spencer Tracy**" [pp. 193-194].

In Michael B. Druxman's play *Gable* (1984), the King of Hollywood speaks a lot about himself, but also a little about others. Here are some of the things he has to say, directly or indirectly, about his three-time co-star:

> That Monty Clift is really something. At times, he acts like he belongs in an institution, but . . .
>
> (*Shrugs, sits at dressing table.*)
>
> I watched him do a scene in a phone booth the other day. Fascinating talent. He's right up there with **Tracy** [p. 9].

Four Hollywood Legends

. . .

The Last Mile? I saw it on Broadway the other day with **Spencer Tracy**.

You want me to play Killer Mears? Are you nuts? I couldn't come close to **Tracy** [p. 22].

At the beginning of Joseph Wambaugh's cop novel *The Secrets of Harry Bright* (1985), there is a lengthy description of Palm Springs which includes references to several movie stars:

> So Palm Springs provided a refuge, a sanctuary between pictures. They all came: **Gable**, Lombard, Cagney, **Tracy**, Hepburn, the Marx Brothers, even Garbo. And no matter how fearful they might be about Time, those people who had to remain changeless, the desert had an answer even for that. The warm dry climate soothed arthritic pain, bursitis, lung disorders. Everyone started feeling more vigorous, playing tennis and golf, swimming, cavorting like Errol Flynn [p. 5].

In another novel by Wambaugh, *Fugitive Nights* (1992), a reference to Tracy and a few other movie stars takes place in a scene where private investigator Breda Burrows goes to a medical building in Palm Springs:

> Breda looked at her watch. Most physicians opened up at 9:00 A.M. In that Clive Devon's urologist was either stonewalling or knew nothing, she decided to take a shot at his G.P.
>
> The medical building wasn't far from Desert Hospital. In the days of **Gable**, **Tracy**, the Marx brothers, Garbo—in Palm Springs's golden age—the hospital had been the city's finest resort hotel, El Mirador [p. 168].

In Wambaugh's *Hollywood Station* (2006), two famous couples of movie stars are mentioned—in a clearly non-sequitur reference—during a conversation between two cops, Nathan Weiss (a.k.a. Hollywood Nate, due to his acting aspirations) and Wesley Drubb:

> "You don't say." Nate was gazing up at the luxurious apartment buildings and condos on both sides of his favorite Los Angeles street.
>
> "They're usually identified by a tattoo of a black hand with an *M* on the palm of it. In the Pelican Bay Maximum Security Prison, an MM gang member had sixty thousand dollars in a trust account before it was frozen by authorities. He was doing deals from inside the strictest prison!"
>
> "Do tell." Nate imagined **Clark Gable** in a black tie and Carole Lombard in sable, both smiling at the doorman as they went off for a night on the town. At the Coconut Grove, maybe.
>
> Then he tailored a fantasy to fit **Tracy** and Hepburn, even though he knew that neither of them had ever lived on the street. But what the hell, it was his fantasy [pp. 241-242].

In Stuart M. Kaminsky's *The Man Who Shot Lewis Vance* (1986), Sergeant John Cawelti, a cop who does not like private eye Peters but hopes to meet his client, John Wayne, who is in danger of being killed, pays an indirect compliment to Tracy:

> Patterson shrugged, but Cawelti didn't see him.
>
> "Wayne's the only damn movie star who means anything except for **Spencer Tracy**," Cawelti explained. "I'll get on it but you better be giving me this straight. And what's it all got to do with you?" [p. 56]

Four Hollywood Legends

In Marcia Muller's mystery *Trophies and Dead Things* (1990), narrator Sharon McCone finds a lot of videos while clearing out the apartment of a murdered client of All Souls Legal Cooperative, a company at which she works as staff investigator:

> There were hundreds of them, stacked against the wall behind the TV: **Bogart, Tracy** and Hepburn, Barbara Stanwyck, William Powell, Cary Grant; a full run of Charlie Chans and Mr. Motos and the Topper series; westerns, comedies, drama. Not one of them had been produced later than the mid-fifties. It made me wonder if Hilderly hadn't been trying to pretend the sixties and seventies and eighties had never happened [p. 12].

John Dandola's *West of Orange* (1990) is a novel in which Spencer Tracy is one of the special guests at the world premiere of *Edison, the Man*, about to take place in four Orange towns in New Jersey. Various forms of the actor's name—Spencer Tracy, Tracy, Mr. Tracy or Spence—appear on numerous pages of this 'mystery set against movie history.' Here are some of the passages worth quoting:

> "Tuxedos, gentlemen," Dietz cautioned.
> "They were fitted this morning," Edie answered for them.
> "How's **Spence**?"
> "*Kvetching* as usual. Strickling's coming in with them on Wednesday morning."
> "So, Louise is coming? They battling?"
> "No, more like one hand doesn't know what the other's doing. She's so wrapped up in her deaf children programs and he's always at the studio. They never seem to talk. The Catholic Church should reconsider divorce" [p. 140].

At ten-twenty, everything came to a sudden stand-still. **Spencer Tracy** appeared through a rear entrance, his wife on his arm, a broad smile on his face, his shock of red hair making him the most noticeable man in the armory.

Spencer Tracy was in complete control of the moment in the way only a master actor or a master politician can be. He went immediately to speak with the widow Edison and her children [pp. 191-192].

William Diehl's mystery *Primal Fear* (1993) contains a reference to several actors from the golden era in a description of a Chicago district as seen by the book's protagonist, defense attorney Martin Vail:

> The main street had changed very little in ten years. The stores all looked the same, except several had been bought out by the big chains, and the Ritz, the movie theater which had shown old classics on Sunday night and introduced him to Cagney, O'Brien, Robinson, **Bogart**, **Tracy** and Busby Berkeley, had been converted into a flea market. He passed Shick Madison's barbershop and a tinge of hurt stung his chest. He stopped for a minute and stared at the sidewalk in front of the shop [p. 189].

The actor's name is also mentioned in Jennifer Lash's Irish novel *Blood Ties* (1997). Here the pretext is an attempt to find the possible connotations of the name given to a newborn and unwanted baby by its mother:

> Dolly slept. Tug came. The baby slept. Everyone said, 'What's his name?' 'He's Spencer,' Dolly said, simply to stop them all asking. It was after the pub. Those thick gold letters which she read every day. Maybe it was after all pubs. And also, Dolby knew that Lumsden had said there was this poet called Spencer. He had told her that in the bar one day. The

nurses thought of **Spencer Tracy**. Tug said it was a bit strange, it should be a saint's name. Tug was still hoping Dolly would come round to the idea of Catholic adoption. 'Bottle or breast,' they said. Dolly said bottle. She feared that damp, crumpled little mouth so close to her [p. 222].

In Stuart Woods's mystery *Dead Eyes* (1994), temporarily blind movie star Chris Calloway and Jon Larsen, a policeman protecting her from a dangerous stalker, have lunch at the Racket Club in Pam Springs, where they talk about movie stars:

> "This place was owned by Charlie Farrell, who was a big-time agent, and the actor Ralph Bellamy," Chris said. "It was *the* place to be seen in the old days. I sometimes wish I had been in Hollywood during the thirties. I think I'd have liked being cossetted by MGM, having all my decisions made for me. The money's better these days, but I think it must be a lot harder that it was."
>
> "My favorite movies were made then," Larsen said. "Fred Astaire and Ginger Rogers, **Gable**, Jimmy Stewart, Cary Grant, Katharine Hepburn, **Spencer Tracy**."
>
> "I'd give anything to have worked with **Spencer Tracy**," she said. "He may be the best actor the movies ever produced."
>
> "I can't disagree" [p. 117].

Another mystery by Woods, *The Prince of Beverly Hills* (2004), is set in Los Angeles, mostly in 1939. In the following passage, Centurion Studio's new chief of security, Rick Barron, and the Studio's main leading man, Clete Barrow, have dinner at (Dave) Chasen's Southern Pit; they meet Hedda Hopper and are surrounded by Hollywood celebrities:

> A waiter brought them a drink and menus, and Rick looked

around. Jack Benny and his wife were across the room, in a booth next to **Spencer Tracy** and a woman Rick assumed to be his wife. "This place must be catching on," he said, nodding toward the two stars.

Clete looked over and waved at **Tracy**. "Evening, **Spence**, Louise." He turned back to Rick. "Yes, word does get around when a place is good, and almost everything on the menu is. I do recommend the chili, though" [p. 84].

In another book by Woods, *Son of Stone* (2011), set in New York but related to the author's L.A. novels through the character of Vance Calder, a megastar now dead, Spencer Tracy, is mentioned, along with two other great actors, in a conversation between two employees of the *New York Post*, Kelli Keane (an ambitious gossip columnist) and Jess (a young movie buff from the Arts section):

"Jess."

"Kelli, how you doing?"

"Okay. You're a film buff, right?"

"Gee, how'd you guess? Could it be because I review them for the paper?"

"Tell me about Vance Calder."

"Hollywood great, up there with Jimmy Stewart, **Spencer Tracy**, and Cary Grant; five Academy Awards, eighteen nominations, both records for an actor. What else do you need to know?" [p. 118]

Loren D. Estleman's novel *Edsel* (1995) contains an extensive reference to *Bad Day at Black Rock* and a brief one to Tracy outside of that context. However, the two references are logically connected as the actor's name is mentioned again in a passage where the protagonist/narrator, journalist

Connie Minor, wonders about the fate of private detective J. W. Pierpont, last seen at the movie show:

> Something else had been absent for more than a year. As suddenly as the scrawny spectre of J. W. Pierpont had appeared in my life, it had just as suddenly left. I had neither seen nor heard from him since that night at the Bel-Air Drive-In when I had sicced him on Carlo Ballista in full view of God and **Spencer Tracy**. For months after that I had expected him to pop up any time [p. 275].

A reference to Tracy and Gable appears in George Baxt's novel *The William Powell and Myrna Loy Murder Case* (1996), in a passage where the narrator expresses Myrna Loy's thoughts about some of her co-stars (and one director):

> Powell yanked her away from the table and led the way to theirs. "Well, Minnie, it's been too long a time since we've lunched."
> "Three days, for God's sake."
> "That's much too long a time." Myrna smiled. She adored her friend. Not once since their first film together in 1934, *Manhattan Melodrama*, had he ever made a pass at her. Unlike **Spencer Tracy** and **Clark Gable** and Victor Fleming, who never ceased to try to force their attention on her. Her marriage to Arthur Hornblow hadn't dampened their enthusiasm, it just heightened the challenge [p. 7].

In John Updike's novel *In the Beauty of the Lilies* (1996), a reference to the actor becomes a part of Essie's thought about the Irish people and their religion:

She knew enough Irishmen—Patrick, for one, and the bachelor algebra teacher back in Basingstoke, Mr. O'Brien, and **Spencer Tracy** and Donald O'Connor, and indeed until the emergence of the Jews hadn't the Irish been the soul of American environment?—to understand how an unflappable charm and wit could enwrap a pinched, rigid private morality, a spoiled priesthood [pp. 353-354].

Tracy is mentioned—as one of the actors that have played priests on the screen—in William Kienzle's mystery *No Greater Love* (1999). The quoted excerpt reveals the thoughts of Bill Cody, a man who missed his vocation but wants to do his best for his son not to repeat his mistake:

As Bill coaxed the infant to wrap his tiny fingers around his father's thumb, he pictured his son the priest. Like the macho men of the past who weren't embarrassed to wear the clerical outfit. Who hung out together. Who hunted and fished on vacation together. Who displayed the pelts, the skins, the heads on their rectory walls. Who were portrayed in movies by the likes of **Spencer Tracy**, Gregory Peck, **Humphrey Bogart**, Barry Fitzgerald, and Bing Crosby. Men's men.

That was Bill's mission—to turn out a priest in this mold [p. 68].

In Adriana Trigiani's novel *Big Stone Gap* (2000), Tracy and some of his peers are mentioned in a passage where the book's narrator/protagonist, Ave Marie Mulligan, reminisces about the interests of her deceased mother:

Mama always took me to the movies over at the Trail Theater, right next to Zackie's. I didn't know it at that time, but Jim Roy Honeycutt, who owned the place, showed movies that were ten, fifteen years old. I never bothered to ask my mother why the people on the screen were wearing funny hats and hairdos; I just accepted it. It wasn't until years later that I found out Mr. Honeycutt saved a lot of money renting old prints. That's how I fell in love with the leading men of the 1930s and '40s: **Clark Gable**, William Powell, **Spencer Tracy**, Robert Taylor, and especially Joel McCrea. Mama loved the actresses, costumed by the great designers Edith Head, Adrian, and Travis Banton [p. 73].

James Ellroy's *The Cold Six Thousand* (2001) is a mystery set in the mid-1960s, with a plot related to John Kennedy's assassination. Tracy's name is mentioned in item #6 of a document insert, dated 2/8/65, of an internal memorandum sent to "Director" from "Blue Rabbit":

> 6 - Per MAIL COVERS. To date, assigned agents have intercepted, logged and remailed numerous letters of support, along with large and small donations to the SCLC, many of them sent by notable leftist-sympathizers, members of Communist front groups and movie stars, among them Danny Kaye, Burt Lancaster, Walter Pidgeon, Burl Ives, **Spencer Tracy**, Rock Hudson, Natalie Wood and numerous folk singers of lesser repute. (See Addendum List #B for details. Per guidelines, please read and burn.) [p. 364]

In Elizabeth Hay's novel *A Student of Weather* (2001), Tracy (along with Gable) is referenced in a series of comparisons initiated by Norma Joyce in a conversation with Maurice Dove:

"Who is more beautiful?" she asked him. "Katharine Hepburn or Carole Lombard?"

"They're both beautiful."

"But which one is *more* beautiful?"

He smiled. "All right. Katherine Hepburn."

"Why?"

"Better bones. But I like Carole Lombard."

"Why?"

"She's more fun, she's more natural." (A distinction she tucked away for future use and comfort; Katharine Hepburn only got **Spencer Tracy** while Carole Lombard got **Clark Gable**.)

"Do you think Katharine Hepburn's more beautiful than Mrs. Simpson?" [p. 87]

In another novel by Elizabeth Hay, *Garbo Laughs* (2003), Tracy is mentioned once in the context of *Woman of the Year* and once independently. The following passage is a part of the chapter in which the Gold family goes on vacation to Havana:

They found Frankie the very first morning, in the Hotel Nacional's Club of Fame, an airy glassed-in terrace overlooking an unused swimming pool. He was with Ava in the mural representing the fifties, and so was John Wayne, Nat King Cole, Mickey Mantle, Lola Flores, Yma Sumac, **Spencer Tracy**, Marlon Brando. But no Jean Simmons. A mural for each decade, with Buster Keaton, **Gary Cooper**, Jack Dempsey, and Meyer Lansky consigned to the thirties; Fred Astaire, Betty Grable, Rita Hayworth, and Churchill in the mural for the forties; García Márquez, Josephine Baker, Yuri Gagarin in the post-revolution sixties, Francis Ford Coppola in the seventies, Muhammed Ali in the eighties, and so on [p. 255].

Martha Sherrill's novel *My Last Movie Star* (2002) includes references to *Captains Courageous* (minor) and *Test Pilot* (major) in the part which is focused on Myrna Loy. While paying a ghostly visit to the book's narrator, journalist Clementine James, Myrna Loy has an opportunity to talk about many aspects of her life and career, including her male co-stars. Here is what she says about Tracy (with a few words thrown in by Dorothy Lamour):

> The old car turned north on Fairfax and began climbing toward Sunset. In the distance, the Hollywood Hills were brown and dotted with scrub brush and patches of green grass. I reached my hand out the window to feel the air.
>
> "So, were you in love with **Spencer Tracy**?" I asked.
>
> "Terrific actor," she replied.
>
> I laughed. "That's it? That's all you have to say?"
>
> . . .
>
> "I was always in love," **Myrna** said, looking at me. "There's really nothing more to add. I had crushes on people. I was always in love. That's just how it was. My first substantial role was in something called *Across the Pacific* with Monte Blue. Remember him?"
>
> . . .
>
> "And **Tracy**?"
>
> "Keeping ahead of him wasn't easy. Chased me for years and then sulked adorably when I married someone else. I think he was still heartbroken when we met—his big affair with Loretta had just ended."
>
> "Loretta Young?"
>
> "It wasn't much of a secret. And I gather she insisted that he do the right thing and return to his wife."
>
> "They didn't even hide it," said Dorothy.
>
> "No?"
>
> "**Spencer** drank," said **Myrna**. "He drank a lot. It seemed romantic then. He used to disappear for days. After a while, I got pretty good at figuring out when he was about to slip away. His eyes got dark and miserable. When we were making *Test Pilot*, he disappeared in the middle of filming. I drove all around

Riverside, where we were shooting, and went into every bar and flophouse I could find, looking for him." She rubbed the side of her face. "People don't seem to understand," she said, "how you can be terribly in love with somebody and not sleep with them. But I do."

"I guess he had a thing for redheads," I said. "Or strong women,"

Myrna didn't say anything, just drove for a while, but I could tell from her face that she was about to say something and trying to figure out how to say it.

"He hit her, you know," she said finally. "He'd hit Kate and yell at her and make cracks and insult her in public. It was very ugly sometimes. She'd just smile and nod. She stuck by him when nobody else wanted to. Strong woman. I guess she was strong, all right. She took it" [p. 250-252].

In the fifth chapter of James Neel White's historical book *I Was a P-51 Fighter Pilot in WWII* (2003), entitled Hollywood Stunt Pilots, Tracy's name appears in a passage listing the actors who portrayed pilots on the screen in the period prior to World War II:

Lead actors appeared as pilots in airplane movies in the late 1930s, but stunt pilots actually did the flying. The actors included James Cagney, Dennis Morgan, John Wayne, Frank Hawks, William Gargan, George Brent, John Payne, **Spencer Tracy**, William Boyd, Robert Young, Ralph Bellamy and Jack Holt. Stunt flyers' careers grew alongside the growth of the movie industry as a whole, but the public did not care if stunt pilots did the flying. The roles that actors played were believable enough [p. 25].

Marisa de los Santos's novel *Love Walked In* (2005) was mentioned earlier in this part of the book because of a reference to *Libeled Lady*, which was triggered by a character's resemblance to William Powell. Nonetheless, Tracy himself is mentioned by Santos just on the following page in a passage where narrator/protagonist Cornelia Brown describes her encounter with Martin Grace:

> This might not sound so earth-shattering to you, so fabulously clever or romantic, but trust me when I tell you that it was. Right from the start, we just had a cadence, and intuitive rhythm that I might possibly compare to the sixth sense that jazz musicians have when they're playing together if I knew the first thing about jazz. You've seen **Tracy**-**Hepburn** movies, yes? It was the conversation I'd been waiting for all my life [p. 10].

Laurence Klavan, in his novel *The Shooting Script* (2005), reminds us about two films that Tracy began shooting and was replaced by other actors:

> I stood there, mortified, I recalled that **Spencer Tracy** had been replaced by Gregory Peck in the movie *The Yearling*. The whole film had been remade from scratch, just like, well, a burnt loaf [p. 10].

> I froze. I remembered that James Cagney had replaced **Spencer Tracy** in Robert Wise's *Tribute to a Bad Man*. Composing myself, I swiveled slowly around [p. 238].

A reference to Tracy and his frequent co-star appears at the end of Sandra Brown's novel *Ricochet* (2006). Once the mystery is solved and justice served, the two protagonists and lovers, Duncan and Elise, are starting to plan their future together. Elise is thinking about reopening an old movie theater:

She frowned at his terminology, but continued her thought. "Not too far from your house, there's an old movie theater."

"Across from Forsyth Park? It's been there since the thirties. Hasn't been in operation for years."

"I was thinking it could be restored," she said hesitantly. "Very nicely. Make it a theater for classic movies only. *Giant, Lawrence of Arabia, Doctor Zhivago*. Big, epic movies like that. Or film noir. **Tracy** and Hepburn. There's an endless list of film festivals. It could host premieres. There could be a wine bar off the lobby, not just your ordinary concessions. It could also be rented for special events or programs, charity fund-raisers, corporate parties, conventions. Think of the convention business it could draw [p. 383].

Two references to Tracy were found in Jeffrey Cohen's *Some Like it Hot – Buttered* (2007). The first one is a part of a passage where Amy Ansella tells narrator/protagonist Elliot Freed about the character and habits of her deceased husband, a man that died in Elliot's Comedy Tonight movie theater:

"Although Vincent was usually a happy sort of guy; not in the annoying way, like one of those chipper little secretaries who is always wearing a pin to commemorate some holiday or another, but just . . . happy. He was glad to be alive. Things were always good for him. He never told jokes—he hated jokes—but he liked banter. He was always using lines from **Tracy** and **Hepburn** movies, or the Marx Brothers." Damn. Now I liked the guy [pp. 52-53].

The other excerpt is related to the previous one as it shows Elliot trying to catalogue the movies from Vincent Ansella's huge collection that he received from Amy:

Once I separated them, I could begin organizing by groups and classifications: all Bob Hopes in one section, all Red Skeltons in another, Cary Grants cross-referenced by **Katharine Hepburn**, who also had to be paired with **Spencer Tracy**. It became more elaborate as time went on, but it was a system that eventually would make sense to me, since I had invented it [pp. 235-236].

There is a clearly flattering reference to the actor in Maureen Johnson's novel *Suite Scarlett* (2008). The context of the scene is the arrival of a new guest, Amy Amberson, to Hopewell Hotel in New York, run by the Martins, whose four children's names are Scarlett, Spenser, Lola and Marlene.

"Amy Amberson," she said, all smiles. "I'm the new guest. I'll be here all summer."

"All summer?" Spencer repeated.

"I think it's adorable how you all do that," she said. "Spencer . . . another wonderful name. All associated with classic films. There's Marlene Dietrich, who played Lola in *The Blue Angel*. Scarlett, of course, is Scarlett O'Hara from **Gone with the Wind**. And Spencer is **Spencer Tracy**, one of the greatest leading men of all time [p. 77].

James Scott Bell's mystery *Try Fear* (2009) has a scene in which attractive District Attorney Kimberly Pincus invites lawyer/narrator Ty Buchanan, after he defeats her in court, to a drink. They talk about courtroom tactics and movies:

"If you were to be yourself, you'd have any jury wating out of your hand. See, the greatest actor of all time was **Spencer Tracy**."

"Yeah?'

"You know his work?"

"Not really."

I did. Jacqueline and I used to watch old movies. A lot. "**Tracy** was the best. **Bogart** said he was. Because you couldn't see the wheels turning. And somebody asked **Tracy** what his secret was, and all he said was, be yourself and listen to the other actor. But lawyers want to get up in court and put a show. If you really want to win, don't make it about Kimberly Pincus. Make it about justice. Make it about the People. Make it about—why am I telling you all this? I'm giving away the store" [p. 47].

Aaron Latham's mystery *Riding with John Wayne* (2006) includes three references to Tracy, all praising his acting method. His name is mentioned for the first time when Jamie Stone, the film director, gives instructions to Sarah, the leading lady:

"But what do I say?" she asks.

"We're not sure yet," Jamie says. "But that's where you stop and turn. If you don't, you'll be out of focus." A dire threat to any leading lady, much less ours. "Sarah, do you remember all those **Spencer Tracy** scenes that begin with his head bowed? Most people think that's because he was humble or contemplative, but that was never it at all. He was just looking for his mark because he didn't want to be fuzzy, and neither do you" [p. 277].

The actor is mentioned again when Jamie rehearses lines with Clyde Goodnight, the screenwriter's father and dialogue coach:

"Well, make believe I'm a tree. Talk tree-talk to me. What about that? Do I remind you of a tree? I mean any particular tree?"

My father studies Jamie, trying to see her as a tree.

"You're not one tree," he says softly, his eyes down. "You're lotsa trees." He looks up at her. "You're a whole forest of them trees."

"What do you mean?" Jamie asks, still reading every word, and sounding like it. Slightly stilted.

My father looks down again, like **Spencer Tracy** searching for his mark, but there isn't any mark. He is pensive [pp. 285-286].

The final reference to the actor's technique appears toward the end of the book, during a conversation between Jamie and screenwriter Chick Goodnight (the narrator of the book) regarding some bad news:

"Did Shelly call you?"
"No, it was Rick Livingston, you know, head of production. Shelley doesn't make this kind of call."

Imitating **Spencer Tracy**, I look down at the floor. I don't see any answers there [p. 313].

Ellen Cooney's *Lambrusco* (2008) is a novel set in Italy during World War II. Tracy is mentioned in it twice in reference to two minor characters: Frank Lamb, an American soldier, truck driver and medic (in the first excerpt), and Tom Tully (Tullio Tomasini), a U.S. Army Intelligence officer (in the second):

It used to be that he vowed to himself, his whole childhood and adolescence, that no matter what happened in his life he'd get married one time, and that would be that, but unfortunately, or very luckily, depending on how you looked at it, God had given him a disposition that was favorable for the ladies. He wasn't trying to be a braggart, but people often told him he resembled the great American actor **Spencer Tracy**.

Did I know who that was? In Hollywood he was a king. The greatest thing about him was that he proved you don't have to be suave or even handsome to have women adore you [p. 141].

And I was furious—*furious*—not at the attackers, whoever they were, but at that officer big shot, a stranger to me, heard of and never seen but looming largely, unexpectedly, in my mind: Tullio Tomasini. What was he doing in Italy? Had he come to be married to his *fidanzata* and spoil my hopes? Why was he involving himself with guns and partisans? Did he imagine himself a hero in a Hollywood movie, an Italo-American **Spencer Tracy**? [p. 160]

A reference almost summarizing all the Tracy-Hepburn films appears in David Rosenfelt's novel *Dog Tags* (2010), in a scene showing attorney Andy Carpenter (the narrator) and his wife Laurie negotiating how to spend the last couple of hours of their evening:

I don't have to be a math major to know that if the movie lasts two hours, we're not going to bed until at least ten thirty. That would be much later than my planned scheduled, which had me in a sexually satisfied sleep by ten o'clock.
"Haven't we seen this one already?" I ask.
"Of course. It's **Tracy** and Hepburn."
"As I recall, they argue and are completely incompatible for ninety minutes of the movie, and then they fall in love. I hope I didn't spoil the ending for you."
The ending is my favorite part," she says. "Let's watch this, okay? We can talk later" [p. 171].

A. D. Scott's debut novel *A Small Death in the Great Glen* (2010) is set in the Scottish Highlands of the 1950s. A reference to the actor is triggered by the resemblance between him and a minor character (a priest, naturally) in the book:

> Leaving a much-mildewed golf umbrella by the door, the man joined them. He requested a Guinness. McAllister looked furtively at the newcomer in the bar mirrors. The next Great White Hope with a good resemblance to **Spencer Tracy**, was McAllister's first impression. He waited a while for the Guinness and his heartbeat to settle, then, balancing three glasses, returned to the table.
>
> "Michael Kelly. You must be John McAllister." The priest stood, holding out a massive ham of hand.
>
> McAllister returned the handshake.
>
> "Sandy has told me some of your story. I'm deeply sorry about your brother [p. 171].

Rachel Shukert's novel *Starstruck* (2013) is, needless to say, set in Hollywood. Among its numerous movie references, there are two passages that include Spencer Tracy's name: one relating a lovers' quarrel and one listing a mixture of real and fictitious movie stars.

> Amanda shook her head. "I can't. It's with a producer over in Max Wineman's division."
>
> "I see." Pushing her away, Harry turned toward his desk. "I see. I'd better get back to work."
>
> "Harry, no! You don't understand—"
>
> "I *do* understand. You've got a date with a bigger fish than me. Well, I hope you hook him. I hope you reel him in real good."
>
> "It's not like that! Come on, the guy is probably old enough to be my father."
>
> "Do you honestly think that makes it *better*?"

"Harry, it's just business, honest!" Amanda pleaded, desperate to make him see. "The guy is looking for a fresh face to put in the new detective picture he's making with **Spencer Tracy** over at **Metro**. Larry Julius's office set it up, for chrissake" [p. 85].

Searchlights combed the sky. Camera flashbulbs popped. The marquee of Grauman's Chinese Theater was ablaze with light.

And the crimson carpet paraded Hollywood's brightest stars.

Clark Gable. Carole Lombard. Joan Crawford and Bette Davis, ignoring each other, as usual. **Spencer Tracy**. Olivia de Havilland, gazing adoringly at Errol Flynn. Gabby Preston in white, beaming on the arm of Jimmy Malloy. Amanda Farraday close behind them, pale and wraithlike in darkest black. John Barrymore, a little unsteady on his feet. Marlene Dietrich in top hat and tails [p. 336].

Shukert's other Hollywood novel, *Love Me* (2014), also contains a multitude of movie references. One of them is presented under *Boys Town*. Below are a couple out of several passages mentioning Tracy; the first one expressing the disappointments of Gabby Preston, an aspiring actress with a drinking problem; the second one focusing on the participants of the eleventh Academy Awards ceremony:

She was supposed to have stacks of congratulatory telegrams from the likes of **Clark Gable** and **Spencer Tracy** and Claudette Colbert, and weeks' worth of consultations with Rex Mandalay, the famously tempestuous (and tight-panted) Australian who was Olympus's most revered costumer, about the gorgeous gown he would design just for her [p. 6].

Clark Gable and Carole Lombard were here, getting the stink eye from Joan Crawford, who was hanging on the arm of Franchot Tone. Katharine Hepburn was whispering something in **Spencer Tracy**'s ear, much to Mrs. Tracy's visible chagrin. Leo Karp was sitting with **Louis B. Mayer,** who wasn't drinking, and Harry Cohn, who was. *Greta Garbo was there.* True, she wasn't actually *speaking* to anybody, but she was *there* [p. 79].

Tracy is clearly not as popular among writers of narrative fiction or nonfiction as the other three legends featured in this book. Still, based on my research only, the actor and/or his films are mentioned in about 120 literary works by more than ninety authors. The writers that keep remembering him most loyally include George Baxt (who mentions Tracy in four of his novels, evoking a total of five of his films), Robert B. Parker (three/three), Adriana Trigiani (three/two), Sam Shepard and Barbara Taylor Bradford (three/one each), and Joseph Wambaugh and Stuart Woods (three books by each and no film mentioned). Michael B. Druxman mentions thirty of his movies in the play *Tracy* and four of them once again in the play *Gable*. The list continues with Thomas Pynchon (two/four), Michael Malone (two/three), Lawrence Sanders, Loren D. Estleman, Fannie Flagg, Elizabeth Hay, Stuart M. Kaminsky, Andrew J. Fenady and Jeffrey Cohen (two/two each), and James Scott Bell and Rachel Shukert (two/one each). James A. Michener references ten of Tracy pictures in a single novel, *The Drifters*. The works that mention Tracy's name in their titles and/or use the actor as a major character include *Tracy: A One-Person Play in Two Acts* (1984) by Michael B. Druxman, Sam Shepard's tale "Spencer Tracy Is Not Dead" (1990), John Dandola's novel *West of Orange* (1990) and Susan Snively's poem "Spencer Tracy" (1997).

The uniqueness of Spencer Tracy's acting talent consists in, among other things, the fact that he was able to create his own, absolutely individual and natural manner of delivering lines, which makes the viewer unaware of the acting part but absorbed in, and almost hypnotized by, the actor's enormously expressive face flawlessly, but unobtrusively, revealing, or reflecting, all pondering processes and emotional changes that take place within the characters he portrays. His responses to either positive or negative acts that occur around him are always deliberate and even delayed, as opposed to, say, Clark Gable's instantaneous reactions, frequently appearing to be hasty or premature. At the same time—thanks to his strong, sometimes overpowering, but always charismatic personality—Tracy dominates nearly in every scene, regardless of the caliber and physical appearance of the other actors in the scene. As a result of such an original and carefully developed persona, Tracy's filmography includes numerous pictures with both intellectual values and intellectual characters—scientists, lawyers, politicians, high-rank officers, reporters, successful businessmen and the like—in the center. (An interesting comment regarding Tracy's technique is made in Aaron Latham's mystery *Riding with John Wayne*.)

While the number of the overall Tracy references is significantly smaller than those of the other three actors, their distribution in time is equally interesting, if not even more striking. For, with no reference found in sources from the 1930s, the total number of his references from the period 1940 through 1979 hardly exceeds ten, and then it drastically rises, reaching about twenty in the 1980s, almost thirty in the 1990s, and nearly fifty in the first decade of the twenty-first century. With about ten allusions already found in works from the current decade, the prognosis for the numbers to keep growing in the near future does not sound stretched or unlikely.

III. LIST OF REFERENCES (FOUND) TO TRACY AND HIS FILMS

While the year after the book title refers to the copyright/publication date (to provide an accurate sense of chronology), the page numbers are taken from the specific editions in which the references were found—as described in the Overall Bibliography (Reference Sources).

Beryl Bainbridge – *Something Happened Yesterday* (1998)
- Tracy – 123
- *Inherit the Wind* – 123

George Baxt – *The Clark Gable and Carole Lombard Murder Case* (1997)
- Tracy – 102
- *A Man's Castle* – 102
- *San Francisco* – 102

George Baxt – *The Humphrey Bogart Murder Case* (1995)
- Tracy – 5
- *Up the River* – 5

George Baxt – *The Tallulah Bankhead Murder Case* (1987)
- *20,000 Years in Sing Sing* – 111

George Baxt – *The William Powell and Myrna Loy Murder Case* (1996)
- Tracy – 7
- *Whipsaw* – 124

James Scott Bell – *Try Darkness* (2008)
- Tracy – 183
- *Boys Town* – 183

James Scott Bell – *Try Fear* (2009)
- Tracy – 47

Betts, June Harman – *Father Was a Caveman* (2007)
- Tracy – 203
- *Boys Town* – 203

Lawrence Block – *Small Town* (2003)
- *Inherit the Wind* – 67

Valerie Block – *Don't Make a Scene* (2007)
- *Woman of the Year* – 314

Steven Bochco – *Death by Hollywood* (2003)
- *Dr. Jekyll and Mr. Hyde* – 147

C. J. Box – *In Plain Sight* (2006)
- Tracy – 7
- *Inherit the Wind* – 7

Barbara Taylor Bradford – *Angel* (1993)
- Tracy – 217
- *Bad Day at Black Rock* – 217

Barbara Taylor Bradford – *Just Rewards* (2006)
- *Bad Day at Black Rock* – 555

Barbara Taylor Bradford – *Where You Belong* (1999)
- *Bad Day at Black Rock* – 206

Sandra Brown – *Ricochet* (2006)
- Tracy – 383

James M. Cain – *Love's Lovely Counterfeit* (1942)
- Tracy – 220

Stephen J. Cannell – *Runaway Heart* (2003)
- Tracy – 107
- *Inherit the Wind* – 107

Colin Campbell – *Montecito Heights: A Resurrection Man Novel* (2014)
- Tracy – 362, 369
- *Bad Day at Black Rock* – 362, 369

Lorenzo Carcaterra – *Sleepers* (1995)
- Tracy – 5
- *Boys' Town* – 5

Harlan Coben – *Deal Breaker* (1995)
- Tracy – 260
- *Adam's Rib* – 260

Jeffrey Cohen – *It Happened One Knife* (2008)
- *Adam's Rib* – 151
- *Guess Who's Coming to Dinner* – 184

Jeffrey Cohen – *Some Like it Hot – Buttered* (2007)
- Tracy – 52, 236

Paula Marantz Cohen – *Jane Austen in Boca* (2002)
- Tracy – 184
- *Inherit the Wind* – 184

Ellen Cooney – *Lambrusco* (2008)
- Tracy – 141, 160

John Dandola – *West of Orange* (as *Dead at the Box Office*) (1990)
- Tracy – 17, 18, 24, 37, 38, 45, 46, 52-54, 140, 142, 180, 181, 188, 189, 191-193, 197, 199, 201-205, 207, 211
- *Stanley and Livingstone* – 51, 52
- *Edison the Man* – 16, 25, 37, 39, 45, 46, 78, 83, 111, 163, 179
- *Boom Town* – 17, 18

Marisa de los Santos – *Love Walked In* (2005)
- Tracy – 10
- *Libeled Lady* – 9

Nelson DeMille – *Word of Honor* **(1985)**
- Tracy – 415
- *Judgment at Nuremberg* – 415

William Diehl – *Primal Fear* **(1993)**
- Tracy – 189

Kirk Douglas – *Dance with the Devil* **(1990)**
- San Francisco – 48, 56

Michael B. Druxman – *Gable: A One-Person Play in Two Acts* **(1984)**
- Tracy – 9, 22-24, 54
- San Francisco – 31
- *Test Pilot* – 24, 39
- *Boom Town* – 10
- *Inherit the Wind* – 23

Michael B. Druxman – *Tracy: A One-Person Play in Two Acts* **(1984)**
- Tracy – 3-67
- *Up the River* – 34
- *Quick Millions* – 35
- *Society Girl* – 37
- *20,000 Years in Sing Sing* – 37
- *Shanghai Madness* – 40
- *Man's Castle* – 37, 38
- *Marie Galante* – 40
- *Fury* – 46
- *San Francisco* – 47, 54
- *Libeled Lady* – 46
- *Captains Courageous* – 49, 50
- *Test Pilot* – 54
- *Boys Town* – 47, 53, 56
- *Northwest Passage* – 53
- *Boom Town* – 53
- *Dr. Jekyll and Mr. Hyde* – 55
- *Woman of the Year* – 55, 56

- *Adam's Rib* – 57
- *Malaya* – 62
- *Father of the Bride* – 62
- *Pat and Mike* – 57
- *Plymouth Adventure* – 62
- *Bad Day at Black Rock* – 24, 62, 64
- *The Mountain* – 66
- *Desk Set* – 66
- *The Old Man and the Sea* – 66
- *Inherit the Wind* – 15, 16
- *Judgment at Nuremberg* – 67
- *It's a Mad, Mad, Mad, Mad World* – 9
- *Guess Who's Coming to Dinner* – 7, 9, 43, 58, 68, 69

John Gregory Dunne – ***True Confessions*** **(1978)**

- *Boys Town* – 122

James Ellroy – ***The Cold Six Thousand*** **(2001)**

- Tracy – 364

Loren D. Estleman – ***Edsel*** **(1995)**

- Tracy – 181-184, 275
- *Bad Day at Black Rock* – 181-184

Loren D. Estleman – ***Downriver*** **(1988)**

- Tracy – 51
- *Thirty Seconds Over Tokyo* – 51

Andrew J. Fenady – ***The Man with Bogart's Face*** **(1977)**

- Tracy – 20, 92

Andrew J. Fenady – ***The Secret of Sam Marlow*** **(1980)**

- Tracy – 17, 118
- *Test Pilot* – 118
- *Boom Town* – 118

F. Scott Fitzgerald – ***The Last Tycoon*** **(1940/41)**

- Tracy – 74, 156

Fannie Flagg – *Can't Wait to Get to Heaven* (2006)
- Tracy – 151
- *Edison, the Man* – 151

Fannie Flagg – *Coming Attractions* (as *Daisy Fay and the Miracle Man*) (1981)
- Tracy – 76
- *Test Pilot* – 76

William Goldman – *Magic* (1976)
- Tracy – 16

W.E.B. Griffin – *Blood and Honor* (1996)
- Tracy – 443
- *Boys Town* – 443

Elizabeth Hay – *Garbo Laughs* (2003)
- Tracy – 42, 255
- *Woman of the Year* – 42, 165
- *Thirty Seconds Over Tokyo* – 165

Elizabeth Hay – *A Student of Weather* (2001)
- Tracy – 87

Oscar Hijuelos – *The Mambo Kings Play Songs of Love* (1989)
- Tracy – 5
- *The Old Man and the Sea* – 5

William Bradford Huie – *Mud on the Stars* (1942)
- Tracy – 188

Maureen Johnson – *Suite Scarlett* (2008)
- Tracy – 77

Stuart M. Kaminsky – *Midnight Pass* (2003)
- *Guess Who's Coming to Dinner* – 73

Stuart M. Kaminsky – *Poor Butterfly* (1990)
- *San Francisco* – 16

Adam Kennedy – *Just Like Humphrey Bogart* (1978)
- Tracy – 108

William X. Kienzle – *No Greater Love* (1999)
- Tracy – 68
- *Guess Who's Coming to Dinner* – 170

Kiernan, Caitlín R. – *The Drowning Girl* (2012)
- Tracy – 52
- *Inherit the Wind* – 52

Stephen King – *Duma Key* (2008)
- *Woman of the Year* – 141, 404
- *Adam's Rib* – 141

Barbara Kingsolver – *Flight Behavior* (2012)
- *Guess Who's Coming to Dinner* – 109

Laurence Klavan – *The Cutting Room* (2004)
- Tracy – 255
- *Adam's Rib* – 255

Laurence Klavan – *The Shooting Script* (2005)
- Tracy – 10, 238

Hank Klimitas - *Twice a Survivor: A Katrina Journal* (2006)
- Tracy – 38
- *Devil at 4 O'Clock* – 38

Herman Koch – *The Dinner* (2009)
- *Guess Who's Coming to Dinner* – 77-80

Jennifer Lash – *Blood Ties* (1997)
- Tracy – 222

Aaron Latham – *Riding with John Wayne* (2006)
- Tracy – 277, 286, 313

Laura Lippman – *In a Strange City* (2001)
- Tracy – 81
- *Inherit the Wind* – 81

Jeff Long – *The Wall* (2006)
- Tracy – 59
- *The Mountain* – 59

Michael Malone – "Blue Cadillac" (2002)
- Tracy – 29
- *Inherit the Wind* – 29

Michael Malone – *The Four Corners of the Sky* **(2009)**
- Tracy – 91
- *Boom Town* – 329
- *Father of the Bride* – 91

Archer Mayor – *Scent of Evil* **(1992)**
- Tracy – 72
- *Inherit the Wind* – 72

Annalena McAfee – *The Spoiler* **(2011)**
- Tracy – 59
- *The Old Man and the Sea* – 59

Robert R. McCammon – *Swan Song* **(1987)**
- Tracy – 235
- *Boys Town* – 235

Ron McCoy - "It Ain't Me, Babe: Working for Richard Nixon"
- Tracy – 292
- *Inherit the Wind* – 292

Sharyn McCrumb – *The Hangman's Beautiful Daughter* **(1992)**
- Tracy – 203
- *Captains Courageous* – 203

Dermot McEvoy – *Our Lady of Greenwich Village* **(2008)**
- Tracy – 51
- *The Last Hurrah* – 51

Larry McMurtry – *All My Friends Are Going to Be Strangers* **(1972)**
- Tracy – 137

Larry McMurtry – *Loop Group* **(2004)**
- *Bad Day at Black Rock* – 71

James A. Michener – *The Drifters* **(1971)**
- Tracy – 461-463, 468, 506, 507, 551, 572
- *Up the River* – 463

- *Captains Courageous* – 462, 506, 507
- *Boys Town* – 506, 507
- *Keeper of the Flame* – 462
- *The Seventh Cross* – 572
- *Father of the Bride* – 462
- *The Old Man and the Sea* – 462, 507
- *Inherit the Wind* – 551
- *It's a Mad, Mad, Mad, Mad World* – 507
- *Guess Who's Coming to Dinner* – 507

John Douglas Miller – *The Greek Summer* (2003)
- Tracy – 141
- *Inherit the Wind* – 141

Marcia Muller – *Trophies and Dead Things* (1990)
- Tracy – 12

Michael P. Naughton – *Deathryde: Rebel Without a Corpse* (2008)
- Tracy – 123, 145
- *It's a Mad, Mad, Mad, Mad World* – 123, 145

John O'Hara – *From the Terrace* (1958)
- Tracy – 957, 959

John O'Hara – "James Francis and the Star"
- Tracy – 183

Robert B. Parker – *Double Play* (2004)
- Tracy – 22
- *Thirty Seconds Over Tokyo* – 22

Robert B. Parker – *Early Autumn* (1981)
- *Captains Courageous* – 154
- *Boys Town* – 153

Robert. B. Parker – *Playmates* (1989)
- *Boys Town* – 194

Andrew Potok – *Ordinary Daylight: Portrait of an Artist Going Blind* (1980)
- Tracy – 139
- *Boys Town* – 139

Richard Price – *Freedomland* (1998)
- *Captains Courageous* – 191

Thomas Pynchon – *Gravity's Rainbow* (1973)
- *Dr. Jekyll and Mr. Hyde* – 712

Thomas Pynchon – *Vineland* (1990)
- *20,000 Years in Sing Sing* – 294
- *San Francisco* – 78
- *Boys Town* – 154

Leigh Riker – *Acts of Passion* (1985)
- Tracy – 247
- *The Old Man and the Sea* – 247

Harold Robbins – *The Carpetbaggers* (1961)
- Tracy – 483, 520

David Rosenfelt – *Dog Tags* (2010)
- Tracy – 171

Philip Roth – *The Plot Against America* (2004)
- Tracy – 349
- *Boys Town* – 349

Mike Sager – "The Temple of Doom" (2003)
- Tracy – 295
- *Boys Town* – 295

Lawrence Sanders – *McNally's Dilemma* (1999)
- *Captains Courageous* – 85

Lawrence Sanders – *The Second Deadly Sin* (1977)
- Tracy – 113
- *Pat and Mike* – 113

Budd Schulberg – *The Harder They Fall* (1947)
- Tracy – 188

Budd Schulberg – *What Makes Sammy Run?* (1941)
- Tracy – 162, 163

A. D. Scott – *A Small Death in the Great Glen* (2010)
- Tracy – 171

Sam Shepard – *Fool for Love* (1983)
- Tracy – 49

Sam Shepard – *Motel Chronicles* (1982)
- *Bad Day at Black Rock* – 86

Sam Shepard – "Spencer Tracy Is Not Dead" (1990)
- Tracy – 181, 192-194

Martha Sherrill – *My Last Movie Star* (2002)
- Tracy – 246, 247, 250-252
- *Captains Courageous* – 246
- *Test Pilot* – 246-248, 251

Rachel Shukert – *Love Me* (2014)
- Tracy – 6, 15, 24, 79, 82, 83
- *Boys Town* – 24

Rachel Shukert – *Starstruck* (2013)
- Tracy – 85, 336

Susan Snively – "Spencer Tracy" (1997)
- Tracy – 6

LaVyrle Spencer – *Then Came Heaven* (1997)
- Tracy – 197
- *Adam's Rib* – 197

Kathryn Stockett – *The Help* (2009)
- Tracy – 212
- *It's a Mad, Mad, Mad, Mad World* – 206, 212

Janet Thornburg – "Chosen" (2005)
- Tracy – 82
- *Desk Set* – 82

Roderick Thorp – *Rainbow Drive* (1986)
- *Adam's Rib* – 84

Adriana Trigiani – *Big Cherry Holler* (2001)
- Tracy – 122
- *Test Pilot* – 122

Adriana Trigiani – *Big Stone Gap* (2000)
- Tracy – 73

Adriana Trigani – *Lucia, Lucia* (2003)
- *Father of the Bride* – 82

Scott Turow – *Personal Injuries* (1999)
- Tracy – 107
- *Adam's Rib* – 107

Daphne Uviller – *Super in the City* (2009)
- Tracy – 162
- *Adam's Rib* – 163

Gore Vidal – *Myra Breckinridge* (1968)
- Tracy – 34
- *Boom Town* – 36
- *The Seventh Cross* – 36
- *Thirty Seconds Over Tokyo* – 147

Kurt Vonnegut – *Bluebeard* (1987)
- Tracy – 16, 19
- *Captains Courageous* – 16, 19

Joseph Wambaugh – *Fugitive Nights* (1992)
- Tracy – 168

Joseph Wambaugh – *Hollywood Station* (2006)
- Tracy – 242

Joseph Wambaugh – *The Secrets of Harry Bright* (1985)
- Tracy – 5

James Neel White – *I Was a P-51 Fighter Pilot in WWII* (2003)
- Tracy – 25

Connie Willis – "At the Rialto" (1989)
- Tracy – 446, 456
- *Woman of the Year* – 446, 456

Stuart Woods – *Dead Eyes* (1994)
- Tracy – 117

Stuart Woods – *The Prince of Beverly Hills* (2004)
- Tracy – 84

Stuart Woods – *Son of Stone* (2011)
- Tracy – 118

IV. CREDITS TO TRACY'S FILMS REFERENCED

1. *Up the River* (Fox, 1930). Sc. Maurice Watkins. Dir. John Ford. Phot. Joseph August. Cast: ST (Saint Louis), Warren Hymer (Dannemora Dan), Claire Luce (Judy), Humphrey Bogart (Steve), Joan Marie Lawes (Jean), William Collier, Sr. (Pop), George MacFarlane (Jessup).

2. *Quick Millions* (Fox, 1931). Sc. Courtney Terrett and Rowland Brown from their story. Dir. Rowland Brown. Phot. Joseph H. August. Cast: ST (Daniel J. "Bugs" Raymond), Marguerite Churchill (Dorothy Stone), Sally Eilers (Daisy De Lisle), Bob Burns ("Arkansas" Smith), John Wray (Kenneth Stone), Warner Richmond ("Nails" Markey), George Raft (Jimmy Kirk).

3. *Society Girl* (Fox, 1932). Sc. Elmer Harris from the play by John Larkin. Dir. Sidney Lanfield. Phot. George Barnes. Cast: James Dunn (Johnny Malone), Peggy Shannon (Judy Gelett), ST (Briscoe), Walter Byron (Warburton), Bert Hanlon (Curly), Marjorie Gateson (Alice Converse), Eula Guy (Miss Halloway).

4. *20,000 Years in Sing Sing* (First National, 1932). Sc. Courtney Terrett, Robert Lord, Wilson Mizner and Brown Holmes from the book by Lewis E. Lawes. Dir. Michael Curtiz. Phot. Barney McGill. Music by Bernhard Kaun. Cast: ST (Tom Connors), Bette Davis (Fay), Lyle Talbot (Bud), Louis Calhern (Finn), Arthur Byron (Warden Long), Warren Hymer (Hype), Grant Mitchell (Dr. Ames).

5. *Shanghai Madness* (Fox, 1993). Sc. Austin Parker and Gordon Wellesley from a story by Frederick Hazlitt Brennan. Dir. John G. Blystone. Phot. Lee Garmes. Cast: ST (Pat Jackson), Fay Wray (Wildeth Christie), Ralph Morgan (Li Po Chang), Eugene Pallette (Lobo Lonergan), Herbert Mundin (Larsen), Reginald Mason (William Christie) Arthur Hoyt (Van Emery).

6. *Man's Castle* (Columbia, 1933). Sc. Jo Swerling from a play by Lawrence Hazard. Dir. Frank Borzage. Phot. Joseph August. Cast: ST (Bill), Loretta Young (Trina), Glenda Farrell (Fay LaRue), Walter Connolly (Ira), Marjorie Rambeau (Flossie), Arthur Hohl (Bragg), Dickie Moore (Joie).

7. *Marie Galante* (Fox, 1934). Sc. Reginald Berkeley from the play by Jacques Deval. Dir. Henry King. Phot. John F. Seitz. Cast: ST (Dr. Crawbett), Ketti Gallian (Marie Galante), Ned Sparks (Plosser), Helen Morgan (Miss Tapia), Sig Ruman (Brogard), Leslie Fenton (General Saki Tenoki), Arthur Byron (General Gerald Phillips).

8. *Whipsaw* (MGM, 1935). Sc. Howard E. Rogers from a story by James Edward Grant. Dir. Sam Wood. Phot. James Wong Howe. Music by William Axt. Cast: Myrna Loy (Vivian Palmer), ST (Ross McBride), Harvey Stephens (Ed Dexter), William Harrigan (Doc Evans), Clay Clement (Harry Ames), Robert Warwick (Wadsworth), Robert Gleckler (Steve Arnold).

9. *Fury* (MGM, 1936). Sc. Bartlett Cormack and Fritz Lang from a story by Norman Krasna. Dir. Fritz Lang. Phot. Joseph Ruttenberg. Music by Franz Waxman. Cast: ST (Joe Wilson), Sylvia Sidney (Katherine Grant),

Walter Abel (District Attorney), Bruce Cabot (Kirby Dawson), Edward Ellis (Sheriff), Walter Brennan ("Bugs" Meyers), Frank Albertson (Charlie).

10. *San Francisco* (MGM, 1936). Sc. Anita Loos from a story by Robert Hopkins. Dir. W.S. Van Dyke. Phot. Oliver T. Marsh. Music by Edward Ward. Cast: Clark Gable (Blackie Norton), Jeanette MacDonald (Mary Blake), ST (Father Mullin), Jack Holt (Jack Burley), Jessie Ralph (Mrs. Burley), Ted Healy (Mat), Shirley Ross (Trixie).

11. *Libeled Lady* (MGM, 1936). Sc. Maurine Watkins, Howard Emmett Rogers and George Oppenheimer from a story by Wallace Sullivan. Dir. Jack Conway. Phot. Norbert Brodine. Music by William Axt. Cast: Jean Harlow (Gladys), William Powell (Bill Chandler), Myrna Loy (Connie Allenbury), ST (Haggerty), Walter Connolly (Mr. Allenbury), Charley Grapewin (Mr. Bane), Cora Witherspoon (Mrs. Burns-Norvell).

12. *Captains Courageous* (MGM, 1937). Sc. John Lee Mahin, Marc Connelly and Dale Van Every from the novel by Rudyard Kipling. Dir. Victor Fleming. Phot. Harold Rosson. Music by Franz Waxman. Cast: ST (Manuel), Freddie Bartholomew (Harvey Cheyne), Lionel Barrymore (Disko), Melvyn Douglas (Mr. Cheyne), Charley Grapewin (Uncle Salters), Mickey Rooney (Dan), John Carradine ("Long Jack").

13. *Test Pilot* (MGM, 1938). Sc. Vincent Lawrence and Waldemar Young from a story by Frank Wead. Dir. Victor Fleming. Phot. Ray June. Music by Franz Waxman. Cast: Clark Gable (Jim), Myrna Loy (Ann), ST (Gunner), Lionel Barrymore Drake), Samuel S. Hinds General Ross), Marjorie Main (Landlady), Ted Pearson (Joe).

14. *Boys Town* (MGM, 1938). Sc. John Meehan and Dore Schary from a story by Dore Schary and Eleanor Griffin. Dir. Norman Taurog. Phot. Sidney Wagner. Music by Edward Ward. Cast: ST (Father E. Flanagan), Mickey Rooney (Whitey Marsh), Henry Hull (Dave Morris), Leslie Fenton

(Dan Farrow), Addison Richards (The Judge), Edward Norris (Joe Marsh), Gene Reynolds (Tony Ponessa).

15. *Stanley and Livingstone* (20th C-F, 1939). Sc. Philip Dunne and Julien Josephson from research material and story outline by Hal Long and Sam Hellman. Dir. Henry King. Phot. George Barnes. Music by Robert R. Bennett, David Buttolph, Louis Silvers, R.H. Bassett, Cyril Mockridge and Rudy Schrager. Cast: ST (Henry M. Stanley), Nancy Kelly (Eve Kingsley), Richard Greene (Gareth Tyce), Walter Brennan (Jeff Slocum), Charles Coburn (Lord Tyce), Sir Cedric Hardwicke (Dr. David Livingstone), Henry Hull (James G. Bennett, Jr.).

16. *I Take This Woman* (MGM, 1940). Sc. James Kevin McGuinness from a story by Charles MacArthur. Dir. W.S. Van Dyke. Phot. Harold Rosson. Music by Bronislau Kaper. Cast: ST (Karl Decker), Hedy Lamarr (Georgi Gragore), Verree Teasdale (Madame Marcesca), Kent Taylor (Phil Mayberry), Laraine Day (Linda Rogers), Jack Carson (Joe), Mona Barrie (Sandra Mayberry).

17. *Edison, the Man* (MGM, 1940). Sc. Talbot Jennings and Bradbury Foote from a story by Dore Schary and Hugo Butler. Dir. Clarence Brown. Phot. Harold Rosson. Music by Herbert Stothart. Cast: ST (Thomas A. Edison), Rita Johnson (Mary Stillwell), Lynne Overman (Bunt Cavat), Charles Coburn (General Powell), Gene Lockhart (Mr. Taggart), Henry Travers (Ben Els), Felix Bressart (Michael Simon).

18. *Northwest Passage* (MGM, 1940). Sc. Laurence Stallings and Talbot Jennings from the novel by Kenneth Roberts. Dir. King Vidor. Phot. William V. Skall and Sidney Wagner. Music by Herbert Stothart. Cast: ST (Major Robert Rogers), Robert Young (Langdon Towne), Walter Brennan ("Hunk" Marriner), Ruth Hussey (Elizabeth Browne), Nat Pendleton ("Cap" Huff), Louise Hector (Reverend Browne), Robert Barrat (Humphrey Towne).

19. *Boom Town* (MGM, 1940). Sc. John Lee Mahin from a story by James Edward Grant. Dir. Jack Conway. Phot. Harold Rosson. Music by Franz Waxman. Cast: Clark Gable (Big John McMasters), ST (Square John Sand), Claudette Colbert (Betsy Bartlett), Hedy Lamarr (Karen Vanmeer), Frank Morgan (Luther Aldrich), Lionel Atwill (Harry Compton), Chill Wills (Harmony Jones).

20. *Dr. Jekyll and Mr. Hyde* (MGM, 1941). Sc. John Lee Mahin from the novel by Robert Louis Stevenson. Dir. Victor Fleming. Phot. Joseph Ruttenberg. Music by Franz Waxman. Cast: ST (Dr. Harry Jekyll), Ingrid Bergman (Ivy Peterson), Lana Turner (Beatrix Emery), Donald Crisp (Sir Charles Emery), Barton MacLane (Sam Higgins), C. Aubrey Smith (The Bishop), Peter Godfrey (Poole).

21. *Woman of the Year* (MGM, 1942). Sc. Ring Lardner, Jr. and Michael Kanin. Dir. George Stevens. Phot. Joseph Ruttenberg. Music by Franx Waxman. Cast: Katharine Hepburn (Tess Harding), ST (Sam Craig), Fay Bainter (Ellen Whitcomb), Reginald Owen (Clayton), Minor Watson (William Harding), William Bendix ("Pinkie" Peters), Ludwig Stoessel (Dr. Lubbeck).

22. *Keeper of the Flame* (MGM, 1942). Sc. Donald Ogden Stewart from a story by I. A. R. Wylie. Dir. George Cukor. Phot. William Daniels. Music by Bronislau Kaper. Cast: ST (Steven O'Malley), Katharine Hepburn (Christine Forrest), Richard Whorf (Clive Kerndon), Margaret Wycherly (Mrs. Forrest), Forrest Tucker (Geoffrey Midford), Frank Craven (Dr. Fielding), Horace McNally (Freddie Ridges).

23. *The Seventh Cross* (MGM, 1944). Sc. Helen Deutsch from the book by Anna Seghers. Dir. Fred Zinnemann. Phot. Karl Freund. Music by Roy Webb. Cast: ST (George Heisler), Signe Hasso (Toni), Hume Cronyn (Paul Roeder), Jessica Tandy (Liesel Roeder), Agnes Moorehead (Madame Marelli), Herbert Rudley (Franz Marnet), Felix Bressart (Poldi Schlamm).

24. *Thirty Seconds Over Tokyo* (MGM, 1944). Sc. Dalton Trumbo from a book by Ted W. Lawson and Robert Considine. Dir. Mervyn LeRoy. Phot. Harold Rosson and Robert Surtees. Music by Herbert Stothart. Cast: Van Johnson (Lieut. Ted Lawson), Robert Walker (David Thatcher), ST (Lieut. Col. James H. Doolittle), Phyllis Thaxter (Ellen Lawson), Tim Murdock (Dean Davenport), Don DeFore (Charles McClure), Robert Mitchum (Bob Gray).

25. *Adam's Rib* (MGM, 1949). Sc. Garson Kanin and Ruth Gordon. Dir. George Cukor. Phot. George J. Folsey. Music by Miklos Rozsa. Cast: ST (Adam Bonner), Katharine Hepburn (Amanda Bonner), Judy Holliday (Doris Attinger), Tom Ewell (Warren Attinger), David Wayne (Kip Lurie), Jean Hagen (Beryl Caighn), Hope Emerson (Olympia La Pere).

26. *Malaya* (MGM, 1950). Sc. Frank Fenton from a story by Manchester Boddy. Dir. Richard Thorpe. Phot. George J. Folsey. Music by Bronislau Kaper. Cast: ST (Carnahan), James Stewart (John Royer), Valentina Cortese (Luana), Sydney Greenstreet (The Dutchman), John Hodiak (Kellar), Lionel Barrymore (John Manchester), Gilbert Roland (Romano).

27. *Father of the Bride* (MGM, 1950). Sc. Frances Goodrich and Albert Hackett from the novel by Edward Streeter. Dir. Vincente Minnelli. Phot. John Alton. Music by Adolph Deutsch. Cast: ST (Stanley T. Banks), Elizabeth Taylor (Kay Banks), Joan Bennett (Ellie Banks), Don Taylor (Buckley Dunstan), Billie Burke (Mrs. Doris Dunstan), Leo G. Carroll (Mr. Massoula), Moroni Olsen (Herbert Dunstan).

28. *Pat and Mike* (MGM, 1952). Sc. Ruth Gordon and Garson Kanin. Dir. George Cukor. Phot. William Daniels. Music by David Raksin. Cast: ST (Mike Conovan), Katharine Hepburn (Pat Pemberton), Aldo Ray (Davie Hucko), William Ching (Collier Weld), Sammy White (Barbey Grau), George Mathews (Sylvester "Spec" Cauley), Loring Smith (Mr. Breminger).

29. *Plymouth Adventure* (MGM, 1952). Sc. Helen Deutsch from the novel by Ernest Gebler. Dir. Clarence Brown. Phot. William H. Daniels. Music by Miklos Rozsa. Cast: ST (Captain Christopher Jones), Gene Tierney (Dorothy Bradford), Van Johnson (John Alden), Leo Genn (William Bradford), Barry Jones (William Brewster), Dawn Addams (Priscilla Mullins), Lloyd Bridges (Coppin).

30. *Bad Day at Black Rock* (MGM, 1955). Sc. Millard Kaufman from Howard Breslin's short story "Bad Time at Honda." Dir. John Sturges. Phot. William C. Mellor. Music by André Previn. Cast: ST (John J. Macreedy), Robert Ryan (Reno Smith), Anne Francis (Liz Wirth), Dean Jagger (Tim Horn), Walter Brennan (Doc Velie), Ernest Borgnine (Coley Trimble), Lee Marvin (Hector David).

31. *The Mountain* (Paramount, 1956). Sc. Ranald MacDougall from the novel by Henri Troyat. Dir. Edward Dmytrtyk. Phot. Franz F. Planer. Music by Daniele Amfitheatrof. Cast: ST (Zachary Teller), Robert Wagner (Chris Teller), Claire Trevor (Marie), William Demarest (Father Belacchi), Barbara Darrow (Simone), E. G. Marshall (Solange), Anna Kashfi (Hindu Girl).

32. *Desk Set* (20th C-T, 1957). Sc. Phoebe and Henry Ephron from a play by Robert Fryer and Lawrence Carr. Dir. Walter lang. Phot. Leon Shamroy. Music by Cyril Mockridge. Cast: ST (Richard Sumner), Katharine Hepburn (Bunny Watson), Gig Young (Mike Cutler), Joan Blondell (Peg Costello), Dina Merrill (Sylvia Blair), Sue Randall (Ruthie Saylor), Neva Patterson (Miss Warriner).

33. *The Old Man and the Sea* (Leland Hayward/WB, 1958). Sc. Paul Viertel from the novella by Ernest Hemingway. Dir. John Sturges. Phot. Floyd Crosby, James Wong Howe. Cast: ST (The Old Man), Felipe Pazos (The Boy), Harry Bellaver (Martin), Don Diamond (Café Proprietor), Don

Blackman (Hand Wrestler), Joey Ray (Gambler), Mary Hemingway (Tourist).

34. *The Last Hurrah* (Columbia, 1958). Sc. Frank Nugent from the novel by Edwin O'Connor. Dir. John Ford. Phot. Charles Lawton, Jr. Cast: ST (Mayor Frank Skeffington), Jeffrey Hunter (Adam Caulfield), Dianne Foster (Maeve Caulfield), Pat O'Brien (John Gorman), Basil Rathbone (Norman Cass, Sr.), Donald Crisp (Cardinal Martin Burke), James Gleason ("Cuke" Gillen).

35. *Inherit the Wind* (UA, 1960). Sc. Nathan E. Douglas and Harold Jacob Smith from the play by Jerome Lawrence and Robert E. Lee. Dir. Stanley Kramer. Phot. Ernest Laszlo. Music by Ernest Gold. Cast: ST (Henry Drummond), Fredric March (Matthew Harrison Brady), Gene Kelly (E.K. Hornbeck), Florence Eldridge (Mrs. Brady), Dick York (Bertram T. Cates), Donna Anderson (Rachel Brown), Harry Morgan (The Judge).

36. *The Devil at Four O'Clock* (Columbia, 1961). Sc. Liam O'Brien from a novel by Max Catto. Dir. Mervyn LeRoy. Phot. Joseph Biroc. Music by George Duning. Cast: ST (Father Matthew Doonan), Frank Sinatra (Harry), Kerwin Mathews (Father Joseph Perreau), Jean-Pierre Aumont (Jacques), Gregoire Aslan (Marcel), Alexander Scourby (The Governor), Barbara Luna (Camille).

37. *Judgment at Nuremberg* (UA, 1961). Sc. Abby Mann from his play. Dir. Stanley Kramer. Phot. Ernest Laszlo. Music by Ernest Gold. Cast: ST (Chief Judge Dan Haywood), Burt Lancaster (Ernst Janning), Richard Widmark (Colonel Tad Lawson), Marlene Dietrich (Mrs. Bertholt), Maximilian Schell (Hans Rolfe), Judy Garland (Irene Hoffman), Montgomery Clift (Rudolf Peterson).

38. *It's a Mad, Mad, Mad, Mad World* (UA, 1963). Sc. William and Tania Rose. Dor. Stanley Kramer. Phot. Ernest Laszlo. Music by Ernest

Gold. Cast: ST (Captain C. G. Culpeper), Milton Berle (J. Russell Finch), Sid Caesar (Melville Crump), Buddy Hackett (Benjy Benjamin), Ethel Merman ((Mrs. Marcus), Mickey Rooney (Ding Bell), Phil Silvers (Otto Meyer).

39. *Guess Who's Coming to Dinner* (Columbia, 1967). Sc. William Rose. Dir. Stanley Kramer. Phot. Sam Leavitt. Music by Frank DeVol. Cast: ST (Matt Drayton), Katharine Hepburn (Christina Drayton), Sidney Poitier (John Prentice), Katharine Houghton (Joey Drayton), Cecil Kellaway (Monsignor Ryan), Beah Richards (Mrs. Prentice), Roy E. Glenn, Sr. (Mr. Prentice).

V. TRACY'S MONOGRAPHIC BIBLIOGRAPHY (BOOKS ONLY)

Andersen, Christopher P. *An Affair to Remember: The Remarkable Love Story of Katharine Hepburn and Spencer Tracy*. New York: William Morrow and Company, 1997.

Curtis, James. *Spencer Tracy: A Biography*. New York: Alfred A. Knopf, 2011.

Davidson, Bill. *Spencer Tracy: Tragic Idol*. New York: E. P. Dutton, 1988.

Deschner, Donald. *The Films of Spencer Tracy*. New York: Citadel, 1968.

Kanin, Garson: *Tracy and Hepburn: An Intimate Memoir*. New York: Viking Press, 1971.

King, Alison. *Spencer Tracy*. New York: Crescent Books, 1992.

Loew, Brenda (ed.). *Spencer Tracy, Fox Film Actor: The Pre-Code Legacy of a Hollywood Legend*. Newton, MA: New England Vintage Film Society, 2008.

Smith, Milburn. *Tracy & Hepburn: The Love Story That Lasted Longer Than Most Marriages*. New York: Barven Publications, 1971.

Swindell, Larry. *Spencer Tracy*. New York: World Publishing Company, 1969.

Tozzi, Romano. *Spencer Tracy*. New York: Pyramid, 1973.

Epilogue:
Final Remarks and Conclusions

As indirectly stated in the Introduction, the primary goal of *Four Hollywood Legends* is to convince the reader about the mythological proportions and the immense impact factor of the four actors concerned. In order to do so, excerpts have been quoted from nearly six hundred literary works by nearly three hundred authors. In order to create a valid and unbiased picture of the subject matter and to guarantee due prestige of the presented material, I tried to avoid both self-published and vanity press books, and I managed to accomplish that goal with a few very well justified exceptions. On the other hand, I made sure that all possible genres are represented. Thus, in addition to my primary personal focus—main stream fiction, mysteries and contemporary westerns—I made sure that also other genres, less favored by my own taste, such as horror, political and espionage techno-thrillers, science fiction and romance, are represented here as well. There are also numerous quotations from plays and scarce from nonfiction—mostly biographical and autobiographical books excluding those focused on movie celebrities. I did not conduct a thorough research of poetry, but at least one poem with a reference to each of the four actors has been found and presented here nonetheless.

It is not surprising—and it is confirmed in the Overall Bibliography—that some authors have been represented here by many more works than others, a disproportion that results from a few different factors. Three writers, for instance, are frequently quoted here due to the fact that they repeatedly focus on Hollywood circles as their setting. They are Stuart (M.) Kaminsky (his middle initial not used consistently), who has as many as eighteen mysteries in the Bibliography, Stuart Woods (with nine titles) and George Baxt (with eight of his books). My personal taste resulted in multiple representations of writers whom I have been enjoying reading for some time now and who, thus, have been researched quite thoroughly. This list includes Robert B. Parker (fourteen works), Elmore Leonard (thirteen), John Updike (nine), Joseph Wambaugh (nine), Charles Bukowski (seven), Lawrence Block (seven), Loren D. Estleman (seven), Evan Hunter /Ed McBain (seven), Larry McMurtry (five), John O'Hara (five), Sam Shepard (five) and Donald E. Westlake/Richard Stark (five). A combination of the above two plus some other criteria explain why certain authors—such as Stephen King (eleven items), Martha Grimes (ten), Michael Malone (ten), Greg Iles (ten), Adriana Trigiani (eight), Barbara Taylor Bradford (eight), Robert K. Tanenbaum (seven), Lawrence Sanders (six), William Goldman (five), Susan Isaacs (five), Fannie Flagg (five) and Marcia Muller (five)—take a substantial portion of the Bibliography, even though they have not been researched entirely.

Unfortunately, some of my very favorite authors—due to the scarceness or lack of required references in their works—are either represented here but modestly (James Jones, Sinclair Lewis and Philip Roth) or not at all (Ernest Hemingway, John Steinbeck, Dashiell Hammett, Raymond Chandler, Cornell Woolrich, Jim Thompson and several others). On the other hand, some insightful and fairly numerous references found, sometimes accidentally, in works by such writers as Don DeLillo, Pete Hamill, Elizabeth Hay, Oscar Hijuelos, Marisa de los Santos, Michael Malone, Jill McCorkle,

Epilogue

Greg Iles and James Scott Bell made me seek the authors' other books and thus discover some new significant literary talents.

A closer study of the Overall Bibliography (Reference Sources) will also indicate an interesting tendency: the number of books with references to the four actors has significantly increased in recent years, which means that if I had written the book, say, fifteen years ago, it would have been a considerably smaller volume and many of the actors' films would not have been even mentioned. On the other hand, we can probably predict with a decent dose of certainty that the subject matter of this book will find more and more data in the next few years—five, ten, or maybe even more. Such a tendency, surprising and thus deserving a separate research, proves once again that Bogart, Cooper, Gable and Tracy do hold a special place in the history of film (and culture in general), that their work cannot be discarded merely because of its age, and that their legends and historical significance will remain or even grow as time goes by.

In my extensive research begun many years ago, I have been taking comprehensive notes of all movie references, and, based on the accumulated data, I can authoritatively conclude that there are no movie stars with literary references surpassing those of the four stars discussed here. The names of Charlie Chaplin, Greta Garbo and Marilyn Monroe do appear in literature almost as frequently, but the number of references to their films is drastically smaller. The few actors that can compete with Spencer Tracy as far as their overall number of references is concerned are John Wayne, Cary Grant, Burt Lancaster and Marlon Brando. Wayne with his westerns (his major references) is presented in my previous book, *Western Movie References in American Literature*. Lancaster and Brando have also their entries in that book, but rather limited, so both of them, just like Cary Grant and maybe a few other, both male and female, movie stars, deserve to be discussed in a separate publication.

The movie references presented throughout the book may appear to be randomly scattered even though they are organized in each part either according to the chronology of the films (all Sections I), or according to the chronology of the sources (all Sections II), with a conscious effort to keep quotations by one author in an uninterrupted sequence everywhere. Occasionally, due to an overwhelming number of references to a single film, which, besides, happens to be memorable through some very well-known lines—like in the case of *Gone with the Wind* and *Casablanca*—the criteria are somewhat different. Consequently, any extra insight or reflection (other than the obvious) resulting from the enormous complexity of the material will be most likely missed by the reader. In an attempt to rectify such an inevitable drawback, I came up with the following list of sample categories (purposes, roles, characters) of movie references with the most typical and poignant example of each. The examples are taken only from references to specific films; the ones covering the most popular lines are intentionally skipped; and—admittedly—the list is far from complete, rather random and subjective as I included some of my very favorite excerpts, quotations of personal significance.

1. An illustration of an actor's performance as inspiration for a young teacher – *The Petrified Forest* (Bogart) in *The Blackboard Jungle* (1955) by Evan Hunter.

2. Juxtaposition in the perception of the American cinema – *Casablanca* and *Beat the Devil* (Bogart) and *Guess Who's Coming to Dinner* (Tracy) in *The Drifters* (1971) by James A. Michener.

3. A particular movie show as a powerful memory of a tragic childhood – *Casablanca* (Bogart) in *Mean High Tide* (1994) by James W. Hall.

4. A comparison between the feelings of the book's characters with the love between characters of a movie – *Casablanca* (Bogart) in *Love Walked In* (2005) by Marisa de los Santos.

5. An open discussion about the lack of clarity in the plot of Chandler's book and Hawks's film – *The Big Sleep* (Bogart) in *The Man with Bog-*

art's Face (1977) by Andrew J. Fenady and *The Burglar Who Thought He Was Bogart* (1995) by Lawrence Block.

6. Film knowledge exchange as a means of a special bonding between two strangers – *In a Lonely Place* and other films (Bogart) in *The Burglar Who Thought He Was Bogart* (1995) by Lawrence Block.

7. The fate of a famous prop as part of a character's story – *The African Queen* (Bogart) in *The Water Is Wide* (1972) by Pat Conroy.

8. An illustration of women's different expectations of their heroes dependent on the times – *The Virginian* (Cooper) in *Calamity Town* (1942) by Ellery Queen.

9. A simile between a character's pose and a painting – *The Texan* (Cooper) in *The Ballad of Ethan Burns* (2013) by James D. Balestrieri.

10. A perfect match between an actor's persona and a character he plays – *Mr. Deeds Goes to Town* (Cooper) in *Murder in the Red Room* (1992) by Elliott Roosevelt.

11. A reference to a funny lexical item as an illustration or evidence of a character's familiarity with film history – *Mr. Deeds Goes to Town* (Cooper) in *Riding with John Wayne* (2006) by Aaron Latham.

12. A dual perception of the same movie at the time of crisis – *Meet John Doe* (Cooper) in *Love Walked In* (2005) by Marisa de los Santos.

13. A metaphor/simile illustrating the mental state of a character – *Distant Drums* (Cooper) in *All My Friends Are Going to Be Strangers* (1972) by Larry McMurtry.

14. An undoubted allusion to a movie not yet released or even made at the time setting of the book used as an unusual example of prolepsis – *High*

Noon (Cooper) in *High Midnight* (1981) by Stuart Kaminski. (The author uses the same device in his novel *The Man Who Shot Lewis Vance*.)

15. A boy's minor sin justified by his fascination with a particular movie – *High Noon* (Cooper) in *The End of the Pier* (1992) by Martha Grimes.

16. An illustration of a clearly negative character's hypocrisy by revealing his pretended support for certain moral/social/political values – *High Noon* (Cooper) in *The Devil's Garden* (1998) by Ralph Peters.

17. A strong praise of the western genre through the convincing presentation of the reasons for the protagonist's attraction to it – *High Noon* (Cooper) in *Betrayed* (2010) by Robert K. Tanenbaum.

18. A fantasy resulting from sexual frustrations – *Love in the Afternoon* (Cooper) in *Starving Hearts* (2000) by Lynn Ruth Miller.

19. An idea for a remake as a focal point in a conflict – *Man of the West* (Cooper) in *Shadow Play* (2004) by David Cole.

20. A source of inspiration – *It Happened One Night* (Gable) in *The Moviegoer* (1960) by Walker Percy.

21. Circumstances of a famous true/historical event – *Manhattan Melodrama* (Gable) in *Gravity's Rainbow* (1973) by Thomas Pynchon, *Libra* (1988) by Don DeLillo, *The Hot Kid* (2005) by Elmore Leonard and *Creole Bell* (2012) by James Lee Burke.

22. An analogy (real or imagined) between a situation in the film and in the book – *Gone with the Wind* (Gable) in *Carolina Moon* (1996) by Jill McCorkle.

23. Background information about a real-life character – *Run Silent,*

Epilogue

Run Deep (Gable) in *Our Lady of Greenwich Village* (2008) by Dermot McEvoy.

24. A specific movie title serving as a means to make an unusual encounter seem authentic – *It Started in Naples* (Gable) in *Very Valentine* (2009) by Adriana Trigiani.

25. A captivating episode built on circumstances derived from a movie reference – *The Misfits* (Gable) in *Hey There (You with the Gun in Your Hand)* (2008) by Robert J. Randisi.

26. An abundance of information about a certain idea – *Boys Town* (Tracy) in *The Plot Against America* (2004) by Philip Roth.

27. A real place offering special food similar to what is made in a movie (Katharine Hepburn's waffles) – *Woman of the Year* (Tracy) in "At the Rialto" (1989) by Connie Willis.

28. A movie show as an extensive circumstance accompanying a complex sequence of events in a book – *Bad Day at Black Rock* (Tracy) in *Edsel* (1995) by Loren D. Estleman.

29. A strong similarity in the behavior/mannerisms of a book character and a movie character – *Inherit the Wind* (Tracy) in *Small Town* (2003) by Lawrence Block.

30. An important voice in a political discussion – *Judgment at Nuremberg* (Tracy) in *Word of Honor* (1985) by Nelson DeMille.

31. An insightful analysis of four major characters through their individual opinions on the same film – *Guess Who's Coming to Dinner* (Tracy) in *The Dinner* (2009) by Herman Koch.

There are hundreds of literary quotations presented in this book, most of them referring to only one of the actors, some to two, and maybe a few to three of them. A quotation that ties all four actors together, and thus appropriate to be used as the conclusion of this publication, was found in Michael B. Druxman's play *Tracy* (1984). Set in 1967, when only Tracy—out of the four—was still around but soon to join the others, the play gives the last of the great four a chance to mourn the other three and the old times in the following way:

> I just can't watch the pictures that **Bogie** and **Gable** and **Coop** made anymore. It takes too much out of me, and there's not much left to take out [p. 68].

Unlike Tracy the character of Druxman's play, a lot of the four actors' cotemporaries, but also numerous representatives of the few generations that came after them, did and have had a great desire to watch the films in which these actors appeared, and all those devoted fans—whether old or young—keep being inspired by the everlasting values that the movies offer, especially if they are willing and able to watch them with a film-historian's eye, and incessantly captivated by the phenomenal talents of their leading men. Despite the enormous social, cultural and political changes that have taken place in the last fifty years, despite the unimaginable technological progress, films like *Casablanca* and *The Caine Mutiny*, *Meet John Doe* and *High Noon*, *It Happened One Night* and *The Misfits*, *Fury* and *Inherit the Wind*—just like the works of Vergil, Shakespeare or Dickens—are and will be repeatedly revisited, discussed and analyzed for both their aesthetic assets and the complex and universal issues that they skillfully raise. That the process has already been going on for some time now has been unquestionably proven by the content of this book.

Overall Bibliography
(Reference Sources)

Following is the list of literary works where references were found to Bogart, Cooper, Gable and Tracy. The information given after the author's name and the title refers to the specific edition from which the quoted excerpts were copied. Thus, the given dates are the publication dates of those editions—not necessarily the years when the works were originally published or copyrighted. The letters B (for Bogart), C (for Cooper), G (for Gable) or T (for Tracy) after the bibliographical information refer to the actor(s) whose name(s) and/or film(s) is/are mentioned in a given work.

Abbott, Jeff. *The Only Good Yankee*. New York: Ballantine Books, 1995. C

Abella, Alex. *The Great American*. New York: Simon & Schuster, 1997. C

Alcorn, Randy. *Edge of Eternity*. Colorado Springs, CO: WaterBrook Press, 2009. C, G

Allen, Woody. *Play It Again, Sam*. New York: Samuel French, 1996. B

Arnold, Wolf. "Farm Work." In *Interlude in Ravenna: Short Stories*. Prospect, CT: Biographical Publishing Company, 2007. G

Atkins, Ace. *Robert B. Parker's Lullaby*. New York: G.P. Putnam's Sons, 2012. B, C

Auster, Paul. "Ghosts." In *The New York Trilogy*. New York: Penguin Books, 1990. B

———. "The Locked Room." In *The New York Trilogy*. New York: Penguin Books, 1990. C

Bachman, Richard (aka Stephen King). *The Regulators*. New York: Dutton/Penguin Group, 1996. C

Bainbridge, Beryl. *Something Happened Yesterday*. New York: Carroll & Graf, 1998. T

Balestrieri, James D. *The Ballad of Ethan Burns*. Lyme, NH: Aisle Seat Books, 2013. C

Barbery, Muriel. *Gourmet Rhapsody*. New York: Europa Editions, 2009, translated from the French by Alison Anderson. B, G

Barnes, Linda. *Deep Pockets*. New York: St. Martin's Minotaur, 2004. B

Barnett, Jill. *Sentimental Journey*. New York: Pocket Books, 2002. C

Baxt, George. *The Alfred Hitchcock Murder Case*. New York: International Polygonics, 1987. G

———. *The Clark Gable and Carole Lombard Murder Case*. New York: St. Martin's Press, 1997. B, G, T

———. *The Greta Garbo Murder Case*. In *Two Great Mysteries: The Dietrich and Garbo Murder Cases*. New York: Barnes & Noble, 2000. B, C, G

———. *The Humphrey Bogart Murder Case*. New York: St. Martin's Press, 1995. B, C, G, T

———. *The Mae West Murder Case*. New York: St. Martin's Press, 1993. C, G

Bibliography

_____. *The Marlene Dietrich Murder Case*. In *Two Great Mysteries: The Dietrich and Garbo Murder Cases*, New York: Barnes & Noble, 2000. C, G

_____. *The Tallulah Bankhead Murder Case*. New York: International Polygonics, 1988). B, C, G, T

_____. *The William Powell and Myrna Loy Murder Case*. New York: St. Martin's Press, 1996. G, T

Beckerman, Ilene. *What We Do for Love*. Chapel Hill, NC: Algonquin Books of Chapel Hill, 1997. B, C

Bell, James Scott. *Final Witness*. Nashville, TN: Broadman & Holman, 1999. B, G

_____. *No Legal Grounds*. Grand Rapids, Michigan: Zondervan, 2007. B

_____. *Try Darkness*. New York: Center Street, 2008. B, C, G, T

_____. *Try Dying*. New York: Center Street, 2007. B, G

_____. *Try Fear*. New York: Center Street, 2009. B, C, T

Bellow, Saul. *More Die of Heartbreak*. New York: William Morrow, 1987. G

Bernhardt, William. *Capitol Murder*. New York: Ballantine Books, 2007. C

_____. *Murder One*. New York: Ballantine Books, 2001. B

_____. *Nemesis: The Final Case of Eliot Ness*. New York: Ballantine Books, 2009. C, G

Betts, June Harman. *Father Was a Caveman*. Bloomington, IN: AuthorHouse, 2007. T

Blatty, William Peter. *Dimiter* .New York: Forge/Tom Doherty Associates, 2010. B

_____. *Legion*. New York: Simon and Schuster, 1983. B

Block, Lawrence. *The Burglar Who Painted Like Mondrian*. New York: Harper Torch, 2005. B

_____. *The Burglar Who Thought He Was Bogart*. New York: Onyx, 1996. B

_____. *The Burglar Who Traded Ted Williams*. New York: Dutton Books, 1994. B

_____. *Hit Parade*. New York: William Morrow/HarperCollins, 2006. B

_____. *Small Town*. New York: William Morrow/HarperCollins, 2003. B, T

_____. "Some Days You Get the Bear." In *Some Days You Get the Bear*. New York: William Morrow, 1993. B

_____. *When the Sacred Ginmill Closes*. New York: Avon Books, 1986. B, C

Block, Valerie. *Don't Make a Scene*. New York: Ballantine Books, 2007. G, T

Bochco, Steven. *Death by Hollywood*. New York: Random House, 2003. G, T

Bogart, Stephen Humphrey. *Play It Again*. New York: Forge/Tom Doherty Associates, 1995. B

_____. *The Remake: As Times Goes By*. New York: Forge/Tom Doherty Associates, 1997. B

Boothe, Clare. *The Women*. In *Sixteen Famous American Plays*. New York: The Modern Library, 1941. G

Box, C. J. *In Plain Sight*. New York: G. P. Putnam's Sons, 2006. T

Bradford, Barbara Taylor. *Act of Will*. Garden City, NY: Doubleday & Company, Inc., 1986, Book Club Edition. G

_____. *Angel*. New York: Random House, 1993. G, T

_____. *Breaking the Rules*. New York: St. Martin's Press, 2009. G

_____. *Her Own Rules*. New York: HarperCollins, 1996. G

_____. *Just Rewards*. New York: Doubleday/St. Martin's Press, 2006, large print. T

_____. *Letter from a Stranger*. New York: St. Martin's Press, 2012. B

_____. *Remember*. New York: Random House, 1991. B, G

_____. *Where You Belong*. New York: Doubleday, 1999. B, G, T

Bram, Christopher. *Lives of the Circus Animals*. New York: Perennial/HarperCollins, 2003. B, C

Brandner, Gary. "Heat Lightning." In *A Hot and Sultry Night for Crime*. Ed. by Jeffrey Deaver. New York: Berkley Prime Crime, 2003. B

Braun, Lilian Jackson. *The Cat Who Brought Down the House*. New York: Jove, 2004. B, G

Breaznell, Gene. *Deadly Divots*. Bridgehampton, NY: Bridge Works, 2003. C

Brooks, Bill. *Bonnie and Clyde: A Love Story*. New York: Forge/Tom Doherty, 2004. C

Brown, Dale. *Chains of Command*. New York: G. P. Putnam's Sons, 1993. C

Brown, Irene Bennett. *Where Gable Slept*. Jefferson, Oregon: Riveredge, 2010. G

Brown, Joe David. *Addie Pray*. New York: Simon & Schuster, 1971) C

Brown, Sandra. *Ricochet*. New York: Simon & Schuster, 2006. T

_____. *Smash Cut* .New York: Simon & Schuster, 2009. B

Bukowski, Charles. "Animal Crackers in My Soup." In *Tales of Ordinary Madness*. San Francisco: City Lights Books, 1983. B

_____. *Factotum*. New York: ECCO/HarperCollins, 2002. B

_____. "The Gut-Wringing Machine." In *The Most Beautiful Woman in Town & Other Stories*. San Francisco: City Lights Books, 1983. G

_____. *Hollywood*. New York: ECCO/HarperCollins, 2002. B, G

_____. "The Murder of Ramon Vasquez." In *The Most Beautiful Woman in Town & Other Stories*. San Francisco: City Lights Books, 1983. B, G

_____. "Night Streets of Madness." In *Tales of Ordinary Madness*. San Francisco: City Lights Books, 1983. B

_____. "A Rain of Women." In *Tales of Ordinary Madness*. San Francisco: City Lights Books, 1983. B

Burke, James Lee. *Bitterroot*. New York: Simon & Schuster, 2001. B

_____. *Creole Belle*. New York: Simon & Schuster, 2012. G

_____. *The Glass Rainbow*. New York: Simon & Schuster, 2010. G

_____. *Rain Gods*. New York: Simon & Schuster, 2009. B

_____. *The Tin Roof Blowdown*. New York: Simon & Schuster, 2007. G

Burnett, Barbara. *Writers of the Purple Sage*. New York: Thomas Dunne/St. Martin's Press, 1994. G

Butler, Robert Olen. *Hell*. New York: Grove Press, 2009. B

Cain, James M. *Double Indemnity*. Vintage Books/Random House, 1978. G

_____. *Love's Lovely Counterfeit*. In *Three by Cain*. New York: Vintage Crime/Random House, 1989. T

_____. *Serenade*. In *Three by Cain*. New York: Vintage Crime/Random House, 1989. G

Callan, Michael Feeney. "Drumcondra." In *An Argument for Sin: A Poetry Excursion*. Dublin: Crysis Press, 2013. C

Campbell, Colin. *Montecito Heights: A Resurrection Man Novel*. Woodbury, MN: Midnight Ink, 2014. G, T

Cannell, Stephen J. *Runaway Heart*. New York: St. Martin' Press, 2003. T

Capote, Truman. *Answered Prayers: The Unfinished Novel*. New York: Plume, 1988. B

Carcaterra, Lorenzo. *Gangsters*. Waterville, ME: G. K. Hall & Co., 2001. B

____. *Sleepers*. New York: Ballantine Books, 1996. B, G, T

Carr, John Dickson. *The Crooked Hinge*. In *Four Complete Dr. Fell Mysteries*. New York: Avenel Books, 1988. C

Carroll, Leslie. *Temporary Insanity*. New York: Avon Trade/HarperCollins, 2004. B, C

Cawood, Hap. *The Miler*. Yellow Spring, OH: Cimarron Books, 2003. C

Clarke, Arthur C. *2010: Odyssey Two*. New York: Del Rey/Ballantine Books, 1982. G

Clements, Arthur L. "Why I Don't Speak Italian." In *Unsettling America: An Anthology of Contemporary Multicultural Poetry*. Ed. by Maria Mazziotti Gillan and Jennifer Gillan. New York: Penguin, 1994. B

Coben, Harlan. *Deal Breaker*. New York: Dell, 2012. B, T

Cohen, Jeffrey. *A Farewell to Legs*. Baltimore, Maryland: Bancroft Press, 2003. B

____. *It Happened One Knife*. New York: Berkley Prime Crime, 2008. B, G, T

____. *Some Like it Hot – Buttered*. New York: Berkley Prime Crime, 2007. B, T

Cohen, Paula Marantz. *Jane Austen in Boca*. New York: St. Marin's Griffin, 2003. G, T

Cole, David. *Butterfly Lost*. New York: Harper, 1999, Book Club Edition. G

____. *Shadow Play*. New York: Avon Books, 2004. C

Collins, Max Allan. *Flying Blind*. New York: Dutton, 1998. C, G

____. *Majic Man*. New York: Dutton, 1999. C, G

_____. *Quarry in the Middle.* New York: Hard Case Crime, Dorchester/Winterfall, 2009. B, G

Condon, Richard. *Prizzi's Family.* Thorndike, ME: Thorndike Press, 1989, large print. B

_____. *Winter Kills.* New York: Dell, 1975. C, G

Conroy, Pat. *Beach Music.* New York: Nan A. Talese/Doubleday, 1995. C

_____. *The Lords of Discipline.* New York: Bantam Books, 1983. G

_____. *The Water Is Wide.* New York: Bantam Books, 2002. B

Cook, Thomas H. *Breakheart Hill.* New York: Bantam Books, 1995. G

_____. *Peril.* New York: Bantam Books, 2004. C

Cooney, Ellen. *Lambrusco.* New York: Pantheon Books, 2008. T

Cornwell, Patricia. *Isle of Dogs.* New York: Berkley Books, 2002. G

Cortázar, Julio. *The Winners.* New York: Pantheon Books/Random House, 1965, translated from the Spanish by Elaine Kerrigan. C, G

Crichton, Michael. *The Andromeda Strain.* New York: Dell, 1971. C

Crider, Bill. *We'll Always Have Murder: A Humphrey Bogart Mystery.* New York: ibooks/Simon & Schuster, 2001. B, C, G

Cussler, Clive. *Sahara.* New York: Simon & Schuster, 1992. B, C

Daheim, Mary. *The Alpine Pursuit.* New York: Ballantine Books, 2004. C

Dandola, John. *West of Orange* (as *Dead at the Box Office*). Glen Ridge, NJ: Jersey Yarns/Tory Corner Editions, 1993. G, T

Dart, Iris Rainer. *Beaches.* New York: Bantam Books, 1988. G

Davis, Bruce. *We're Dead, Com on In.* Gretna, LA: Pelican, 2005. C, G

Deaver, Jeffrey. *The Bone Collector.* New York: Signet, 1999. B

DeLillo, Don. *Libra.* New York: Viking Penguin, 1988. G

_____. *Underworld.* New York: Scribner, 1997. B

_____. *White Noise.* New York: Penguin, 1999. G

de los Santos, Marisa. *Belong to Me.* New York: William Morrow/HarperCollins, 2008. C

_____. *Falling Together.* New York: William Morrow/HarperCollins, 2011. B

_____. *Love Walked In.* New York: Plume/Penguin, 2006. B, C, G, T

DeMille, Nelson. *The General's Daughter*. New York: Warner Books, 1999. B

———. *Word of Honor*. New York: Warner Books, 1998. T

Dickey, Eric Jerome. *Resurrecting Midnight*. New York: Dutton, 2009. B

Diehl, William. *Primal Fear*. New York: Ballantine Books, 1994. B, C, G, T

Doctorow, E. L. *Daniel*. New York: Signet/New American Library, 1972. B

Douglas, Kirk. *Dance with the Devil*. New York: Random House, 1990. B, G

Druxman, Michael B. *Gable: A One-Person Play in Two Acts*. Austin, TX: CreateSpace Independent Publishing Platform, 2011. C, G, T

———. *Tracy: A One-Person Play in Two Acts*. Austin, TX: CreateSpace Independent Publishing Platform, 2011. B, C, G, T

Duffe, Mary. *The Summer Gary Cooper Won the War*. St. Louis, MO: S & R Press, 1974. C

Dunne, Dominick. *Another City, Not My Own*. New York: Crown, 1998. B, G

Dunne, John Gregory. *True Confessions*. New York: Pocket Books, 1978. B, C, G, **T**

Dunning, John. *Two O'Clock, Eastern Time*. New York: Scribner, 2001. C

Ellroy, James. *The Cold Six Thousand*. New York: Alfred A. Knopf, 2001. T

———. *L. A. Confidential*. New York: Mysterious Press/Warner Books, 1991. C, G

Eco, Umberto. *Foucault's Pendulum*. San Diego: Harcourt Brace Jovanovich, 1989, translated from the Italian by William Weaver. B, G

Edgerton, Clyde. *The Bible Salesman*. New York: Little, Brown and Company, 2008. G

Edwards, Murray H. "With a Lot of Help from My Friends." In *Looking for Lucy Gilligan and Other Stories*. Abilene, TX: The Old Weather Bureau, 2009. T

Estleman, Loren D. *Downriver*. New York: ibooks/Simon & Schuster, 2002. C, T

———. *Edsel*. New York: Warner Books, 1995. B, G, T

———. *The Hours of the Virgin*. New York: Warner Books, 2000. B

———. *Jitterbug*. New York: Tom Doherty Associates, 1998. B, G

———. *Retro*. New York: Tom Doherty Associates, 2004. B, G

———. *Something Borrowed, Something Black*. New York: Tom Doherty Associates, 2002. B, C, G

———. *The Witchfinder*. New York: Warner Books, 1999. C

Esstman, Barbara. *Night Ride Home*. New York: Perennial/HarperCollins, 2001. C

Evans, Elizabeth. *The Blue Hour*. Chapel Hill, NC: Algonquin Books, 1994. G

Fast, Howard. *The Dinner Party*. New York: Dell, 1987. C

Favorite, Eileen. *The Heroines*. New York: Scribner, 2008. G

Fenady, Andrew J. *The Man with Bogart's Face*. Waterville, ME, and Bath, England: Thorndike Press/Chivers Press, 2002, Large Print. B, C, G, T

———. *The Secret of Sam Marlow: The Further Adventures of the Man with Bogart's Face*. Chicago: Contemporary Books, 1980. B, C, G, T

Fitzgerald, F. Scott. *The Last Tycoon*. New York: Bantam Books, 1976. C, T

Flagg, Fannie. *The All-Girl Filling Station's Last Reunion*. New York: Random House, 2013. G

———. *Can't Wait to Get to Heaven*. New York: Random House, 2006. T

———. *Coming Attractions* (as *Daisy Fay and the Miracle Man*). New York: Warner Books, 1981. B, G, T

———. *I Still Dream About You*. New York: Random House, 2010. B

———. *Standing in the Rainbow*. New York: Ballantine Books, 2003. G

Fonseca, Isabel. *Attachment*. New York: Alfred A. Knopf, 2008. G

Ford, Richard. *Independence Day*. Boston: Little, Brown and Company, 1995. C, G

Forstchen, William R. *One Second After*. New York: Forge/Tom Doherty Associates, 2009. C

Fowle, Herb 'Chick.' *Against All Odds*. Lincoln, NE: iUniverse, 2006. C

Friedman, Kinky. *God Bless John Wayne*. New York: Bantam, 1996. B, C

Furutani, Dale. *The Toyotomi Blades*. New York: St. Martin's Paperbacks, 1998. B, C

Gann, Ernest K. *The High and the Mighty*. Garden City, New York: Permabooks, 1954. G

Garfield, Brian. *Death Wish*. Greenwich, CT: Fawcett Crest, 1974. C, G

Gary, Romain. *The Ski Bum*. New York: Harper & Row, 1965. C

Gibson, William. *The Cobweb*. New York: Bantam, 1967 C

Goldman, William. *Control*. New York: Delacorte, 1982. B

_____. *Magic*. New York: Dell, 1977. T

_____. *Marathon Man*. New York: Dell, 1975. B, C

_____. *Father's Day*. New York: Bantam Books, 1972. G

_____. *Your Turn to Curtsy, My Turn to Bow*. New York: Bantam Books, 1965. G

Gorman, Ed. "The Alibi." In *Raymond Chandler's Philip Marlowe: A Centennial Celebration*. New York: ibooks, 1999. G

Grady, James. *Thunder*. New York: Warner Books, 1994. B, C

Green, Gerald. *The Last Angry Man*. New York: Charles Scribner's Sons, 1956. G

Griffin, S. A. "America Poem." In *Poems from Penny Lane*. Ed. by Gary Parrish, Jr. and LeAnn Bifoss. Boulder, CO: Farfalla Press/McMillan & Parrish, 2003. C, G

Griffin, W.E.B. *Blood and Honor*. New York: Jove Books, 1997. B, T

Grimes, Martha. *Belle Ruin*. New York: Viking/Penguin, 2005. C, G

_____. *The Case Has Altered*. New York: Henry Holt and Company, 1977. B

_____. *Cold Flat Junction*. New York: Viking/Penguin, 2001. B, G

_____. *The End of the Pier*. New York: Alfred A. Knopf, 1992. C

_____. *The Five Bells and Bladebone*. Boston: Little, Brown and Company, 1987. B, C

_____. *The Grave Maurice*. New York: Onyx/New American Library, 2003. B, C

_____. *Help the Struggler*. Boston: Little, Brown and Company, 1985. B

_____. *Jerusalem Inn*. Boston: Little, Brown and Company, 1984. C

_____. *The Man with a Load of Mischief*. New York: Onyx/New American Library, 2003. C

_____. *The Old Wine Shades*. New York: Viking/Penguin, 2006. B
Grisham, John. *The Brethren*. New York: Doubleday, 2000. B
_____. *The Firm*. New York: Island Books/Dell, 1992. G
Hall, James W. *Mean High Tide*. New York, Dell, 1995. B
Hamill, Denis. *Fork in the Road*. New York: Washington Square Press, 2001. B, G
Hamill, Pete. *The Gift*. New York, Boston: Little, Brown and Company: 2005. G
_____. *The Guns of Heaven*. New York: Hard Case Crime, Dorchester/Winterfall, 2006. B
_____. *Snow in August*. Boston, New York: Little, Brown and Company, 1997. B, C
_____. *Tabloid City*. New York: Little, Brown and Company: 2011. B
Hamilton, Donald. *The Terminators*. Greenwich, CT: Fawcett, 1975. C
Hamner, Jr., Earl. *Spencer's Mountain*. New York: Dell, 1973. B
Harris, Joanne. *Chocolat*. New York: Penguin, 2000. B
Harris, Thomas. *Red Dragon*. New York: Dutton/Penguin Group, 1981. C
Hay, Elizabeth. *Garbo Laughs*. New York: Counterpoint, 2003. B, C, G, T
_____. "Sayonara." In *Small Change*. Washington D.C.: Counterpoint, 2001. B
_____. *A Student of Weather*. New York: Counterpoint, 2001. C, G, T
Healy, Jeremiah. "In the Line of Duty." In *Raymond Chandler's Philip Marlowe*. New York: ibooks/Simon & Schuster, 1999. C
_____. *Yesterday's News*. New York: Pocket Books, 1990. C
Hendricks, Judith Ryan. *Bread Alone*. New York: William Morrow/HarperCollins, 2001. B, C, G
Herlihy, James Leo. *Midnight Cowboy*. New York: Simon & Schuster, 1965. C
Hijuelos, Oscar. *Beautiful María of My Soul*. New York: Hyperion, 2010. B
_____. *The Fourteen Sisters of Emilio Montez O'Brien*. New York: Farrar, Straus and Giroux, 1993. C, G

_____. *The Mambo Kings Play Songs of Love*. New York: Farrar, Straus and Giroux, 1989. B, T

_____. *A Simple Habana Melody*. New York: HarperCollins, 2002. C

Hillerman, Tony. *Skeleton Man*. New York: HarperCollins, 2004. G

Hłasko, Marek. *Sowa, córka piekarza* (*Owl, the Baker's Daughter*). Poland: Wydawnictwo Da Capo, 1999, in Polish. B

Holmes, Rupert. *Where the Truth Lies*. New York: Random House, 2003. B

Hosseini, Khaled. *The Kite Runner*. New York: Riverhead Books, 2003. G

Huie, William Bradford. *Mud on the Stars*. New York: Signet Books/New American Library, 1955. T

Hunter, Evan (also as Ed McBain). *The Blackboard Jungle*. London: Constable, 1955. B

_____. *Fat Ollie's Book* (see Ed McBain)

_____. *Gladly the Cross-Eyed Bear* (see Ed McBain)

_____. *Jack and the Beanstalk* (see Ed McBain)

_____. *Jigsaw* (see Ed McBain)

_____. *The Moment She Was Gone*. New York: Simon & Schuster, 2002. B

_____. *Strangers When We Meet*. New York: Dell, 1958. G

Iles, Greg. *Black Cross*. New York: Dutton, 1995. G

_____. *Blood Memory*. New York: Scribner, 2005. C, G

_____. *Dead Sleep*. New York: G. P. Putnam's Sons, 2001. B

_____. *The Devil's Punchbowl*. New York: Scribner, 2009. B, G

_____. *Mortal Fear*. New York: Dutton, 1997. C

_____. *Natchez Burning*. New York: William Morrow/HarperCollins, 2014. B

_____. *The Quiet Game*. New York: Dutton, 1999. G

_____. *Sleep No More*. New York: G. P. Putnam's Sons, 2002. B

_____. *Turning Angel*. New York: Scribner, 2005. G

_____. *24 Hours*. New York: G. P. Putnam's Sons, 2000. B

Infante, Guillermo Cabrera. *Three Trapped Tigers*. Normal, London: Dalkey Archive Press, 2015, translated from the Spanish by Donald Gardner and Suzanne Jill Levine. C

Irving, John. *A Prayer for Owen Meany*. New York: Ballantine Books, 1990. B

Isaacs, Susan. *After All These Years*. New York: HarperCollins, 1993. B, G

_____. *Any Place I Hang My Hat*. New York: Scribner, 2004. G

_____. *Goldberg Variations*. New York: Scribner, 2012. B

_____. *Red, White & Blue*. New York: HarperCollins, 1998. B, C, G

_____. *Shining Through*. New York: Ballantine Books, 1989. C, G

Jackson, Joe. *Leavenworth Train: A Fugitive's Search for Justice in the Vanishing West*. New York: Carroll & Graf, 2002. C

Janis, Byron, with Maria Cooper Janis. *Chopin and Beyond: My Extraordinary Life in Music and the Paranormal*. Hoboken, NJ: John Wiley & Sons, 2010. C, G

Jeffries, Donald. *The Unreals*. Danville, CA: StoneGarden, 2007. B, C

Johnson, Maureen. *Suite Scarlett*. New York: Point, 2008. G, T

Jones, James. *From Here to Eternity*. New York: Charles Scribner's Sons, 1951. C, G

_____. *Go to the Widow-Maker*. New York: Delacorte, 1967. G

_____. *Some Came Running*. New York: Signet, 1957. C, G

Jong, Erica. *Any Woman's Blues*. New York: Harper & Row, 1990. C, G

_____. *Inventing Memory*. New York: HarperCollins, 1997. B

Kaminsky, Stuart (M.). *Bright Futures*. New York: Forge/Tom Doherty Associates, 2008). G

_____. *Bullet for a Star*. New York: St. Martin's Press, 1977. B, C, G

_____. *The Dead Don't Lie*. New York: Forge/Tom Doherty Associates, 2007. B

_____. *Denial*. New York: Forge/Tom Doherty Associates, 2005. B

_____. *The Devil Met a Lady*. New York: The Mysterious Press/Warner Books, 1993. B, G

_____. *High Midnight*. New York: St. Martin's Press, 1981. B, C, G, T

_____. *Lieberman's Thief*. New York: Henry Holt and Company, 1995. B, G

_____. *The Man Who Shot Lewis Vance*. New York: St. Martin's Press, 1986. B, C, T

———. *Midnight Pass*. New York: Forge/Tom Doherty Associates, 2003. B, T
———. *Mildred Pierced*. New York: Otto Penzler/Carroll & Graf, 2003. B, G
———. *Murder on the Yellow Brick Road*. New York: St. Martin's Press, 1977. B, G, T
———. *Poor Butterfly*. New York: The Mysterious Press, 1990. T
———. *Retribution*. New York: Forge/Tom Doherty Associates, 2001. C, G
———. *Smart Moves*. New York: Thomas Dunne/St. Martin's Press, 1986. B, G
———. *Think Fast, Mr. Peters*. New York: Thomas Dunne/St. Martin's Press, 1987. B, C, G
———. *To Catch a Spy*. New York: Otto Penzler/Carroll & Graf, 2002. B
———. *Tomorrow Is Another Day*. New York: The Mysterious Press/Warner Books, 1995. B, C, G
———. *Vengeance*. New York: Forge/Tom Doherty Associates, 1999. B, C
Kaufman, Sue. *Diary of a Mad Housewife*. New York: Bantam Books, 1972. B, C
Kazan, Elia. *The Assassins*. Greenwich, CT: Fawcett Crest, 1973. B
Keillor, Garrison. *Lake Wobegon Summer 1956*. New York: Viking Penguin, 2001. G
Kennedy, Adam. *Just Like Humphrey Bogart*. New York: Signet/New American Library, 1979. B, C, G, T
Kerouac, Jack. *Desolation Angels*. New York: Perigee Books/G. P. Putnam's Sons, 1980. B, C, G
———. *On the Road*. New York: Penguin, 2007. C
———. *Satori in Paris*. In *Satori in Paris and Pic: Two Novels by Jack Kerouac*. New York: Grove Press, 1988. B, G
Kerr, Jean. *Please Don't Eat the Daisies*. Greenwich, CT: Crest/Fawcett, 1959. C
William X. Kienzle. *No Greater Love*. New York: Fawcett Books/Ballantine Books, 2000. B, T
Kiernan, Caitlín R. *The Drowning Girl*. New York: ROC/New American Library, 2012. T

King, Stephen (also as Richard Bachman). *Bag of Bones*. New York: Pocket Books, 1999. B

———. *Christine*. New York: The Viking Press, 1983, Book Club Edition. B

———. *Dolores Claiborne*. New York: Signet, 1993. C

———. *Duma Key*. New York: Scribner, 2008. G, T

———. *11/22/63*. New York: Scribner, 2011. B, C, G

———. *The Green Mile*. New York: Pocket Books, 1999. G

———. "The Langoliers." In *Four Past Midnight*. New York: Signet, 2004. C

———. *Lisey's Story*. New York: Scribner, 2006. G

———. *The Regulators* (see Richard Bachman)

———. *The Stand*. New York: Signet/New American Library, 1991. B

———. "What Is It in French?" In *Everything's Eventual: 14 Dark Tales*. New York: Pocket Books, 2003. G

Kingsolver, Barbara. *The Bean Tree*. New York: Harper/Perennial, 2003. C

———. *Flight Behavior*. New York: HarperCollins, 2012. T

Klavan, Laurence. *The Cutting Room*. New York: Ballantine Books, 2005. C, G, T

———. *The Shooting Script*. New York: Fawcett Books, 2006. G, T

Klimitas, Hank. *Twice a Survivor: A Katrina Journal*. New York, Lincoln, NE: iUniverse, 2006. T

Kober, Arthur. "*Having Wonderful Time*." In *Sixteen Famous American Plays*. New York: The Modern Library, 1941. C

Koch, Herman. *The Dinner*. London, New York: Hogarth, 2012, translated from the Dutch by Sam Garrett. T

Kohler, Heinz. *My Name Was Five*. Minneapolis, MN: Mill City Press, 2009. C

Lankford, Terrill Lee. *Earthquake Weather*. New York: Ballantine Books, 2004. B

Lardo, Vincent. *McNally's Alibi*. New York: G. P. Putnam's Sons, 2002. B

Larsson, Stieg. *The Girl with the Dragon Tattoo*. New York: Vintage Crime/Black Lizard/Random House, 2009, translated from the Swedish by Reg Keeland. G

Lash, Jennifer. *Blood Ties*. New York: Bloomsbury, 1999. T

Latham, Aaron. *Riding with John Wayne*. New York: Simon & Schuster, 2006. C, G, T

Lawrence, E. Duke. *The $trip*. New York: Bloomsbury, 2009. G

Laymon, Richard. *Endless Night*. New York: Leisure Books/Dorchester Publishing, 2004. C

_____. *The Lake*. New York: Leisure Books/Dorchester Publishing, 2004. B

Lehane, Dennis. *A Drink Before the War*. New York: HarperTorch, 2001. B

Leigh, Janet. *House of Destiny*. Don Mills, Ont., Canada: Mira Books, 1995. B, C, G

Leonard, Elmore. *Be Cool*. New York: Dell, 2000. B, C

_____. *City Primeval: High Noon in Detroit*. New York: HarperTorch, 2002. C

_____. "Comfort to the Enemy" in *Comfort to the Enemy and Other Carl Webster Stories*. New York: Harper, 2010. B

_____. *Djibouti*. New York: Harper, 2011. B

_____. *52 Pick Up*. New York: HarperTorch, 2002. C

_____. *The Hot Kid*. New York: HarperTorch, 2006. G

_____. *LaBrava*. New York: Harper, 2009. B

_____. *Maximum Bob*. New York: Delacorte, 1991. G

_____. *The Moonshine War*. New York: Dell, 1985. C

_____. *Out of Sight*. New York: Dell, 1997. C

_____. *Pronto*. New York: Delacorte, 1993. C

_____. "Tenkiller." In *When the Women Come Out to Dance*. New York: William Morrow/HarperCollins, 2002. G

_____. *Tishomingo Blues* New York: William Morrow, 2002. C

_____. *Up in Honey's Room*. New York: Harper, 2008. B, G

Levin, Ira. *Rosemary's Baby*. New York: Dell, 1968. C

Lewis, Sinclair. *Kingsblood Royal*. New York: Random House, 1947. G

Lippman, Laura. *Another Thing to Fall*. New York: William Morrow/HarperCollins, 2008. B, C

_____. *In a Strange City*. New York: William Morrow/HarperCollins, 2001. G, T.

Littlefield, Sophie. *A Bad Day for Sorry*. New York: Minotaur Books, 2009. C

Long, Jeff. *The Wall* (New York: Atria Books, 2006. T

Lovesey, Peter. *Diamond Solitaire*. New York: The Mysterious Press/Warner Books, 1993. B

_____. *The Summons*. New York: Soho Press, 2004. C

Ludlum, Robert. *The Bourne Ultimatum*. New York: Random House, 1990. C

_____. *The Matlock Paper*. New York: Dell, 1986. B

MacDonald, John D. *The Executioners* (as *Cape Fear*). New York: Random House, 2014. G

Malone, Michael. "Blue Cadillac." In: *Red Clay, Blue Cadillac: Stories of Twelve Southern Women* Naperville, IL: Sourcebooks Landmark, 2002. T

_____. *The Delectable Mountains or, Entertaining Stranger*. Naperville, IL: Sourcebooks, 2002. G

_____. *Dingley Falls*. Naperville, IL: Sourcebooks, 2002. B

_____. *First Lady*. Naperville, IL: Sourcebooks Landmark, 2001. B

_____. *Foolscap or, The Stages of Love*. Naperville, IL: Sourcebooks, 2002. C

_____. *The Four Corners of the Sky*. Naperville, IL: Sourcebooks Landmark, 2009. B, C, G, T

_____. *Handling Sin*. Naperville, IL: Sourcebooks, 2004. G

_____. "Invitation to the Ball." In: *Red Clay, Blue Cadillac: Stories of Twelve Southern Women*. Naperville, IL: Sourcebooks Landmark, 2002. B

_____. "Love and Other Crimes." In: *Red Clay, Blue Cadillac: Stories of Twelve Southern Women*. Naperville, IL: Sourcebooks Landmark, 2002. G

_____. *Time's Witness*. Naperville, IL: Sourcebooks, 2002. B, C, G

Marquand, John P. *Wickford Point*. New York: P. F. Collier and Son, 1939. C

Martin, Charles. *Maggie*. In: *Down Where My Love Lives*. Nashville: Thomas Nelson, 2008. G

Mayor, Archer. *Scent of Evil*. New York: Mysterious Press/Warner Books, 1996. T

McAfee, Annalena. *The Spoiler*. New York: Vintage Books/Random House, 2012. B, T

McBain, Ed (aka Evan Hunter). *Fat Ollie's Book*. New York: Simon & Schuster, 2002. B

_____. *Gladly the Cross-Eyed Bear*. New York: Warner Books, 1996. B

_____. *Jack and the Beanstalk*. New York: Holt, Rinehart and Winston, 1984. C, G

_____. *Jigsaw*. In *Three from the 87th*. Garden City, NY: Nelson Doubleday, 1971. B

McBride, Mary. *Say It Again, Sam*. New York: Warner Books, 2004. B, C

McCammon, Robert R. "I Scream Man!" In *Blue World*. New York: Pocket Books, 1990. C

_____. *Swan Song*. New York: Pocket Books, 1987. C, T

McCorkle, Jill. *Carolina Moon*. Chapel Hill, Algonquin Books of Chapel Hill, 1996. G

_____. *Life After Life*. Chapel Hill, Algonquin Books of Chapel Hill, 2013. B, G

McCoy, Horace. *They Shoot Horses, Don't They?* New York: Avon/Hearst, 1969; c-t 1935. C

McCoy, Ron. "It Ain't Me, Babe: Working for Richard Nixon." In *Time It Was: American Stories from the Sixties*. Ed. by Karen Manners Smith and Tim Koster. Upper Saddle River, NJ: Pearson Prentice Hall, 2007. T

McCrumb, Sharyn. *The Hangman's Beautiful Daughter*. New York: Charles Scribner's Sons/Macmillan, 1992. T

_____. *Lovely in Her Bones*. New York: Ballantine Books, 1990. C

McEvoy, Dermot. *Our Lady of Greenwich Village*. New York: Skyhorse, 2008. B, G, T

McGivern, William P. *The Caper of the Golden Bulls*. New York: Pocket Books, 1967. C

McGuane, Thomas. *The Cadence of Grass*. New York: Vintage Contemporaries, 2002. C

McMurtry, Larry. *All My Friends Are Going to Be Strangers.* New York: Touchstone, 1989. C, G, T

———. *Loop Group.* New York: Simon & Schuster, 2004. T

———. *Moving On.* New York: Simon & Schuster, 1987. C

———. *Rhino Ranch.* New York: Simon & Schuster, 2009. G

———. *Somebody's Darling.* New York: Scribner Paperback Fiction/Simon & Schuster, 2002. C

Michener, James A. "Australia." In *Return to Paradise.* New York: Bantam Books, 1964. B

———. *The Drifters.* New York: Fawcett, 1982. B, T

———. *Iberia.* New York: Fawcett, 1969. C

———. "Polynesia." In *Return to Paradise.* New York: Bantam Books, 1964. G

Miles, Keith. *Double Eagle.* Scottsdale, AZ: Poisoned Pen Press, 2002. C

Miller, John Douglas. *The Greek Summer.* London and Lincoln, NE: iUniverse, 2003. G, T

Miller, Linda Lael. *The Legacy.* New York: Pocket Books, 1994, large print. C

Miller, Lynn Ruth. *Starving Hearts.* Pacifica, CA: excentrix press, 2000. C

Miller, Rebecca. *The Private Lives of Pippa Lee.* New York: Farrar, Straus and Giroux, 2008. G

Muller, Marcia. *Coming Back.* New York: Grand Central, 2010. B

———. *The Ever-Running Man.* New York: Warner Books/Hachette Book Group, 2007). G

———. *Trophies and Dead Things.* New York: Mysterious Press/Warner Books, 1990. B, T

———. *Where Echoes Live.* New York: Mysterious Press/Warner Books, 1991. B

———. *While Other People Sleep.* Mysterious Press/Warner Books, 1998. B

Nadelson, Reggie. *Red Hot Blues.* New York: St. Martin's Press, 1998. C

Nadler, Stuart. *Wise Men.* New York: Reagan Arthur Books/Little, Brown and Company, 2013. C, G

Naughton, Michael P. *Deathryde: Rebel Without a Corpse.* Los Angeles: Gilded Hearse Press, 2008. B, G, T

Neiderman, Andrew. *Curse*. New York: Pocket Books, 2000. C

_____. *The Hunted*. London: Pocket Books, 2006. C

Nichols, John. *The Sterile Cuckoo*. New York: Avon Books, 1966. G

O'Brien, Tim. "The Ghost Soldiers." In *The Things They Carried*. New York: Houghton Mifflin Harcourt, 1990. C

_____. *If I Die in a Combat Zone, Box Me Up and Ship Me Home*. New York: Broadway Books, 1999. B

_____. "On the Rainy River." In *The Things They Carried*. New York: Houghton Mifflin Harcourt, 1990. C

O'Callaghan, Thomas. *Bone Thief*. New York: Pinnacle Books, 2006. C

O'Connor, Flannery. "A Good Man Is Hard to Find." In *Three by Flannery O'Connor: Wise Blood, A Good Man Is Hard to Find, The Violent Bear It Away*. New York: Signet/New American Library, 1964. G

Odets, Clifford. *Golden Boy*. In *Waiting for Lefty and Other Plays*. New York: Grove Press, 1993. C

_____. *Waiting for Lefty*. In *Waiting for Lefty and Other Plays*. New York: Grove Press, 1993. G

O'Hara, John. "Can I Stay Here?" In *Collected Stories of John O'Hara*. New York: Random House, 1984. C

_____. *From the Terrace*. New York: Carroll & Graf, 1984. C, T

_____. "James Francis and the Star." In *Waiting for Winter: A Collection of 21 New Stories by John O'Hara*. New York: Random House, 1966. G, T

_____. "Natica Jackson." In *Collected Stories of John O'Hara*. New York: Random House, 1984. G

_____. *Pal Joey*. New York: Vintage Books/Random House, 1983. G

Olasky, Marvin. *Scimitar's Edge*. Nashville, TN: Broadman & Holman, 2006. C

Palmer, Michael. *Political Suicide*. New York: St. Martin's Press, 2013. C

Paretsky, Sara. *Tunnel Vision*. New York: Delacorte, 1994. C

Paris, Iris. *Once Upon a Chariot*. Mustang, OK: Tate Pub & Enterprises, 2008. C

Parker, Robert B. *Bad Business*. New York: G. P. Putnam's Sons, 2004. G

_____. *Blue Screen*. New York: G. P. Putnam's Sons, 2006. G

_____. *Cold Service*. New York: G. P. Putnam's Sons, 2005. C

_____. *Crimson Joy*. New York: Delacorte, 1988. G

_____. *Double Deuce*. New York: Berkley Books, 1993. C

_____. *Double Play*. New York: Berkley Books, 2005. B, T

_____. *Early Autumn*. New York: Dell, 1992. T

_____. *God Save the Child*. In *The Early Spenser: Three Complete Novels*. New York: Delacorte/Seymour Lawrence, 1989. B

_____. *Hush Money*. New York: G. P. Putnam's Sons, 1999. B

_____. *The Judas Goat*. New York: Dell, 1987. B, C

_____. *Mortal Stakes*. New York: Dell, 1987. C, G

_____. *Pale Kings and Princes*. New York: Dell, 1988. B

_____. *Playmates*. New York: G. P. Putnam's Sons, 1989. B, T

_____. *Sea Change*. New York: Berkley Books, 2007. B

Patterson, James. *Along Came a Spider*. New York: Warner Books, 1993. C

_____. *Maximum Ride: School's Out Forever*. New York: Warner Vision Books, 2007. G

Patterson, James and Howard Roughan. *Sail*. New York: Little, Brown and Company, 2008. C

Percy, Walker. *Love in the Ruins*. New York: Picador/Farrar, Straus and Giroux, 1999. G

_____. *The Moviegoer*. New York: Avon Books/Bard, 1982. G

Peters, Ralph. *The Devil's Garden*. New York: Avon Books, 1999. B, C, **G**

_____. *Traitor*. New York: Avon Books, 1999. C

Petrakis, Harry Mark. "Legends of Glory." In *Legends of Glory and Other Stories*. Carbondale, IL: Southern Illinois University Press, 2007. C

Phillips, Jayne Anne. *Machine Dreams*. New York: Vintage Contemporaries/Random House, 1999. G

Picoult, Jodi. *House Rules*. New York: Atria Books, 2010. B

_____. *Picture Perfect*. New York: G. P. Putnam's Sons, 1995. G

_____. *Songs of the Humpback Whale*. New York: Washington Square Press, 2001. G

Potok, Andrew. *Ordinary Daylight: Portrait of an Artist Going Blind.* New York: Bantam Books, 2003. T

Price, Richard. *Freedomland.* New York: Dell, 2005. T

Pronzini, Bill. *Shackles.* New York: Dell, 1990. G

Puzo, Mario. *The Fourth K.* New York: Random House, 1990. C, G

Pynchon, Thomas. *Gravity's Rainbow.* New York: Viking: 1973. G, T

_____. *Inherent Vice.* New York: Penguin, 2009. B

_____. *Vineland.* Boston: Little, Brown & Company, 1990. B, G, T

Queen, Ellery. *Calamity Town.* New York: ImPress/Reader's Digest, 2003. C

Randisi, Robert J. *Hey There (You with the Gun in Your Hand).* New York: Minotaur Books, 2008. B, G

_____. *You're Nobody 'Til Somebody Kills You.* New York: Minotaur Books, 2009. G

Rankin, Ian. *Mortal Causes.* London: Orion, 2005. B, C

Raucher, Herman. *A Glimpse of Tiger.* Greenwich Village, CT: Fawcett Crest, 1975. G

_____. *Ode to Billy Joe.* New York: Dell, 1976. G

_____. *Summer of '42.* New York: Dell, 1971. B, C

_____. *There Should Have Been Castles.* New York: Dell, 1979. G

Riker, Leigh. *Acts of Passion.* Lincoln, NE: iUniverse, 2001. T

Robbins, Harold. *The Carpetbaggers.* New York: Kangaroo/Pocket Books, 1962. B, G, T

_____. *Never Leave Me.* New York: Avon Books, 1968. G

_____. *Where Love Has Gone.* New York: Giant Cardinal/Pocket Books, 1963. G

Roberts, Les. *Deep Shaker.* New York: Thomas Dunne/St. Martin's Press, 1991. C

Roberts, Nora. *High Noon.* New York: G. P. Putnam's Sons, 2007. C

_____. *Holding the Dream.* New York: Berkley Books, 2012. C

_____. *Northern Lights.* New York: G. P. Putnam's Sons, 2004. C

Roosevelt, Elliott. *Murder in Georgetown.* New York: Thomas Dunne Books/St. Martin's Minotaur, 1999. G

_____. *Murder in the Lincoln Bedroom.* New York: Thomas Dunne Books/St. Martin's Minotaur, 2000. B, G

_____. *Murder in the Red Room.* New York: Avon Books, 1994. C

Rosenfelt, David. *Dog Tags.* New York: Grand Central, 2010. T

Rossner, Judith. *Looking for Mr. Goodbar.* New York: Simon & Schuster, 1975. G

Roth, Philip. *American Pastoral.* Boston: Houghton Mifflin, 1997. G

_____. *Our Gang.* New York: Random House, 1971. G

_____. *The Plot Against America.* New York: Vintage International, 2005. T

_____. *Portnoy's Complaint.* New York: Bantam, 1970. C

Roubaud, Jacques. *The Loop.* Champaign, IL: Dalkey Archive Press, 2009, translated from the French by Jeff Fort. C

Rucker, Rudy. *Saucer Wisdom.* New York: Forge/Tom Doherty Associates, 1999. C

Sager, Mike. "The Temple of Doom." In *Scary Monsters and Super Freaks: Stories of Sex, Drugs, Rock 'N' Roll and Murder.* New York: Thunder's Mouth Press, 2003. T

Salinger, J. D. *The Catcher in the Rye.* Boston: Little, Brown and Company, 1991. C

Samway, Patrick. *Walker Percy: A Life.* Chicago: Loyola Press, 1999. C

Sanders, Lawrence. *The Case of Lucy Bending.* New York: Berkley Books, 1987. G

_____. *McNally's Alibi.* New York: G. P. Putnam's Sons, 2002. B

_____. *McNally's Dilemma.* New York: G. P. Putnam's Sons, 1999. T

_____. *McNally's Risk.* New York: G. P. Putnam's Sons, 1993. B

_____. *The Second Deadly Sin.* New York: Berkley Books, 1985. T

_____. *The Sixth Commandment.* New York: Berkley Books, 1987. B, C, G

_____. *The Timothy Files.* In *Three Complete Novels.* New York: G. P. Putnam's Sons, 1999. C

Sandford, John. *Silent Prey.* New York: Berkley Books, 2008. B

_____. *Winter Prey.* New York: Berkley Books, 1994. C

Saporta, Lionel R. "Gifts." In *Gifts*. New York and Lincoln, NE: iUniverse, 2006. C

Schulberg, Budd. *The Disenchanted*. New York: Random House, 1950. C, G

_____. *The Harder They Fall*. New York: Random House, 1947. B, G, T

_____. *What Makes Sammy Run?* New York: Vintage Books/Random House, 1993. G, T

Scott, A. D. *A Small Death in the Great Glen*. New York: ATRIA/Simon & Schuster, 2010. C, T

Sebold, Alice. *The Almost Moon*. New York: Little, Brown and Company, 2007. G

Shagan, Steve. *City of Angels* (as *Hustle*). London: Star Books/W. H. Allen, 1976. B

_____. *Save the Tiger*. New York: Dell, 1973. B, C

Shaw, Irwin. *Rich Man, Poor Man*. New York: Delacorte, 1970. B

Sheldon, Sidney. *A Stranger in the Mirror*. New York: Warner Books, 1981. G

Shepard, Sam. *Fool for Love*. In *Fool for Love and Other Plays*. New York: Bantam Books, 1988. T

_____. "Gary Cooper, Or the Landscape." In *Cruising Paradise*, New York: Vintage/Random House, 1996. C

_____. "Lost in Ruins." In *Cruising Paradise*, New York: Vintage/Random House, 1996. B

_____. *Motel Chronicles*. San Francisco: City Lights Books, 1982. B, C, T

_____. "Spencer Tracy Is Not Dead." In *Cruising Paradise*, New York: Vintage/Random House, 1996. T

Sherrill, Martha. *My Last Movie Star*. New York: Random House, 2002. B, C, G, T

Shukert, Rachel. *Love Me*. New York: Delacorte, 2014. B, C, G, T

_____. *Starstruck*. New York: Delacorte, 2013. B, G, T

Sillitoe, Alan. "The Decline and Fall of Frankie Buller." In: *The Loneliness of the Long-Distance Runner*. New York: Vintage International/Random House, 2010. C

Simon, Neil. *Plaza Suite*. In *The Comedy of Neil Simon*. New York: Equinox Books/Avon, 1973. B

Simon, Roger L. "Summer in Idle Valley." In *Raymond Chandler's Philip Marlowe: A Centennial Celebration*. New York: ibooks, 1999. B

Skye, Christina. *Going Overboard*. New York: Island Books/Bantam Dell, 2001. B, C, **T**

Smith, Barbara Burnett. *Writers of the Purple Sage*. New York: Thomas Dunne Books/St. Martin's Press, 1994. G

Snively, Susan. "Spencer Tracy." In: *The Undertow*. Gainesville, University Press of Florida, 1997. T

Sparks, Nicholas. *The Choice*. New York: Grand Central Publishing, 2007. B

Spencer, LaVyrle. *Then Came Heaven*. New York: G. P. Putnam's Sons, 1997. B, T

Spewack, Bella & Samuel. *Boy Meets Girl*. In *Sixteen Famous American Plays*. New York: The Modern Library, 1941. C, G

Spiro, Bernard. *The Other War: Letters from a GI in India in 1944& 1945*. Lincoln, NE: iUniverse, 2001. B, C, G

Sprinkle, Patricia. *Who Left That Body in the Rain?* New York: Signet/New American Library, 2002. C

Stark, Richard (aka Donald A. Westlake). *The Seventh*. Chicago: The University of Chicago Press, 2009. B

Stevens, Laurie. *The Dark Before Dawn*. Northridge, CA: Follow Your Dreams productions, 2001. C

Stockett, Kathryn. *The Help*. New York: Berkley Books, 2011. G, T

Styron, William. *Sophie's Choice*. New York: Random House, 1979. B, G

Talton, Jon. *Deadline Man*. Scottsdale, AZ: Poisoned Pen Press, 2010. B

Tanenbaum, Robert K. *Absolute Rage*. New York: Atria Books, 2002. C

———. *Bad Faith*: New York: Gallery Books, 2012. B

———. *Betrayed*. New York: Gallery Books, 2010. C, B

———. *Depraved Indifference*. New York: Signet/New American Library, 1900. C

———. *Enemy Within*. New York: Pocket Books, 2001. B

_____. *Falsely Accused*. New York: Dutton, 1996. B

_____. *Fury*. New York: Atria Books, 2005. B

Theroux, Paul. *Saint Jack*. Boston: Houghton Mifflin, 1973. G

Thornburg, Janet. "Chosen." In *Rhubarb Pie*. Eugene, OR: Thunderegg Press, 2005. T

_____. "Lucky Lady." In *Rhubarb Pie*. Eugene, OR: Thunderegg Press, 2005. G

Thorp, Roderick. *Rainbow Drive*. New York: Summit Books, 1986. B, T

Traver, Robert. *Anatomy of a Murder*. New York: St. Martin's Press, 1958. C

Trigiani, Adriana. *Big Cherry Holler*. New York: Ballantine Books, 2002. C, G, T

_____. *Big Stone Gap*. New York: Random House, 2000. G, T

_____. *Home to Big Stone Gap*. New York: Random House, 2006. G

_____. *Lucia, Lucia*. New York: Random House, 2003. G, T

_____. *Milk Glass Moon*. New York: Random House, 2002. G

_____. *Rococo*. New York: Random House, 2005. G

_____. *The Queen of the Big Time*. New York: Random House, 2004. G

_____. *Very Valentine*. New York: Harper, 2009. G

Trocheck, Kathy Hogan. *Every Crooked Nanny*. New York: Avon Books, 2000. C, G

Truman, Margaret. *Murder at the Washington Tribune*. New York: Ballantine Books, 2005. B

Turow, Scott. *The Burden of Proof*. New York: Farrar, Straus and Giroux, 1990. C

_____. *Personal Injuries*. New York: Farrar, Straus and Giroux, 1999. T

Updike, John. *Bech: A Book*. Greenwich, CT: Fawcett Crest/Alfred A. Knopf, 1965. B, G

_____. *Brazil*. New York: Alfred A. Knopf, 1994. C

_____. "Cruise." In *The Afterlife and Other Stories*. New York: Alfred A. Knopf, 1994. B

_____. "Gesturing." In *The Early Stories*. New York, Alfred Knopf, 2003. B

_____. *In the Beauty of the Lilies.* New York: Borzoi/Alfred A. Knopf, 1996. B, C, G, T

_____. "Morocco." In *My Father's Tears and Other Stories.* New York: Alfred A. Knopf, 2009. B

_____. "Packed Dirt, Churchgoing, a Dying Cat, a Traded Car." In *The Early Stories.* New York, Alfred Knopf, 2003. B

_____. *Rabbit at Rest.* New York: Alfred A. Knopf, 1990. C

_____. "Tristan and Iseult." In *The Afterlife and Other Stories.* New York: Alfred A. Knopf, 1994. B

Uviller, Daphne. *Super in the City.* New York: Bantam Books, 2009. T

Vidal, Gore. *Myra Breckinridge.* New York: Bantam Books, 1968. B, C, G, T

Viets, Elaine. *Murder Between the Covers.* New York: Signet/New American Library, 2003. C

Vincent, E. Duke. *The $trip.* New York: Bloomsbury, 2009. G

Vonnegut (Jr.), Kurt. *Bluebeard.* New York: Dial Press/Random House, 2006. T

_____. *Breakfast of Champions.* New York: Dell, 1975. C

Walsh, Michael. *As Time Goes By.* New York: Warner Books, 1998. B

Wambaugh, Joseph. *The Choirboys.* New York: Dell, 1976. G

_____. *Finnegan's Week.* New York: Bantam Books, 1994. B, G

_____. *Floaters.* New York: Bantam Books, 1997. G

_____. *Fugitive Nights.* New York: Bantam Books/Perigord Press, 1993. B, G, T

_____. *The Glitter Dome.* New York: William Morrow, 1981. B, G

_____. *Hollywood Crows.* New York: Little, Brown and Company, 2008. B

_____. *Hollywood Hills.* New York: Little, Brown and Company, 2010. G

_____. *Hollywood Station.* New York: Little, Brown, 2006. B, G, T

_____. *The Secrets of Harry Bright.* Toronto, New York: Bantam Books, 1986. B, C, G, T

Weisman, John. *SOAR.* New York: Harper/Collins, 2003. C

Wells, Rebecca Wells. *Divine Secrets of the Ya-Ya Sisterhood.* New York: HarperTorch, 2002. B, G

West, Nathanael. *The Day of the Locust*. New York: Time Reading Program, 1965. C

Westlake, Donald E. (also as Richard Stark) *The Hot Rock*. New York: Warner Books, 2001. C

———. *Jimmy the Kid*. New York: M. Evans & Company, 1974. B

———. *The Road to Ruin*. New York: Mysterious Press/Warner Books, 2004. G

———. *The Seventh* (see Richard Stark)

———. *Smoke*. New York: The Mysterious Press/Warner Books, 1995. B

White, James Neel. *I Was a P-51 Fighter Pilot in WWII*. New York: iUniverse, 2003. B, C, G, T

Wideman, John Edgar. "Across the Wide Missouri." In *Damballah*. New York: Mariner Books, 1998. G

Williams, Tennessee. *The Glass Menagerie*. In *The Glass Menagerie, A Streetcar Named Desire, Cat on a Hot Tin Roof, Suddenly Last Summer*. New York: Quality Paperback Book Club, 1994. G

Willis, Connie. "At the Rialto." In *Impossible Things*. New York: Bantam Books, 1994. G, T

———. "Even the Queen." In *Impossible Things*. New York: Bantam Books, 1994. B

Wilson, F. Paul. *Infernal*. New York: Tom Doherty Associates, 2005. B, G

Wolfe, Tom Wolfe. *A Man in Full*. New York: Bantam Books, 2001. G

Wolff, Isabel. *Out of the Blue*. Don Mills, ON: MIRA Books, 2012. C

Woods, Stuart. *Bel-Air Dead*. New York: G. P. Putnam's Sons, 2011. G

———. *Beverly Hills Dead*. New York: G. P. Putnam's Sons, 2008. G

———. *Dead Eyes*. New York: HarperCollins, 1994. G, T

———. *L.A. Times*. New York: HarperCollins, 1993. B, C

———. *Mounting Fears*. New York: G. P. Putnam's Sons, 2009. B

———. *The Prince of Beverly Hills*. New York: G. P. Putnam's Sons, 2004. G, T

———. *Short Straw*. New York: G. P. Putnam's Sons, 2006. B

———. *Son of Stone*. New York: G. P. Putnam's Sons, 2011. G, T

———. *Strategic Moves*. New York: G. P. Putnam's Sons, 2011. B

Wouk, Herman. *Marjorie Morningstar*. New York: Signet Books/New American Library, 1964. C, G
____. *War and Remembrance*. New York: Pocket Books, 1980. B
____. *The Winds of War*. New York: Pocket Books, 1973. C
____. *Youngblood Hawke*. Garden City, NY: Doubleday, 1962. G
Zusak, Markus. *I Am the Messenger*. New York: Alfred A. Knopf, 2010. B

Index

Numbers in bold indicate photographs

Abbott, Jeff 329, 475
Abella, Alex 406, 475
Absolute Rage 492
"Across the Wide Missouri" (1981) 711
Across the Wide Missouri 600-602, **601**, 697, 711, 719
Action in the North Atlantic 122, 260, 272-273
Act of Will 568, 693
Acts of Passion 787-788, 856
Adam's Rib 766, 770-775, **771**, 810, 849, 851, 853, 857, 858, 866
Addie Pray 439-440, 477
Adventure 596-597, 599-600, 697, 718
Adventures of Marco Polo, The 313-315, 454, 475, 476, 499
African Queen, The xvi, 2, 14, 75, 159, 169-174, **172**, 179, 191, 198, 241-242, 243, 246, 247, 249, 250, 251, 252, 253, 259, 260, 266, 276, 877
After All These Years 157-158, 255, 654-655, 701
Against All Odds 342, 480

Alcorn, Randy 381, 475, 691
Alfred Hitchcock Murder Case, The 649-650, 691
"Alibi, The" 653, 699
Allen, Woody 38-40, 75, 125-126, 143, 169, 239, 243
All-Girl Filling Station's Last Reunion, The 592, 699
All My Friends Are Going to Be Strangers 352-353, 487, 641, 705, 818-819, 854, 877
All Through the Night 59-60, 256, 260, 272
Almost Moon, The 708
Along Came a Spider 369-370, 489
Along Came Jones 293, 344, 489, 502
Alpine Pursuit, The 391, 478
Amazing Dr. Clitterhouse, The 14-15, 25, 249, 269
American Pastoral 659, 708
"America Poem" 388-389, 481, 699
Anatomy of a Murder 353-354, 493
Andromeda Strain, The 439, 478
Angel 657, 693, 781, 848
Angels with Dirty Faces 15-18, 191, 230, 247, 248, 256, 259, 263, 265, 269, 542, 755
"Animal Crackers in My Soup" 207, 247
Another City, Not My Own 219-220, 250, 660, 697
Answered Prayers: The Unfinished Novel 20, 248
Any Number Can Play 600, 697, 719
Any Place I Hang My Hat 701
Any Woman's Blues 369, 483, 701
Arnold, Wolf 612, 691
Assassins, The 256
As Time Goes By 37, 54-55, 82-83, 240, 265
Atkins, Ace 84, 243, 400, 475
Attachment 699
"At the Rialto" 525, 712, 762-764, 858, 879
Auster, Paul xviii, 143-144, 243, 313, 475
"Australia" 260

Bad Business 706

Bad Day at Black Rock 726, 778-783, **779**, 810, 829-830, 848, 849, 851, 854, 857, 867, 879
Bad Day for Sorry, A 397, 486
Bag of Bones 158, 257
Bainbridge, Beryl 793, 847
Balestrieri, James D. 292, 401, 415, 476, 877
Ballad of Ethan Burns, The 292, 401-402, 415-416, 476, 877
Ball of Fire xv, **331**, 332-333, 491, 501
Barbery, Muriel 109-110, 244, 583-584, 691
Barefoot Contessa, The 184-186, 220, 254, 256, 259, 260, 277
Barnes, Linda 111-112, 244
Barnett, Jill 320, 476
Baxt, George xix, 2, 3, 7-8, 10-11, 19, 25, 26, 34-36, 38, 52-54, 85, 212-216, 239, 240, 244, 293, 298, 303, 308, 313-315, 335-336, 364, 453-454, 467, 476, 512-514, 515-516, 519-520, 526, 535, 537-538, 540-541, 542-543, 549, 580-581, 606, 649-652, 686, 688, 691-693, 727, 729-730, 731-732, 830, 844, 847-848, 874
Beaches 567-568, 696
Beach Music 374-375, 478
Bean Trees, The 444, 485
Beat the Devil 176-179, 246, 255, 260, 263, 276, 876
Beau Geste xvii, 316-320, **317**, 354, 420, 433, 444, 470, 476, 478, 479, 480, 484, 485, 486, 489, 500
Beautiful Maria of My Soul 222, 254, 788
Bech: A Book 264, 710
Beckerman, Ilene 81-82, 219, 244, 347, 349, 408, 476
Be Cool 46, 108, 258, 341, 485
Bel-Air Dead 672-673, 712
Belle Ruin 481, 699
Bell, James Scott xix, 65, 71-72, 86-87, 154, 234-235, 239, 244-245, 395-396, 465, 476-477, 530, 680-681, 693, 754, 838-839, 844, 848, 875
Bellow, Saul 570-571, 693
Belong to Me 310, 479
Bernhardt, William xix, 310, 394-395, 467, 477, 531-532, 693
Betrayal (as *Betrayed*) 289, 291, 479, 496
Betrayed 59, 88, 264, 398-399, 492, 878

Betts, June Harman 753-754, 848
Beverly Hills Dead 584-585, 671, 672, 712
Bible Salesman, The 682-683, 698
Big Cherry Holler 462, 493, 521-525, 544, 709, 746, 857
Big Shot, The 61, 246, 272
Big Sleep, The 48, 127, 133, 134-141, **135, 139**, 165, 182, 191, 202, 203-204, 222, **240**, 241, 246, 249, 251, 252, 257, 259, 261, 264, 265, 274, 681, 876-877
Big Stone Gap 544, 553-554, 590, 676, 709, 831-832, 858
Bitterroot 149-150, 248
Blackboard Jungle, The 3-4, 254, 876
Black Cross 700
Black Legion 10, 245, 268
Blatty, William Peter 120-121, 245
Block, Lawrence 2, 10, 11, 13-14, 18-19, 25-26, 27, 28, 36-37, 50-51, 61, 67-69, 76-79, 86, 124-125, 130-131, 133-134, 138, 161-162, 164-166, 177-178, 184, 186-187, 217-219, 239, 245-247, 363-364, 477, 795, 848, 874, 877, 879
Block, Valerie 679-680, 693, 765-766, 848
Blood and Honor 224-225, 252, 751, 852
Blood Memory 482, 700
Blood Ties 827-828, 853
Bluebeard 740-741, 858
Bluebeard's Eighth Wife **312**, 312-313, 490, 499
"Blue Cadillac" 793, 854
Blue Hour, The 614-615, 658, 698
Blue Screen 572-574, 706
Bochco, Steven 693, 848
Bogart, Stephen Humphrey xxi, 51-52, 79-81, 192, 223, 240, 247
Bone Collector, The 103, 249
Bone Thief 392, 488
Bonnie and Clyde: A Love Story 294-296, 477
Boom Town 592-593, **593**, 625, 643, 696, 697, 698, 704, 710, 718, 759, 768, 810, 817, 849, 850, 851, 854, 858, 865
Boothe, Clare 629-630, 693
Bourne Ultimatum, The 366, 486

INDEX

Boy Meets Girl 299, 425, 492, 629, 709
Boys Town xiv, xiv, 726, 747-755, **749**, 810, 843, 848, 849, 850, 851, 852, 854, 855, 856, 857, 863-864, 879
Box, C. J. 796, 848
Bradford, Barbara Taylor 96-97, 247, 568-570, 594-596, 657, 686, 693-694, 781-782, 844, 848, 874
Bram, Christopher 247, 346-347, 477
Brandner, Gary 17, 247
Braun, Lilian Jackson 172-173, 231-232, 247, 679, 694
Brazil 447, 493
Bread Alone 129, 254, 410, 482, 700
Breakfast of Champions 440-441, 493
Breakheart Hill 695
Breaking the Rules 570, 693
Breaznell, Gene 477
Brethren, The 159-160, 253
Bright Futures 565, 701
Bright Leaf 350-351, **351**, 490, 502-503
Brooks, Bill 294-296, 477
Brother Orchid 27, 134, 187, 245, 271
Brown, Dale 372, 477,
Brown, Irene Bennett 533-534, 591-592, 623-624, 684-685, 688, 694
Brown, Joe David 439-440, 477
Brown, Sandra 91, 247, 836-837, 848
Bukowski, Charles xviii, 206-208, 239, 247-248, 645, 646, 694, 874
Bullet for a Star 8-9, 11-12, 29-31, 42-43, 209-210, 239, 255, 321-322, 483, 646, 701
Bullets or Ballots 8-9, **9**, 255, 267-268
Burden of Proof, The 448, 493
Burke, James Lee 149-152, 248, 539, 586-587, 694, 878
Burglar Who Painted Like Mondrian, The 76, 245
Burglar Who Thought He Was Bogart, The 10, 11, 13-14, 18-19, 25-26, 27, 28, 36, 50-51, 61, 77-78, 86, 124-125, 133-134, 138, 161-162, 164-166, 177-178, 184, 186-187, 217-219, 239, 245-246, 877
Burglar Who Traded Ted Williams, The 68, 246
Burnett, Barbara 657-658, 694, 709

915

Butler, Robert Olen 236-238, 248
Butterfly Lost 615-616, 695

Cadence of Grass, The 463, 487
Caine Mutiny, The 2, 13-14, **179**, 179-183, 186, 191, 241, 246, 250, 253, 256, 257, 259, 277, 880
Cain, James M. 630, 694, 814, 848
Calamity Town 291, 490, 877
Callan, Michael Feeney 417, 477
Call of the Wild, The 542-546, **543**, 692, 695, 697, 705, 709, 710, 716
Campbell, Colin 694, 782-783, 849
"Can I Stay Here?" 435-436, 488
Cannell, Stephen J. 794-795, 849
Can't Wait to Get to Heaven 758, 852
Caper of the Golden Bulls, The 437-438, 487
Capitol Murder 394-395, 477
Capote, Truman 20, 176, 177, 248, 276
Captains Courageous 555, 726, 737-743, **739**, 747, 786, 810, 833, 850, 854, 855, 856, 857, 858, 863
Carcaterra, Lorenzo 16-17, 229-230, 248, 542, 695, 750-751, 849
Carolina Moon 579-580, 705, 878
Carpetbaggers, The 262, 707, 816-817, 856
Carr, John Dickson 426, 477
Carroll, Leslie 248, 336, 477
Casablanca xiv, xvi, 2, 14, 37, 50, 61-121, **63, 74**, 124, 125-126, 128, 137, 138, 143, 154, 159, 165, 171, 176, 190, 191, 198, 201, 202, 204, 206, 219, 232, 239, 241, 243, 244, 245, 246, 247, 248, 249, 250, 251, 252, 253, 254, 255, 256, 257, 258, 259, 260, 261, 262, 263, 264, 265, 266, 272, 340, 346, 569, 764, 876, 880
Casanova Brown 342-343, **343**, 461, 480, 492, 501
Case Has Altered, The 252
Case of Lucy Bending, The 708
Catcher in the Rye, The 428, 491
Cat Who Brought Down the House, The 172-173, 231-232, 247, 679, 694
Cawood, Hap 388, 478
Chain Lightning 161, 162, 246, 275

Chains of Command 372, 477
China Seas 516, 692, 716
Chocolat 253
Choice, The 263
Choirboys, The 599, 710
Chopin and Beyond 347, 465-466, 483, 701
"Chosen" 785-786, 857
Christine 179-180, 257
City of Angels (as *Hustle*) 62, 262
City Streets xiv, **419**, 420
Clarke Arthur C. 548-549, 695
Clark Gable and Carole Lombard Murder Case, The 26, 215-216, 244, 542-543, 580-581, 691-692, 847
Clements, Arthur L. 123, 248
Coben, Harlan 248, 849
Cobweb, The 430, 480
Cohen, Jeffrey 114-115, 235-236, 248-249, 530-531, 596, 683, 688, 695, 774-775, 805, 837-838, 844, 849
Cohen, Paula Marantz 678, 695, 794, 849
Cold Flat Junction 252, 699
Cold Service 357, 489
Cold Six Thousand, The 832, 851
Cole, David 389-390, 413, 469, 478, 615-616, 695, 878
Collins, Max Allan 249, 286, 460, 478, 527, 582-583, 662-665, 695
"Comfort to the Enemy" 131-132, 258
Coming Attractions (as *Daisy Fay and the Miracle Man*) 171-172, 251, 645, 699, 745, 852
Coming Back 119, 144-145, 260
Command Decision **598**, 598-600, 697, 698, 710, 719
Condon, Richard 249, 441, 478, 695
Conflict 133-134, 241, 246, 274
Conroy, Pat 170-171, 249, 374-375, 478, 695, 877
Control 95-96, 252
Cook, Thomas H. 412-413, 478, 695
Cooney, Ellen 840-841, 849
Cornwell, Patricia 695

Cortázar, Julio 434, 478, 695
Cowboy and the Lady, The **315**, 316, 483, 499-500
Creole Belle 694
Crichton, Michael 439, 478
Crider, Bill 8, 14-15, 19-20, 24, 25, 37-38, 56-57, 70-71, 83-84, 128-129, 140-143, 145, 160, 239, 240, 249, 462, 478, 674, 696
Crimson Joy 572, 706
Crooked Hinge, The 426, 477
"Cruise" 99, 264
Curse 383, 488
Cussler, Clive 148, 249, 318-320, 478
Cutting Room, The 324, 485, 703, 773, 853

Daheim, Mary 391, 478
Dance with the Devil 223, 250, 525, 575, 656, 696, 734-736, 850
Dancing Lady **521**, 521-522, 709, 715
Dandola, John 553, 574-575, 655-656, 696, 755-756, 757-758, 759, 826-827, 844, 849
Daniel 250
Dark Before Dawn, The 400, 492
Dark Passage 143-145, 191, 222, 243, 249, 257, 260, 274
Dark Victory 20-22, 248, 255, 270
Dart, Iris Rainer 567-568, 696
Davis, Bruce 391-392, 479, 696
Day of the Locust, The 426, 494
Dead Don't Lie, The 160, 255
Dead End 11-13, **12**, 191, 230, 244, 245, 255, 268
Dead Eyes 665-666, 712, 828, 858
Deadline Man 175, 264
Deadline – U.S.A 174-175, 260, 276
Deadly Divots 477
Dead Sleep 254
Deal Breaker 248, 849
Death by Hollywood 693, 848
Deathryde: Rebel Without a Corpse 133, 166, 260, 681, 705, 800-801, 855
Death Wish 440, 480, 699

Deaver, Jeffrey 103, 249
"Decline and Fall of Frankie Buller, The " 299-300, 344-346, 492
Deep Pockets 111-112, 244
Deep Shaker 350, 490
Delectable Mountains or, Entertaining Stranger, The 642, 704
DeLillo, Don xviii, 225, 249, 537, 649, 696, 874, 878
De los Santos, Marisa xix, 115-117, 233-234, 250, 310, 324-325, 467, 479, 530, 541-542, 585, 696, 736-737, 836, 849, 874, 876, 877
DeMille, Nelson 90, 250, 798-799, 850, 879
Denial 178-179, 255
Depraved Indifference 397-398, 492
Desire xv, 303-305, **304**, 463, 481, 498
Desk Set 784-786, **785**, 851, 857, 867
Desolation Angels 145-146, 257, 316, 354, 433, 484, 516-517, 635-636, 702
Desperate Hours, The **187**, 187-188, 241, 255, 277-278
Devil and the Deep, The 298, 453, 476, 497-498
Devil at 4 O'Clock 797-798, 853
Devil Met a Lady, The 211, 647, 701
Devil's Garden, The 107, 261, 382, 489, 706, 878
Devil's Punchbowl, The 254, 700
Diamond Solitaire 216-217, 258
Diary of a Mad Housewife 72-73, 256, 438, 484
Dickey, Eric Jerome 250
Diehl, William 250, 827, 850
Dimiter 120-121, 245
Dingley Falls 258
Dinner, The 805-807, 853, 879
Dinner Party, The 480
Disenchanted, The 306, 491, 631-632, 708
Distant Drums 352-353, 487, 503, 877
Divine Secrets of the Ya-Ya Sisterhood 266, 578-579, 711
Djibouti 108-109, 258
Doctorow, E. L. 250
Dog Tags 841, 856
Dolores Claiborne 416-417
Don't Make a Scene 679-680, 693, 765-766, 848

Double Deuce 356, 489
Double Eagle 364-365, 488
Double Indemnity 630, 694
Double Play 261, 770, 855
Douglas, Kirk 223, 250, 406, 525, 575, 656, 696, 734-736, 850
Downriver 443-444, 479, 769-770, 851
Drifters, The 2, 6, 27, 40-41, 91-92, 122, 126, 162-164, 169-170, 175, 176, 184-185, 189, 197-198, 239, 260, 727, 738, 748, 766-767, 768, 775-776, 786, 790-791, 799-800, 802-803, 817-818, 844, 854, 876
Drink Before the War, A 49-50, 217, 258
Dr. Jekyll and Mr. Hyde 759-762, **760**, 809, 848, 850, 856, 865
Drowning Girl, The 797, 853
Drumcondra 417-418, 477
Druxman, Michael B. xix, 250, 443, 479, 510-512, 518, 552-553, 555-556, 594, 596-597, 599-600, 602, 603-606, 610-612, 613-614, 648-649, 686, 688, 696, 697, 728-729, 730-731, 732-734, 736, 740, 745-746, 759, 761, 762, 770-771, 775, 777, 778, 783, 784, 786-787, 791-792, 798, 800, 803-804, 823-824, 844, 850, 880
Duffe, Mary 289, 291, 468, 479
Duma Key 703, 766, 774, 853
Dunne, Dominick 219-220, 250, 660, 697
Dunne, John Gregory xix, 94, 250, 442, 479, 548, 566, 697, 851
Dunning, John 460-461, 479

Early Autumn 738, 740, 855
Earthquake Weather 58, 257
Eco, Umberto 97, 250, 698
Edge of Eternity 381-382, 475, 691
Edgerton, Clyde 682-683, 698
Edison the Man 553, 574, 756, 757-758, 759, 826-827, 849, 852, 864
Edsel 180-181, 250, 660-661, 698, 779-780, 829-830, 851, 879
11/22/63 121, 257, 412, 484, 685
Ellroy, James 479, 698, 832, 851
Endless Night 341-342, 485
End of the Pier, The 370-371, 481, 878
Enemy Within 264

INDEX

Enforcer, The 133, 166-169, **167**, 261, 263, 276
Esstman, Barbara 330, 479
Estleman, Loren D. xix, 22-23, 71, 124, 180-181, 189-190, 231, 239, 250-251, 301-302, 443-444, 467, 479, 660-665, 686, 698, 769-770, 779-781, 829-830, 844, 851, 874, 879
Evans, Elizabeth 614-615, 658, 698
"Even the Queen" 172, 266
Ever-Running Man, The 587, 705
Every Crooked Nanny 407-408, 493, 710
Executioners, The 634, 704

Factotum 206, 247
Falling Together 116-117, 250
Falsely Accused 264
Farewell to Legs, A 114-115, 248
"Farm Work" 691
Fast, Howard 480
Father of the Bride 726, 775-776, 778, 810, 851, 854, 855, 858, 866
Father's Day 606-609, 699
Father Was a Caveman 753-754, 848
Fat Ollie's Book 259
Favorite, Eileen 588-589, 698
Fenady, Andrew J. xix, 31-32, 41-42, 62-63, 95, 135-136, 146, 156, 160-161, 202-206, 239, 251, 317-318, 480, 599, 602-603, 643-644, 698, 743-744, 820-821, 844, 851, 877
52 Pick Up 486
Fighting Caravans 296, **297**, 491, 497
Final Witness 71-72, 86-87, 244
Finnegan's Week 48, 265, 711
Firm, The 576, 700
First Lady 258
Fitzgerald, F. Scott xviii, 306, 427, 480, 631, 811, 851
Five Bells and Bladebone, The 252, 371, 481
Flagg, Fannie xix, 119, 171-172, 251-252, 592, 645, 699, 745, 758, 844, 852, 874
Flight Behavior 807-808, 853

Floaters 711
Flying Blind 286-287, 478, 527, 662, 695
Fonseca, Isabel 699
Fool for Love 822, 857
Foolscap or, The Stages of Love 449-450, 486
Ford, Richard 457, 480, 658, 699
Fork in the Road 557, 700
Forsaking All Others xv, 540-542, **540**, 692, 693, 696, 715-716
Forstchen, William R. 396-397, 480
For Whom the Bell Tolls xv, 69, 284, 337-342, **338**, **340**, 420, **468**, 480, 483, 485, 491, 494, 501
Foucault's Pendulum 97, 250, 698
Fountainhead, The 347-349, **348**, 476, 486, 502
Four Corners of the Sky, The 55-56, 154-155, 173-174, 186, 239, 258, 287-288, 297-298, 299, 337, 486, 532-533, 592-593, 643, 704, 775, 776, 854
Fourteen Sisters of Emilio Montez O'Brien, The 451, 482, 656-657, 700
Fourth K, The 448-449, 490, 707
Fowle, Herb "Chick" 342, 480
Freedomland 742, 856
Free Soul, A xiv, 511-515, **513**, 625, 692, 696, 710, 713
Friedman, Kinky 102-103, 252, 457, 480
Friendly Persuasion 284, **407**, 407-408, 473, 493, 504
From Here to Eternity 428-429, 483, 551, 565, 701
From the Terrace 435, 489, 815, 855
Fugitive Nights 97-98, 265, 711, 824, 858
Furutani, Dale 220, 252, 381, 480
Fury xv, 732-733, **733**, 810, 850, 862-863, 880
Fury (2005) 264

Gable: A One-Person Play in Two Acts 443, 479, 510-511, 555-556, 688, 696, 850
Gangsters 248
Gann, Ernest K. 606, 699, 720
Garbo Laughs 104-107, 173, 232-233, 253, 303, 305, 385-387, 411-412, 463-464, 481, 584, 700, 764-765, 833, 852
Garfield, Brian 440, 480, 699

"Gary Cooper, Or the Landscape" 454-455, 468, 491
Gary, Romain 436-437, 469, 480
General's Daughter, The 90, 250
"Gesturing" 200-201, 264
"Ghosts" 143-144, 243
"Ghost Soldiers, The " 445-446, 448
Gibson, William 430, 480
"Gifts" 491
Gift, The 253
Girl with the Dragon Tattoo, The 585, 703
Gladly the Cross-Eyed Bear 148-149, 181, 259
Glass Menagerie, The 632, 711
Glass Rainbow, The 694
Glimpse of Tiger, A 523-524, 707
Glitter Dome, The 85, 265, 556-557, 711
God Bless John Wayne 102-103, 252, 457, 480
God Save the Child 201, 261
Going Overboard 64-65, 85-86, 128, 263, 384-385, 492
Goldberg Variations 255
Golden Boy 488
Goldman, William xix, 95-96, 171, 198-200, 252, 338-339, 480, 606-609, 634-635, 699, 819-820, 852, 874
Gone with the Wind xiv, xvi, xvii, 85, 117, 191, 389, 443, 510, 516, 518, 534, 555, 556-592, **559, 573**, 614, 624, 626, 651, 653, 656, 671, 674, 684, **687**, 689, 691, 692, 693, 694, 695, 696, 697, 698, 699, 700, 701, 702, 703, 704, 705, 706, 707, 708, 709, 710, 711, 712, 717-718, 838, 876, 878
"Good Man Is Hard to Find, A " 705
Good Sam 347, 486, 502
Gorman, Ed 653, 699
Go to the Widow-Maker 638-640, 701
Gourmet Rhapsody 109-110, 244, 583-584, 691
Grady, James 137-138, 252, 372, 481
Grave Maurice, The 252, 371, 481
Gravity's Rainbow 535, 641-642, 707, 759-760, 856, 878
Great American, The 406, 475

Greek Summer, The 546, 705, 795-796, 855
Green, Gerald 633-634, 699
Green Mile, The 703
Greta Garbo Murder Case, The 85, 213, 244, 335-336, 476, 515-516, 520, 692
Griffin, S. A. 388-389, 481, 699
Griffin, W.E.B. 224-225, 252, 751, 852
Grimes, Martha 239, 252, 253, 370-371, 467, 481, 699, 874, 878
Grisham, John 159-160, 253, 576, 700
Guess Who's Coming to Dinner xvi, 726, 802-808, **803**, 810, 849, 851, 852, 853, 855, 869, 876, 879
Guns of Heaven, The 253
"Gut-Wringing Machine, The " 645-646, 694

Hall, James W. 100-102, 180, 253, 876
Hamill, Denis 557, 700
Hamill, Pete 103, 225-226, 239, 253, 459-460, 481, 874
Hamilton, Donald 356, 481
Hamner, Jr., Earl 253
Handling Sin 704
Hangman's Beautiful Daughter, The 741-742, 854
Harder They Fall, The 188-190, **189**, 193, 241, 251, 260, 262, 278, 708, 814, 856
Harris, Joanne 253
Harris, Thomas 361, 481
"Having Wonderful Time" 425-426, 485
Hay, Elizabeth xix, 104-107, 173, 232-233, 253-254, 303, 305, 385-387, 411-412, 463-464, 467, 481-482, 527-528, 584, 673-674, 700, 764-765, 832-833, 844, 852, 874
Healy, Jeremiah 365-366, 482
"Heat Lightning" 17, 247
Hell 236-238, 248
Hell Divers (as *Hell Below*) 516, 692, 713
Help, The 709, 801-802, 857
Help the Struggler 253
Hendricks, Judith Ryan 129, 254, 410, 482, 700
Herlihy, James Leo 437, 482

INDEX

Heroines, The 588-589, 698
Her Own Rules 568-569, 693
Hey There (You with the Gun in Your Hand) 58-59, 262, 616-619, 707, 879
High and the Mighty, The 699
High Midnight 211, 255, 288, 290, 316, 326-327, 333-334, 339, 361-362, 468, 483, 518, 701, 756-757, 878
High Noon xiv, xvi, xx, 128, 284, 288, 292, 353-402, **355, 360, 368**, 420, 433, 441, 446, 463, 464, 468, 471, 473, 475, 476, 477, 478, 479, 480, 481, 482, 483, 484, 485, 486, 487, 488, 489, 490, 491, 492, 493, 494, 503, 878, 880
High Sierra 28-38, **33, 35**, 42, 156, 191, 204, 209, 241, 244, 246, 247, 249, 251, 255, 258, 265, 266, 271
Hijuelos, Oscar xix, 185-186, 220-222, 254, 451-453, 482, 656-657, 700, 788, 852, 874
Hillerman, Tony 700
Hit Parade 78-79, 246
Hłasko, Marek 254
Holding the Dream 376-377, 490
Hollywood 206, 247, 646, 694
Hollywood Crows 48, 265
Hollywood Hills 711
Hollywood Station 234, 265, 585-586, 711, 825, 858
Holmes, Rupert 112-113, 254
Honky Tonk 594, **594**, 697, 718
Hosseini, Khaled 700
Hot Kid, The 538-539, 703, 878
Hot Rock, The 350, 494
Hours of the Virgin, The 189-190, 251
House of Destiny 127-128, 223-224, 258, 284-285, 320, 351-352, 456, 485, 597-598, 703
House Rules 89-90, 261
Hucksters, The 597-598, 703, 718-719
Huie, William Bradford 814-815, 852
Humphrey Bogart Murder Case, The 3, 7-8, 10-11, 19, 25, 34-36, 38, 52-54, 212-215, 239, 244, 308, 313-315, 454, 476, 514, 652, 692, 727, 847
Hunted, The 384, 488

Hunter, Evan 3-5, 148-149, 181, 239, 254, 363, 482, 635, 700, 874, 876
Hush Money 261

I Am the Messenger 112, 266
Iberia 438-439, 487
If I Die in a Combat Zone 93-94, 261
Iles, Greg xix, 188, 239, 254-255, 482, 686, 700, 874, 875
In a Lonely Place 162-166, **164**, 192, 241, 246, 260, 276, 877
In a Strange City 704, 853
Independence Day 457, 480, 658, 699
Infante, Guillermo Cabrera 354-355, 482, 701
Infernal 117, 266, 712
Inherent Vice 118-119, 236, 261
Inherit the Wind 726, 790-797, **791**, 809, 810, 847, 848, 849, 850, 851, 853, 854, 855, 868, 879, 880
In Plain Sight 796, 848
Insomnia 367, 485
In the Beauty of the Lilies 99-100, 138, 201, 264, 285, 308, 376, 447-448, 493, 577-578, 615, 659-660, 710, 772, 830-831
"In the Line of Duty" 482
Inventing Memory 226-227, 255
Invisible Stripes 14, 245, 270-271
"Invitation to the Ball"
Irving, John 20-22, 255
Isaacs, Susan xix, 107-108, 157-158, 255, 328, 335, 382-383, 467, 482, 571-572, 653-655, 686, 701, 874
"I Scream Man!" 367-368, 487
Isle of Dogs 695
I Still Dream About You 119, 252
"It Ain't Me, Babe: Working for Richard Nixon" 854
It Happened One Knife 235-236, 248, 530-531, 596, 683, 688, 695, 774-775, 805, 849
It Happened One Night xv, 510, 522-535, **523**, **529**, 561, 624, 626, 627, 640-641, 643, 656, 662, 673, 683, 684, 689, 692, 693, 694, 695, 696, 697, 700, 702, 704, 705, 706, 707, 709, 710, 712, 715, 878, 880
It's a Big Country 351-352, 456, 485, 503

INDEX

It's a Mad, Mad, Mad, Mad World 799-802, 810, 851, 855, 857, 868-869
It Started in Naples xv, 613, 710, 721, 879
I Was a P-51 Fighter Pilot in WWII 113-114, 232, 266, 285, 288-289, 494, 520, 677, 711, 835, 858

Jack and the Beanstalk 363, 482, 704
Jackson, Joe 320-321, 483
"James Francis and the Star" 637-638, 706, 816, 855
Jane Austen in Boca 678, 695, 794, 849
Janis, Byron 347, 465, 483, 701
Janis, Maria Cooper xxi, 347, 450, 465, 483, 701
Jeffries, Donald 255, 325-326, 464-465, 483
Jerusalem Inn 371, 481
Jigsaw 196-197, 259
Jimmy the Kid 92-93, 266
Jitterbug 22-23, 124, 251, 661-662, 698
Johnson, Maureen 701, 838, 852
Jones, James xviii, 428-430, 483, 551, 638-640, 701, 874
Jong, Erica 226-227, 255, 369, 483, 701
Judas Goat, The 45-46, 63-64, 94-95, 201-202, 261, 316-317, 489
Judgment at Nuremberg 726, 798-799, 810, 850, 851, 868, 879
Just Like Humphrey Bogart 126-127, 208-209, 239, 257, 484, 567, 702, 821-822, 852
Just Rewards 782, 848

Kaminsky, Stuart M. xix, 2, 7, 8-9, 11-12, 15-16, 29-31, 42-45, 59-60, 111, 122, 152-153, 160, 178-179, 181-182, 186, 209-212, 239, 255-256, 288, 290, 310-311, 316, 321-322, 326-327, 333-334, 339, 361-363, 458-459, 466-467, 468, 483-484, 518, 524-525, 560-561, 562-565, 646-647, 686, 688, 701-702, 734, 756-757, 760-761, 805, 825, 844, 852, 874
Kaufman, Sue 72-73, 256, 438, 484
Kazan, Elia 256, 810, 814
Keeper of the Flame 766-767, **767**, 855, 865
Keillor, Garrison 674-675, 702

927

Kennedy, Adam xix, 126-127, 208-209, 239, 257, 484, 567, 702, 821-822, 852
Kerouac, Jack xviii, xix, 145-146, 257, 316, 354, 433, 484, 516-517, 635-637, 702-703
Kerr, Jean 434, 484
Key Largo 31, 64, 156-160, **157**, 191, 204, 241, 249, 251, 252, 253, 255, 257, 264, 265, 275
Kid Galahad 11, 244, 268, 271
Kienzle, William X. 257, 804, 831, 853
Kiernan, Caitlín R. 797, 853
King of the Underworld 18-19, 245, 269
Kingsblood Royal 704
Kingsolver, Barbara 444, 485, 807-808, 853
King, Stephen xix, 121, 143, 158, 179-180, 239, 257, 367, 412, 416-417, 446, 467, 484-485, 685, 686, 703, 766, 774, 853, 874
Kite Runner, The 700
Klavan, Laurence 324, 485, 703, 773, 836, 853
Klimitas, Hank 798, 853
Kober, Arthur 425, 485, 497
Koch, Herman 805-807, 853, 879
Kohler, Heinz 358-359, 485

LaBrava 32-33, 46, 258
L.A. Confidential 479, 698
Lake, The 257
Lake Wobegon Summer 1956 674-675, 702
Lambrusco 840-841, 849
Langoliers, The 367, 446, 485
Lankford, Terrill Lee 58, 257
Lardo, Vincent 110, 257
Larsson, Stieg 585, 703
Lash, Jennifer 827-828, 853
Last Angry Man, The 633-634, 699
Last Hurrah, The xv, 727, 789-790, 854, 868
Last Tycoon, The 427, 480, 811, 851
Latham, Aaron 308-309, 464, 485, 557-559, 703, 839-840, 845, 853, 877

L.A. Times 69-70, 266, 340, 494
Lawrence, E. Duke 703
Laymon, Richard 257, 341-342, 485
Leavenworth Train: A Fugitive's Search for Justice in the Vanishing West 320-321, 483
Left Hand of God, The 186-187, 246, 277
Legacy, The 373, 488
"Legends of Glory" 395, 489
Legion 245
Legion of the Condemned 288, 483, 496
Lehane, Dennis 49-50, 217, 258
Leigh, Janet 127-128, 223-224, 258, 284-285, 320, 351-352, 456, 485, 503, 597, 703
Leonard, Elmore xix, 2, 32-33, 46, 108, 131-132, 239, 258, 291-292, 300-301, 341, 347, 359-360, 467, 468, 485-486, 538-539, 576-577, 686, 703-704, 874, 878
Letter from a Stranger 96-97, 247
Levin, Ira 347-348, 486
Lewis, Sinclair 704, 874
Libeled Lady xv, 736-737, **737**, 836, 849, 850, 863
Libra 537, 696, 878
Lieberman's Thief 44-45, 256, 702
Life After Life 174, 259, 534-535, 561-562, 705
Lilac Time 288-289, 494, 496
Lippman, Laura xix, 704, 853
Lisey's Story 703
Littlefield, Sophie 397, 486
Lives of a Bengal Lancer, The 299-302, **301**, 326, 420, 479, 486, 492, 493, 498
Lives of the Circus Animals 247, 346-347, 477
"Locked Room, The" 313, 475
Lone Star 602, 697, 719
Long , Jeff 783-784, 853
Looking for Mr. Goodbar 708
Loop, The 312-313, 490
Loop Group 782, 854
Lords of Discipline, The 695

"Lost in Ruins" 263
"Love and Other Crimes" 643, 704
Love in the Afternoon xv, 408-412, **409, 411**, 420, 463, 476, 482, 484, 488, 504, 878
Lovely in Her Bones 363, 487
Love in the Ruins 706
Love Me 263, 466, 492, 686, 709, 754-755, 843-844, 857
Lovesey, Peter 216-217, 258, 376, 486
Love's Lovely Counterfeit 814, 848
Love Walked In 115-116, 233-234, 250, 324-325, 479, 530, 541-542, 585, 696, 736-737, 836, 849, 876, 877
Lucia, Lucia 528-529, 710, 775, 776, 858
"Lucky Lady" 709
Ludlum, Robert 66-67, 258, 366, 486

MacDonald, John D. 634, 704
Machine Dreams 706
Mae West Murder Case, The 453-454, 476, 651-652, 692
Maggie 704
Magic 819-820, 852
Majic Man 460, 478, 582, 665, 695
Make Me a Star 296-298, 486, 497
Malaya 778, 851, 866
Malone, Michael xix, 55-56, 65-66, 154-155, 173-174, 186, 239, 258-259, 287-288, 297-298, 299, 322, 336-337, 449-450, 467, 486-487, 532-533, 592-593, 642-643, 686, 704, 775, 793, 844, 854, 874
Maltese Falcon, The xvi, 7, 14, 29, 38-59, **40, 45**, 75, 117, 128, 137, 156, 165, 182, 191, 201, 202, 204, **240**, 241, 243, 244, 245, 246, 247, 249, 250, 251, 252, 255, 256, 257, 258, 259, 260, 261, 262, 263, 264, 265, 266, 272
Mambo Kings Play Songs of Love, The 185-186, 220-221, 254, 788, 852
Manhattan Melodrama 535-539, **536**, 625, 692, 694, 696, 703, 707, 715, 830, 878
Man in Full, A 581-582, 712
Man of the West 292, 389, 412-416, 470, 476, 478, 504, 878
Man's Castle, A 731-732, 847, 850, 862

Man Who Shot Lewis Vance, The 256, 484, 825, 878
Man with a Load Mischief, The 481
Man with Bogart's Face, The xvii, 41, 62-63, 135-136, 146, 161, 202-204, 239, 251, 317-318, 480, 602-603, 643-644, 698, 820, 851
Marathon Man 171, 198-200, 252, 338-339, 480
Marie Galante 731, 850, 862
Marjorie Morningstar 430-431, 494, 632-633, 712
Marked Woman 10-11, 244, 268
Marlene Dietrich Murder Case, The 293-294, 298, 453, 476, 512-513, 650-651, 692
Marquand, John P. 289, 487
Martin, Charles 704
Matlock Paper, The 66-67, 258
Maximum Bob 576, 704
Maximum Ride: School's Out Forever 587-588, 706
Mayor, Archer 792-793, 854
McAfee, Annalena 238-239, 259, 789, 854
McBain, Ed 129-130, 148-149, 181, 196-197, 239, 259, 363, 704, 874
McBride, Mary 240, 259, 390-391, 487
McCammon, Robert 367-368, 487, 748-749, 854
McCorkle, Jill 174, 259, 534-535, 561-562, 579-580, 705, 874, 878
McCoy, Horace 423-424, 487
McCoy, Ron 796-797, 854
McCrumb, Sharyn 363, 487, 741-742, 854
McEvoy, Dermot 17-18, 118, 182, 239, 259, 609-610, 682, 705, 789-780, 854, 879
McGivern, William P. 437-438, 487
McGuane, Thomas 463, 487
McMurtry, Larry xix, 352-353, 403-404, 442-443, 467, 487, 589-590, 641, 705, 782, 818-819, 854, 874, 877
McNally's Alibi 110, 257
McNally's Dilemma 743, 856
McNally's Risk 262
Mean High Tide 100-102, 180, 253, 876
Meet John Doe 284, 321-326, **323**, 420, 464, 479, 483, 485, 487, 500, 877, 880

Men Are Such Fools 14, 245, 269
Men in White 535, 693, 715
Michener, James A. xviii, xix, 2-3, 6, 27, 40-41, 91-92, 122, 126, 162-164, 169-170, 175, 176, 184-185, 189, 197-198, 239, 260, 438-439, 487, 547, 705, 727-728, 738, 748, 766-767, 768, 775-776, 786, 790-791, 799-800, 802-803, 817-818, 844, 854, 876
Midnight Cowboy 437, 444, 482
Midnight Pass 152-153, 186, 256, 805, 852
Mildred Pierced 111, 256, 647, 702
Miler, The 388, 478
Miles, Keith 364-365, 488
Milk Glass Moon 675, 710
Miller, John Douglas 546, 705, 795-796, 855
Miller, Linda Lael 373, 488
Miller, Lynn Ruth 878, 409-410, 488
Miller, Rebecca 589, 705
Misfits, The xv, 613-624, **614, 619**, 625, 626, 658, 684, **688**, 689, 694, 695, 697, 698, 707, 710, 721, 879, 880
Mogambo xv, 364, 603-606, **605**, 692, 697, 720
Moment She Was Gone, The 149, 254
Montecito Heights: A Resurrection Man Novel 694, 782-783, 849
Moonshine War, The 300-301, 486
More Die of Heartbreak 570-571, 693
Morocco 293-296, **295**, 444, 453, 476, 477, 485, 497
"Morocco" (1979) 98-99, 265
Mortal Causes 100, 262, 374, 490
Mortal Fear 482
Mortal Stakes 356, 441-442, 489, 642, 706
Motel Chronicles 146-147, 263, 405-406, 491, 778-779, 857
Mountain, The 783-784, 851, 853, 867
Mounting Fears 70, 266
Moviegoer, The 296, 522, 706
Moving On 403-404, 487
Mr. Deeds Goes to Town x, xv, 284, 305-310, **307, 309**, 313, 420, 454, 464, **467**, 476, 477, 479, 485, 490, 491, 493, 498-499, 531, 877
Mud on the Stars 814-815, 852

Muller, Marcia 2, 27-28, 60, 119, 144-145, 239, 260, 587, 705, 826, 855, 874
Murder at the Washington Tribune 264
Murder Between the Covers 493
Murder in Georgetown 708
Murder in the Lincoln Bedroom 227-229, 262, 673, 708
Murder in the Red Room 306-307, 490, 877
"Murder of Ramon Vasquez, The" 208, 247, 645-646, 694
Murder on the Yellow Brick Road 210, 256, 563, 688, 702, 760-761
Mutiny on the Bounty xvi, 124, 510, 534, 547-549, **547**, 625, 626, 684, 689, 692, 694, 695, 697, 698, 705, 708, 716
My Last Movie Star 57-58, 110-111, 149, 230-231, 263, 463, 492, 551-552, 554-555, 677-678, 708, 747, 833-835, 857
My Name Was Five 358-359, 485
Myra Breckinridge 195, 265, 300, 326, 493, 640, 710, 767-768, 769, 817, 858

Nadelson, Reggie 375-376, 488
Nadler, Stuart 401, 488, 705
Naked Edge, The xiv, **417**, 417-418, 470, 477, 504-505
Natchez Burning 254
"Natica Jackson" 638, 706
Naughton, Michael P. 133, 166-169, 260, 681, 705, 800-801, 855
Neiderman, Andrew 383-384, 488
Nemesis: The Final Case of Eliot Ness 310, 477, 531-532, 693
Never Leave Me 707
Never Let Me Go 602-603, 643, 698, 720
Nichols, John 637, 705
Night Flight 520, 677, 711, 714
Night Ride Home 330, 479
"Night Streets of Madness" 207, 248
No Greater Love 257, 804, 831, 853
No Legal Grounds 87, 245
No Man of Her Own 518-520, 692, 697, 714
Northern Lights 377-378, 464, 490
Northwest Mounted Police 320-321, 483, 485, 500
Northwest Passage 759, 850, 864

Now and Forever **298**, 299, 486, 498

O'Brien, Tim xviii, 93-94, 261, 445-446, 488
O'Callaghan, Thomas 392, 488
O'Connor, Flannery 705
Ode to Billy Joe 707
Odets, Clifford 425-426, 488, 627, 705
O'Hara, John xviii, xix, 420, 435-436, 488-489, 637-638, 706, 815-816, 855, 874
Oklahoma Kid, The 15, 19-20, 244, 249, 270
Olasky, Marvin 392-394, 489
One Second After 396-397, 480
Old Man and the Sea, The xv, 726, 786-789, **787**, 810, 851, 852, 854, 855, 856, 867-868
Old Wine Shades, The 253
Once Upon a Chariot 344, 489, 706
Only Good Yankee, The 329-330, 475
"On the Rainy River" 445, 488
On the Road 433, 484
Ordinary Daylight: Portrait of an Artist Going Blind 748, 855
Other War: Letters from a GI in India in 1944 & 1945, The 264, 342-343, 461-462, 492, 709
Our Gang 708
Our Lady of Greenwich Village 17-18, 118, 182, 239, 259, 609-610, 682, 705, 789-790, 854, 879
Out of Sight 291-292, 486
Out of the Blue 387-388, 494

"Packed Dirt, Churchgoing, a Dying Cat, a Traded Car" 15, 265
Painted Desert, The 510-511, 696, 713
Pale Kings and Princes 261
Pal Joey 706
Palmer, Michael 402, 489
Paretsky, Sara 373-374, 489
Paris, Iris 344, 489, 706

Parker, Robert B. xix, 2, 45-46, 63-64, 84, 94-95, 201-202, 239, 243, 261, 316-317, 356-357, 362, 400-401, 441-442, 467, 475, 489, 572-574, 642, 686, 706, 736, 738, 770, 844, 855, 874

Parnell 552-553, 697, 717

Passage to Marseille 10, 124-125, 246, 273

Pat and Mike 776-777, **777**, 851, 856, 866

Patterson, James 369-370, 489, 587-588, 706

Percy, Walker 296, 491, 522, 706, 878

Peril 412-413, 478

Personal Injuries 773, 858

Peter Ibbetson 302-303, 476, 498

Peters, Ralph 107, 261, 382, 489, 706, 878

Petrakis, Harry Mark 395, 489

Petrified Forest, The 3-8, **5**, 24, 156, 191, 204, 230, 244, 249, 251, 254, 256, 260, 263, 264, 267, 876

Phillips, Jayne Anne 706

Picoult, Jodi 89-90, 261, 706

Picture Perfect 706

Plainsman, The 310-311, **311**, 459, 484, 499

Play It Again 51-52, 79, 223, 240, 247

Play It Again, Sam xvii, 38-40, 75, 125, 143, 169, 239, 243

Playmates 261, 855

Plaza Suite 195-196, 263

Please Don't Eat the Daisies 434, 484

Plot Against America, The 752-753, 856, 879

Plymouth Adventure 778, 851, 867

Political Suicide 402, 489

"Polynesia" 547, 705

Poor Butterfly 702, 734, 852

Portnoy's Complaint 438, 490

Potok, Andrew 748, 855

Prayer for Owen Meany, A 20-22, 255

Price, Richard 742, 856

Pride of the Yankees, The xvi, 284, 326, 333-337, **335**, 420, 458, 476, 478, 482, 483, 484, 486, 490, 501

Primal Fear 250, 827, 850

935

Primeval: High Noon in Detroit 359-360, 468, 486
Prince of Beverly Hills, The 584, 666-672, 712, 828-829, 859
Private Lives of Pippa Lee, The 589, 705
Prizzi's Family 249
Pronto 486
Pronzini, Bill 707
Puzo, Mario 448-449, 490, 707
Pynchon, Thomas xviii, xix, 49, 79, 118-119, 236, 261-262, 535-536, 549-550, 641-642, 707, 730, 750, 759-760, 844, 856, 878

Quarry in the Middle 249, 583, 695
Queen, Ellery 291, 490, 877
Queen of the Big Time, The 514-515, 710
Quick Millions 728-729, 850, 861
Quiet Game, The 700

Rabbit at Rest 446-447, 493
Rainbow Drive 48-49, 136-137, 147-148, 264, 772, 857
Rain Gods 150-152, 248
"Rain of Women, A" 206-207, 248
Randisi, Robert J. 58-59, 262, 616-623, 707, 879
Rankin, Ian 100, 262, 374, 490
Raucher, Herman 73, 262, 333, 490, 523-524, 640-641, 707
Red Dragon 361, 481
Red Dust 516-518, **517**, 603, 606, 625, 635, 692, 697, 702, 714
Red Hot Blues 375-376, 488
Red, White & Blue 255, 482, 701
Regulators, The 485
Remake: As Time Goes By, The 80-81, 240, 247
Remember 96, 247, 594-596, 693
Resurrecting Midnight 250
Retribution 362-363, 484, 565, 702
Retro 251, 662, 698
Return of Dr. X, The 24-25, 244, 249
Rhino Ranch 589-590, 705
Rich Man, Poor Man 6, 263

Ricochet 836-837, 848

Riding with John Wayne 308-309, 464, 485, 557-559, 703, 839-840, 845, 853, 877

Riker, Leigh 787-788, 856

Road to Ruin, The 711

Roaring Twenties, The 22-24, **23**, 134, 191, 230, 245, 249, 251, 270

Robbins, Harold 262, 707, 816-817, 856

Robert B. Parker's Lullaby 84, 243, 400-401, 475

Roberts, Nora 376-381, 464, 467, 468, 490

Roberts, Les 350, 490

Rococo 675-676, 710

Roosevelt, Elliott 227-229, 262, 306-307, 490, 673, 708, 877

Rosemary's Baby 347-348, 486

Rosenfelt, David 841, 856

Rossner, Judith 708

Roth, Philip xviii, 438, 490, 659, 708, 752-753, 856, 874, 879

Roubaud, Jacques 312-313, 490

Roughan, Howard 370, 489

Rucker, Rudy 332-333, 491

Runaway Heart 794-795, 849

Run Silent, Run Deep 609-610, **610, 611**, 682, 705, 720

Sabrina xv, 25, **183**, 184, 191, 241, 246, 253, 255, 260, 277, 411

Sager, Mike 752, 856

Sahara 122-124, 248, 251, 262, 273

Sahara (1992) 148, 249, 318-320, 478

Sail 370, 489

Saint Jack 709

Salinger, J. D. xviii, 428, 491

Samway, Patrick 296, 491

Sanders, Lawrence xix, 110, 212, 262, 357-358, 491, 647-648, 708, 743, 776-777, 844, 856, 874

Sandford, John 262, 371-372, 491

San Francisco 549-550, **550**, 625, 656, 692, 696, 697, 702, 707, 716, 726, 732, 733-736, **735**, 810, 847, 850, 852, 856, 863

Saporta, Lionel R. 394, 491

Saratoga 553, 696, 717
Saratoga Trunk 344-347, **345**, 477, 483, 492, 501-502
Satori in Paris 257, 636-637, 703
Saucer Wisdom 332-333, 491
Save the Tiger 75-76, 122-123, 262, 337, 491
Say It Again, Sam 240, 259, 390-391, 487
"Sayonara" 104, 254
Scent of Evil 792-793, 854
Schulberg, Budd xviii, xix, 189, 193, 262, 278, 306, 491, 631-632, 708, 813-814, 856
Scimitar's Edge 392-394, 489
Scott, A.D. 491, 841-842, 856
Sea Change 261
Sebold, Alice 708
Second Deadly Sin, The 776-777, 856
Secret of Sam Marlow, The 31-32, 41-42, 95, 136, 156, 160-161, 202, 204-206, 239, 251, 318, 480, 599, 644, 698, 743-744, 821, 851
Secrets of Harry Bright, The 47, 265, 327-328, 493, 711, 824, 858
Sentimental Journey 320, 476
Serenade 630, 694
Sergeant York 284, 326-331, **328**, 334, 420, 458, 475, 480, 482, 483, 484, 493, 494, 500
Seventh Cross, The xv, 767-768, 817, 855, 858, 865
Shackles 707
Shadow Play 389-390, 413-415, 469, 478, 878
Shagan, Steve 62, 75-76, 122-123, 262, 337, 491
Shanghai Madness 730-731, 850, 862
Shaw, Irwin 6, 263
Sheldon, Sidney 565-566, 708
Shepard, Sam 146-147, 176-177, 263, 405-406, 454-455, 468, 491, 778-779, 822-823, 844, 857, 874
Sherrill, Martha xix, 57-58, 110-111, 149, 230-231, 263, 463, 492, 551-552, 554-555, 556, 677-678, 708, 747, 833-835, 857
Shining Through 328, 335, 482, 571-572, 653-654, 701
Shooting Script, The 703, 836, 853
Short Straw 153-154, 266

Shukert, Rachel xix, 263, 466, 492, 686, 709, 754-755, 842-844, 857
Silent Prey 262
Sillitoe, Alan 299-300, 344-346, 492
Simon, Neil 195-196, 263
Simon, Roger L.263
Simple Habana Melody, A 451-453, 482
Sixth Commandment, The 212, 262, 357-358, 491, 647-648, 708
Skeleton Man 700
Ski Bum, The 436-437, 469, 480
Skye, Christina 64-65, 85-86, 128, 263, 384-385, 492
Sleep No More 254
Sleepers 16, 248, 542, 695, 750-751, 849
Small Death in the Great Glen, A 399-400, 491, 841-842, 856
Small Town 130-131, 246, 795, 848, 879
Smart Moves 7, 256, 564, 702
Smash Cut 91, 247
Smoke 266
Snively, Susan 761-762, 844, 857
Snow in August 103, 225-226, 253, 459-460, 481
SOAR 330-331, 494
Society Girl 729, 850, 861
Soldier of Fortune xv, 606-609, **607**, 699, 720
Somebody's Darling 442-443, 487
Some Came Running 429-430, 483, 701
"Some Days You Get the Bear" 246
Some Like it Hot – Buttered 235, 249, 837-838, 849
Something Borrowed, Something Black 71, 231, 251, 444, 479, 698
Something Happened Yesterday 847
Somewhere I'll Find You 96, 594-596, 683, 693, 718
Songs of the Humpback Whale 706
Son of Stone 673, 712, 829, 859
Sophie's Choice 6-7, 264, 644-645, 709
Sowa, córka piekarza (*Owl, the Baker's Daughter*) 254
Sparks, Nicholas 263
Spencer, LaVyrle 166, 263, 772-773, 857
Spencer's Mountain 253

"Spencer Tracy" 761-762, 844, 857
"Spencer Tracy Is Not Dead" 822-823, 844, 857
Spewack, Bella & Samuel 425, 492, 629, 709
Spiro, Bernard 264, 342-343, 461-462, 492, 709
Spoiler, The 238-239, 259, 789, 854
Sprinkle, Patricia 387, 492
Stand, The 143, 257
Standing in the Rainbow 699
Stanley and Livingstone 755-756, 849, 864
Starstruck 263, 686, 709, 842-843, 857
Starving Hearts 409-410, 488, 878
Sterile Cuckoo, The 637, 705
Stevens, Laurie 400, 492
Stockett, Kathryn 709, 801-802, 857
Stranger in the Mirror, A 565-566, 708
Strangers When We Meet 635, 700
Strategic Moves 98, 266
$trip, The 683-684, 703, 710
Student of Weather, A 385, 482, 527-528, 673-674, 700, 832-833, 852
Styron, William xviii, 6-7, 264, 644-645, 709
Suite Scarlett 701, 838, 852
Summer Gary Cooper Won the War, The 289, 291, 468, 479
"Summer in Idle Valley" 263
Summer of '42 73-74, 262, 333, 490
Summons, The 376, 486
Super in the City 775, 858
Swan Song 487, 748-750, 854
Swing Your Lady xv, 13-14, 245, 268-269

Tabloid City 253
Tallulah Bankhead Murder Case, The 212, 244, 303, 364, 476, 540, 606, 692, 729-730, 847
Talton, Jon 175, 264
Tanenbaum, Robert K. 59, 88-89, 264, 397-399, 492, 874, 878
Task Force **349**, 349-350, 494, 502
Teacher's Pet xv, 510, 610-612, 625, 691, 697, 720

"Temple of Doom, The " 752, 856
Temporary Insanity 248, 336, 477
"Tenkiller" 704
Terminators, The 356, 481
Test Pilot 518, 553-555, 625, 697, 698, 699, 708, 709, 717, 743-747, **744**, 810, 833, 834, 850, 851, 852, 857, 863
Texan, The 292-293, 476, 497, 877
Thank Your Lucky Stars 122, 256, 273
Then Came Heaven 166, 263, 772-773, 857
There Should Have Been Castles 524, 707
Theroux, Paul 709
They Came to Cordura 416-417, 470, 484, 504
They Drive by Night 27-28, 36, 246, 260, 271
They Shoot Horses Don't They 423-424, 487
Think Fast, Mr. Peters 44, 256, 484, 524-525, 647, 702
Thirty Seconds Over Tokyo 765, 768-770, **769**, 810, 851, 852, 855, 858, 866
Thornburg, Janet 709, 785-786, 857
Thorp, Roderick 48-49, 136-137, 147-148, 264, 772, 857
Three Trapped Tigers 354-355, 482, 701
Thunder 137-138, 252, 372, 481
Time's Witness 65-66, 259, 322, 487, 704
Timothy Files, The 358, 491
Tin Roof Blowdown, The 586-587, 694
Tishomingo Blues 359-360, 486
To Catch a Spy 122, 256
Tokyo Joe 161-162, 246, 275
To Have and Have Not xvi, 75, 125-133, 134, 137, 191, 208, 222, 243, 246, 249, 252, 254, 255, 257, 258, 259, 260, 261, 263, 273-274
Tomorrow Is Another Day 15-16, 256, 334, 458-459, 484, 560-561, 688, 702
Too Hot to Handle 555-556, 697, 708, 717
Toyotomi Blades, The 220, 252, 381, 480
Tracy: A One-Person Play in Two Acts 250, 479, 697, 728, 844, 850
Traver, Robert 353-354, 493
Treasure of the Sierra Madre, The xvi, 48, 145-155, **147**, **152**, 165, 191, 202, 241, 245, 246, 248, 249, 251, 253, 254, 256, 257, 259, 263, 264, 266, 275, 772

Trigiani, Adriana xix, 462, 493, 514-515, 521-522, 544-546, 553-554, 590-591, 613, 675-676, 686, 709-710, 746, 831-832, 844, 857-858, 874, 879
"Tristan and Iseult" 64, 265
Trocheck, Kathy Hogan 407-408, 493, 710
Trophies and Dead Things 60, 260, 826, 855
True Confessions 94, 250, 442, 479, 548, 566, 697, 851
Truman, Margaret 264
Try Darkness 65, 234-235, 245, 395-396, 476, 681, 693, 754, 848
Try Dying 154, 234, 245, 530, 680-681, 693
Try Fear 245, 465, 477, 838-839, 848
Tunnel Vision 373-374, 489
Turning Angel 254, 700
Turow, Scott 448, 493, 773, 858
24 Hours 188, 255
20,000 Years in Sing Sing xv, 729-730, 847, 850, 856, 861-862
2010: Odyssey Two 695
Twice a Survivor: A Katrina Journal 798, 853
Two O'Clock, Eastern Time 479
Two Mrs. Carrolls, The 141-142, 249, 274

Underworld 225, 249
Unreals, The 255, 325-326, 464-465, 483
Updike, John xviii, xix, 2, 15, 64, 98-100, 138, 200-201, 239, 264-265, 285-286, 308, 376, 446-448, 467, 493, 577-578, 615, 659-660, 710, 772, 830-831, 874
Up in Honey's Room 131, 258, 577, 704
Up the River 2-3, 7, 240, 244, 250, 260, 267, 727-728, 818, 847, 850, 854, 861
Uviller, Daphne 775, 858

Vengeance 181-182, 256, 310-311, 459, 484
Vera Cruz **355**, 402-406, **403**, **405**, 475, 487, 491, 503
Very Valentine 544-546, 590-591, 613, 676, 710, 879
Vidal, Gore xix, 195, 265, 300, 326, 493, 640, 710, 767-768, 769, 817, 858
Viets, Elaine 493
Vineland 49, 79, 262, 549-550, 707, 730, 750, 856

Virginia City 18, 25-26, 184, 215, 244, 245, 271
Virginian, The 289-292, **290**, 420, 479, 480, 483, 486, 487, 490, 496, 877
Vonnegut, Jr., Kurt xviii, 440-441, 493, 740-741, 858

Wagons Roll at Night, The 11, 38, 53, 244, 271-272
Waiting for Lefty 627-628, 705
Walker Percy: A Life 296, 491
Wall, The 783-784, 853
Walsh, Michael 37, 54-55, 82-83, 240, 265
Wambaugh, Joseph xix, 2, 47-48, 85, 97-98, 234, 239, 265, 327-328, 493, 556-557, 585-586, 599, 686, 710-711, 824-825, 844, 858, 874
War and Remembrance 266
Water Is Wide, The 170-171, 249, 877
Weisman, John 330-331, 494
We'll Always Have Murder 8, 14-15, 19-20, 24, 25, 37-38, 56-57, 70-71, 83-84, 128-129, 140-143, 145, 160, 239, 240, 249, 462, 478, 674, 696
Wells, Rebecca 266, 578-579, 711
We're Dead, Come on In 391-392, 479, 696
Westlake, Donald E. xix, 92-93, 266, 349-350, 494, 711, 874
West, Nathanael 426, 494
West of Orange (as *Dead at the Box Office*) 553, 574-575, 655-656, 696, 755-756, 757-758, 759, 826-827, 844, 849
"What Is It in French?" 703
What Makes Sammy Run? 631, 708, 813-814, 856
What We Do for Love 81-82, 219, 244, 347, 349, 408, 476
When the Sacred Ginmill Closes 36-37, 77, 246, 363-364, 477
Where Echoes Live 27-28, 260
Where Gable Slept 533-534, 591-592, 623-624, 684-685, 688, 694
Where Love Has Gone 707
Where the Truth Lies 112-113, 254
Where You Belong 247, 569-570, 694, 781-782, 848
While Other People Sleep 144, 260
Whipsaw 732, 848, 862
White, James Neel xix, 113-114, 232, 266, 285, 288-289, 494, 520, 677, 711, 835, 858
White Noise 649, 696

White Sister, The 520, 692, 714
Who Left That Body in the Rain? 387, 492
"Why I Don't Speak Italian" 123, 248
Wickford Point 289, 487
Wideman, John Edgar 600-601, 711
William Powell and Myrna Loy Murder Case, The 526, 535, 537-538, 541, 652, 692, 732, 830, 848
Williams, Tennessee 632, 711
Willis, Connie 712, 762-764, 858, 879
Wilson, F. Paul 117, 266, 712
Winds of War, The 431-433, 494
Wings 285-288, 478, 486, 493, 495-496
Winners, The 434-435, 478, 695
Winning of Barbara Worth, The 284-285, 456, 471, 485, 495
Winter Kills 441, 478, 695
Winter Prey 371-372, 491
Wise Men 401, 488, 705
Witchfinder, The 301-302, 479
Wolfe, Tom 581-582, 712
Wolff, Isabel 387-388, 494
Woman of the Year 104, 762-766, **763**, 774, 810, 833, 848, 850, 852, 853, 858, 865, 879
Women, The 629-630, 693, 746
Woods, Stuart xix, 69-70, 98, 153-154, 239, 266, 340, 494, 584-585, 665-671, 672-673, 686, 712, 828-829, 844, 858-859, 874
Word of Honor 798-799, 850, 879
Wouk, Herman xviii, xix, 179, 181, 266, 277, 430-433, 494, 632-633, 712
Writers of the Purple Sage 657-658, 694, 709

Yesterday's News 482
Youngblood Hawke 712
You're Nobody 'Til Somebody Kills You 620-623, 707
Your Turn to Curtsy, My Turn to Bow 634-635, 699

Zusak, Markus 112, 266

www.ingramcontent.com/pod-product-compliance
Lightning Source LLC
Chambersburg PA
CBHW071211290426
44108CB00013B/1160